TOUGH 'OMBRES IN NORMANDY

THE RISE OF THE 90TH INFANTRY DIVISION IN WORLD WAR II

RICHARD C. ANDERSON JR.

STACKPOLE
BOOKS
Essex, Connecticut
Blue Ridge Summit, Pennsylvania

STACKPOLE BOOKS
An imprint of The Globe Pequot Publishing Group, Inc.
64 South Main Steet
Essex, CT 06426
www.globepequot.com

British Library Cataloguing in Publication Information available

Library of Congress Cataloging-in-Publication Data available

ISBN 978-0-8117-7833-6 (hardback)
ISBN 978-0-8117-7834-3 (electronic)

CONTENTS

Acknowledgments v
Notes on Terminology ix
Introduction xiii

Chapter 1: Dad and the War 1
Chapter 2: The 90th Infantry Division 27
Chapter 3: Baptism of Fire 55
Chapter 4: Change of Mission .90
Chapter 5: Calvary on Mont Castré 115
Chapter 6: Victory on Mont Castré 157
Chapter 7: "They Got the Wrong Man" 179
Chapter 8: Collapse on the Island 190
Chapter 9: Problem Division? 218
Chapter 10: Task Force Weaver 237
Chapter 11: Solid Shoulder or Broken Neck? 277
Chapter 12: The Battle of Le Bourg-Saint-Léonard 306
Chapter 13: Closing the Chambois-Falaise Pocket 327
Chapter 14: Epilogue 367

Notes 393

ACKNOWLEDGMENTS

I WOULD LIKE TO THANK ALL THE ARCHIVISTS AND LIBRARIANS AT THE MANY FEDeral and state facilities I have had the pleasure of working with on this and my previous titles. You are the often unsung heroes of history, preserving the records of the past. I wish I could thank all of you individually but can only single out a few that especially helped with this project.

I am deeply indebted to the staff of the Donovan Research Library of the Maneuver Center of Excellence, U.S. Army, at Fort Benning, Georgia. Part of the collections they hold include the Student Monographs from the Advanced Infantry Officers Course of the Infantry School Library. The Monographs, many of them written by the actual participants in the actions they describe, are an invaluable resource for those interested in the U.S. Army in World War II. Many of them also include maps, which help to clarify what happened. Some of those are included in this work. Nichole J. Copeland, Genoa R. Stanford, and Rebekka Bernotat, Donovan Research Library reference librarians, have been especially helpful.

I must also acknowledge the hard work of the archivists and staff of the Modern Military Branch at the National Archives, Archives II, at College Park, Maryland. Over the years their assistance has been invaluable.

A huge thanks goes to Lore Oehmichen. She has kindly allowed me to include photographs taken by her father, Captain Herbert Karl Oehmichen, during the war. Herbert was born in 1915 in New York City to German parents, Paul, born in Leipzig, and Erna Israelzik, a German Jew born in Berlin. Paul was a conscientious objector who had left Germany in 1910 to avoid the draft and only returned in 1913 to marry Erna, after which they moved to New York, where Paul and his younger sister, Elinor, were born. After the end of World War I in 1920, the family returned to Germany, first to Naumburg and then to Gera in 1928, where Herbert graduated from high school in 1934. With the Nazis in power, Herbert's parents managed to send him back to New York with the intention of following, but they and his younger sister were not allowed to leave.

On 16 October 1940, Herbert registered for the draft as required by the new Selective Service Act but was not drafted until the following year on 23 October. He entered service at the Camp Grant Army Reception Center at Rockford, Illinois, and was assigned to the Field Artillery. He completed basic training at Fort Sill, Oklahoma, on 29 December 1941 and was initially posted as a private with the Artillery School Mess as a mess sergeant.[1] Herbert was accepted at Officer Candidates School in April 1942 and was commissioned as a 2d lieutenant in the Field Artillery on 21 July 1942. He initially served with the 333d Field Artillery Regiment and was promoted to 1st lieutenant on 16 November 1942 and captain on 30 November 1943. By then he was commander of Battery C, 777th Field Artillery, but on 24 December 1943 he was recruited by the Office of Strategic Services for the Military Intelligence Service program at Camp Ritchie, Maryland. His fluency in German—he also had some French—made him an obvious candidate for the prisoner-of-war interrogation program.

Oehmichen graduated from Ritchie on 6 April 1944 and by 10 April was on his way to England, arriving on 17 April. On 30 April, Herbert and his Military Intelligence Service men were attached to the 90th Infantry Division as the Interrogation Prisoner of War Team No. 49 (Provisional). What was most interesting is that he was allowed to carry a camera, and during the war he took numerous snapshots, which were probably processed by the 90th Infantry Division's attached Signal Corps Photography Detachment. A selection of those photographs, none published until now, are included in this work. The complete selection of photos taken during the war by Captain Oehmichen may be found on Lore's Facebook blog at https://www.facebook.com/HKO90THWWII.

At the end of the war, sometime between when the 90th Infantry Division was in Czechoslovakia or when it occupied Riga Kaserne in Deggendorf Bavaria, Captain Oehmichen somehow managed to make his way to the "model" concentration camp at Theresienstadt, where he rescued his mother. Then, in an even more extraordinary feat, he managed to find his father, who had lived in hiding in Gera for nearly ten years, and his sister, Elinor, who as an American citizen had been forced to work in a nearby labor camp. Sadly, though, Erna's sister was murdered in Auschwitz and her brother-in-law died in Theresienstadt.

After the war, Herbert, his wife Bette, and his daughters Cynthia and Lore settled in Milwaukee where he had a long career as brewmaster for Miller Brewing Company, before retiring to California. He died in 1990, just two weeks shy of his seventy-fifth birthday, and is buried at Academy Cemetery in Clovis, California.

A special thanks also goes to Geoff Gentilini, Director/Lead Researcher at Golden Arrow Research, LLC, for his work in locating and copying the Morning Reports (MR) of the various units. His work is impeccable and was invaluable in answering some of the questions I had about Dad's exact whereabouts at different times and the confusing changes of command in the regiments and battalions of the 90th Infantry Division during the intense fighting in Normandy.[2]

All historians interested in the European Theater of Operations U.S. Army (ETOUSA) in World War II owe thanks to Thierry Arsicaud, creator of the Coordinates Translator and webmaster of "Notes on the Modified British System of coordinates used on the European Theatre of Operations during the WWII." His Coordinates Translator enables one to find specific locations referenced in wartime military reports on Google Maps and MapQuest.[3]

Another huge debt is owed to those sites preserving history by maintaining high-resolution online digital versions of the maps used by the British and American armies in Europe. Normandy War Guide and the Perry-Castañeda Library Map Collection at the University of Texas are two of the better-known ones, but there are many other private and institutional sites available.

Thank you to the 90th Infantry Division Association for keeping alive the memory of the officers and men of the 90th Infantry Division in both world wars. The Association website, http://www.90thdivisionassoc.org/index.html, also contains a large repository of unit histories, After-Action Reports, and General Orders related to the 90th and its associated units, which is invaluable for anyone researching the division.

So many people have helped me over the years with questions related to the Normandy Campaign that it is impossible to name more than a few. One is a good friend, Niels Henkemans. Early in the writing of this book, he read some passages and provided invaluable corrections and insights on the Germans facing the 90th. His multivolume study of the German Army in Normandy, *Defending Normandy*, just began publishing in 2024 and is the most complete and accurate work on the subject available.

For my three sons—Alex, Sebastian, and Galen—this is your family history too; I hope you enjoy reading about your Granddad's part in the war.

As always, to Jolly, for loving me, putting up with my strange obsession, and keeping me on the straight and narrow. I may never write the bestseller historical romance you want me to, but I hope you know I love you forever and always.

And of course to Mom and Dad.

NOTES ON TERMINOLOGY

I have tried to describe the roads and terrain in this study as they existed in the summer of 1944. However, much has changed in the intervening seventy-eight years. Most noticeably, towns have expanded their urban footprint, roadways have been widened and more are paved, and the extensive system of small farming fields surrounded by the famous hedgerows—the bocage—has changed as farmers expanded their fields for more efficient farming. That said, in general the roads follow similar routes, the names of towns are the same, and the course of rivers and streams are the same.

Both before and after the war, the French periodically changed the letter and number designations of roads in France, which otherwise makes little difference, because American reports habitually gave the route of a road rather than its designator. I have followed that convention but when possible have added the road designation or name as found on modern maps in parenthesis, with (RN) for Routes Nationales or (D) for Routes Départementales: for example, the Barneville-Carteret to La-Haye-du-Puits Road (D903). Note there were no Autoroutes (A) in France in 1944.

Another complication is that American soldiers at the time of the battle tended to mangle French place-names and their proper spellings when writing reports. For example, Le Hameau Dupré became "Dupreys" to the 357th Infantry. Wherever possible I have corrected those spellings. The identification of place-names on American maps also tended to be haphazard. Reference was often made to localities, such as "Lithaire," as if they were individual towns because of how they appeared on maps. In this case, what was called "Lithaire" was actually the hamlet of La Martinerie in the commune of Lithaire. Even more confusing, the World War II commune of Lithaire is now merged into the modern commune of Montsenelle. Whenever possible I have tried to use the actual place-name if it is clear that is what was meant.

NOTES ON TERMINOLOGY

Locations in U.S. Army records refer to Army Map Service (AMS) maps, which were almost always direct copies of British Geographical Section, General Staff (GSGS) maps. They were created using the Modified British System of map coordinates based upon a Cassini projection of the European continent, which was then split into ten zones. Each zone was then divided into squares, each 500 by 500 kilometers, which were assigned a lowercase letter in alphabetical sequence. Each of those were then further subdivided into twenty-five squares, each 100 by 100 kilometers, which were assigned an uppercase letter from A to Z, omitting I. In turn, each of those were divided into one-kilometer-square blocks, which were numbered from 00 to 99 west to east and from 00 to 99 south to north. A specific location could then be described by its map square and a numerical reference that consisted of four, six, or eight digits, depending on the degree of accuracy. For example, vZ3383 was a point 33 kilometers east and 83 kilometers north in square vZ of the Lambert Zone 1, which describes the location of Alençon.

One peculiarity is that while the Allied military maps used by both the Americans and British were metric, American unit records commonly expressed distances as miles, yards, and feet rather than as kilometers and meters. The Germans of course used metric measurements. I have chosen to give distances throughout as they were expressed in the original record with a parenthetical clarification when necessary.

Most of the operations described in this work occurred in Lambert Zone 1, covering northwestern France including the coast from the mouth of the Seine to Quiberon Bay, the Brittany Peninsula, the Cotentin Peninsula, Calvados, and Normandy. In June and July, the 90th Infantry Division operated almost entirely in square vT, before moving to vY and vZ and then into the Nord de Guerre Zone in August. For those readers who would like to better follow the description of the actions, many of the GSGS 1:50,000 and 1:100,000 series maps are available online from various sources.

I have tried to use abbreviations sparingly, especially those for military terms, because they may be confusing for some readers. When I do use abbreviations, the first occurrence follows the term in parentheses.

American unit designations are normally given in full, without abbreviation. Note that the traditional American Army ordinal designation of "d" rather than "nd" and "rd," as in 2d and 3d for second and third, are used throughout, although even during the war its use was inconsistent. The traditional American Army wartime spellings of "ponton" for pontoon, "indorsement" for endorsement, and "inclosure" for enclosure are also followed.

NOTES ON TERMINOLOGY

German unit designations are given in italics and follow the standard German military naming conventions of the time, followed in parenthesis by an English translation in the first occurrence, with any additional information given as a footnote as in: *I/Grenadier-Regiment 1050.* (1st Battalion, 1050th Infantry Regiment) of the *77. Infanterie-Division.* (77th Infantry Division). Note that a period in German unit designations serve the same purpose as English ordinals, such as "st," "th," and "nd."

The time of events are as given or as I have inferred from the original records. For clarity, all times are designated using the twenty-four-hour clock as "HHMM" unless I quote from an original report when the full military date-time entry is used. In that case for example "061240 July 1944" would be 1240 (12:40 P.M.) on 6 July 1944.

Last, unless otherwise indicated, all references to daily events involving units of the 90th Infantry Division and its superiors and subordinates during the campaign are taken directly from primary sources, including those units' After-Action Reports, Field Orders, Operational Reports, Journals, and Journal Files, and so are not otherwise referenced in endnotes. I also have not included a separate bibliography due to space considerations. It, along with a number of appendices that otherwise would have appeared in this book, including extended biographies of some of the officers of the 90th Infantry Division, are available on my website, andersonmilitaryhistory.com.

INTRODUCTION

In the winter of 1968–1969, my family was living in Darmstadt, Germany, where my Dad, a lieutenant colonel in the U.S. Army, was the Assistant G-2 (Intelligence Officer) of the Seventh U.S. Army's V Corps Artillery Headquarters. A veteran of World War II, like millions of other American soldiers Dad was discharged at the end of the war and returned to civilian life. However, unlike most others, after two years struggling to find meaningful work in postwar America, he applied for a Regular Army (RA) commission and was accepted. His tour of duty at Darmstadt was the end of a twenty-seven-year career as an Army officer, which took my family to Germany twice, as well as Japan, Oklahoma, Michigan, Kentucky, and numerous other places. . . . Mom and Dad lived in at least twenty-two different addresses in twenty-two years.

With just a few months left of his final tour, Dad decided it was a perfect opportunity for him to retrace the course of his route as a young 2d lieutenant across Europe during World War II, going from the end in Czechoslovakia in May 1945 to the beginning in France in June 1944. Darmstadt was conveniently close to one location of particular significance, Oppenheim, a small town on the Rhine River, which is where on the night of 22/23 March 1945 the Third U.S. Army—commonly known as "TUSA"—crossed that historic military barrier. Unfortunately, the end of his trail was in Pilsen, which in 1969 was part of Communist Czechoslovakia, so not accessible to us. Instead Dad drove us to the Saarland, where he and the TUSA were stalemated from October through December 1944. He planned then for us to visit the Normandy beaches when we left Germany to return to the States. We would leave in early July, just after the twenty-fifth anniversary of D-Day, take the train to Paris and then rent a car and tour Normandy, before heading to Le Havre and our ship home.

Unfortunately, or perhaps fortunately from my parents' point of view, that plan did not play out. When we arrived in Paris from Frankfurt, Mom and Dad looked up a friend, who was the French wife of a warrant officer who had served under Dad at the V Corps Artillery Headquarters. Her husband was on a one-year tour in Vietnam, and she decided to spend the year with their children at her parents' home in Paris. What derailed Dad's plans was her parents, who turned out to be wealthy, sophisticated Parisians, who insisted on showing Mom and Dad the city, wining and dining them at the Folies Bergère, the Lido Club, and at their country chateau, which they described as a "cottage." It had a wine cellar. I still fondly remember the fabulous multicourse meal we enjoyed at their favorite restaurant in Fontainebleau, where they had to call ahead to make sure the soufflé would be ready for our dessert. So instead of spending a day or two in Paris, we spent most of the week, and the trip to Normandy was placed on hold for another time. We returned to the States, where my parents began second careers as real estate agents in Northern Virginia.

I attended high school and then graduated from college in Virginia and moved out to live on my own. After they got me out of the house, Mom and Dad fully retired to the Sea Islands of South Carolina in 1977 and began to travel the world. They went to Yugoslavia, Russia, China, and did a cruise around the world, but somehow they never got back to France, which meant Dad's plan for retracing his steps in Normandy remained on hold. Then in 1995, Mom had to have major heart surgery and, in the aftermath, decided her traveling days were over. However, Dad still had that hankering, like so many veterans, of returning to Normandy. So in late 1999 he made me an extraordinary offer—he would pay for a weeklong trip to France and would include myself and my two older boys, Alex and Sebastian, who at that time were seventeen and fourteen, so long as I agreed to do the driving. Of course I said yes.

In late April 2000 I met my Dad at Dulles International Airport outside of D.C. in the countryside of Virginia. I flew ahead to London, while he met my two sons, who flew in from Chicago, where they lived with my ex-wife. We rendezvoused in London, where we did a day of touring, before taking the Eurostar train via the Chunnel to Paris. After a day in Paris, we rented a car and spent an extraordinary week traveling the same route my Dad followed from June through September 1944, ending at Château-Thierry. From there Dad and the boys flew home via Charles De Gaulle International Airport and I returned to London, where I spent a week working and musing about the book I might one day write about our travels.

However, I am not a quick writer, and just five years later, at a family Christmas in 2005, Mom and Dad told the family of Dad's deadly diagnosis. He had amyotrophic lateral sclerosis, "Lou Gehrig's disease," and had likely less than a year left to live. Sadly, I am an idiot and did not think to ask Dad to write down what he remembered of those years he could speak of with such clarity. . . . He always kept track of places and dates for us all. Ten months later it was too late. My dad died on 22 October 2006, just a few weeks shy of his eighty-fifth birthday. So I set the book idea aside and mourned his passing.

In 2024, after I finished my last book, *American Thunder*, I decided that if I was going to tell my dad's story, it was now or never. I ordered copies of the MR for his Battery A, 537th Antiaircraft Automatic Weapons Battalion, and for most of the other units of the 90th Infantry Division, which the 537th was attached to. I added those to the collection of operational reports I already had for the 90th, my collection of books written about the 90th Infantry Division, as well as various memoirs, including what I can remember of what Dad told me of his experiences. Sadly, only a few of the letters Dad wrote to Mom during the war survived, most of them written while he was still in the States. However, he meticulously kept copies of his personnel file documents as well as numerous souvenirs—matchbox covers, bills, tickets, identity cards, and so forth—that made it possible to track most of his movements and activities during the war. Finally, I had the notes that I wrote up in the evening on every day of our trip across France. Nevertheless, I still wish I had thought to quiz Dad on so many details, but I hope this retelling is enough.

CHAPTER 1

DAD AND THE WAR

In the spring of 1939 my Dad, Richard "Dick" Anderson, was a seventeen-year-old high school graduate from New Kensington, Pennsylvania. New Kensington was a small industrial town fifteen miles up the Alleghany River from Pittsburgh. Dad's father, Dudley "Dud" Hulings Anderson, worked as a manager for the Aluminum Company of America—Alcoa—and was a Republican city councilman in what was otherwise a staunchly Democratic town. Dad's mother, Margaret "Peg" Virginia Kendlehart Anderson, was a housewife.

Peg and Dud's families were solidly Pennsylvanian. Dud's maternal family, the Hulings, settled in Amity Township, near Pottstown in eastern Pennsylvania, sometime before 1713, and were French Huguenot in origin. During the eighteenth and nineteenth centuries they migrated west as Pennsylvania was settled to Lewistown in Mifflin County and northwest Pennsylvania in Venango County. Dud's maternal second cousin, Willis James Hulings, was commissioned a Colonel of Volunteers in the Spanish-American War, served briefly in Puerto Rico, and was a one-term U.S. representative, while an even more distant second cousin, Colonel Thomas Marcus Hulings, was killed in action on 10 May 1864 while leading the 49th Pennsylvania Volunteers in Upton's Assault on the Mule Shoe at Spottsylvania during the Civil War.

Dud's paternal side were slightly more recent immigrants to the United States: Dud's great-great-grandfather John H. Anderson was born in Glasgow and arrived in Pennsylvania as a teenage immigrant from Scotland just after the end of the Revolutionary War. He settled in Clarion County and the adjacent Armstrong County. John's grandson, Lott Miles Anderson, enlisted in the Union Army, Company E, 62d Pennsylvania Volunteers, on 25 July 1861. Lott was severely wounded in action—"shot through left shoulder"—at the Battle of Gaines' Mill on 27 June 1862 and was discharged for disability on 17 November 1862.[1]

Peg's paternal family were Pennsylvania "Dutch"—Germans from Göttingen in Lower Saxony—Johann Ludwig Kantelhardt and Dorothea Elisabeth Flentgen. They emigrated to Baltimore in 1804, where their names were Anglicized to John Lewis and Dorothy Elizabeth Kendlehart. John Lewis was a shoemaker by profession and sometime between 1806 and 1810 moved to the town of Gettysburg, where he opened a shoe store. Peg's grandfather, David—his full name was actually Johann David, but he never used Johann, and most people did not realize it was his first name—was born in Gettysburg in 1813. He too was a shoemaker by trade, apprenticing with his father.[2]

By the 1860s, David was a prominent citizen in Gettysburg, with a boot and shoe store at the family home at 110 Baltimore Street. He was a director of the Gettysburg National Bank, and in the spring of 1863 he became president of the city council, shortly before the Confederate Army arrived in town on the afternoon of 26 June 1863.

On that day, Confederate General Jubal Early tied his horse to a wooden pump on Baltimore Street and issued a demand to "the borough authorities for 60 barrels of flour, 7,000 pounds of pork or bacon, 1,200 pounds of sugar, 600 pounds of coffee, 1,000 pounds of salt, 40 bushels of onions, 1,000 pairs of shoes, 500 hats, or $5,000 in money," a sum that was impossible for the small town of two-thousand-odd persons to fulfill. Because the mayor had fled town on news of the rebels' arrival, responsibility for a reply to Early fell on David. With some courage and probably considerably more trepidation, he approached the rebel commander with a reply.

> *GETTYSBURG, JUNE 26, 1863*
> *Gen. Erley [sic],*
> *Sir: The authorities of the borough of Gettysburg, in answer to the demand made upon the same borough and county by you, say their authority extends but to the borough; that the requisition asked for can not be given, because it is utterly impossible to comply. The quantities required are far beyond that in our possession. In compliance, however, to the demand, we will request the stores to be opened and the citizens to furnish whatever they can of such provisions, etc., as may be asked. Further we can not promise. By authority of the council of the borough of Gettysburg, I hereunto, as president of said board, attach my name.*
>
> *D. Kendlehart*[3]

Early did not press the matter and next day he and his division left and marched on to York. Three days later, on 30 June, Union troops from Brigadier General John Buford's 1st Cavalry Division of the Army of the Potomac marched into Gettysburg. Many of the town's boys, including David's sons, thirteen-year-old John Lewis and nine-year-old James William—Peg's father—helped water and feed the troopers horses. On the morning of 1 July, as the battle developed north and west of town, John Lawrence Burns, a sixty-nine-year-old veteran of the War of 1812 and part-time cobbler at David's boot and shoe store, shouldered his musket and marched off to join the Union Army in battle. Burns was slightly wounded but managed to return home and was later lauded by the Union press for his bravery. Burns later met Abraham Lincoln when the president came to Gettysburg for the dedication of the Soldier's National Cemetery, where Lincoln delivered his "Gettysburg Address."[4]

Later that morning of 1 July, David's twenty-one-year-old daughter, Mary Cecilia, joined a group of friends on the corner of Washington Street and High Street passing refreshments to the soldiers of the Union Eleventh Corps as it marched through town, serenading them with the song "Our Union Forever."[5]

When the Confederate Army occupied Gettysburg on the evening of 1 July, David feared the rebels might take him hostage and so he fled, leaving his wife and five children to flee to McAllister's Mill southeast of town. He first made his way to Christ Lutheran Church and later the McAllister house on Chambersburg Road. After four harrowing days, early on 5 July, David's eldest son, John Lewis, and a family friend, George Arnold, managed to find him in town. The three men discovered the Confederates had surreptitiously withdrawn under cover of a ferocious thunderstorm during the previous night. They cautiously made their way into the Union lines, where they were taken to the headquarters of the commander of the Union Army of the Potomac, Major General George Gordon Meade, bringing him the first conformation the Confederates had retreated.[6]

Except for Lott Anderson and Thomas Hulings, Dad's family had little military experience. Dud was drafted into the Army in World War I, but not until summer 1918. He was mustered into the Field Artillery on 23 August and went to Camp Breckenridge, Kentucky, for training. However, the "Great War" ended with the Armistice of 11 November 1918 and Dud was discharged a month later on 10 December, without ever leaving the States.

Despite that distinct lack of familial martial history, Dad applied to and was accepted by the Virginia Agricultural and Mechanical College and Polytechnic Institute at Blacksburg, which was better known as Virginia Polytechnic Institute or "VPI" and is now known as Virginia Tech. Dad's family was solidly middle class but like most Americans had felt the effects of the Great Depression of 1929 and the Great Recession of 1937. Dad entering VPI was a significant savings for the Anderson family. Freshmen at VPI were members of the Corps of Cadets with a mandatory two-year commitment to the ROTC program, which covered much of their tuition.[7]

For the class of 1940 in the fall of 1939, the VPI Corps of Cadets was organized as a regiment of five battalions. The 1st Battalion consisted of Company A, B, and C, which were organized as Infantry. The 2d Battalion, Company E, F, and G, were organized as Engineers. The 3d Battalion, Battery I, K, and L, were organized as Coast Artillery, as were the 4th Battalion's, Battery M, N, and O, and the 5th Battalion's, Battery R, S, and T. The 4th and 5th Battalion staffs and Battery R, S, and T were newly organized for the class of 1940, which was an indication of the expansion of the military in the United States after nearly twenty years of decreasing military spending and stagnant personnel strength.

Like other ROTC programs, the Corps of Cadets was affiliated with units of the Army's Organized Reserve. VPI was a primary feeder school for the Reserve's 317th and 318th Infantry Regiment, the 305th Engineer Regiment of the 80th Division, and the nondivisional 343d Engineer Regiment (General Service, GS), 375th Engineer Regiment (GS), and the 622d Coast Artillery Regiment (Harbor Defense).[8]

Dad was assigned to Battery K of the 3d Battalion as a cadet private; he held that rank quite simply because all freshman cadets were privates. He became one of 1,850 members of the Corps of Cadets, just as the world was going to war. Like most freshman entering VPI's Corps of Cadets, Dad arrived on campus about a week before the school year started for his initial cadet orientation and training. Cadets were issued uniforms, then taught rudimentary drill including how to "brace," which was a highly exaggerated position of attention with the chin forced back, wrinkling the skin of the neck. It was their first introduction to the disciplined life of a VPI Cadet.

It was during this time, when Dad transitioned from civilian to cadet life, that Nazi Germany invaded Poland on 1 September 1939. The United Kingdom and France declared war on Germany two days later. Within a few weeks the Germans triumphed, conquering Poland, and then dividing the territory with their new ally, the Soviet Union, while the still mobilizing British and French looked helplessly on.

Despite those momentous events, life at VPI remained little changed. On 23 September, the VPI "Gobblers" beat Randolph Macon College 26–0 in the first game of the college football season, but then they lost two games straight, as well as the final game against arch rival VMI. VPI ended the season 4-5-1.[9]

In the spring of 1940, the VPI freshman left their "Rat" year to spend five weeks at ROTC summer camps as rising upperclassmen. Dad went to Fort Monroe, Virginia, which was the Headquarters of the Coast Artillery. There the VPI cadets practiced on a multitude of Army weapons, from the .45 Caliber M1911 Pistol to the massive 12-inch M1895 Coast Artillery Gun. It was during this time that Europe slipped deeper into war and a crisis developed in the Pacific. The United States also tried to exert diplomatic pressure to stem Japanese aggression against China.[10]

In April, Germany seized Denmark and Norway. Then, in May, they invaded the Netherlands, Belgium, Luxembourg, and France, forcing the British to evacuate the remains of their army from the beaches of Dunkirk. France capitulated in June, accepting a humiliating armistice that left the northern two-thirds of the country under German occupation. Britain managed to hang on to the end of the year, fighting the German Luftwaffe (Air Force) to a standstill in the Battle of Britain while relying on the Royal Navy to protect them from a German cross-Channel invasion. In the Far East Japan entered its fourth year of war with China, ignoring American attempts at diplomacy. In retaliation the United States embargoed the export of machine tools to Japan in June.

The course of Dad's sophomore year that began in September 1940 was little different from his freshman year, although as a sophomore he was automatically promoted to cadet private first class. Football and classes dominated the fall and winter of 1940. VPI improved its record slightly to 5–5 but again lost its final game to VMI, this time 0–14. Classroom study was followed again by ROTC summer camp and then a few weeks of leave at home. At the same time the world war continued to expand. On 22 June 1941, the Germans invaded the Soviet Union and swiftly seized the Soviet Baltic States and much of European Russia in what appeared to be an unstoppable onslaught. In the Far East on 25 July, Japan occupied French Cochinchina, what is now the southern half of Vietnam. In retaliation President Roosevelt immediately ordered the freezing of Japanese assets in the United States, which led the Japanese warlords to decide on an attack on American, British, and Dutch possessions in the Pacific.

When Dad began his junior year as a cadet corporal in the fall of 1941, the United States and Japan were on a collision course to war. VPI ended with a winning 6–4 football season but lost yet again to VMI. When VPI won its final game 13–0 against Richmond University at Miles Stadium in Blacksburg on 29 November, the

VPI Cadet Richard C. Anderson. Dad's first cadet photo was processed by Roanoke, Virginia Photo Finishing on 10 May 1940, the same day that Nazi Germany invaded the Netherlands, Belgium, Luxembourg, and France.

Japanese fleet was en route across the north Pacific to attack the American fleet at anchor at Pearl Harbor.

The Japanese attack on Pearl Harbor on 7 December 1941 was followed the next day by the American declaration of war. Hitler in turn declared war on the United States on 11 December. Dad's quiet campus routine was quickly upended as the nation mobilized. The leisurely five weeks of ROTC summer camp, followed by five weeks of summer vacation, were replaced by more intensive study in the classroom and field. The War Department directed that instead of June 1943, Dad's class would graduate three months early in March 1943. The 1943 football season was canceled, and Dad began his senior year as a cadet sergeant, on 23 June 1942. In the seven months since the Japanese attack, American forces suffered defeat after

VPI Cadet Richard C. Anderson, fall 1941.

defeat in the Pacific. Garrisons in the Philippines, Wake, and Guam were defeated and marched into captivity, while America's ally Britain lost its Pacific stronghold of Singapore. In Europe, Britain seemed on the verge of defeat in North Africa and the Soviet Union appeared to be collapsing by the summer of 1942.

Allied fortunes improved remarkably by the time Dad graduated on 19 March 1943. The Battle of Midway in the Pacific in June 1942 ended the string of Japanese victories, while the British in North Africa defeated Erwin Rommel's German-Italian army at El Alamein in October 1942. Then, on 7 November 1942, the U.S. Army entered the ground war against Germany when an Anglo-American force landed in French Morocco and Algeria. However, Continental Europe was still dominated by the Nazis and the campaign to push back the Japanese had barely begun. The Army was still expanding rapidly, inducting and training officers and men as rapidly as possible.

After graduation, Dad was granted ten days' leave at home before reporting for Officer Candidate Training at Camp Davis, North Carolina. Some of the time he spent getting to know Dorothy Ann "Dottie" Gibbs, who was the sister of his brother's wife. Dad's older brother Bill had married Betty Jane Gibbs, his high school sweetheart, the previous November. Betty Jane's younger sister Dottie was also the best friend of Bill and Dad's younger sister Helen. Dottie Gibbs was tiny, barely five feet tall, but vivacious and the swingiest jitterbug dancer at New Kensington High. She was also a year and a half younger than Dad but quickly captured his interest. During Dad's short leave she recalled many years later that she "let him drive her home one night after a dance," but for a time she remained his little sister's best friend.

Dad reported to the Antiaircraft Artillery Officer Candidate Division of the Antiaircraft Artillery School at Camp Davis on 1 April and after orientation his training began on 5 April. Training continued until 12 August 1943, when he was commissioned as a 2d Lieutenant, Coast Artillery Corps (Antiaircraft Artillery). Far from being "90 Day Wonders," the young officers commissioned into the Coast Artillery had 129 days' service as enlisted OCS candidates, and many also had ROTC experience in college, although few had gone through cadet military training like Dad. Then as now, VPI was one of a small number of senior military colleges in the United States, besides West Point, which trained college students to become officers. By war's end, VPI contributed 7,285 alumni to the uniformed services. The Army and Army Air Corps received 5,941 men, the Navy 1,059 men, the Marines 110, the Merchant Marines 29, the Coast Guard 23, and one "Techman" even served in the Royal Air Force. VPI graduates included ten brigadier generals, five major generals, and a rear admiral. Three hundred and twenty-three alumni died in the war, 4.5 percent of those who served. Three received the Medal of Honor, seven the Distinguished Service Cross, two the Navy Cross, at least seventy-three the Silver Star, and ninety-four the Distinguished Flying Cross, while an uncounted number received the Bronze Star, including Dad.[11]

Sometime during those 129 days, Dottie Gibbs and Helen Anderson decided to take the train from Pittsburgh to Jacksonville, North Carolina, to visit Betty Jane and Bill. Betty Jane was working at the USO there while Bill was now a Marine stationed at nearby Camp Lejeune. Helen later said, "we went there because we wanted to buck up the troops!" Apparently it worked, because by the time Dottie and Helen returned to Pittsburgh, Dick Anderson and Dottie Gibbs were engaged.

After graduation on 12 August, Dad was granted another ten days of leave. The highlight was five days later when he and Dottie were married at the Parnassus (now Logans Ferry) Presbyterian Church in New Kensington, by Reverend J. Clarence Pinkerton, D.D. The bride wore a blue velvet dress, while the groom was in uniform.

Engagement photo, Dottie and Dick Anderson, 27 August 1943.

The reception was at the bride's home in Valley Heights. From then on, they were Dick and Dottie Anderson.[12]

Their honeymoon was a single night at the William Penn Hotel in downtown Pittsburgh, after which they took the train to Camp Davis, where Dad was assigned to Battery C, 115th Antiaircraft Artillery (AAA) Gun Battalion, Mobile, on 23 August. Mom found a room in a boardinghouse, first in Wilmington and then closer to Camp Davis on Wrightsville Beach.[13]

The 115th AAA Gun Battalion had been activated at Camp Davis on 20 March 1943 and began organizing on 4 April, just as Dad was beginning his Officer Candidate Course. When he reported for duty Battery C already had six months of basic and advanced training. Dad had a lot of catching up to do in his position as a Battery Officer, a title that basically meant he did anything and everything his Platoon Leader and Battery Commander told him to do.

There was not much time for Dad to settle in at Camp Davis or for Mom to make a home at Wrightsville Beach. On 17 September, Dad and the 115th left Camp Davis for Camp Pickett, Virginia. Mom settled into another rooming house in Kenbridge, about 14 miles away. The Battalion began amphibious training and learned the intricacies of the highly advanced and top-secret SCR 584 gun-laying radar. The battalion then moved temporarily to Camp Bradford, near the Norfolk Navy Base, on 29 September for amphibious maneuvers.[14]

Training was tough in the hot and humid fall of the Virginia Tidewater. On 27 September Dad got a dressing-down from his commanding officer after he led his battery on an 8-mile-long speed march in just one hour and fifty minutes. While the temperature was just 75 degrees, the humidity had been high. The march began with 137 men and ended with just 40, including Dad, who had four blisters on one foot and two on the other. The captain commanding Battery C, who did not take part in the march, gave Dad "hell" afterward because so many men had dropped out. However, as Dad observed in a letter to Mom, "It was supposed to be a speed march and I was determined to do it in the required time or bust. We bust."

On 20 October, the 115th crossed the James River Bridge and then the York River at Yorktown on their way to New Port Comfort, east of Gloucester, on Virginia's Middle Peninsula, where they practiced with the SCR 584. By 25 October, they were back at Camp Pickett, where they were given orders for another and more permanent move, to Fort Dix where they would prepare for overseas movement (POM).

On 2 November, the 115th left by train for Fort Dix. Mom followed and set up house with two other officers' wives in a rented home in Bordentown, New Jersey, about 12 miles from Fort Dix. Fort Dix at this time was designated a Reprocessing Center, where a unit in POM turned in all its heavy equipment: artillery guns, machine guns, vehicles, and the like because new equipment would be issued from depots in Britain when they arrived. Units then drew new uniforms and personal equipment, packed and crated the minimum unit equipment allowance, and then ensured all billets in the unit Table of Organization (T/O) were filled by qualified personnel because a unit was required to be 100 percent of T/O strength when they were loaded aboard ship. On 25 November, Thanksgiving Day, the 115th AAA Battalion marched to the Fort Dix railroad station for its 110-mile trip to Camp Shanks, New York, which was the Port of Embarkation (POE) where they would load aboard ship for the journey to Europe. However, Dad was not with them.

Dad had run afoul of the last requirement for a unit POM. With just three months of experience as an officer in the 115th AAA Battalion, he was considered

Dottie and Dick Anderson in a photo booth, probably fall 1943.

too green to go overseas. Instead he was relieved from assignment to the 115th on 24 November and temporarily assigned to the 4th Headquarters and Headquarters Detachment, Special Troops, XIII Corps, at Fort Du Pont, Delaware. Unfortunately, Mom had already left for New Kensington under the assumption Dad was shipping out to Europe, so their first Thanksgiving was spent apart.

On 29 November, Dad was reassigned to a different unit, the 537th AAA Automatic Weapons (AW), Battalion, Mobile, commanded by Lieutenant Colonel Beo Wallace Recer, an Organized Reserve (OR) officer from Texas. The 537th was activated 15 July 1942 in the Army of the United States (AUS) at Camp Hulen, Texas. Once organized and with basic training completed, the 537th moved to Camp Atterbury, Indiana, in April 1943, before heading to Fort Jackson, South Carolina, on 3 May 1943 for unit maneuvers. From there they moved to Nashville and the Tennessee Maneuver Area on 13 July 1943 for corps maneuvers. The 537th returned to Camp Atterbury in August, then left permanently on 1 September 1943, heading for Camp Pickett, where it began the same amphibious training course the 115th went through. Upon completing that course, the battalion moved to Camp Davis, then left for Fort Dix at 1300 1 November, arriving at 0515 2 November, where it was attached to the 124th AA Group. However, even though it was an older and more experienced unit, it was not scheduled to POM until February 1944. As a result, Dad got an extra three months of experience before leaving the United States. He would need it, considering his three months of experience as an officer were with 115th Battalion's massive 90mm guns rather than the very different guns equipping the 537th Battalion.[15]

As an Automatic Weapons Battalion the 537th was supposed to be armed with thirty-two 40mm AA Guns M1 and thirty-two trailer-mounted Cal. .50 Machine-Gun Mounts M51—also known as the "Multiple Cal. 50 Machine-Gun Mount, M45, on Trailer Mount M17." However, production of the Trailer Mount M51 had just begun in August 1943 and only 2,195 were manufactured by the end of the year, which was not even close to the 7,680 needed for the 240-odd Automatic Weapons battalions authorized by then. Many of those produced were immediately shipped overseas, except for those used for training. Thus, in 1942 the War Department decreed that units in training would have to make do with a 50 percent allowance of basic equipment.[16]

Just before Christmas on 15 December, Dad and the 537th were sent off to a firing range at Wellfleet on Cape Cod, which duty was supposed to extend to 29 December. Mom and Dad would spend their first Christmas as a married couple apart, so they decided she would take the train home to New Kensington as she had done for Thanksgiving. However, when Dad and Battery A got to Massachusetts, they found December conditions on Cape Cod were unsurprisingly less than ideal. When they arrived on 16 December and settled into tent quarters, the high temperature was just 24 degrees and the low was 10 degrees. It warmed up for the first day of firing on 17 December to all of 33 degrees, but then the exercise was

Lieutenant Colonel Beo W. Recer in Germany after VE Day.

cut short as a thunderstorm blew into the area, so only a few trial shots with the 40mm guns were fired. Temperatures plummeted to 7 degrees that night. Dad remembered thinking it was the coldest he had been in his life and continued to think so until he encountered even more intense cold at the Battle of the Bulge in January 1945.

From 18 through 22 December, the weather was barely tolerable with daytime highs in the low 40s, but the nighttime temperatures were well below freezing. On 18 December they fired trial shots with the 40mm guns again and then from 19 through 22 December they were finally able to fire full programs against target sleeves with both the 40mm and .50 caliber mounts.

However, on the evening of 22 December they were ordered to cancel the rest of the planned program. A nor'easter was roaring in with temperatures expected to average from 8 to 30 degrees for the next four days and near-zero visibility from intermittent rain and snow showers. Those conditions were anticipated to last through at least 28 December. On the morning of 23 December, they fled Cape Cod and headed back to Fort Dix. Dad got back to the rental house in Bordentown late that evening, but their room was dark. Mom was not there. Because they had not expected him to be back in time for Christmas, Mom had taken the train to New

Kensington days earlier just as they had planned. There she spent the holidays with Dad's family—her mom and dad had moved to Phoenix, Arizona, earlier that year.

The Army and fickle weather meant the first Christmas of Mom and Dad's marriage was spent apart, but it would not be the last time. While Mom had Christmas at home, Dad spent Christmas in High Bridge, New Jersey, with his Aunt Helen Grant Kendlehart and her husband Paul C. Carling.

Mom and Dad did not get together again in Bordentown until after the new year. No sooner were they reunited than they found out the 537th was ordered to POM. Dad was granted a three-day preembarkation furlough on 6 January and planned to take Mom to visit with family in New Kensington, but their bad luck continued. They got on the Pennsylvania Turnpike in the used Ford sedan Dad had bought for $250, which was nearly two months' pay for a 2d lieutenant, only to have it break down after just 50 miles on the road. Stuck in the middle of nowhere, they finally managed to get the car towed back to the used car lot, which of course was closed. Luckily, the tow truck driver agreed to drop them off at their rented house in Bordentown. A few days later, when the used car outfit called to ask what they should do with the car, Dad told them to just keep it because he was soon on his way overseas. It was the last Ford Dad ever owned.

At the end of January, the 537th was alerted for movement from Fort Dix to Camp Kilmer, New Jersey, which was the POE. They would soon be on their way to England. Mom left Bordentown by train for New Kensington, where she would stay with Peg and Dud. She did not know it, but when she left Bordentown, she was pregnant with their first child, my older sister Connie.

On 3 February, Battery A moved to Camp Kilmer in final preparation for boarding a troopship bound for Britain. However, Dad and the other officers of the 537th still had opportunities to spend a few hours in nearby New York City. About this time Dad joined his boss, the 1st Platoon Leader, 1st Lieutenant Jack Wesley Lindell, and a battalion medical officer, at the "World Famous Ubangi Club." The Ubangi Club was at 1678 Broadway in midtown Manhattan. It had gained fame in Harlem during the 1930s as the venue for its gender-bending headliner, African American vocalist and pianist Gladys Bentley, who performed suggestive lyrics while dressed in a cream-colored tuxedo and top hat. However, the club moved downtown in 1937 after the city banned cross-dressing acts and became a more conventional jazz club. The Ubangi Club, and many other similar clubs, closed later in 1944, after the Federal Revenue Act of 1943 increased the "Cabaret Tax" on live music performances from 5 to 30 percent on 1 April. Although after considerable protest

Dad at the Ubangi Club, New York City, early February 1944. Left to right, the Battalion Surgeon Captain Noah Gray, Dad, and 1st Lieutenant Jack W. Lindell.

Congress decreased the tax to 20 percent it has still been credited as one of the reasons the live Big Band Swing era ended in the United States.[17]

The last weeks of February were spent turning in heavy equipment and packing personnel gear in final preparation for embarkation. On 28 February the 537th climbed up the gangways to the Steamship *NY 225*, which was code for the British ocean liner *Queen Mary*. The *Queen Mary*, like her near sister ship, the *Queen Elizabeth*, had been fitted out in 1940 as a fast troop transport. The 801 officers, warrant officers, and men of the 537th were joined aboard by another 11,149 soldiers from other units and the great liner's 1,190 crewmen. It took most of the next day, 29 February, to get everyone aboard. Dad remembered that it was stifling belowdecks and the stench of unwashed men (showers were not allowed to conserve water), many of whom were seasick, and overtaxed toilets made it almost unbearable. Luckily, though, the gun crews of the 537th were allowed to rotate topside to help man the antiaircraft guns mounted on the ship, which was a pleasant relief.

The *Queen Mary* left New York Harbor on 1 March 1944 without escort as the sole ship of Convoy AT 97 and headed into the Atlantic, making an average speed of 26.51 knots per hour. Her speed was the reason she had no escort; she was so fast that it was calculated it was extremely unlikely a German U-boat could ever get

Queen Mary as a troopship in New York Harbor at the end of the war, 20 June 1945. U.S. Coast Guard photo.

into position to fire a torpedo at her, let alone hit her. Five days, twelve hours, and twelve minutes later she put into Gourock, Scotland, after covering 3,504 miles.[18]

Battery A debarked at 1135 on 8 March. Once processed the battalion entrained for Okehampton, almost 500 miles to the south in Devonshire, where they arrived at 1115 on 9 March. Battery A, with the rest of the battalion, settled into a tented camp at the Okehampton Showground, a mile west of town in the English countryside.

Few of the American soldiers had ever been overseas in their lives. Certainly Dad had not been. All officers and men suffered a certain culture shock; the British spoke English, but it was not "American" English. The scarce food available when they visited the local pubs was unpalatable to most Americans, and they thought the cask-aged British ales and beer were served "warm," but they eventually got used to it. The hardest part was the lack of communication with family in the States. There was no overseas telephone access for them, while access to radiograms and cable telegrams was extremely limited and heavily censored. That left the mail and Victory Mail or "V-mail." V-mail was written on a special form as a single-sided letter, then was microfilmed and sent by air to the States, where they were blown up again to letter size, copied, and sent to the recipient. Writing letters and V-mails was a huge outlet for soldiers overseas but were also required reading for officers appointed as unit censors, which was a role Dad had to undertake on occasion.

Every officer and enlisted man was issued a four-page War Department pamphlet titled "When You Are Overseas" as guidance for what was permitted. There were ten subjects that were prohibited, but the chief worry for many was that they might write about sensitive personal subjects that the unit censor would become aware of. For them, the Army thoughtfully provided the use of a "blue envelope,"

"In the main mess hall (formerly the First Class dining saloon) where more than 2,000 troops can be fed at one sitting. In peacetime it used to take 800 First Class passengers but now sittings go on from 6 a.m. till 9 p.m. The wall map at the end used to be illuminated to show diners the course and position of the ship." Photo from the 28 September 1944 sailing of the *Queen Mary* from Greenock, Scotland, to New York carrying wounded American personnel. IWM.

which a soldier could request so that their letter bypassed the unit censor and instead went directly to an anonymous censor at a central Base Post Office.

Even before leaving the States the 537th was assigned to TUSA and was attached to the 113th AAA Group of the VIII Corps. However, many TUSA units, including the 537th AAA, were attached to the First U.S. Army—commonly known as "FUSA"—for Operation NEPTUNE, the assault on Hitler's Fortress Europe. FUSA placed them under the command of the 11th AAA Group of the VII Corps, which in turn attached them to the 90th Infantry Division, which began

"First Class cabin, once with only one bed, now has 12 bunks in it. Occupants are US Army Air Corps heavy bomber crews, who are gathered round a map on the deck discussing their various missions while in the European Theatre of War. They are (on the deck): Sergeants R T Riskey of Florida; M E Medway of New York; J S Fetrow of Philadelphia; C R Vankirk of New Jersey; G M Craig of Philadelphia; J P Jordan of Philadelphia; and F E Eubik of Philadelphia. On the bunks are: Sergeants W R Tasker of New Jersey; B Davey of New Jersey; D S Collins of New Jersey; and M Sim of Philadelphia." Photo from the 28 September 1944 sailing of the *Queen Mary*. IWM.

an association that would continue, with only a few short interruptions, until the end of the war.

The 90th Infantry Division attached each of the 537th's batteries individually to one of its four Field Artillery battalions. Dad's Battery A was attached to the 343d Field Artillery Battalion (105mm Howitzer), Battery B to the 344th Field Artillery Battalion (105mm Howitzer), Battery C to the 345th Field Artillery Battalion (155mm Howitzer), and Battery D to the 915th Field Artillery Battalion (105mm Howitzer). However, at this point the attachment was entirely theoretical because the artillery battalions were about 28 miles away at Davenport House in Shropshire.

At Okehampton the 537th AAA drew vehicles and heavy weapons from the many depots in the surrounding countryside. On 17 March, Dad was ordered by the

"U.S. gunners manning a twin Bofors during gun drill." Photo from the 28 September 1944 sailing of the *Queen Mary.* IWM.

Battery A commander, Captain Alfred L. Lea, to lead a detachment of ten enlisted men on temporary duty to General Depot G-25 at Ashchurch, 145 miles to the north in Gloucestershire. At the depot they were issued four new half-track vehicles, were hastily trained in their operation and maintenance, and then drove them back to Okehampton on 20 March.

The new vehicle was required because of a decision made by the planning staffs for Operation NEPTUNE, the amphibious invasion of Hitler's Fortress Europe. One invasion requirement was to keep the number of wheeled vehicles in the assault and follow-on combat formations to a minimum. In other landings in North Africa and Italy it was found that wheeled vehicles got stuck too easily in the sand and clay of the beaches, which created havoc and required too much effort to extract them in the critical early hours of an invasion. Thus, the British and American planners substituted full-track and half-track vehicles for wheeled vehicles in organizations whenever possible.

However, only the nine Self-Propelled AAA AW battalions then in England were equipped with half-track vehicles, while there were twenty-six Mobile AW battalions, like the 537th, which used 6x6 2.5-ton trucks to tow their 40mm guns and trailer mounts. A solution was found through the initiative of two FUSA staff officers, Antiaircraft Officer, Colonel Charles G. Patterson and Ordnance Officer, Colonel John B. Medaris. They had Ordnance troops fit 332 M51 mounts on surplus

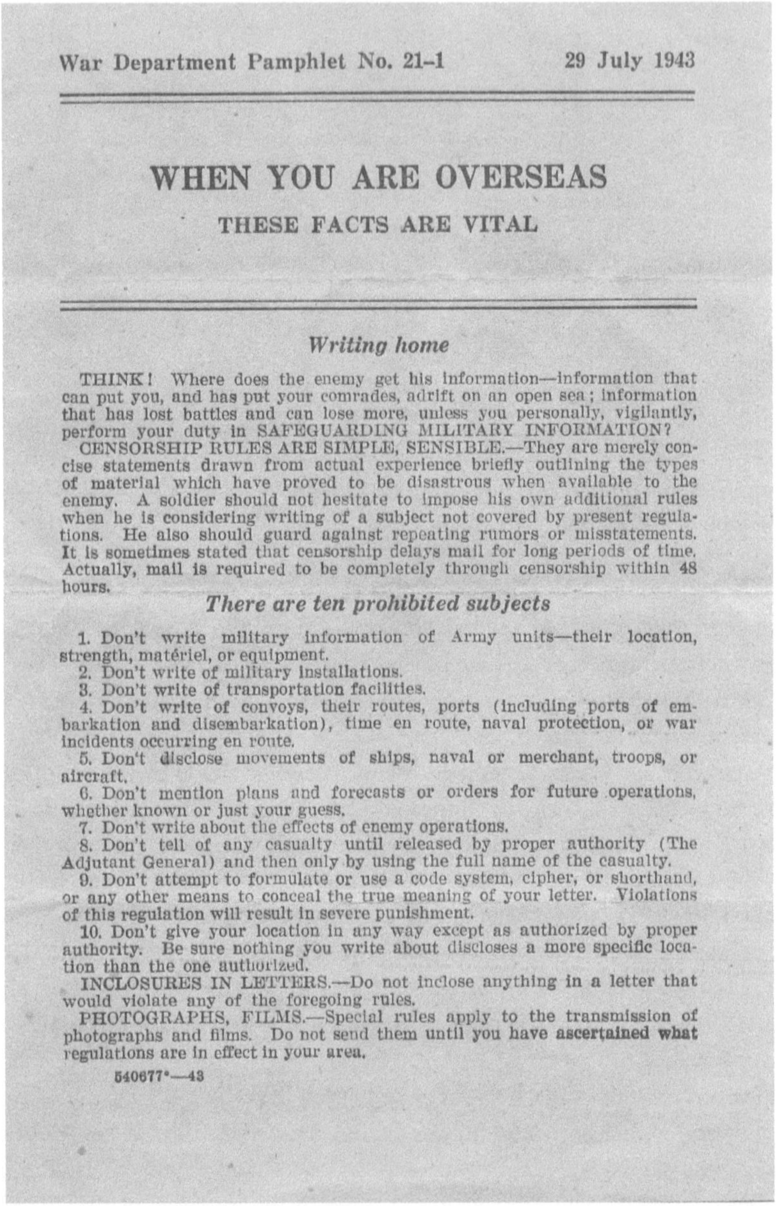

War Department Pamphlet No. 21-1 29 July 1943

WHEN YOU ARE OVERSEAS

THESE FACTS ARE VITAL

Writing home

THINK! Where does the enemy get his information—information that can put you, and has put your comrades, adrift on an open sea; information that has lost battles and can lose more, unless you personally, vigilantly, perform your duty in SAFEGUARDING MILITARY INFORMATION?

CENSORSHIP RULES ARE SIMPLE, SENSIBLE.—They are merely concise statements drawn from actual experience briefly outlining the types of material which have proved to be disastrous when available to the enemy. A soldier should not hesitate to impose his own additional rules when he is considering writing of a subject not covered by present regulations. He also should guard against repeating rumors or misstatements. It is sometimes stated that censorship delays mail for long periods of time. Actually, mail is required to be completely through censorship within 48 hours.

There are ten prohibited subjects

1. Don't write military information of Army units—their location, strength, matériel, or equipment.
2. Don't write of military installations.
3. Don't write of transportation facilities.
4. Don't write of convoys, their routes, ports (including ports of embarkation and disembarkation), time en route, naval protection, or war incidents occurring en route.
5. Don't disclose movements of ships, naval or merchant, troops, or aircraft.
6. Don't mention plans and forecasts or orders for future operations, whether known or just your guess.
7. Don't write about the effects of enemy operations.
8. Don't tell of any casualty until released by proper authority (The Adjutant General) and then only by using the full name of the casualty.
9. Don't attempt to formulate or use a code system, cipher, or shorthand, or any other means to conceal the true meaning of your letter. Violations of this regulation will result in severe punishment.
10. Don't give your location in any way except as authorized by proper authority. Be sure nothing you write about discloses a more specific location than the one authorized.

INCLOSURES IN LETTERS.—Do not inclose anything in a letter that would violate any of the foregoing rules.

PHOTOGRAPHS, FILMS.—Special rules apply to the transmission of photographs and films. Do not send them until you have **ascertained what** regulations are in effect in your area.

540677°—43

Crucial information for a soldier overseas. The War Department's four-page instruction pamphlet on important things to know when serving overseas.

2d Lieutenant Anderson in England. Range practice with the .45 Caliber Pistol M1911. He is being shown the finer points of the classic offhand firing stance.

M2 Half-Track Personnel Carriers, which were then designated the Multiple Gun Motor Carriage (MGMC) M16B. Sixteen each were issued to twenty of the mobile AAA AW battalions in Britain (twelve were kept as spares). The 537th assigned four to each of the battalion's four batteries. In Battery A, each of the two platoons received two of the vehicles that Dad's detachment had driven to Okehampton. Jack Lindell assigned Dad to supervise the two in the 1st Platoon, which were each organized as a provisional Machine Gun Squad.[19]

Dad was fascinated by the new weapon. The four machine guns on the mount could be selectively fired, the gunner choosing to fire the upper or lower pair separately or all four simultaneously. That enabled the gun crew to reload, clear stoppages, or let the barrel cool while maintaining sustained fire. While the cyclic rate of fire of the .50 Caliber M2 machine gun was 450 to 575 rounds per minute, normally it was only fired in short bursts to prevent overheating. As many as 100 to 150 rounds could be fired in a single burst from a cool gun, giving the well-trained MGMC gunner the ability to fire up to 600 continuous rounds in as little as a minute by rotating the firing of the guns. Otherwise, the M16Bs rate of fire was only limited by the time it took to change the heavy and bulky 200-round drums that fed the machine guns.[20]

Dad left on temporary duty on 2 April for further training in aircraft recognition. On 18 April he graduated from the VII Corps Aircraft Recognition School "some where [*sic*] in England," which likely meant Weston Super Mare in Somerset, the location of the 11th AAA Group's headquarters. The end of the course also apparently entitled him to a forty-eight-hour pass; he later recalled visiting London about this time. He probably arrived the night of 18/19 April, during one of the last raids of the "Little Blitz," which was a German night-bombing campaign during the late winter and spring of 1944. He remembered that getting around in the blacked-out city streets at night was the hardest part of his visit, but he still enjoyed himself and even recalled having a decent dinner at a restaurant.[21]

On 17 April, the 537th moved again, making a sustained motor-march of 195 miles north to Birmingham in Warwickshire, where they settled in by the end of the month. They remained there until the battalion embarked for the landing in France. When Dad returned from his leave in London on 20 April, he was billeted at Mr. and Mrs. A. Caldwell's Hydro Private Hotel at 37 & 39 School Road, Hall Green, Birmingham 29.[22]

The next move by the 537th AAA was to Burley Manor, Hampshire, on 22 May.[23] On 11 June, five days after D-Day, they moved to Marshaling Area D, Section 14 at Charlestown, just outside of Weymouth. Marshaling Area D, Section 14, was a Marshalling Camp—one of the "Sausage Camps," so called because of their shape on planning maps. The Sausage Camps were the reception areas for units preparing to land in France. The 537th AAA spent its few days in the camp waterproofing vehicles and equipment. The men were also issued new uniforms for the invasion, which were impregnated with a chemical intended to make the cloth impervious to poison gas. It also stank and kept the cloth from wicking moisture away from the soldiers' bodies, so it quickly turned them into a sweating, smelly mess. On 12 June, they drove to the hardstands, which were concrete ramps constructed on the beaches around Plymouth, and began loading. The four lettered batteries embarked first, one each to a Landing Ship Tank (LST) for the slow voyage across the Channel. The Battalion Headquarters Battery loaded and landed later, arriving on 17 June.

An M16B from an unknown AAA battalion, probably spring 1945, possibly the Moselle or Rhine River. The M16B was distinctive because it did not have the folding flaps on the armored sides of the vehicle, and it stood up higher on its platform in the bed of the half-track. U.S. Army Signal Corps (SC).

The convoy left Plymouth early on 13 June and took about sixteen hours to get to UTAH Beach. For the officers and men of the 537th it was a miserable passage as the tension of heading into combat, the wallowing of the flat-bottomed LST, and the stench of their impregnated clothing combined in making many of them violently seasick. They arrived about 4,000 yards offshore in the late morning, probably around 1230 on 14 June. About four and a half hours later they were directed to close the beach and began unloading around 2130. Sporadic German artillery fire, probably observed from Mont Castré (Hill 122), which they would come to know too well, was hitting the beach as they drove down the ramp of the LST. The beachmaster urged them to clear the beach as rapidly as possible, and military police directed them a few thousand yards inland to a bivouac in a field bounded by the Norman hedgerows they would also come to know so well. Waterproofing was removed from vehicles and weapons, and it was well after midnight when the exhausted men collapsed around their vehicles and slept. No man, neither officer nor enlisted, dug shelters under the assumption that none were probably needed

VII Corps Aircraft Recognition School Graduation Certificate. Surprisingly, it appears that the commander of the VII Corps, Major General J. Lawton Collins, took the time to sign the certificate.

and that in any case they were scheduled to move out at dawn to join their assigned artillery battalion.[24]

Their sleep only lasted for a few minutes though. As Dad remembered it, he had barely closed his eyes when a series of loud explosions erupted from the field next to theirs. It turned out it was occupied by a 90mm AAA battery, which opened fire on approaching German aircraft. The deafening rapid fire of the 90mm guns was shortly followed by even more deafening explosions as German bombs began hitting the beach and among the ships offshore. No one in the 537th was hit and the raid was quickly over, but that was the end of sleep for the night as officers and men scrambled to find entrenching tools and frantically dug in for the first time in earnest. They had just encountered "Bed Check Charlie," one of the nightly German air raids that continued until 17 August.[25]

During that long night and in the early morning hours of 15 June, the four batteries contacted the artillery battalion each were scheduled to support. By early afternoon they were on their way, moving slowly through the crowded beachhead area, to the frontlines. Sometime during the late afternoon of 15 June, Battery A, 537th AAA AW Battalion went into position "Somewhere in France" beside the firing batteries of the 343d Field Artillery Battalion near Amfreville. Dad was officially in combat.[26]

****

On 20 April 2000, we left our hotel in Caen early in the morning, driving the N13 to Isigny-sur-Mer, where we crossed the Vire River, then the Vire-Taute Canal at Carentan, and finally the Douve River. At Saint-Côme-du-Mont we turned northeast on the D913 to Sainte-Marie-du-Mont and the Musée du Débarquement de Utah Beach—the Utah Beach Landing Museum. The D913 was known as "Exit 2" to the VII Corps planners and was one of seven roads traversing the marshy country inland from the beaches and was the principal hard-surface exit from the beaches used on D-Day. Unfortunately, the museum was closed. Instead we decided to walk on the beach. The German positions were eagerly explored, as were the 4th and 90th Infantry Division memorials.

From there we drove north along the coast toward Grand Hameau des Dunes, trying to establish exactly where Dad may have landed because he and Battery A did not actually land on TARE GREEN or UNCLE RED, the two beaches established on D-Day. He recalled they landed under sporadic German artillery fire, which meant it was almost certainly SUGAR RED beach, which was opened on D+1. SUGAR RED ran from a point just east of the intersection of the beachfront road (D421) and Exit 4 (D423), near the modern Mémorial Leclerc beach exit, and extended west to Grand Hameau des Dunes. By 14 June, it was the only beach still under German fire from their positions to the northwest. The field they turned into for the night was probably somewhere off Exit 4, between Saint-Germain-de-Varreville and La Selleraie. The Battery A MR for 14 June only noted their position was "Somewhere in France."[27]

Dad's impressions of these early movements remained vividly imprinted in his memory as we explored the roads around UTAH Beach. A minor thing he noted were the telephone and power poles along the roads, which were the exact same, distinctively shaped concrete pylons he remembered. There was also a major difference; there were no dead cows in the fields. The least pleasant memory and the first thing that hit them as they exited their LST was the stench. It wafted from inland to the water, permeating everything. He recalled it as a combination of the smell of unwashed bodies, decaying flesh, thousands of latrines, and hundreds of thousands of hasty "cat holes" men had dug to defecate in, but also overlaid with a strange sickly sweet smell of burnt sugar and vanilla. That last scent, reminiscent of cotton candy, was produced from the widespread use by American combat engineers of a British-developed explosive known as "Composition C," which was an early form of "plastic explosive" incorporating nitrocellulose. The officers and men of Battery A saw, heard, and smelled the reality of war as they advanced inland.

CHAPTER 2

THE 90TH INFANTRY DIVISION

The wartime experiences of Dad and the 537th AAA AW Battalion were inextricably linked to that of the 90th Infantry Division. The 90th was originally constituted in the Great War on 5 August 1917 as the 90th Division of the National Army, at Camp Travis, Fort Sam Houston, Texas. It was formed from recruits mostly drawn from Texas and Oklahoma so became known as the "Texas and Oklahoma Division." After completing organization, the division shipped to France between 13 June and 6 July 1918, setting up headquarters at Aignay-le-Duc. It first entered the trenches in Lorraine at Villers-en-Haye and Puvenelle and after gaining combat experience took part in the St. Mihiel and Meuse-Argonne offensives. After serving with distinction the 90th returned to the United States on 7 June 1919 and was demobilized on 17 June 1919 at Camp Bowie, Texas.

The War Department reconstituted the 90th Division in the OR on 24 June 1921 as part of the postwar Army. It was allocated to the Eighth Corps Area assigned to the XVIII Corps. Its recruiting area was Texas, although it kept its Great War "T-O" shoulder patch. Division Headquarters was organized on 8 August 1921 and established its first offices in the Eighth Corps Area HQ Library at Fort Sam Houston, before relocating to rooms in the Gunter Hotel at San Antonio on 14 September 1921. The headquarters moved again in June 1923 to Building 42-T at Fort Sam Houston, before it made its final move before World War II in July 1926 to the Alamo Building in San Antonio, which led to its other nickname, the "Alamo Division."

The new division's recruiting drive proved popular enough that by January 1924 it was at 99 percent of its authorized officer strength: 896 of 905 officers were assigned to the division. However, pressure from the State National Guard (NG) offices, which were worried about maintaining the strength of their own units, ensured that the National Defense Act of 1921 included legislation forbidding OR units from recruiting more than 33 percent of its authorized enlisted personnel and prohibited any enlistment or pay incentives for the Enlisted Reserve Corps (ERC). Consequently, the OR was heavy on officers but light on enlisted strength. By 30 June 1926, the entire OR establishment of the U.S. Army consisted of 103,829 officers, but only 5,775 enlisted men. By 30 June 1939, officer strength increased to 116,719, but enlisted strength fell to just 3,054. Thus, on average the 33 OR divisions had fewer than 100 of its legal maximum strength of 6,292 enlisted men present. The 90th Division, like all OR divisions, was a unit in name only.[1]

Nevertheless, the division's officers were very active through the 1920s, assigned to conduct Civilian Military Training Camp (CMTC) courses during the spring and summer, and did annual training with the RA 2d Division's Headquarters, 9th Infantry, and 23d Infantry at Fort Sam Houston and nearby Camp Bullis. However, in common with the rest of the Army, beginning in October 1929 the Great Depression hit the 90th Division hard. The ensuing fiscal austerity meant opportunities for meaningful training of officers became rare. Typically, officers were fortunate if they received a two-week tour of active duty every four of five years. By 1934, only one in seven ORC officers actively participated in the summer training camps.[2]

Stringent financial limitations were also placed on administrative meetings during those lean years. By the early 1930s, the only other unit activities other than the infrequent training camps were "Inactive Training Period" meetings of unit officers. For example, the 179th Infantry Brigade (357th and 358th Infantry) meetings were held at the Texas Hotel in Fort Worth, while the 180th Infantry Brigade (359th and 360th Infantry) met at the Federal Building in Houston. However, the division did not meet as a complete unit. In common with the other OR divisions, the 90th did not take part as a unit in any of the occasional Corps Area maneuvers during the 1920s and early 1930s or in the large Army Maneuvers of 1940 and 1941. Instead the division contributed teams of officers who served as umpires or support personnel to other divisions. For example, 138 officers were contributed to the 2d Division and 66 to the 36th Division in the 1938 Eighth Corps Area maneuver at Camp Bullis.[3]

After the Japanese attack on Pearl Harbor, the division was finally activated on 25 March 1942 at Camp Barkeley, Texas. It was an entirely new unit, comprised mostly of newly commissioned OCS officers and enlisted draftees. By the time the division was activated, most, if not all, of the prewar officers and enlisted OR personnel had been drafted into other units or had been retired, leaving the 90th

Division essentially an empty shell. The cadre for the new organization was supplied by the 6th Division, an RA unit, which itself was reactivated 12 October 1939, and the 33d Division of the Illinois NG, which had been inducted into federal service on 5 March 1941.

In theory the cadre system was tightly regulated. Mobilizing a new division required a well-trained and experienced cadre of 172 officers and 1,190 enlisted men who would initially train and command a large influx of 452 OCS officers and 13,425 enlisted draftees. However, the reality was considerably different. Typically, the units providing cadre used the system to dump its "bad apples" on another unit. That and the overall lack of experienced manpower in the Army due to the prewar limitations on its size meant that typically fewer than 200 of the enlisted cadre in newly activated divisions had been in service for longer than three years. Nor were the numbers expected on paper always forthcoming. Typically, there were some shortfalls in the cadre strength, and it was not uncommon that as few as two-thirds of the enlisted cadre were actually available at activation. Thus, the 90th Division's 315th Engineer Battalion received its planned 17 officers from the Engineer Replacement Training Center at Fort Leonard Wood, Missouri, but only 52 of the 86 enlisted men it was supposed to draw from the 6th Division's 6th Engineer Battalion.[4]

However, none of these issues were unique to the 90th Division. Rather, they were a commonplace problem in an Army that expanded from just 174,000 enlisted personnel, including 17,000 in the Army Air Corps, on 1 July 1939 to about 2,750,000 by the time the 90th was activated. The 90th Division's experience was not unique. It was just one of 29 infantry divisions activated during 1942, and its problems mirrored those of the Army as a whole.

The 90th Division also underwent a major reorganization when it was activated. The 19,997-strong post–Great War "square" organization of two infantry brigades, each of two infantry regiments was discarded for a more modern, streamlined "triangular" organization. On 20 February 1942, before the division was activated, the 360th Infantry, present since the division was first organized in 1917, was relieved from assignment to the 90th Division and was concurrently withdrawn from the OR and allotted to the AUS as an inactive unit.[5] It was formally disbanded on 11 November 1944 without ever being activated and saw no service in World War II. The 165th Field Artillery Brigade was reorganized as the Headquarters and Headquarters Battery, 90th Division Artillery, and its assigned regiments, the 343d, 344th, and 345th, were reorganized as battalions, while the 315th Ammunition Train was reorganized as the 915th Field Artillery Battalion. The 315th Engineer

Camp Barkeley, Texas, date unknown. University of North Texas Libraries, the Portal to Texas History, Hardin-Simmons University Library, Abilene, Texas.

Regiment was reorganized on 25 February as the 315th Engineer Combat Battalion, and many other adjustments were made to the divisional organization. The reorganization left the division with a theoretical initial T/O strength of 15,514 officers and men, but it would be some time before that strength was achieved. On 20 May 1942, the division was formally redesignated as the 90th Infantry Division to distinguish it from the other specialized division types then in existence or being considered (Cavalry, Armored, Motorized, and Airborne).[6]

Perhaps the most important cadre assigned to the 90th Division was its first commander, Major General Henry Terrell Jr. He was promoted to major general, AUS, on 15 February 1942 and was assigned as commanding general of the 90th Division.[7]

According to the mobilization planning in effect, General Terrell and twelve officers of his staff should have been at Camp Barkeley at least thirty-seven days before the division was constituted. The rest of the initial officer and all the enlisted cadre were to arrive thirty days ahead of time. Given that Terrell was present at Barkeley no later than 15 February, it would appear at least the initial schedule was kept.

Major General Henry Terrell Jr. U.S. Army SC.

One crucial decision made early on by the War Department with regard to divisional mobilization was that all training would be done within the division itself. That meant that except for the cadre, all enlisted personnel arrived at the division directly from Selective Service reception centers in the Corps Area the division was mobilized in. None of those men had completed the most basic of training. Thus, the first phase in forming the division was Basic and Individual Training of the enlisted men, which was expected to take seventeen weeks. The cadre would first divide the men into units and then would teach them the basics of military courtesy, drill, sanitation and first aid, care and firing of individual weapons, and the care of equipment and clothing. The final week was spent in Mobilization Training Program (MTP) tests, written and oral examinations that evaluated the state of training.[8]

Assuming the schedule was kept, the 90th Infantry Division would have completed the first phase on 22 July 1942 and would have advanced to the next unit training phase, which was expected to last thirteen weeks. Unit training began with company training drills. A basic series of company maneuvers were practiced. In the offense, the company learned how to conduct an approach march; how to conduct the reconnaissance, planning, and ordering of an attack; the forms of attack maneuvers, such as envelopments and penetrations; how to act as a reserve; and the form of attack in specific types of terrain, such as woods, villages, across streams and rivers, and on fortified positions. They practiced preparing defensive positions, acting as a reserve, and executing retrogrades, either delaying or retreating. The next step was to assemble the companies to practice similar maneuvers as battalions, and then finally, in the case of the infantry regiments, to assemble the battalions to execute the maneuvers as a complete regiment. As in the earlier phase, the final week was allocated for MTP tests. All infantry and cavalry platoons took combat-firing proficiency tests for all organic weapons, while artillery units were given battery and battalion firing tests.

Again, assuming the schedule was kept, the second phase would have been completed on 14 October 1942, and the division would have advanced to the final phase, combined arms training, which was expected to last fourteen weeks. Combined arms training practiced offensive and defensive maneuvers of the entire division, which required coordinating artillery fires—but not tanks—with infantry maneuver. The last week was taken up with more MTP tests and infantry battalion field exercises.

If on schedule, the third phase would have ended on 20 January 1943. The final phase was a period of large-scale maneuvers, which the division participated in as part of a corps. The maneuvers introduced air and mechanized units (armored divisions and tank battalions) to the division. In the last week AGF evaluation teams graded the performance of the division and its constituent parts in the maneuvers. Eight weeks were allotted to the final phase of training.

Final preparations for deployment, including personnel adjustments, deployment leave, turning in training equipment, and packing necessary unit equipment for shipment, were allotted a generous four months. Thus, in theory, the 90th should have been fully trained by 17 March 1943, not quite a year after it was activated. In this perfect scenario, the division would be ready to POM, going overseas to a theater of war prepared to fight the enemy, four months later in July 1943. However, the 90th did not actually POM until February 1944 and did not leave the United States until 23 March 1944, almost exactly two years after activation and at least eight months later than planned.

Obviously, the precisely timed one-year plan did not work for the 90th Infantry Division. Indeed, it did not work for most of the divisions that were mobilized. Of the twenty OR divisions activated in 1942 only one, the 88th, managed to complete its training and POM on schedule. For the nineteen others, including the 90th, the average time lost to various causes was seven months. So what happened that so slowed the mobilization of the divisions?

Thirty-seven years later, one junior 2nd lieutenant in the 357th Infantry, who was one of the original cadre officers sent to the 90th from the 20th Infantry of the 6th Division, described the training problems endemic in the MTP. He did so with the benefit of considerable experience because he was General William E. DePuy, U.S. Army, Retired, who was the first commanding general of the U.S. Army Training and Doctrine Command (TRADOC) from 30 June 1973 until his retirement on 1 July 1977. He described the reality of the MTP in 1979 as

> *A time-oriented process. A unit spent so many hours or days on each subject. . . . The goal or object was to complete the training—get it done! Never mind whether or not the troops learned anything. The process completely obscured the product. If a soldier missed first aid training he must make it up so that 100 percent of the unit went through the prescribed [MTP]. . . . The learning function was obscured and secondary to the scheduling function. Few took training seriously.*[9]

Dupuy initially joined the 90th Infantry Division as a 1st lieutenant and was assigned as a communications officer with the Headquarters Company, 357th Infantry. Later he was what was known at the time as a liaison officer, a role that was essentially an Assistant Regimental S-3 (Operations). On 12 June 1944, he was reassigned as the 1st Battalion, 357th Infantry S-3. By then, he was a captain.[10]

Unfortunately, there were other problems as well. Little allowance was made in the MTP for minor or major issues that could derail the training process. For example, the MTP required that six months after activation the division would form a cadre for another division that was mobilizing. Of course, because the original cadre was considered an overstrength, in theory creating a cadre should not have been a problem, except that the War Department also increased the size of the cadre between March and September 1942 to 216 officers and 1,460 enlisted. Meanwhile, the War Department also required that units give up personnel for specialist training, while soldiers who showed leadership and initiative were selected for noncommissioned officer (NCO) or officer candidate schools. Others volunteered for parachute training in the new airborne forces. The result was a steady drain of personnel from the division who were replaced by new officers and men who needed to be integrated into the division and who often also required basic training.

Normal attrition of personnel was also a problem. Officers and men became sick, injured, and died during training. Some were not up to the physical and mental stresses they met and were transferred to other units and duties or were discharged from the Army. That attrition was exacerbated by conflicts within the War Department requirements for POM. One such requirement was that the unit be at full T/O strength before it went overseas. However, in January 1942, the War Department had also decided to activate new divisions without an overstrength or an allowance for extra "basic privates," who were "men included in tables of organization over and above all specified job assignments as an advance provision for replacements" because the emphasis was on activating as many new units as possible.[11]

Thus, from the start of mobilization until it went overseas, divisions were constantly bleeding manpower and trying to find trained replacements without ever being in combat. The replacements had to come from somewhere. Because replacements could not be drawn from within the division through an overstrength, they had to be found externally, either by taking trained personnel from other units, which simply further exacerbated the problem, or by drawing untrained personnel from induction centers and attempting to quickly train them up to the standards of the rest of the unit.

The consequence of the conflicting requirements all too often was units with variable standards of individual training, many of whom then failed the individual MTP tests, which in turn could mean the unit would have to repeat the phase, delaying the deployment of the entire division. Or it could result in a unit at the end of a training phase that was forced to suspend advancing to the next phase while they ran large numbers of replacement personnel through basic training. Similarly, units that failed unit or combined arms training were required to recycle through part of the training and be retested. As Colonel Joseph H. Rustemeyer, the first commander of the 358th Infantry, put it years later,

> *I had good NCOs, but with the Army's need for officers, many of my best NCOs left for OCS. To fill vacant NCO positions it was necessary to develop NCOs from men of the lower ranks. As they developed, then they too would go to OCS. So, you see, it took a long time to shake down the regiment.*[12]

Rustemeyer was relieved of command in the spring of 1943 before the division deployed because General Marshall decreed regimental commanders could not be older than fifty-one when sent into combat. Rustemeyer was instead sent to another regiment in training. The first commanding officers of the other two infantry regiments also did not take them into combat. Colonel Edwin D. Patrick, commander of the 357th Infantry, was relieved on 20 November 1942, returned to the 6th Infantry Division—he was part of the original cadre from that division—and was promoted to brigadier general and then major general. He was killed in action leading the 6th Infantry Division in the Philippines on 16 March 1945. Patrick was succeeded by Lieutenant Colonel John W. Sheehy. Colonel Alfred E. Dedicke, the first commander of the 359th Infantry, died of a heart attack on 8 October 1942 and was succeeded by Lieutenant Colonel Frank K. Fales, who was promoted to colonel on 6 November 1942.[13]

There was also a considerable turnover of officers in other senior positions of the division. The first Assistant Division Commander, Brigadier General Charles W. Ryder, was appointed and then left almost at once, in May 1942, to take the same post with the 34th Infantry Division, before he took command of that division in June 1942. His replacement, Colonel Alan W. Jones, was promoted to brigadier general on 24 June 1942, after Ryder left the division. He later commanded the 106th Infantry Division in its disastrous defeat in the battle of the Bulge. In turn, when Jones was relieved to organize the 106th Infantry Division on 3 February 1943, he was replaced by Brigadier General Samuel Tankersley Williams, who landed in Normandy with the forward elements of the 90th on 7 June 1944. Williams had commanded Company I, 359th Infantry in World War I. Williams had acquired the nickname "Hanging Sam" after remarking at a court-martial in 1943 that the defendant's guilt was not in doubt, and he deserved to be hanged.[14]

Similarly, command of the Division Artillery Headquarters turned over three times before the division landed in Normandy. The first commander, Brigadier General John E. Lewis, left the division to organize the X Corps Artillery Headquarters in July 1942 and was replaced by Brigadier General George D. Shea, who in turn left the division in September 1943 to assume command of the 141st Field Artillery Brigade. Shea was replaced by Brigadier General John M. Devine on 25 September 1943. Devine remained in command of the 90th Division Artillery until 16 September 1944, when he left to take command of Combat Command B, 7th Armored Division.[15]

Just like Dad's 537th AAA AW Battalion, another problem with the training plan was a lack of equipment. The War Department decision that units in training would make do with a 50 percent allowance of basic equipment applied to divisions too. By early 1943, divisions were experiencing postponements of up to six weeks in various training phases due to lack of equipment, ammunition, and the limited number of weapons, which meant the "groups working single weapons were so large

Samuel T. Williams as a lieutenant general in 1955, when he was Commanding General of the Fourth Army at Fort Sam Houston, Texas. U.S. Army SC.

that individuals were receiving scant instruction." On 12 April 1943, a report on the 90th said there were problems getting ammunition for both artillery and infantry unit training, although postwar Colonel Rustemeyer could not recall any significant shortages.[16]

The 90th Infantry Division experienced all these problems, but they were problems endemic to the mobilization process and were not unique to the 90th. Postwar, Colonel Rustemeyer, and other officers and men of the division believed the 90th was at least as well trained as the other American divisions mobilized that served in Europe. However, the 90th was also subjected to some stresses most other divisions did not run into.[17]

For example, on 15 September 1942, the War Department ordered the division redesignated and reorganized as the 90th Motorized Division. The Motorized Division was the second version of an organization first tested by the 4th Infantry

Brigadier General John M. Devine postwar, when he was Commanding General of the 8th Armored Division. U.S. Army SC.

Division in the fall of 1941 and was intended to partner with the armored division in an armored corps. As such, the 90th expanded to a nominal strength of 16,689 officers and men, adding about 1,200 personnel, mostly vehicle drivers, mechanics, and reconnaissance (the Mechanized Cavalry Troop tripled in size and a reconnaissance company was added to the 915th Engineer Battalion), as well as adding about 400 motor vehicles to the division. Notably, this occurred about the same time the division lost 1,676 officers and men to cadre the 104th Infantry Division. Three other RA divisions, the 6th, 7th, and 8th, also joined the 4th and 90th as motorized divisions.[18] All then went through a new unit training phase focused on developing the specific tactics and techniques required for the new organization.

Four months later, on 28 January 1943, the reorganized division completed unit training and moved to the Louisiana Maneuver Area for six weeks of combined arms training, followed by two weeks of divisional maneuvers against the 77th Infantry

Division. The postexercise evaluation of both divisions was damning for units supposedly in the last stages of training. The report remarked both units demonstrated "laxity in training during the basic unit and combined arms periods," there was "a lack of control on the part of commanders," and there was "a general failure on the part of officers to correct errors and deficiencies on the spot; and a failure to conform to tactical doctrine." Other problems were found that were typical in other divisions running through the exercises: troops failed to properly use cover and concealment, they bunched up too much while moving, and they exhibited only fair march discipline.[19]

However, even before the 90th Motorized Division reached the maneuver area, Army Ground Forces (AGF), which was responsible for mobilization, organization, doctrine, and training in the Army, was already reconsidering the utility of the motorized infantry concept. Testing in maneuvers showed that a standard infantry division could just as easily be motorized simply by the attachment of six Quartermaster Truck Companies. On 12 March 1943, the War Department approved converting the test motorized divisions, including the 90th, back to the standard infantry division organization. The month after the 90th returned to Camp Barkeley it was redesignated and reorganized again on 1 May 1943 as the 90th Infantry Division.[20]

Excess personnel were again siphoned away from the division at Camp Barkeley. Also, at about this time another draft of personnel for training of officers and NCOs was drawn from the division. Both further exacerbated the turnover of personnel and the constant retraining and testing associated with it. Once reorganization as a standard infantry division was completed the 90th again concentrated on reviewing the individual and unit training phases of the MTP. However, the constant personnel turnover continued on 6 August 1943, when fifty newly commissioned 2d lieutenants joined the division.

On 12 September 1943, the division deployed to the Desert Training Center at Indio, California, where it stayed for three months, engaged in maneuvers with the 93d Infantry Division (Cld) in an extended version of the eight-week final training phase.[21] From there it entrained and headed for Fort Dix, New Jersey, beginning the movement 26 December 1943 and ending 8 January 1944. The 90th was finally in POM and from Fort Dix the division's next destination was the ETOUSA.[22]

What followed was one of the worst aspects of the Army mobilization and deployment planning in World War II. The division remained camped at Fort Dix for the next seventy days—over two months—waiting for shipment to Europe. During this hiatus there were no opportunities for unit training or practice and,

"Camp Polk, Louisiana. Lieutenants Heim, Highberger, Compton, Montgomery and Pinnock eat some G.I. chow after a day in the field. 26 January, 1943. 90th Signal Company, 90th Infantry Division." U.S. Army SC 171746.

indeed, little for the officers and men to do other than wait. Possibly more disruptive though was that when the division arrived at Fort Dix, General Terrell left it. The War Department decided he would be better used in organizing and training another unit instead of taking the division he had commanded for nearly two years into combat. Upon arriving at Fort Dix, Terrell was relieved of command of the 90th on 23 January and was reassigned as the first commanding general of the newly organized—it was activated on 15 January—XXII Corps. Terrell left at once for Fort Campbell, Kentucky. The promotion shows that Terrell, despite the training problems his division had experienced, was still considered a sound and up-and-coming officer by the War Department. On the same day General Terrell left, Brigadier General Jay Ward MacKelvie assumed command of the 90th Infantry Division.

Finally, on 5 March 1944, the 90th Infantry Division was officially assigned to the ETOUSA and TUSA and made final preparations for the voyage to Britain. From 13 to 17 March, the division's units staged by train to Camp Kilmer, New Jersey, the New York POE. Troops began the embarkation process on 21 March by Regimental Combat Team (RCT).

The meeting of the War Plans Division, War Department General Staff in 1942. From left to right: William K. Harrison Jr., Leonard S. Gerow, Robert W. Crawford, Dwight D. Eisenhower, Leonard T. Gerow, Thomas T. Handy, Stephen H. Sherrill, John L. McKee, and Jay W. MacKelvie. MacKelvie apparently ingratiated himself with both Eisenhower and Leonard Gerow, which may have been a factor in his receiving command of the 90th Infantry Division and the decision to place it in the immediate buildup after D-Day. U.S. Army SC.

The 357th Infantry and 343d Field Artillery boarded Hired Military Transport (HMT) *Dominion Monarch*, a British ocean liner designed to carry 525 first-class passengers in luxury from Britain to Australia and New Zealand. She was converted in August 1940 to carry 142 officers and 1,341 enlisted men and was later modified again to carry 3,663 officers and men but actually carried more than that. She had 4,322 officers and men aboard of the 90th Infantry Division and other units.[23]

The 358th Infantry, 344th Field Artillery, 315th Engineer Combat Battalion, 90th Quartermaster Company, and 790th Ordnance Light Maintenance Company boarded the S.S. *John Ericsson*. She was another ocean liner, formerly the Swedish-America Lines's MV *Kungsholm*. She was requisitioned by the U.S. War Shipping

Brigadier General Jay W. MacKelvie. U.S. Army SC.

Administration (WSA) on 31 December 1941 and converted to carry 5,461 officers and men, nearly four times her civilian capacity of 1,428 passengers. She too exceeded her designed capacity and had 5,540 officers and men embarked.[24]

Division Headquarters, the 90th Reconnaissance Troop, 359th Infantry, and 345th and 915th Field Artillery boarded HMT *Athlone Castle*. She was another former British ocean liner designed to carry 245 first-class and 538 cabin-class passengers and was converted to carry 4,395 officers and men. She too was overcrowded with 5,111 officers and men actually embarked.[25]

Two other transport ships in the convoy may have carried troops from the 90th Infantry Division. They were the USAT *Edmund B. Alexander* and HMT *Stirling Castle*.[26]

On 23 March, the 90th Infantry Division was attached to FUSA and on the same day departed from the New York POE on Convoy UT-10. It was primarily a troop convoy and consisted of twenty-five ships—eighteen troop transports—including the *Dominion Monarch*, *John Ericsson*, *Athlone Castle*, *Edmund B. Alexander*, and the *Stirling Castle*; three general cargo ships; two refrigerated cargo ships; one armored vehicle transport ship, and one aircraft ferry. The entire convoy had about sixty thousand officers and enlisted men of the AGF and Army Air Forces (AAF) embarked.[27]

The size and precious value of the convoy required a large escort, which was provided by U.S. Navy Task Force 68, comprised 14 warships: the light cruiser U.S.S. *Cincinnati* (CL-6); five destroyers: U.S.S. *Mervine* (DD-489), U.S.S. *Quick* (DD-490), U.S.S. *Davison* (DD-618), U.S.S. *Tillman* (DD-641), and U.S.S. *Robinson* (DD-562); and seven destroyer escorts: U.S.S. *Fogg* (DE-57), U.S.S. *Foss* (DE-59), U.S.S. *Gantner* (DE-60), U.S.S. *George Washington Ingram* (DE 62), U.S.S. *Ira Jeffery* (DE-63), U.S.S. *Lee Fox* (DE-65), and U.S.S. *Jenks* (DE 665), and the fleet oiler U.S.S. *Chemung* (AO-30).[28]

When the convoy reached the Irish Sea, it split up. Seven ships with the 90th Infantry Division embarked, including the *Dominion Monarch*, *Athlone Castle*, *Edmund B. Alexander*, and the *Stirling Castle*, headed for Liverpool, where they arrived on 3 April. The 90th Infantry Division began disembarking there on the morning of 4 April 1944. However, it arrived short of about one-third of its strength. When she was barely outside New York Harbor the *Ericsson* developed engine trouble and had to turn back. After three days of repairs, she departed again as part of Convoy CU-19, which was a mix of troop transport ships, cargo ships, colliers, and oil tankers. The convoy, and the *John Ericsson*, arrived at Liverpool on 8 April and completed unloading on 9 April.

When all its elements finally arrived, the 90th Infantry Division moved to its initial cantonment areas with Division Headquarters at Birmingham in the Midlands. The 357th Infantry was to the west with the 1st Battalion at Gatacre Hall, Wolverhampton in Shropshire, and the rest of the regiment at Kinlet, near Bewdley. The late-arriving passengers from the *John Ericsson*, the 790th Ordnance Light Maintenance Company, 90th Quartermaster Company, and the 1st Battalion, 358th Infantry settled into Coton Hall in Shropshire, with the rest of the 358th Infantry far to the south in Sturt Common, also near Bewdley. The 359th Infantry was farther west, with the 1st Battalion in Wales, at Willey Moor, near Knighton in Shropshire and the rest of the regiment at Leominster in Herefordshire. Unlike the rest of the division, all four Field Artillery battalions, as well as General Devine with a detachment of his Division Artillery Headquarters, were concentrated at

Davenport House, Shropshire.[29] Once settled in the division began preparing in earnest for its role in the invasion:

> *A period of intensive training followed, consisting of mine detection, village fighting, assault on fortified positions, hedgerow fighting, artillery firing problems, road marches and obstacle course. The rough edges were polished off, and "coordination" between units became more than a word, more than a goal, but an accomplished fact.*[30]

While en route on 27 March, the FUSA had ordered the 90th Infantry Division attached to the VII Corps as part of the immediate invasion follow-on force. Once he arrived in England, General MacKelvie was informed his division had been selected as the immediate follow-on division supporting the VII Corps landing on UTAH Beach on D-Day. The division would land in three increments over the first three days of the invasion, which would leave it somewhat fragmented until it could be reassembled on the far shore.

A detachment of the 359th Infantry Regimental Headquarters—the Headquarters, part of Headquarters Company, and attached liaison officers from other organizations—along with the Forward Echelons of the Headquarters of its 1st and 3d Battalions with half the vehicles of the 1st and 3d Battalion were designated "Group AA." The rest of the 359th Infantry Regimental Headquarters, the 1st and 3d Battalion minus vehicles, the Mine Platoon of Antitank Company, and a detachment of Service Company were designated "Group A." Both Group AA and A were attached to the 4th Infantry Division. Group AA was to land on D-Day in the morning assault waves, while Group A would land in the afternoon. They would remain in 4th Infantry Division reserve until they passed to the control of the Advance Detachment of the 90th Infantry Division when it landed on D+1.

The Advance Detachment was led by General Williams and included Group B of the 359th Infantry, with its 2d Battalion, Cannon Company, Antitank Company (less its Mine Platoon), Service Company (minus its detachment with Group A), and the other half of the 1st and 3d Battalion vehicles. Also attached to Group B were Company B, 315th Engineer Combat Battalion, Company B, 315th Medical Battalion, elements of the Division HQ and HQ Company the bulk of the 90th Signal Company, the 90th Reconnaissance Troop, four liaison officers from Division Artillery, and liaison parties from other units of the division and VII Corps. The Advance Detachment would establish liaison with the VII Corps and 4th Infantry Division HQ and prepare assembly areas for the arrival of the 90th Infantry Division, while continuing to act as a reserve for the 4th Infantry Division.

One of the more peculiar and inexplicable command decisions made by General MacKelvie in the planning of the invasion was to attach the commander of the 1st Battalion, 359th Infantry, Lieutenant Colonel George H. Lawrence, to the Headquarters, 359th Infantry. That left the 1st Battalion commanded by its Executive Officer, Major Robert P. Booth. Why MacKelvie created such a command arrangement is unknown, but in the end it meant Colonel Lawrence never led in combat the 1st Battalion he had trained with for months.

The bulk of the combat strength of the division, the 357th and 358th Infantry, the rest of HQ and HQ Battery, Division Artillery with two artillery battalions, the 343d and 344th Field Artillery, and parts of the 915th Field Artillery, Company A and B, 315th Engineer Combat Battalion, and Company A and B, 315th Medical Battalion, were not scheduled to land until D+2. General MacKelvie and the rest of Division HQ would land then as well, along with the leading elements of the division logistic support elements, the 790th Ordnance Light Maintenance Company and 90th Quartermaster Service Company. Finally, the division's 155mm howitzer battalion, the 345th, would also land on D+2, but in a separate convoy. Once it completed landing and assembled, the mission of the division was to drive to Cherbourg in conjunction with the 4th Infantry Division.[31]

While this intricate planning was going on problems within the division were cropping up. In England, MacKelvie

> *Quickly gained a reputation as a stickler for protocol, concentrating on petty discipline rather than combat readiness. He remained aloof from his staff and subordinate officers and often ignored advice from his assistant and his artillery commander.*[32]

On 15 May, with invasion preparations accelerating, General MacKelvie created greater resentment when he relieved Colonel Sheehy of command of the 357th Infantry. Sheehy was directed to report to Division HQ as a supernumerary officer. In his place, General MacKelvie assigned the former division Chief of Staff, Colonel Philip H. Ginder, as the new commander of the 357th. Controversially, MacKelvie did not have Sheehy take Ginder's place as Chief of Staff, and he did not actually replace Ginder until 18 May, with Colonel Robert Lynn Bacon. Nor was that the only command shakeup in the division. Colonel Ginder himself had only been Chief of Staff for a few days when he took over the 357th; he had taken the position on 2 May when the previous Chief of Staff, Colonel Gustave C. Dittmar, was assigned to FUSA as its G-5 (Civil Affairs) Executive Officer. However, the division G-2, Lieutenant Colonel James O. Boswell, and G-3, Lieutenant Colonel Richard G.

Stilwell, were both solid officers, who stayed in their respective positions throughout the campaign.[33]

General MacKelvie's relief of the popular Colonel Sheehy led to a crisis of confidence within the division and apparently started a whispering campaign by the officers and men denigrating the division commander. Rumor had it that Ginder, who had ingratiated himself with MacKelvie, had cajoled the general into placing him in command of the 357th Infantry. General Omar N. Bradley, commanding the First U.S. Army, later commented to General Eisenhower after a preinvasion review of the 90th Infantry Division that he was concerned with MacKelvie's demeanor and indecisiveness, but "plans were progressed too far to make any change in divisions especially as the number of divisions who were fully equipped at that time was limited." MacKelvie made things worse when he addressed the officers and men of the division just prior to the embarkation. Traveling from battalion to battalion, he read a speech "in an uncertain voice" that was "ineptly phrased and filled with clichés such as 'don't fire until you see the whites of their eyes.'" These were the first hints of a major rift in the leadership of the division, which would have devastating consequences in combat.[34]

With D-Day originally planned for 5 June, the division began moving from its cantonment to its designated sausage camps near its embarkation areas in late May. The main body of the 90th Infantry Division—the Division Advance Detachment, Detachment 2, and Group B—moved to camps "generally north and east of the cities of Cardiff and Newport, Wales." Group A and AA moved to marshalling camps in Devonshire near the camps of the 4th Infantry Division. A few elements, such as the 790th Ordnance Light Maintenance Company, were located as much as 175 miles away at Arundel Castle in Sussex on the south coast of England. The Division Rear, with detachments of officers and men from all elements of the division, was established at Bournemouth.

Officers and men of the Advance Detachment, 357th Infantry left their Marshaling Camp at the Chepstow Racecourse in Monmouthshire at 1430 on 3 June and boarded the S.S. *Explorer* at Cardiff at 1615. Detachments of personnel of Headquarters Company, Service Company, Antitank Company, and Cannon Company, 357th Infantry, with the vehicles, weapons, and equipment of the regiment left their Marshaling Camp at Sedbury in Gloucestershire at 1900 on 3 June and went by train to the embarkation area at Newport. By 2300, they completed loading all vehicles, weapons, and equipment onto S.S. *Charles Morgan* (MT 223) and S.S. *Clara Barton* (MT 224). The remaining personnel of the 1st, 2d, and 3d Battalion and Medical Detachment, 357th Infantry left the Chepstow Racecourse

Marshaling Camp at 0325 on foot and train and began embarking at Cardiff at 0630 on 4 June. They were aboard by 1600. The 3d Battalion embarked on the S.S. *Bienville*, while the personnel of the 1st and 2d Battalion, Regimental Headquarters Company, Service Company, Antitank Company, and Cannon Company were on the S.S. *Explorer*.[35]

The 343d Field Artillery Battalion, which was the normal attachment to the 357th Infantry RCT, and the 344th Field Artillery Battalion, which was normally part of the 358th Infantry RCT, were also at the Chepstow Racetrack Marshalling Camp. On 3 June, the personnel of the two Field Artillery battalions boarded the *Bienville* and *Explorer* at Cardiff, while the howitzers, vehicles, and drivers boarded MT at Newport.[36]

The 358th Infantry, which was at Camp Llangatock in Brecknockshire, embarked its 3d Battalion on the S.S. *Bienville* at Cardiff on 3 June as well. The remainder of the 358th RCT, along with General MacKelvie and part of the Division Staff and Special Troops, boarded the S.S. *Excelsior* at Newport. The Headquarters and Service Battery, Battery A, and Battery B, 345th Field Artillery, embarked at Cardiff on S.S. *Charles C. Jones* (MT 209), while Battery C boarded the S.S. *Charles D. Poston* (MT 210). Final loading of Detachment 2 was completed on 4 June and all ships transporting the Division Main Body anchored in the Bristol Channel waiting for the movement to the beaches.

Group A and AA began embarking on 1 June, but at Devonshire ports on the southwest coast of England. Group AA loaded vehicles and men on Landing Craft Tank, LCT (5) 2130 and 2438 at Dartmouth. The HQ and HQ Company and 1st Battalion, 359th Infantry of Group A loaded on Landing Craft Infantry, Large: LCI (L) 231, 325, 326, 349, and 350 at Plymouth. The 3d Battalion, 359th Infantry of Group A loaded on LCI (L) 524, 527, 528, and 552 at Dartmouth. Group A completed loading on 2 June and moved to an anchorage off Salcombe Bay in the English Channel on 3 June.

Group B and the Division Advance Detachment personnel embarked on the troopship U.S.S. *Susan B. Anthony* at Newport on 3 June, which moved into the Bristol Channel at 1800, where she anchored. Also on board were personnel detachments from the 321st and 907th Glider Field Artillery Battalion of the 101st Airborne Division as well as from other VII Corps units. A total of 2,317 Army personnel and 418 Navy crewmen were aboard. The vehicles, weapons, and personnel of Cannon Company and Antitank Company, 359th Infantry, and the other personnel and vehicles of the Advance Detachment were loaded on four MT at Newport. Cannon Company was on the S.S. *George E. Pickett* (MT 227) and AT Company was on the S.S. *Josiah Nelson Cushing* (MT 229). The 359th Infantry's attached 915th Field Artillery Battalion was loaded on the S.S. *Frank R. Stockton* (MT 226) and the S.S. *Jedediah S. Smith* (MT 228), along with the vehicles and drivers of the 90th Infantry Division Reconnaissance Troop.[37]

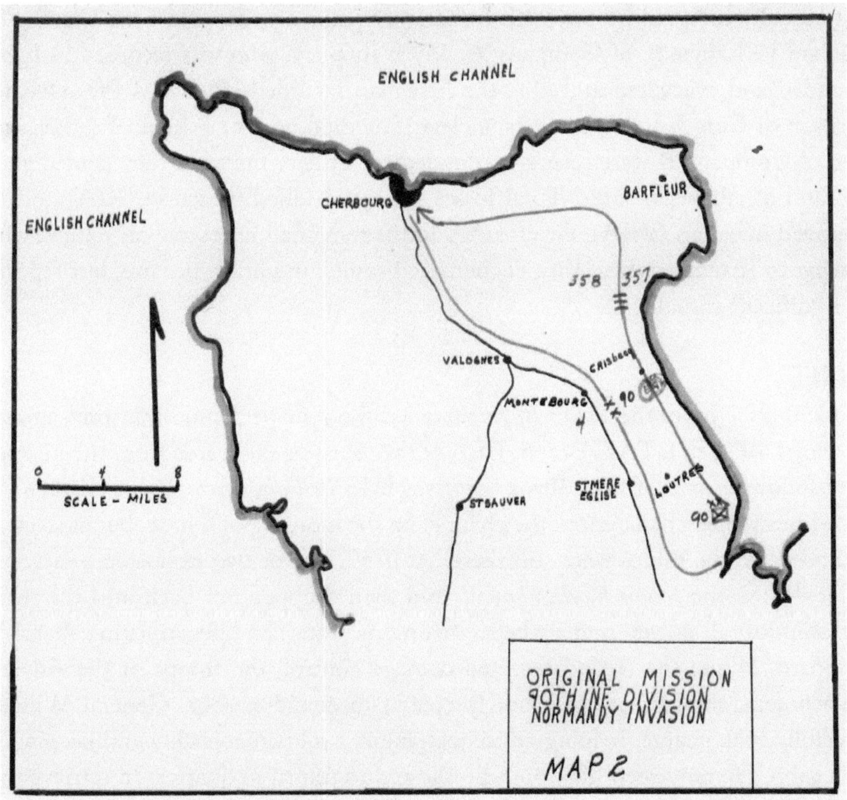

Map 1. Original Mission of the 90th Infantry Division. Major Charles E. Ronan, Infantry, *The Operations of the 3rd Battalion, 357th Infantry (90th Infantry Division) in the Hedgerow Battle of Normandy, 8–11 June 1944 (Normandy Campaign) (Personal Experience of a Battalion Executive Officer)* (Fort Benning, GA: The Infantry School, Advanced Infantry Officers Course, 1948–1949), Map 2.

6 JUNE

The Division Advance Detachment and Groups A and AA sailed with the invasion convoy on 5 June, while the Division Main Body set sail on 6 June. Group AA began landing on UTAH Beach at 1000 on 6 June. Group A began landing from its LCI (L) at 1400, assembled, and then about 2045 moved to a bivouac area just south of St. Martin-de-Varreville, where they settled in for the night at about 2330. Landing Groups AA and A were reportedly heavily shelled by German artillery. Probably the first casualty incurred by the 90th Infantry Division was Private First Class (Pfc.) William L. Langston of Company A, 359th Infantry, who was recorded as lightly wounded and evacuated at 1400. The first man recorded killed was Pfc. David F. Atcuson of Company M, but it is unclear if he died on 6 or 7 June. Another three men of Company B were severely wounded by artillery fire after they landed about two and a half hours later. Total losses were one killed in action (KIA) and ten wounded in action (WIA). Groups AA and A remained in reserve on 7 June, while moving to Reuville, where they encountered some random sniper fire, but reported no significant casualties.[38]

7 JUNE

At 0750 on 7 June, the *Susan B. Anthony* led the four personnel transport ships of Convoy LBP 1 to UTAH Beach. Each of the four was 600 yards from the next and were following one of the convoy escorts, HMS *Pelican*, down swept channel No. 34. Minesweepers had cleared the channel on the morning of 6 June, but at least one and possibly two mines were still there. At 0757, one or two explosions—accounts differ—lifted the *Susan B. Anthony* up and then dropped her back into the water. The ship lost all power, quickly began taking on water, and began listing sharply to starboard. While the crew attempted damage control, the troops of the Advance Detachment climbed on deck and prepared to abandon ship. General Williams forcefully took charge, helping get sixteen injured soldiers to safety and keeping his men calm. He requested his troops be allowed to return to quarters to retrieve their weapons and gear, but permission was denied, given the lack of light and the damage below.[39]

Within 30 minutes the situation got much worse. Fuel from broken tanks leaked into the engine firerooms and ignited, and by 0840 the fire was out of control. With water continuing to rise it was obvious the ship could not be saved, and at 0850 other vessels began coming alongside to rescue the troops and crew. By 0943 all the troops and crew, except for a small salvage party, were aboard a half dozen assorted

Company B, 359th Infantry of Group A on LCI (L) 326 waiting to go ashore on 6 June 1944. In the background, three more LCI (L) of Group A are visible. U.S. Army SC.

rescue ships and at about 1000 the last of the salvage party and the commanding officers abandoned ship.

At 1010, the *Susan B. Anthony* sank about nine miles from the Normandy coast, taking down with her all the equipment of the Advanced Detachment and Group B, as well as the heavy weapons and ammunition of the 2d Battalion, 359th Infantry and many of the 2d Battalion troops' individual weapons. However, all Navy and Army personnel aboard were saved. Fifteen Navy and sixteen Army personnel were injured, mostly with broken bones and contusions, but none seriously. Adding to the confusion, the survivors were landed in scattered groups all along the American beachhead area, some on UTAH and others on OMAHA beach.

Officer and men of one of the heavy weapons companies of the 359th Infantry, ashore in Normandy on 6 June 1944, moving inland from UNCLE RED UTAH Beach. The men are closely bunched up on each side of the road, which was an often fatal tendency followed by green troops. U.S. Army SC.

Four officers on board the *Susan B. Anthony* were awarded the Soldier's Medal for "heroism not involving actual conflict with the enemy."

> *LT COL James O. Boswell O19188, GSC, Hq, 90th Inf Div, United States Army. On 7 June when the* Susan B. Anthony *was fatally damaged off the coast of France, Lt Col Boswell, at great risk to his own life, voluntarily made repeated trips to the various troop compartments of the ship, some of which were fast flooding, in order to insure that*

all troops aboard were safely evacuated. As the result of Lt Col Boswell's heroic efforts, together with those of other officers, all of the troops aboard were safely evacuated in the one and one-half hours before the doomed ship sank. Entered service from the District of Columbia.[40]

Major Gilbert E. Strickland, Captain Richard F. Lynch, and 1st Lieutenant Carl B. Everett received the exact same citation and award. Boswell was the Division G-2, Strickland was the Deputy Division G-3, Lynch was part of the Division General Staff, and Everett was General Williams's aide-de-camp.

General Williams and his staff evacuated the *Susan B. Anthony* onto a British frigate, HMS *Narborough*, of the 15th Escort Group. Williams then cajoled the British captain into dropping them off at UTAH Beach. When none of the other

Portside view of the U.S.S. *Susan B. Anthony* (AP-72) sinking by the stern off UTAH Beach, 7 June 1944. The photograph was taken from LCT (6) 544. LCI (L) 496 may be seen to the left, tied up to the portside next to the No. 1, 2, and 3 Hatch. To the center right, the bow of the U.S.S. *Pinto* (ATF 90) may be seen tied up portside amidships. The photo was taken by Quartermaster 2d Class William T. O'Neill. Courtesy of the Library of Virginia, William T. O'Neill Records.

Men of the 359th Infantry, 90th Infantry Division, attached to the 12th Infantry, 4th Infantry Division, rest at the Café J. Philippe in Baudienville, France, on 7 June 1944. U.S. Army SC.

rescue vessels followed suit, General Williams's group became the only part of the 90th Division troops embarked on the *Susan B. Anthony* to land on the correct beach on 7 June. Meanwhile, the Division Main Body sailed eastward along the coast of England before turning south toward UTAH Beach, and the 1st and 3d Battalion, 359th Infantry, remained in 4th Infantry Division reserve.[41]

8 JUNE

The three personnel transport ships with Detachment 2 arrived off UTAH Beach at mid-morning on 8 June and began unloading at 1200. By midnight, all personnel closed into an assembly area in the vicinity of Turqueville-Reuville-Audouville-la-Hubert-Écoquenéauville. However, unloading vehicles and heavy equipment lagged far behind schedule. By the end of the day only 5 percent of vehicles were present in the assembly area.

The Division Artillery was in slightly better shape. Although the Field Artillery Advance Detachment on the *Susan B. Anthony* did not get ashore until 2200 on 7 June and soon found out its planned assembly area at St. Marcouf was still in enemy hands, it established a new one in the vicinity of Leutres. The division's Field Artillery assets quickly began coalescing there. General Devine arrived at 1300 on 8 June and was later joined by the 1st Howitzer Section of Battery C, 344th Field Artillery and the two sections of Battery B, 915th Field Artillery, which landed at 1850. During the night of 8/9 June, more elements of the Division Artillery came ashore and by the morning of 9 June the 343d, 344th, 345th, and part of the 915th Field Artillery were all complete and ashore.

The 359th Infantry experienced its first serious contact with the enemy during the day. When the 1st Battalion, 12th Infantry of the 4th Infantry Division assaulted the German line between Azeville and Saint-Marcouf it found itself pinned down by heavy German fire on its left flank from the direction of Azeville. To distract the Germans, at 1500, Company B of the 359th was attached to the 12th Infantry and sent directly toward Azeville, receiving casualties described as "heavy," although in fact only one enlisted man was recorded as wounded on that day. The engagement continued the next day until 1920, when the 22d Infantry passed through the 1st Battalion, 359th, which withdrew to Reuville and rejoined the rest of the regiment. On 9 June, the 1st Battalion, 359th captured twenty-five prisoners from the *243. Infanterie-Division*, mostly from its *Ersatz-Batallion* (Replacement Battalion). Two men from the communications section of Company C alone reportedly captured eleven Germans. This time casualties were substantial; the 1st Battalion suffered seven killed and twenty-two wounded on 9 June, and then another twelve on 10 June from air attacks and artillery.

9 JUNE

General Devine did not wait for orders or the arrival of the rest of the division to find a role for his artillery. On the evening of 8 June, he told Lieutenant Colonel Frank W. Norris, the commander of the 345th Field Artillery, he intended to locate an old friend, Major General Matthew B. Ridgway, commander of the 82d Airborne Division, to offer him the services of the 90th Division Artillery. At 0600 on 9 June, Devine and Norris tracked down Ridgway, who was happy to accept the offer because most of his artillery was lost in the airborne drops on the night of 5/6 June. At 1050 the 345th Field Artillery fired its first rounds of the war, and possibly the first fired by the 90th Infantry Division, in a fifteen-minute concentration supporting Ridgway's paratroopers. Although none of the artillery battalion's L-4 Liaison and Observation aircraft—nicknamed "Cubs"—were available, the fires were later assessed as on target and helpful to the airborne units. The "Cubs" had in fact already come ashore, disassembled, and loaded in 2.5-ton trucks, but were accidentally diverted to the 4th Infantry Division Artillery and did not join their respective 90th Division Artillery battalions until late on 9 June.[42]

Meanwhile, the Division Main Body completed assembly and prepared to execute its first attack. On 9 June, the 82d Airborne Division, supported by the

345th Field Artillery Battalion, established a bridgehead on the west side of the Merderet. Before dark, the 90th moved forward to its jump-off positions for the next day's attack.

****

Dad recalled one of the most disconcerting things about the fighting in Normandy. To the men fighting there it seemed as if it was always daytime, and the night lasted no time at all.

Allied forces in Normandy used British Double Daylight Savings Time; their clocks were set forward two hours from Greenwich Mean Time. That meant that in mid-June, sunset was at about 11:12 PM (2312), civil twilight ended at 11:56 PM (2356), just four minutes before midnight, civil twilight began at 6:14 AM (0614), and sunrise was at 6:58 AM (0658). Daylight lasted for almost sixteen hours and fifteen minutes. Civil twilight is the time during the day when enough natural light remains that artificial light is not needed. However, the military is more concerned with nautical twilight, which is generally considered to be when military operations may begin with minimal difficulty. In mid-June 1944 in Normandy, nautical twilight began at 5:12 AM (0512) and ended well after midnight at 12:59 PM (0059).

What that meant for the soldiers fighting in Normandy was their "night" lasted for as little as four hours. The result was chronic exhaustion, especially for inexperienced troops who had not yet learned to take every possible opportunity for foxhole catnaps. It also meant coffee and cigarettes were critical stimulants for the troops. My Dad, already a social smoker like most men of the era, developed a two- to three-pack-a-day cigarette habit he kept until he finally quit in the 1960s. Until then, his morning ritual was to light up before getting out of bed, followed by a cup of hot, black coffee.

The Germans, who because of the Allied blockades had almost no access to coffee and little access to tobacco, fell back on Ersatz—substitutes—such as "coffee" made from acorns, chicory, or roasted grains, and "tobacco" that normally contained a small quantity of real tobacco mixed with beech, cherry, grapevine, chestnut, raspberry, oak, blackberry, and hop leaves, with or without perfumed flavor additives. One other widespread stimulant for the German soldier, which reputedly made them fearless and even cheerful in combat and enabled them to spend more than three days without sleep and march up to 60 kilometers without rest, was Pervitin. First issued to the German Wehrmacht (Armed Forces) in large quantities in Poland in 1939 and France in 1940, up to 17.5-million doses per month were manufactured in the Third Reich. However, widespread use of Pervitin also led to addiction, heart problems, psychoses, and suicide because Pervitin was a methamphetamine.[43]

CHAPTER 3

BAPTISM OF FIRE

The VII Corps was tasked by FUSA on D-Day with landing on the eastern coast of the Cotentin Peninsula, then attacking north, securing the port of Cherbourg. The Cotentin extends northwest into the English Channel from mainland France as part of the northern coast of France. West of the peninsula are the Channel Islands in the Bay of Saint Malo and to the southwest is the base of the Brittany Peninsula. The eastern coast of the Cotentin consists of low, sandy beaches, backed by a belt of low-lying meadowland several miles wide, bordered to the west by a rising ridge of higher ground. Much of the meadowland had been deliberately inundated by the Germans as defensive measures and many of the roads leading inland from the coast were underwater. A major terrain feature in the southern Cotentin was the Douvre River and its tributary, the Merderet, which drained a major part of the peninsula, running south and southeast, then northeast to the sea. German control of the drainage system meant that like the meadows much of these river valleys were inundated, turning the road system into what were essentially raised causeways. Combined with the natural swampland of the Prairies Marecageuses de Gorges between Saint-Jores and Carentan, these inundations largely closed off the peninsula from the French mainland, except for the roads running from Carentan and Pont l'Abbé east to Isigny (N13) and south to Vire (D674) on the eastern side of the peninsula, and the roads (D2 and D971) running generally north to south from Le Haye to Coutances and Avranches along a narrow strip of land inland from the fortified western coast.[1]

The German defenses of the Cotentin Peninsula until mid-May 1944 only counted two divisions, the *243.* and *709. Infanterie-Division* (Infantry Division), with the former defending the west coast and Cherbourg and the latter the east coast and Cap de La Hougue. The VII Corps planners initially sought to exploit what was perceived as a weakness in the German defenses by dropping an airborne bridgehead from UTAH Beach westward that would interdict reinforcements moving from the west and south into the Cotentin, while movement from the east would be blocked by the landing on OMAHA Beach. The plan envisaged the 101st Airborne Division landing southeast of Ste. Mère-Eglise, where it would destroy the bridges in the vicinity of Carentan and seize the crossings over the Douve at Pont l'Abbé and Beuzeville-la Bastille, while the 82d Airborne Division landed west of St. Sauveur-le Vicomte, extending American control nearly to the Cotentin's west coast. However, the plan was hurriedly revised on 27 May when a new German division, the *91. Infanterie-Division (LL)*, was discovered deploying in the center of the peninsula from Valognes to St. Sauveur-le Vicomte and La Haye-du-Puits. The change reined in the 82d Airborne Division. It would be dropped astride the Merderet and north of the Douve, one regiment between Gourbesville and Amfreville, one regiment north of Picauville, and one regiment near Sainte-Mère-Église. The change meant cutting off Cherbourg and the Cotentin from reinforcements and would require a deliberate attack by the VII Corps sometime after the landing.[2]

As the various units of the 90th Division assembled near UTAH Beach, General MacKelvie and his staff landed early on the morning of 8 June. At about noon the first Division Command Post (CP) was established in France at Hameau des Loutres and MacKelvie and his staff prepared to execute the planned division mission. Under the original plan, the 90th Division was supposed to land in support of the 4th Infantry Division. Then, once the beachhead was secured, the two divisions would drive north to seize Cherbourg, while their left and rear was protected by an advance of the 82d and 101st Airborne west to cut the peninsula. However, the late change to the airborne plan combined with the badly scattered airborne landing meant the paratroopers were barely able to hang on to the positions they had seized and were in no position to execute a major attack west across the Merderet River.

Consequently, the VII Corps commander, Major General J. Lawton "Lightning Joe" Collins, was forced to hastily revise the plan again. When General Williams arrived at the VII Corps CP in the late evening of 8 June, the Assistant Corps Commander, Major General Eugene M. Landrum, informed him the 90th Infantry Division was no longer tasked to capture Cherbourg. Instead Williams was instructed to prepare a plan for the division to drive west with the mission of cutting off the German forces in the Cotentin Peninsula from the rest of the German army in France. General Williams delivered the warning order from the VII Corps HQ to MacKelvie late on the evening of 8 June. The 90th Infantry Division was tasked with the major job of driving west from the beachhead to cut off the peninsula. The division, minus the 359th Infantry, which remained attached to the 4th Infantry Division, would attack across the Merderet through the lines of the 82d Airborne Division on 10 June. The division would have to rely solely on the support of its organic Field Artillery, and no tank support was available. Worse, none of the maps issued to the division covered the new attack area and no replacement maps were at hand. The division was forced to make do with a few large-scale maps, which did not give enough detail of the roads or terrain in the area and led to considerable confusion and misdirection as units moved forward.[3]

MacKelvie's odd reaction to the changed orders was later remarked upon by at least one of the participants at the initial conference. MacKelvie appeared disturbed at the change but left the CP to make a quick reconnaissance of the Merderet River crossings with his G-3, Lieutenant Colonel Richard G. Stilwell. After returning, Williams, Stilwell, and other members of the staff worked feverishly to recast the division's plans, but MacKelvie simply sat quietly in a corner of the farmhouse headquarters and stared into the distance, rarely saying anything, and not adding to the discussions or decision making. It was another indication General MacKelvie may have been out of his depth as a division commander. Colonel Harold Meyer, General Williams's biographer, speculated that MacKelvie, as an artilleryman, was more used to "algebraic functions, logarithm tables, firing charts, and the displacement of field pieces" than he was to the "art of infantry command" and that his Army training "had not taught him the importance of command adaptability and the need to quick adjustment to battlefield situations."[4]

However, Meyer's analysis of MacKelvie failed to account for all the other Field Artillerymen who served admirably as division commanders during the war. For example, the fourth commander of the 90th Infantry Division, Brigadier General Raymond Stallings McLain, first gained recognition in the war as the 45th Infantry Division Artillery Commander in Italy. Several other highly distinguished commanders were artillerymen. Another was Brigadier General Anthony C. McAuliffe, the commander of the 101st Airborne Division Artillery who took command of the division in the defense of Bastogne during the Battle of the Bulge when its commander, Major General Maxwell D. Taylor, also an artilleryman, was absent at a conference in Washington. McAuliffe famously replied "NUTS!" to the German demand for surrender of the surrounded division. McAuliffe was promoted to major general after the battle and was given command of the 103d Infantry Division. Other generals who were artillerymen in the Normandy Campaign included Major

General Edward H. Brooks, commanding the 2d Armored Division; Major General Robert W. Grow, commanding the 6th Armored Division; and Major General Ira T. Wyche, commanding the 79th Infantry Division, all of whom had distinguished careers as division commanders.[5]

It seems more likely that MacKelvie's faults as a general had little to do with his branch of service but were more a part of his personality. MacKelvie had risen from the ranks after enlisting as a private in the famed 7th Cavalry in January 1913 before he was offered a commission and transferred to the Field Artillery after the United States declared war on Germany in April 1917.[6] He saw little or no action in the Great War but stayed in the Army. He taught ROTC, was an instructor at the Field Artillery School, and attended the Command and General Staff School and Army War College before receiving an assignment in the Office of the Chief of Staff in February 1941. Then just before Pearl Harbor was attacked he was assigned to the Office of the Assistant Chief of Staff, War Plans Division (WPD), first under Brigadier General Leonard T. Gerow and then under Eisenhower. Just why General Marshall chose MacKelvie to command the 90th is unknown, but it seems likely that MacKelvie made a good impression on the Chief of Staff as well as Eisenhower and Gerow during his service on the War Department General Staff.

10 JUNE

Early in the morning of 10 June, the 358th Infantry, minus its 2d Battalion, which was in division reserve, crossed the Merderet at Chef du Pont on the division left (south) and assembled in the bridgehead held by the 508th Parachute Infantry, south of Hill 30. The 357th Infantry on the division right (north) crossed the river at La Fiere and began advancing toward Amfreville and Le Motey, passing through the lines of the 507th Parachute Infantry and 325th Glider Infantry at Cauquigny.[7]

The 357th Infantry advance was slowed initially because it was unable to locate the 82d Airborne Division units in the positions briefed to the regiment the day before. The lack of accurate maps also led to units taking wrong turns and losing contact with the main body. Some casualties were also incurred by sporadic German artillery fire on the La Fiere bridge. The 357th finally advanced with the 3d Battalion on the right, the 2d Battalion on the left, and 1st Battalion in reserve. The difficulties experienced by the American infantry in the unfamiliar terrain were well expressed by then Major Charles E. Ronan, the 3d Battalion Executive Officer:

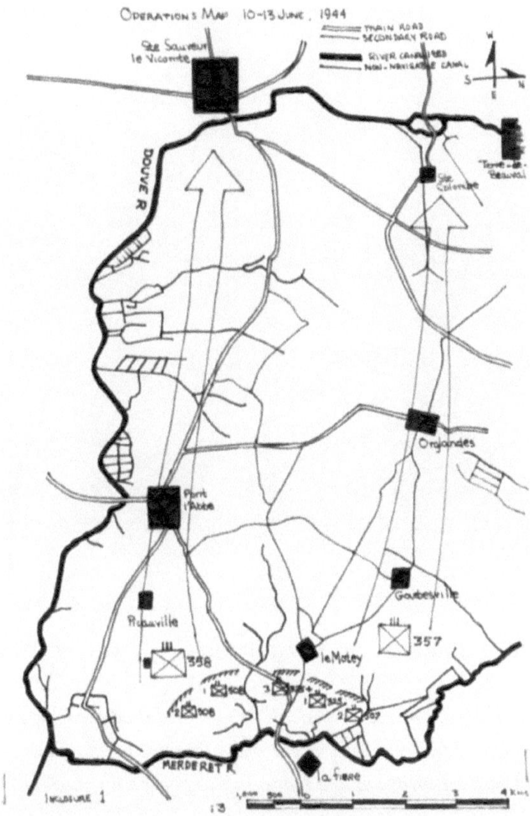

Map 2. Scheme of maneuver, 90th Infantry Division, 10–13 June 1944. Blastos, Inclosure 1.

The Battalion area was broken up by innumerable hedgerows. The Battalion Commander directed that all Company commanders thoroughly orient unit guides before darkness so they would be familiar with their routes to the initial point. The Battalion Executive, prior to darkness, checked with each company as to guides and was informed that all were well oriented and there would be no trouble.[8]

Confusion began when the Battalion moved forward. K Company crossed the initial point on schedule. L Company was not present. I Company was ordered to follow K Company. L Company arrived at the initial point as the last of I Company crossed. The unit guides had become lost in the maze of hedgerows and oriented themselves through the sound of the other elements marching down the road. No other difficulties were experienced at that time.

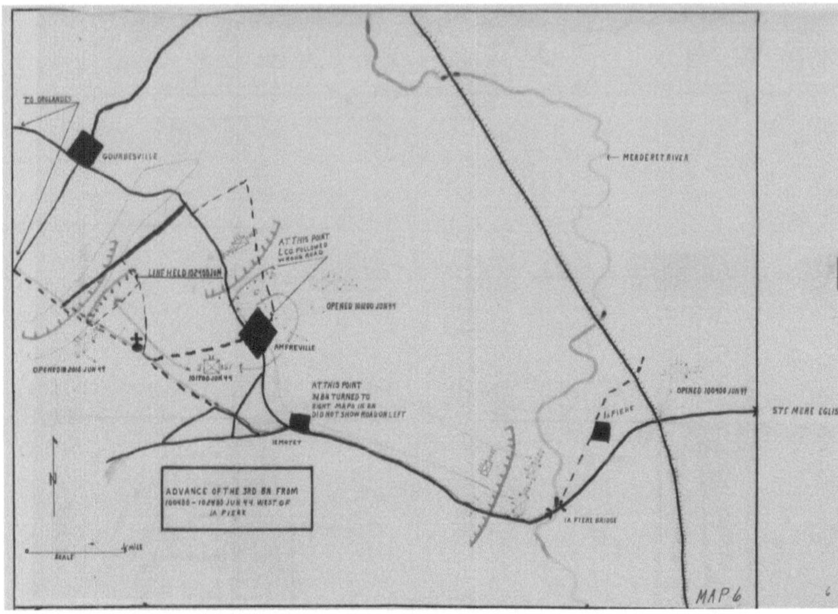

Map 3. Advance of the 3d Battalion, 357th Infantry on 10 June 1944. Ronan, Map 6.

> *The sudden changing of the Division's mission resulted in a very serious handicap to subordinate units. There were insufficient maps for issue to all officers and key noncommissioned officers in the Battalion. The maps, which had been issued for the invasion and initial mission, did not cover the new area over which the Division was now to attack. What maps were issued were not of uniform scale. Certain roads did not appear on all maps. This later resulted in the 3rd Battalion and L Company following wrong roads in the vicinity of AMFREVILLE. [Company L was out of contact with the rest of the battalion from 1200 to 1530.]*[9]

The advance was slow but steady against light resistance until 1240 when the 2d Battalion was held up by a German strongpoint. About this time, the 2d Battalion commander, Lieutenant Colonel LeRoy F. Lester, went forward to make a reconnaissance of the situation and promptly disappeared for nearly three hours. Lester finally turned up at the Regimental Headquarters at around 1530 where he proclaimed his battalion had suffered 50 percent casualties. Shortly afterward, Lester, who was thoroughly despised by his officers and enlisted men—he was later described as a "big, potbellied, coarse blowhard" who "walked like an ape, sported a prominent beer belly, had beetle brows, and was much more feared than respected"—claimed he had gone blind and was taken to the rear where he was relieved of his command. Lester was replaced by his Executive Officer, Major Stanley F. Jastre, a quiet officer well regarded by the officers and men of the 2d Battalion for his study and practice of tactics.[10]

The holdup of the 2d Battalion led the 3d Battalion to halt as well. Colonel Ginder attempted to get the 2d Battalion moving again by sending a company from the 1st Battalion forward as reinforcement, but without success. At 1530, the rest of the 1st Battalion went forward to relieve the 2d Battalion, which withdrew into reserve to reorganize. At 2130, the 1st and 3d Battalions moved forward again, but the advance was halted almost immediately by intense German fire and the battalions withdrew to their original positions. Again, Major Ronan's postwar account of the attack by the 3d Battalion illustrates how difficult it was for green troops to maneuver in the hedgerows.

> *The Battalion Executive arrived in the 3rd Battalion area [at around 1900] and found them preparing to move out. The S-3 informed him that the Battalion was to attack at 2000 hours and that the Battalion Commander had gone to the Regimental Command Post to secure the attack order. If he did not return in time additional information would be furnished by the Regimental S-2, who was somewhere along the line of march.*
>
> *The 3rd Battalion moved out in Battalion column preceded by the Battalion Executive and the S-3. Where the Battalion was going, the line of departure, supporting fires, adjacent units, direction of attack, and other similar matters were unknown.*
>
> *The Regimental S-2 was met after the Battalion had marched some 300 yards north, he explained that Regiment was to continue the attack on GOURBESVILLE, with the 1st Battalion on the left, and the 3rd Battalion on the right. The present road [the D126] was to be the boundary between the battalions. The time of attack was 2000 hours and the line of departure was a poorly defined line forward of an open field. A 10 minute artillery preparation was to be fired at 1950. The artillery preparation commenced as the S-2 finished his brief and fragmentary instructions.*
>
> *After receiving the order the Battalion Executive informed Captain Thompson, of L Company, of the order and stated L Company would attack on the Battalion's right. He then instructed the S-3 to get all Company Commanders forward at once. He hurried forward to locate the vaguely defined line of departure and to select an assembly area for last-minute orders and coordination. The area was located and the Battalion moved in. As the Company Commanders arrived they were informed of the situation. The artillery fire ceased before the Battalion had closed into the area.*
>
> *Before the attack moved out, the Battalion Commander arrived in the Battalion area but he had little additional information. There was no time for Company Commanders to*

properly orient their Platoon Leaders. Maps were critical. Had they been available there would have been no time for a map study. The Regimental order stressed speed. The terrain would be the same as the Battalion had encountered all day, continuous hedgerows.

The attack commenced at 2030 hours. After moving forward about 150 yards the Battalion encountered a murderous band of small arms and mortar fire. It seemed impossible for anyone to survive it. The Battalion assault troops answered with a withering fire. Despite this, all was in favor of the defenders. From their prepared positions, in the hedgerows, they could observe our advancing men. Our men fired blindly. Our fires sweeping the area struck the hedgerows doing little damage and fires directed at the top of the hedgerows were also ineffective. The Battalion CP was under small arms and mortar fire for the next two hours, however no casualties were suffered by this group.

The attack continued until 2300 hours. No appreciable gain was made. Company commanders and platoon leaders exposed themselves almost needlessly trying to lead their units forward. Captain James Thompson, of L Company, was killed in this attack. Lt. Thomas Maguire, L Company Executive was critically wounded. Captain Richard Shaw, of I Company, was critically injured and litter bearers were unable to get to them until late the next morning. This was also a severe blow as Lt. Howard, Executive Officer of I Company, had been killed earlier in the day.

Gradually the attack broke off, and at 2330 hours the Battalion pulled back to the line of departure. L Company remained in position to provide security during the night for the remainder of the Battalion.[11]

The 358th Infantry fared a little better. Its 1st Battalion led off the advance at 0400, under the gaze of General MacKelvie and his staff, as well as the regimental commander, Colonel James V. Thompson. By 0530 they crossed the Merderet on the D70 at Chef du Pont with just two casualties from mines. The 1st Battalion bypassed a German strongpoint in the Chateau de L'Isle Marie, about 1,100 yards south of the bridge, which they decided had been destroyed by fire from the supporting 345th Field Artillery, and continued to advance south, reaching the bridge over the Douve at Beuzeville-la-Bastille at 0545, before turning west toward Picauville, which they reported capturing at 0945.

However, in the meantime the German position at the Chateau de L'Isle Marie turned out to be very much not destroyed. After the 1st Battalion bypassed it, German small arms fire from the Chateau began harassing the advance of the rest of the regiment. At 0820, Company I, supported by the 345th Field Artillery, was ordered to seize the Chateau. This attack jumped off at 0930 and successfully occupied the Chateau, but sporadic sniper fire continued from the vicinity. The 3d Battalion then went on to secure the bridge at Beuzeville-la-Bastille and prepared it for demolition. While that was done, the 1st Battalion halted at Picauville while the Germans withdrew and established a new line 600 yards west of the village, which they stubbornly held on to when the 1st Battalion advance continued at 1300. Later in the afternoon, the 3d Battalion, after finishing its mission at Beuzeville, came up on the right (north) of the 1st Battalion. At 1645, Colonel Thompson ordered the two battalions to attack westward in line abreast toward Pont l'Abbe, supported by three battalions of artillery, but the attack petered out after advancing some 300 yards to the edge of the village.

The Germans initially opposing the 90th were identified by Division G-2 as elements of the *1058. Grenadier-Regiment* facing the 358th Infantry and the *1057. Grenadier-Regiment* facing the 357th Infantry. Both were from the *91. Infanterie-Division (LL)* and were supported by elements of the *1. Fallschirmjäger Ersatz-und-Ausbildungs-Regiment* (1st Parachute Infantry Replacement Training Regiment). The *91. Infanterie-Division* had suffered heavy losses in fighting the American airborne on D-Day, including the division commander, Generalmajor (literally major general, but equivalent to a U.S. Army brigadier general) Wilhelm Falley who was killed by troopers of the 82d Airborne in the early morning hours of D-Day. By 12 June, the *91. Infanterie-Division* recorded the loss of 2,212 men killed, wounded, and missing.[12]

The Germans made full use of the terrain and their considerable experience in defensive tactics to slow the American advance to a crawl. Small German elements, dug into the hedgerows, used their automatic weapons and mortars to full advantage, falling back to a new preplanned position when heavily pressed. Their camouflage and fire discipline tended to be excellent, frequently allowing them to fire into the flanks and rear of American troops that had unknowingly bypassed them. George Patton later characterized the tactics in his diary entry on 6 July:

> *[Lieutenant General Courtney H.] Hodges came in at supper and gave me some good first hand [sic] information of how the Germans are fighting. They use small groups of 8 to 14 men with a M.G. two Auto Pistols [submachine guns] and some riflemen also an observer who has a wire to the Mortars which are set up some 2000 yds further to the rear. And fire on targets designated by the observer. When things get too hot the whole group falls back to the next hedge a few hundred yards to the rear. They move one at a time well spread.*[13]

Unfortunately, American tactics at this stage of the war were not nearly as sophisticated as the German tactics. Typically, American units were caught in the open by German mortars and automatic weapons as they advanced across the hedged fields in regulation "Infantry School" formation where battalions deployed with two companies in line and one in reserve, typically using a road to guide the direction of advance. The tactics taught in training were essentially a carryover from lessons learned in the Great War and were only marginally modified by lessons from the battles in North Africa, Sicily, and Italy. Rather than carefully emplacing heavy weapons—mortars, heavy machine guns, infantry cannon, and Field Artillery—to maintain suppressing fire on the German front lines during the advance, the American infantry instead was taught to use "marching fire" in the attack.[14]

Marching fire was based on the Great War development of the submachine gun and the automatic rifle, which were expected to suppress the enemy trench line while the troops advanced in the assault. In theory, spraying the enemy front, along with mortar and artillery fire, would keep the enemy's heads down until the advancing troops were on top of them. The problems were the Germans had learned not to use simple linear defenses, and they were experts at camouflage in terrain that made camouflage relatively simple. The result was there was no linear front line and no obvious targets for the American infantry to focus on. As General DePuy reflected many years later,

> *As you know, the problem with infantry is that while you may get fire superiority through suppression, just at the time when you need it the most, during the assault, when the troops all rise up out of their foxholes or from behind a hedgerow and move forward, you lose it. So, the enemy then comes up out of his holes and starts to fire at you, and you lose the suppression.*
>
> *So, marching fire obviously was designed to overcome that problem, but somewhere in the transmission between the lessons learned and our unit, marching fire became the tactic through which you attacked, In other words, we lined up two battalions with two companies up and they went across the line of departure, using marching fire. It might have worked if the enemy was not well dug in, not well camouflaged, and very weak; but, if the enemy was professional, as the Germans usually were, was well-hidden, and was in very good positions, marching fire as often as not, just wasn't sufficient. We marched into their killing zones. We didn't learn about overwatch suppression until later in the war.*[15]

Worse, the extended formations made command and control extremely difficult in the broken and confusing terrain of the bocage, where visual observation was limited sometimes to less than 50 yards. It was especially problematic for the inexperienced American battalion, company, and platoon leadership. Movements slowed even more as American regimental and battalion commanders tried to make decisions. At the end of the day, the 357th Infantry reported 82 battle casualties and the 358th 134 battle casualties, which was a steep price for the limited ground gained.

Typical bocage in the Cotentin Peninsula. Aerial reconnaissance photograph from June or July 1944. U.S. Army SC.

German losses are unknown, other than the 90th Division G-2 reporting the capture of eight German prisoners on 10 June. The number of prisoners captured by the division was probably the best measure of its progress, given estimates of enemy killed and wounded were at best problematic and at worst highly exaggerated. The number of prisoners taken in were always more or less accurate and were reported daily by Division G-1 (Personnel) and G-2.[16]

At midnight German aircraft overflew the division, drawing heavy but ineffectual machine-gun fire from various units. Unfortunately, the machine-gun tracers also apparently revealed positions to the Luftwaffe, who bombed the Division Artillery Headquarters and 344th Field Artillery areas, killing three and wounding twenty-six.

11 JUNE

The two regiments of the 90th Infantry Division resumed the attack on 11 June, supported by effective fires from the supporting Division Artillery, as well as fighter-bomber strikes by the IX Tactical Air Command (TAC). However, the attacks were poorly coordinated. The 357th Infantry jumped off at 0800, but the 358th attack did not begin until five hours later. Worse, although the 746th Tank Battalion was

Typical bocage at ground level. U.S. Army SC.

released from attachment to the 4th Infantry Division and attached to the 90th at 0001, only two of its companies were available because it had suffered significant losses and required considerable maintenance after four hectic days of intense combat. The 746th Tank Battalion was also not enthusiastic regarding its attachment to the 90th, commenting,

> *Furthermore, the Battalion, having had its main baptism of fire with the 4th Infantry Division and having worked out plans for coordination between the two arms, was a bit skeptical as to operation with the 90th. Elements of the 90th had previously bivouacked near the Battalion at St Martin and they were recognized as being green troops by the manner in which they conducted themselves during the hours of darkness in their local security areas. At that time our Battalion had been in action approximately 4 days and was itself green, but the troops liked to consider themselves as veterans.*

Captain Asher K. Pay, commanding Company B, 746th Tank Battalion, reached the 357th Infantry at 0800 and attempted to get a sense of the tactical situation and what Colonel Ginder required of the tankers. What Pay found was confusion, a sense of defeat, and a lack of decisiveness. Ginder could not decide what to do with the tanks, and when Pay suggested a specific tactical deployment, he was rebuffed by the colonel. With no decision made for its employment, the tank company assembled under cover of a nearby orchard.

The 357th Infantry attack was preceded by a ten-minute artillery bombardment of the suspected German positions, which began at 0750. Unfortunately, the 3d Battalion commander, Lieutenant Colonel Thomas T. Kilday, did not return from Regimental Headquarters with the attack order until 0800, which was when the attack was to jump off. As Major Ronan noted,

> *Again, the Company Commanders had no time to brief their Platoon Leaders. Two junior lieutenants found themselves in command of companies. Platoon Sergeants were now leading platoons in several cases.*
>
> *The attack moved off about 0830 hours with K Company replacing L Company in the assault. The attack bogged down as it had the previous evening.*
>
> *. . . Radio conversations between the Battalion Commander and the Company Commanders disclosed to the command post that the attack was making little progress. Artillery fire was limited. The impossibility of forward observers to adjust fire was attributed to the fact that their field of observation was limited to the width or length of fields, which seldom extended 150 yards. A great amount of mortar fire was used. Platoon Leaders were handicapped by their lack of maps. Locations were hard to report as each field and hedgerow looked alike. There was very little direct communications between the Battalion Command Post and the Battalion Observation Post during the morning of 11 June.*[17]

Both the 1st and 3d Battalions reported they were halted by German mortar fire by 0930. At 1000, Colonel Ginder ordered one company from the 2d Battalion attached to the 3d Battalion to reinforce the attack, but in a grim comedy of errors, the 3d Battalion was told Company E was the attachment, only to have instead the Company F commander report with his men to the 3d Battalion Headquarters for orders. Then, after further back-and-forth between the regiment and the battalion, it was decided to keep Company F and that when Company E arrived, they would be told to return to the 2d Battalion, only for the hapless 3d Battalion Executive Officer to discover in the meantime the Company F commander and his troops had wandered away and were nowhere to be found. The upshot was that neither company ended up supporting the renewed effort by the 3d Battalion.[18]

During this time Major Ronan noticed that there was an increased number of men wandering to the rear down the road that divided the 1st and 3d Battalion. Some were wounded, but most were not and were only "helping" the wounded to the rear. In one case, a soldier who was wounded in the buttocks by a mortar fragment was being helped by a second unwounded man, while a third unwounded man carried the rifles and equipment of the other two, and all were shepherded by a fourth

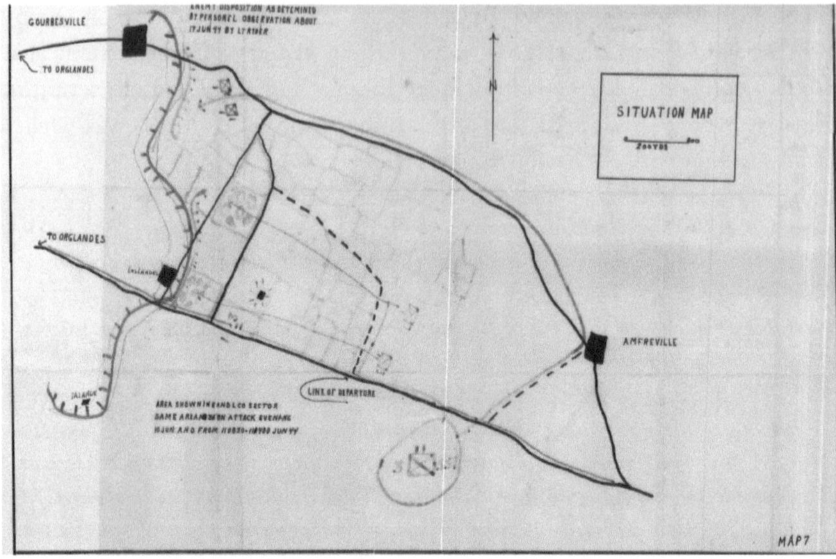

Map 4. Situation map, 357th Infantry, 11 June 1944. Ronan,Map 7.

unwounded man, a K Company platoon sergeant, who was there to "see that the other two men returned to their unit." Major Ronan ordered the three unwounded men back to K Company and assigned guards to watch for any others drifting to the rear.[19]

At 1320, another ten-minute artillery barrage was fired without any effect on German resistance and at 1400 the two battalions were ordered to withdraw 400 yards to an assembly area where they would reorganize and prepare for another advance. Water, K rations, and ammunition were issued to each company, and company commanders and platoon leaders reorganized and filled vacancies caused by the day's losses. The respite was welcome, but this habit of withdrawing to reorganize often meant the Germans would move forward to occupy the unoccupied ground, which created further havoc.

While all this activity was going on, at 1445 General Collins suddenly appeared at the 3d Battalion CP. Doubtless irate at the lack of offensive action, Collins first demanded to speak to the Battalion Commander, who had just left for the Regimental CP. He then asked Major Ronan what the battalion was doing and who had ordered them back from the front lines. Ronan explained that they had been ordered to reorganize but could not say who gave the order. Dissatisfied, Collins asked where the Regimental CP was and promptly left.

Meanwhile, supported by heavy artillery fire, the 1st Battalion was finally able to clear Amfreville at 1420. The 357th Infantry's CP moved there shortly after, and then a few minutes later General Collins arrived following his interrogation of Major Ronan. A doubtless frustrated Collins urged Ginder to immediately press the attack. A harried Ginder split up his 2d Battalion to reinforce the attack, attaching Company F, 2d Battalion, to the 1st Battalion, and Company E and G, 2d Battalion, to the 3d Battalion.

The 3d Battalion commander returned to his CP at around 1500 with orders for the renewed attack. The line of departure was the same as earlier in the day as was the axis of advance: the battalion would advance along the right of the Amfreville-Orglandes Road (D325), bypassing Gourbesville, which would be to the right (north). The dispositions of the companies and supporting platoons would also remain the same. However, when told the attack would jump off at 1530, the Company K commander refused to lead his men forward.

> *He said the time between the present and the hour of attack was insufficient to clear the assembly area, let alone march to a line of departure. He further stated he had personally led his company forward twice in the past 18 hours over the same terrain and under the same circumstances. The orders in all attacks had arrived so late that not one of his Platoon Leaders or noncommissioned officers had been briefed beyond a few words as they were advancing to the line of departure. The failure of the Battalion to achieve success in the two previous attacks, over the same area, had driven the men's morale and spirit to a breaking point. He stated he was not physically afraid and would serve as a rifleman but he felt he was failing his men if he ordered them into another attack that was destined for failure before it started.*[20]

Colonel Kilday immediately relieved the Company K commander, appointing the Regimental S-2 in his stead, then directed the company commanders to rejoin their units. However, Major Ronan intervened, making some of the same points as Company K's commander and suggesting if it was possible to delay the start of the attack, they could finally have a chance to get the battalion better set to break the enemy's defensive line. Ronan appealed to the Regimental S-3 who was present, asking if he thought Colonel Ginder might agree to postpone the attack, especially given they still had had no chance to contact or coordinate with the attached Company E. The S-3 agreed, hurriedly made his way to the Regimental CP, and returned at 1530, just as the companies were moving out, with the welcome news that the attack was delayed until 1800.

The delay allowed Kilday and Ronan time to plan a coordinated attack on the German position. Kilday would lead Company I and K in a wide flanking movement to the right, while Ronan would pin the German front with Company L and E. No artillery preparation would be fired in the hope of surprise. Kilday sensibly restored the former commander of Company K to his position before the flanking force moved out.[21]

Meanwhile, at 1600 the tanks of Company B's 3d Platoon finally rolled out in support of the 1st Battalion attack. They mopped up several machine-gun nests and reportedly "killed many infantryman." The tanks and additional infantry strength allowed Company C to reach the road running through Les Landes, the D69, about 2,000 yards west of Amfreville, but at dark the tanks were pulled back by Captain Pay to refuel and reammunition, ending the attack.[22]

The attack of the 3d Battalion jumped off at 1720, when Kilday's flanking force moved out. Ronan's pinning force began its advance twenty minutes later and gained 300 yards against sporadic small arms fire, until exploding German ammunition in a stone barn spooked Company E, which went to ground until Ronan was able to urge them forward. By then, Ronan's force was out of contact with the flanking force but had advanced across four hedgerow-lined fields and could hear firing far to their right. Then

> *The ground dropped to a well traveled narrow sunken road [probably the Rue Maison Neuve]. On the far side of the road, in E Company's area, was a rather large woods. To the right of this there was an open field, which was bounded on the forward and rear side by the usual hedgerow. On the right of this field was another woods of about equal size to that in front of E Company. This woods on the right was directly in the line of advance for L Company.*[23]

Major Ronan assessed the open field was a perfect killing zone for German mortars and artillery, so he ordered Company E and L into the woods. Both were well into the trees when heavy German small arms fire opened up, panicking some men who ran into the field, only to encounter the expected German shelling. Ronan managed to stem the panic and get the men back into the woods, but in the process, he was wounded and evacuated. The loss of his leadership effectively ended the advance after the woods were finally cleared.

Colonel Kilday's flanking element on the right made no progress and by nightfall the attack was over. Regimental casualties for the day were heavy, reported as 303 killed, wounded, and missing.[24]

In the zone of the 358th Infantry, Lieutenant Colonel Christian H. Clarke Jr., commanding the 2d Battalion, was informed at 0600 his battalion was released from division reserve as of 1000 and he should immediately report to the Regimental CP. When he arrived, he found Lieutenant Colonel William L. "Spike" Nave of the 1st Battalion and was given a quick lesson in the circumstances the green American troops were facing. When Clarke asked Nave how they were supposed to get through the hedgerows, he apparently got an earful. Nave replied that most of his battalion's casualties the previous day were incurred by artillery and mortars, which were accurately ranged in on the hedgerows. German fire discipline was excellent. "Snipers" (likely the well-camouflaged German fighting positions) waited until the Americans passed before shooting them from the rear, while the uncontrolled American fire in response served only to pinpoint the Americans' location for the German artillery and mortars. Communications were also problematic: telephone wire was constantly cut, radios did not function well in the deep hedge-lined fields, and message runners were prime targets for German snipers so were routinely escorted by entire patrols, which likely only served to further slow them down.

At 1055, the 358th Infantry finally received orders to resume its attack, again with two battalions abreast, to seize Pont l'Abbe and advance on to Étienville. The regiment's advance would be supported by all four divisional artillery battalions as well as a tactical air bombardment. However, the confused terrain was making support by American fighter-bombers problematic as well. At 1044, the Regimental S-3, Major Arthur L. Nichols, called Nave to complain he had received reports the 1st Battalion had fired on American aircraft four minutes earlier and ordered his men to cease firing on them. However, at 1050, Nave called Nichols back to tell him in fact the fire was German and was coming from Pont l'Abbe, which was not in American hands. To make matters worse, the attack was delayed until 1300 in order to prepare the artillery and air support and to get the 2d Battalion into position on the right (north) of the 3d Battalion.

Both General MacKelvie and General Williams visited the 358th Infantry CP during the morning and apparently met with General Collins, who went there too after his visit to the 357th Infantry CP. Collins was unimpressed with the performance of the 90th, later recalling encountering a group of soldiers in a ditch far from the front line who gave him evasive answers when he asked what they were doing. When Collins mentioned the incident to MacKelvie the Division Commander made no excuses but seemed bewildered about what could be done about the division's lack of aggressiveness.[25]

The Germans took advantage of the long lull to begin working troops around the right flank of Company L, which was the right-hand company of the 3d Battalion. The German infiltration complicated the 2d Battalion's approach march as they tried to avoid them. The march ended with the left of the 2d Battalion coming up behind the right of the 3d, which required an hour to straighten out, all the time harassed by fire from the German infiltrators. Nevertheless, the attack jumped off at 1300, but by 1400 Company A, leading the 1st Battalion, was halted by German machine-gun fire and was then forced to go around a heavily mined and booby-trapped field. By 1600, the 1st and 3d Battalions were on their initial objectives with the 2d Battalion moving up on their right rear. By 1640, the Germans had fallen back to Pont l'Abbe and were again holding firm against the advance of the 1st and 3d Battalion despite heavy supporting American artillery fire, while the 2d Battalion was attempting to envelope the town to the north against increasing resistance. At 1855, the Germans surprised the Rear CP of the 358th Infantry with an accurate mortar barrage that severely wounded the Regimental XO, Lieutenant Colonel Blair C. Stouffer, which sowed additional confusion in the American ranks. Shortly afterward the American attack petered out. Regimental casualties were again heavy, reportedly 194 killed, wounded, and missing, most of them, like the previous day, in the 1st and 3d Battalion.

The 359th Infantry, minus its 1st Battalion, which remained under 4th Infantry Division control containing a German force at Chateau de Fontenay, was released from attachment to the 4th Infantry Division and reverted to control of the 90th Infantry Division at 0140 on 11 June. It moved into 90th Division reserve near Haut Guetteville by 1330. However, the 2d Battalion, which was still lacking half its heavy weapons and equipment and 30 percent of its small arms after the sinking of the *Susan B. Anthony*, remained ineffective. The 1st Battalion finally was released back to the regiment and division at 2000, while the Regimental AT, Cannon, and Service Company finally rejoined the regiment as well. Although the Divisional After-Action Report implies the 359th was fully committed to the attack that evening and suffered heavy shelling while moving to a position near Picauville, there is little evidence from the regimental reports that such occurred—only two KIA and forty-one WIA were lost to artillery fire in the regiment. It was not until the morning of 12 June that the complete regiment was committed to action under command of the 90th.[26]

Once more, little had been accomplished by the division other than the loss of significant numbers of officers and men. Approximately six hundred to seven hundred casualties were incurred, which was about 6 to 7 percent of the division strength committed to action, a significantly high level of intensity.[27]

One 90th Infantry Division casualty on 11 June was recognized by the award of the Distinguished Service Cross.

First Lieutenant (Infantry) Rufus N. Garrett (ASN: 0-339882), United States Army, was awarded the Distinguished Service Cross (Posthumously) for extraordinary heroism in connection with military operations against an armed enemy while serving with the 90th Infantry Division, in action against enemy forces on 11 June 1944. First Lieutenant Garrett's intrepid actions, personal bravery and zealous devotion to duty at the cost of his life, exemplify the highest traditions of the military forces of the United States and reflect great credit upon himself, the 90th Infantry Division, and the United States Army.[28]

Garrett, thirty years old, was from El Dorado, Arkansas. He was the son of Rufus Napoleon Garrett, a banking, oil, and foundry owner in El Dorado, who had died in 1942. A ROTC graduate of the University of Arkansas, Captain Garrett was an OR officer called up in February 1942. His wife, Agnes Soule, received his last letter, written while crossing the Channel on 7 June, shortly after she received notice of his death from the wife of a fellow officer in Texas. The official War Department notification was not until 6 July. In addition to his wife, he left behind an eighteen-month-old daughter, Penny. Reflecting again the confusion found in the 90th Infantry Division, Lieutenant Garret's unit was not identified, nor were the exact circumstances of his heroism. He was Assistant S-2 in the 2d Battalion, 358th Infantry but the Morning Report only records his death.

12 JUNE

By the morning of 12 June, the 90th Infantry Division was finally able to deploy its third infantry regiment in the attack and was able to support that attack with tanks as well as artillery, but to little avail. The 357th was ordered to continue its push toward Amfreville, while the 358th advanced on Gourbesville, and the 359th joined in by attacking from Picauville into the gap between the 357th and 358th Infantry. However, there was no attempt by MacKelvie to mass forces against any part of the German position, little attempt at reconnaissance to seek out weak points, and no attempt to develop a main effort. Instead the division pushed forward with seven battalions on a line spread over a front about 5 miles long. The results were predictable.

The 357th Infantry prepared to advance with the same deployment it had ended the previous day. The 3d Battalion was on the right, with Company E and G attached, and the 1st Battalion was on the left, with Company F attached. Ginder's deployment effectively took the Regiment's 2d Battalion out of the battle as a maneuver element and instead used it to reinforce the other two in the attempt to batter forward through the German defenses by sheer mass. Even the elements of Company M—the Battalion Weapons Company—not attached to the forward companies was committed, helping the Regimental Intelligence and Reconnaissance (I&R) Platoon protect the Regimental CP near La Pesquerie, about 1,500 yards east of Gourbesville, from a German patrol that had approached within about 500 yards.

While Colonel Ginder was working out this plan of attack, General MacKelvie suddenly appeared in the CP and began to loudly criticize Ginder and his assembled battalion commanders for their failure to carry out his attack orders on time. Then, in yet another sign of the inexperience and disarray in the division, a runner arrived from Division Headquarters with the order MacKelvie was criticizing his officers for not carrying out. Even so, MacKelvie did not delay the time of execution of the order and demanded it be carried out. The attack began at 1050.[29]

At least this time Colonel Ginder finally decided to make use of the attached tanks. Company B, 746th Tank Battalion moved up and assembled in its orchard again at 0700 ready to support the advance. However, only the 1st Platoon, under 1st Lieutenant Irving N. Hurley, with five M4 Medium Tanks, was chosen initially to support the advance of the 1st Battalion on the left. Hurley was given the mission of suppressing a German strongpoint west of the D69 at Les Landes. The strongpoint, dug into a farmhouse and its surrounding fields, consisted of numerous machine-gun positions supported by mortars. The rest of the tank company remained in reserve.

Coordination between tanks and infantry remained poor, negating the effects of the tank support. The infantry advanced, but Hurley's platoon did not move until 1345, according to the 357th Infantry, or 1400, according to Company B, 746th Tank Battalion. The reason for the delay is unknown. The tanks pushed forward, crossing the highway, and advancing into the German strongpoint, but Lieutenant Hurley reported his infantry support was weak and would not advance. While the tank attack was going on, General Landrum appeared at the 357th Infantry CP and asked Captain Pay why the infantry was not advancing while praising the performance of Pay's tankers. Shortly after, Pay committed his 2d Platoon, under Lieutenant Frank Kogut, which had been reduced to just two tanks earlier in the week. Kogut's tanks reached the German strongpoint about 1700, just as a German "bazooka" round hit Lieutenant Hurley's tank turret, killing him instantly and wounding three of his crew. Shortly after, an intense German artillery and mortar bombardment was unleashed on the area, completely separating the remaining American tanks from their infantry support. Lieutenant Colonel Clarence G. Hupfer, the commander of the 746th Tank Battalion, who was listening in by radio was able to get a counter bombardment directed on Gourbesville, which covered the withdrawal of the tanks.[30]

While the 357th Infantry's attack gained no additional ground, a mission of mercy did accidentally discover an alternative to attacking the German positions at Gourbesville head-on. A French civilian appeared at the Regimental CP with news of wounded American paratroopers sheltered in a barn southeast of Gourbesville. Lt. Charles Ryder Jr., Assistant Regimental S-2, guided by the Frenchman, was dispatched with a patrol to rescue them. En route he found a sheltered and apparently unguarded approach leading to the village from the east.[31]

By 1800, the infantry and tanks were back at the start line of the attack, with only heavy casualty to show as the result of four hours of intense combat. At about the same time, General Williams, Lieutenant Colonel Hupfer, and Colonel Francis F. Fainter, commander of the 6th Tank Group, made a quick visit to the front lines, reconnoitering and formulating a plan to carry on the attack. However, the next attack by the 357th Infantry would not be led by Colonel Ginder. He was relieved of his command at 1730, probably in person by General Williams, but certainly with the agreement of General MacKelvie. Colonel Sheehy, who was at the 358th Infantry CP at the time, was ordered to assume command of the regiment again.

One 357th Infantry soldier's action on 12 June resulted in the award of a Distinguished Service Cross.

> *Second Lieutenant Charles C. Wetzel (ASN: 0-1320206), United States Army, was awarded the Distinguished Service Cross (Posthumously) for extraordinary heroism in connection with military operations against an armed enemy while serving with the 357th Infantry Regiment, 90th Infantry Division, in action against enemy forces on 12 June 1944. Second Lieutenant Wetzel's intrepid actions, personal bravery and zealous devotion to duty at the cost of his life, exemplify the highest traditions of the military forces of the United States and reflect great credit upon himself, the 90th Infantry Division, and the United States Army.*[32]

2d Lieutenant Wetzel was in Company I, but curiously his death was recorded by the 357th Infantry on 16 June rather than 12 June. It is yet another example of the slow reporting and errors inherent in the introduction of an inexperienced division into combat.

It was probably when General Williams returned to the Division CP that he reportedly encountered General MacKelvie huddling in a shallow ditch next to a hedgerow. According to an often repeated account, Williams lost his temper at what he supposed was MacKelvie's timidity and inaction. Williams verbally lambasted his commander:

> *Goddammit General, you can't lead this division hiding in that goddam hole. Go back to the CP. Get the hell out of that hole and go to your vehicle. Walk to it, or you'll have this goddam division wading in the English Channel.*[33]

Williams's intemperance was beginning to get the better of him. A combat veteran in World War I with the 359th Infantry, Williams had zero tolerance for what he perceived as MacKelvie's temerity.

The 359th Infantry finally entered battle on 12 June. It was inserted in the center of the line into the yawning gap between the 357th and 358th Infantry. The 1st Battalion, 359th Infantry closed in the vicinity of Haut Geutteville at 0315 and remained in division reserve until 16 June. The rest of the regiment, including the partly reorganized and reequipped 2d Battalion, was ordered to attack "on an azimuth of 240 degrees." In other words, it was to advance approximately southwest by west, toward its objective, which was the blacktop D69 road south of Les Landes.

Two platoons of the 746th Tank Battalion's Company A furnished ten medium tanks to support the advance, with one platoon attached to each infantry battalion. The company commander and his two platoon commanders went forward from the 90th Division Forward CP to the 359th Infantry CP at 0600 where they were able to attend a meeting of the regiment's commanders. They also were able to make a foot reconnaissance of the approach to the line of departure, which was along a narrow sunken road, and spent a short time coordinating plans for the use of the tanks. With that the advance began at 0800.

Unfortunately, the cooperation between tanks and infantry again quickly broke down. While the tanks were able to get forward to the line of departure, the 1st Platoon struggled to find an exit from the sunken lane across boggy and rough terrain. The 2d Platoon did jump off on time, but both tank platoons found the German defensive fire quickly pinned down the infantry, leaving them alone in the advance. Nevertheless, the tankers reported inflicting significant casualties on the defenders, and they managed to advance some 1,700 yards, just short of the D69 Road.

The infantry, separated again from the tanks, struggled against intense mortar and machine-gun fire. Worse, in the confusion the two battalions veered nearly 90 degrees off the planned line of advance and spent six hours driving nearly due north. At around 1400 the error was finally realized, and the two battalions paused to reorganize, with the 2d Battalion about 200 yards short of the D69 road and the 3d Battalion about 700 yards away. At 2150, the 3d Battalion resumed its attack, closing with the 2d Battalion about 100 yards short of its objective as night fell.[34]

The operations of the 358th Infantry began on a sour note on 12 June. Apparently spooked by a reference in the nightly Division G-2 Report that read, "the enemy is capable of counter-attacking with either tanks or SP guns reported moving N into the vicinity of ETIENVILLE [about 4,500 yards west of the regimental front line]," at 0130 Colonel Thompson ordered the 2d and 3d Battalion to withdraw to the east of the road running northeast out of Pont L'Abbe, the D15, and prepare for an "impending enemy tank attack." After a call for fire at 0310, a four-battalion artillery concentration was fired at 0325 on a location about 3,000 yards north of Pont L'Abbe, so somewhat south of the 357th Infantry positions at Les Landes, "where the sound of tanks had been reported." Five volleys, about 240 rounds, were fired on "fifty tanks" and nothing further came of the supposed German tank attack. By 0500, the two battalions completed their withdrawal to positions along the D15.

In fact, it is doubtful there were many, if any, German armored vehicles opposing the division. The *709. Infanterie-Division* had nine 7.5cm s.Pak Sfl. auf Lorraine-Schlepper, which was an open-topped German self-propelled antitank gun mounted on ex-French tracked armored personnel carriers but were 20 kilometers away at Valognes on D-Day. By 12 June they were likely far to the north, trying to slow the advance by the 4th Infantry Division on Cherbourg. The *243. Infanterie-Division* deployed the *2. Kompanie* of *Panzerjäger-Abteilung 243.* with twelve Sturmgeschütz (7.5cm assault guns) at Le Pont aux Moines, 1 kilometer south of St. Jacques, about 20 kilometers to the west, and its *1. Kompanie* with fourteen 7.5cm s.Pak Sfl. Marder III 4 kilometers north of Barneville, and about 25 kilometers away. They engaged the 82d Airborne at Sainte-Mère-Église, attacking from the north, and losing at least two Sturmgeschutz and three Marders, but by 12 June the main body was probably farther north, opposing the 4th Infantry Division, although some elements may have been opposing the 90th Infantry Division.

The most likely culprit was the remnants of the *Panzer-Ersatz-und-Ausbildungs-Abeilung 100*, which was attached to the *91. Infanterie-Division*. It originally consisted of twenty-nine aging French tanks, captured by the Germans in 1940, and three or more obsolescent German tanks. Its headquarters was at Franquetot, with companies at Baupte, Coigny, and Auvers. On 6 June it advanced toward Sainte-Mère-Église and was heavily engaged by the 508th Parachute Infantry at La Fière and Cauquigny, losing at least four tanks there. It remained engaged farther south with the 505th Parachute Infantry of the 82d Airborne Division at Beuzeville la Bastille, Cretteville, Francquetot, and Coigny-Houtteville-La Prieure, but it is possible some of its vehicles could have been seen and heard, spooking the 358th Infantry.[35]

In any event, no German tank attack transpired, and at 0615 Colonel Thompson issued orders to Lieutenant Colonel Clarke, commanding the 2d Battalion and Lieutenant Colonel Jacob Bealke, commanding the 3d Battalion, to resume the attack at 0800. The 1st Battalion would contain the German position at Pont L'Abbe on the north and east, while the 3d Battalion on the far right and the 2d Battalion in the center bypassed the town and drove to the high ground farther west. They were supported by ten light tanks of the 1st and 3d Platoon, Company D, 746th Tank Battalion, which advanced to the outskirts of Étienville where they halted, unable to continue against intense artillery and antitank gun fire. It is not entirely clear from the record, but it appears the light tanks attacked with little or no infantry support and by evening they withdrew to the 746th Tank Battalion bivouac near Ste. Mère-Eglise. Again, there had been no combined arms cooperation between the infantry and tanks.

The 358th Infantry jumped off on time, but neither the 2d or 3d Battalion were initially able to cross the line of departure as they were hit by heavy mortar, machine-gun, and sniper fire. By 1040, Company G advanced slightly, but then quickly bogged down again. Five minutes later, Spike Nave, commanding the 1st Battalion, was wounded in the stomach and evacuated to the regimental aid station. Major Albert Seeger, the Battalion Executive Officer, took command. Then at 1050, Colonel Thompson, who had come forward attempting to prod forward Company F, was severely wounded. Company F soon fell back badly disorganized, leaving Colonel Thompson and several other wounded officers and men behind. It took forty minutes before Company F was reorganized and renewed the attack, reinforced by Company I. They were able to advance to where Thompson and the others were lying wounded and evacuate them.

The Germans quickly capitalized on the stalled American advance, and at 1110 the 1st Battalion reported it was being heavily counterattacked. With both regiment and battalion commander out of action, Lieutenant Colonel Clarke took command of the regiment, while his Executive Officer, Major Marion C. L. Baldwin, took over the 2d Battalion. At 1125, heavy German artillery fire forced the Regimental CP to withdraw, but it remained under periodic artillery and sniper fire in its new position.

By noon, the 2d and 3d Battalions had finally inched forward, but only by committing everything except Company E and even its commander, Captain Underwood, was out of action after being shot in the foot by a sniper. At 1310,

Colonel Sheehy arrived from Division Headquarters with orders for the regiment to hold in place and reorganize. Clarke was told to resume the attack on Pont L'Abbe after the Air Corps hit it with a fighter-bomber attack. While at the 358th Infantry CP, Colonel Sheehy received word he was to take command of the 357th Infantry and he immediately left in his jeep for the reported location of the Regiment's 1st Battalion.

The Air Force's P-47s hit the town at 1710. The first bombing pass was short to the north of town and bomb fragments killed at least one American, 2d Lieutenant Thomas W. Lasher, a liaison officer from Division Artillery. However, the rest of the bombs were direct hits on the town, and when the regiment advanced again at 2037 there was no resistance and Pont L'Abbe was finally secured.[36]

During the day, the teamwork and bravery of two soldiers of the 358th Infantry earned them both Distinguished Service Crosses.

> *The President of the United States of America, authorized by Act of Congress July 9, 1918, takes pleasure in presenting the Distinguished Service Cross to Staff Sergeant Gus Hampl (ASN: 37156279), United States Army, for extraordinary heroism in connection with military operations against an armed enemy while serving with Headquarters and Headquarters Company, 358th Infantry Regiment, 90th Infantry Division. On 12 June 1944, in the vicinity of Picauville, France, the attack of Company L, 358 Infantry, encountered the direct fire of an enemy 75 mm gun which was strongly emplaced and protected by small arms fire and mortar fire. Sergeant Hampl and one other man, members of a demolition team attached to the rifle company, volunteered to attempt the destruction of the gun. A friendly mortar barrage drove the enemy gun crew to shelter in a nearby building while Sergeant Hampl and his companion worked their way forward. They reached the gun and, although under enemy observation and fire, placed an explosive charge in the breach and demolished it. They then threw incendiary grenades into the building in which the enemy had taken cover, setting it afire and forcing them to surrender. The heroic actions of Sergeant Hampl, and his courageous devotion to duty exemplified the highest traditions of the military forces of United States.*
>
> *Private First Class Eduardo F. Ramirez (ASN 38000897), Headquarters Co., 358th Infantry Regiment, 90th Infantry Division, United States Army. For extraordinary heroism in connection with military operations against an armed enemy. On 12 June 1944, in the vicinity of Picauville, France, the attack of Company L, 358 Infantry, encountered the direct fire of an enemy 75mm gun which was strongly emplaced and protected by small arms fire and mortar fire. Private Ramirez and one other man, members of a demolition team attached to the rifle company, volunteered to attempt the destruction of the gun. A friendly mortar barrage drove the enemy gun crew to shelter in a nearby*

building while Private Ramirez and his companion worked their way forward. They reached the gun and, although under enemy observation and fire, placed an explosive charge in the breach and demolished it. They then threw incendiary grenades into the building in which the enemy had taken cover, setting it afire and forcing them to surrender. The heroic actions of Private Ramirez, and his courageous devotion to duty exemplified the highest traditions of the military forces of United States.[37]

For yet a third day losses in the 90th Infantry Division were very high. While the division reported only 185 casualties, the two regiments principally engaged, the 357th and 358th, reported over 400. Although it is likely that some of those regimental casualties were "catching up" from the previous days of combat, it is still evident that attrition in the division was averaging about 3 percent per day, a very high level of intensity.

Worse, adding armored support to the infantry and artillery combined arms team had not resulted in any significant improvement in the division's performance. After two days of fighting with the division, the 746th Tank Battalion was relieved from attachment to the 90th and attached instead to the 82d Airborne Division. However, the poor infantry-armor coordination exhibited between the 90th Infantry Division and 746th Tank Battalion was not a fault of either; instead it was a problem endemic to the U.S. Army. Four years after the creation of the Armored Force, the AGF had failed to ensure tank-infantry combined arms training was a standard element in the mobilization training program.

At no point in its training in the United States is it evident the 90th spent any time practicing coordination with tanks. Then, after arriving in England on 9 April, it trained in "mine detection, village fighting, assault on fortified positions, hedgerow fighting, artillery firing problems, road marches and obstacle courses," but again no time was spent training with tanks.[38]

The dearth of infantry-tank combined arms training was made worse by the lack of a field manual and doctrine specifically meant for the separate tank battalion, which was intended to provide that support for the infantry division. In May and June 1943, representatives of the Armored Force, AGF, and the Army Command and General Staff School met at Fort Knox to write the long-delayed field manual expressly for the separate tank battalion but were forced to delay until new Tank Battalion Tables of Organization and Equipment were published on 15 August 1943. The Adjutant General finally published the first edition of *FM 17-36 Employment of Tanks with Infantry (Tentative)* in September 1943. Although an AGF directive of 16 October 1943 mandated training separate tank battalions with infantry divisions during the combined arms maneuver cycle, the demands of war constantly disrupted that effort. By then it was also unlikely to have much effect because most of the separate tank battalions were at the end of the training cycle, were preparing to deploy, or were already deployed overseas.[39] Then in March 1944, *FM 17-36* was updated with the provisory *(Tentative)* removed from the title. The update finally gave cognizance to the idea of attaching the separate tank battalion to an infantry division and for task organizing company-size and smaller elements of the tank battalion with smaller units within the infantry division. However, by then it was much too late to have any effect on the units preparing for the invasion.[40]

Worse still, AGF failed to organize, train, and equip enough separate tank battalions that one could be regularly paired with each infantry division in theater. The initial troop basis for NEPTUNE only included eight separate tank battalions (including two light tank) for the seven infantry and two airborne divisions committed to the assault. Nine other tank battalions were present in England as of 1 June, but four were special units equipped with the top-secret Canal Defense Light (CDL) and were incapable of acting as a standard infantry-support tank battalion. Another, the 707th, was assigned to the ETOUSA Ground Forces Replacement Center, and the remaining four were assigned to TUSA as the initial follow-on to the assault forces. Worse, while the War Department allocated thirty-four infantry divisions to the ETOUSA through the end of 1944, they planned for only thirty separate tank battalions, including the six CDL and two light tank battalions. Under that scenario only two-thirds of the infantry divisions could have a permanent separate tank battalion as attachment. Put another way, there was only one medium tank battalion for every 1.5 divisions intended for the ETOUSA.[41]

The 746th Tank Battalion was well aware of the problem and after its initial experience in combat with the 4th Infantry Division attempted to create its own solution, which was later mentioned in its June After-Action Report.

> *The development of the new [tank-infantry] liaison plan was tried for the first time during the Battalions attachment to the 90th. During this action the command tanks of company commanders of both A and B companies were kept in the vicinity of regimental CP's for personal liaison with the regimental commander and for radio liaison with the tank platoon [tank and infantry units used different radios that did not normally net]. Quarter ton truck [sic] was also maintained at the regiment CP and frequent trips during the day were made forward to contact the platoons.*

Unfortunately, this fix had little effect on the battle. As the 746th Tank Battalion June After-Action Report also said,

The operations were not too successful due to difficult and restricted terrain. The infantry suffered heavy casualties from mortars and artillery as well as from lack of battle experience.

One of the more interesting exploits during the evening of 12 June was led by none other than Captain Oehmichen, the commander of the Interrogation Prisoner of War Team No. 49. He received information from prisoners that led him to organize a patrol that rescued four wounded American paratroopers from behind German lines near Amfreville. He then led the patrol two miles into German-held countryside and supervised the safe evacuation of wounded men back to the American lines. Captain Oehmichen was awarded the Bronze Star for heroic service for this action.[42]

The day had been hard for the Germans as well. In the morning, the staff car of General der Infanterie (Lieutenant General) Erich Marcks was strafed by Allied fighters near Hébécrevon, west of Saint-Lô. Marcks, his aid, and driver scrambled out of the car and made for a ditch, but the one-legged Marcks—he had lost his left leg on the Eastern Front in 1941—was hit by a 20mm cannon shell fragment before he reached cover. The fragment severed his femoral artery, and he bled to death at 0945. General der Flieger Eugen Meindl, commander of the *II. Fallschirm-Jäger-Korps*, which was moving to the front from Quintin in Brittany, took temporary command of the *LXXXIV Armee-Korps* before Generalfeldmarschall (Field Marshal) Erwin Rommel, commander of *Heeresgruppe B* (Army Group B), ordered the commander of the *XXV Armee-Korps*, General der Artillerie Wilhelm Fahrmbacher, to take command later that evening. Rommel and Fahrmbacher decided to divide the German forces facing the Americans into two Kampfgruppe (Combat Group, abbreviated *KG*). One, *KG Hellmich*, placed the defenses of the Cotentin into a single group under the command of Generalleutnant Heinz Hellmich, commander of the *243. Infanterie-Division*. His command consisted of his own *243. Infanterie-Division*, *91. Infanterie-Division*, *77. Infanterie-Division*, and *709. Infanterie-Division*, which would defend the Cotentin north of the Douve River. The second, *KG Meindl*, consisted of the forward elements of his own corps headquarters with the badly battered remnants of the *352. Infanterie-Division* and *Fallschirm-Jäger-Regiment 6*. Meindl also received the newly arrived *KG Heintz* (a reinforced regiment of *275. Infanterie-Division*) and *17. SS-Panzergrenadier-Division "Götz von Berlichingen"* (*SS-GvB*). Additional reinforcements on their way to oppose the Americans were the *3. Fallschirm-Jäger*

Division, *353. Infanterie-Division*, and another regimental-size Kampfgruppe from *265. Infanterie-Division*.[43]

During the day, the Germans reinforced their line opposing the 359th Infantry with elements of the *243. Infanterie-Division*. By evening, the *1.*, *3.*, *6.*, and *7. Kompanie* of *Grenadier-Regiment 920.* and the *Regimentstroß* (Service Company) of *Grenadier-Regiment 922.* were identified, implying that probably two battalions of one regiment and elements of another were present. In addition, on 11 June the *9. Kompanie* of *Fallschirm-Jäger-Ausbildungs-Regiment 1.* was also identified in front of the 358th Infantry.

13 JUNE

Sometime in the late evening of 12 June or early morning of 13 June, General Collins relieved General MacKelvie of command of the 90th Infantry Division without prejudice and ordered General Landrum to take command of the division. Collins apparently had been contemplating relieving MacKelvie for some time, possibly since 11 June, when he was touring the division zone. General Landrum's visit to the division on 12 June probably confirmed Collins's decision, and he received Bradley's agreement that same day. When General Williams heard of MacKelvie's relief, he wondered if news of his tirade of the previous day had gotten to Collins and was a factor in his decision.[44]

John Colby, who was a Weapons Platoon Leader and then Company Commander in the 357th Infantry, gave the most succinct analysis of MacKelvie's effect on the division:

> *He was, at best, a neutral factor, he was, in most instances, a distinctly negative factor for the Division and its performance. Shortfalls included: no apparent knowledge of infantry tactics or battlefield leadership; unwillingness to accept sound advice from his knowledgeable subordinates (Williams and Devine); delayed all orders for nit-picking review; issued orders so late his subordinates had no time to coordinate essential details before the designated "H-Hour," which resulted in disastrous loss of life; was distant, cold, and remote in personality, even with his personal staff and major subordinate commands.*[45]

General Landrum, like MacKelvie, entered the Army as an enlisted man before the Great War. Landrum too did not serve in combat during that war; he spent the war in Utah, the Hawaiian Department, and the Philippines. He too stayed in the Army and attended the Command and General Staff School, the War College, and the Infantry School, where he became Executive Officer in December 1940.

Major General Eugene M. Landrum. U.S. Army SC.

He commanded the 7th Infantry Division in the invasion of Attu in the Aleutians in May 1943 and commanded the 87th Infantry Division in training in the States before he was assigned as Collins's deputy.[46]

Physically, the division's new commander, Landrum, was short and rotund; in photos his trousers dragged on the ground and his overcoat reached down nearly to his ankles, making him look even shorter and stouter than he was. His round, jowly face was usually obscured by the large pipe he habitually clasped in his teeth, and he quickly developed the bad habit of commanding the division while sitting in a wicker chair in his cellar headquarters. Altogether he made a poor impression on the beleaguered staff officers of the 90th Infantry Division but after the chaos of MacKelvie's tenure it seemed unlikely that he could be worse.[47]

The attack of the 357th Infantry continued at 0700 with Colonel Sheehy now commanding. The 1st and 2d Battalion advanced to the northwest with Orglandes as the objective, but the pace remained slow. The 3d Battalion, reorganized overnight, remained in reserve until 0945 when Sheehy ordered it to the right flank and across the Amfreville-Gourbesville Road. The 3d Battalion was ordered to attack Gourbesville from the northeast using the covered route discovered by Lieutenant Ryder the previous day, in order to relieve the pressure on the other two battalions. However, the hope the new approach was unguarded was dashed when the 3d Battalion met the same unrelenting heavy mortar and artillery fire. Its attack stalled by 1220, well short of the village.[48]

During the afternoon, Lieutenant John Colby, the Weapons Platoon Leader of Company E, took command of the company when its commander was evacuated with battle fatigue. Colby was able to get the company forward past "Coffin Corner," a road intersection near Gourbesville that was zeroed in by German artillery and mortars, only to be ordered to withdraw from his exposed position by the Battalion Commander, Major Jastre. Colby, irate at the order to withdraw after the effort to get to the position, refused and was relieved by Jastre, who was killed moments later by the German artillery fire. Colby managed to get back to Battalion Headquarters, where he informed the senior officer there, Captain Ernest C. Magnuson, that he was now the battalion commander. Magnuson ordered Colby to forget Jastre's orders and sent him back to his company with orders to hold its position. In turn, Magnuson later turned over command to Captain William Louis Domries, the commander of Company G, who was his senior in rank. The 2d Battalion had been through four commanding officers in as many days.[49]

The 359th Infantry was supposed to jump off to the attack at 0500, but orders from the division were not received by then, so the attack was postponed to 0745. It continued to advance cross country on a compass azimuth of 258 degrees (west southwest), with the objective—Reigneville-Bocage—about 2.5 miles distant.

The 359th advanced in a column of battalions with the 3d leading, followed by the 2d 500 yards behind. The 1st Battalion remained in division reserve. The 3d Battalion advanced 500 yards when it was halted by German machine-gun, mortar, and artillery fire at 0905. The 2d Battalion was ordered to continue advancing on an "azimuth of 285 degrees" (west northwest) around the right of the 3d Battalion but only managed to gain another 200 yards before it too was halted.

Colonel Clarke was relieved of responsibility for commanding the 358th Infantry when Spike Nave, who was senior to him, arrived at the Regimental CP. Although Nave was still recovering from the stomach wound he suffered the previous day, when he heard Colonel Thompson was wounded, he insisted on leaving the regimental aid station and returning to duty. The regiment mopped up Etienville in the morning and secured the area south to the Douvre River with the 3d Battalion, which had not yet been in action. At 1045, the quiet was punctured by a "tank attack" reported from the southwest, which was repelled without difficulty by the Regimental Antitank Company. It seems likely the German tanks were simply the remnants of whatever forces that caused the tank scare the previous day. The 2d Battalion, 358th Infantry spent the day in its position's northeast of Etienville and suffered casualties from a bombing strike during the day. Generals Ridgway and Gavin of the 82d Airborne Division met with Colonel Clarke at the Regimental CP at Etienville as they developed a plan to pass the 82d Airborne Division through to relieve the regiment.

During the day the fires of the 90th Infantry Division were heavily reinforced. In addition to the attached 980th Field Artillery Battalion, the 9th Infantry Division and 82d Airborne Division Artillery fired in support.

14 JUNE

Impatient with the lack of progress by the 90th Infantry Division, General Collins ordered elements of the 82d Airborne Division and newly landed 9th Infantry Division to pass through the 358th Infantry to secure the line of the Douvre River to the west at Saint-Sauveur-le-Vicomte and Sainte-Colombe. The 358th Infantry would execute a limited attack to cover the movement and then assemble at Pont l'Abbe, while the 359th Infantry would shift its attack toward Orglandes and the 357th Infantry would continue its attack on Gourbesville.

The 3d Battalion, 357th Infantry spent the morning of 14 June reorganizing in its positions north of the Amfreville-Gourbesville Road (D126) while it prepared to renew the assault on Gourbesville from the east. The 2d and 3d Battalions remained on a line extending south of the Amfreville-Gourbesville Road to positions near Les Landes.

The initial plan was for a carefully coordinated attack following a bombing of the German positions around Gourbesville at 1345, which fell apart when the aircraft failed to show up. Instead a heavy artillery concentration was plotted that would mark the locations for a rescheduled bombing attack with the infantry to jump off at 1930. However at 1700, that plan was scrapped as well when it turned out the artillery had not been issued with the proper colored smoke shells to mark the target for the AAF. In the end, a doubtless frustrated General Williams personally led the 3d Battalion into the attack at 1930. The attack he led slowly worked its way into Gourbesville from the east against fierce resistance. At 2020, the Americans got into the town but were forced back to the outskirts by a German counterattack shortly afterward.

Lieutenant Colby's Company G, 357th Infantry, spent the day securing the fields around "Coffin Corner." In one field they found the evidence that confirmed his suspicion that a German headquarters had been there. Vehicles, chairs, tables, and other gear were scattered about, including one truck that contained a regimental payroll. Colby's men amused themselves for a while by lighting cigarettes with ten- and twenty-Reichsmark bills and began a craps game that was only interrupted when a German "light tank" suddenly appeared on the road. After firing into the surprised Americans and causing a momentary excitement until the company mail orderly grabbed a bazooka and fired at the "tank." Apparently undamaged, it quickly drove off back toward Gourbesville.

Later that evening, Colby was ordered to advance toward Gourbesville in support of the 3d Battalion attack. Believing the Battalion S-2 report that there were no Germans along the route, Colby foolishly chose to lead the advance himself and was nearly killed when he tried to push through a hedgerow only to have a German fire a submachine gun at him at pointblank range. Luckily the German missed and fled from the terrified Colby.

After recovering from his fright, Colby ordered scouts forward and finally reached the Amfreville-Gourbesville Road, just south of the Les Seurelles Road. Suddenly an American jeep drove past them from the direction of Amfreville, headed toward Gourbesville. Before they could stop it, the jeep drove on and a few moments later Colby heard a burst of German machine-gun fire. When Colby and his men moved toward the firing, they encountered the shaken driver of the jeep. He told them he was driving Colonel Sheehy and Lieutenant Killough of Regimental Cannon Company to the 3d Battalion Headquarters and that both Sheehy and Killough were dead.[50]

The 359th Infantry began its attack at 0845. The 3d Battalion made slow progress, but the 2d Battalion was immediately pinned down by intense small arms fire. Colonel Fales ordered the 3d Battalion to hold in place while the 2d Battalion closed up, but Germans quickly infiltrated between the two battalions creating more confusion and alarm. Fearing the 3d Battalion would be isolated, Colonel Fales ordered them to set up all around defenses and hold the battalion in place until the next day. That evening the 60th Infantry of the 9th Infantry Division moved up as planned and contacted the left flank of the 359th Infantry.

The 358th Infantry continued its attack north and west of Etienville with all three battalions at 0850. The 1st Battalion on the left was to support the attack by fire, while the 2d and 3d Battalion advanced to its right. After advancing a few hundred yards the attack ended at 1700 when the 507th Parachute Infantry and

325th Parachute Infantry of the 82d Airborne Division passed through and reached Bonneville. The 358th then marched to an assembly area and embarked in trucks for Amfreville. After debarking the trucks, the regiment advanced by a circuitous route to the right of the 357th Infantry and occupied a position running generally along the road (D69) from Les Blaisots to the Merderet River. However, one company of the 2d Battalion managed to get lost and somehow wandered in front of the positions the 3d Battalion, 357th Infantry had occupied after withdrawing from its foothold in Gourbesville.[51]

Interrogation of twenty-nine prisoners of war captured during 14 June indicated the Germans were bringing up additional troops to oppose the westward advance of the VII Corps. *Grenadier-Regiment 1050.* of the *77. Infanterie-Division* was identified facing the 359th Infantry, while more elements of the *243. Infanterie-Division*, including parts of *Grenadier-Regiment 920.*, *921.*, and *922.*, and *Ersatz-Bataillon 243.*, moved up to support the battered units of the *91. Infanterie-Division* that had been fighting the VII Corps since 6 June.

On the German side on 14 June, Generalfeldmarschall Rommel discussed the perilous situation with General der Artillerie Fahrmbacher at the latter's headquarters. The two were clear that their own units were unlikely to withstand the major American attack they expected would strike the tenuous line connecting the defenders at Cherbourg with the main German defense line at the base of the Cotentin Peninsula. They realized their units in the Cotentin were too disorganized and lacked the ammunition to defend a north-south line through the middle of the Cotentin after the collapse of their defense of the Douve River. All three of the divisions that originally defended the peninsula, the *91.*, *243.*, and *709.* were considered fought out, and only one division, the newly arriving *77. Infanterie-Division* was more or less intact.[52]

The *77. Infanterie-Division* had been defending the area around St. Malo on D-Day but was alerted to reinforce the defenses on the Cotentin on 7 June, as soon as its units could be relieved by the *5. Fallschirm-Jäger-Division* (Parachute Infantry Division). Motorized elements of the division, probably parts of *Grenadier-Regiment 1050.*, *III./Artillerie-Regiment 177.*, and *Panzerjäger-Abteilung 177.*, were at Granville by 8 June, and by 10 June were at Valognes. Five of the division's six infantry battalions followed on bicycles and assembled between Valognes and Saint-Sauveur-le-Vicomte by the morning of 14 June. The first prisoner from the division was captured on 13 June.[53]

One German prisoner provided a succinct commentary on the tactics of the American troops he had encountered.

An intelligent observation was made by a rather intelligent German non com with several years of combat experience, who more or less deserted yesterday. He described our Infantry as being "hesitant," he also criticized them for shooting blindly and starting their fire as far as 1000 yds away from the enemy, which discloses their positions. They also bunch up and the PW claimed that he could have killed 20 of them yesterday, but did not fire his MG in order to not draw any arty.

****

After we left the closed UTAH Beach Museum, we wandered north along the coast before turning inland at Ravenoville, likely following a route similar to that of Dad's Battery A. We followed signs to Sainte-Mère-Église where we visited the excellent Airborne Museum that commemorates the 82d and 101st Airborne Division. Driving west on the D15 we stopped briefly at the La Fière Bridge and the "Iron Mike" Monument.

From there we wandered confusing country lanes from Cauquigny to Gourbesville. We drove through the intersection where Colonel Sheehy was killed almost before we knew we were there. It quickly became obvious why it proved so difficult for American units to navigate in the bocage. Much of the roadway was sunken, making it impossible to see beyond the next bend where the road would twist and turn, sometimes seeming to double back on itself. The terrain was very broken, characterized by low, steep hills, narrow curving lanes, and tiny stone villages and farmhouses. After driving through Gourbesville we made our way to Saint-Sauveur-le-Vicomte before turning east again to Picauville, then south, crossing the Douve River and driving on to Prétot-Sainte-Suzanne.

CHAPTER 4

CHANGE OF MISSION

15 JUNE

Five days after the VII Corps changed the mission of the 90th Infantry Division it was changed again. The division was ordered to shift its axis farther north and advance to a line running from the railroad station at Le Ham (La Gare de Montebourg), tying in with the 1st Battalion, 359th Infantry on the east side of the Merderet, then running west about 6 miles to Terre-de-Beauval on the Douve River northwest of Golleville. When it reached this objective, it would revert to the defensive and reorganize.[1]

The 358th Infantry completed its march from Amfreville during the morning and went into line north and east of the 357th Infantry, with the 3d Battalion on the right and the 2d Battalion on the left. The 3d Battalion reconnoitered a ridgeline north of Gourbesville overlooking the Merderet River and protected the right flank of the division, while maintaining contact with the 2d Battalion. Intense German artillery concentrations fell on both battalions during the day, which could not have been an easy one for Colonel Nave because both Generals Collins and Landrum spent most of the afternoon at his CP following the progress of the advance. At 2030, they ordered the 358th to halt for the night.[2]

The 357th Infantry CP received word of the ambush of Colonel Sheehy at 0200. Patrols were sent out to find him at 0700, but without success. Then in the early afternoon, as the 3d Battalion continued probing at the German defenses, word of a second ambush was received when General Devine, the Division Artillery Commander, appeared alone at the 357th Infantry CP. Devine had attempted to reach the 3d Battalion early in the day, but his jeep ran into German machine-gun fire at the intersection of the D126 and the Les Surelles Road, just south of the site of Sheehy's ambush. Devine escaped on foot up the Les Surelles Road to the 3d Battalion CP, but Major James C. Buchanan Jr., the Division Artillery Supply Officer, was killed and Devine's driver, Tech 5 Earl C. Bender, was severely wounded.[3]

Despite the close call, General Devine, assisted by Lieutenant Colonel Ken Reimers, commander of the 343d Field Artillery, immediately went to work coordinating fires supporting the 3d Battalion as it again prepared to assault Gourbesville from the east. Reimers later partially blamed General Williams for the slowness and poor planning of the final attack on Gourbesville. According to Reimers, General Williams insisted the town be taken quickly but did not allow enough time for artillery and infantry coordination. He also refused the offer of air support and insisted the attack begin at 1715 even though planning had only begun at 1700. Finally, Reimers was able to persuade him to delay the attack to 1745.[4]

However, another unexpected problem cropped up. Devine ordered a number of check rounds fired in order to ensure the main barrage would strike in front of American lines, only to have word come to the CP to cease fire because the rounds were impacting on friendly troops. Confused, Colonel Kilday confirmed none of his men were there and General Williams was told by Colonel Clarke that none of the 358th Infantry's men were there, so fire recommenced only to hear cries of cease fire again. This time, 1st Lieutenant Eames L. Yates, one of General Williams's aides, was sent forward and discovered the troops hit by friendly fire were the errant company from the 2d Battalion, 358th Infantry, which had gotten lost the night before.

> *A number of officers were dead. Their still-smoking bodies were clustered around a map, in a hedgerow corner, as if they were trying to figure out their positions. A young sergeant was the only one there who seemed to be in command.*[5]

The survivors of the errant company were hustled out of the way and the 3d Battalion, 357th Infantry began its final assault on Gourbesville, only to have it halted because the artillery preparation was again hitting American troops. Extraordinarily, Colonel Ginder, even though he had been relieved three days earlier, was still present in the 357th Infantry's area. Ginder had spent the day harassing Colonel Kilday and eventually forced him to push the 3d Battalion lines forward 150 yards, so that the artillery preparation again crashed into American positions, forcing another pause to the attack. The troops were hastily reorganized again, the barrage finally went in without hitting American troops, and the 3d Battalion advanced, only to discover most of the Germans were gone, leaving only a thin covering force to cover the withdrawal. The town was finally secured at 2330.[6]

The final action at Gourbesville resulted in another award of a Distinguished Service Cross to a soldier from Company I, 357th Infantry, although it took nearly a year for the act of heroism to be recognized.

> *Private First Class Arnold F. Beckman, United States Army, was awarded the Distinguished Service Cross for extraordinary heroism in connection with military operations against an armed enemy while serving with Company I, 357th Infantry Regiment, 90th Infantry Division, in action against enemy forces on 15 June 1944. Private First Class Beckman's intrepid actions, personal bravery and zealous devotion to duty exemplify the highest traditions of the military forces of the United States and reflect great credit upon himself, the 90th Infantry Division, and the United States Army.*[7]

While the 3d Battalion completed the capture of Gourbesville, the rest of the 357th Infantry withdrew to an assembly area in reserve near Amfreville. At 0920 the 2d Battalion moved to the right to relieve the 1st Battalion, 359th Infantry at Magneville on the eastern side of the Douvre River.

The 359th Infantry resumed its attack to seize the bridge at Orglandes at 0500, leading off with the 3d Battalion. The 2d Battalion jumped off at 0755 and when it came up parallel to the 3d the two halted to reorganize and prepare for a second coordinated push. The attack continued at 1600 against strong mortar and automatic weapons fire. By nightfall the regiment had gained nearly 1,000 yards and made contact on the left with the 47th Infantry of the 9th Infantry Division. At 1935, General Landrum messaged Colonel Fales that the 359th was attached to the 9th Infantry Division as of 0800 the next day.

However, the success of the 359th Infantry was at a heavy cost for the Field Artillery. During the early morning, 1st Lieutenant Ross Novelli of Battery C, 915th Field Artillery, which was in direct support of the 359th Infantry, went forward to act as forward observer with one of the rifle companies of the 3d Battalion. He stopped at the 3d Battalion CP where its commander, Lieutenant Colonel George H. Lawrence, told him the two leading companies, I and K, were far ahead of the rest of the battalion and were out of contact with each other and the battalion. Lawrence suggested Novelli wait until the lines were consolidated and contact was restored with the forward companies so he could then move forward with the Battalion CP so as to be better protected if they ran into bypassed German units in the bocage.

Novelli took Lawrence's advice and was waiting when his battalion commander, Lieutenant Colonel James A. Costain, arrived, accompanied by 2d Lieutenant

Ralph Schmidt, a forward observer from Battery A. Costain listened impatiently to Novelli's explanation for why he had not joined the forward infantry and then impulsively started on foot down one of the narrow hedgerow lanes leading to the front lines. Costain was followed by his radio operator, Corporal Max Shaffer. After a slight hesitation because Costain had given no orders or instructions, Novelli followed when Colonel Lawrence told him contact with his forward infantry had been restored and he should tell Costain. Novelli, accompanied by Schmidt, soon caught up with Costain with the news, but the colonel barely acknowledged him and kept going on. About 75 yards farther on, the group ran into a friend of Novelli's, 1st Lieutenant Benjamin R. Respass, commander of the 359th's I&R Platoon and one of Respass's men, Sergeant Ray Jackson, who also joined the impromptu patrol.[8]

The mismatched group of four officers and two enlisted men had continued on for another 600 yards when the path reached a small, enclosed field. They entered the field and when the small, well-dispersed group was all through the gate a German machine gun fired on them. They all went to ground concealed in the four-foot-high grass that covered the field. None were injured and they were able to slightly raise up and fire back briefly before the German fire forced them down again into the grass. Uncertain what to do, Novelli then saw Costain stand erect, cry out "let's get the yellow bastards," and move forward firing, quickly joined by Respass, before both were cut down by the German fire. Respass was able to stumble past Novelli, blood streaming from a severe head wound, but Costain was killed, probably instantly. His body fell hidden in the tall grass, leaving the rest unaware if he was alive or dead.

Slowly the survivors of the group worked their way out of the field and helped Respass to an aid station. The artillerymen managed to return to the 915th's CP with the news and spent some time trying to adjust fire onto the German-occupied hedgerow so they could rescue their colonel, but without success. It is unclear when Colonel Costain's body was recovered and it was not until 0930, when a wounded Corporal Shaffer got back to the 3d Battalion CP, that Costain's death was confirmed. He was replaced as commander of the 915th by Major Eric Peach, Executive Officer of the 344th Field Artillery. Both Costain and Respass received the Silver Star and Purple Heart for their actions that day.[9]

The commander of Company E, 359th Infantry was awarded a Distinguished Service Cross for his bravery, which sadly culminated with his death on 15 June.

Captain (Infantry) James R. Harvey (ASN: 0-24588), United States Army, was awarded the Distinguished Service Cross (Posthumously) for extraordinary heroism in connection with military operations against an armed enemy while serving with the 90th

Infantry Division, in action against enemy forces from 12 to 15 June 1944. Captain Harvey's outstanding leadership, personal bravery and zealous devotion to duty at the cost of his life, exemplify the highest traditions of the military forces of the United States and reflect great credit upon himself, the 90th Infantry Division, and the United States Army.[10]

Company E also lost two other enlisted men killed and one officer and eleven enlisted men that day, while losses for the entire regiment were twelve killed and twenty-six wounded.

Operations on 15 June netted another fifty-one German prisoners of war captured by the 90th, forty of them by the 357th Infantry alone. Nineteen were from the *Grenadier-Regiment 1049.* of the *77. Infanterie-Division*, thirty-one were from the three regiments of the *243. Infanterie-Division*, and just one was from the 90th's initial opponent, the *91. Infanterie-Division.* All indications were that the Germans too were suffering severe casualties and from 10 June through midnight 15 June the 90th Infantry Division had rounded up a total of 108 prisoners. The division later reported 448 PW for the period from 8 to 15 June 1944, but that likely included large numbers of stragglers in the beach defenses rounded up by the 359th Infantry from 6 to 10 June that were not counted in the prisoner interrogation reports.

16 JUNE

After receiving much-needed rest, rations, and water, the 358th Infantry resumed the attack to the northwest in column of battalions at 0800, bypassing Le Culais to the right (east). However, Colonel Spike Nave was killed almost immediately as he led the 3d Battalion forward.

The President of the United States of America, authorized by Act of Congress, July 9, 1918, takes pride in presenting the Distinguished Service Cross (Posthumously) to Lieutenant Colonel (Infantry) William Lester Nave (ASN: 0-17737), United States Army, for extraordinary heroism in connection with military operations against an armed enemy while serving with Headquarters, 358th Infantry Regiment, 90th Infantry Division, in action against enemy forces in France, on 16 June 1944. While leading his regiment in an attack against strong enemy defensive positions near Gourbesville, France, Colonel Nave assumed personal command of a leaderless rifle company. He reorganized the men and led them forward, inspiring them by his bold, fearless leadership. When the attack was halted by machine-gun crossfire, Colonel Nave boldly stood erect and walked calmly along the line of men encouraging them to advance. Then, still in the lead he ran towards the enemy but was hit as he crossed a stream. He fell, still shouting to his men

> *to go forward, and died almost immediately. Inspired by his example the troops overran the enemy position. Lieutenant Colonel Nave's fearless courage and his supreme devotion to duty at the cost of his life, exemplify the highest traditions of the military forces of the United States and reflect great credit upon himself, the 90th Infantry Division, and the United States Army.*[11]

After Nave was killed, Colonel Clarke again took command of the 358th and ordered the 1st Battalion to take up the attack, but it soon stalled at the stream. In turn, the 2d Battalion was committed to the right of the 1st Battalion and crossed the stream under intense automatic weapons fire. Worse, it appeared supporting American artillery was firing short into friendly troops.

Captain William J. Falvey, the 358th Infantry S-2, recounted years later at a 358th Infantry Regiment annual luncheon how he was sent forward by Colonel Partridge to confirm Nave's death and find his body. When he returned to Regimental Headquarters, he took shelter in a foxhole as intense artillery fire fell on the front lines just a few hundred yards away. Falvey believed the artillery fire was American and called General Williams to halt it. Williams refused, telling Falvey, "we've been trying to take Gubersville for several days, and we're not stopping shelling for anybody." Then General Landrum, who was visiting the 358th Headquarters and was pinned down in the same foxhole with Falvey, took the phone and told Williams, "Sam, stop the god damn artillery." The incident sheds a different light on the generally negative views of Landrum. Falvey maintained that Landrum "was a great guy to be there [in a foxhole] with."[12]

Nevertheless, with the support of heavy weapons, the 2d Battalion was able to drive the Germans back and secure the right flank of the division along the Merderet River. At 1335, Colonel Richard C. Partridge arrived to take command of the 358th. By 1843 all three battalions were across the stream and firmly entrenched along the ridge running northeast from Le Culais.

The 357th Infantry spent a day that was relatively quiet after the intensity of the previous week. The 1st Battalion relieved the 3d Battalion at Gourbesville, which moved to a position southwest of town before moving to an assembly area east of town to reorganize. During these movements at 0800, the body of Colonel Sheehy was found in the Gourbesville Church. Shortly afterward, a search party organized and led by General Devine found Major Buchanan's body in a field outside of town and also determined that Devine's wounded driver had survived the ambush and was evacuated to an aid station. Meanwhile, the 2d Battalion, 357th Infantry completed the relief of the 2d Battalion, 359th Infantry at Montebourg and secured the division right flank along the Merderet River. At 0900, Colonel George B. Barth assumed command of the 357th Infantry, relieving Lieutenant Colonel Charles M. Schwab, who resumed his post as Regimental Executive Officer.[13]

The 1st Battalion, 359th Infantry reverted to regimental control at 0030 when it was relieved by the 2d Battalion, 357th Infantry at Magneville, and it began a long march in the dark to a position in regimental reserve. The 359th Infantry resumed its attack at 0800 attached to the 9th Infantry Division. The 2d Battalion led and the 3d Battalion protected the right and rear. The objective was the bridge crossing the marshy stream north of Orglandes on the Orglandes-Urville Road (D24). At 1440 the 2d Battalion reached the Rue les Tourelles (D325) west of Gourbesville, when Major General Manton S. Eddy, commanding the 9th Infantry Division, ordered the regiment halt at its present location and go into division reserve. Colonel Fales was then told at 1630 that the 359th would be notified when to continue the attack. Eddy directed the 1st Battalion pass through the 2d Battalion, which would go into reserve, when the 9th Division took Orglandes. In anticipation of a new attack order from the 9th Infantry Division, at 1920 Colonel Fales ordered the 3d Battalion to wait until the 1st Battalion came up abreast of them to their left before launching a coordinated attack at 2020. However, the 1st Battalion was delayed, so the attack time was changed first to 2100 and then 2140, but then the 39th Infantry of the 9th Infantry Division failed to clear Orglandes so the attack was canceled entirely.

The end of the day on 16 June was also the end of the first week of combat by the 90th Infantry Division as a unit. The results were decidedly disappointing. The division had averaged an advance of less than 1,000 yards per day; overall a total of between 3.75 and 4 miles (6 to 6.4 kilometers) was gained. The cost was staggering, probably over 2,000 killed, wounded, missing, and captured, plus a large, but unknown, number of battle injuries, sick, and battle fatigue. Well over 16 percent of the division's committed strength were casualties, and the average daily casualty rate amounted to about 2.3 percent, which was more than twice the expected average for a division-sized element in combat. The toll on officers was particularly high: the 357th Infantry alone had lost nearly one-third of the officers present on 30 May 1944; most of its original company commanders and platoon leaders were casualties.[14]

The division received 2,451 officers and men as replacements between 12 and 19 June 1944. Most were destined for the infantry regiments. For example, the 357th Infantry recorded receiving 16 officers and 144 enlisted men on 12 June, 1 officer and 89 enlisted men on 13 June, 26 officers and 422 enlisted men on 14 June, 16 officers and 286 enlisted men on 15 June, 1 officer on 16 June (Colonel Barth), and

1 officer on 17 June, for a total of 61 officers and 941 enlisted men. Replacements more than made up for the 824 battle casualties and probably covered nonbattle casualties as well.

Unfortunately, while rapid individual replacement kept the personnel strength of units up, it did little to foster unit cohesion. Worse, replacements made the same mistakes that caused the high casualties. They tended to seek comfort from fellow soldiers by bunching up under fire, failed to go to ground when under direct fire, were slow to move quickly when needed, could not distinguish between friendly and enemy fire, and failed to dig in adequately when halted. The result was they suffered casualties at higher rates than experienced men, which fed a vicious cycle where new replacements quickly became casualties that required replacement. It was months before most units began to find better ways to integrate replacements into combat units other than simply telling them which company they were assigned to and then letting them fend for themselves.[15]

Senior leadership in the division also failed to perform well. General MacKelvie's failures are well documented, but there is little evidence that General Landrum did much better. General Williams did his best to hold the division together in the absence of higher leadership and personally led many of the attacks on the ground, but as was seen on 15 June he also seemed prone to the excessive haste in planning and execution that plagued early operations. The division staff were competent but were unable to perform well given General MacKelvie's penchant for micromanagement.

Regimental leadership too was, at best, mediocre. In the 357th Infantry, Colonel Ginder did nothing to negate the distrust of his subordinates, Colonel Thompson was wounded too soon to make an impression on the 358th Infantry, and after his loss the revolving door of leadership in the regiment—first Nave then Clarke then Partridge—four commanders over the space of five days, prevented that regiment from settling into a solid routine, while in the 359th Infantry, Colonel Fales provided stolid but uninspiring leadership.

Of the initial nine infantry battalion commanders, one, Lester, was an immediate failure, another, Kilday, allowed himself to be bullied by Ginder, who had no authority over him, a third, Nave was killed early on, and three others, Homer R. Jensen, 1st Battalion, 357th Infantry; Donald G. Gorton, 2d Battalion, 359th Infantry; and James R. Casey, 3d Battalion, 359th Infantry, left virtually no mark on the records. Jensen was relieved on 23 June, Gorton became the 359th Executive Officer on 13 August, and Casey was relieved by Lawrence on 13 June, while Lawrence was relieved on 17 June by Clyde R. Benbrook who was killed on 4 July.

Only Christian Clarke, 2d Battalion, 358th Infantry, and Jacob Bealke, 3d Battalion, 358th Infantry turned in solid performances at battalion.[16]

However, except for the loss of Colonel Costain, leadership in the Division Artillery was intact and proved highly competent. General Devine and his battalion commanders demonstrated the professionalism that has historically been a hallmark of the U.S. Army Field Artillery. Similarly, the commander of the 315th Engineer Combat Battalion, Lieutenant Colonel Frank Gilchrist, proved quietly competent in the best tradition of the Corps of Engineers.[17]

17 JUNE

The 90th Infantry Division continued its efforts to close up to the line Gare de Montebourg–Terre-de-Beauval throughout the day.

The 359th Infantry on the division left was relieved from attachment to the 9th Infantry Division at 0630. It continued its advance to an objective north of Orglandes at 0730, with the 1st Battalion on the left, the 3d Battalion on the right, and the 2d Battalion echeloned to the left rear. The 1st Battalion reached its objective at 0830 and the 3d Battalion at 0847 against sporadic sniper and machine-gun fire, while the 2d Battalion settled in at Biniville. All battalions then consolidated a defensive position in place.

Headquarters and Headquarters Battery, 537th AAA AW Battalion, landed on the morning of 17 June and opened a CP in the vicinity of the 90th Division Artillery CP at 1000. By this time all the battalion's batteries were deployed as planned with the artillery battalions of the 90th. Dad's Battery A was with the 343d Field Artillery, Battery B with the 344th Field Artillery, Battery C with the 345th Field Artillery, and Battery D with the 915th Field Artillery.

By the morning of 17 June, the situations of *KG Helmich* and the *77. Infanterie-Division* were critical. Hitler had forbidden a request they withdraw south while *KG Schlieben* withdrew north into the Cherbourg fortifications the previous day, but Feldmarschall Rommel and General Fahrmbacher had contrived to begin preparations for such a movement despite interference from the staff of *7. Armee*. Finally, Hitler relaxed his edict—slightly—and authorized the withdrawal of *KG Schlieben*, which gave Rommel the opening to freely interpret those orders and direct *KG Helmich* to concentrate near La-Haye-du-Puits, effectively ordering them to break out south.[18]

18 JUNE

The 90th Infantry Division continued to occupy defensive positions and came under command of Major General Troy Houston Middleton's VIII Corps. The next six days until 23 June would be relatively quiet for most of the division as replacements were taken in and shattered squad, platoon, and company organizations were rebuilt.

However, the 357th Infantry RCT was not as lucky. It was detached at 1400 as a separate Task Force under the command of Colonel Barth and was placed directly under VIII Corps control. Dad's Battery A and the 1st Platoon, Battery C were also part of TF Barth, along with the 343d and 345th Field Artillery and the 1st Platoon, 90th Reconnaissance Troop. Company B, 899th Tank Destroyer Battalion, which was 400 yards north of Biniville, was also attached at 1230. TF Barth was motorized and given the mission of preventing German movement north or south between Saint-Sauveur-de-Pierrepont and Port-Bail-sur-Mer, along the western coast of the Cotentin. The 357th would relieve the 47th Infantry, 9th Infantry Division, battalion for battalion, so that the 47th could move north to reinforce its parent division in the assault on Cherbourg.

The motor march of the task force went smoothly until a reconnaissance by the battalion commanders led to the realization that most of the 47th Infantry was not in the positions designated in the relief order. Only the 1st Battalion found the 1st Battalion, 47th Infantry in the position described in the relief order, north of the St. Sauveur-le-Vicomte to Port-Bail-sur-Mer road (D15) at the end of a low ridge 600 yards north of La Grande Huanville and just east of the main road from Barneville-Carteret to La-Haye-du-Puits (D903). The other battalions were north and east of the expected positions. The 2d Battalion, 47th Infantry was at Canville-la-Rocque about 1,000 yards from the intersection of the two roads and the 3d Battalion. 47th Infantry was nearly a mile from where it was supposed to be at Saint-Sauveur-de-Pierrepont. Both the 47th and 357th Infantry may have confused a culvert over an unnamed stream south of La Croix Bâton with the bridge over the Le Gorget stream 1,600 yards farther south. The upshot was the 2d and 3d Battalion had to execute a night relief of those units, in unfamiliar terrain, while they were still in contact with Germans attempting to move north to Cherbourg and south to Bretteville-sur-Ay in order to escape the developing trap on the Cotentin. Nevertheless, the 357th displayed an unexpected measure of competence as it successfully completed the relief without major incident or casualties. Only three men were wounded and two injured during the day.[19]

The Germans suffered two major losses during the day. At 0600, Generalleutnant Rudolph Stegmann, commanding the *77. Infanterie-Division*, was killed near the village of Les Perques, southwest of Bricquebec-en-Cotentin, possibly by two American paratroopers who had been hiding in the area since D-Day, although the accepted version is he was killed by fragments from a bomb dropped nearby by

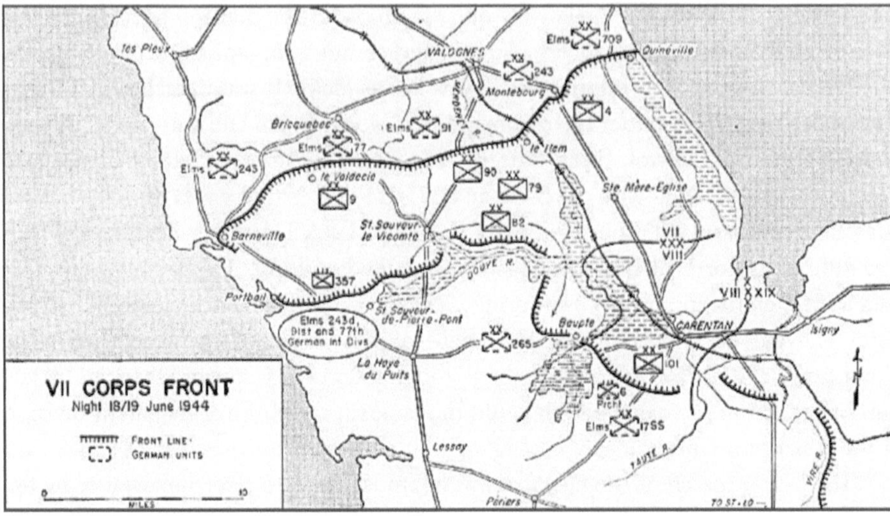

Map 5. VII Corps Front Night 18/19 June 1944. *UTAH Beach to Cherbourg,* Map 25.

Allied aircraft. Generalleutnant Hellmich, commanding *KG Hellmich*, was killed near Canville-la-Rocque when his vehicle was strafed by Allied planes. The two were attempting to find retreat routes south for their commands before the Americans managed to cut through to the west coast of the Cotentin.[20]

19 JUNE

Shortly after midnight, the 90th Infantry Division was relieved from attachment to the VII Corps and attached to the VIII Corps. It remained in place, minus Task Force Barth, while the newly arrived 79th Infantry Division passed through its lines to reinforce the attack on Cherbourg. The 90th Division Artillery reinforced the artillery of the 79th until its units moved out of range. The 358th Infantry began moving to a new assembly area north of Reigneville at 0845, after the 315th Infantry of the 79th Infantry moved through it. The 358th closed in its new area by 1630 and prepared to defend in place.

By 19 June, the German defenses of the Cotentin Peninsula had been split in two by the American advance. One battalion of the *77. Infanterie-Division, I./Grenadier-Regiment 1050.*, had left the division's former positions at St. Malo last—it was the only infantry battalion of the division not equipped with bicycles, so marched on foot—and reached Denneville, 2 miles southeast of Port-Bail-sur-Mer, on the morning of 19 June. Another battalion, *II./Grenadier-Regiment 1049*, was diverted east and joined *KG Eitner* under Major Volkhard Eitner, formerly commander of *Grenadier-Regiment 1057* of *91. Infanterie-Division* near Baupte.[21]

The other four infantry battalions of the division and most of its artillery and heavy weapons were on the other side of the tenuous American line. Minor elements of the division, about 70 men, ended up in Cherbourg and were lost there. The remainder, along with elements of *243. Infanterie-Division*, estimated by the 90th Infantry Division's G-2 Section as 1,200 to 1,400 men but probably considerably more than that, attempted to break out to the south, under the command of Oberst (Colonel) Rudolf Bacherer, formerly commander of *Grenadier-Regiment 1049.*, who was in command of *77. Infanterie-Division* since the death of Generalleutnant Stegmann the day before. At the same time, various elements of *243. Infanterie-Division* and other miscellaneous units cut off from Cherbourg were also trying to escape.[22]

At 0330 Colonel Barth ordered the 357th Infantry to seize the positions facing south as described in the relief order of the previous day. The result was a confused clash as *I./Grenadier-Regiment 1050.* resisted the American advance and other German elements attempted to break out southward.

Because the 47th Infantry had not seized the high ground south of Port-Bail-sur-Mer along the L'Olonde River valley, Colonel Barth ordered the 2d Battalion to advance south from Canville-la-Rocque, cross the D903, and secure the high ground at Le Hameau Dupré and the railroad halt at Denneville. The 1st Platoon, 90th Reconnaissance Troop would assist and a platoon of Company B, 899th Tank Destroyer Battalion would be in support about 200 yards north of the intersection of the D15 and D903. The 3d Battalion would secure Saint-Sauveur-de-Pierrepont. The attack was to begin no later than 0630 and the two battalions jumped off as scheduled.

On the right, the 1st Battalion remained in place, prepared to defend the regiment's right rear from German units moving north to south along the main coast road from Barneville-Carteret to La-Haye-du-Puits (D903). By 1100, a force of 299 Germans fleeing south was working around the flank of battalion, which attempted to extend its lines to cut them off, while bringing the Germans under mortar and artillery fire.

The 2d Battalion jumped off on time but was stopped just north of Les Yons and Denneville when it collided with the fresh *I./Grenadier-Regiment 1050.* The Germans were supported by "four or five tanks" that periodically pushed into the 2d Battalion area. At 1130, the American infantry tried to chase off the German armor with bazookas, antitank grenades, and 57mm antitank guns, but with little success;

only one German vehicle was reported knocked out. At 1145 the situation became even more serious when a group of 400 Germans attempting to escape south threatened to overrun the 2d Battalion CP. It hastily withdrew to the intersection of the D15 and D903 where it was protected by the platoon of the 899th Tank Destroyer Battalion. Shortly afterward at 1210 the Battalion Motor Pool came under small arms fire from another group of wandering Germans and then twenty minutes later reported they were threatened by German tanks and armored cars approaching from the south. Nevertheless, Company F attempted to advance, infiltrating onto the high ground to their front along the Rue Baton, which ran north-south to the west of Les Yons. However, they too were struck by German tanks and infantry and at 1700 fell back north to Saint-Lô-d'Ourville.

The 2d Battalion was roughly handled by the Germans, especially Company F. Of the 20 KIA recorded that day in the 2d Battalion, 16 were in Company F, as were 14 of 17 WIA, and 67 of 79 MIA. The extraordinarily high ratio of killed to wounded is probably explained by the large number of missing, many of whom were likely wounded. A possible confirmation is that three men of the Regimental Medical Detachment were listed as captured that day and later freed on 19 September. They may well have been captured tending to the missing men who were wounded. The casualties in Company F alone accounted for 49 percent of the regiment's losses for the day and probably left the battered company with no more than a few dozen men fit for combat.

By 0730 the 3d Battalion reported it was on its objective, but it appears it was still well short of Saint-Sauveur-de-Pierrepont and at the most had outposts observing that village. At 1100 Company K was hit on its right flank by mortar and machine-gun fire. The fighting that followed was obviously intense, but oddly enough got little mention in the Regimental After-Action Report and postwar *Short History of the 357th Infantry Regiment*. The 3d Battalion recorded a loss of 25 KIA, 52 WIA, and 17 MIA during the day, mostly from Company I and K, which was 44 percent of the loss incurred by the entire regiment.

The 2d Battalion, 359th Infantry and the 359th Antitank Company (less one platoon) were attached to the 357th at 1425 to hold the area from Neuville-en-Beaumont to the Douve River south of Saint-Sauveur-le-Vicomte. They relieved the 90th Reconnaissance Troop (-), which then moved to establish an outpost line southeast of Barneville-Carteret to act as a tripwire warning of German groups attempting to escape south.

Which German armored vehicles gave the 357th so much trouble is something of a mystery. On 18 June, one German captured by the 358th Infantry at

The destroyed center of Valognes. The photograph was taken by Captain Oehmichen, probably around 20 June 1944.

Hémevez, south of Valognes, was identified as a member of *Panzer-Abteilung 206*, which like the *Panzer-Ersatz-und-Ausbildungs-Abeilung 100* was equipped with captured French tanks. On 6 June it was in the far northeast corner of the Cotentin at Beaumont-Hague but had been dispatched south early in the battle to oppose the VII Corps advance. However, it seems unlikely it opposed the 357th Infantry around Port-Bail-sur-Mer. It fell back onto Fortress Cherbourg in front of the advance of the VII Corps and was destroyed there. A more likely candidate is *Sturmgeschütz-Brigade 902*, which was at Tours on 6 June with twenty-five operational Sturmgeschütz (armored assault guns) and six more in short-term repair. Its movements and actions in June are somewhat unclear. On 8 June it was attached to *SS-GvB* for the movement to Normandy, but by 11 June it was attached instead to *LXXXIV. Armee-Korps*. By 13 June it was engaged near Valognes. It was supposedly part of the Cherbourg garrison on 19 June, but two days later was at La Haye-du-Puits with thirteen operational Sturmgeschütz. It seems likely it managed to escape the trap at Cherbourg because by 1 July it was still full strength with thirty Sturmgeschütz operational and another in repair.

Identifying the origin of the "armored cars" is even more difficult. There were none with *Sturmgeschütz-Brigade 902*. and none with *77.* or *91. Infanterie-Division*. They may well have been self-propelled 20mm antiaircraft guns (2cm Flak auf Selbstfahrlafette), which were often identified as armored vehicles by American forces. If that was so, then the most likely candidate would have been

243. Infanterie-Division. The *3. Kompanie* of its *Panzerjäger-Abteilung 243* had four such vehicles.

Apparently FUSA never took the threat of the German tanks too seriously. Sometime during the day, Company B, 899th Tank Destroyer Battalion was relieved from attachment to the 357th Infantry and attached instead to the 60th Infantry, 9th Infantry Division, as it advanced north along the west coast of the Cotentin from Barneville towards Le Pieux.

20 JUNE

Throughout the day Task Force Barth made minor adjustments to its positions and took no major offensive action. The Germans continued to harass the Task Force with mortar and artillery fire, while making occasional jabs at the American lines with a few "tanks."

At 1030, the 343d and 345th Field Artillery fired concentrations on German positions at the railroad halt at Deneville in front of the 2d Battalion. Then at 1115 they fired again on Germans fleeing south of Barneville, who were observed by the 90th Reconnaissance Troop. Otherwise, it was another fairly quiet day for the 1st Battalion, although Company B was struck by mortar fire on its positions on the D903 south of Huanville at 1425.

The 3d Battalion north of Saint-Sauveur-de-Pierrepont was counterattacked at 1234 by a German force of unknown size. Three hours later at 1520 Company L was hit by four "Panzers" at the "bridge at Saint-Sauveur-de-Pierrepont"—they may have been confusing the culvert over the unnamed stream south of La Croix Bâton with the bridge over the Le Gorget 1,600 yards farther south. Twenty minutes later they were reported "holding firmly." Nevertheless, an antitank strongpoint composed of a platoon of the 315th Engineers and two 57mm antitank guns was set up in the rear of the battalion at La Hardellerie[?], which was probably near Besneville.[23] The 607th Tank Destroyer Battalion (3-inch gun—towed) was attached to the 90th Infantry Division at 1800 to bolster its antitank defenses.

21 JUNE

At dawn elements of both *Grenadier-Regiment 1049.* and *1050.*, along with elements of other German units, attempted to break through the positions of the 1st Battalion, 357th Infantry. Company B was hard hit, suffering eighteen casualties, but capturing twenty Germans. Company C fared better though, mostly through the efforts of a single rifleman. Private Ralph F. Pomeroy executed a single-handed bayonet charge that netted him 44 German prisoners, an extraordinary feat of arms that perversely earned him no formal recognition. His gallantry was probably the reason Company C recorded just a single man killed during the day. In all, the 1st Battalion, 357th Infantry captured 101 of an estimated 174 Germans, mostly from *77. Infanterie-Division*, attempting to flee south. Another 37 German dead and 36 wounded evacuated to American hospitals were accounted for, with none escaping. Otherwise, the day was relatively quiet compared to the previous three and was taken up mostly by patrolling and improving positions.[24] The 2d Battalion, 359th Infantry was relieved from attachment to Task Force Barth at 0620 and moved to a new assembly area in the vicinity of Cretteville.

22 JUNE

The 357th Infantry spent the day consolidating and reinforcing its positions while continuing active patrolling. Its lack of tank support continued to hamper its offensive capability.

The 1st Battalion unsuccessfully tried to knock out two pillboxes near Saint-Lô-d'Ourville that were part of the German beach defenses at Port-Bail-sur-Mer. Company A, 315th Engineers relieved Company A, 357th Infantry at 1400 so the 1st Battalion defenses could be extended farther to the left (south).

At 0800, the 2d Battalion made another attempt to regain the area between Les Yons and Le Hameau Dupré lost by Company F on 19 June, but without success. Again, the threat of German armor held the advance to a crawl. By 1700 the battalion had only managed to gain 200 yards as it tried to deal with four German "tanks." As late as 2100 as many as six German "tanks" continued to press the 2d Battalion near Les Yons, before the fighting petered out.

The 3d Battalion, 357th Infantry spent the day quietly as it prepared to move west, closing up to the beleaguered 2d Battalion. The 3d Battalion, 359th Infantry was attached to Task Force Barth at 1900 and was ordered to relieve the 3d Battalion, 357th Infantry during the morning of 23 June. The 315th Engineers (-) were attached to Task Force Barth as well, relieving the last platoon of the 90th Reconnaissance Troop southwest of Saint-Sauveur-le-Vicomte, which moved to join the rest of the troop.

Most of the day's losses again fell on the 2d Battalion, which suffered 8 KIA, 25 WIA, and 2 MIA, a total of 35 of the 50 casualties incurred by the 357th Infantry. The 1st Battalion suffered most of the remaining casualties, except for one man killed in the Regimental Medical Detachment. The 3d Battalion was untouched.

After 1100 German aircraft became very active over the division zone. Both Battery C (-) and D, 537th AAA AW Battalion reported firing on four German FW 190 fighter planes southeast of Cretteville but made no claims of success. Dad's Battery A and the 1st Platoon, Battery C, which were attached to Task Force Barth, did not see or engage any planes.

23 JUNE

The 358th and 359th Infantry moved to relieve the 507th Parachute Infantry south of the Douve. The new division positions extended from Baupte to northwest of Prétot-Sainte-Suzanne where it abutted the positions of the 82d Airborne Division.[25]

Task Force Barth was reinforced again during the day as the VIII Corps built up the line cutting the Cotentin in two. At 1100, Troop B, 4th Cavalry Squadron (Mechanized) and Company B, 607th Tank Destroyer Battalion were attached. Troop B reinforced the picket line of the 90th Reconnaissance Troop (-) screening the north of the task force in the vicinity of Saint-Lô-d'Ourville, Barneville, Besneville, and Saint-Maurice-en-Cotentin.

While the day was relatively quiet for the 357th Infantry, one man was recognized for his heroism.

> *The President of the United States of America, authorized by Act of Congress, July 9, 1918, takes pleasure in presenting the Distinguished Service Cross to Staff Sergeant John M. Gabbamonte, United States Army, for extraordinary heroism in connection with military operations against an armed enemy while serving with Company F, 357th Infantry Regiment, 90th Infantry Division, in action against enemy forces on 23 June 1944, near Dupreys [sic Le Hameau Dupré, near Port-Bail-sur-Mer], France. When fire from an enemy tank severely wounded a soldier firing a rocket launcher near his position, Staff Sergeant Gabbamonte quickly recovered the rocket launcher and fired upon the tank, forcing it to retreat. When a second tank approached, the intrepid sergeant held his position and placed such effective fire upon the tank that he set it on fire. A third tank moved up and opened fire upon the sergeant, but he forced it to withdraw by scoring a direct hit. His conspicuous courage, heroic determination to engage the enemy and his supreme devotion to duty exemplify the highest traditions of the military forces of the United States and reflect great credit upon himself, the 90th Infantry Division, and the United States Army.*[26]

Another Distinguished Service Cross was awarded to an officer of the 359th Infantry.

Second Lieutenant Barney B. Taylor, United States Army, was awarded the Distinguished Service Cross for extraordinary heroism in connection with military operations against an armed enemy while serving with Company G, 359th Infantry Regiment, 90th Infantry Division, in action against enemy forces on 23 June 1944. Second Lieutenant Taylor's intrepid actions, personal bravery and zealous devotion to duty exemplify the highest traditions of the military forces of the United States and reflect great credit upon himself, the 90th Infantry Division, and the United States Army.[27]

Given how quiet this day was it seems quite possible these awards were misdated. Sergeant Gabbamonte's actions seem to fit in well with the 2d Battalion's battle on 19 June, while Lieutenant Taylor's also seem out of place given the lack of activity in the 359th Infantry that day. Company G, 359th Infantry recorded no casualties on 23 June, and no mention of such an action was made in the Record of Events of its MR.

24–30 JUNE

The last week of the month passed relatively quietly for the division, not because FUSA felt there was a need to rest the division, but simply because bad weather intervened to delay operations all along the Allied front. For nearly seventy-two hours, from the evening of 19 June through the evening of 22 June, a storm swept into the English Channel, battering the Allied beaches. Sustained 5-foot waves halted unloading during the entire period, while for three hours, from 1800 to 2100, on 20 June the waves exceeded 8 feet and severely damaged the American artificial harbor—MULBERRY "A"—at Arromanches-les-Bains. All supply deliveries, but especially ammunition, were curtailed, as were offensive plans. For FUSA it meant the planned VIII Corps offensive south, set for 22 June, was first delayed, and then canceled.[28]

In the zones of the 358th and 359th Infantry, defensive positions were improved, and active patrolling of the German lines took place every night. The 357th Infantry was slightly more active, including the repulse of a company-sized German probe on the 3d Battalion on the night of 25/26 June, which was played up a bit more in the Division After-Action Report than it was by the 357th Infantry. The division reported,

During the night of the 25th and the morning of the 26th, an enemy patrol struck in force in the area of the OPLR [outpost line of resistance] of the 357th and made slight penetration. Hand grenades were used extensively between our units and the enemy patrols.

The enemy was destroyed or taken prisoner. The 357th's lines were restored. 40 prisoners including one Regimental Commander and two Lieutenants were taken. 357th suffered 13 casualties.[29]

All of that was very dramatic but was not reflected in any way by the 357th Infantry's report for the day. It merely noted, One hundred and fifty Germans approached the 3d Battalion position but were dispersed and driven off by mortar and artillery fire."

The 357th Infantry reported capturing just "four Russians" on 25 June and five more on 26 June. Nor did the 357th record the capture of any German officers between 2400 23 June and 2400 30 June. It is unclear why the division's report on the day's activities would vary so greatly from the regiment's, but it seems as if the description of the day's events by the division was closer to what happened on the evening of 18/19 or 19/20 June. Even more confusing, the 357th Infantry said the five reported captured on 26 June were by a gun crew of Dad's Battery A near the 357th Infantry Regimental CP, but Battery A said it was six men they captured, and it was on 25 June at 1600.

The lackluster performance of his 1st Battalion led Colonel Barth to relieve its commander, Lieutenant Colonel Homer E. Jensen. Barth directed Major Edward S. Hamilton to assume command of the 1st Battalion on 27 June. Hamilton had been assigned to the 357th Infantry on 1 January 1944 but was immediately placed on detached duty as Assistant Division G-3 and had just rejoined the regiment on 24 June. Barth's first question to Hamilton was "are you my man?" Hamilton's reply, "yes, sir," apparently satisfied Barth, who confided he had no confidence in Jensen because he lacked aggressiveness, fortitude, and leadership, while the battalion's morale was at low ebb.[30]

When Hamilton arrived at the 1st Battalion CP, he found Jensen lying in a foxhole. Worse, according to Hamilton's estimate, the CP was nearly a mile from the forward companies. Hamilton quickly put his stamp on the battalion, moving the CP to within 500 yards of the front lines. He then relieved one of his company commanders, who claimed he could not bear the responsibility of having his men killed and wounded. Hamilton, newly appointed to the responsibility of battalion command, was unimpressed with the captain's argument and told him,

As you are not personally afraid, I am going to recommend that you be stripped of your rank and be reduced to the grade of private, in which position you will have no

responsibility for others, and be assigned to a front-line combat company in which you will have full opportunity to demonstrate your personal courage.[31]

Dad's Battery A finally recorded its location as other than "Somewhere in France" on 24 June, but it remained somewhat cryptic. The Battery MR stated its location as "Gde Haunville 1/2S T0990, Manche, France," which could be interpreted as a half mile south of the map grid vT0990, but that would have placed them in Saint-Lô-d'Ourville. Then on 28 June, the location was given as "Gde Haunville 1 Mile NE T1092," which was more legible but just as mystifying, because it would have placed them even farther away from the place marked "Gde Huanville" on maps. However, La Grande Huanville is not really a place but rather an area between Huanville, which was a tiny village north of the D903 highway, and Saint-Lô-d'Ourville and is now the name of a country road. It was not the first nor the last time that Americans were confused by French place-names.

Battery A also spotted its first enemy aircraft on 24 June, two "ME 109 [*sic*, Bf 109]" fighters, but they were out of range. Dad and Battery A were also under direct enemy fire for the first time on 27 June but had suffered no battle casualties.[32]

On 29 June, the 357th Infantry prepared for relief by the 315th Infantry of the 79th Infantry Division, which began at 1000 and was completed by 2200. Beginning at 1600, the 357th Infantry began marching to an assembly area near Hautteville-Bocage west of Orglandes and closed there at 0500 30 June, ending its semiindependent existence. The 343d Field Artillery, with Dad's Battery A, moved to Gruchy, just north of Appeville.

Before they left, Captain Oehmichen supervised the surrender of a large number of Osttruppen (former Soviet POW pressed into German service) from Port-Bail, which effectively completed the liberation of that town. On 28 June, twelve Russians from the *Wolga-Tatarisches Infanterie-Bataillon 627*, led by a corporal, Sandar Waliulin, surrendered to the 357th in the vicinity of "Yons." Waliulin convinced Oehmichen that more of the Osttrupen wanted to surrender, and the two worked up a surrender leaflet that was fired into the town. The next day, some of its Osttruppen ambushed and wounded the battalion commander, Rittmeister Sörensen, and then fled to American lines. Captain Oehmichen supervised the surrender of thirty-four more men from the *1. Kompanie* and fifteen from the *4. Kompanie* of *Wolga-Tatarisches Infanterie-Bataillon 627*, along with fifteen men from the *2. Kompanie* of *Georgeisches Infanterie-Bataillon 797*, which was at St. Lô

The surrender of the Russians at the farmhouse of Le Maugerie. Sandar Waliulin is in the center and Captain Oehmichem is on the right. Master Sergeant Theodore W. Henning is on the left. Oehmichen and Henning are wearing pieces of parachute silk as scarves. U.S. Army SC.

d'Ourville, surrendered to the 357th Infantry. A photo opportunity was set up for propaganda purposes documenting the surrender at the farmhouse of Le Maugerie. Another 112 men from the *Wolga-Tatarisches Infanterie-Bataillon 627* surrendered between 30 June and 3 July to the 315th Infantry.[33]

The end of the month also saw a welcome addition to the combat power of the 90th Infantry Division. On 28 June, the 712th Tank Battalion, commanded by Lieutenant Colonel George B. Randolph, was attached to the division. That was somewhat in anticipation of its arrival because it did not began landing on UTAH until 29 June and did not complete unloading until 30 June. Randolph, a forty-year-old OR officer and former Alabama high school mathematics teacher, was given command of the 712th Tank Battalion on 6 June 1944 when its previous commander, Lieutenant Colonel Samuel Whitside Miller, was relieved.

The story of Miller's relief is a good example of the problems the expanding American Army had finding and promoting good officers. On paper, "Whit" Miller was an excellent choice to command a tank battalion. He was the son of a Medal

The surrender of the Russians at the farmhouse of Le Maugerie. Sandar Waliulin is speaking with another of Captain Oehmichen's team and a 90th Division MP is watching and sharing cigarettes. U.S. Army SC.

of Honor winner, grandson of a U.S. Army brigadier general, and a relative of U.S. president William Henry Harrison. He graduated from West Point as a 2d lieutenant, Infantry, but served in the Quartermaster Corps until 1936, when he transferred to the Cavalry. By August 1942, Miller was a lieutenant colonel commanding the 2d Battalion, 11th Armored in the 10th Armored Division. When the armored divisions were reorganized in 1943, the 3d Battalion, 11th Armored became the 712th Tank Battalion and Miller was transferred from the 2d Battalion to command it.[34]

By the time the battalion arrived in England in March 1944, Miller had gained a reputation as a crazed martinet with his battalion's officers and men. One of the battalion medical officers, Captain Jack Reiff, later wrote that Miller "was an inadequate, obsessive compulsive neurotic, replete with facial tics and picking at his fingernails." Years later Reiff was reminded of Miller after watching Humphrey Bogart's character, Captain Queeg, in the movie the *Caine Mutiny*.[35] Whether or not Miller was truly obsessive-compulsive, he certainly had other problems. Trying

The Russians relaxing at the farmhouse of Le Maugerie. U.S. Army SC.

to live up to his illustrious forebears may have been part of it. He was married and then quickly divorced in the 1930s, then remarried shortly before Pearl Harbor. In the obituary written by his daughter, Janet Miller Simkins, his alcoholism was acknowledged as a near lifelong problem. Perhaps tellingly too, Miller apparently later told his family it was a "sad day of his life was when he had to give up 'Danavar,' his private mount, in 1942 and become a tank commander." It seems possible that in addition to his private demons, he was also indifferent to his role as commander of a tank battalion.[36]

Once in England, Miller's actions became more and more erratic. He publicly humiliated his executive officer, Major Baxter Davis, by ordering him to double-time in front of enlisted men when Miller decided Davis had not responded to a command quickly enough. He also threatened the battalion maintenance officer, Captain Forrest Dixon, with court-martial after he failed to mount blackout lights on the tanks as ordered in an VIII Corps directive, even though the directive specified the lights were only to be mounted on general purpose vehicles and not ordnance vehicles like tanks. At their wits' end, the men of the 712th finally took an exceptional step and sent a petition to the VIII Corps G-1 asking for Miller's relief. Although such a course was normally anathema to the Army's ethos, apparently

Miller's conduct was considered so egregious that the request was granted, and Randolph was given command of the battalion.[37] Miller was transferred to the 29th Infantry Division G-3 staff. On 21 July his rank was terminated, and he reverted to the rank of major, possibly another indication the performance of his duties was considered problematic. It was not until 1949 that Miller was promoted back to lieutenant colonel, and he retired in 1957.[38]

Colonel Randolph soon did what he could to develop the coordination between his tanks and the infantry that had proved so lacking in the division's earlier experience with the 746th Tank Battalion. On 30 June, Randolph held a conference at the 358th Infantry CP, with several of the regiment's commanders and staff. "During this conference the limitations and possibilities of Tank-Infantry support were developed." While there is no record of similar conferences with the 357th or 359th Infantry, it is likely Randolph did something similar with them.

However, there was little time available to the 90th and 712th for practical demonstrations, practice, or training in the proposed tactics. On 26 June the attention of Omar Bradley turned southward again when Cherbourg surrendered and operations in the northern Cotentin began to wrap up. He directed the VIII Corps commander, General Middleton, to begin planning for an advance on Coutances beginning on or about 1 July. The main effort of the attack would be by the 90th Infantry Division on the left (east), which would attack south and west, and by the 79th Infantry Division on the right (west), which would attack south and east, pinching out the 82d Airborne Division between them after that division had attacked south to its objective. The 90th and 79th would then join forces near La Haye-du-Puits and would push south to Lessay and then Coutances. Farther east, the VII Corps, fresh from its conquest of Cherbourg, would pick up the attack a day or so later on the axis Carentan-Périers, followed by the XIX Corps on the axis Villiers Fossard-Saint-Lô with the V Corps in support, until all four of First U.S. Army's corps were hammering on the German defenses.

****

Our route skipped Port-Bail-sur-Mer and Besneville, where Dad spent the end of June with Task Force Barth. However, he did recall one distinct incident that probably occurred during their time near Besneville. On one stretch of the road, quite possibly the D15 from Saint-Sauveur-le-Vicomte to Port-Bail-sur-Mer, they drove past a wrecked German vehicle column, the aftermath of either an air or artillery strike. A work party from a "Colored" Quartermaster Service Company was clearing German corpses from the wreckage. The men would take a corpse and roll it onto a canvas shelter half and then manhandle it into the back of a truck for transfer to one of the many cemeteries sprouting around the Norman countryside. As Dad's Platoon passed, one of the bodies heaved into the truck split into two, cascading putrefying flesh and human offal over the road, the truck, and the men loading the bodies. The obscenities and screams of disgust may be imagined.[39]

CHAPTER 5

CALVARY ON MONT CASTRÉ

Early on the morning of 1 July, Bradley's planned attack was delayed again. The VII Corps needed time to orient itself in its new position and the arrival of units intended for the XIX Corps farther east, and to reinforce the other corps, were delayed by the shipping backlog caused by the "Great Storm" of 19–22 June. The new time set by FUSA for the VIII Corps attack was 3 July at 0530, following an intense fifteen-minute artillery barrage. The VII Corps attack would begin on 4 July, and the XIX Corps later still. The line Coutances-Caumont would be the immediate FUSA objective, while the initial objective for the VIII Corps was to reach a line running northeast from Lessay to Gorges. The 90th Infantry Division objective on that line ran from Pissot to Le Hameau Perrey and Gorges, an advance of over 8 miles, which would leave it facing east-southeast.[1]

General Landrum's plan for the 90th Infantry Division was an attack by two regiments abreast, with the third in reserve. The 537th AAA AW Battalion, 712th Tank Battalion (less Company A attached to the 82d Airborne Division), 607th Tank Destroyer Battalion, and Company A, 86th Chemical Mortar Battalion were attached in direct support of the division. In general support of the 90th Infantry Division Artillery was the 333d Field Artillery Group (Cld) with the 333d Field Artillery Battalion (Cld, 155mm howitzer) and the 733d Field Artillery Battalion (155mm gun), which was moving into position having just landed on 29 June. Additional, albeit temporary, artillery support was provided by the 4th Infantry Division Artillery (until 6 July when the 4th began its own attack) and four battalions of 155mm howitzers from the VII Corps under the 142d Field Artillery Group, the 951st, 955th, 980th, and 981st Field Artillery (also only until the VII Corps began its attack). The 90th Division Artillery could also call on the support of the VIII Corps heavy artillery, which consisted of two battalions of massive 240mm howitzers, the 551st and 552d Field Artillery, and two more battalions of 155mm guns, the 559th and 561st Field Artillery. Yet more support was given to General Middleton on the afternoon of 2 July, when General Eisenhower told him, "You can get all [the airpower] you desire."[2]

The 359th Infantry with Company C, 712th Tank Battalion and Company A (less one platoon), 86th Chemical Mortar Battalion on the right (west) would seize and consolidate a position in the Forêt de Mont-Castré. Then it would continue the attack southward when ordered. The 359th would initially have priority for supporting artillery fire.

The 358th Infantry with Company B, 712th Tank Battalion and one platoon of Company A, 86th Chemical Mortar Battalion on the left (east) would force the corridor between the Forêt de Mont-Castré and the Prairies Marecageuses de Gorges (hereafter Prairies), blocking German counterattacks from the east and south of the Prairies and support the 359th Infantry in seizing Mont Castré.

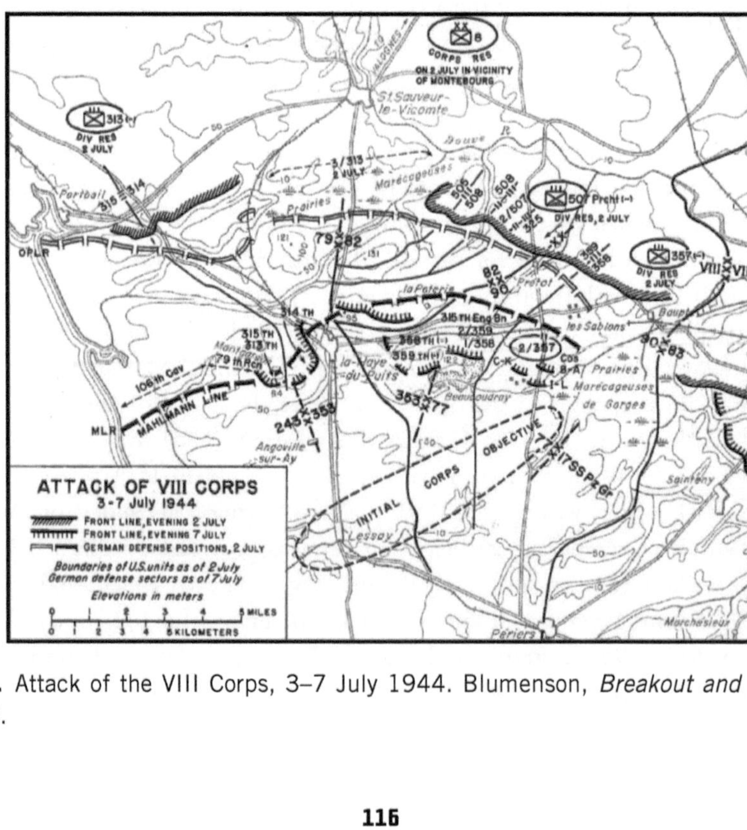

Map 6. Attack of the VIII Corps, 3–7 July 1944. Blumenson, *Breakout and Pursuit*, Map 3.

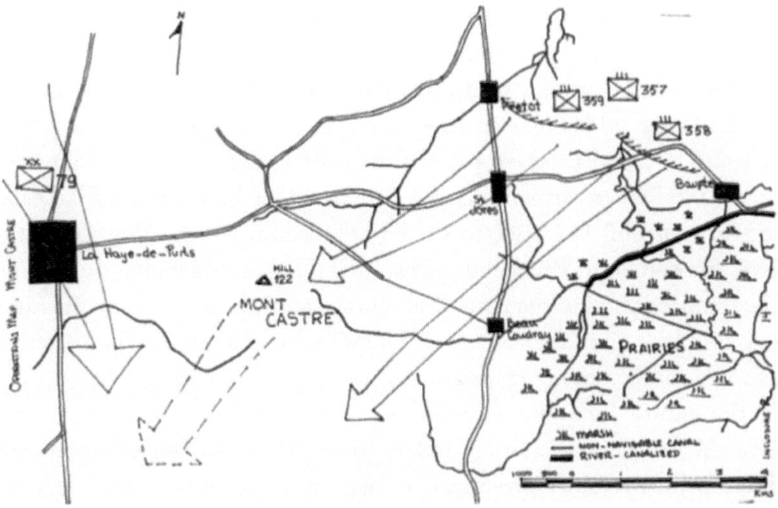

Map 7. Scheme of maneuver of the 90th Infantry Division, 3 July 1944. Blastos, Inclosure 7.

The 357th Infantry was in division reserve and would prepare to pass through the 358th Infantry to seize the final division objective.

The two dominating terrain features that concerned the 90th Infantry Division were the forested hill known as Mont Castré and the marshy lowlands of the Prairies. At an average height of 84 meters and a peak of 122 meters above sea level, Hill 122 was named for the castle ruins on the north side, just below its peak. It dominated the surrounding countryside. The height gave a clear view extending east and west to the sea and north to the Douve River, providing almost perfect observation of the attack routes available to the 90th Infantry Division. The hill was heavily forested, mostly in oak, beech, and hornbeam, with occasionally dense undergrowth. The ridgeline of which Mont Castré is a part extends west where it was known as Montgardon Ridge to the Americans, the dominating feature of which, Hill 84, was the objective of the 79th Infantry Division. The contiguous hill mass shielding the town and road intersection of La Haye-du-Puits provided an almost perfect defensive system for the Germans.[3]

In contrast to the Mont Castré-Montgardon highlands, much of the Prairies lay below sea level. It is just one of five such "prairies" in the Cotentin. Four follow the courses of the major rivers in the Cotentin, the Merderet, the Douve, the Vire, and the Taute, while the fifth, the Prairies is a twelve square mile basin draining into the other four. The Prairies are flat peat bogs, dotted with numerous sinkholes, springs, streams, and ponds, as well as numerous irrigation ditches and canals. Crossing the bogs on foot was hazardous, while crossing it in vehicles, wheeled or tracked, was impossible. In the 90th Division zone, the Prairies extended from the left flank at Baupte south to Gorges and left parts of the main road from Prétot-Sainte-Suzanne to Gorges, the D24, a virtual causeway. The corridor between the Prairies and the forested mass of Hill 112 bisected by the D24 leading to the 359th Infantry's first objective, the hamlet of Beaucoudray, was less than 2 miles wide.[4]

The temporary lull in the American attacks southward caused by the June storm was a godsend for the German forces defending the Cotentin. The battered forces that had fled south were reorganized and strongly reinforced.

By the end of June, the western part of the *LXXXIV Armee-Korps* front line extended 27 kilometers (16.75 miles) from Port-Bail-sur-Mer–Saint-Sauveu r-de-Pierrepont–Prétot-Sainte-Suzanne–Baupte, south of an east-west arm of the Prairies. The defenders comprised *Gruppe König*, under Oberst Eugen König, who had taken command of the *91. Infanterie-Division* on 10 June. *Gruppe König* had four subgroups, each varying in strength from roughly a battalion to a regiment. On the right was *KG Mecklenburg* (*KG 265. Infanterie-Division*) with two medium-strength and one weak infantry battalion. To its left was *KG Lewandowski* with two weak infantry battalions from *91. Infanterie-Division* and one weak infantry battalion from *265. Infanterie-Division*. To *KG Lewandowski's* left was *Ost-Regiments-Gruppe Bunjatschenko* with one weak infantry battalion of Osttruppen in the outpost line and another in support. Finally, to *Gruppe Bunjatschenko's* left was *KG Simon* with one strong Osttruppen battalion and two medium-strength infantry battalions from *243. Infanterie-Division*. Supporting them were thirty Sturmgeschütz of *902 Sturmgeschütz-Brigade*, along with ten 7.5cm s.Pak Sfl. Marder, three towed 7.5cm Pak, and all the surviving artillery pieces of the *91*, *243*, and *265 Infanterie-Division*: probably thirty-four light guns and forty heavier guns and howitzers of nine different types, German, Soviet, Belgian, and Czech in origin.[5]

In corps reserve along the Montgardon-Mont Castré line was the fresh *353. Infanterie-Division* (minus *KG Böhm*, which was attached to *352. Infanterie-Division* of *II. Fallschirm-Korps* farther east) under Generalleutnant Paul Mahlmann with five strong infantry battalions and the remnants of *77. Infanterie-Division* with one medium-strength and three weak infantry battalions. Between them, the two divisions had about ten Sturmgeschütz, fourteen 7.5cm s.Pak Sfl. Marder, nine towed 7.5cm Pak, six 8.8cm Pak, and sixty German Field Artillery pieces. Mahlmann's division also had a fully organized *Feldersatz-Bataillon* (Field Replacement

Battalion) and a full *Marsch-Batallion-Infanterie* (Infantry Replacement Battalion, a temporary unit composed of infantry replacements), which gave him a reserve of about 1,500 men that could immediately replace casualties. The Montgardon-Mont Castré position quickly became known as the Mahlmann Linie (Mahlmann Line).

The combined German strength was formidable, especially given they were fighting on the defensive. All told they had managed to amass about 134 pieces of Field Artillery, 40 Sturmgeschütz, and 42 towed and self-propelled heavy antitank guns, which was a respectable total to oppose the VIII Corps's 252 artillery pieces and 118 medium and 69 light tanks. However, except for the *353. Infanterie-Division*, the German infantry units were weak, and ammunition was scarce. On 27 June, *77. Infanterie-Division*, *353. Infanterie-Division*, and *Gruppe König* reported only 35 percent of its artillery Erst-Ausstattung (initial ammunition issue) on hand, although *353. Infanterie-Division* did have 87 percent of its 10.5cm howitzer ammunition. In terms of small arms ammunition, *77. Infanterie-Division* and *Gruppe König* only had 36 percent of its machine gun Erst-Ausstattung, while *353. Infanterie-Division* was in better condition with 92 percent.[6]

More problematic for American fortunes, two other German formations were assembling in the area behind the *LXXXIV Armee-Korps*. By the end of June, *Fallschirmjäger-Regiment 15* and *I./Fallschirm-Artillerie-Regiment 5* (18 10.5cm leFH) of *5. Fallschirmjäger-Division* completed its movement from Rennes to the village of Saint-Sébastien-de-Raids, northeast of Périers, and went into corps reserve. While the division had only begun forming on 1 April, the *I. Bataillon* and *III. Bataillon* had drawn cadre from combat veterans of the formidable *1. Fallschirmjäger-Division* in Italy and were filled out by select recruits. Although as late as 22 May units of *5. Fallschirmjäger-Division* were still lacking three-quarters of authorized light and heavy infantry weapons and only had 9 percent of the planned number of motor vehicles, it is likely that *Fallschirmjäger-Regiment 15* and *I./Fallschirm-Artillerie-Regiment 5* were nearly full strength in terms of manpower.[7]

The other new unit was the *2. SS-Panzer-Division "Das Reich"* It had been ordered to move to Normandy on 12 June but was in relatively poor shape after severe losses in the Soviet 1943–1944 winter offensive. The first elements of the division were transferred to Bordeaux for rebuilding beginning 2 February 1944, but the last did not leave the Eastern Front until 25 March. By late June, the combat-ready elements of the division were assembled in the area Torigny-sur-Vire–Canisy–Beaucoudray. One KG was committed on 26 June to stem the British Operation EPSOM and was not ordered to rejoin the division until the night of 1–2 July so was probably still en route. However, about half the division strength, most of two

Panzer battalions and three Panzer-Grenadier battalions, and all the available artillery, were in *Heeresgruppe-B* reserve and were assembling in the vicinity of Torigni-sur-Vire–Canisy–Beaucoudray, south of Saint-Lô. The first wheeled elements of the division began arriving in the assembly area on 16 June and the first tanks on 18 June, but major elements of the division were still moving from Southern France and did not arrive until late July.[8]

Although the Germans had managed to assemble a significant force to oppose the VIII Corps, their defense was complicated by conflicts within the German high command facing the Americans, which had suffered considerable upheaval. On 18 June, General Fahrmbacher relinquished his temporary command of the *LXXXIV Armee-Korps* to Generalleutnant Dietrich von Choltitz. At the same time, *II. Fallschirm-Korps* under General der Flieger Eugen Meindl, which had been committed on the eastern half of the *7. Armee* front on 11 June temporarily under Fahrmbacher's command, came directly under *7. Armee* command. However, overnight on 28/29 June the commander of *7. Armee*, Generaloberst Friedrich Dollmann, died of a heart attack and was succeeded by SS-Oberstgruppenführer Paul Hausser. Hausser was commanding *II. SS-Panzer-Korps* at the time, which was then embroiled in a major battle containing the British Army's Operation EPSOM, so it is questionable how well acquainted he was with the issues *7. Armee* was facing.[9]

Immediately after taking command of the *LXXXIV Armee-Korps*, von Choltitz assessed *Gruppe König* could not hold the overextended line from Port-Bail-sur-Mer–Saint-Sauveur-de-Pierrepont–Prétot-Sainte-Suzanne–Baupte because it was too weak, which is why he placed the corps reserve, *77.* and *353. Infanterie-Division*, along the Mahlmann Linie, which he considered more defensible terrain. By this arrangement *Gruppe König* became an outpost line, while *KG Mahlmann* became the main line of resistance. When attacked *König* would resist as long as possible before falling back behind the Mahlmann Linie where they could reorganize.

However, Feldmarschall Gerd von Runstedt, commanding *Oberbefehlshaber West* (High Command in the West), recommended defending even farther back along the line of the Ay and Sèves Rivers. Choltitz felt the Ay–Sèves line was an excellent fall-back position but did not place any of his scarce troops there. Then Hitler intervened. He was temperamentally opposed to any sort of defensive position prepared to the rear of a main line of resistance. As a result, he designated König's position the main line of resistance, which made the *353. Infanterie-Division* troops appear idle, in turn leading to orders moving them eastward to relieve *SS-GvB* so it could reassemble and reconstitute as a mobile reserve. As a further measure to begin the reconstitution of the divisions shattered in the battle for the Cotentin, *Gruppe König* was dissolved, and its various constituent parts began to reorganize under their original divisional headquarters. The *77. Infanterie-Division* took command of the eastern end of the Mahlmann Linie, which was considered more important than the western end of the line, while the weaker *243. Infanterie-Division* took command of the left (west) of the line, and the remnants of *Gruppe König* (*91. Infanterie-Division*) continued to command the hodgepodge of units holding the outpost line. However, by the morning of 3 July when the VIII Corps was about to begin its attack, the Division Headquarters, three infantry battalions, and nearly half the artillery regiment of *353. Infanterie-Division* were en route to an assembly area near Périers That left just two infantry battalions and the *Pionier-Batallion* (minus one company) of the *353. Infanterie-Division*, along with some artillery and elements of *Panzer-Jäger-Abteilung 353*, with four weak battalions of the *77. Infanterie-Division* to man the Mahlmann Linie.[10]

This mistake on the part of the Germans nearly granted the VIII Corps the opportunity for a major success if they could punch through the outpost line and seize the weakly held Mahlmann Linie before the Germans could bring up reinforcements. However, that fleeting chance ended when a drenching downpour began early in the morning of 3 July. While the Ninth U.S. Air Force recorded flying five missions totaling 275 fighter-bomber sorties that strafed and bombed defended areas, gun positions, fuel dumps, roads, and bridges in the vicinity of Lessay and Périers in support of the VIII Corps, it is doubtful if any were effective. As the Ninth Air Force summarized the day, "Bombs fell in all the target areas, but the results were unobserved." Worse, the Field Artillery's "Cubs" could not fly, which severely reduced the capabilities of the mass of artillery made available to the VIII Corps, and especially the 90th Infantry Division.[11]

3 JULY

The division attacked in the heavy rain at 0530 following the preplanned fifteen-minute preparation by the 90th and 4th Division Artillery. The heavy weapons of the 357th Infantry and the two reserve battalions of the 358th and 359th Infantry joined in reinforcing the artillery fire.

On the right (west) the 359th Infantry was concentrated on a 700-yard line of departure running east from the road to Le Carrefour Saint-Jores (D24), about 500 yards south of Le Ruisseau and Vindefontaine. Connection with the 82d Airborne Division, about 700 yards farther west, was maintained by patrols. The regiment attacked to the south-southwest with two battalions abreast, the 1st Battalion on the right and the 2d Battalion on the left. They immediately ran into heavy resistance from the German positions in Prétot-Sainte-Suzanne.

The 1st Battalion, 359th Infantry got into a "vicious close quarter fight" in orchards southwest of Prétot-Sainte-Suzanne and ended the day badly disorganized and weakened by casualties—it reported the loss of 41 KIA, 147 WIA, and 1 MIA, about a quarter of its effective strength. However, the battalion claimed to have annihilated the defending German battalion, which from the identification of prisoners was possibly elements of *II./Grenadier-Regiment 894* of *KG Mecklenburg*. In the afternoon resistance weakened and by 1600 the 1st Battalion reached a hill about 660 yards north of the Château de Sainte Suzanne and the Église Sainte-Suzanne (Church of Sainte-Suzanne) midway between the road to La Haye du Puits (D67) and the road to Saint-Jores (D24). It had advanced by about 1.5 miles, which was a credible performance after the slow advances in June.[12]

The 2d Battalion, 359th Infantry initially faced less resistance and advanced rapidly south but then began taking heavy casualties from accurate observed fire from the direction of Mont Castré. Nevertheless, with the support of Company C, 712th Tank Battalion, which lost a 105mm howitzer-armed Medium Tank M4 when it skidded off the road and threw a track, the 2d Battalion reached the outskirts of the Château and Église by 1600 after an advance of nearly 2.25 miles and the loss of 100 officers and men. Its left extended east across the Saint Jores-Le Plessis road (D24) where it loosely tied in with the 358th Infantry. Meanwhile the reserve 3d Battalion moved in behind the 1st Battalion and established contact patrols between the two forward battalions. It lost just ten men during the day, but one was the commander of Company K, Captain Edwin L. Ross. One indication of the confusion and lack of cohesion in the 359th Infantry at this time was that Captain Ross's death in action was not noted in the Company K MR until 6 July. In the evening, the 359th was ordered to resume the attack at 0600 the next day with the 3d Battalion passing through the 1st Battalion, which would reorganize.

On the left (east) the 358th Infantry line of departure extended east about a mile from the left of the 359th Infantry to just east of Francquetot. It also attacked southeast with its 1st Battalion on the right (west), 2d Battalion on the left (east), and 3d Battalion in reserve behind the 2d. The advance met no resistance until 0715 when the 2d Battalion reported contact near Les Sablons. At 0830 a total of twenty-five prisoners were reported captured and by 0945 another twenty Germans had been rounded up.

The 1st Battalion, 358th Infantry, with one platoon of medium tanks of Company B, 712th Tank Battalion in support, advanced quickly about 1.75 miles, reaching Le Carrefour (crossroads) Saint-Jores at around 0900. Then as the battalion turned south astride the D24 and advanced on Saint-Jores 500 yards away it was hit at 1330 by a "Boche infantry-tank assault" on its right flank, which knocked out two of Company B's tanks and drove the battalion back to the crossroads. A third Company B tank was lost when it tipped over on its side while driving parallel with a hedgerow. The rest of the day was a seesaw of advances and retreats as the battalion captured and then lost Saint-Jores three times. Finally, the advance of the 2d Battalion, 359th Infantry to Église Sainte-Suzanne on its right relieved the pressure on the 1st Battalion and it was able to secure Saint-Jores before nightfall.

The 2d Battalion, 358th Infantry, also with one platoon of medium tanks of Company B, 712th Tank Battalion in support, advanced rapidly and by 0700 reported it was 100 yards east of Les Sablons. However, at 0725 the battalion began receiving heavy fire from machine guns, mortars, and artillery. At 0900, the Battalion CP was hit by machine-gun, mortar, artillery, and "88" fire. It wounded all the battalion wiremen who laid and repaired field telephone cable, which was vital in maintaining communications. Also wounded was Lieutenant Colonel Merton E. Munson, commander of the supporting 344th Field Artillery Battalion, who was observing from the 2d Battalion CP. Nevertheless, by 0915 Company G reported it had reached the east-west railroad line south of Les Sablons. Then at 1155, a "tank" attack struck Company F, completely disorganizing it, and forcing it to withdraw because it claimed to have no bazooka ammunition. At the same time contact with Company E was lost. At 1230, the 2d Battalion was ordered into reserve in place, with the 3d Battalion committed between the right of the 2d and left of the 1st Battalion to restore the situation. The 2d Battalion settled in for the night along the railroad line south of Les Sablons.

The 3d Battalion, 358th Infantry met considerable resistance when it moved into line. At 1310, a platoon of Company B, 607th Tank Destroyer Battalion was brought into position 500 yards west of Les Sablons but did not report engaging any German armored vehicles. Then, between 1500 and 1530, two squads of the attached Company B, 315th Engineers reported "tangling" with a German "tank" in Les Sablons. Then Company I, in Sablons along with the Assault Gun Platoon and a platoon of Light Tanks M5A1 of Company D, 712th Tank Battalion in support, reported one "tank" and two half-tracks—or possibly they were "assault guns"—were threatening them from a position 500 yards to the south. The three American assault guns reported knocking out one of the German vehicles, describing it as a "Mark IV," while losing one of its own tanks and another one put out of action by a hit on its track. Company B, 712th Tank Battalion also lost two tanks and seven men during the day. Company K finally secured Les Sablons at 1730 but were hammered by a German artillery barrage—it was German habit to hit their own positions after they withdrew with a carefully preregistered artillery or mortar fire to unsettle the new occupants. The Americans then faced a German counterattack at 2100, but Lieutenant Colonel Bealke committed Company L to repel the attack and by 2130 all was more or less quiet.

Notably, this action was one of the first engagements by the 105mm-armed Medium Tank M4 "Assault Gun" in Normandy. The Tank Battalion Assault Gun Platoon of three tanks was part of the Tank Battalion Headquarters and Headquarters Company. Each of the three Medium Tank Companies also had one Assault Gun. In yet another sign of confusion and inexperience in tank-infantry cooperation by the Americans in Normandy, the 712th Tank Battalion reported its Assault Gun Platoon was attached to the 359th Infantry although it is clear it was actually the 358th.

One of the Company K, 358th Infantry's officers received the Distinguished Service Cross for his bravery at Les Sablons.

First Lieutenant William J. Henry, 0461526. Company K, 358th Infantry, 90th Division, United States Army.

> *For extraordinary heroism in connection with military operations against an armed enemy in France. On July 3, 1944, Company "K," 3rd Battalion 358th Infantry was attacking south in the vicinity of Les Sablons, France, when they were stopped by extremely heavy enemy mortar and automatic weapons fire. Lieutenant Henry, heavy weapons platoon leader, went forward under fire with a sound-powered telephone to adjust the fire of his platoon. As he reached the hedge from which he was to observe he was severely wounded by enemy mortar and small arms fire. Despite these wounds he stayed at his position directing fire, with complete disregard for his own safety, and would not accept evacuation until his mission was accomplished.*
>
> *The conspicuous gallantry of Lieutenant Henry and his courageous devotion to duty exemplify the highest traditions of the military service of the United States.*[13]

The identity of the German "tanks" that caused so many problems for the two regiments of the 90th Infantry Division on 3 July is not positively known. First it has to be acknowledged that identification of German armor by American tankers was frequently inaccurate, although they generally were able to distinguish a "tank" from an "assault gun" or a "halftrack." It may be that in their first engagement the men of the 712th Tank Battalion simply did not yet have the experience to make a correct identification. One remote possibility in the vicinity was the *SS-Panzer-Aufklärungs-Abteilung 17.* (armored reconnaissance battalion) (minus its *2. Kompanie*) of the *SS-GvB*, but it only had light armored cars and halftracks and was probably not committed until the next day. The most likely candidates were either *Sturmgeschütz-Brigade 902*, which had two companies in support of the right of *LXXXIV Armee-Korps* and one in support of the left, or elements of *Panzer-Jäger-Abteilung 353*.[14] Adding to the mystery, the 90th Infantry Division G-2 Report for 3 July noted that

> *A destroyed Mark III [tank] was found to have 1/4" armor plate 6" from the main part of the hull. This would detonate AT rocket grenades and HE shells.*

That perfectly describes the Schürzen (skirts) found on late production Panzer III—albeit the original intent was to protect the weak side armor and suspension from Soviet antitank rifle fire—but very few Panzer III were actually in France. Just six were operational and five were in short-term repair in France as of 1 June. Curiously though, *Panzer-Ersatz-und-Ausbildungs-Abteilung 100* had its headquarters at Franquetot on 6 June, so it is possible it was one of the three to eight assigned to them. However, it could also describe the Sturmgeschütz, which was based on the Panzer III chassis. Further support for the assumption they were assault guns rather than tanks also came from a "reliable" German prisoner interrogated by the 82d Airborne Division who stated there were only assault guns and no tanks west of the road running north-south from Prétot-Sainte-Suzanne through Saint-Jores (D24). Given the 90th also captured men from the *I./Grenadier-Regiment 942* during the day it seems likely the German combined arms counterattacks on the 358th and 359th Infantry were by that battalion coming up from its reserve position near Mont Castré.[15]

While the battle was raging west of it, the 357th Infantry remained quietly in reserve. On 1 July, the 3d Battalion was ordered to relieve the 2d Battalion, 358th Infantry at Baupte and became the Division Reserve. On 2 July, minus the 3d Battalion, the regiment stealthily crossed the Pont l'Abbé, which was still under German observation and subject to harassing fire, and marched 9.25 miles south to an assembly area 500 yards south of Les Creveuils, which it reached at 2000 suffering just one wounded and one injured in the process. It remained there until 1515 on 3 July, when General Landrum called and ordered the regiment to Pont Auny 3.50 miles to the southwest. The regiment closed in its new area by 1845 when General Landrum called again at 2000. This time he directed Colonel Barth to move the 3d Battalion to establish outposts between Baupte and Pont Auny, while Company L, with the battalion Antitank Platoon, a section of 81mm mortars, and a section of heavy machine guns would remain at Baupte to maintain contact with the 90th Reconnaissance Troop, which was patrolling the north edge of the Prairies. The 3d

Battalion completed its movement at 2330 and the regiment settled in for the night having lost just three men wounded during the day.

The 90th Infantry Division reported "over 600 casualties" for the day, while the daily casualty report stated it was 80 killed and 302 wounded, which seems a gross underestimate. The 358th Infantry reported 30 killed, 229 wounded, and 11 missing; the 359th Infantry 59 killed, 240 wounded, and 1 missing; and the 357th Infantry just 3 wounded. The Division After-Action Report also stated it made an "average advance of 1200 yards," which may have been an underestimate.

One noticeable issue highlighted during the day's events was Landrum's repeated calls to Colonel Barth micromanaging the movements of the 357th Infantry. This habit later became one of the chief complaints about his command style. Landrum frequently bypassed his regimental commanders and gave specific orders to their battalion commanders, ignoring the chain of command and existing regimental plans.[16]

The rest of the VIII Corps's attack to the right (west) of the 90th Infantry Division also met with mixed results. Immediately to the right of the 90th, the 82d Airborne Division attack was more successful. The 325th Glider Infantry, advancing to the right of the 359th Infantry, complained that the 359th's failure to advance exposed the left flank of the 325th to German fire. However, it seems more likely the 700-yard gap between the two regiments and poor coordination between the two divisions were the actual culprits. Nevertheless, the 325th seized the eastern end of the La Poterie ridge but were unable to secure the village of La Poterie. Farther west, the 505th Infantry infiltrated a battalion into the German rear and quickly seized most of Hill 131, while the 508th Infantry seized the southern slope of Hill 131 and prepared to take Hill 95 on 4 July. By evening, the paratroopers had shattered *Gruppe Bunjatschenko*, which collapsed despite a valiant attempt at a counterattack by its commander.[17]

The 82d Airborne Division's attack displayed a tactical finesse hard won in combat in Sicily and Italy. Experience taught the paratroopers that careful reconnaissance before an attack, infiltration into the enemy flank and rear, attacking in columns of companies and battalions or combinations of columns and lines disposed according to the terrain, and strict fire discipline worked better against the German defenses than did the conventional linear tactics employed by the 90th's infantry battalions.

On the VIII Corps right, the 79th Infantry Division advance mirrored the partial success of the 90th. It seized parts of Hill 121 northwest of La Haye-du-Puits in a well-thought-out maneuver by its 314th Infantry, while its 315th Infantry captured Denneville. However, fierce German resistance stalled the division short of its main objective, the crossroads at Le Haye-du-Puits.[18]

4 JULY

Two maps recovered the previous day by the 505th Parachute Infantry from the body of a German officer, probably from *Pionier-Batallion 353*, revealed the extent of the German defenses facing the VIII Corps attack. They confirmed that the first day's battle for Mont Castré had only pushed in the German outpost line. The maps showed the trace of the German main line of resistance—the Mahlmann Linie—was from Beau Coudray to the Forêt de Mont Castré and then on to the coast. It also confirmed the presence of major elements of the *353. Infanterie-Division* and other units and hinted that the Germans would attempt to hold the line "whatever the price." However, it gave no hints of how the officers and men of the 90th Infantry Division could force the Germans from their strong positions.

Those officers and men spent hours in the dark after midnight readjusting battalion positions into defensive positions before attempting to rest, resupply, and reorganize. However, the Germans gave them no respite. The excellent observation afforded by Mont Castré over the 90th's positions allowed the Germans to pinpoint the American dispositions. The German observers were aided by a nearly full moon, the extended twilight hours, and a brief break in the constant rain—the weather turned clear and warm overnight before the rain began again in the morning. Making the night even shorter, General Landrum ordered all units to "stand-to to repel counter-attacks from 0430 to 0530" and to resume the attack at 0600 after a ten-minute artillery preparation.

The 359th Infantry jumped off on the division right (west) at 0600, again with two battalions abreast, the 3d on the right and the 2d on the left. The 1st Platoon, Company C, 712th Tank Battalion supported the 1st Battalion, the 2nd Platoon, the 3d Battalion, and the 3d Platoon, the 2d Battalion, 359th Infantry.

The 3d Battalion passed through the 1st Battalion to reach its line of departure and immediately met stiff resistance including heavy machine-gun, mortar, and artillery fire from high ground to the west and south. Just west of Le Fry an unnamed creek in a deep ravine ran into the Senelle River, which paralleled the Carrefour Saint-Jores Road (D903) to the south. The 3d Battalion was thrown into confusion after its commander Major Benbrook, an OR officer and 1926 graduate of the University of Arkansas, was killed when his command group ran into a German patrol. His Executive Officer, Captain John Forrest Smith, took command. Under heavy fire the battalion was stalled by midday, unable to move either south to the

D903 or west against the strong German position on the other side of the ravine. By the end of the day, it had suffered losses of twelve dead and forty-two wounded. One soldier of the 3d Battalion was awarded the Distinguished Service Cross for his actions on 4 July.[19]

Private Barney H. Prosser, United States Army, was awarded the Distinguished Service Cross for extraordinary heroism in connection with military operations against an armed enemy while serving with Company I, 359th Infantry Regiment, 90th Infantry Division, in action against enemy forces on 4 July 1944. Private Prosser's intrepid actions, personal bravery and zealous devotion to duty exemplify the highest traditions of the military forces of the United States and reflect great credit upon himself, the 90th Infantry Division, and the United States Army.[20]

The 2d Battalion advance was also subjected to heavy fire and at 1155 was hit by a strong counterattack spearheaded by three "tanks" that drove the battalion back to its starting positions around the Église Sainte-Suzanne, despite the support of the 3d Platoon, Company C, 712th Tank Battalion. The Germans kept up the assault there until late in the afternoon when they withdrew. The 2d Battalion was able to follow up and by dark it reached the D903 where its patrols contacted the 1st Battalion, 357th Infantry farther east at Saint-Jores. It suffered nine dead, fifty-one wounded, and two missing. One 2d Battalion soldier received the second Distinguished Service Cross awarded in the 359th Infantry on 4 July.

The President of the United States of America, authorized by Act of Congress, July 9, 1918, takes pleasure in presenting the Distinguished Service Cross to Technical Sergeant [then Staff Sergeant] Abraham Jamail (ASN: 18114594), United States Army, for extraordinary heroism in connection with military operations against an armed enemy while serving was Section Sergeant of Weapons Platoon, Company G, 359th Infantry Regiment, 90th Infantry Division, in action against enemy forces on 4 July 1944, in the vicinity of St. Suzanne, France. Locating an enemy machine gun which was holding up the company's advance, Technical Sergeant Jamail fired a rifle grenade into the position, routing the crew of three which he then killed by rifle fire. Receiving fire from the left, he then crossed a heavily mined field to a hedgerow which had been cleared by the enemy to give them better fields of fire. Moving along its embankment, he destroyed another machine gun with grenades and forced the surrender of four others. Reaching the enemy command post, Sergeant Jamail killed, wounded, and captured the remainder of the group. Technical Sergeant Jamail's intrepid actions, personal bravery and zealous devotion to duty exemplify the highest traditions of the military forces of the United States and reflect great credit upon himself, the 90th Infantry Division, and the United States Army.[21]

When the German counterattack pushed back the 2d Battalion a dangerous gap opened up between it and the 3d Battalion. Colonel Fales committed the 1st Battalion with the 1st Platoon, Company C, 712th Tank Battalion to attack into the gap and toward the D903 to relieve the pressure on both battalions. The 1st Battalion passed around the left of the 3d Battalion, spearheaded by Company A whose commander, Captain Leroy Pond, was an OR officer from the University of Arkansas, class of 1938. Pond's twenty-seventh birthday was on D-Day and he proved an inspiring and gifted officer. His red hair and intensity earned him the nickname of "Fireball" long before he entered combat, but the nickname proved appropriate. Pond received his first of two awards of the Distinguished Service Cross for his actions on 4 July, which was also the third Distinguished Service Cross awarded in the 359th Infantry that day.

> *The President of the United States of America, authorized by Act of Congress July 9, 1918, takes pleasure in presenting the Distinguished Service Cross to Captain (Infantry) Leroy R. Pond (ASN: 0-370275), United States Army, for extraordinary heroism in connection with military operations against an armed enemy while serving with the 1st Battalion, 359th Infantry Regiment, 90th Infantry Division, in action against enemy forces on 4 July 1944. Captain Pond's outstanding leadership, personal bravery and zealous devotion to duty exemplify the highest traditions of the military forces of the United States and reflect great credit upon himself, the 90th Infantry Division, and the United States Army.*[22]

Pond's attack pushed down the ravine of the Senelle and crossed the D903. Company A and B drove south while Company C pushed west, clearing the Germans from in front of the 3d Battalion. By midnight, the 1st Battalion was established firmly across the road and was tied in with the 3d Battalion on its right and the 2d Battalion on its left. The day's battle under the skillful leadership of "Fireball" Pond had cost the 1st Battalion just twenty-six casualties: four killed, twenty-one wounded, and one missing.

The author of the 358th Infantry's wartime *History*—probably the Regimental S-3 Major William T. Wallace—began his entry for 4 July with the comment that there were "more fireworks than any of us had ever seen in the States! And Rain!" He then added, "a not so secondary thought in the minds of all was 'doesn't it ever stop raining in Normandy!'" He also discovered that the map overlay accompanying the division's orders for the day gave an incorrect tracing for the line-of-departure for the regiment, a potentially dangerous error that reflected poorly on the work done by the division staff. A mismarked line-of-departure could have ended with American artillery fire falling on its own frontline infantry as they prepared to advance. Luckily there was time to warn the units involved and correct the error.[23]

However, when the 358th with Company B, 712th Tank Battalion and the sole remaining operational tank of the Battalion Assault Gun Platoon jumped off behind an artillery "blanket of fire" they encountered a new surprise—the Germans simultaneously launched their own counterattack. It struck the 2d Battalion on its exposed left (east) and drove between Company E and G, completely disrupting the battalion's attack. German mortar and artillery fire observed from Mont Castré was particularly effective and it was 1700 before the battalion was reorganized and capable of advancing again. Nevertheless, by 2200 it was digging in around La Butte, although there were still some worries about German elements that had been bypassed and were now in the American rear.

On the right the 1st Battalion drove forward against strong resistance and reached the east-west railroad line by 0700. Shortly after 0810, the 1st Battalion, with the addition of Company B, 712th Tank Battalion, continued to press forward until 1100. At that point, the 3d Battalion passed through and took up the attack. At around 1250, Colonel Partridge ordered the 358th halt in place to reorganize and prepare for a further attack at 1400, which was later postponed to 1700. The 1st Battalion advanced in this new attack for about 400 yards before it was pinned down by German artillery fire at 1832. However, it had managed to fight its way across the railroad tracks and into the village of Les Belles Croix south of Saint-Jores.

The 3d Battalion's mission in the center was to make a limited advance to seize the high ground to its immediate front. From there it would support the advances of the 1st and 2d Battalion until they moved past it, at which time the 3d Battalion would revert to regimental reserve. However, the other two battalions were unable to contact one another, so the 3d Battalion remained in the line. During this action, another Distinguished Service Cross was awarded to a member of the 358th Infantry.

> *The President of the United States of America, authorized by Act of Congress, July 9, 1918, takes pleasure in presenting the Distinguished Service Cross to Captain (Infantry) Phillip H. Carroll, United States Army, for extraordinary heroism in connection with military operations against an armed enemy while serving as Commanding Officer of Company K, 358th Infantry Regiment, 90th Infantry Division, in action against enemy forces on 4 July 1944, in the vicinity of Les Sablons, France. On that date, Company K was ordered to attack through lines held by another company to secure a strong enemy position. Other attacking troops had twice been thrown back, suffering heavy casualties. Captain Carroll*

personally led his company forward, across a deep railroad cut, through intense enemy mortar, machine-gun, automatic weapons and artillery fire, fearlessly exposing himself to the enemy in order to encourage his men. Despite a painful shell-fragment wound which blinded him in one eye, Captain Carroll continued his courageous advance inspiring his men to capture the objective, and not until he had assured the defense of the position did he seek medical aid. Even then he walked to the aid station so that another wounded soldier of his company could be evacuated by litter. Captain Carroll's fearless leadership, personal bravery and zealous devotion to duty exemplify the highest traditions of the military forces of the United States and reflect great credit upon himself, the 90th Infantry Division, and the United States Army.[24]

During the day, the advance of the 83d Infantry Division east of the Prairies secured the crossing of the Sèves River and Canal d'Auvers at Baupte from the threat of a German attack from the southeast, releasing L Company, 357th Infantry to rejoin its regiment. It also allowed General Landrum to finally order the 357th Infantry into the battle. At 1500, he ordered the 1st Battalion, 357th Infantry to Saint-Jores to fill in the gap between the 2d Battalion, 359th Infantry and the 1st Battalion, 358th Infantry. The rest of the regiment was alerted to prepare to pass through the 358th Infantry and continue the attack south through Beau Coudray.

According to the narrative in the 90th Division Report of Operations, casualties on 4 July "were considerably higher" than the previous day. However, the casualties reported by the Division G-3 were just 549, which were fewer than the 600 reported in the Division Report of Operations for 3 July but still more than the 382 reported in the G-3 report for 3 July. Meanwhile the total casualties reported by the three regiments was just 309. Confusion over the number of friendly casualties may have left General Landrum and his staff unaware that the slow-moving attack was steadily grinding through the German defenses. The 359th Infantry in particular were now just 1,000 yards from its objective in the Forêt de Mont Castré. However, at this crucial point, General Landrum inexplicably decided to use his uncommitted division reserve, the fresh 357th Infantry, to drive south to Baupte rather than passing it through the 359th Infantry and onto Mont Castré. This, even though the Division Report of Operations cogently commented,

The rapid capture of the Forêt de Mont Castré loomed increasingly important—without it we had no observation; with it the Boche had too much.

Farther west on the VIII Corps front, the 82d Airborne Division also continued to hammer at the German outpost line. In the morning, the 1st and 3d

Battalion, 505th Parachute Infantry seized the northern slope of Hill 95. Then the 2d Battalion, 508th Parachute Infantry passed through and seized the crest of Hill 95 until a German counterattack at 1400 by *I./Grenadier-Regiment 943* of *353. Infanterie-Division* forced them back. However, the paratroopers did not give up and by midnight the crest of the hill was again in American hands. The village of La Poterie on the ridgeline east of Hill 95 was seized by the 3d Battalion, 507th Parachute Infantry and the 325th Glider Infantry by afternoon. The 2d Battalion, 507th Infantry completed the occupation of the La Poterie ridgeline west of Hill 95 with an attack at 2000, although fighting went on into the early hours of 5 July.[25]

The 79th Infantry Division also continued its attack on the right of the VIII Corps line. The 2d Battalion, 314th Infantry joined the 3d Battalion on Hill 121 and by 0830 the position was declared secure. The 1st Battalion, 314th Infantry followed up and seized Bolleville against heavy resistance, while the 3d Battalion advanced to the west end of Hill 95 to relieve pressure on the 82d Airborne Division. Farther to the right the 315th Infantry had less success, advancing until 1600 when a fierce German counterattack struck the two leading companies of the 1st Battalion and halted the advance.[26]

The deteriorating situation on the *LXXXIV. Armee-Korps* front led to Feldmarschall Rommel agreeing with SS-Oberstgruppenführer Hausser's order shifting a *KG SS-Das Reich* to Périers where it would be available to counterattack north towards Le Haye-du-Puits or northeast toward Carentan. *Fallschirmjäger Regiment 15* was also released from *LXXXIV. Armee-Korps* reserve and held ready for a counterattack. The *KG SS-Das Reich* sent to support the *LXXXIV. Armee-Korps* consisted of the *SS-Panzeraufklärungs-Abteilung 2.* (minus the *1. Kompanie*), *III./SS-Panzer-Grenadier-Regiment 3.*, *III./SS-Panzer-Grenadier-Regiment 4.*, two companies of *SS-Sturmgeschütz-Abteilung 2.*, and *II./SS-Panzer-Artillerie-Regiment 2.* The main body of *SS-Das Reich* remained in the vicinity of Torigni-sur-Vire–Canisy–Beaucoudray.[27]

5 JULY

The 90th Infantry Division resumed its attack at 0845 in a light rain, although the weather turned clear and warm later in the day. Soldiers used to the heat of Camp Barkeley in Texas shivered in the cool dampness—the temperature never got above 65 degrees Fahrenheit.

The 359th Infantry was ordered to continue attacking to the south and west to seize Lithaire, Hill 122, and the ridge that ran east through the Forêt de Mont Castré to the secondary road that ran along the east edge of the forest. The 357th

Infantry with the 1st Battalion, 358th Infantry and Company B, 712th Tank Battalion attached would pass through the 358th Infantry and attack south to seize Beau Coudray. The sole operational Assault Gun Platoon tank remained attached to Company B, 712th Tank Battalion as well. After Beau Coudray was secured one battalion of the 357th would turn west to support the 359th attack on the Forêt de Mont Castré, while the rest of the regiment advanced south toward Le Plessis. The 358th Infantry would hold in place until the 357th Infantry seized Beau Coudry and then would withdraw to the area of Les Belles Croix–Saint-Jores as division reserve.

The 359th Infantry attacked at 0845 with the 3d Battalion on the right, the 2d Battalion on the left, and Company C, 712th Tank Battalion in support. The light tanks of Company D, 712th Tank Battalion were also supposedly in support but spent the day idling near the 3d Battalion, 359th Infantry's Observation Post (OP). The 3d Battalion reached the crossroads known as La Peignerie about 1,200 meters east of Lithaire after breaking through German resistance at the line of departure and the 1st Battalion moved forward as the regimental reserve. The 2d Battalion's advance was slower as it met heavy resistance at the crossroads southwest of La Rivagerie on the Lithaire-Beau-Coudray Road (D140) east of Hill 122 at the end of the ridgeline near the ancient ruin known as the "Camp de Cesar." Two medium tanks were knocked out by German antitank guns and "bazooka fire" (Panzerschreck) and one bogged down between the lines and was abandoned.[28]

At 1930, the 1st Battalion, 358th Infantry jumped off to support the attack of the 359th Infantry and at 2015 it was attached to the 359th. The 1st Battalion was ordered to come up on the left rear of the 2d Battalion, 359th Infantry and soon reported it was "in a hot spot already." However, by 2100 Captain Bennett, the 1st Battalion Liaison Officer, told the regiment the 1st Battalion was moving along, were encountering just "some" resistance, and were "taking many prisoners"—thirty were reported taken during the night. They were instructed to continue to reinforce the attack on 6 July.

The 1st Battalion, 357th Infantry waited until 0930 to jump off, then advanced in a column of companies—A, B, C—and gained 400 yards before they were halted by German resistance. By 1010, Company B, 712th Tank Battalion eliminated the pocket of resistance and the advance continued. The 3d Battalion was ordered to move up to the left of the 1st Battalion behind a fresh artillery preparation. By 1120 the 1st Battalion "knocked out one 88 mm gun" and was just 1,000 yards short of the Beau-Coudray crossroads but at 1200 reported meeting stiff resistance about 100 yards from the crossroads. Company A, still in the lead, was ordered at 1240 to hold where it was to avoid unnecessary casualties.

Company B was ordered to come up on the right of Company A, take over the supporting armor of Company B, 712th Tank Battalion, and continue the attack, which it did at 1330. Then at 1410 the rest of the 1st Battalion was ordered to clear off the road so the 3d Battalion, with Company B, 712th Tank Battalion, could come up and move to the right as well. The problem was the marshy terrain about 1,000 yards north of Beau-Coudray on either side of the road (D24) and the steeply banked stream known as the Ruisseau de l'Issue Courte, running west to east draining the high ground of Mont Castré into the Prairies. Combined with high stone walls on either side of the road, it created a bottleneck for the 357th Infantry as it attempted to move south. Company B, 712th Tank Battalion lost three tanks bogged down and only one to German action during the day, which was a good indication of just how difficult the terrain was.

With the tail of the 1st Battalion struggling to move off the road to the right it was 1835 before the 3d Battalion was able to close up behind it. Company B finally managed to reach a point just 50 yards from the road running west from Beau-Coudray but were counterattacked at 2230 and fell back to the main north-south road. At the same time, the leading platoon of Company A was hit by heavy fire from German positions southeast of the crossroads and fell back 200 yards to the rest of the company.

Private Thomas T. Flynn, United States Army, was awarded the Distinguished Service Cross for extraordinary heroism in connection with military operations against an armed enemy while serving with the 357th Infantry Regiment, 90th Infantry Division, in action against enemy forces on 5 July 1944. Private Flynn's intrepid actions, personal bravery and zealous devotion to duty exemplify the highest traditions of the military forces of the United States and reflect great credit upon himself, the 90th Infantry Division, and the United States Army.[29]

The 358th Infantry (minus the 1st Battalion) remained in division reserve throughout the day, prepared to advance south in rear of the 357th Infantry on order. It was also assigned responsibility at 2200 for screening the division left along the Prairies, which were slowly drying out as American engineers repaired the drainage system sabotaged by the Germans. Initially, Colonel Partridge assigned two platoons of the 3d Battalion to guard that flank but then decided to send all of Company L. However, no sooner was that done than at 2330 the Division G-3, Lieutenant Colonel Stillwell, telephoned to say the flank patrols could be withdrawn at 0800 the next morning. The rest of the regiment settled in for the night in positions just east of les Belles Croix.

By midnight, the 90th Infantry Division appeared to be within striking distance of capturing Hill 122, the Forêt de Mont Castré, and the Beau-Coudray crossroads. While the VIII Corps advance from 3 through 5 July was slow, it was causing major damage to the German units opposing it. The total VIII Corps prisoner-of-war haul alone was significant with at least 1,245 collected from the morning of 3 July through midnight on 5 July. The 90th Infantry Division accounted for 487 of them.

Most of the German units manning the outpost line were at best no longer effective and at worst were effectively destroyed. *II./Grenadier-Regiment 895* of *KG 265. Infanterie-Division* was essentially wiped out with only 40 officers and men of a reported Gefechtsstärke (combat strength) of 617 escaping from their positions near Vindefontaine. The other three battalions of *KG 265. Infanterie-Division* were also roughly handled, and each were probably now no stronger than a weak company. *77. Infanterie-Division* was also in dire straits, having suffered severe casualties since its commitment in June. A few days earlier, *Heeresgruppe-B* had assigned a replacement battalion to the battered division, but it appears most of the 1,000 replacements in the battalion were already casualties so an ad hoc replacement company of perhaps 200 men stripped from the fortified ports in Brittany was sent to the division as well.[30]

Perhaps worst of all from the German perspective was the loss of the Sturmgeschütz of *Panzer-Jäger-Abteilung 353*, which were a vital part of their infantry's offensive and defensive combat power. At least one was probably knocked by the 712th Tank Battalion near Les Sablons on 3 July. Possibly eight others were reported destroyed by German engineers on 5 July because they were not recoverable. A German prisoner claimed they were lost because a "lack of ammunition made them a liability," but other reports indicate the tremendous volume of American artillery fire damaged most of them by 4 July. The losses may have left just one operational Sturmgeschütz facing the 90th Infantry Division. One German "tank" was also positively identified destroyed by the 82d Airborne Division near La Fieffé as a Sturmgeschütz III. It was overrun and captured on 5 June and was probably from *Sturmgeschütz-Brigade 902*. Significantly, the 90th Infantry Division did not report any contact with this unit until 12 July when one of its officers was captured by the 359th Infantry near Lastelle.

In response to the American advance, the *LXXXIV. Armee-Korps* released the *I./Grenadier-Regiment 941* during the day and committed it against the advance of the 357th Infantry from Saint-Jores, which was the pressure that forced the 1st Battalion to halt and stymied the attempts by the 2d and 3d Battalion to move west off the road (D24). The *II./Grenadier-Regiment 941* was also brought up during the day and prepared to counterattack toward La Poterie and the 359th Infantry on the 90th's right (west) on 6 July. The *Fallschirmjäger-Regiment 15* also came up from reserve to a position along the south edge of the Forêt de Mont Castré from where it could attack north to secure Hill 122 and the northeastern nose of the ridge. Finally, on the evening of 5 July, *7. Armee* contemplated moving the *KG SS-Das Reich* from Périers to the area north of Lessay so it could conduct a concentrated counterattack north during the night of 6/7 July.[31]

The 90th Infantry Division had made good progress again on 5 July advancing its frontline nearly 2,000 yards. Casualties were still said to be heavy: 488 battle casualties were reported by the Division G-3. But in fact, the infantry regiments only reported losing 280: 85 in the 357th Infantry, 59 in the 358th Infantry, and 136 in the 359th Infantry. Again, Landrum's lack of understanding of what was happening to his division, fostered by his tendency to remain isolated in his Division Headquarters, was obscuring the division's success. Worse, the advance was simply not rapid enough to satisfy the American high command.

On 5 July, General Eisenhower expressed reservations about Landrum as a division commander in a letter to General Marshall. Eisenhower had just returned to SHAEF Headquarters at Camp Griffiss, which was located at Bushy Park in Teddington, Middlesex, on the outskirts of London after four days visiting the beachhead in France. Eisenhower blamed three things for the slow going by the VIII and VII Corps attacks that were then in progress.[32]

> *The first of these, as always, is the fighting quality of the German soldier. The second is the nature of the country. Our whole attack has to fight its way out of very narrow bottlenecks, flanked by marshes and against an enemy who has a double hedgerow and an intervening ditch almost every fifty yards as a ready-made strong points. The third cause is the weather. Our air has been unable to operate at maximum efficiency and on top of this the rain and mud were so bad during my visit that I was reminded of Tunisian wintertime.*[33]

Next, Eisenhower addressed the leadership of the American forces in the beachhead. He extolled the performance of the corps commanders, except for Middleton, commanding the VIII Corps, who he damned with faint praise. He "does not display the enthusiasm in his leadership that do the others but he is tactically sound and a very straightforward workman." Then he touched on division leadership.

> *Among the Division Commanders we still have a few doubts. Strangely enough, all of us (Bradley, Hodges and myself) are much concerned about Landrum. I*

sincerely hope he makes good because we have been counting on him very much. Nevertheless, he seems quite negative. One point to remember, however, is that he is commanding the 90th Division. Collins and our other Commanders agree that this unit is less well prepared for battle than almost any other Division they have seen. I do not know who its original commander was, but our seniors are quite sure the Division was not well brought up.[34]

6 JULY

General Landrum's orders for the day repeated those of the previous three days. The 359th Infantry, with the 1st Battalion, 358th Infantry attached, and the 357th Infantry would both continue the attack south in their respective zones. The 358th Infantry (-) would guard the division right rear with the 3d Battalion at Saint-Jores ready to support the 1st Battalion and the 359th Infantry in "mop[ping] up FORÊT DE MONT CASTRÉ" and the 2d Battalion in division reserve. At least the weather report predicted an end to the incessant rain—although there were intermittent showers during the day, it was mostly clear and warm.

On the division right (west), the day began with a surprise for the 359th Infantry. At 0630, the 359th's commanding officer, Colonel Fales, was relieved of duty by Colonel Bacon, the Division Chief of Staff. Bacon was a forty-eight-year-old graduate of West Point, class of 1917, who had made no secret of his desire to command an infantry regiment in combat. Unfortunately, it does not appear his desire was matched by his ability. While unquestionably brave—he was awarded two Silver Stars during the war—according to his contemporaries Bacon lacked the drive, charisma, and leadership needed to command an infantry regiment and was relieved of command on 3 November by Brigadier General James A. Van Fleet, who assumed command of the 90th on 15 October 1944. Bacon was then transferred to the 95th Infantry Division and became commanding officer of the 379th Infantry on 24 November.[35]

Despite the change of command, the 1st Battalion, 359th Infantry jumped off on time at 0800, climbed the slopes of the ridge west of Hill 122, and secured a dominant position on the high ground north and northwest of La Ville against sporadic German resistance by 1037. The 3d Battalion, 359th Infantry attacked at 0900 to the left of the 1st Battalion and immediately encountered strong resistance. Nevertheless, by 1910 they seized the high ground to the left (east) of the 1st Battalion's positions, which was Hill 122. The 2d Battalion, 359th Infantry and attached 1st Battalion, 358th Infantry jumped off at 0930 and by 0925 reported they had "seized Hill 122" and began to dig in. However, they were not actually on Hill

122. Instead they occupied the "NE nose of the Forêt" and the Camp de Cesar about 1,500 yards to the east-southeast of Hill 122.

Why the 359th Infantry was unable to correctly identify the high ground designated as Hill 122 remains a mystery. It is clearly marked on the maps used by the 90th Infantry Division and was clearly the area occupied by the 3d Battalion, 359th Infantry. The area seized by the 2d Battalion, 359th and 1st Battalion, 358th Infantry is also clearly marked as the Camp de Cesar and is along the 100- and 110-meter contour line, but it is obviously not "Hill 122."[36]

Unfortunately, the 1st and 3d Battalion were unable to firmly link up as the Germans maintained a position on the high ground between them. Worse, there was a 700- to 800-yard gap between the 3d Battalion, 359th on Hill 122 and the 2d Battalion, 359th and 1st Battalion, 358th farther east. By 2000 the 1st and 3d Battalion, 359th Infantry reported German counterattacks were developing and at 2045 the Germans began hitting the 2d Battalion, 359th as well. By 2400 the counterattacks spread to the 1st Battalion, 358th Infantry. The Germans exploited the gaps between the American battalions to infiltrate into the American rear, causing considerable confusion. Worse, the steep slopes on the north side of Mont Castré and the lack of roads made it difficult for armor to move up in support or for supplies to get forward. The 1st Platoon of Company C, 712th Tank Battalion attempted to move forward supplies on the decks of its tanks but without success, while the 2d and 3d Platoons remained in the Company assembly area to the north.

The rest of the 358th Infantry spent most of the early hours of the day in reserve. At 1050, Lieutenant Colonel Bealke's 3d Battalion was alerted for a move west, behind the 358th Infantry, to La Peignerie and Colonel Partridge and Bealke were ordered to report to Division Headquarters for instructions. They did not return to the 358th's CP until about 1400 when Partridge told his staff the 3d Battalion would not be committed "right away" before he left for the Regimental OP on the front line. The men of the Regiment were stunned to hear at 1610 that when Partridge got to the OP he was severely wounded in the chest by mortar fragments. Lieutenant Colonel Clarke took command of the regiment for the third time in as many weeks and almost simultaneously received the order to send the 3d Battalion toward La Peignerie.

However, Clarke had not gone with Partridge and Bealke to Division Headquarters to receive orders. Nor apparently had Partridge confided to him the plans that had been made, which meant Clarke had to phone Division Headquarters for orders, further delaying the attack. General Landrum instructed Clarke to use both the 1st and 3d Battalion to clear up the rear of the 359th. Of course, that plan was problematic because by then the 1st Battalion was already committed with the 359th Infantry on Mont Castré. It seems likely Landrum meant the 2d Battalion, 358th Infantry rather than the 1st Battalion and is yet another indication the senior leadership of the 90th Infantry Division did not have a firm grip on the situation.

Despite the confusion, by 1652 Clarke prepared two plans for the 3d Battalion. In the first it would sweep forward to the southwest on an overextended 1,400-yard front with Company I on the right astride the trail leading from les Belles Croix through les Bois toward Mont Castré and the gap between the 2d and 3d Battalion, 359th Infantry. Company K on the left, followed by Company L, would sweep through the numerous orchards and woodlots that dotted the slopes north and northeast of Mont Castré that were infested by German stragglers and bypassed outposts. The second plan was similar but was oriented as a westward sweep toward Lithaire.

By 1705, the 3d Battalion was making progress but was instructed by Clarke that they were not to get engaged if they met a sizable German force. At that point Clarke left the Regimental CP and went forward to locate the 1st Battalion positions on Mont Castré. Colonel Bealke conferred with Colonel Bacon who asked him to push the 3d Battalion westward another 800 to 900 yards to cover the 359th's supply route on the St Jores to Lithaire road. Bealke agreed so long as he did not encounter resistance greater than company sized and by 1748 Company I was about 500 yards west of the crossroads of the La Poterie-Beau Coudray and St Jores-Lithaire roads where they contacted a German machine gun firing from the eastern outskirts of Lithaire. Company L was in the woods just north of the railroad crossing to the east of Company I and Company K was farther east at Le Fry.

Two minutes later, General Landrum called Colonel Clarke to tell him he decided to switch the emphasis of the division advance from the 357th Infantry on the left to the 358th Infantry on the right. The 3d Battalion was to reassemble at Le Fry and then advance west, followed by the 1st and 2d Battalion. That order indicates Landrum was unaware the 3d Battalion had already advanced well west of Le Fry and that the 1st Battalion was heavily engaged with the 359th Infantry near the Camp de Cesar. Nevertheless, at 1800 the 2d Battalion was alerted to be ready to move to the high ground south of Le Fry.

Colonel Clarke arrived at the 3d Battalion CP at 1905 where he was briefed on its situation, which he passed on to Division G-3. In return, at 1937 Colonel Stillwell ordered Clarke to "Attack to West. Vertical grid 20.5 [roughly 1,300 yards farther west of the 3d Battalion's position]—go that far West—clear those trails East and West and turn South so that 359 can use them." The 3d Battalion duly advanced west but by 2115 encountered heavy resistance and was unable to make any further progress.

Shortly after, at 2133, the 2d Battalion Liaison Officer was sent off from the Regimental CP with the message, "Hurry to the top of the hill. Definite threat from the South." Minutes later the 2d Battalion was instructed to "dig in and hold after securing the hill (120)." At 2200, the leading patrol of the 2d Battalion reported it had reached Hill 122 fifteen minutes earlier, but they were now hearing the approach of a mechanized column 2,000 to 3,000 yards to their south. Ominously, after that the telephone line to the patrol went dead. Finally at 2300, the forward elements of the 2d Battalion reached the lower slopes northeast of Hill 122.[37]

The column heard by the 2d Battalion, 358th Infantry patrol was probably the approach from the southwest of elements of the *KG SS-Das Reich*, which reported its counterattack was badly delayed by the extraordinarily heavy American artillery fire. Nevertheless, by twilight, which began at 1920, the leading SS elements reached a point northeast of Mobecq, opposite the 1st Battalion, 359th Infantry. The units counterattacking the Americans on Hill 122 and at the Camp de Cesar probably also included *II./Grenadier-Regiment 941* and elements of *Fallschirmjäger-Regiment 15*. The German Fallschirmjäger reported they recaptured Hill 122 during the night, demonstrating they could be as confused by the terrain as the Americans because the German counterattacks that began at 2045 as reported by the 1st Battalion, 358th Infantry and 2d Battalion, 359th Infantry struck well east of Hill 122. The attack pushed the 1st Battalion, 358th Infantry onto the reverse slope of the nose of the ridge east of the Camp du Cesar, which allowed the Germans to infiltrate down into the valley between the 357th and 359th Infantry. However, it appears the 3d Battalion, 359th Infantry held onto the crest of Hill 122 throughout the night against German attacks from the south and east.[38]

Farther east on the division left, the 357th Infantry continued to struggle to push past Beau Coudray and cross the deep streambed that drained west to east into the Prairies. At 0900, the 1st Battalion, 357th Infantry attacked south. Company C crossed the Les Belles Croix-Le Plessis road (D24) and reached Beau Coudray at 0930. The rest of the battalion was halted without gaining any ground, Company B to the west of the road and Company A to the east where it had fallen back the previous day. A German counterattack on the right of Company C at 1020 was repulsed and ten Germans were reported taken prisoner, which allowed Company C to advance another 100 yards, securing the west end of the village. The 3d Battalion was then ordered forward past the stalled Company B and into the gap between Company C and Company A at 1135 and reached Beau Coudray

Deadly enemies I. An 8cm Granatwerfer (mortar) 34 with Fallschirmjäger crew in Normandy, June 1944. BAMA Bild 101I-582-2106-32.

with Company L on the right, Company I on the left, and Company K in reserve behind Company C.

The Germans continued to counterattack sporadically, but by 1520 Company I and L had advanced another 150 yards and were overlooking the stream. The Americans then paused to reorganize and reconnoiter the creek and the 2d Battalion passed to division reserve at 1900 replacing the 2d Battalion, 358th Infantry in that role. Company E, which had been sent to a blocking position on the Saint Jores-Plessis road behind Company A at 1700, was withdrawn north back to Les Belles Croix at the same time. An hour later, Company A was ordered to withdraw north past the bottleneck to join Company B in reorganizing. Critically, according to his postwar account Colonel Barth was unaware Company A had already withdrawn 200 yards north up the road after they were counterattacked the previous evening, which meant the new movement badly exposed the left flank of Company L.[39]

Deadly enemies II. An MG 42 manned by a Fallschirmjäger in Normandy, 21 June 1944. BAMA Bild 101I-582-2106-23.

The advance of Company B, 712th Tank Battalion near Saint Jores, 6 July 1944. Still taken from a film shot of the attack by the Signal Corps. *Tank Support Near St Jores 90th Div.* Sergeant Burton Hartman, Det M, 165th Signal Corps Photo Company. Sergeant Hartman was scheduled to land on D-Day with the 2d Rangers at Pointe du Hoc, but the DUKW he was on sank and he lost two of his three cameras, finally making it ashore later in the day.

The advance of Company B, 712th Tank Battalion near Saint Jores, 6 July 1944. Another still taken from Sergeant Hartman's film.

Two officers of the 357th Infantry try to orient themselves on the map. Another still from Sergeant Hartman's film.

The minimal gains made during the day by the 357th Infantry were lost when a violent German counterattack began at 2315. The attackers were later identified as *II./Fallschirmjäger-Regiment 15*, which were supported by strong mortar and artillery fire. The German Fallschirmjäger slipped through the gap where Company A was thought to be and enveloped the left of Company I and L, which held firm in an all-around defense. However, when Company C was ordered to withdraw under heavy pressure it got intermingled with Company K and in the confusion both companies broke and headed for the rear. The Company K commander, Captain Woodrow Radford Allen, of Comanche, Texas, was finally able to halt the two companies 300 yards north of Beau Coudray, where he reorganized them as a single unit. However, Company I and L remained surrounded.[40]

The day's fighting on Mont Castré only cost the 359th Infantry ninety-seven casualties but it was considerably disorganized by the broken terrain. The toing and froing by the 358th Infantry resulted in seven killed and forty-five wounded, including Colonel Partridge, for little result. Including the 204 casualties incurred by the 357th Infantry, the 90th Infantry Division suffered around 353 battle casualties during the day, which closely matched the 337 estimated by the Division G-3. Overall, nothing much was accomplished by General Landrum other than to

Men of the 357th Infantry along a hedgerow. The man in the center is about to fire a rifle grenade. Another still from Sergeant Hartman's film.

Lieutenant General George S. Patton Jr., Lieutenant General Omar N. Bradley, and General Bernard L. Montgomery meet at Montgomery's headquarters near Blay, Normandy, France, 7 July 1944. Note this was one of the few times during the day when it was not pouring rain. U.S. Army SC.

further confuse the situation as he again failed to leave his CP and go forward to assess the situation.

There was also a new arrival at the Normandy front on 6 July: Lieutenant General George Smith Patton Junior. Patton arrived to begin setting up the headquarters of TUSA. Notably that night he complained in his diary about the rain.[41]

7 JULY

By the late evening of 6 July, the VIII Corps concluded its attack was in danger of coming to a standstill. The 79th Infantry Division was exhausted after two weeks of fighting north toward Cherbourg and then south toward Le Haye-du-Puits through what seemed to be an endless series of hedgerows. It had lost over 2,000 battle casualties and hundreds more through illness and injury, mostly in its rifle companies, which the VIII Corps remarked "were filled with about 40% replacements." The 82d Airborne Division was in worse shape with cumulative losses since D-Day of more than 5,400 officers and men to all causes, nearly half its effective starting strength on D-Day—and unlike the 79th and 90th, it had received no replacements since D-Day. Most of its rifle companies were reduced to platoon size or smaller. The 90th Infantry Division's advance had virtually ground to a standstill against the tough German resistance and its cumulative battle casualties were about 3,400 with uncounted numbers sick, injured, or suffering from battle fatigue.

General Middleton resolved that night to employ the Corps reserve, the 8th Infantry Division, to spark a new impetus to the attack. The 8th had completed landing in France on 4 July and assembled at Montebourg on 5 July. It would pass through the 82d Airborne Division, which would go into reserve, and the left of the 79th Infantry Division, to secure a new frontline from La Haye-du-Puits to the Forêt de Mont Castré. The 8th Infantry Division would then follow up with an attack south as the corps' main effort. It was also intended the attack would pinch out the 90th Infantry Division, which would also then go into reserve to reconstitute. The right (west) boundary of the 90th shifted from a northeast to southwest orientation to north to northwest and moved slightly east, shortening the front of the division.[42]

General Landrum's field order issued at 2100 on 6 July was again essentially a repeat of the previous days. The division's main effort would be made on the right, resuming the attack at 0900 with the 359th Infantry driving south from Hill 122. The 358th Infantry was to secure the right and rear of the division along the new boundary with the 8th Infantry Division with one battalion, while the rest of the regiment mopped up the Forêt de Mont Castré and secured the rear of the 359th Infantry. The 357th Infantry would continue to attack Beau Coudray, while its 2d Battalion withdrew to Les Belles Croix and prepared to counterattack any German attempt to exploit the gap between the left of the 358th and the right of the 357th. The weather remained warm but was increasingly cloudy and rainy during the day. Rain and cloud cover again forced the cancelation of all close air support for the 83d Infantry Division of the VII Corps to the east during the day and likely had the same effect on the front of the VIII Corps.[43]

However, the ongoing German counterattacks on the tenuous American positions on Mont Castré and Beau Coudray during the night led Landrum to revise the orders for the day at 0400. Instead of attacking, all divisional units "would mop up rear areas, consolidate and improve positions and continue pressure [on the Germans] with patrols and fire, but that a resumption of the general attack would be delayed." Nevertheless, the revised orders ended up only affecting the men of the 1st and 3d Battalions of the 359th Infantry as they clung to their precarious hold on the ridge of Mont Castré. It reached them at 0550 while they were still struggling with the aftermath of the previous night's battle. They maintained and improved their positions as best they could while under nearly constant attack from the German forces concentrated in the valley to their southwest around the hamlet of Mobecq. The 359th counted five large-scale attacks on their positions during the day, but now the shoe was on the other foot—they had near perfect observation of the German movements for nearly 3 kilometers down the valley to the town of Vesly and were able to hammer the German attackers with artillery fire. Massed fires of the division and corps artillery kept the Germans at bay throughout the day and probably inflicted significant casualties on the Germans.

Meanwhile, the 2d Battalion, 359th and Company B, 315th Combat Engineer Battalion were attached to the 358th Infantry at 1017, while at the same time the 2d Battalion, 358th was attached to the 359th Infantry. The Engineers occupied and held the ground vacated when the 2d Battalion, 358th Infantry moved up from its positions near Le Fry and advanced into the gap between the 1st and 3d Battalion, 359th Infantry at 1527. By 2250, they had seized the high ground northeast of the village of La Ville. Earlier, at 2200, the remainder of the 315th Combat Engineer Battalion was attached to the 358th Infantry as well.

The 3d Battalion, 358th Infantry at La Peignerie was also attached to the 359th Infantry at 1345. It had been attacking west toward Lithaire since 0900. In turn, the 90th Reconnaissance Troop was attached to the 3d Battalion, 359th Infantry to assist in mopping up the valley north of Mont Castré and farther west toward Lithaire and La Rue du Bocage. By 1800, they had seized Lithaire and captured between fifty and seventy-five Germans.

At 1645, the 1st Battalion, 358th Infantry, supported by the fire of the 2d Battalion, 359th Infantry, attempted to regain the ground it had lost east of the Camp du Cesar. It launched two frontal attacks, reaching the crest of the hill twice, but each time they were beaten back. By midnight they halted to reorganize in place.

The 357th Infantry spent a fruitless day attempting to restore its position at Beau Coudray. Company B, which was attached to Colonel Kilday's 3d Battalion, supported by a platoon of Company B, 712th Tank Battalion, was ordered at 0800 to attack to relieve the encircled Company I and L, which were cut off south of the blacktop road that ran west to east through Beau Coudray. The tanks came under "88 mm fire" at 1055 and although none were hit, they were ordered to cease fire and fall back if they were unable to return the fire. Shortly after, at 1100, Company B reached a position overlooking the village and by 1130 were described as "one hedgerow from town" but were under intense mortar fire. At 1405, a strong German infantry force was reported approaching the town from the southwest and artillery and mortar fire was placed on the ford crossing the stream south of Le Renault, but without apparent effect. At 1430, Company B was just 50 yards from Beau Coudray but twenty minutes later was struck in the right flank by German infantry attacking from the west. The German attack was supported by a heavy artillery concentration at 1545, which supposedly resulted in all officers and most of the company NCOs becoming casualties. Perhaps tellingly, that narrative is not supported by the casualty report for the day, which counted a single NCO killed, and one NCO and twelve enlisted men wounded in Company B. However, the artillery did force the withdrawal of the supporting tanks, which led to the Company B attack collapsing as its men broke for the rear. They were reformed near the position of Company A, which had failed to advance to support the flank of Company B.

In fact, Major Hamilton, who had a reputation as a skilled and pugnacious commander of the 1st Battalion, does not appear to have done anything that day with his force, which was composed of Company A, C, and K, 357th Infantry, with the 712th Tank Battalion Mortar Platoon, and the other two platoons of Company B, 712th Tank Battalion. However, there is contradiction and confusion here as well. The 712th Tank Battalion noted Company B was instead occupied with firing in support of the 358th Infantry on 7 July and not the 357th at all! It only remarked that the Battalion Mortar Platoon was in support of the 357th and only fired "several rounds" at targets of opportunity in Beau Coudray. The lack of communication and control over the tank support was evidence that tank-infantry coordination between the 90th Infantry Division and the 712th Tank Battalion remained poor.

Another measure of the disarray in the 357th Infantry is that it was believed another of the platoons of the 712th Tank Battalion was with Captain Allen's force that consisted of Company C and K. They had been subjected to repeated German attacks beginning at 1612 and at 1740 was hit by a German infantry force west of Beau Coudray that supposedly included a Panther tank. The tank platoon assumed to be with Allen's force was ordered to counterattack, but unfortunately the 357th reported the platoon had been "sent to the rear for servicing and the attack did not materialize." However, there is no indication in the reports of the 712th Tank

Battalion that any other platoon had ever been attached to the 357th Infantry, which means the platoon in question was the one already attached to Company B that had been engaged all day long and that had withdrawn with Company B after 1545.

Altogether, the Germans hit Captain Allen's force with fourteen distinct attacks. Only intense artillery supporting fire prevented the collapse of the American line. At 2100, radio communications with Company I failed and shortly afterward a runner reported that the Germans had overrun the Company CP, killing, wounding, or capturing the entire Company Headquarters and forcing the remnants of the company to surrender.

Colonel Barth immediately requested General Landrum release one company of the 2d Battalion, which was then in division reserve, for an attack to relieve Company I and L 1 mile north of the stream. Permission was granted and Company E was released, moving into the line on the right of Company B at 2150, but by then it was too late. Colonel Barth realized that assembling the forces, unscrambling the intermingled companies, and organizing an attack would take too long before darkness fell and postponed the attack to the next day. Two more German attacks struck Captain Allen's combined Company C and K at 2215 and 2230.

Shortly before midnight, Colonel Kilday reached Barth's CP. Kilday told Barth he thought Company L could withdraw from its position back to friendly lines before dawn. With that encouragement, Barth ordered Kilday to send an officer patrol to contact Company L and order them to do so if conditions were feasible. He then insisted Kilday follow with an attack at dawn with all the available strength of the 1st and 3d Battalion, supported by two platoons of Company B, 712th Tank Battalion.

At midnight, Colonel Barth reported the situation of the 357th Infantry as: Company I and L remained isolated south of the east-west blacktop road; Company A was astride the main north-south road, in other words, 1,200 to 1,300 meters north of the Beau Coudray crossroads; Company B was on the right of Company A; Company A and Allen's combined C/K were still just north of the blacktop near Beau Coudray; Company E with one platoon of Company B, 712th Tank Battalion was behind Company A and B; and the 2d Battalion (- E) was in division reserve along the railroad track at Les Belles Croix.

During the day, Battery A, 537th AAA was relieved of its attachment to the 90th Infantry Division and the 357th RCT and reassigned to support the 8th Infantry Division's 28th Field Artillery. The battery moved to new positions near La Dranguerie and in the process suffered its first battle casualties. Five enlisted men were wounded by a "mustard pot" antipersonnel mine at 2000. Two were evacuated, one with serious wounds, and the others were treated and returned to duty.

The day's action had cost the 358th Infantry a reported 118 casualties, while the 359th Infantry only reported 43. The 357th Infantry though had been roughly handled. It reported 373 casualties, including a staggering 244 missing alone: 91 from Company I, 117 from Company L, 27 from Company M, and the rest from Company C, K, and the Regimental Medical Detachment.

An incident also occurred later that night that would eventually result in the loss of the two highest-ranking officers in the division, but not because of wounds or death. General Williams had spent much of the day in what had become a routine for him—visiting the frontline regimental and battalion CPs and OPs, assessing the situation, and advising commanders—especially the young lieutenants that were taking up company command positions because of the heavy losses in company grade officers. On 7 July, General Williams visited the CPs on the division right. At about noon he was at the 1st Battalion, 358th Infantry CP, and at 1245 he arrived at the 358th Regimental CP where he discussed the situation with Colonel Clarke and spoke by phone to Division G-3 Colonel Stillwell. At 1315, Williams ordered Clarke to send the exhausted commander of the 1st Battalion, Major Seeger, to the rear for a rest, replacing him temporarily with the 358th Infantry's Executive Officer, Lieutenant Colonel Frederick W. Loomis. General Williams then went out but returned to the Regimental CP to discuss attack options and artillery preparation with Colonel Clarke before leaving for the 1st Battalion CP again at 1520. From there his movements are unclear, but he returned to the Division CP sometime in the late evening.

According to General Williams's aide, 1st Lieutenant Yates, it was not until they arrived at the Division CP that Williams was aware of the disaster that had fallen on the 357th Infantry at Beau Coudray. When he joined Colonel Stillwell, the G-3, to discuss operations he noticed that the situation map showed Company I and L of the 357th Infantry were surrounded. Stillwell told Williams that communications with the isolated companies was sporadic, the companies' situation was desperate—most officers were wounded or dead, overall casualties were heavy, soldiers were abandoning their weapons and surrendering, and that General Landrum had not acted to release the division reserve to Colonel Barth for a counterattack to restore the situation.

General Williams became furious. He had pledged to the men of the division during training in 1943 that he would never abandon them and that if they were cut off, he would commit troops to rescue them. The enraged Williams found Landrum, dismissed everyone in earshot, then delivered a blistering rebuke of Landrum's failures, similar to the tirade he had given MacKelvie earlier in June. Williams condemned Landrum's habit of command by radio and telephone while sheltered in his dugout and accused him of causing too many unnecessary deaths because of his "Goddamn stupidness" since he assumed command.

When he finished, Williams left Landrum and then—doubtless exhausted himself—made the mistake that nearly ended his career. Still angry, he told his aides, Lieutenants Yates and Everett what he had said to Landrum but, unbeknownst to Williams, Landrum had followed him and overheard. Talking to his commander like that in private might have been forgiven, but telling subordinates what had gone on was unforgivable.[44]

8 JULY

General Landrum planned that when the 121st Infantry of the 8th Infantry Division came up, the 359th Infantry with its 3d Battalion and the 2d Battalion, 358th Infantry would slip eastward off Hill 122, relinquishing the position to the fresh troops. Then, with the 1st Battalion, 359th Infantry following in reserve, they would attack to the southeast through the Forêt toward Lastelle. In turn, the 358th Infantry with the 3d Battalion, 358th Infantry and 2d Battalion 359th Infantry would initiate an attack to the southwest toward Le Plessis when the 359th Infantry group came alongside. The 1st Battalion, 358th Infantry would consolidate on the "Nose" and reorganize as a reserve for the 358th Infantry group. It was expected the attacks would pinch out the 357th Infantry, allowing it to reorganize as division reserve and considerably narrow the division front, eliminating much of the problem of Germans infiltrating through gaps between the regiments. However, the failure of the 8th Infantry Division to move up and clear the front of the division right postponed the planned attack. Worse, the rain returned at 0700 before shifting to scattered showers in the afternoon.

As planned, in the early morning of 8 July the 8th Infantry Division attempted to pass through the 82d Airborne and 79th Infantry Division on the right of the 90th Infantry Division to execute a fresh attack to the south. Given that the 8th was rated as one of the best trained divisions assembled in England before D-Day, much was expected of its commitment to the battle. Unfortunately, it suffered all the usual problems of a "green" division, and its movements were exceedingly slow and hesitant. On the left, the 121st Infantry was supposed to advance to the "West nose of the Forêt de Mont Castré," that is, Hill 122, to relieve the elements of the 358th and 359th Infantry holding there.

However, instead of moving up behind the right of the 359th and passing through the American lines guided by the troops in place, the 121st Infantry attempted to advance around the right of the 359th and immediately ran into German resistance.

> *Although our guides and liaison officers were in contact with the left element of the 121st Inf (left assault regiment of the 8th Div) and the area between their left front and the rear of our hilltop position was clear, scattered enemy resistance remained in the right of the 12st Inf zone and slowed their progress. Thus at midnight the 8th Div had not yet passed through our lines and our resumption of the offensive was postponed.*

The result was confusion, loss of control by the commander of the 121st Infantry, and a complete failure to advance, which left the exhausted men of the 90th alone for another day on Mont Castré.

As the 8th Infantry Division slowly moved up the 82d Airborne remained in position and went into corps reserve. At 1145 on 11 July, it was released from attachment to the VII Corps and moved to UTAH Beach where they embarked on seventeen LST for their return to England. Unfortunately, in the exchange between the 82d and the 8th the 90th Infantry Division temporarily lost part of the attached 712th Tank Battalion, which was instead attached to the 8th Infantry Division. However, the tanks of Company B remained attached to the 357th Infantry and those of Company C remained attached to the 90th, with its 3d Platoon supporting the infantry on Hill 122.[45]

The 2d Battalion, 358th Infantry in the center of the 359th Infantry line on the western end of the division front was attacked at 0330 by what was believed to be a German battalion. The attack was finally repulsed at dawn, but heavy pressure continued through the morning and early afternoon. Another strong attack at 1500 penetrated the line between the 1st Battalion, 359th and the 2d Battalion, 358th Infantry, but was neutralized by a counterattack that restored the line. At 1930, another attack, supported by heavy artillery fire, struck the front of all three battalions. Friendly artillery fire and a dogged infantry defense repelled the German attack by midnight on 8 July.

Farther east, from midnight on 7 July until dawn on 8 July, the Germans continued to probe the positions of the 358th Infantry in the center of the 90th Division line in the woods around the Camp de Cesar. At 1045, the 3d Battalion, 359th Infantry, nearly 3 kilometers to the northwest at Lithaire, was finally relieved from attachment to the 359th Infantry by the 121st Infantry moving across its front. It moved west to the positions north of the 315th Engineer Combat Battalion in the valley and prepared to attack through the Engineers and up the hill to firmly reestablish the connection between the 358th and 359th Infantry. The postponement of the attack due to the lack of movement by the 8th Infantry Division led the 3d Battalion, 359th Infantry to instead relieve the Engineers during the night. During the night of 8/9 July, VIII Corps and 90th Division Artillery pounded suspected German positions on the southern hillsides of Mont Castré.

The 357th Infantry spent the day of 8 July recovering and reorganizing from the previous days' disaster. The regiment had lost about 700 known casualties and had an uncounted number of men who were stragglers, sick, suffering from battle fatigue, or simply exhausted. Although the 2d Battalion was intact, the regiment overall had fewer than 2,400 effectives. The remnants of the 1st and 3d Battalion combined, now under the overall command of Colonel Kilday, probably had fewer than 1,000 officers and men effective. Only the attached Company E was fully effective.

Two hours after dawn, Colonel Barth found that Colonel Kilday had failed to send the patrol to contact Company L and that the attack ordered at dawn had

Sketch of the 357th Infantry in battle near Beau Coudray. The original caption reads: "357 Inf. G Co. 90th Div at the 'Misty Hell' of Foret de Mont Castré, Beau Coudray Normandy, July 2–8, 1944. Finished drawing made from a sketch during the action." U.S. Army.

not taken place. Colonel Barth immediately relieved Kilday of command of the 3d Battalion, 357th Infantry. Kilday was replaced as commander of the 3d Battalion by the Battalion XO, Major John H. Mason, and as commander of the combined force by Major Hamilton. Barth blamed Kilday's lack of leadership and his general exhaustion for the loss of Company I and L the previous day. Major Mason reported at 1310 that about fifty men from Company I and L had managed to reach the Company B lines, while a few were reported reaching other units along the line, but the 3d Battalion was essentially combat ineffective until it could receive replacements and reorganize. The 3d Battalion MR recorded Kilday's relief on 17 July as due to illness. On 24 July, he was returned to duty and on 25 July was relieved from assignment to the 3d Battalion and reassigned to the Headquarters, 90th Infantry Division.[46]

During the morning it became evident the Germans were continuing to infiltrate north and east of the position at Beau Coudray through the marshes. With the infantry strength of the regiment badly weakened, at 1845 Barth ordered the Service Company commander, Captain Thomas C. Wilson Jr., to organize "Jig" Company as a provisional infantry unit using 120 officers and men from his company. It deployed late in the day to positions south and east of La Belle Croix and established contact with the 121st Cavalry Reconnaissance Squadron at Baupte.[47]

By 1615, the 3d Battalion was reporting a German buildup opposite Company E on the west end of the tenuous American line. At 1730, German tanks were observed, and they were brought under artillery fire. The artillery fire was redirected onto Beau Coudray at 1855 and reinforced by fire from 4.2-inch mortars during the remaining hours of daylight. As further protection from a possible German tank attack, a battery of the attached 343d Field Artillery was brought up and placed to fire on the north-south road south of the stream at La Butte. However, except for artillery and mortar fire the Germans remained quiet and there were no major attacks during the day.

The day ended without much accomplishment, but with not much lost either. The positions on the heights of Mont Castré and in the woods were a little more secure than on the previous day. However, casualties continued to mount. The division reported 374 battle casualties for the day, as well as 24 injured and sick, but it may have been catching up with previous days' reporting. The 357th Infantry reported only 26 battle casualties for the day, along with just 1 injured. The 358th reported 98 battle casualties and the 359th another 83 for a total of just 207. Of course, it is also possible that the fractured nature of the two latter regiments affected the accuracy of their reporting to division.

9 JULY

The expected resumption of the attack by the 90th Infantry Division was delayed yet again, as the 8th Infantry Division continued its struggle to get into position.

> *Guides were still waiting for the 121st Inf, but that unit was having difficulties on its right front. As of midnight [9 July], the 121st was no nearer our lines than 24 hours previously.*

George Patton noted in his diary that evening that General Middleton's opinion of the 83d and 90th Infantry Division was they were "really bad" and that the 8th Infantry Division, which Patton had thought was very good in training in Ireland, "showed great timidity in action to day [*sic*] in moving up at night dug fox holes every time they halted." The officers of the 90th probably would have endorsed Middleton's assessment of the 8th after waiting for days for them to secure the right flank.[48]

For the 359th Infantry, the slow approach of the 8th Infantry Division meant another day spent holding in place on its hilltop strongpoint under almost continuous German probing and attacks, intermittent mortar and artillery shelling, and a return of the seemingly endless rain showers. A strong German patrol managed to drive a wedge between the 2d Battalion, 358th Infantry and the 3d Battalion, 359th Infantry at 1930, but a counterattack restored the lines before midnight.

To the left rear of the 2d Battalion, 358th Infantry, Colonel Bacon filled the gap between the left of the 359th Infantry and the right of the 358th Infantry with a provisional company composed of a miscellany of cooks, drivers, and clerks from the 359th, and the dismounted 90th Reconnaissance Troop. They guarded against German infiltrators and secured communications from the rear to the nearly isolated battalions on the ridge. The 3d Battalion 359th Infantry continued to hold its position on the west side of Hill 122 overlooking La Ville, while the 2d Battalion, 358th Infantry clung to the reverse slope to the east of the hill.

At dawn, in the adjacent section of the 358th Infantry line, the 3d Battalion, 358th Infantry completed the relief of the 315th Engineer Combat Battalion, which reverted to divisional control. However, a gap remained between the right of the 3d Battalion, 358th and the left of the 3d Battalion, 359th Infantry that the Germans continued to probe. At 1700, a powerful attack struck the right front and flank of the 3d Battalion, 358th Infantry. It was repulsed, but Germans continued to infiltrate into the gap, so Company B, 315th Engineer Combat Battalion was attached to the 358th Infantry again and moved onto the right flank of the 3d Battalion, 358th

Infantry to help plug the gap. When the infiltration continued into the evening, the rest of the 315th Engineer Combat Battalion was brought up again, and its Company C moved into the line with the Engineers of Company B.

Farther east, the 1st Battalion, 358th Infantry and the 2d Battalion, 359th Infantry established close contact with each other and prepared to continue the attack. Forward observers with the 2d Battalion, 359th Infantry on the eastern edge of the woods used their position to direct punishing artillery fire onto German positions around Beau Coudray.

The 357th Infantry had a quiet day, adjusting and improving positions, while absorbing 209 replacements and reorganizing the shattered companies of the regiment. "JIG" Company extended its lines to the southeast and firmed up its connection with the 121st Cavalry Squadron at Baupte, which was patrolling the marshes between the 90th and the 4th Infantry Division of the VII Corps to the east. The regiment's 2d Battalion remained in division reserve.

Casualties for the day were light. Although the division reported 336, the losses were just twenty-seven for the 357th Infantry, forty-seven for the 358th Infantry, and forty-nine for the 359th Infantry. It seems certain that the Division G-1 and G-3 were still catching up on its casualty accounting.

For Dad, the battle for Mont Castré was mostly about moving from one position to another, supporting Field Artillery batteries that fired incessantly at targets far to the south. Battery A moved again, this time to the tiny hamlet of la Dupinerie, about 5 kilometers north of Mont Castré. What seemed to be a never-ending stream of casualties, walking wounded, severely wounded carried on jeeps and in ambulances, and the dead, stacked like cordwood in trucks, passed their position heading to the rear, And there was the never-ending rain and misery of wet bivouacs.

CHAPTER 6

VICTORY ON MONT CASTRÉ

10 JULY

The seemingly never-ending rain continued throughout the day as the 90th prepared to renew its advance as the 8th Infantry Division slowly closed to the front. On the right (west), the 359th Infantry held in place until 1600, when the 121st Infantry finally passed through the lines of the 2d Battalion, 358th Infantry and the 3d Battalion, 359th Infantry. As soon as their positions were relieved, they moved to the rear and then obliqued to the left as the division boundary shifted eastward. Both battalions encountered problems with the rocky, steep-sided terrain and German resistance but by dark had advanced nearly 1,000 meters and secured the southern slopes of the ridge and the far edge of the woods on the western end of Mont Castré. However, the lack of trails or roads leading south and the continued presence of bypassed groups of German defenders made communications and supply to the forward troops a difficult and hazardous problem. The 1st Battalion, 359th Infantry also remained in place until relieved by the reserve battalion of the 121st Infantry. It too then moved east and assembled in regimental reserve.

The 315th Engineer Combat Battalion regrouped its companies and then moved up onto the high ground vacated by the 3d Battalion, 358th Infantry. The 90th Reconnaissance Troop also reassembled and remounted its vehicles in the valley north of Mont Castré and went into division reserve.

The line held by the 358th Infantry—in order from right (west) to left (east) 3d Battalion, 358th, 2d Battalion, 359th, and 1st Battalion, 358th—maintained their positions on division orders during the early part of the day. Colonel Clarke directed the 1st Battalion, 358th and 2d Battalion, 359th to clear out the remaining German positions in the woods on the eastern end of the ridge. The 2d Battalion,

Wounded helped down from the summit of Mont Castré. They may be from either the 358th or 359th Infantry. U.S. Army SC.

359th was then to move southeast with Company G on the right (west) flank of the battalion contacting the left of the 3d Battalion, 358th Infantry. Patrols from the 3d Battalion, 358th Infantry went forward 300 to 400 yards early in the morning and reported the Germans had withdrawn. In retrospect, it was realized that they had simply not found the well-camouflaged German positions as the well-disciplined Fallschirmjäger held their fire on the American scouts.

The slow relief of the 359th Infantry by the 8th Infantry Division led General Landrum at 1200 to issue a warning order to the 358th Infantry, ordering them to attack when they were ready without waiting for the 359th to move. At 1345, Colonel Clarke announced that H-Hour would be 1500 and an hour later he established his CP near the front line. Colonel Bealke was ordered to advance to an initial phase line along the southern edge of the forest before advancing to seize the hamlet of Lastelle, about 900 yards to the southeast.

Bealke's 3d Battalion, 358th Infantry jumped off at 1400, advancing southeast into the heavily wooded reverse slope of Mont Castré. Colonel Gorton's 2d Battalion, 359th Infantry moved off when the 3d Battalion, 358th came abreast of its position but quickly lost contact in the dense terrain. The action that followed was typical of the confused fighting in the heavily wooded rough terrain of Mont Castré and was chronicled in occasionally conflicting detail in no less than three After-Action Reports as well as the regimental postwar history.

The 3d Battalion was significantly weakened from a week of near continuous fighting. Frontline strength was 18 officers and 567 enlisted men, compared to the nominal strength of an Infantry Battalion, which was 35 officers and 836 enlisted men. Partly that was because Bealke's command group consisted of just himself and six enlisted men, while another 10 officers and 103 enlisted men of the Headquarters and Headquarters Company remained in the rear. However, most of the shortfall was in the three Rifle companies, I, K, and L, which averaged just 4 officers and 145 enlisted men each, rather than the 6 officers and 187 enlisted men called for by T/O&E 7-17. Company I had 5 officers and 143 enlisted men, Company K had 5 officers and 152 enlisted men, and Company L had 3 officers and 139 enlisted men. Company M, the Weapons Company, had 4 officers, including its commander Captain John W. Marsh, and 129 enlisted men, rather than the 8 officers and 158 enlisted men called for in T/O&E 7-18.[1]

The advance began without an artillery preparation in hope the Germans might be caught unawares. Initially, the forested hillside crossed by the battalion sloped gently from northeast to southeast. The forest floor was covered with a dense undergrowth of matted bushes and tangled vines, taller than a man's head. Officers in the 3d Battalion described the action as "more like jungle fighting than ordinary fighting in woods." The vegetation limited visibility to as little as five yards and at most 25 yards. There was no road south from the Forêt, but a single dirt trail ran generally northwest to southeast through a firebreak just east of the small Le Mouloir stream.[2] Company I on the left guided on the firebreak with Company L on the right, with Company K to the right rear in reserve. Company I and L each advanced with two platoons in front deployed as skirmishers with the third platoon behind them in column. Colonel Bealke and the six enlisted men of the command group moved behind the left platoon of Company L, about 100 to 200 yards behind the advancing line.

After advancing about 600 yards, Colonel Bealke halted the battalion so the companies could regain contact with one another. The dense undergrowth had not impeded movement significantly, but it was nearly impossible for the companies to maintain contact and direction. The Company I platoons were all in contact with one another and were in contact with the left platoon of Company L, but the rest of Company L had fallen behind and were out of contact to the right rear. Company K had also lost contact with the forward companies and Battalion Headquarters, except by radio.

Colonel Bealke later said he requested supporting artillery fire, a "purple smoke shell" at a preregistered concentration he believed was close by and then adjusted the rounds until they were directly in front of him. From there, the artillery was able to

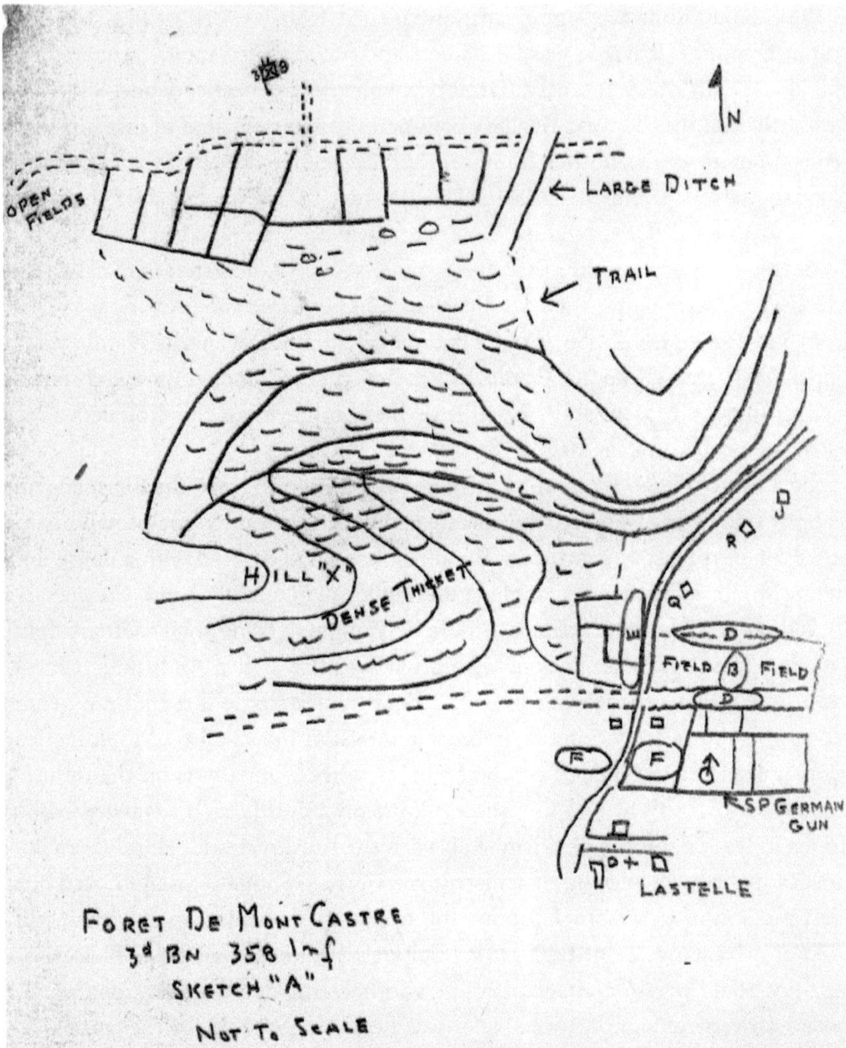

Map 8. The terrain over which Bealke's battalion advanced from north to south. Taylor, Sketch A.

identify the closest coordinate they were firing on, which enabled Bealke to locate the battalion. In the meantime, the companies had managed to regain contact and so Bealke ordered the advance to continue.

After advancing another 400 yards, at about 1700, Fallschirmjäger in carefully camouflaged, dug-in positions opened an intense fire on the left flank of Company I.

The Germans threw dozens of hand grenades and fired into the surprised Americans at point-blank range. A German prisoner later said they were ordered to wait until the Americans were within 10 to 15 yards before opening fire, and the American reports state the combatants were no more than 10 to 15 *feet* apart and in some cases engaged in hand-to-hand combat with "trench knives" as well as exchanging volleys of grenades.[3]

Continuing to push forward, Company I ran into a German strongpoint based on a rocky knoll or hillock 15 to 25 feet high. The knoll completely dominated the last quarter mile (400 meters) of the slope down the Mouloir valley. The two leading platoons of Company I were met by a volley of grenades and fire from three machine guns that caused heavy casualties and practically wiped out its light machine-gun section, pinning the company down. Undaunted, the company commander, Lieutenant Hubert G. Miller, and another soldier grabbed one of the light machine guns and continued the advance. On his own initiative, Pfc. William L. Smiley crawled forward and climbed the rocky hill, where he fired in the Germans before he was mortally wounded.[4]

Smiley's example was followed by Pfc. Theodore Wagner, who also worked his way forward to the hilltop and began throwing hand grenades onto the German positions below him. The German fire temporarily ceased, and Wagner returned to his platoon, grabbed a prisoner that had been captured in the meantime, and forced him onto the top of the hill. Wagner then ordered the German to call for his comrades to surrender and eight Germans, three of them wounded, came out and laid down their arms. Nine others were found dead in the position. The firefight lasted about forty-five minutes to an hour.

The capture of the rocky knoll finally gave the battalion a position where they could observe for some distance in all directions. They could now plainly see the open fields to the south. The vantage point meant they could turn the tables on the Germans and hammer them with observed mortar and artillery fire, just as the Germans had been hammering them.

Meanwhile, Company L on the right had also run into heavy machine-gun fire and volleys of hand grenades. Here too the company commander, 1st Lieutenant George M. Bird, made the difference. Despite a wounded leg, Lieutenant Bird pushed on, killing two Germans and routing others who were holding up the advance. He then reorganized his company while under fire and ordered them to continue the advance, before finally allowing himself to be evacuated.

Ten minutes later, at around 1800, both Company I and L, despite heavy casualties, had cleared the German opposition to their front and were on the verge

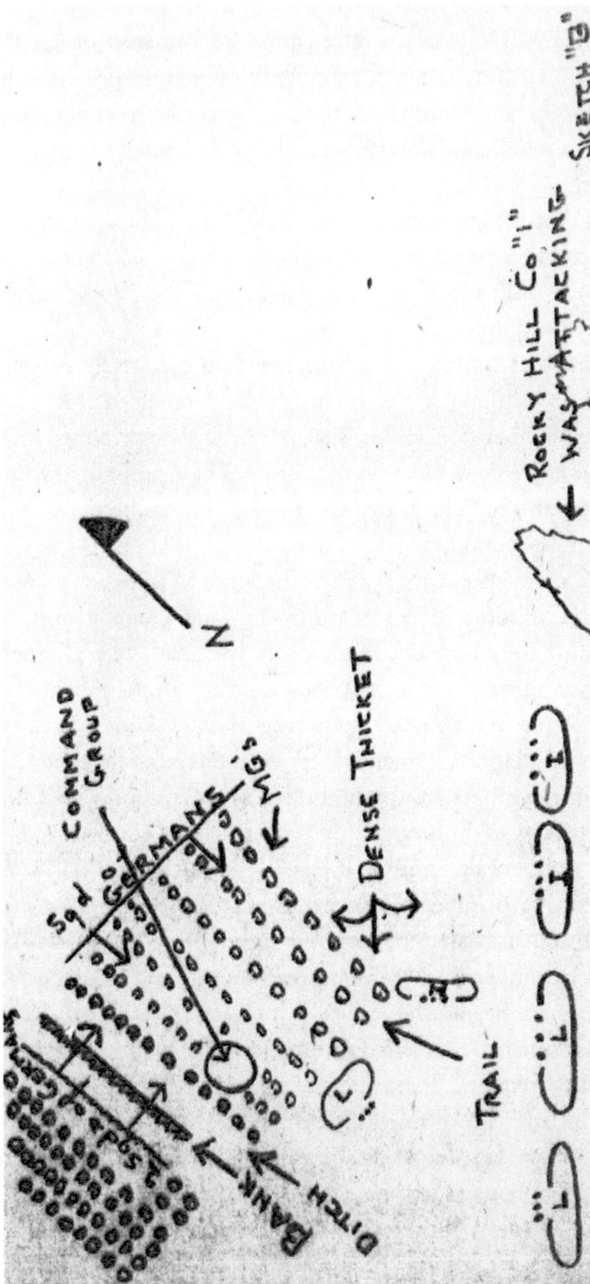

Map 9. The German ambush. Taylor, Sketch B.

of advancing out of the forest. At that point, Colonel Bealke's command group was attacked by a squad of Germans who came in from the west, behind the right of Company L. The command group by now had expanded to about twenty men including telephone linesmen, radio operators, stragglers from Company I, and Captain Marsh, the commander of Company M. Marsh had rushed up from the rear to help Bealke lead the less experienced junior officers commanding the rifle platoons reorganize and he arrived just before the German counterattack. The command group was still about 100 yards behind the left platoon of Company L when the attack was heralded by another barrage of grenades, automatic weapons fire, and a rush of yelling Germans. Although outnumbered, the command group was able to beat off the German attack

However, no sooner was one German attack dealt with than another one hit the command group from the rear, this time by an estimated two squads. The command group was pinned down behind an embankment, with the Germans on the other side throwing an estimated twenty hand grenades at them. It soon got worse when the German squad that had fallen back returned and opened fire again with machine guns, enfilading the command group. Luckily, the reserve platoon of Company L came up from the right rear and was able to outflank both German groups, first rolling up the German line to the north while they were fixated on the command group, and then turning and doing the same to the Germans on the other side of the embankment. Many Germans were killed or captured, while the few survivors fled to the west. Four prisoners later revealed the total size of the German force engaged by the command group was about fifty men.

After the end of this brief, fierce battle, Colonel Bealke again ordered the battalion to halt so the companies could regain contact. Then he placed them in an all-around defense by moving Company K up from the rear, where it had been untouched. However, as they settled in the Germans began mortaring them heavily from another rocky hill west of them on the other side of the La Mouloir stream. The men of the battalion took what shelter they could.

At this same time, between about 1800 and 1830, Major Julius Oehlesen, the Battalion Executive Officer, arrived with four medium tanks of the 2d Platoon, Company C, 712th Tank Battalion. The tanks had followed the rough trail and, in the process, had bulldozed a route through the thicket that was passable to vehicles. They were followed by the battalion litter bearers and ammunition vehicles, which brought a welcome resupply. Shortly after, Company B, 358th Infantry was led up the trail by Lieutenant Colonel Frederick W. Loomis, the Regimental Executive Officer, who was temporarily commanding the 1st Battalion. Company B was attached to the 3d Battalion as a welcome reinforcement. Wire communications to the rear and the all-important artillery support, which had gone out during the fighting for the rocky hill, were also reestablished. Colonel Clarke informed Bealke that the 3d Battalion, 359th Infantry on the right was coming up and the 2d Battalion, 359th Infantry on the left was reporting the German defenses were weakening and it was starting to make progress on the eastern nose of the ridge as well. However, Bealke's men still had no direct contact with either friendly battalion on the right or left; the battalion was effectively isolated about 600 yards ahead of them.[5]

The attack resumed at about 1830 to 1900. Colonel Bealke's plan was to use Company K with the tank platoon to make the battalion's main effort breaking out into the open fields to the south. Company I would defend the rocky knoll against a possible counterattack from the northeast until Company G came up on its left, while advancing in echelon to the left of Company K. However, because the 3d Battalion's position was still so exposed, Bealke decided to deploy Company L to oppose the Germans on the rocky hill to the west, while Company B remained in reserve. Shortly afterward, Company I made visual contact with Company G but was unable to gain physical contact.

The Company K attack was initially very successful. It advanced about 250 yards to the edge of the forest and found an unoccupied German position consisting of dugouts and deep foxholes that looked like an assembly area. From there, they spotted a column of about thirty Germans "coming down the road just to the SE, marching south." The Germans were probably on the "blacktop road' (D138) Rue de Bois that runs from La Rivagerie to Lastelle—and were likely only about 250 yards away, although the range was estimated as 450 yards. The Germans were completely unaware of the American presence until Company K opened fire, killing or wounding all but two of the Germans.

After this brief fusillade, Company K crossed the D138 with the three supporting tanks. However, two of the tanks were quickly disabled by a self-propelled gun firing from an orchard about 400 yards to the south. A third got stuck in a marshy field a little farther on and the fourth had been retained as a reserve to support the battalion rear, so that was the end of the tank support. Nevertheless, Company K pushed on under fire from both flanks until about 2000 hours, when it could go no farther. The company commander, Lieutenant John Hylton, lost contact with Colonel Bealke and so attempted to make his way back to the Battalion CP to request permission to withdraw but was severely wounded en route and never made it. He was found and evacuated by another regiment two days later. A second company officer, Lieutenant Hansen, also tried to get to Bealke but also did not make it.

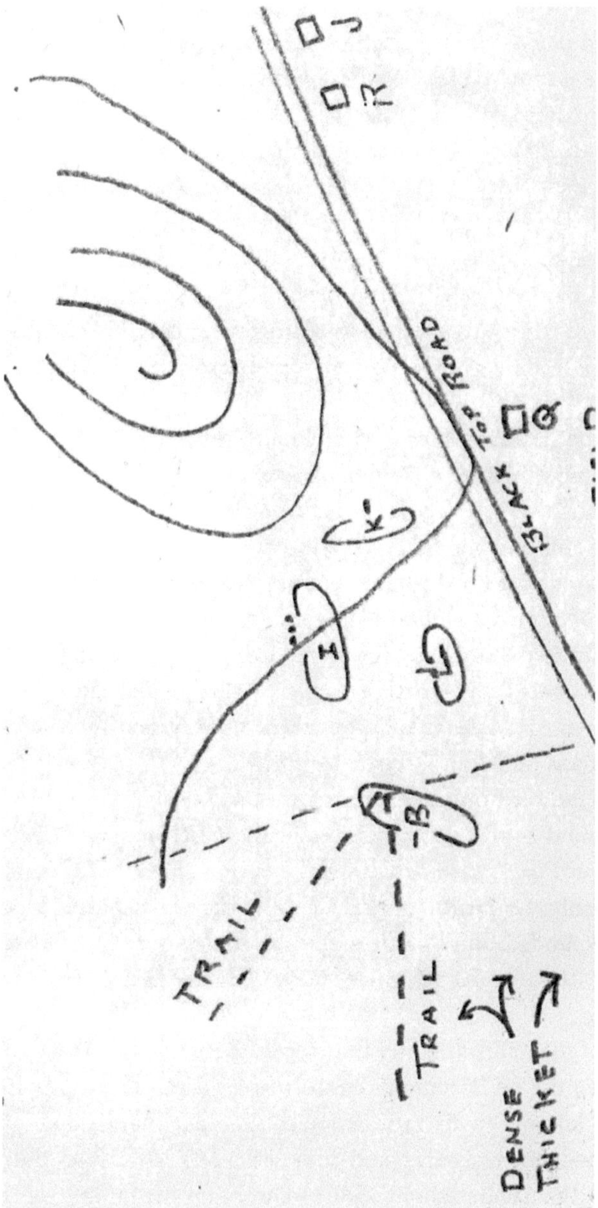

Map 10. Final positions of Bealke's battalion on 10 July 1944. Taylor, Sketch of Final Positions.

He too was severely wounded and did not make it either. About 2100, the battered company withdrew without orders to regain contact with the battalion, which went into an all-around defense on the edge of the forest. The withdrawal was supported by heavy American artillery fire, called in by Colonel Bealke from the rocky knoll.

Meanwhile, Company L held off the Germans to the west, while the 2d and 3d Battalion, 359th Infantry slowly came up in support on either flank. During this time Captain Marsh, the Company M commander, was mortally wounded by a mortar blast while helping again to organize the defense.

During the night, until 0430 the next day, the battalion litter bearers and Ammunition and Pioneer (A&P) Platoon worked ceaselessly, moving up rations and ammunition and moving back casualties.[6] Altogether, about 85 wounded men were evacuated to the Battalion Aid Station on the reverse slope of Mont Castré and 48 dead were collected on 11 July. Colonel Bealke, suffering from a grenade concussion inflicted during the Battalion Headquarters fight, was ordered to the rear for a rest. Colonel Loomis took temporary command of the battalion. The three rifle companies were temporarily reorganized as a single battle group under Lieutenant Miller; the senior officer still unwounded. Many more Company K casualties were evacuated by the Germans after it withdrew from its exposed position. The final count was 11 officers and 343 enlisted men killed, wounded, and missing, over 60 percent of the strength committed. Company K was reduced to 1 officer and 31 enlisted men, while Company L was only slightly stronger with 1 officer and 48 enlisted men. However, unknown to the survivors, the attack had cracked the last defensive line held by the Germans on Mont Castré.

The damage inflicted on the Germans was also severe. German casualties and prisoners were found from four companies of the *Fallschirmjäger Regiment 15.* and one *Fallschirmjäger Pionier Kompanie*, and "four truck loads" of German dead were evacuated—probably around 100 of them. Of 18 prisoners captured by the battalion, only 2 were not wounded. In its battle with the 90th Infantry Division since 15 June, it was later estimated that 70 percent of the *Fallschirmjäger Regiment 15.* had been killed or wounded.

On the left of the 358th Infantry line, the 2d Battalion, 359th Infantry did initiate its attack when the 3d Battalion, 358th Infantry came abreast, but it met strong resistance on the left and made little progress. Company G on the right was eventually able to bypass the resistance and come up alongside the 3d Battalion, 358th Infantry by dark. The 1st Battalion, 358th Infantry on the far left was held in place and supported the two other battalions by fire. By the end of the day, the advance of the 3d Battalion, 358th Infantry and Company G, 359th Infantry had completely outflanked the German position at the eastern end of the Mont Castré ridgeline and left the defenders there badly exposed.

Colonel Bealke, Captain Marsh, and Pfc. Wagner were all awarded the Distinguished Service Cross for their actions in the battle of 10 July, although Pfc. Wagner's citation incorrectly gave the date as 11 July.

Lieutenant Colonel JACOB W. BEALKE, JR., 0305676, Infantry, 3rd Battalion, 358th Infantry Regiment, 90th Infantry Division, United States Army. For extraordinary heroism in connection with military operations against an armed enemy. On 10 July 1944, Lt. Colonel BEALKE, commanding the 3rd Battalion, 358 Infantry, 90 Infantry Division, with 6 men of his battalion headquarters was advancing through the dense under growth of the FORÊT DE MONT CASTRÉ, FRANCE, between his two assault companies. The Battalion mission was to clear the forest of the enemy. After advancing some 400 yards into the forest approximately 20 paratroopers from the elite 5th German Parachute Division, attacked fanatically, screaming, throwing hand grenades and firing machine pistols. Colonel BEALKE, killed two of the enemy with hand grenades, wounded a third and took two others prisoner. The enemy formation broke. A second German group then attacked from the right flank, but Colonel BEALKE killed two with his pistol, one falling at his feet. Twenty additional soldiers arrived as reinforcement just before a third enemy group attacked from the rear of Colonel BEALKE's group. Of the 3rd attacking party 3 were killed, 8 taken prisoner and the remainder disappeared. Colonel BEALKE then continued advancing through the forest. About 200 yards deeper into the timber three enemy grenade launcher teams opened fire. Colonel BEALKE wounded the German officer commanding the position, and the rest of his Detachment killed, wounded or dispersed the enemy crews. Receiving word by radio, that a company of enemy infantry, in column, was proceeding across his front, Colonel BEALKE with an Artillery observer and one wireman swung to the left to reach high ground for observation. The observer was wounded and wireman killed. Colonel BEALKE laid his own wire line to the observation point and from their directed artillery fire against the enemy column for more than an hour until it was destroyed or dispersed. Throughout this action Colonel BEALKE was under heavy mortar and small arms fire. From the observation post he ordered by radio the reorganization and employment of his Battalion and directed the completion of the mission—occupation of the woods. Through the extraordinary heroism, aggressive leadership and dogged determination, in spite of heavy casualties among his officers and men, Colonel BEALKE led his men to a brilliant victory, one of the most outstanding in the operations of his Division in NORMANDY. His actions were in the highest traditions of the military service of United States.

Captain JOHN W. MARSH, 0364376, Company "M," 358th Infantry Regiment, 90th Infantry Division, United States Army. For extraordinary heroism in connection with military operations against an armed enemy in FRANCE. On 10 July 1944, Captain MARSH was commanding Company "M," 358th Infantry Regiment, advancing against a strong enemy position in the vicinity of the FORÊT DE MONT CASTRÉ, FRANCE when the rifle companies of the 3rd Battalion became disorganized and separated in the face of intense enemy fire. Captain MARSH, realizing that many of the officers were replacements with little combat experience, left his heavy weapons company in the control of the second in command and went forward to assist the battalion commander in organizing a hasty defense. With utter disregard of enemy fire coming from the front and both flanks, he led small groups of riflemen forward to close the gaps in the line, boldly directing their fire until the enemy was forced to retire. Before a complete reorganization could be effected, the enemy counter-attacked and again Captain MARSH left his company to proceed to the foremost front line troops to give his assistance. As he directed fire on the enemy he took up arms of the wounded and inspired his men to drive off the enemy. Even after suffering the wounds which resulted in his death he continued to lead his men until he fell, unable to go further. The inspired leadership of Captain MARSH, his courage and complete devotion to duty, exemplify the highest traditions of the Armed Forces of the United States.

Private First Class THEODORE G. WAGNER, 18103681, 3rd Battalion, 358th Infantry, 90th Infantry Division, United States Army. For extraordinary heroism in connection with military operations against an armed enemy. On 11 [sic 11] July 1944, Private First Class WAGNER'S company was attacking in the densely wooded terrain of the FORÊT DE MONT CASTRÉ, FRANCE, when terrific close-range fire was encountered from enemy machine-guns and rifles. This soldier, on his own initiative, worked his way forward scaling a 25-foot rocky hill, in order to reach the enemy strong point from which the fire was coming. At great risk he attained his objective and silenced the enemy guns by throwing several hand grenades into the position. He then forced eight enemy soldiers to surrender to him; nine others were found dead behind the hill. By his courage, gallantry, and intrepid action, Private First Class WAGNER eliminated a serious obstacle in the path of his company's advance.

The 357th Infantry began the day under continuous shelling by German 15cm howitzers from 0100 to 0500. Both the Regimental and 1st Battalion CP were targeted. Despite this indicator, at 1145 General Landrum ordered the 357th Infantry to send out strong patrols to determine if the Germans had withdrawn from their front. Unlike the similar patrols sent out by the 358th Infantry, by 1200 those of the 357th Infantry all reported they had immediately drawn heavy fire. As the 90th Infantry Division After-Action Report laconically noted, "the Boche was still there."

General Williams arrived at the 357th Regiment CP sometime after 1200 to discuss plans for the day. The plan as completed at 1300, called for Company K, with five tanks, to advance again to the east-west blacktop road. Company C would move up into the gap between K and Company B. Company B, supported by five tanks, and Company A would also advance and attempt to seize Beau Coudray again. Company I and L, each reduced to about twenty men, would hold in place just south of the bottleneck and continue to reorganize.

The planned H-Hour for the attack was set for 1530, but when communicated to General Landrum he insisted it jump off an hour early. Company A advanced to within 200 yards of the Beau Coudray crossroads when it was pinned down by intense machine-gun fire coming in from its left (east). Company B, C, and K advanced about 200 yards, but Company B and C then lost direction and veered sharply to the west, coming in behind Company K, which had halted just short of the blacktop road. Major Hamilton then ordered Company K to turn and drive left (east) astride the blacktop, in front of where it was thought Company B and C would be. Instead it received fire from the front and both flanks and made no progress. All three companies then fell back to their start lines, separated by about 500 yards from Company A, I, and L on the left.

Losses were heavy again, particularly for officers. Captain Allen was killed while commanding the combined Company C and K. Four companies had no officers at the end of the day and after shuffling all available ones to those units, none of the six rifle companies had more than two officers. Losses in NCOs were also heavy. As many as four other officers were killed and one wounded in the action on 10 July.

One man in the 357th Infantry was awarded a Distinguished Service Cross for his action on 10 July.

The President of the United States of America, authorized by Act of Congress, July 9, 1918, takes pleasure in presenting the Distinguished Service Cross to Technician Fifth Grade [then Private] Jack L. Evans, United States Army, for extraordinary heroism in connection with military operations against an armed enemy while serving with Company K, 357th Infantry Regiment, 90th Infantry Division, in action against enemy forces on 10 July 1944, near Beau Caudrey [sic], France. Although severely wounded, Technician Fifth Grade Evans refused evacuation to remain in defense of his company's hard-pressed position. Under enemy fire, and in complete disregard for his own safety, he crawled between the lines to bring one of his wounded comrades to safety. When a heavy German attack forced his company to withdraw to the next hedgerow, he remained in his forward position and continued to fire on the advancing enemy, even though he was week from exertion and loss of blood. Feigning death, he succeeded in evading capture and after dark crawled to the protection of his company's new position. The courage, determination, and devotion to duty displayed by Technician Fifth Grade Evans exemplify the highest traditions of the military forces of the United States and reflect great credit upon himself, the 90th Infantry Division, and the United States Army.[7]

The 90th Infantry Division recorded 241 casualties for the day, which was probably more accurate than the regimental reports. The 357th recorded 90 casualties, but it is clear many, like the officers, were recorded late. The 358th reported just 64 casualties, which was just a fraction of the 354 reported lost by its 2d Battalion alone, However, many of the losses reported by the 2d Battalion were actually stragglers. The 359th reported losing just 28 men, which may have been correct. It seems likely the confused nature of the fighting, exhaustion, and the haphazard attachment of battalions to regiments badly affected the accuracy of the reporting.

Dad's Battery A moved again, still attached to the 8th Infantry Division Artillery. It ended the day near the village of Bolleville, about a mile west of La Haye-du-Puits. The Battery MR complained about the heavily mined roads and fields in the area.

11 JULY

For the 359th Infantry on the right of the division, the biggest problem of the day was getting supplies forward across the ridge of Mont Castré to the 3d Battalion, 359th Infantry and the 2d Battalion, 358th Infantry on the southern slopes. It was 1400 before the task was completed and the two battalions were ready to advance. When they did, they quickly reached the Rue de Nerduit (D97) and continued south a short distance. At that point they came under extremely heavy fire from German positions farther south on Hill 92 and halted. The 1st Battalion, 359th Infantry was then brought up through the woods to the left rear of the 3d Battalion, 359th Infantry. At 1930, the 1st Battalion, 359th Infantry executed a coordinated attack with the 3d Battalion, 358th Infantry to seize Lastelle.

In the zone of the 358th Infantry, the 3d Battalion, now commanded temporarily by Colonel Loomis, spent the morning reorganizing and did not resume its attack until midafternoon. Passing over the same ground so hard fought over the previous night, it reached the north-south D138 and turned south, capturing the bridge over the Mouloir north of Lastelle at dusk. At 1930, when the 1st Battalion, 359th Infantry came up on its right, the 3d Battalion advanced and occupied Lastelle shortly after midnight. Farther to the left, the 1st Battalion, 358th Infantry and 2d

Battalion, 359th Infantry began mopping up the now untenable German salient between them at 0600. Four hours later they finished the task and finally gained full control of the eastern "Nose" of Mont Castré and the eastern part of the Forêt. While the 1st Battalion, 358th Infantry fell back to the Nose to regroup, at 1030, the 2d Battalion, 359th Infantry continued the attack. It drove east from the Nose, crossed the D138 and attacked southeastward into a series of hedgerows to outflank the Germans bedeviling the 357th Infantry around Beau Coudray. The zone of attack was narrow, just under 250 yards wide, and was flanked to north and south by open, marshy meadows. The objective, the Rue de la Lande, which ran west-to-east toward La Calvaire and Beau Coudray, was about 550 yards away. Progress was slow and at 1500 the battalion was stopped completely after only making it about halfway to the road.

However, after a week of keeping them in division reserve at Les Belles Croix, General Landrum finally decided to commit the 2d Battalion, 357th Infantry. The plan originally was for it to come up on the left of the 2d Battalion, 359th Infantry when they finished clearing the hedgerows to their front and reached the Rue de la Lande and then advance to outflank the Germans at Beau Coudray. The loss of momentum by the 2d Battalion, 359th Infantry meant instead the 2d Battalion, 357th would attack in column of companies, passing through the left company of the 2d Battalion, 359th.

The 2d Battalion, 357th attacked promptly at 1500. Although the Germans continued to contest the position, the fresh battalion added too much weight to the attack. By dark, they had reached the last hedgerow and reached the road where they were well placed to continue the attack into the flank and rear of the Germans at Beau Coudray.

Although the 90th Infantry Division reported 273 battle casualties for the day, it appears many of those were actually incurred the previous day. The reported regimental casualties totaled just 151, which may have been closer to the actual total.

Dad's Battery A suffered another casualty, this time from the heavy German shelling of the area. One enlisted man was lightly wounded by shell fragments and evacuated.

They also engaged their first German aircraft, two planes identified as "ME 109," which dropped two bombs nearby them at 1725. The Battery Record of Events noted laconically, "No hits. No Casualties. Opened fire at too great a range. Scared target off." The battery remained at Bolleville attached to the 8th Infantry Division Artillery.

12–13 JULY

The German resistance on 11 July was the last gasp of their defense of Mont Castré and the Mahlmann Linie. During the early morning of 12 July, the Germans began a planned withdrawal to a new line about 3,000 meters to the south. The 90th Infantry Division followed to maintain contact while reorganizing from the effects of nine days of continuous and intense battle.

On the right of the division, in the zone of the 359th Infantry, the 1st Battalion moved from Lastelle at 0800 and followed the right rear of the 3d Battalion, 358th Infantry to its left. There was virtually no resistance until the 1st Battalion, 359th reached a point midway between La Salmonnerie and Petit St. Germain where it encountered a strongpoint in a sunken road. Although some tanks came up in support, the battalion was unable to reduce the position, so the battalion commander, "Fireball" Pond, elected to mask the position with a single company and tied the rest of the battalion in with the 3d Battalion, 358th Infantry, which was at Petit St. Germain. The 2d Battalion, 359th was placed in division reserve and ordered to an assembly area at the crossroads near La Bagotterie at 1400. The 3d Battalion, 359th was designated the regimental reserve and moved in echelon to the right rear of the 2d Battalion, 358th Infantry. Then the 2d Battalion, 358th Infantry, still attached to the 359th Infantry, moved due east to Lastelle from where it had encountered the German resistance at Hill 92. From Lastelle it moved south to La Bagotterie and then turned southeast to come abreast of the 1st Battalion, 359th Infantry. There it hit an extension of the strongpoint that held up Captain Pond's Battalion just south of Pierrepont and could advance no farther.

In the 358th Infantry zone in the division center, the 1st Battalion relieved the 2d Battalion, 359th Infantry shortly after midnight of 11 July and the 2d Battalion, 359th Infantry reverted to division reserve. At 0800, the 1st Battalion on the left and thc 3d Battalion on the right advanced to the southeast with negligible resistance. The 1st Battalion reached the stream north of Gorges—the Mouloir again, in its north-to-south run from Baupte—with its left on the Prairies. Patrols attempted a crossing but drew heavy fire, which soon drew in the entire battalion. All attempts to cross the stream were repulsed and the battalion halted in place for the night, side-slipping to the right to allow the 2d Battalion, 357th Infantry to come up on its left. The 3d Battalion, still organized as a single battlegroup of 4 officers and 122 enlisted men led by Lieutenant Miller and under the overall command of Colonel Loomis, advanced from Lastelle to La Salmonnerie and attempted to seize the crossroads at Petit St. Germaine. It encountered fierce resistance from machine guns and a

Replacements assembling and preparing gear near Prétot-Sainte-Suzanne. One column visible to the left rear has already been organized and is marching off. Mid-July 1944.

reported tank (probably an assault gun) but by late evening had forced the Germans out of their position. Casualties included all officers except Miller and about 40 men, killed or wounded. The remnants organized their own defense in the former German position and were reinforced by two platoons of the Regimental Antitank Company but were unable to establish contact with the 1st Battalion to their left.

Both Colonel Loomis and Lieutenant Miller received the Distinguished Service Cross for their actions at the Petit St. Germain crossroads.

> *Lieutenant Colonel Frederick H. Loomis, United States Army, was awarded the Distinguished Service Cross for extraordinary heroism in connection with military operations against an armed enemy while serving with the 90th Infantry Division, in action against enemy forces on 12 July 1944. Lieutenant Colonel Loomis' intrepid actions, personal bravery and zealous devotion to duty exemplify the highest traditions of the military forces of the United States and reflect great credit upon himself, the 90th Infantry Division, and the United States Army.*[8]

First Lieutenant HUBERT G. MILLER, 01295925, Infantry, Company I, 358th Infantry regiment, 90th Infantry Division, United States Army. For extraordinary heroism in connection with military operations against armed enemy. On 12 July 1944 near LA VALAISSERIE, FRANCE while the 3rd Battalion, 358th Infantry was attacking through hedgerows, Lieutenant MILLER, as commanding officer of Company I, was severely and painfully wounded when the Battalion was pinned down by intense enemy machine-gun fire. Learning that all the other officers of Companies I, K, and L had become casualties, Lieutenant. MILLER refused to be evacuated and took command of the reorganization of the three companies under heavy enemy fire. With disregard of his injuries and personal safety, he then moved forward in direct line of fire from the enemy and brought back to safety a severely wounded enlisted man. Lieutenant MILLER remained in command of his troops until relieved by another officer some three hours later. The gallant example set by this officer inspired the troops which he commanded to strive more aggressively for success in all their combat missions.[9]

The 3d Battalion, 358th Infantry, was awarded a Meritorious Unit Citation on 24 February 1945 for its actions from 10 to 12 July 1944 on Mont Castré.

UNIT CITATION

Under the provisions of Section IV, Circular 333, War Department, 22 December 1943, and pursuant to the authority contained in 4th Indorsement, Headquarters Third United States Army, File AG 200.6 (5 November 1944) GHMCA-4, dated 14 February 1945, the following unit is cited:

The Third Battalion, 358th Infantry, is cited for extraordinary heroism in the face of enemy in France. During the period 10–12 July 1944, the officers and men of this organization displayed great courage, endurance and dogged determination in the attack through the dense Forêt de Mont Castré, France. The position known as the "Mahlman [sic] Line" was part of the main enemy defensive line. It consisted of dug-in positions, cunningly camouflaged in the tangled underbrush and other devices which utilized to the fullest the natural defensive qualities of the area. Despite repeated fierce enemy counterattacks the Battalion relentlessly drove forward and eliminated a battalion of parachute infantry and a company of parachute engineers, both of which were part of the elite 5th German Parachute Division. By the end of the first day the Battalion Commander and 11 of the 17 officers were casualties but the advance had progressed to within 75 yards of the initial objective. The following day the remnants of the three rifle companies, one of which had 20 men, were reorganized into one composite company with a strength of 126 men and commanded by a lieutenant. In a renewed charge the depleted Battalion overran the objective, killed 40 enemy, captured 8 machine guns, bazookas and mortars. On 12

July 1944 as it left the forest the Battalion, retaining its aggressiveness, fought with exceptional daring and great skill and took successive objectives. The Battalion's break through the enemy's main position contributed materially to the Division's advance. The inspiring leadership of its officers and the gallantry displayed by all ranks were in accordance with the highest military tradition.

By command of Major General ROOKS

On the left of the division, the 1st and 3d Battalion, 357th Infantry spent much of the day reorganizing and refitting after the rough handling they had suffered north of Beau Coudray. Only 219 replacements were received by 10 July, and none arrived on 11 or 12 July. They remained in the vicinity north of Beau Coudray in division reserve. The 2d Battalion continued its attack at 0800 and met almost no resistance. It reached Le Plessis and mopped up a few German stragglers before moving south along the west edge of the Prairies until it was halted in the vicinity of La Coutrie by the 1st Battalion, 358th Infantry moving across its front. It was after dark before they were able to move forward and tie in with the left of the 1st Battalion, 358th infantry along the Mouloir Stream.

Overall, the day saw the entire VIII Corps advance as the Germans fell back to their next delaying positions. To the right of the 90th, the 8th Infantry Division moved forward until it hit the German position on Hill 92 where it halted for the night. On the VIII Corps right, the 79th Infantry Division advanced abreast of the 8th Infantry Division. To the east, in the VII Corps zone, the 4th Infantry Division also was able to finally advance south along the narrow neck of relatively dry land east of the Prairies.

On 13 July, General Landrum planned on renewing the attack along the line with all three regiments jumping off simultaneously. Although the glacial pace of the 8th Infantry Division had resulted in the relief of its commander, Major General William C. McMahon, the previous day, the 8th Infantry Division was again slow in coming up alongside the 359th Infantry on the division right. As a result, the only action by the 359th Infantry was to eliminate the strongpoint that had halted progress the previous day. In the center and on the left, the 357th and 358th Infantry spent the day forcing the Mouloir Stream and capturing Gorges. One soldier of the 357th Infantry received an award of the Distinguished Service Cross for his actions on 13 July.

The President of the United States of America, authorized by Act of Congress July 9, 1918, takes pleasure in presenting the Distinguished Service Cross to Technical Sergeant

Howard Wesley Trego (ASN: 38148986), United States Army, for extraordinary heroism in connection with military operations against an armed enemy while serving with Company B, 1st Battalion, 357th Infantry Regiment, 90th Infantry Division, in action against enemy forces in the vicinity of Gorges, France, on 13 July 1944. Technical Sergeant Trego was reconnoitering an enemy machine gun position, the fire from which was delaying the advance of the infantry companies. His movements were covered by fire support from his platoon leader and one other soldier. As Technical Sergeant Trego advanced he came upon and killed an enemy soldier with his carbine. Taking the dead soldier's machine pistol he moved near the machine gun position, killing more of the enemy on the way. When his machine pistol ran out of ammunition he used in success an automatic rifle, an enemy rifle, and an M1 rifle. His platoon leader and the other soldier then came forward and their combined fire caused the disorganized enemy group to come out of their position and surrender. Although Technical Sergeant Trego and his party were out of ammunition, their bold front hid this face from the enemy. As a result of this action eight prisoners were taken, eight enemy killed, a machine gun captured, and the battalion's advance was allowed to continue. Technical Sergeant Trego's extraordinary heroism, personal bravery and zealous devotion to duty exemplify the highest traditions of the military forces of the United States and reflect great credit upon himself, the 90th Infantry Division, and the United States Army.[10]

The following day, 14 July, the 90th Infantry Division finally reached the objectives it had been assigned eleven days earlier. The 359th Infantry, still on the division right, advanced without any resistance to a crossroads just north of the village of Sèves on the Sèves River. To the left of the 359th the 358th Infantry also advanced rapidly, against slight resistance, to the high ground overlooking the Sèves River from the village of Ney west to contact with the 359th Infantry. On the division left, the 357th Infantry advanced without resistance to the vicinity of Gorges and La Cellerie. For the next week they held in place reorganizing and filling up depleted units with replacements while the VII Corps remained inactive.

The assessment made by the 90th Infantry Division of the Battle of Mont Castré was written sometime after the fact but was generally accurate.

The battle of the Forêt de Mont Castré had been won. Blood, guts and superior equipment had finally broken the Mahlman [sic] Line. The cost to the 90th Div had been high; some 5000 had been killed, wounded or captured. But the German losses were heavier. The 90th Div, drained as it was of key officers and non-commissioned officers had undisputedly proven its combat effectiveness. For 9 continuous days and nights it had fought without respite against a seasoned and entrenched enemy, and its wounds notwithstanding, emerged from the fight victorious and high spirited.

A complete assessment of how well the 90th Infantry Division performed in the Battle of Mont Castré is difficult to make. The estimate made in 1944 of the cost to the division was probably exaggerated. The actual loss in terms of battle casualties—killed, wounded, and missing/captured—was likely closer to 3,523 than 5,000. However, the loss due to sickness and injuries, as well as neuropsychiatric casualties—battle fatigue, combat exhaustion, shell shock, and other similar terms were also used—probably brought the total to well over 5,000, although the official figures for the period from 3 to 12 July only counted 310 due to those causes.

The number of casualties inflicted on the Germans by the 90th infantry Division is even more difficult to assess. Many of the wartime German records were lost in the retreat from France or later in the collapse of the Third Reich. Reports for the individual German infantry formations opposing the Americans in the Cotentin Peninsula are almost nonexistent. However, some records from *7. Armee* still exist. Those are the consolidated "10-day" reports for July. They show that the *LXXXIV. Armee-Korps* reported 6,043 casualties for 1–10 July 1944: 880 killed, 3,682 wounded, and 1,481 missing. During the same period, the 90th Infantry Division reported the capture of 949 Germans, plus an additional unknown number who were captured wounded. Given that captured reported by one side in battle are a subset of missing-in-action reported by the opposing side, it may be speculated that the number of killed and wounded suffered by the Germans opposing the 90th Infantry Division were proportional. That would imply that possibly 64.1 percent of the 880 killed and 3,682 wounded reported by the Germans were also lost versus the 90th Infantry Division. Thus, it could be estimated the Germans lost about 564 killed, 2,360 wounded, and 949 captured, a total of about 3,873.[11]

However, it is also evident the *LXXXIV. Armee-Korps* report underestimated casualties. The 82d Airborne Division alone reported capturing 772 prisoners during the same period, for a total of 1,721 captured by the two divisions. Nor does that include prisoners captured by the 8th or 79th Infantry Division. Part of the discrepancy was likely caused by losses in units not reported by the *LXXXIV. Armee-Korps*. For example, the *Fallschirmjäger Regiment 15* likely reported its casualties through *II. Fallschirm-Korps*. *SS-Das Reich* may also have reported casualties separately.[12]

Nevertheless, even given these uncertainties and caveats, it seems likely that the 90th Infantry Division inflicted about as many casualties as they suffered. They also reached their objective of pushing the Germans out of the Mahlmann Linie defenses and off Mont Castré. That they were late in achieving their objective is moot; none of the Allied offensives planned for the first week of July achieved their objectives. Farther east, the 4th Infantry Division under the VII Corps attacked in succession on 4 July following the VIII Corps. It also failed to reach its objective, even after the 83d Infantry Division was added to the attack on 7 July. The same occurred to the XIX Corps farther east along the River Vire. Its two divisions, the 29th and 30th Infantry, failed to reach its objective even after the XIX Corps committed the 3d Armored Division to the attack. The XIX Corps's primary objective, Saint-Lô, was not reached until 18 July.

Nevertheless, the perception to this day is that the 90th Infantry Division uniquely failed in its mission. It is singled out as a "problem division," even though most of the other divisions of FUSA suffered similar problems. Ultimately, General Bradley's perception of unique failure in the 90th Infantry Division led to the relief of General Landrum and General Sam Williams.

As the Battle for Mont Castré began winding down, Dad's Battery A and the rest of the 537th AAA AW Battalion except for Battery D were relieved from attachment to the 8th Infantry Division and reattached to the 90th Infantry Division. Battery A was attached again to the 343d Field Artillery and the 537th RCT in the vicinity of Beau Coudray.

****

Leaving Prétot-Sainte-Suzanne we headed south before turning west at Saint-Jores to Montsenelle, heading almost due west toward La Haye-du-Puits. As we approached Montsenelle we could see the ridge of Mont Castré on the southern horizon.

It is immediately obvious why Mont Castré was such a critical terrain feature to both the Germans and the Americans. It dominates everything around it. The steep, heavily wooded hillside is forbidding even today. We would have liked to stop, but about midway between Prétot-Sainte-Suzanne and Montsenelle the sun disappeared, and the rain began again. We decided to press onward, as Dad muttered, "it never stops raining in this damned country."

CHAPTER 7

"THEY GOT THE WRONG MAN"

As early as 12 July, General Bradley was losing patience with Landrum's command of the 90th Infantry Division. Bradley had little patience in any case with division commanders who did not meet his expectations. He had already relieved MacKelvie, and on 12 July he relieved Major General William C. McMahon, the commander of the 8th Infantry Division. On 13 July, Bradley noted to his aide, Captain Chester B. Hansen, that

> *Every time I went to see [Landrum], he was in his command post, which was usually in the basement of some building. He never got outside of it. And he had no way to inspire his division. You got to get out there and show you are interested and are willing to take a chance with them.*[1]

Although the course of these events is not well documented, by the morning of 13 July, it seems both Eisenhower and Bradley were finished with Landrum. The replacement they agreed upon was Brigadier General Theodore Roosevelt Jr. Roosevelt's performance as a "Supernumerary General Officer" with the 4th Infantry Division on D-Day had been stellar, earning him a recommendation for the Medal of Honor. Bradley may have had some qualms because he had relieved Roosevelt of duty as Assistant Division Commander of the 1st Infantry Division in 1943 along with Major General Terry de la Mesa Allen, the Big Red One's commander, because of what Bradley had perceived as rampant indiscipline in the division in the North African and Sicilian campaigns. However, Eisenhower's opinion prevailed, and Bradley changed his mind. However, that same morning Eisenhower and Bradley were shocked to learn that Roosevelt was dead. He had died late the previous night in his tent at Meutis, outside Cherbourg where he was serving as the Town Commander. Roosevelt had been stricken by a massive heart attack in his sleep.

After Roosevelt's death, Eisenhower confirmed to Roosevelt's widow, Eleanor Butler Alexander Roosevelt, that "his work was so outstanding that he was to be assigned to Division Command the day after his death."[2] Postwar, Bradley justified his change of heart about Roosevelt by saying,

> *"He's too short-hearted to take a division—too much like one of the boys." But it was not a disciplinarian the 90th needed now. It called for a man with vitality and courage, a man who could pick up the division single-handedly and give it confidence in itself. . . . With a thick skinned disciplinarian as his second in command, Ted would have the 90th brawling with Germans in a couple of weeks.*[3]

The news of Roosevelt's death left Eisenhower and Bradley in a quandary. Bradley had already used who he believed was his only other good candidate as a replacement division commander, Brigadier General Donald Stroh, to replace McMahon as commander of the 8th Infantry Division. Other potential candidates may have been present in Normandy but were needed in their current positions. For example, Brigadier General Raymond S. McLain, who eventually took command of the 90th on 28 July, was commander of the 30th Division Artillery, which was scheduled to enter combat with the XIX Corps in two days.

Nor did Eisenhower and Bradley consider Brigadier General Williams a candidate to replace General Landrum, despite Williams's sterling performance as a combat leader in the campaign to date. Williams outburst at Landrum on 7 July meant the relationship between the two was cool at best, but it was made worse by another incident around 13 or 14 July. The new commander of the 8th Infantry Division, General Stroh, visited the 90th Infantry Division to coordinate operations and reportedly told Landrum and Williams that he was hesitant to push his own division while the 90th was in a weakened condition after ten days of intense fighting. Stroh innocuously asked, "are you people doing any better now?" which led Williams to lose his temper and become "ill-mannered." Later Landrum confronted Williams, telling him that "he should avoid similar comments to other senior officers." In response, Williams requested a transfer to another division.[4]

Instead General Landrum composed the following message to General Middleton, the commander of the VIII Corps.

14 July 1944
Subject: Assistant Division Commander
To: Commanding General VIII Corps, A.P.O. 308, U.S. Army

1. *I request that a Brigadier General with combat experience in this war be assigned to this division as Assistant Division Commander at the earliest practicable time and that the present Assistant Division commander, Brigadier General Sam T. Williams, U.S. Army, be given another assignment.*
2. *While General Williams has discharged the many specific missions that I have assigned to him promptly, I feel that a general officer of a more optimistic and calming attitude would be more beneficial to this division at this time.*
3. *I believe that a general officer who was not connected with this division during its training period would be of greater assistance to me in the elimination of the training deficiencies that exist in this division.*

E. M. Landrum
Major General, U.S. Army, Commanding

On Sunday, 16 July 1944, at 1145, General Williams was visiting an outpost of Company G, 357th Infantry, along the Sèves River near the village of Nay, when he received a message ordering him to report to VIII Corps Headquarters outside La Haye du Puits. When he arrived, General Middleton handed him Landrum's message and an endorsement Middleton had written to Bradley. Middleton's message to Bradley read,

16 July 1944
To: Commanding General, First U.S. Army, A.P.O. 230

1. *Approved.*
2. *General Williams has been directed to report to your headquarters, there being no appropriate assignment for him in the VIII Corps.3. I do not know General Williams well, however, the fact that the 90th Division has not come up to expectations in combat is common knowledge. The Division Commander who brought the division to France has been relieved. I believe that new life and an improved attitude in the division can be developed by the assignment of a man as Assistant Division Commander who has proven himself in combat in this war, and who has had no relations with the division in the past.Troy H. Middleton*

Major General, U.S. Army, Commanding

General Williams was summarily relieved and sent to report to Major General William B. Kean, Chief of Staff, FUSA. There he waited for two days, before he was given a second, more damning letter written by Landrum and dated the same as the previous one. It enumerated Williams's supposed faults, including his excitability, indiscretion, intemperance of speech, defensive attitude regarding training deficiencies, and expressed Landrum's loss of confidence in Williams's capacity to fulfill the duties of an Assistant Division Commander. Worst of all, Landrum recommended Williams's reduction to his permanent grade of Lieutenant Colonel with an appointment as colonel, AUS. Middleton too had rewritten his endorsement to match Landrum's.

General Williams's relief was perhaps the least deserved of any of those made of General officers during the Normandy Campaign. The various remarks made regarding the state of training of the 90th Infantry Division were simply specious—its state of training was no better and no worse than any other division sent to Europe. The files of the AGF Inspector General, its G-3 Training Division, and its history do not contain any indication that the 90th suffered from training deficiencies that were not corrected in the mobilization process. Its activation, organization, and training program were no different from other divisions, except for its experiment with motorization, which was an experience shared by the 4th, 6th, 7th, and 8th Infantry Divisions, none of which were assessed as poorly trained. Notably, it was the 8th Infantry Division in Normandy that had demonstrated many of the same problems as the 90th, while the 4th Infantry Division had not.

It is all too evident that General Williams was a scapegoat for the failings of other officers, like many other officers in the U.S. Army during the war. His performance was probably better than that of either of the other two brigadier generals serving as Assistant Division Commanders in Normandy who were relieved of duty. They were Brigadier General Henry A. Barber Jr., 4th Infantry Division, relieved 2 July 1944, and Brigadier General Thomas L. Martin, 2d Infantry Division, relieved 4 July 1944. As General DePuy said in 1979,

> *Landrum was not visible to the fighting troops. The man who was felt was "Hanging Sam." And that is a tragic story because "Hanging Sam" was fired. They got the wrong man. Williams was the ADC and he was with us all the time and was helpful and a very brave and powerful man as later everyone found out.*[5]

Curiously, while Eisenhower, Bradley, and Middleton all expressed discontent with the performance of the 90th Infantry Division, the American public were told a far different story. On 19 July, The *New York Times* published a story authorized by the FUSA and ETOUSA Public Affairs Sections.

> *Ever since D-day, when they stormed up the beaches, thousands of officers and men fought their hearts out as anonymous entities. They were unknown soldiers whose name and unit were military secrets. For reasons of security, not even their families were permitted to know where they were or what they were doing.*
>
> *A division may have established the greatest record of war and any number of Sergeant Yorks and any number of heroes, but until the army decides that the unit be identified, these men fight on without recognition. One such division on this front was the Ninetieth, which arrived here on D plus 1, and has been in contact with the enemy almost every day since then. Only today was its existence acknowledged. This outfit is so good that even three members of the infantry band received Silver Stars for gallantry in action.*
>
> *BUCK PRIVATE TAKES COMMAND*
>
> *One buck private led a platoon for four days through wild combat after a company commander and three platoon leaders had been killed. He took command at the dying request of the last platoon leader to fall, and carried on through some of the bitterest fighting of the war around St. Suzanne until he too was wounded. He was made a sergeant and has been recommended for a lieutenancy. Because he was wounded, army regulations forbid the mention of his name until formal notification has been made.*
>
> *The Ninetieth Division arrived in France on June 7 and had its first taste of beachhead. Fortunately all were rescued.*
>
> *GENERAL IN STREET FIGHTING*
>
> *In the fighting rank meant little. At Gourbesville, the assistant divisional commander fought off snipers in the street and was in the direct line of possible fire from the four hidden Germans. They were apparently unaware that a general was in range, but they held their fire rather than disclose their position.*
>
> *With the 82nd Airborne Division, the 90th defended the southern flank while other troops moved northward to take Cherbourg. This division was the principle factor in setting the trap for the Germans caught between Cherbourg and the southern line of the peninsula. One hundred and sixty-one Germans were killed while attempting to flee, one company of one infantry regiment.*
>
> *One of the division's outstanding feats was the capture of the Forêt de Mont Castré, known to the army as Hill 122. This high spot was the anchor of the main line of resistance in this sector. The hill, which was heavily mined, was taken after four days that those who lived to tell it will never forget.*
>
> *Captain Leroy (Fireball) Pond, whose battalion was completely surrounded moved within 400 yards of the German position, carrying a portable radio, and relayed*

> *information of the enemy position to the artillery. From a perch in a tree he directed the fire that cleaned out the enemy and freed his battalion. His helmet was knocked off by shrapnel and some bent his radio antenna during the three hours that he stayed at his post, but he remained until every enemy gun had been stilled and his men were again on the offensive.*
>
> *The division went into action on June 10th, fighting yard by yard through some of the most difficult terrain that veteran soldiers had ever seen. Before them fell such towns as Pont 'Abbe, Amfreville and Gourbesville. Their losses were heavy as they battled through the streets in hand-to-hand combat, fought desperately from behind murderous hedgerows while the enemy waited on the other side to pick them off, and struggled waist deep through swamps to reach their objectives.*[6]

It is interesting that one of the reasons cited for the low morale and lack of esprit de corps in the 90th Infantry Division at this time was attributed directly to the tardy release of public information regarding the division's participation in the Normandy Campaign. It appears this article was the first news account released that informed the public the division was fighting in France, over a month after it first entered combat. In contrast, the role of the Army Rangers, 1st and 29th Infantry and the 82d and 101st Airborne divisions was publicized within days of the invasion.[7]

14-21 JULY

From 14 to 21 July, the 90th Infantry Division remained in position along the Sèves River, with the 358th Infantry in the center, overlooking the area nicknamed the "Island" at Saint-Germain-sur-Sèves. The Island was so named because on American maps it appeared as an area of slightly elevated terrain about 3 kilometers long and 1 kilometer wide, amid marshes, that was bordered to the northwest by the Sèves River and to the southeast by the L'Holerotte River. By 19 July, the 357th Infantry was on the division left with the 1st Battalion on the right, the 2d Battalion on the left, and the 3d Battalion in regimental reserve at Gonfreville. The 359th Infantry was on the division right with the 2d Battalion on the right, the 1st Battalion on the left, and the 3d Battalion in reserve east of Haute Perrey.

The rest of the VIII Corps remained inactive as well during this period. General Bradley's latest plan for FUSA, developing since 13 July, was for a main effort by VII Corps known as Operation COBRA. On the left of the 90th Infantry Division the 4th Armored Division moved up on 18 July and relieved the 4th Infantry Division, which moved east to join the VII Corps for COBRA. On the left of the 4th Armored Division was the 83d Infantry Division, with the VII Corps east of it. On the right of the 90th were the 8th and then the 79th Infantry Division, stretching the VIII Corps line west to the sea.

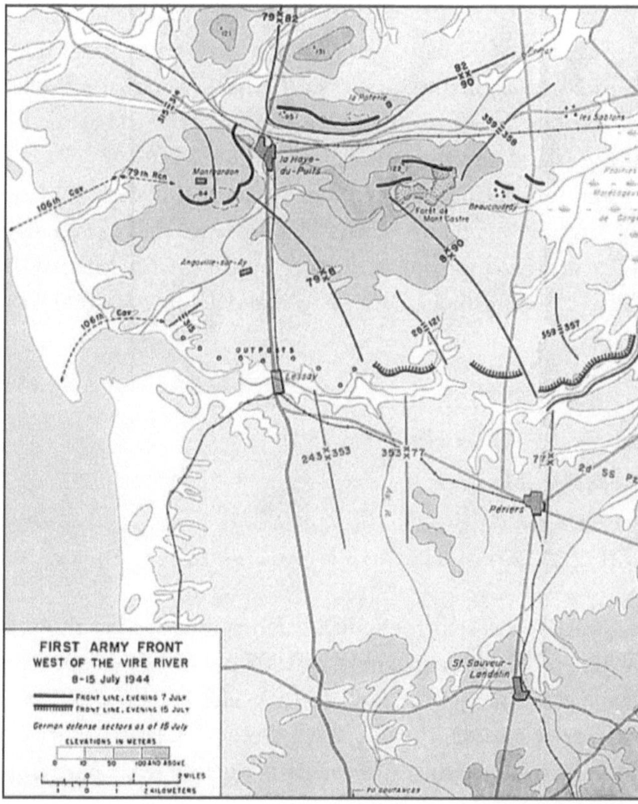

Map 11. The FUSA Front West of the Vire River, 8–15 July 1944. Blumenson, Map II.

The VIII Corps attack that would follow up Operation COBRA was planned as a simple frontal assault by all four divisions abreast to seize the high ground around Coutances 20 kilometers to the south. Unfortunately for the 90th Infantry Division, the Island presented a major obstacle for its attack south. All the approaches to the Sèves River in the division zone were "devoid of cover and swept by enemy fire." A patrol from the 358th Infantry reported at 1015 on 19 July that the river itself was only 10 to 15 feet wide (3 to 4.5 meters), 1.5 feet deep (less than 0.5 meters), and was fordable by personnel along much of its length. However, the marshy ground limited the areas where vehicles, especially tanks, could approach the river, while the high, soft banks limited where they could cross. The sole bridge crossing the river at the west end of the Island on the Gonfreville-Périers Road (D140) known as the "3 Arch Stone" bridge was confirmed destroyed by a patrol from the 3d Battalion,

358th Infantry at 1245 hours 21 July. The only ford reported passable by tanks or other vehicles was about 600 meters east of the bridge site and 1,400 meters west of the church in Saint-Germain-sur Sèves. Perhaps worst of all, relatively higher ground farther south at Le Buisson and La Parmenter provided the Germans with observation of the Island and the American approaches.

General Landrum decided that it was necessary for the 90th to first capture the Island as a jumping-off point for the main offensive. He presented the idea to General Middleton who approved an attack by the 358th Infantry scheduled for dawn on 19 July.[8] Division Field Order #15 dated 17 July at 2000 was duly issued, which read in part,

> *358th Infantry*
> *Atchd: Co B and Assault Gun Plat, 712th Tk Bn*
> *Co A 86th Cml Bn*
>
> *Attacks 190530 in column of Bns to seize and hold Obj and contain the enemy on the Island E of Grid 30. The rear Bn will not be committed except on Division order.*

One complication was that the 358th Infantry was cycling through commanders. Colonel William W. Cornog arrived at 1907 on 15 July to take command from Colonel Clarke, just as the regiment was settling into its new positions in the center of the division line overlooking the Island. Colonel Clarke reverted again to his position as Regimental Executive Officer. It is unclear what part Colonel Cornog had in planning the operation though, because at 1230 on 17 July he was relieved of command and ordered away again! Colonel Clarke again assumed command of the regiment.[9]

The next problem was artillery ammunition supply. The ongoing issues supplying the Allied armies over the beaches of Normandy still plagued the 90th Infantry Division. At 1400 on 18 July, Colonel Clarke was notified by Corps that the attack would be postponed for twenty-four hours because of shortages of ammunition and at 2055 on 19 July the attack was postponed again "to permit acquisition of the artillery ammunitions necessary for the support of the operation."

Yet another complication was replacements. From 15 through 21 July on the eve of the planned attack, a total of 1,010 officers and enlisted replacements were received by the 358th Infantry, nearly one-third of the total regimental strength and equivalent to the strength of five of the nine rifle companies of the regiment. The Division After-Action Report noted for the period from 16 to 18 July that

Critical supporting weapon for the U.S. Army's Infantry: Artillery. This is a 105mm howitzer M1A1 of the 344th Field Artillery Battalion in firing positions, sometime in July 1944. Photo from Combat History 344 FA BN.

> *All units continued training and rehabilitation. Particular stress was placed on Infantry-Tank training, familiarization firing with all weapons and the indoctrination of infantry officers in field artillery forward observer methods.*[10]

Whether or not that was sufficient to mold a cohesive unit so soon after the heavy losses at Mont Castré was questionable. The problem of introducing green units to combat was highlighted again at 1730 on 19 July, when the newly arrived 4th Armored Division launched a limited objective attack—a "strong combat patrol"—directed at the church in the village of Nay. Unfortunately, Nay had been occupied by American troops of Company I, 3d Battalion, 357th Infantry for five days. Before proper identification was made and the shooting stopped, three enlisted men of Company I had been wounded. The 4th Armored Division, under the command of Major General John S. "P" Wood, had been in line for just a day and had only been in France since 13 July.[11]

However, perhaps the most serious complication was that as planned the attack by the 358th Infantry would be the only significant American offensive operation along the front of the VIII Corps and the adjacent VII Corps. Only the XIX and V Corps farther east were still engaged in offensive operations. That meant that every German mortar, artillery piece, and rocket launcher that could be brought to bear on the attackers would be largely untroubled by requests for support from other German units.

On 20 July at 1855, Division HQ notified Colonel Clarke that the attack would be postponed again because of the poor weather, which had caused a delay in the VII Corps attack as well. However, instead of the early morning attack as originally planned, Clarke was informed the "attack would probably be 1200 or 1500 21 July [and that] a four hour notice would be given." That timing did not hold either; at 1420 on 21 July, General Landrum called and told Clarke the attack would be postponed again to 22 July. Finally, at 2000 on 21 July, H-Hour was set to 0630 the following morning. As the 358th *History* put it,

> *All was now coordinated and planned for the coming battle, which was to go down in 358th Infantry annals as a splendid example of heroism, doggedness and loyalty—of heartache and disappointment.*

In fact, the coming battle would be a disaster for the 358th Infantry.

Much of this interplay was largely unknown to most of the officers and men of the 90th Infantry Division and its attached units. For Dad's Battery A, the period was again one of miserable, rainy weather, and sporadic German mortar and artillery fire that was rarely deadly but always nerve-racking.

Dad's Battery A moved with the 343d Field Artillery to a position near Gorges on 14 July. On 19 July, they engaged five of "6 or 7 ME 109s strafing over area." One plane was reported Category I—shot down—and one Category II—damaged. The pilot of the shot down plane was captured by personnel of the 90th Reconnaissance Troop and 315th Engineers. It was the first "confirmed kill" of the war for Battery A.[12]

****

Our route west from Montsenelle to La Haye-du-Puits paralleled the ridge of Mont Castré. It took less than twenty minutes in the rain to drive from Picauville to Le Haye-du-Puits, which was a journey that took the Americans days in 1944.

Dad remembered the first victory claimed by Battery A very well. He recalled that the German plane was hit by one of the 40mm guns rather than by the .50 calibers of one of "his" M16B. Surprisingly, though, it was a different event the next day that he remembered as vividly, perhaps because it was the subject of a lot of comment and speculation by the officers and men of the Allied armies at the time.

At 1242 Berlin time on 20 July, a bomb exploded during a briefing at Hitler's field headquarters, the Wolfsschanze (Wolf's Lair) at Görlitz (modern Gierłoż,

Poland), about 8 kilometers east of the East Prussian town of Rastenburg, which injured Adolf Hitler and nineteen other men, three of whom later died. One man, a stenographer, was killed instantly. Hitler's right leg was burned from the blast and peppered with splinters from the heavy table leg that had partially shielded him from the full effect of the explosion. His right eardrum was perforated, and he suffered from conjunctivitis of his right eye, but he survived.

The plotters were a group of Wehrmacht officers, mostly Heer, who believed that assassinating Hitler and seizing power from the Nazis was the only way possible for Germany to negotiate an end to the war. Hitler exacted a terrible revenge against the plotters and their families. The assassin, Claus Philipp Maria Justinian Schenk Graf von Stauffenberg, and his coconspirators were captured and summarily executed late that night at the headquarters of the *Ersatzheer* (Replacement Army) in Berlin when the coup attempt collapsed. As many as 7,000 others were arrested and an estimated 4,980 were executed.[13]

What is most surprising is that the Allied armies in Normandy were aware of the coup attempt as early as 1900, just six hours and eighteen minutes after the bomb exploded. The 90th Division Artillery After-Action Report noted that "everyone was thoroughly disgusted when they received the report about 1900 that an attempt has been made on Hitler and that he had only been slightly wounded." That news of the attempt had reached the Allies so soon is fascinating, but what is even more fascinating is that Hitler's survival was not actually confirmed until very early the next morning, when Hitler made a six-minute radio speech to the German people at 0100 Berlin time on 21 July. Perhaps even more fascinating is that two days later, prisoners captured from the *Fallschirmjäger Regiment 6* said they had heard of the attempt on Hitler "but didn't attach much importance to it."[14]

CHAPTER 8

COLLAPSE ON THE ISLAND

Colonel Clarke's plan for the 358th Infantry's seizure of the Island was relatively straightforward. It was to be an attack by two battalions advancing abreast in a column of companies on a front of 2,000 meters centered on the ford on the Sèves. Bealke's 3d Battalion would secure the line of departure and provide fire support for Lieutenant Colonel Albert Seeger's 1st Battalion, which would assault to the right of the ford. Major C. Stedman Chandler's 2d Battalion would attack to the left of the ford. Yet another indication of the confusion rampant in the division at this time is that the original division attack order specified an assault in column of battalions. Why it was changed to two battalions abreast is unknown.

The attack would be supported by all four organic divisional artillery battalions, the attached 687th Field Artillery (105mm howitzer), the supporting 333d Field Artillery (Cld) (155mm howitzer), and three supporting 4th Armored Division Artillery battalions (only one of which would remain in support after firing the preparation). In addition, the 607th Tank Destroyer Battalion would use its towed 3-inch guns in the preparation and then would move up to provide additional anti-tank support. Finally, the twelve 4.2-inch mortars of Company A, 86th Chemical Mortar Battalion, would fire high explosive (HE) in the preparation and then switch to chemical smoke on call to provide concealment for the crossing units. In all, the artillery and mortars would fire 48 4.2-inch, 360 105mm, and 48 155mm rounds in the two minutes before the infantry jumped off. Then they would increase the range and another 48 4.2-inch, 198 105mm, and 48 155mm rounds would follow in the two minutes after the infantry jumped off. The tank destroyers would add another 120 rounds of 3-inch from H-2 minutes to H+4 minutes. However, ammunition restrictions meant that after firing the preparation, the artillery was rationed to 17 rounds per piece. Theoretically that was 1,530 rounds from the seven battalions.

Other support for the attack was provided by the 712th Tank Battalion and the 315th Engineer Combat Battalion. Company A and B, 712th Tank Battalion, were placed in direct support of the 358th Infantry. Company A was in direct fire support to accompany the infantry assault, while Company B was used for indirect fire, reinforcing the fires of the 915th Field Artillery. The Battalion Assault Gun Platoon also fired as artillery, but against targets in the vicinity of Périers. Company C and D remained in reserve. The division order tasked the 315th Engineers to "provide close support to assault Regts with particular attention to prompt construction of vehicular and tank crossings across swamp barriers." The 358th Infantry After-Action Report remarked that the "Engineers will make two crossings—and will take all size trucks," but it is unclear exactly how they planned to do so because no additional attached engineer or bridging assets were provided by the VIII Corps. The 315th Combat Engineer Battalion only had access to fourteen Assault Boats M2, which was a plywood scow capable of carrying up to fifteen infantrymen. The boats could be linked together and used as an expedient raft or assault bridge, but such a raft or bridge could only support very light loads of about two tons.

The greatest shortfall was intelligence on the German defenses. Little was known of the strength or location of German forces on the Island. The last prisoners captured and interrogated by the 90th Infantry Division were five enlisted men of the *4. Kompanie* of *Fallschirm-Pionier Abteilung 5* near Nay on 15 July. They provided little information and what they did have was a week old by the time the 358th Infantry made its attack. In the end, the 870 rounds of artillery and mortar ammunition expended on the Island were essentially fired blindly at what were suspected to be defensive positions. After the war, soldiers of *Fallschirmjäger-Regiment 6.* who survived the battle on the Island said that the American artillery fired well beyond the German positions and did little or no damage.[1]

The defenders from *Fallschirmjäger-Regiment 6.* were under the command of Major Freiherr Freidrich-August von der Heydte. On the eve of the Allied invasion, it was a very strong unit of about 3,500 to 4,500 well-equipped, well-trained, and highly motivated men, but by late July only a remnant was left. It suffered extremely heavy casualties in June; its *I. Batallion* was virtually destroyed by the evening of 7 June and was disbanded. By 22 June, the regiment had a combat strength of between 700 and 1,200 officers and men, including about 300 recently arrived recruits who were poorly armed and equipped. The *III. Batallion* was on the western end of the island, with *9. Kompanie* astride the D140 Road guarding the bridge site and *11. Kompanie* on its right extending the line to Saint-Germain-sur-Sèves. The *10. Kompanie* was in reserve and *12. Kompanie*, the battalion heavy weapons company, was farther south, on the other side of the Holerotte River manning the battalion's mortars. The *II. Bataillon* was on the eastern end of the Island with *7. Kompanie* defending Saint-Germain-sur-Sèves, but the location of its other companies to the right and in reserve are unknown. The companies averaged a strength of about ninety officers and enlisted men each.[2]

Each battalion had constructed a main line of resistance manned by two forward companies, which were within observation and direct fire range of the Sèves. However, based upon his experience so far in Normandy, Major von der Heydte instructed his men to construct a second strong line of resistance 300 to 800 meters to the rear, essentially running down the center of the Island, that was manned by the weaker reserve companies. The two positions were connected by communications tranches that made it possible to move troops from one position to the other while concealed and undercover.[3]

Major von der Heydte's Gefechtsstand (command post) was in a farmhouse near the Carentan-Périers road (D971). Nearby in regimental reserve was the regiment's *16. Kompanie*. It was originally a bicycle-mounted reconnaissance unit with about 140 to 160 officers and men, but by 22 July was reduced to just five NCOs and twenty-seven enlisted men, led by Oberfeldwebel Alexander Uhlig, a twenty-five-year-old veteran of nearly eight years with the German Fallschirmjäger. Uhlig had jumped into Dombas and Narvik in April of 1940 in the Norwegian Campaign, jumped into the hell that was Crete, and had fought in North Africa, Italy, and now France, and had been awarded both the Iron Cross 1st and 2nd Class. He was to prove a fearsome enemy to the Americans in the coming battle.[4]

Critically, a second and much more powerful reserve element was also available to the Germans. While the 90th was battering through the Mahlmann Linie, the *KG SS-Das Reich* was withdrawn from its assembly area south of Mont Castré and rejoined the main body of the division at Périers. On 11 July, the division moved northeast to reinforce the badly battered *SS-GvB*. The presence of the fresh troops blunted the advance of the 4th and 83d Infantry Division south astride the Carentan-Périers road at Saintenay to the east of Saint-Germain-sur-Sèves. *Fallschirmjäger-Regiment 6.* was attached to *SS-Das Reich* and at least one platoon of four Panzer IV from the *II. Abteilung* of *SS-Panzer-Regiment 2.* were placed at the disposal of Major von der Heydte. In addition, as many as eleven batteries of artillery were available to support Heydte's Fallschirmjäger, a formidable array of firepower for the Germans at this stage in the war.[5]

The Americans had known *SS-Das Reich* was in the area for some time. The VIII Corps and 90th Infantry Division had been in contact with them on Mont

Castré as recently as 9 July. Concern over the location of *SS-Das Reich* is evident in the G-2 reports of the 90th Infantry Division during the period. However, confirmation of the presence of the *SS-Das Reich* in the vicinity of the Island did not come until the evening of 22 July, when a captured German overlay dated 8 July, showing it moving to the area, was distributed to American units. Until then, it seems little thought was given to the possibility the Germans would commit its tanks to counter the American attack.[6]

22 JULY

At 0100 on 22 July, in near total darkness—the moon was waxing crescent that morning and provided little light, especially in the pouring rain—the 1st and 2nd Battalion, 358th Infantry began moving from the vicinity of Gorges to the line of departure. German artillery fire harassed the movement from the beginning. Sound and flash ranging attempted to fix the German positions so American artillery could fire counterbattery, but without much success. The Germans were well versed in tactics to minimize counterfire and that and the sheer number of German batteries able to fire were already complicating the operation. Nevertheless, by 0325 the 2d Battalion had closed into the assembly area. The 1st Battalion began moving to the line of departure at 0545 and the 2d Battalion followed ten minutes later.

The artillery preparation began exactly on time and lifted on schedule at 0630, which was also time for the battalions to jump off. Instead the Germans, as if on cue, immediately began the "most intense and sustained counterpreparation [*sic*] fire that the Division had experienced to date" along the length of the American side of the river. One thing that may have saved the Americans from even greater losses in the coming battle was the extraordinarily high frequency of "duds" experienced from the German artillery fire. On 21 July, the 90th Division Artillery noted that 60 of 106 rounds fired at the 90th were duds or low-order bursts, and on 26 July the 83d Infantry Division reported 285 of 300 rounds fired at them were duds. Nevertheless, the unrelenting German artillery barrage was soon augmented by mortar and machine-gun fire. Company A, 712th Tank Battalion, was hit by mortar and artillery fire as it moved up to support the infantry and lost one tank to a high-velocity round just twenty-five minutes into the attack. After nearly an hour, Company F had committed its reserve platoon. They were fired on by "everything the enemy had" but were still 50 yards from the river, while two company commanders in the 2d Battalion were out of action. By 0755, no crossing had been made and both infantry battalions were stuck in place. General Landrum, who had arrived at Colonel Clarke's forward OP near the planned crossing point, ordered the artillery

Map 12. The "Island," 23 July 1944. Blastos, Inclosure 3.

preparation fired again to try to jump-start the assault. The artillery's "Cubs" were ordered up into the overcast to spot targets, but the low overcast made it impossible for them to see anything.[7]

The second artillery preparation opened fire at 0840 and at 0845 increased the range, working over the same areas. Three minutes later an artillery observer reported that the 2d Battalion still had not moved. However, at 0855 elements of Company E reached the river. At the same time, Colonel Clarke went forward to confer with Colonel Seeger of the 1st Battalion. When he returned, Clarke said "they were continuously being shot at." At 0910, Company G was committed to the left of Company E, but still no real progress was made. The 4.2-inch chemical mortars were ordered to fire more smoke at 0945 to provide some concealment for the infantry, but without effect. Company E was forced to withdraw after suffering thirty-five casualties, including the company commander, and Company G moved up in its place at 1000.[8]

General Landrum, still at Clarke's OP, notified Division Headquarters at 1010 that they were under heavy long-range German fire and again ordered up the "Cubs" "when the weather broke." At 1017, he ordered the Division G-3 to request air support to knock out the German artillery and three minutes later got a "promise" that armed air reconnaissance would be forthcoming, but the atrocious weather kept them grounded as well. Landrum then contacted General Devine at Division Artillery and told him to review the concentrations they had fired to look for any "likely mortar positions" that may have been missed and gave him permission to fire on the "Chateau," which was about 1 kilometer north of the village. It had been left out of the fire plan, probably because it was so far from the crossing points—nearly 2 kilometers—that it was considered unimportant, but by this time Landrum was desperately looking for any targets that could be seen and hit.[9]

Nearly four and a half hours into the battle at 1055, still no one had crossed the river. Colonel Clarke suggested Seeger rush the 1st Battalion across in small groups, but nothing came of the attempt. By this time, Company B was alongside Company G, so from right to left, three companies, F, G, and B, were along the river's edge.

Major Falvey, the 358th Infantry S-2, sometime during the morning encountered two Signal Corps men trying to get forward to photograph the attack. He told them where a good location was overlooking where Company E was trying to cross under heavy mortar and artillery fire. Falvey also advised the photographers to meanwhile take shelter from the incessant fire in two deep holes. After Falvey left, the photographers were both killed by artillery or mortar fire before they could find shelter. One of the two, 1st Lieutenant Everett W. Shadden, was awarded the Silver Star.[10]

> *The President of the United States of America, authorized by Act of Congress, July 9, 1918, takes pride in presenting the Silver Star (Posthumously) to First Lieutenant (Signal Corps) Everett W. Shadden (ASN: 0-496183), United States Army, for gallantry in action while serving with Detachment 7, 166th Signal Photographic Company, 90th Infantry Division. The conspicuous courage Lieutenant Shadden displayed while photographing an engagement of the 90th Infantry Division on 22 July 1944, near Nay, France, distinguishes him as an outstanding officer. Lieutenant Shadden was killed by an exploding enemy mortar round while performing his mission. His determination and supreme devotion to duty were in keeping with the highest traditions of military service and reflect great credit upon himself, his unit, and the United States Army.*[11]

Finally, at 1101, Bealke's Company I reported they could see men of Company F on the opposite bank. At the same time, Major Robert H. Schulz, the 2d Battalion Executive Officer, reported he did not believe there were "many Germans on the Island" and that Company F had managed to get into some of the buildings on the far side of the ford. Over an hour later at 1215, Colonel Seeger declared his 1st Battalion was "about ready" to cross the Sèves. Forty-five minutes later, the 1st Battalion was reported to have advanced 100 yards, which should have put them on the far bank of the river. Twenty-five minutes after that it was confirmed that Company B and C had both crossed and captured some German prisoners.[12]

However, at 1338, just a few minutes after the last message, Major Chandler complained he could not get his 2d Battalion to move forward. General Landrum discussed emplacing bridges to get tanks onto the Island, but the commander of Company B, 315th Engineers, Captain Wilson M. Midyett, replied that the tanks could cross without bridges and the matter rested there for the moment.

Next an obviously impatient Landrum "suggested" General Devine was not "pushing his observers enough," a suggestion that was unlikely to have been well received by Devine or by Colonel Munson who's 344th Field Artillery was in direct support of the 358th Infantry. Munson was "pushing" his observers. He had assigned four forward observer teams to the infantry battalions: 1st Lieutenant Saul Bauer of Battery A was with the 1st Battalion, 2d Lieutenant C. Fishbein and 1st Lieutenant Leon J. Lisecki of Battery B were with the 2d Battalion, and 1st Lieutenant J. W. Coleman of Battery C was with the 3d Battalion. In addition, 1st Lieutenant Sheridan T. Dowling from the 687th Field Artillery was also attached to the 1st Battalion. However, the major problem with the artillery remained poor visibility. The rain and low cloud cover made ground observation and identification of targets very difficult and air observation nearly impossible.[13]

Major Chandler continued to have problems getting his men forward. At 1425, the 2d Battalion was halted again by the heavy German fire. All three companies were reported to be completely disorganized. Ten minutes later Chandler reported he was still trying to get Company G across to join Company F and Seeger's 1st Battalion. Colonel Clarke reached Chandler by field telephone shortly after 1500 to ask if tanks could help in getting Company G across the Sèves. After some discussion, Clarke directly ordered him to get Company E and G across the river with tanks, then move them to the left of the 1st Battalion. Chandler agreed and said he believed he could get them across by following the 1st Battalion's route. Chandler thought he could then move northeast behind the 1st Battalion, before turning east, coming up on the 1st Battalion's left.

Nearly an hour later, at 1550, Colonel Clarke had a similar conversation with Colonel Seeger. Oddly, the commander of the 1st Battalion told Clarke he did not want to move tanks onto the Island until he had "more room"! Seeger also told Clarke he was "working on" some buildings that were causing trouble for the advance, but he seemed unaware of the help tanks could provide him in that task. A half hour later, Seeger informed Clarke that Company F was down to just fifty men. They had been trying to subdue the German-held buildings that were giving so much trouble and finally withdrew to allow the tanks on the other side of the river to work them over. However, the tank fire also had no effect.

Nearly an hour later, at 1643, Company A finally crossed the river, while Company B and C advanced to the east. Clarke asked Seeger if the 1st Battalion had any visibility on the whereabouts of the 2d Battalion, but the answer was "no." It was 1700, twelve and a half hours after the attack began, before Major Chandler reported that Company G was crossing onto the Island and that he was about to take Company E over himself. At 1810, Company F withdrew back across the ford to resupply with ammunition.

At this point, General Landrum directed Colonel Clarke to order the battalions to get their stragglers together in the rear and then move them to their units. At 1838, Colonel Clarke finally reached the limits of his frustration with the slowness and poor performance of the 2d Battalion and relieved Major Chandler. The Regimental Executive Officer, Colonel Loomis, took temporary command of the 2d Battalion and tried to sort it out. In the process, he discovered that Company E had not in fact crossed the river at all.

Meanwhile at 1945 a German counterattack was made on the 1st Battalion, but it was repulsed without much effort. Shortly afterward, at 2105, Bealke's 3d Battalion S-3 reported that a patrol was sent to the bridge site, but "every time it moved it received small arms fire from buildings." The Germans had obviously not fallen back at any point.

Confusion continued to grow as the exhausted troops fought on in the continual rain and increasing darkness. At 2025, Colonel Clarke ordered the 2d Platoon, Company A, 712th Tank Battalion committed from reserve. However, eighteen minutes later the platoon leader told Clarke his platoon was unavailable in the rear, refueling and rearming, which is what Major Schulz, the 2d Battalion Executive Officer, had ordered him to do. Nor had his platoon been in "reserve" during the day; it had fired 100 rounds in support of the 2d Battalion. None of the tanks of Company A in fact had been in reserve, they had all been firing in support during the day. However, all of Company C, 712th Tank Battalion, was in reserve and unused, as were the light tanks of Company D, while Company B had spent the entire day firing indirectly. In fact, they spent the entire time from 22 to 26 July firing 5,560 rounds of 75mm HE at targets reinforcing the fire of the 915th Field Artillery Battalion. Three weeks after the 712th Tank Battalion was first attached to the 90th, infantry-tank coordination remained a major problem in the 90th's operations.

The 358th Infantry was also confused regarding whether any of the tanks had crossed onto the Island. At various times during the day the answer appeared to be yes, and at other times no. The 358th Infantry After-Action Report confidently stated,

> *At 2115 Major Falvey was informed by 1st Bn that five tanks had crossed the stream. . . . By 2230 the 2d Platoon of tanks had crossed the stream and were promptly surrounded. They were in radio contact and were told to "stay put" and not to withdraw. There were now 2 platoons of tanks on the Island.*[14]

Except that was all fantasy. No tanks had crossed the Sèves and none were on the Island. The After-Action Report of the 712th Tank Battalion succinctly stated, "2d platoon attempted to make crossing, but too much mud and too much concentrated enemy fire. Platoons spent night in position under all kinds and calibers of heavy enemy fire."

By 2300, things had quieted down a bit. Colonel Loomis reported there had been no small arms fire for thirty minutes in the 2d Battalion area, but they were still "receiving spasmodic artillery and mortar fire." He was still trying to get the balance of the 2d Battalion across the stream and into position and was still rounding up stragglers from the 1st and 2d Battalion as late as 2345. At midnight, the defense was "buttoned up."

By then, the 1st Battalion had captured ten Germans—two from *9. Kompanie* and eight from *11. Kompanie*—and sent them back for interrogation. The results of the interrogation were the first inkling that the 90th Infantry Division had of what they were encountering on the Island: the 358th Infantry, over 3,000 strong, was facing three companies of German Fallschirmjäger totaling about 270 officers and men. Major Schulz was correct; there weren't many Germans on the Island.

Unknown to the Americans, the 1st Battalion attack, even as slow as it had moved, combined with the crushing American artillery fire—General Devine's organic, attached, and reinforcing battalions had fired a total of 5,290 rounds from 0630 to 2400—had severely compromised the German defenses. When Company B and C had finally advanced and crossed the river, they had struck the seam between the two forward German companies and inflicted severe casualties on the German defenders. The *11. Kompanie*, which was already weak—it only had two platoons totaling about sixty to eighty men—had fallen back to the secondary line of resistance, allowing the 1st Battalion to advance about 600 meters, threatening the flank of the *9. Kompanie* to the west defending the bridge area as well as the flank of *7. Kompanie* to the east in Saint Germain-sur-Sèves. In response, Major von der Heydte, thinking the American attack was only a strong patrol, ordered Oberfeldwebel Uhlig to take the thirty-two men of *16. Kompanie*, clarify the situation, and take some prisoners. On the way, one NCO and three men were wounded by American artillery fire, and two men were detailed to help them to the rear, leaving Uhlig with just twenty-six men. However, as they moved up, he also collected some additional men, probably from *11. Kompanie*, raising his strength to about fifty. By early evening, his little band had stealthily advanced to the right of the American position.[15]

As he got closer to the American, Uhlig quickly realized that they were not just a "strong patrol"; he estimated them as at least three hundred men. Nevertheless, Uhlig decided to attack, which was the counterattack reported by Colonel Seeger at 1945. Uhlig recalled pushing back the Americans about 320 meters (350 yards) but was disappointed that his men were unable to capture any of the prisoners Major von der Heydte wanted. On the other hand, from the American point of view Uhlig's counterattack was quite different. Two American medics and a wounded soldier who were interviewed later said,

> *The front lines were approximately 150 yards East of town [the village of Sèves near the site of the bridge, not Saint-Germain-sur-Sèves, which was about 2,000 meters east of Sèves] Capt. Moore of Co B was in charge. The enemy put down a terrific artillery barrage and followed it up with an assault of tanks [Uhlig had no tanks with him at this time] and troops on foot. They literally caught our men in their fox holes. The American troops withdrew about 500 yards [457 meters]. The Germans threw hand grenades in house that held our troops. Capt. Moore and Lt. Spyde organized and tied in for the night.*[16]

The Americans "buttoned up," forming a shallow, crescent-shaped line that was about 200 yards deep and 800 to 1,000 yards across in front of the ford. The 1st Battalion formed the bulk of the defensive arc, with Company B and C in line and Company A in reserve, while the elements of the 2d Battalion—mostly the remnants of Company G and possibly a few men from Company F—occupied the left and rear nearer the ford. Seeger set up his Battalion CP close to the front line in the shallow bridgehead. The two battalions, each about 700 strong at the beginning of the operation, after losses—estimated later as 2 officers and 7 enlisted men killed, 10 officers and 180 enlisted men wounded, and 6 enlisted men missing, along with uncounted hundreds of stragglers and the bulk of the 2d Battalion that had not crossed—probably numbered not much more than Uhlig's estimate of 300: perhaps 400 officers and men at most. The extended perimeter was much more lightly manned than it would appear. Worse, the 1st Battalion and Company G were badly disorganized, the morale of their men was shaky, and the command and control exerted by their officers and NCOs was uncertain.[17]

23 JULY

Early on 23 July, at 0140, Major Wallace, the 358th Infantry's G-3, called Colonel Seeger to tell him to expect the tanks to arrive in his area around 0530. Seeger was also told to "take full advantage of any opportunities that might occur," but he was given no definite order to attack. Trucks tried to move forward to resupply the troops on the other side of the river at 0445 but were driven back by artillery and mortar fire. Major Michael Knouf, the 358th Infantry's S-4, crossed the river at about 0830 and initiated a resupply of ammunition and rations by hand, carrying them across the river, with limited success.

At 0900, Colonel Clarkson D. McNary, a West Pointer from the class of 1918, arrived at the 358th Infantry CP from the 90th Infantry Division Headquarters. General Landrum had sent him to assume command of the 358th Infantry, which was a curious thing to do in the middle of a battle. It is difficult to tell for sure, but his arrival was likely a sign of displeasure on the part of Landrum for Clarke's handling of the battle. However, McNary sensibly refused to take over from Clarke in the middle of the operation and did not assume command until 1620.

General Landrum arrived at the 358th Infantry CP at 0907—again belying the notion he always commanded from a basement bunker far in the rear. Five minutes later, Company F was reported crossing into the bridgehead again at the same time another German attack supported by tanks struck the 1st Battalion. Ominously, the 1st Battalion requested more bazookas be sent to them. Clarke ordered the 2d Battalion to get all possible strength across as soon as possible and then went forward with Colonel McNary to the Regimental OP.

At 0930, Colonel Seeger reported the German tanks intended to "push us off the island," which was rather an obvious inference. He requested the fire of two or three artillery batteries in support of the 1st Battalion, but, problematically, the 344th Field Artillery had last had contact with its observers at 2200 on 22 July. It was later noted that 97 percent of the artillery missions fired were unobserved and it is unlikely any more were observed on 23 July. To help combat the tank threat, a bazooka team from the 3d Battalion was ordered to move out and Colonel Clarke also notified the Regimental Antitank Company to get ready to move forward. However, by then it was far too late; no wheeled vehicles or guns were able to get onto the Island on 23 July.

The effect of the near-constant rainfall of the past days was felt early in the morning of 23 July, when the Sèves began to overflow its banks. The weather had been stormy on 20 July, and rain continued to fall intermittently during 21 July and steadily for much of 22 July. By first light on 23 July, it was evident that most of the length of the river was unfordable to vehicles and men. At 0810, Major Howard A. Stotler, the 1st Battalion S-3, reported the river in his area could only be crossed by swimming and where the battalion had crossed the previous day at the ford was now neck deep in water. No tanks had been able to cross onto the Island, and no progress had been made on building a bridge as the prospective bridge site remained under German fire.

The situation on the Island quickly became critical. At 0948, eighteen minutes after his last conversation with Clarke, Seeger called and said he was "getting hit hard and did not know if he could hold out any longer." He asked again for artillery support, but by then it was too late. At 1000 hours, Colonel Clarke called from the OP and said he could see about twenty-five American soldiers on the Island with their hands above their heads. He followed up with a call to General Landrum, telling him that he had seen fifty men surrendering to a single German. Clarke told Landrum that men were still crossing back from the Island and that it appeared to be a complete withdrawal. In turn, General Landrum passed the bad news to VIII Corps, telling General Middleton at 1032 that it was a "terrific counter-attack" and that the men on the Island were surrendering.

Major Ralph L. LaForge, the 1st Battalion Executive Officer, managed to get back across the river at 1045 and took temporary command of the remnants of the 1st Battalion. Some men were being collected by a straggler line formed by the 1st Battalion S-1, Captain Thomas W. Caldecott, using the personnel of the 1st Battalion and 3d Battalion who had not crossed the river. LaForge told Clarke at 1230 that Colonel Seeger was still missing but that they had managed to collect 17 officers and 315 enlisted men of the battalion. Two company commanders and many other officers and men were missing and presumed captured. Major Knouf had also managed to get off the Island as well but was wounded and evacuated.

Lieutenant Dowling of the 687th Field Artillery was the only artillery observer that had managed to get to the Island and had remained there overnight. His radio was smashed, but he continued to fight on and tried to restore telephone communications with the rear without success as lines laid across the river kept breaking or were swept away. He managed to escape the debacle of the morning surrender and made it back across the river to safety. He was awarded a Silver Star for his actions on 23 July. Curiously, the General Order for his citation was from the 8th Infantry Division rather than the 90th Infantry Division, although his battalion was attached to the 90th from 20 to 30 July.[18]

What had happened in the bridgehead that caused such a collapse? The previous night, Oberfeldwebel Uhlig had been stymied. He had attacked the American bridgehead from the south, hitting the 1st Battalion, but made no real gains and had suffered casualties that reduced his command to twenty-eight men. Determined to continue the attack the next day, Uhlig spent the night finding reinforcements. He managed to acquire two MG42 heavy machine guns and crews and about sixteen more riflemen, most of whom were replacements. They brought the strength of his little KG back up to fifty. He next got the support of the platoon of *SS-Das Reich* tanks placed at Major von der Heytde's disposal.[19]

Uhlig decided to place the relatively immobile, but lethal, pair of MG42 in a well-camouflaged and well-protected position in a sunken road east of the bridge site at Sèves. From there they were within about 300 to 400 meters of the ford and could interdict any attempt to reinforce or retreat from the Island. However, to protect the crews from counterfire by exposing them too soon, Uhlig gave them strict orders not to fire before the main assault by his group. His original scheme for the tank support was to create four small assault groups consisting of a NCOs and seven men, each sheltering behind a tank until they got close to the American lines, but the leader of the SS tank platoon refused. The tanker complained the Americans had too many bazookas and insisted Uhlig's men would have to go first. Without a choice, Uhlig agreed. Then, to top that off, one of the tanks broke down before it could join Uhlig's group, leaving him with three. Then, as the three remaining tanks approached Uhlig's position, one accidentally rammed the wall of a farmhouse and got trapped when the roof collapsed onto it, which left him with just two tanks for the attack.

Nevertheless, the intrepid Uhlig carried on with just the two tanks in support. At 0700, they advanced northeast from Sèves toward the American bridgehead and struck the right of the 1st Battalion. This initial attack was repulsed by artillery and fire from the tanks of Company B, 712th Tank Battalion across the river, but neither of the German tanks were hit. Uhlig shifted his group east and attacked again at around 0800 from the southeast toward the track leading from Saint-Germain-sur-Sèves to the ford. Again, they were unsuccessful.[20]

Undeterred, Uhlig attacked a third time at 0912 and managed to penetrate the American line. This was the attack that caused Colonel Seeger so much concern at 0930. Uhlig's attack broke through the American lines and advanced into the area of the 1st Battalion CP. At that point Seeger ordered his men at the CP to cease fire, and they surrendered. Major Knouf was within 30 yards of Seeger but refused to surrender, ordering the men with him to make a break for the ford. At that point Uhlig's two machine guns opened fire, interdicting the withdrawal route and wounding Knouf, who was carried across the ford by his jeep driver. From then on, it was every man for himself. Those who could not bring themselves to chance the machine-gun fire interdicting the path across the ford surrendered.

Uhlig was astonished at the sudden collapse of the American resistance and quickly became concerned. He started by assigning one or two of his man to every group of 20 to 25 American prisoners, but then quickly realized he was running short of men. By Uhlig's calculation, 11 American officers and 200 enlisted men were his prisoners, more than four times the strength of his attack group.

Once the American prisoners were sent to the rear with their escorts, Uhlig reorganized the German main line of resistance with the two machine guns and the 30 or so men he had left. He then returned to Heydte's Gefechtsstand at about 1500 to report his mission accomplished. There he witnessed something almost as extraordinary as his own battlefield victory. Major von der Heydte formally introduced Uhlig to the eleven captured American officers, who were having tea with the Major. While it might seem like a "war story," Major von der Heydte was well known as an old-school, aristocratic officer with a somewhat mischievous sense of humor even in wartime. After defeating the attack by the 83d Infantry Division on the 4th of July, he had returned several captured American medics to the American lines during a truce. He also sent a note with them telling the American commander he thought the Americans were more in need of the medics than he was but that if their position was reversed in the future, he hoped the Americans would extend him the same courtesy.[21]

Meanwhile, Colonel Bealke reported at 1240 that the 3d Battalion had evacuated all the men that had been able to make it to the friendly side of the Sèves. He believed that unless a truce was somehow called with the Germans that none of the wounded still on the opposite bank could be evacuated. Surprisingly, less than two hours later that is exactly what happened. At 1130, Major Falvey, who was at the Regimental Aid Station visiting his friend Major Knouf, overheard two chaplains of the 358th Infantry, Captain Joseph J. Esser, a Catholic, and Captain Edgar H. Stohler, a Protestant, talking about attempting to help the wounded.[22] Falvey later recalled,

> *I remember telling them that it might be all right for them to go out into that bullet-filled area because if they got killed they would surely go to heaven, but me, I could not take a chance like that.*[23]

Sometime before 1430, the two chaplains, with Stohler prominently carrying a large Red Cross flag, led a party of medics and litter bearers down to the river, where they began searching for the wounded. Perhaps surprisingly, the Germans did not shoot at them. When they crossed the Sèves to look for more casualties they were met by a German officer, described by Stohler as a "captain." Captain Stohler, who spoke some German, negotiated with the officer who agreed to contact Major von der Heydte. Heydte, who had held a similar truce with the 83d Infantry Division earlier in July, agreed to a three-hour local ceasefire. During the truce, some wounded Germans in American hands were turned over to the Germans and some American wounded in German hands were turned over to the Americans.[24]

However, it turned out that German fire was not what the two chaplains, the medics, and their litter bearers should have feared. The weather had cleared enough that the IX TAC could finally fly missions in support of the 90th Infantry Division. At 1310, the division notified the 358th Infantry that three bombing and strafing missions were planned for the division front line. They were scheduled for the afternoon, at 1330, 1440, and 1500, during the truce negotiated by Stohler and Esser. Chaplain Stohler later described what happened.

> *At times we were waist deep in mud and water, but we went on until we gained the opposite shore of the Seves River just fifty yards from the German front. We found our first wounded man and strangely enough, as we were talking to him, there came a lull in the German fire and we were able to get him back safely.*
>
> *Then we went on and when we would find a wounded man we would signal to stretcher-bearers who would come across and get him. When we were half through with the job, we heard planes overhead, and suddenly our own fighters dived down and began staffing and bombing. You see, we were so close to the Germans that we were almost in their midst. Esser and I dived into a wet ditch and lay in mud and water. When the planes left we continued our work, but then another bunch of planes came back.*
>
> *This time when we hit the ditch we found a German medic also dodging the plane fire. I speak some German, so we talked and found that he was Catholic but hadn't been*

to church in a long time. Father Esser then gave him his own rosary which he had carried for fifteen years and told me to tell him to learn to pray again.

The firing stopped, the medic disappeared, and we finished our job. In all, we rescued seventy-six wounded men.[25]

The dramatic rescue of the soldiers and selfless bravery of the chaplains, medics, and litter bearers was captured in print by Associated Press War Correspondent Edward D. Ball and by Associated Press sketch artist Howell Dodd of the *Atlanta Journal* newspaper and was reprinted by newspapers across the United States. After the war, the Salvation Army commissioned Leslie Michaelson to paint an allegorical portrait of the event titled *Dawn of a New Hope* that hung for some years in the Pentagon's Office of the Chief of Chaplains, U.S. Army.[26]

It was about 1725 when the stories of the two medics and one wounded man who managed to escape got to Colonel Clarke. They described the events of the morning as follows:

One tank attacked from one direction and two tanks from another direction. Some of the American troops wanted to surrender. Others told them they would shoot them if they did! A rumor started that we would withdraw to the creek. Some men did. At 1000 this morning Lt. Col. Seeger, who was surrounded, issued the order to "cease firing." Major Knouf then ordered about 50 men to infiltrate back across the stream. He was hit in an attempt to make an escape back from the island. An aid man pulled him back to the North side of the creek, but due to the persistent MG fire [Uhlig's two heavy MG 42] was unable to evacuate him. Major Knouf was only 30 yards from Lt. Col. Seeger when he surrendered. Co F was with the 1st Bn.

The full extent of the disaster was only realized late that evening as the 358th Infantry S-3, Major Wallace, tallied up the loss reports. One officer and 68 enlisted men had been killed, 5 officers and 99 enlisted men were wounded, and 11 officers and 254 enlisted men were missing. With the 205 lost the previous day, the regiment had lost 643 officers and enlisted men, about 20 percent of its effective strength. Chaplain Stohler reported at 1822 that the "German Officer stated he had captured 200 of our men, 11 officers (one a Lt. Col.)." Postwar, Major von der Heydte claimed that his men captured "more than three hundred prisoners, among them thirteen officers including a battalion commander" and ended with "more than five hundred prisoners, including wounded." Both figures were incorrect and exaggerated. Captain Esser and Captain Stohler were both awarded the Silver Star for their actions on 23 July.[27]

One of Howell Dodd's sketches "in no man's land" of the chaplains evacuating the wounded on 23 July 1944.

24 JULY

The next day was spent reorganizing the shattered 358th Infantry and assessing the causes of the failure. No enlisted replacements and only a single officer replacement were recorded joining the 358th Infantry on 23 July. However, in fact two officers joined the 358th, Colonel McNary and Major Cleveland A. Lytle. Lytle arrived at 2325 on 23 July but was not entered in the MR until 4 August.

Major Lytle joined the 90th Infantry Division while under something of a cloud with regard to his war record. An elementary school principal, Cleveland "Cleve" Lytle was a South Carolina NG officer who entered service when his unit, Company K, 118th Infantry, was federalized in September 1940. On the eve of D-Day, Lytle was appointed Executive Officer of the 2d Ranger Infantry Battalion on 26 March 1944 when the former Executive, Major Max Schneider, left to take command of the 5th Ranger Infantry Battalion. Shortly before D-Day Lytle was promoted to major.

As a Ranger, Lytle was a highly respected, spit-and-polish officer, who was a hard-charger on duty and was well liked by his fellow officers and the men under his

Presentation by Brigadier General James A. Van Fleet of the Silver Star Medal to Captain (Chaplain) Edgar H. Stohler. It is likely this was taken between 15 October and 15 November 1944 at the presentation of Stohler's second award of the Silver Star Medal. U.S. Army SC.

command. Unfortunately, he was also a heavy drinker. When the 2d Rangers were organizing and training at Camp Forrest, Tennessee, in late 1943, one of his Platoon Leaders would stay sober and drive Lytle and a British Commando officer who was attached to the battalion to the bars in Tullahoma. Prior to D-Day in England, Lytle was given command of Force A, composed of three companies of the 2d Rangers, which were tasked to storm the cliffs at Pointe du Hoe to disable the German coast artillery battery there. However, on the eve of the invasion, 5 June 1944, Lytle and the other officers of Force A were on their transport, the British assault ship *Ben My Chree* celebrating the promotion of another officer. Unfortunately for Lytle, British Navy ships, unlike American, were not "dry." Lytle was drinking—some accounts claim he drank more than a quart of gin or whiskey—and suddenly became belligerent. He had discovered that the last intelligence estimate doubted the German guns were there and he began to loudly question the sense and utility of the operation, declaring it a suicide mission. When some officers tried to hustle him out of the compartment he lashed out and struck the Battalion Surgeon, Captain Walter

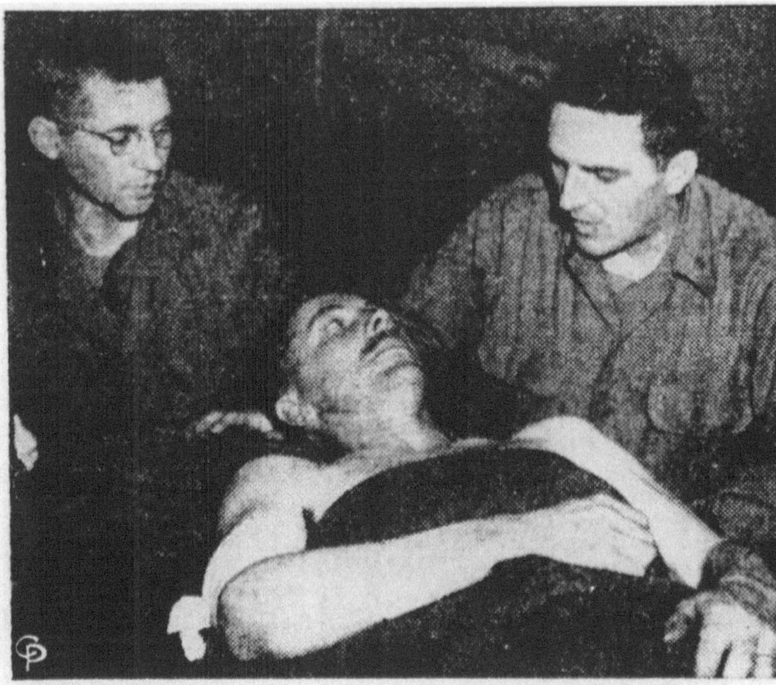

RISKING THEIR LIVES to evacuate wounded soldiers from a No-Man's-Land on the Seves River front in Normandy, American chaplains headed a stretcher bearer unit, entered into a four-hour truce agreement with the Germans, and worked tirelessly between the battle lines. Two of these "heroes of the cloth", shown above, are Capt. Joseph Esser (left), Cleveland, Minn., and Chaplain Edgar Stohler, Ipava, Ill., attending Sgt. Frederick Peterson, Paynesville, Minn. *(International)*

Captain (Chaplain) Esser, left, and Captain (Chaplain) Stohler, right, minister to Sergeant Frederick Peterson. U.S. Army SC.

Block, with his fist. Colonel Rudder relieved Lytle of duty and took over command of Force A himself. Except for his drunken lapse in judgment, Lytle would have been the hero of Pointe du Hoe rather than Rudder.[28]

Lytle was relieved from duty and assignment to the 2d Ranger Battalion and reassigned to the 10th Replacement Depot on 7 June 1944. It is unclear when he was assigned to the 90th Infantry Division or what he was doing between 7 June and 23 July 1944. It is also unclear what if anything other than rumors that Landrum, McNary, or Clarke knew of his background. When McNary and Clarke reshuffled officer assignments to fill the holes in the battalion command created by the capture of Seeger and the other officers, they decided to make the 2d Battalion Executive Officer, Major Schulz, the Battalion Commanding Officer and gave him Lytle as his Executive Officer. Colonel Loomis moved to take command of the 1st Battalion in Seeger's place, with Major Ralph L. La Forge as Executive Officer. The 3d Battalion remained unchanged, with Colonel Bealke as commander and Major Oehlesen as Executive Officer.[29]

However, it would be some time before the two shattered battalions would be fully combat effective. The men who escaped from the Island and those collected by the straggler line were withdrawn on the evening of 23 July to the vicinity of Gonfreville where they waited the arrival of replacements. Those were slow in coming though. By the end of the month just 4 officers and 90 enlisted men were assigned to the regiment, bringing its effective strength up to just 121 officers and 2,421 enlisted men, almost exactly three-quarters of its 3,360-man T/O&E strength.

General Landrum quickly tried to explain the reasons for the failure of the attack to his superiors. Although this passage was inserted into the Division After-Action Report for 23 July, it was likely written a few days later. Reading between the lines, it appears the explanation was in response to questions raised by higher headquarters, most like General Middleton, but also possibly General Bradley.

> *The battle of the "ISLAND" had been a costly failure, shattering as it had 2 battalions of infantry. In the case of higher headquarters the Division setback was inexplicable but in vindication of the officers and men who had fought, bled and died in a heroic attempt to make the attack a success it must be stated that a curious series of cumulative circumstances had combined to deny success.*
>
> (1) *Except in the narrow zone of the attack, the entire Army front was inactive and the Boche was able to give undivided attention to this sole threat to the integrity of his front. While its infantry strength could not be diverted to the extent of opposing us with numerical superiority, all artillery within range could be and was directed at us.*
>
> (2) *During both days of the attack weather conditions deprived us of air support and, of more immediate concern, prevented the use of artillery liaison planes to find and adjust on counterbattery targets.*
>
> (3) *The success of the attack was contingent upon the element of surprise to the extent of rushing the open ground N of the "ISLAND" before the Boche could react to the sudden pressure. However, the infantry was not at the LD at the prescribed hour and the preparation fires were not followed up. The enemy emerging from cover after the completion of the preparation and not finding*

himself attacked at close quarters was alerted to and ready for the attack when finally launched.

(4) *Although Regt entered the battle at full strength, well over 50% of its Bn strengths were replacements for whom this was their first fight. Caught at the LD by heavy enemy fire, and unable to fight back effectively, they could not be expected to react like seasoned veterans. The instinct for self-preservation outweighed obedience to orders and posed insurmountable obstacles to rapid reorganization.*

(5) *The inability to cross supporting weapons to effectively engage enemy tanks had a definite psychological reaction on the infantry me up front.*

Landrum's "explanation" raises as many questions as it answers.

(1) Why if it was known the attack of the 358th Infantry would be the sole regimental-sized attack of the day was the attack even attempted? No effort was made to distract the attention of the Germans to any other section of the line; no diversionary or feint attacks were made by other 90th Infantry Division or adjacent units.

(2) In World War II, the strength and professionalism of the American Field Artillery was often a decisive factor in battle. The support given to the 358th Infantry attack was reasonable; ten battalions were available for the preparation and as many as eight thereafter. That is commensurate with the support given to the VII Corps in Operation COBRA, where the three divisions attacking were supported by as many as thirty-six battalions. The difference was observation—the artillery support in COBRA was primarily observed fire from aerial and forward observers in communication with the Fire Direction Centers; on the Island more than 90 percent of the fire was unobserved and communications to the rear was almost nonexistent.

That raises the question of why the attempt was made when the weather was known to be poor. The next day, 24 July, was the scheduled time for Operation COBRA, but it was delayed to 25 July because the poor weather interfered with the execution of the massive air bombardment and artillery plan. In that case the artillery was to fire extensively on known and suspect flak locations to facilitate the bombing, before switching over to a conventional artillery support program. If a massive operation like COBRA could be delayed, then why not do the same with the relatively minor operation by the 90th Infantry Division?

(3) There is no evidence that the infantry was late to the line-of-departure for the attack. There is no mention of such a problem in the 358th Infantry's

After-Action Report. Instead the problem appears to have been where the line-of-departure was and when the attack was executed. The line-of-departure was about 100 yards from the riverbank. In average circumstances, infantry was expected to march cross-country at a pace of about 1.5 miles per hour. With 100 yards to cover, that meant that in good circumstances it would take two minutes for the leading elements to reach the river. Given that nautical twilight on 22 July began at 0540 and sunrise was at 0619, even with the overcast it was daylight at H-Hour of 0630, which meant the troops were fully exposed in the nearly barren meadowland when they jumped off. The best evidence is that most of the artillery preparation did not strike the German front lines, so there was nothing inducing the Germans to shelter deep in their fighting holes. The reports indicate that the leading American elements advanced about 50 yards, so for about one minute, before the German fire became so severe that they ceased to advance and went to ground.

(4) Given that about half of the troops were replacements and unfamiliar with their units and leaders, it is unsurprising that they went to ground 50 yards before they reached the river. However, because that was a known factor, what is surprising is that so little effort was made to overcome that obstacle. Clarke's original concept was for a night attack, which in general were anathema to American planners at the time, due to what they perceived as the problems with controlling units and observing supporting artillery fires. In this case, though, given the greenness of the troops and the lack of means to conduct observed artillery fire, which was known in advance, it must be asked why a night attack was not attempted anyway. Although the evidence is not clear for who ordered it, the change from an attack by a column of battalions to one of two battalions abreast is another indication that Clarke's hands may have been tied when it came to the tactics employed. It is possible that it was Landrum who ordered the change, given his alleged tendency to micromanage his units.

(5) The inability to get tanks into close support of the infantry after the division had been in combat for six weeks is inexplicable. The ford was considered passable by the engineers, but little effort was expended to get the tanks across the river and onto the Island to provide direct support for the Infantry. Worse, two companies of medium tanks and one of light tanks were completely unused. One company sat in the rear and was wasted firing as artillery, when there was plenty of artillery to be had. Another company sat in the rear and conducted routine vehicle maintenance. The failure to use the tanks in mass in support of the infantry was possibly the single major failing of the division.

It is difficult not to infer that the attack by the 358th Infantry was carried out partly because General Landrum felt that he needed to show his leadership of the division was sound after its performance at Mont Castré and the dismissal of General Williams. Unfortunately, any leadership qualities Landrum displayed on the Island by spending time at Clarke's CP were overshadowed by the inept tactics he employed. Like too may operations in Normandy, the attack was a simple, straightforward and unimaginative frontal attack, over unfavorable terrain, in unfavorable weather conditions, with an ill-prepared unit.

Within a few days of the failed attack by the 358th Infantry, the Germans were forced to withdraw from the Island when their right flank was unhinged by the success of Operation COBRA. So why did Landrum, Middleton, and Bradley feel the attack by the 358th Infantry was necessary? None of these questions can be answered other than by inference, but it seems certain the attack by the 358th Infantry was an unnecessary and reckless waste of manpower.

25 JULY

Operation COBRA began at 1100 on 25 July, following a tremendous bombardment by heavy, medium, and light bombers. Initially, going was slow, due both to German resistance and to the heavily cratered roads and fields that slowed progress. Later that evening Bradley ordered the offensive expanded, directing General Middleton to attack the next day. Middleton set H-Hour for the VIII Corps as 0530 on 26 July.

For the 90th Infantry Division the day was spent gawking at the spectacle of the Allied air assault to the east. The 358th Infantry received a paltry fifteen men as replacements for the heavy losses it had suffered.

The disaster on the Island did result in a revision to the plan of attack by the 90th Infantry Division when the VIII Corps joined in the attack with the VII Corps. The 359th Infantry's orders remained essentially unchanged. They were directed to drive south toward Périers along the division right boundary. The battered 358th Infantry would extend to the left and with the 90th Reconnaissance Troop would relieve the 357th Infantry and would contain the Island. The 357th Infantry would attack southwest along the Carentan-Périers Road, cutting off the Island and contacting the 359th Infantry north of Périers. When that maneuver concluded, the 358th Infantry would mop up the Island. H-Hour for the attack by the VIII Corps was set at 0530 on 26 July.

26 JULY

The 357th Infantry attacked as ordered on the division left, adjacent to the 83d Infantry Division's 329th Infantry, which attacked south from Sainteny toward Saint-Sébastien-de-Raids. Unfortunately for the 357th, the 4th Armored Division was also deployed in the area along with the 83d, prepared to exploit any advantage gained. Units of the two divisions were tightly stacked up in the narrow peninsula of dry land extending on either side of the Carentan-Périers road, which simply left no room for the 357th to deploy, other than on an even narrower spit of dry land running north to south just east of Nay. The 357th Infantry was thus only able to attack on a single company front and met heavy resistance immediately after jumping off. The 329th Infantry to their left also made little progress as the German unleashed a storm of mortar and artillery fire. By noon it was obvious the attack was stalled. Plans were made to slip the 329th Infantry east, allowing the entire 2d Battalion, 357th Infantry to get into line for a new attack at 1900. However, repositioning the two regiments under fire took so much time that the renewal of the attack was delayed until the morning of 27 July.

The experience of the 359th Infantry was similar to but not as disastrous as that of the 358th Infantry four days earlier. Colonel Bacon elected to attack in a column of battalions as Colonel Clarke had originally planned. The attack jumped off as scheduled at 0530, with the 2d Battalion leading the assault in a column of companies and the 3d Battalion ready to follow. The 1st Battalion extended the line of the regiment west about 1,000 yards to the boundary with the 8th Infantry Division.

Unlike the previous attempt, Company G crossed the river at 0620 without coming under fire and quickly overran the first German line of entrenchments about 100 yards south of the riverbank. However, when they tried to advance farther, they were stopped by machine-gun and mortar fire. Company F came up on the left and attempted to get the advance going again, but at 0900 a counterattack supported by tanks and artillery fire struck between the two companies and forced them back to the captured German entrenchments. They managed to hold on there, but German fire kept the engineers from moving up and preparing a fording site for tanks and other vehicles.

The German tanks settled into concealed, defiladed positions on either flank of the 2d Battalion bridgehead and continued to harass the infantry and engineers throughout the rest of the day. The Fallschirmjäger attempted counterattacks at 1200 and 1300, but both were repulsed. Company E crossed into the bridgehead at 1430 and filled in the gap between the two companies then helped repulse yet another attack at 1500 that ended with a close-range exchange of hand grenades before the Germans fell back. However, the Germans kept hammering at the American line, attacking again at 1600. German infantry supported by two tanks hit the left and infantry supported by three tanks hit the right of the American line at 1600 and again at 1800, but still without success. The 2d Battalion claimed five German tanks were knocked out: three by its bazookas and two by artillery fire. At 2115, the 3d Battalion was ordered to relieve the 2d Battalion, which had suffered heavy casualties in the bridgehead, while the 1st Battalion sent patrols across the river in its zone to try to discover if the Germans were withdrawing.

One officer distinguished himself during the second battle on the Island and received the Silver Star:

> *The President of the United States of America, authorized by Act of Congress, July 9, 1918, takes pleasure in presenting the Silver Star to Captain (Infantry) Hobby H. McCall (ASN: 0-422737), United States Army, for gallantry in action while serving with Headquarters, 2d Battalion, 359th Infantry Regiment, 90th Infantry Division, on 26 July 1944, near Gonfreville, France. On that date, a company in Captain McCall's Battalion suffered exceptionally heavy casualties when crossing the Sèves River. All of the officers of the company with the exception of a second lieutenant became casualties. Captain McCall, S-3 of the Battalion, was sent forward to assume command of the company, reorganize it and continue the attack. Without regard for his own safety and while still under heavy enemy artillery, mortar fire and fire from tanks, he joined the company and went about, personally exposing himself to fire, regrouping the men and encouraging them in the attack. After reorganizing the unit he placed himself at the head of the company and led it in an assault which finally gained the objective although nearly 50% of the effective strength of the company had become casualties in the effort. Captain McCall was wounded in the action and later evacuated but not until the company had reached its objective. This gallant action was a fine example of outstanding courage and devotion to duty and was a fine example of the best traditions of the military spirit.*[30]

Surprisingly, the reaction of the Germans west of the VII Corps attack was initially nonchalant. When Major von der Heydte queried *SS-Das Reich* about its effect, the reply was reassuring, "the forces in the forward line had been struck only lightly." However, on the afternoon of 26 July, Major von der Heydte received much more disturbing news:

> *The Americans have effected a breakthrough in the sectors of the [5. Fallschirmjäger] and the Panzer Lehr Division. The front has collapsed in these sectors. American*

tanks have crossed the Périers-Saint-Lô road and, advancing via Marigny, are approaching the Saint-Lô-Coutances road. The [SS-Das Reich] will accordingly fall back this very night [the night of 26/27 July] to a reconnoitered position south of Périers, near St. Sauveur-Lendelin. [Fallschirmjäger-Regiment 6.] will be committed at the northern edge and west of St. Sauveur-Lendelin, with its greatest strength along the Périers-Coutances road.[31]

27 JULY

On the night of 26/27 July, Heydte ordered Uhlig to take the *16. Kompanie*, which had received enough replacements to bring it up to a strength of about 100 men, and cover the withdrawal of the regiment from the Island. Uhlig did so, feigning a strong front in the early morning of 27 July and preventing American patrols from detecting the extent of the overnight withdrawal. However, by 0540 on 27 July, it was evident to the Americans that the Germans were in fact pulling out as the threat of envelopment by the successful VII Corps attack to the east threatened their right flank and rear.

On the 90th Infantry Division right, about 1,000 yards east of the Périers-Coutances Road, the 3d Battalion, 359th Infantry passed through the 2d Battalion at 0900 and advanced due south. The 1st Battalion followed before swinging east to Gruchy and coming abreast of the 3d Battalion. Both met resistance from a German detachment—probably Uhlig's—blocking the approaches to the Périers-Coutances Road from the east later that evening and halted for the night. The 2d Battalion followed later at 1600 and occupied Périers—the ultimate objective assigned to the division nearly a month earlier.

On the division left, the 357th Infantry completely failed to discover the German withdrawal and jumped off as planned at 0900—"into thin air." The 2d Battalion advance was only delayed by scattered mines. It was followed by the 1st Battalion, which came up on its right rear, and the 3d Battalion, which did the same to its left rear. The 357th reached its objective, the Périers-Carentan Road 2 kilometers southwest of raids before noon. It then turned south on division orders to cross the Taute River and seize the high ground south of Saint-Sébastien-de-Raids. The 2d Battalion crossed the Taute at La Fossairie and then advanced south toward the Périers-Saint-Lo Road, where it overwhelmed a small blocking force. The 3d Battalion completed crossing the river and closed up with the 2d Battalion by dark, while the 1st Battalion waited to cross the river at first light.

The battered 358th Infantry spent the day searching the Island for German stragglers with the 2d and 3d Battalions but only found numerous mines. Two routes across the Island were cleared by 2000 and the regiment moved south to an assembly area near Gruchy.

28 JULY

The rapidly accelerating American advance continued on 28 July. The 90th Infantry Division headed south with all elements east of the Périers-Coutances Road, which had been allocated to the 4th and 6th Armored Divisions. The two armored divisions were followed by the 8th and 79th Infantry Division, while later that day the 90th and 83d Division were ordered to maintain their positions and await further orders. The 90th Infantry Division settled into an assembly area with the 357th Infantry in the vicinity of Saint-Sauveur-Lendelin, the 358th Infantry at L'hôtel Cathelinais, and the 359th Infantry in the vicinity of La Houssaye. Contact was established with elements of the 1st Infantry Division to the east, but for the first time in fifty-three days there was no reported contact with German units on the ground—the only Germans encountered were stragglers, who quickly surrendered.

However, Battery A and the rest of the 537th AAA did not have the luxury of being out of contact with the Luftwaffe. On 28 July, after the division had settled into its assembly area, an "ME 109" dropped bombs in the Battery A area and got away. The next evening at 1910, a single FW 190 attacked Battery A from the north and did not get away. One of Dad's M16Bs and at least one 40mm gun were observed obtaining multiple hits. The German plane crashed about 2,500 meters east of its position at La Sellerie, which was east of Saint-Sauveur-Lendelin. The German pilot parachuted to safety and was captured. A little later, just fifteen minutes before midnight on 29 July, another "ME 109" attacked Battery A, which again obtained hits on the plane, but this time the German got away.

A significant change in the command arrangements of the U.S. Army in Normandy also occurred on 28 July. As the COBRA breakthrough began developing into a breakout, General Bradley asked George Patton, who was waiting for his TUSA Headquarters to become operational as scheduled at 1200 on 1 August, to take over supervision of the VIII Corps on the right of the breakthrough. That evening, Patton changed the planned execution of Bradley's orders for the exploitation phase of COBRA, assigning the attack to the 4th and 6th Armored Division instead of to the 79th and 90th Infantry Division.[32]

Perhaps fittingly, one of the seventy-two German prisoners captured by the 90th Infantry Division sometime during 28–30 July 1944 was Oberfeldwebel Alexander Uhlig. After executing Heydte's order to delay the American advance to the best of his ability, Uhlig tried to rejoin the regiment near Saint-Sauveur-Lendelin, but *16.*

Kompanie got split up trying to avoid the onrushing 4th Armored Division. Uhlig was captured by the 357th Infantry, near Saint-Michel-de-la-Pierre. He was sent to the VIII Corps cage at Périers, then evacuated across UTAH Beach to England where he was sent to the Le Marchant Prisoner-of-War Transit Camp in Devizes, Wiltshire, as one of its first inmates. After interrogation, he was sent to Liverpool and then by ship to New York and finally Camp Clark in Missouri. On 29 October 1944, he was awarded the Ritterkreuz (Knight's Cross). After the war, Uhlig was returned to England, still a prisoner, but managed to escape on the night of 22/23 April 1947 and made his way home to Leipzig. He died 1 November 2008 in Essen, Germany, at the age of eighty-eight.[33]

****

From Le Haye-du-Puits we turned south again and then from Lessay went east to Périers. The rain still came down, incessantly. It took just seventeen minutes to make the drive to Périers, which took the 90th Infantry Division a week to accomplish, including the debacle on the Island. Because of the rain we decided not to stop at the Island and instead pressed on. From Périers, the drive to Saint-Sauveur-Lendelin took us about eight minutes. In 1944, it took the 90th two days to cover those 4 miles against weakening German opposition.

CHAPTER 9

PROBLEM DIVISION?

FOLLOWING THE DEBACLE ON THE ISLAND, GENERAL BRADLEY'S STAFF ADVISED him to break up the 90th Infantry Division and cannibalize its manpower for urgently needed replacements. They believed the division was combat ineffective and past rehabilitation. Bradley later claimed he still continued to believe the division could be turned around with the right commanders, but it may have been Patton and Middleton who got the relief of Landrum moving. Patton noted in his diary entry of 23 July,

> *A Bn. of the 90th Div ran today. I talked to Middleton and we are going to relieve Gen [blank—Patton probably did not recall Landrum's name when he wrote the entry] and put in McClain and Weaver and I hope it do [sic] some good it is a very bad div.*[1]

On 25 July, Bradley met with Brigadier General McLain, the 30th Division Artillery Commander. Bradley confided his concerns with the performance of the 90th to McLain and assigned him to the position of Assistant Division Commander, which had been vacant since General Williams was relieved nine days earlier. The initial task Bradley gave McLain was to do a thorough survey of the division's condition, talking to whomever he wanted, before reporting back to Bradley whether he believed the division could be made effective again.

According to Bradley, McLain asked him, "can you help me get rid of those officers I may not want and give me replacements?" Bradley replied, "Anything you want, Ray, Go down there and look around for 48 hours. Then come back to me with a list and we'll get rid of every man on it."[2]

McLain was one of those unique general officers of the U.S. Army in World War II who, just like MacKelvie and Landrum, originally entered the Army as an enlisted man. However, there the resemblance ended. MacKelvie and Landrum were both RA officers, but McLain was a Guard officer.

Raymond McLain was born on 4 April 1890 in Kentucky. The family was poor and after his father died in 1903, Raymond was forced to leave school and find work. Four years later, he moved to Oklahoma City to work as a bookkeeper at a real estate office. By 1911, he opened his own title business and in 1912 enlisted in the Oklahoma NG. He was commissioned as an Infantry officer in 1914 and entered federal service when the Guard was mobilized to defend the southern border from incursions by Mexican rebels after Pancho Villa's attack on Columbus, New Mexico, in 1916. When the NG was federalized for the Great War, McLain went with the 36th Division to France in July 1918 where he saw service commanding a Machine Gun Company.[3] He remained in the Guard after the war and by 1937 was a brigadier general commanding the 70th Field Artillery Brigade of the 45th Division. When his brigade was federalized on 16 September 1940, McLain went to Fort Sill for field training, where a friend of McLain's recalled that one night after seeing lights in McLain's tent, he went in to find him studying various field manuals. When asked why he did not get some sleep after the long day. McLain replied, "I've got some smart young men in this brigade, and I have to stay ahead of them."[4]

However, McLain's career was nearly stillborn following the Louisiana Maneuvers of September 1941. The Commanding General of the VIII Corps, of which the 45th Division was a part, Major General George V. Strong, gave McLain an indifferent performance review, which was passed to General Marshall by the G-1 of the War Department General Staff, Brigadier General Wade Haislip. McLain was rated "satisfactory," which indicated average at best, but it was the statement that Strong believed McLain had "neither the physical stamina nor the reserve necessary for extended field service" that was most damning. Worse, his own 45th Division commander, Major General William S. Key, who he had been serving with for four years, rated McLain "excellent" but then said he could "not recommend [him] for duty in the event of war."[5]

In the second phase of the maneuvers, McLain took command of the 86th Infantry Brigade when its commander fell ill and performed brilliantly, attracting favorable commentary from Lieutenant General Walter Krueger, then commander of TUSA. It may have helped too that Lieutenant General Lesley J. McNair, Marshall's Chief of Staff during the maneuvers, damned General Key with faint praise as "forceful, impressive, and that's about all. Dubious for the long pull." In the end, Key was replaced by Major General Troy Middleton in October 1942, and

McLain went with him and the 45th Infantry Division to Sicily and Italy. Ironically, neither Strong nor Key served in combat in the war.[6]

In Sicily, McLain's quiet competence impressed George Patton, who commanded the Seventh U.S. Army. McLain was awarded the Distinguished Service Cross for his handling of the 45th Division Artillery. Later, in February 1944 at Anzio, his command of the 45th Division Artillery played a decisive role in stopping the major German counteroffensive known as FISCHFANG, which threatened to overwhelm the Allied beachhead.

General Eisenhower cabled General Marshall on 27 March 1944 to specifically request McLain be transferred to the ETOUSA as an "extra candidate to insure [*sic*] against eventualities"—if the "Army commanders recommend the relief of any division commanders." By 10 May, McLain was in England and had assumed command of the 30th Division Artillery.[7]

Formal portrait photo of Raymond McLain as an Oklahoma National Guard Brigadier General, circa 1937. U.S. Army NG.

General McLain landed on OMAHA Beach on 10 June 1944 with his 30th Division Artillery Headquarters. On the run into the beach an explosion caused McLain's landing craft to lurch sharply, throwing him against the hull. When they reached shore, he was in great pain but refused treatment for three days as there was so much that needed to be done. When he finally went to the aid station, he found out he had broken three ribs. He ordered the medic to "tape 'em up, I've got things to do."[8]

Earlier in July, when General Bradley was contemplating replacing McMahon of the 8th Infantry Division and Landrum of the 90th Infantry Division, he went over the possibilities with George Patton, who was then in France waiting for the activation of his TUSA. During the discussion Bradley asked Patton who he should select for the 90th. Patton's laconic reply was "McLain." At the end of the discussion, Bradley, apparently dissatisfied with Patton's earlier reply, repeated, "George, you haven't commented on any of these officers. This division is going to belong to you: you had better speak up." An impatient Patton responded, "hell, damn it, I told you McLain and that is what I meant."[9]

On 27 July, General Bradley appointed General McLain Assistant Division Commander of the 90th Infantry Division, eleven days after General Williams was relieved. As early as 1335 on 27 July, General McLain was at the 358th Infantry CP where he was appraised of the situation on the Island. Over the next two days McLain visited every unit in the division.

29 JULY

On 29 July, General Middleton wrote to Bradley recommending the relief without prejudice of Landrum. Middleton told Bradley.

> *The Ninetieth Division has given me much concern. I have, therefore, watched it closely in order that I might determine the basic reasons for its failure to perform up to standard.*[10]

The decision Bradley had deferred two weeks earlier with the death of General Roosevelt was upon them again.

30 JULY

General McLain completed his assessment of the 90th Infantry Division and its unit commanders and returned to Bradley's HQ. He handed Bradley a list of sixteen officers and told him, "If you can help me get rid of these people we can make the 90th a going unit." Bradley passed the names to his FUSA G-1, Colonel Joseph J. O'Hare, and told him to give McLain the officers he asked for as replacements. Then

Bradley told McLain he was making him division commander. At 1130 on 30 July, McLain took command of the 90th Infantry Division.[11]

Curiously, it is unknown who the sixteen officers listed by McLain were. None of the senior General Staff officers or the regimental and battalion commanders in the 90th Infantry Division were replaced at this time. The sixteen were likely regimental and battalion staff officers and deputy assistant chiefs of staff at Division HQ. There are mention in the regimental and battalion MR of several officer transfers within the 90th, as well out of the division to FUSA and 12th Army Group in August, but it is unclear if any of them were numbered among these sixteen.[12]

Even more curious is that one senior officer evidently left out of the loop on General Bradley's decision was General Eisenhower. Although both Eisenhower and Bradley later implied that they had worked closely together on the decision to replace Landrum, there is actually little evidence for that. It was not until 2 August that Eisenhower dispatched a cable to General Marshall requesting the assignment of a new commander for the 90th. In the cable, Eisenhower said that it was Generals Bradley and Middleton who believed they needed a commander for the 90th Infantry Division "of more color and one who had not been associated with any of the unpleasant experiences of the division." Of course, by then, General McLain had already taken over the division.[13]

One other replacement officer arrived at the division on 31 July 1944. He was the second officer mentioned by Patton in his diary entry on 23 July, Brigadier General William Gaulbert Weaver. Weaver was assigned to take McLain's place as Assistant Division Commander.

Weaver, unlike Generals MacKelvie, Landrum, McLain, and Williams, was a West Pointer, class of 1912. He was also a veteran of the Great War in France, where he was awarded the Distinguished Service Cross and the Purple Heart Medal and received the apt nickname of "Wild Bill" because of his combative nature. However, in July 1944, Weaver was not in a combat assignment; instead he was working as a logistician, with the title of Field Deputy Commander of the Services of Supply, ETOUSA.

When Bradley began looking for an officer to serve as a replacement Assistant Division Commander for the 90th Infantry Division, General Middleton recommended Weaver and McLain seconded the request. Both had known Weaver in the Great War and knew he was a fighter. Wild Bill was given a farewell party on 26 July at the Services of Supply, ETOUSA Headquarters and the next day was on his way to France. On the morning of 31 July, he reported to General McLain at the 90th Infantry Division Headquarters at the Chateau du Perron near

William G. Weaver as a colonel while commanding the 38th Infantry in 1942—he is wearing the Fourragère aux couleurs de la Croix de guerre, which is the braided cord worn on his left shoulder to signify he was a member of the unit awarded the Croix de guerre during World War I. U.S. Army SC.

Saint-Sauveuer-Lendelin. Ironically, Weaver's replacement as the ETOUSA Field Deputy Commander was Brigadier General Jay MacKelvie.[14]

In Generals McLain and Weaver, the 90th Infantry Division finally got a combination of commanders who could command, inspire, and lead the division in battle.

McLain's experience as a citizen soldier working with other citizen soldiers of the NG in peace and war, combined with his frontline battle experience in both the World War I and World War II, well prepared him to rehabilitate the 90th Infantry Division. Unlike the remote MacKelvie or the blustery Landrum, he was calm and methodical in dealing with problems, evaluating the strengths and weaknesses of his officers and men and inspiring them to win. The history of one of his 30th Infantry Division Artillery units captured his qualities well:

Other generals inspected the Battalion in training. General McLain, commanding general of the 30th Division Artillery, informally spoke to us, and answered questions. His quiet humor and common sense did much to steady us, then and later in combat.[15]

Although he appeared somewhat mild-mannered and affable, General McLain was also a fighting man, as he had proven in World War I and would demonstrate again in World War II. On at least three different occasions during the war, when McLain moved with his Advanced Headquarters toward the front they ran into bypassed German troops or roadblocks and had to fight their way out. McLain would routinely man the jeep-mounted machine gun and on two occasions personally captured a dozen German soldiers.[16]

Weaver was closer to Hanging Sam Williams in personality. Despite his age—he was five years older than Bradley, two years older than Eisenhower and McLain, and a year older than Middleton—Weaver was an energetic, youthful officer. Later in the war, after the capture of Fort de Koenigsmacker near Metz on 12 November 1944, when General Weaver introduced his new aide, Captain Van R. Mayhall, to General Patton, Patton's sole remark was "Mayhall, you got your Goddam work cut out for you." As Mayhall wrote years later in his memoir,

I only knew General Weaver at that time as a fighting general, a good boss, and a very considerate man to be around. It was later that I began to understand what General Patton might have been talking about. General Weaver didn't like to stay still. He hated the Germans from the first World War. He liked to wander around where the action was going on. He liked to see how the soldiers were making out. On the personal side, he liked to drink not a little bit but a whole lot.[17]

During the period from 29 to 31 July, while the 90th Division's leadership was shuffled, its units rested in the areas they had secured on 28 July. Reorganization, rehabilitation, and training, overseen by McLain and Weaver, were the order of the day. Notably, during this period of rest, General McLain ordered the unit kitchens brought forward, and by 0900 on 29 July, they were with their respective companies serving hot meals.

The experience of the 358th Infantry during this period was probably typical and was the best documented. Hot meals were ready that evening and hot breakfasts and dinners were served on 30 and 31 July. Also, during the evening of 29 July, officers were redistributed within and between units of the regiment. The Regimental Field Train with the personal baggage of the officers and men was ordered to join the

358th south of the Saint-Lô-Périers Road by 0700 on 30 July. On 30 July, at 1200, Colonel McNary returned from a conference of the regimental commanders with the new division commander, and reported,

> *The General does not want any officers reclassified* [polite Army language for demoted]*—he wants them to be given a specific job. The General had changed the award board and wanted recommendations in immediately. Short, fast road marches were to be the thing in the future. (For physical hardening, Col. McNary suggested that it be done over hedge-rows, with short rushes.) Bn Comdrs were urged to perfect their men in regards to their individual weapons. The General directed that artillery be used more. He stated we seldom use artillery during a counter-attack by the enemy. The General added "When I was ordered to the 90th Inf Div, I was told that there was a lack of alertness in REGIMENTS and DIVISION."*

Colonel McNary added,

> *Men should dig deeper foxholes and not under trees* [where artillery and mortar rounds bursting in the treetops could cause serious casualties below them]. *"B" Rations* [the B Ration was prepared by trained cooks and had greater variety than the "C" Rations carried and prepared by the individual solder] *for an indefinite period. Men be given their blanket rolls so they could get a change of clothing. That a reconnaissance be made for a swimming hole or a bathing spot of some sort.*

During the day of 30 July, all troops were instructed in and practiced firing the bazooka. General Weaver arrived at 1430 and inspected the 2d Battalion. He also arranged to bring up a Quartermaster shower unit so all the officers and men could get clean. Fresh uniforms were issued, and a bathing schedule was set up, which was carried out. On 31 July, the day was spent cleaning up personnel and equipment and orienting replacements on the arms and mission of the regiment. General Weaver was at the Regimental CP again by 1030 to confer with McNary and Clarke. That evening, all regimental commanders were called again to meet McLain at Division Headquarters to discuss plans for the next operation.

31 JULY

Although the number of officers and men arriving as replacements were small, only about 106 for the 357th and 358th Infantry—the 359th did not track replacements daily—it was finally possible for the units to fit them in with some attention paid to unit cohesion rather than treating them just as warm bodies. It also appears that a significant number of wounded and sick officers and men were returned to units from hospitals at this time. During the month a total of 537 experienced officers and enlisted men were returned to duty in the division. The 358th Infantry remained weak, with only about 72 percent of its T/O&E strength reported as effective, while the 357th Infantry strength was reported as about 92 percent effective. The 359th Infantry effective strength was not reported but was likely closer to that of the 357th Infantry than the hard-hit 358th Infantry. Overall, the 90th Division's effective strength was at about 92 percent of T/O&E as of the evening of 31 July.

General McLain's first assessment of the division was recorded in the final entry of the July After-Action Report:

> *The first phase of the battle for FRANCE has ended. During it the 90th Inf Div played a vitally important part. It had met the best the German could offer by way of resistance and although bloodied, had beaten him. It had developed battle experience and equally important, battle confidence. And the brief respite afforded in the last few days of July had permitted revitalization of both individuals and units. Thus on the eve of August the 90th Div was spiritually and physically ready for the stellar role it was about to be given.*

At 1900 on 31 July, General McLean met the officers of the 357th and 359th Infantry to discuss the overall situation—they were put into the "Big Picture." That was a new phrase that began popping up in various reports after General McLain assumed command of the 90th Infantry Division. It spoke to a new attitude and relationship between the Division Commander and his Staff and the Commanders and Staffs of the combat elements of the division. The taciturn General MacKelvie never took his subordinates into his confidence and General Landrum rarely did. Their Field Orders were directives, with little or no context given regarding the overall course of the campaign. In contrast, General McLain's first Field Order began with a paragraph describing exactly what the "Big Picture" was:

> 1. a. *The enemy is withdrawing to the SOUTH and SOUTHEAST towards MAYENNE. Reports indicate reinforcements may reach undetermined parts of the line and they may be expected to counterattack in order to relieve pressure on his hard pressed troops. Only small groups have been contacted in the area to be occupied. Unconfirmed reports indicate possibility of Panzer troops EAST of AVRANCHES.*

The "Big Picture" had changed considerably in the aftermath of Operation COBRA. That attack had begun inauspiciously on 24 July, when bad weather had caused a twenty-four-hour delay, but not before some of the American heavy bombers had mistakenly bombed friendly units, killing 70 and wounding 358 in the 4th, 9th, and 30th Infantry Division. Worse, the aborted bombing was believed to have alerted the Germans to the coming offensive, and further casualties were incurred taking back the ground that had been relinquished when troops had pulled back from the bomb line. Things did not improve, at least initially, when Operation COBRA final got underway on 25 July. Although the weather and visibility were much better, dust and smoke from the first bombs dropped accumulated and obscured aiming points. Combined with human error, it led again to bombs landing in American positions. This time 111 Americans were killed and 490 wounded. One of the dead was General McNair, notional commander of the First U.S. Army Group and, until 13 July, Chief of the AGF directly under General Marshall.[18]

Nevertheless, the three divisions assigned to break through the German front line—9th, 4th, and 30th Infantry Division from right to left (west to east)—pushed ahead in the wake of the bombing. Resistance varied from moderate to heavy, but by evening the advance began to accelerate. Only 200 German prisoners were collected, but General Collins gambled that the Germans were beginning to give way and committed his mobile reserve consisting of the 2d and 3d Armored Division and 1st Infantry Division (motorized) to exploit the opening breach. The next day, 945 more Germans were captured, then 1,443 on 27 July, and 1,476 on 28 July.

As mentioned earlier, in attempting to blunt the attack by the VII Corps, the German *LXXXIV Armee-Korps* withdrew the *SS-Das Reich*, *SS-GvB*, and *Fallschirmjäger-Regiment 6.* from their positions facing the left wing of the VIII Corps on 27 July and attempted to establish a new position east of Saint-Sauveur-Lendelin, extending east to Montpinchon and Cerisy-la-Salle, where they tried to contact the 5. *Fallschirmjäger-Division.* Instead they were nearly surrounded in a pocket between Montpinchon and Roncey by the onrush of the 2d and 3d Armored Division. Only fragments of the German units managed to escape to the east and south.[19]

The withdrawal of the mobile SS units also unhinged the German line running westward to the coast. The right of the *KG 91. Infanterie-Division* west of the Périers-Coutances highway was struck by the 4th Armored Division, which attacked southwest from Sainteny to Périers into the vacuum following the withdrawal of the SS. Farther west the remnants of the *243. Infanterie-Division* were routed by the 6th Armored Division pushing south from Lessay. By the evening of 28 July, the leading elements of the 4th Armored Division were still 30 miles from Avranches, where five highways converged from the north and the east—two from Granville, and one each from Coutances, Villedieu-les-Poëles, and Brécey. From that intersection two bridges crossed the Sée River into Avranches. From the city, a single highway then ran 4 miles to the south where it crossed the Sélune River at a bridge near Pontaubault. From Pontaubault, highways ran west into Brittany, south to the Loire, and east toward Paris.

Early in the evening of 30 July, a column of CCB, 4th Armored Division under Brigadier General Holmes E. Dager, found the bridges north of Avranches intact and secured them. Then they seized the town without opposition. In the interest of speed and coordination, General Wood decided to attach all the 4th Armored combat assets in the vicinity, including Colonel Bruce Clarke's CCA, to Dager's CCB. After a brief and confusing fight with German remnants trying to escape through Avranches on the night of 30/31 July, General Dager sent elements of CCA, 4th Armored Division south and east to secure Pontaubault. Against all odds, after expecting the Germans to destroy the crucial bridge on the Sélune River, a Task Force of CCA captured the bridge intact on the late afternoon of 31 July.[20]

The capture, intact, of the bridges at Avranches and Pontaubault was one of the main "Big Picture" items briefed by General McLain to his senior commanders on the evening of 31 July. Capturing and holding the bridges would allow the three divisions of the VIII Corps to drive south and west into Brittany and hopefully all the way to the port city of Brest at the west end of the Brittany Peninsula. Capturing Brest was considered a key part of the logistical planning supporting the future operations of American forces in France. General Middleton in the first week of August would drive the 4th and 6th Armored Division relentlessly west and south with the objective of Brest paramount in his mind.

That left the XV Corps under Wade Haislip, now a major general, as the next major unit available to push south and east from the Cotentin into the breach opened by Operation COBRA. Under the original NEPTUNE planning it was expected that all of TUSA would be committed to operations in Brittany as its corps arrived in the beachhead. That plan was essentially unchanged as of the eve of TUSA becoming fully operational and the VIII Corps was already making a dash for Brest. In early planning in July before COBRA, the XV Corps had been expected to push west onto the Brittany Peninsula alongside the VIII Corps. By 29 July, that changed to a commitment on the left of the VIII Corps with an objective of driving southwest from Avranches to Fougères, then Rennes, and finally Quiberon Bay. The XX and XII Corps would follow in succession to secure TUSA's left to the FUSA's right. However, the results of COBRA changed Bradley's thinking just as he was about to assume operational command of the 12th Army Group.[21]

1–4 AUGUST

At 1000 on 1 August, General Haislip was notified that "the projected operation of the Corps toward the southwest had been cancelled, and that [a] new operation would be [started] towards the southeast." The new corps mission was to protect and expand the narrow corridor leading south from the Cotentin through the Avranches-Pontaubault bottleneck. The Corps would be committed into the gap opening between the VIII Corps, which was heading west and south, and the VII Corps, which was heading south and east. The initial zone of the XV Corps would be between the VII Corps right, which was currently near Brécy, and the VIII Corps left at Rennes. Instead of attacking southwest toward Rennes, the XV Corps would attack southeast toward Saint Hilaire-du-Harcouët.

The XV Corps would lead with the 79th and 90th Infantry Division, which would be followed by the newly arrived 5th Armored Division, and then the 83d Infantry Division. At noon on 1 August, the 90th Infantry Division passed from attachment to the VIII Corps and FUSA to the XV Corps and TUSA. Already at 1000 the division had received warning orders from the XV Corps to prepare to move by motor to Saint Hilaire-du-Harcouët, approximately 50 miles to the south. The initial missions assigned to the division by the XV Corps were:

(1) *To seize and secure the bridge over the SELUNE River near ST HILAIRE,*
(2) *Block the advance of enemy to the WEST on AVRANCHES, between the SELUNE RIVER and the SEE RIVER,*
(3) *Relieve elements of VIII Corps and protect the DAMS on the SELUNE RIVER between ST HILAIRE and AVRANCHES,*
(4) *Be prepared to move EAST, NORTHEAST, or NORTH.*

A fifth mission was added later that night: "(5) To capture the town of LOUVIGNE and extend the zone to the SOUTH to connect with the 79th Infantry Division operating on our right."

At 2300 on 1 August, the 90th Infantry Division began moving, led by Task Force Randolph, under Lieutenant Colonel Randolph, the commander of the 712th Tank Battalion. It was composed of the Assault Gun Platoon and Company D, 712th Tank Battalion and the 90th Reconnaissance Troop. Task Force Randolph was followed at 2330 by Task Force Clarke, under Lieutenant Colonel Clarke, who was still serving as Executive Officer of the 358th Infantry. It comprised Jake Bealke's 3d Battalion, 358th Infantry, a detachment of the 90th Signal Company, the 344th FA Battalion, one platoon of Company B, 315th Engineer Combat

Battalion, Company A (minus one platoon), 607th Tank Destroyer Battalion, and Battery B, 537th AAA Battalion.

Randolph's and Clarke's mission was to cover the advance of the division by establishing roadblocks between the Sélune and Sée rivers to the north of Saint-Hilaire. If the bridge over the Sélune northwest of Saint-Hilaire was undefended Randolph would seize it. If the bridge was defended, then Task Force Clarke, following a half hour behind Randolph, would seize it, along with another crossing north of the town. The main body of the division would follow Randolph and Clarke in turn. Combat Team (CT) 7 (357th Infantry; 343d Field Artillery Battalion; Co A, 315th Engineer Combat Battalion; Company A, 315th Medical Battalion; Company B and 1 platoon of Company A, 607th Tank Destroyer Battalion; and Battery A, 537th AAA Battalion) would advance at 0130 on 2 August, two hours after Clarke. CT 8 (358th Infantry (-TF Clarke); Company B, 315th Engineer Combat Battalion; Company B, 315th Medical Battalion; and the 693d Field Artillery Battalion) would follow at 0400. The 345th and 915th Field Artillery Battalion, 607th Tank Destroyer Battalion (-), and C and D Battery, 537th AAA Battalion, would move next at 0630. The 359th Infantry and Company C, 315th Medical Battalion would be the Division Reserve and would not move until 0745. The Division Headquarters and Headquarters Company, Division Artillery Headquarters and Headquarters Battery, 90th Signal Company (-), the 315th Engineer Combat Battalion (-), the 790th Ordnance Company, the 90th Quartermaster Company, and Headquarters and Headquarters Battery, 537th AAA Battalion would leave at 0900. Bringing up the rear at 1030 was the 712th Tank Battalion.

The 90th Infantry Division was fully motorized for this movement by the attachment of six Quartermaster Truck companies; everyone in the division would ride on a vehicle and no one would walk. Also, in the interest of speed, most of Randolph's medium tanks were left behind to catch up later so they would not block the faster moving trucks on the roads. The route ran from an Initial Point [IP] on the Périers-Coutances Road (D971) at Monthuchon through Coutances-Lengronne-La Haye-Pesnel-Avranches to a "de-trucking area" in the vicinity between Isigny-le-Buat and Montgothier. Battery A, 537th AAA Battalion with the CT 7 would follow Task Force Clarke and was given the mission of protecting the detrucking area until all units closed in the area, when it would revert to its normal role protecting the 343d Field Artillery Battalion.

Task Force Randolph and Clarke moved out of Cathelmais as scheduled. The convoy speed was set initially at 15 to 25 miles per hour until 0500 on 2 August when they sped up to 25 to 35 miles per hour. Minor resistance was easily pushed aside or bypassed until the 3d Battalion, 358th Infantry reached Isigny-le-Buat and detrucked. From there, Company I advanced rapidly to the southeast and reached the Sélune River by 1100.

Company I discovered the railroad bridge northwest of town was destroyed by the Germans, but the road bridge there was intact, as was the road bridge leading into town from the north. The road leading to the northwest road bridge came under heavy artillery fire as Company I approached, so Colonel Bealke decided to simultaneously rush the bridge from front and left flank with Company K while moving Company I onto the high ground to the right as a base of fire. Moving quickly, because it was feared the Germans would blow up the bridge, Company I quickly took position and opened fire on the German-held side of the bridge. The 344th Field Artillery went into battery and fired a short artillery preparation, while the light tanks of the 1st Platoon, Company D, 712th Tank Battalion raced across the bridge with the lead platoon of Company K close behind them. The fire of the light tanks and Company I forced the German defenders to keep their heads down and resistance quickly collapsed. By 1500 the town was secured, and outposts were sent to the north, east, and south. The two task forces settled in and prepared to hold in place overnight, but at 1800 orders were received to move out to Louvigne-du-Désert about 15 kilometers to the south, which was secured without resistance by 0100 on 3 August. The 1st Battalion, 358th Infantry took over the defense of Saint-Hilaire.

The contrast between this attack by the 3d Battalion, 358th Infantry and those conducted earlier in June and July cannot be more obvious. The infantry, artillery, and tanks of the two task forces acted swiftly and in close cooperation. Colonel Bealke quickly decided on a course of action after an initial reconnaissance, counting on the obvious confusion on the part of the Germans to make the assault successful. However, he also reinforced the possibility of success by establishing a supporting fire position with Company I and made good use of the American artillery's capability of firing quickly and accurately. The light tanks made excellent use of defilade from the few German high-velocity guns on the far side of the river while approaching the bridge, then used their speed to cross the last 100 yards safely. Once across the bridge their firepower suppressed the Germans trying to stop the infantry crossing. The infantry moved quickly, did not bunch up, and did not go immediately to ground when the Germans opened fire. It was a near textbook tactical success.

While only about eight prisoners were captured by TF Randolph and Clarke at Saint-Hilaire, the division reported the capture of a total of seventy-four Germans on 2 August. What was astonishing was the variety of units the prisoners came from. Men from six different German divisions and fourteen different units of those divisions were identified. The prisoners were rounded up from all the way to the rear at Avranches, as well as along the entire 30-kilometer division front, from Reffuveille in the north, to Saint-Hilaire in the center, to Saint-Georges-de-Reintembault in the south. Casualties in Task Force Clarke were one man killed and one wounded. Colonel Clarke noted later that day that the ease with which the bridge and town were taken had "helped immeasurably to build up the morale of the troops."

Although the division had done well on 2 August, one distinguished observer of the march was not completely happy. Sometime before Clarke captured the bridge at Sainte-Hilaire, George Patton joined the marching column of the division somewhere between Avranches and Sainte-Hilaire:

> *We caught up with the 90[th Infantry Division] which is advancing between the SEE & the SELUNE. The discipline is bad the men filthy and the officers apathetic many have removed the insignia from their helmets and collars. I saw one Lt of Artillery jump out of a peep [Patton's preferred term for "jeep"] and head for a ditch when a plane flew over firing a little. I corrected these acts.*
>
> *I walked for a couple of miles in the column the men seemed normal but not in hard condition. Some were getting rides on guns and the others made no comment. I called them babies and they dismounted. We came on Haislip and McClane [McLain] the new div commander just north of ST. HILAIRE-DU HARCOUET. There were some Germans in the town which was being attacked.*[22]

Patton's displeasure is understandable, but it is also perplexing. It is unlikely that McLain's influence had yet percolated down to things such as uniform cleanliness and proper wear of insignia. The officers and men were barely a week from the wet misery of floundering in the rain in the flooded marshes of the Island after all. The 90th's esprit de corps took a while to develop, but it was growing, even if George Patton did not see it yet. Just a few weeks later, when Captain Mayhall joined General Weaver as his aide, his first experience at Division Headquarters was to be "branded" with the famous division insignia, the T-O,

> *A guy with a paintbrush and stencil came up to me and said "Captain, let me have your left shoulder." I turned my left side toward him and before I knew what he was doing, I had a T and O painted on my shirt. The man said, "Captain, you are now a Tough 'Ombre."*[23]

This is possibly the earliest reference to the division's best-known nickname but is from a postwar memoir. Curiously enough, although "Tough 'Ombres" is probably now the best-known nickname for the 90th, it is difficult to say exactly when it started being used and who coined it. It may not have gained currency until the end of 1944, when the *Stars and Stripes* published the first edition of a pamphlet extolling the accomplishments of the "Tough 'Ombres" in one of the publications meant to boost morale.[24] Some attribute the nickname to Patton, but mention of the nickname does not appear in his original diary entries. The nickname was also not that common within the division and only appeared twice in the division history. Not even the division's daily mimeographed news sheet *The Sniper* used the nickname. Nevertheless, by the end of the war the nickname "Tough 'Ombres" was firmly in place.[25]

Patton's remark about troops riding on vehicles and gun carriages rather than marching may have had more to do with his short temper and desire to find fault than anything substantial. The 90th Infantry Division was on a motor march after all, where speed of advance was key, so Patton's ire at troops riding on vehicles is inexplicable.

At 2050 on 2 August, Colonel Clarke resumed command of the 358th Infantry when Colonel McNary was forced to relinquish command due to what was first thought to be a severe attack of sinusitis. In fact, it was a flare-up of tuberculosis, which he had suffered from since serving a tour of duty in the Panama Canal with the 14th Infantry in the 1930s. He left the regiment and did not return. Colonel Loomis resumed his duties as Regimental Executive Officer and Major Lytle received command of the 1st Battalion. Colonel Bealke took command of Task Force Clarke, which continued to nominally exist under Bealke's command until 1640 3 August when it was officially dissolved.

The main body of the division followed Task Force Clarke as scheduled but was delayed by congestion on the roads leading south out of Périers. The 90th was supposed to have had road priority according to the XV Corps orders, but the reality was that the division was following the same route used by four divisions—the 4th and 6th Armored and the 8th and 79th Infantry—and was followed by the 5th Armored Division, all of which were vying for the same road space. Congestion was so bad through Avranches that the 5th Armored Division, which Haislip wanted to lead the XV Corps advance, was held on the north bank of the Sée River for two days before crossing and assembling at Vitré on 5 August. The movement of the 90th turned into what was later described as a "very ragged march," but nevertheless the division's units closed into the detrucking area on the night of 2/3 August with "reasonable expeditiousness" and its combat elements moved promptly into their designated positions.

By 1415 on 2 August, CT 7 had detrucked at Montgothier, protected from the Luftwaffe by Battery A, 537th AAA Battalion. From the detrucking area, the CT 7 infantry marched on foot to their designated locations. The 1st Battalion was at Reffeuville, the 2d Battalion in reserve at La Mancellière, and the 3d Battalion at Naftel. CT 8 (- TF Clarke) detrucked and established its headquarters at Isigny-le-Buat. The 2d Battalion guarded a dam on the Sélune River south of Bardet and the river running south. During the night of 2/3 August, the 3d Battalion (Task Force Clarke) marched 7 miles south of Saint-Hilaire to Louvigné-du-Désert with Company K at Landivy 4 miles to the east. The 359th Infantry assembled in division reserve with Headquarters and the 2d Battalion on the Rue Bourget in Isigny-le-Buat, the 1st Battalion at Ducey, and the 3d Battalion at Vezins. Headquarters and Headquarters Company and Company A and C, 712th Tank Battalion moved through Avranches overnight and assembled at Le Bourget. They were bombed and strafed by the Luftwaffe en route, but the only damage was an ammunition truck set on fire and abandoned.

On 3 August, General Haislip ordered his two divisions to maintain the defense of the line Fougères–Mortain. The 90th remained in place except for some minor jockeying of units. On the far left of the division, the 2d Battalion, 357th Infantry moved east 11.5 kilometers from La Mancellière to La Bazoge, 4.5 kilometers south of Juvigny, in the wake of the 1st Infantry Division advance. The 343d Field Artillery of CT 7, with Battery A, 537th AAA Battalion, displaced from Montgothier about 6 miles to new firing positions at Chasseguey. On the road, they were overflown by a massive wave of German aircraft, estimated as forty to fifty planes. The planes were flying from west to east and may have been using the road the column was on (D48) for navigation.

> *During the march the largest fleet of enemy planes witnessed to date, appeared. At first, a number the men thought them to be P-51's. There were too many to be enemy. Then they attacked. Undo Able and other ack-ack outfits kept them away from our column but other installation's got a fair working over before friendly planes came and drove them away. Famous last words—keep going, those are P-51's.*

The 1st Platoon of Battery A opened fire on the German aerial armada when it attacked and claimed one plane destroyed. As the Germans flew down the length of the column, the 2d Platoon also opened fire and claimed a second aircraft. Most likely given the speed with which the situation developed, at least the first and possibly the second aircraft downed were by the M16B mounts because it took two to three minutes to prepare the 40mm guns to fire. The handheld .50 caliber on the vehicles of the 343d Field Artillery also opened fire but were likely just a deterrent because they lacked the accuracy and volume of fire of the M16B.

In the new positions the division units continued to round up German stragglers—one was collected by the men of Battery A, 537th Antiaircraft Battalion—while the division suffered only a few casualties. The pause extended through 4 August, as the traffic jams at Avranches and Pontaubault continued to hinder the deployment of the XV Corps. Finally, at 2135 on 4 August, a warning order was called to all units of the 90th Infantry Division: "Be prepared to move 0600 [5 August]."

The new mission given to the division was an advance east to the Mayenne River. The zone of advance designated for the division was bounded on the right by a line extending to north of Laval, which would be in the 79th Infantry Division's zone of advance to the right (south) of the division. The boundary on the left of the division zone, which was also the boundary between FUSA and TUSA as well as the VII and XV Corps, was dependent on the movements of the 1st Infantry Division. As of the early morning of 5 August, if the 1st Infantry Division advanced to the town of Mayenne and seized crossings on the river there, the 90th Infantry Division would move south of it to find river crossings south of Mayenne. However, in the contingency of the 1st Infantry Division remaining at Mortain or advancing farther north, the 90th Infantry Division would swing north and take on the mission of seizing the bridge at Mayenne.

General McLain reacted to General Haislip's warning order by calling his staff and commanders to the Division CP near Launay, about 5.5 miles northwest of Saint Hilaire, just before midnight on 4 August. McLain ordered the formation of a fast, hard-hitting, mobile strike force, under the Assistant Division Commander. The Headquarters of Task Force Weaver would consist of detachments of the Division Headquarters, the 90th Division Signals, and the 90th Division MP Platoon. Its combat elements would include Task Force Randolph, still with the 90th Reconnaissance Troop and Company D, 712th Tank Battalion, along with the rest of the 712th Tank Battalion, Colonel Barth's CT 7 with the 357th Infantry (motorized), the 343d Field Artillery Battalion, Company A, 315th Engineer Combat Battalion, Company A, 315th Medical Battalion, Company A, 607th Tank Destroyer Battalion, and Battery A, 537th AAA Battalion.[26]

At 0300 on 5 August, Major General Clarence R. Huebner, commander of the 1st Infantry Division, notified the XV Corps and 90th Infantry Division that he did not intend to advance on Mayenne for a few days. General Bradley temporarily shifted the boundary between the FUSA and TUSA to north of Mayenne and gave Haislip and McLain permission to go ahead. The decision by General Huebner and the delay getting the 5th Armored Division across the Sée River forced General Haislip to give the mission of leading the XV Corps advance east to the 90th Infantry Division. Because of those two decisions the mission of expanding the American breakout was given to the "Problem Division." The spearhead of the breakout would be the 90th Infantry Division. The spearhead of the spearhead would be Task Force Weaver.

****

From Saint-Sauveur-Lendelin we headed south as the rainstorm continued. We quickly drove through Coutances, Gavray, and Avranches to our next overnight stop at Ducey. The next day we spent some time exploring the area where TUSA became operational and the 90th Infantry Division began its thrust east into France. The capture of the bridges at Pontaubault is commemorated by a lonely Bailey Bridge placed as a monument in an empty field. The Brittany American Cemetery at Saint James is stunningly beautiful and poignant. Its 28 acres contain the remains of 4,404 American war dead. From there we visited Mont-Saint-Michel, before turning east to follow the route of Task Force Weaver. Returning to Ducey, we drove to Saint-Hilaire-du-Harcouët.

Dad well remembered the exhilarating drive south from the Cotentin and through Coutances, Cérences, La Haye-Pesnel, and Avranches to Saint-Hilaire-du-Harcouët. After weeks of near-constant rain, frequent harassment from German mortar and artillery fire, and short moves of a few hundred yards from one hedgerow-enclosed field to another, the full mobility of the American Army could finally be exploited. They were moving and the few Germans they encountered no longer resisted so stoutly but instead meekly surrendered, many of them appearing completely bewildered that the Americans were in their rear.

Dad also remembered well the sudden appearance of the large swarm of German aircraft on 3 August. However, he did not recall shooting down either of the two aircraft claimed. The four M16B typically were dispersed along the length of the march column rather than concentrated at one point, because it was realized that opening fire quickly at fleeting targets was more important than accuracy in terms of deterring an aircraft attack. Unlike the others, the M16B Dad was riding on did not have enough time to react because the Germans overflew them so quickly.

CHAPTER 10

TASK FORCE WEAVER

5 AUGUST

When Colonel Barth returned from the meeting at Division Headquarters at 0200 on 5 August, he immediately notified his Battalion, Antitank Company, Cannon Company, and Supply Company commanders to report to the Regimental CP at 0300 hours for march orders and a briefing. Task Force Weaver was quickly organized and began moving south, crossing the IP at La Richardiere at 0600.[1]

The column was led by the 2d Platoon, 90th Reconnaissance Troop. The main body of Task Force Randolph followed as the reconnaissance echelon of Task Force Weaver, with the rest of the 90th Reconnaissance Troop, and the Reconnaissance Platoon and Company D of the 712th Tank Battalion. Its mission was to advance on the designated route and reconnoiter parallel and lateral routes at road intersections. If they met resistance they were to "close with fire" and "discover [the] enemy position." If they could not overwhelm the resistance immediately, they were to find alternate routes around the flanks, operating on foot as necessary.[2]

The reconnaissance element was followed immediately by General Weaver's command group, composed of the detachments from the Division Headquarters, including an Air Support Party, as well as Signals, and Military Police. The Signals Detachment maintained communications between the different parts of the Task Force, mostly by radio because the movement was planned to be too quick and the distances moved too far for the maintenance of telephone wire. The MPs were kept busy marking routes for following units and providing guides where needed.

One of the most important elements of the Task Force Headquarters was the Division Air Support Party. Its mission was to maintain communications and liaison with squadrons of P-47 fighter-bombers from the XIX TAC, which were to support

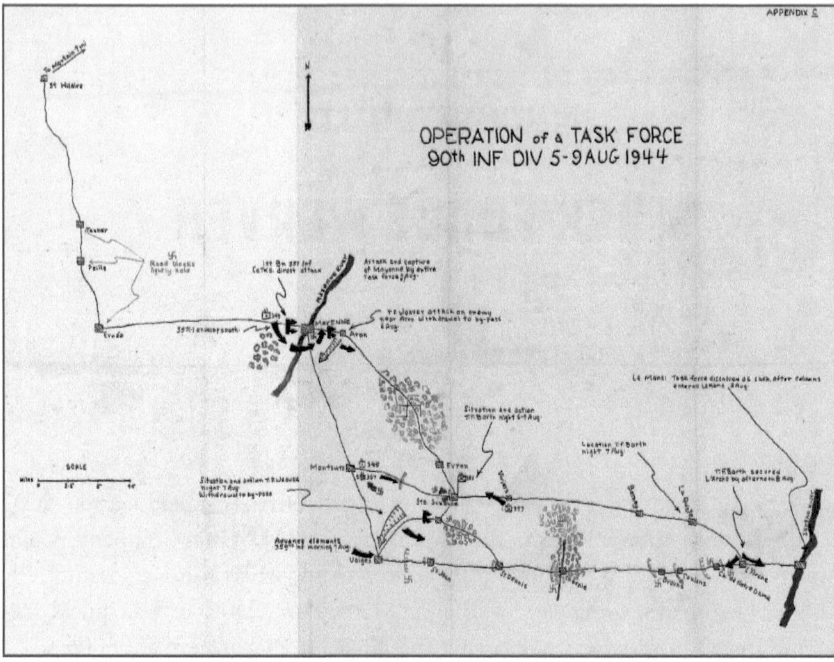

Map 13. Operations of Task Force Weaver from St. Hilaire to Le Mans, 5–9 August 1944. Major Francis S. Kelly, *The Operations of Task Force Weaver (Reinforced RCT 90th Infantry Division) from St Hilaire du Harcoeut to Le Mans France, 5–9 August 1944* (Fort Benning, GA: The Infantry School, Advanced Infantry Officers Course, 1947–1948), Appendix C. Major Kelly commanded the 90th Division MP Platoon and was Division and Task Force Provost Marshal.

the advance. The Air Support Parties were provisionally organized before the invasion with personnel attached from the Ninth Air Force. The 90th's Air Support Party initially consisted of eleven officers and enlisted men with four vehicles. It was equipped with both SCR-299 and SCR-522 radios so it could communicate with both ground and air units within range. The system had steadily improved since early June, when the Air Support Party requests were sent through a highly centralized control system at Ninth Air Force Headquarters in Uxbridge, England, which typically took four to eight hours or more to process. Then on 18 June, the Ninth Air Force authorized the establishment of a communications and control headquarters in France, collocated with FUSA Headquarters, to speed up close air support requests. That system was further improved and by mid-July, immediate air support missions could be executed within sixty to eighty minutes.[3]

However, even faster times were desired, which led to the development of "Armored Column Cover" for Operation COBRA. Under Armored Column Cover, air groups and squadrons were assigned daily to different ground units as on call support. The P-47 squadrons rotated missions during the daylight hours so that a flight was always available. They ranged ahead of the column, up to 35 miles to the front and flanks, looking for the enemy. When they found German positions, they reported them directly to an air controller from the Air Support Party, who was with the column, via a USAAF VHF SCR-522 radio mounted in a tank or jeep. The controller was also usually an experienced fighter bomber pilot from the group providing the column cover. The controller could then authorize the attack or alternately direct the aircraft to another target and could pass strike results to the supported ground unit via the SCR-299.[4]

The maturation of the Air Support Party and Armored Column Cover placed a powerful weapon in the hands of General Weaver and the commanders of the other American columns driving deep into German-held territory. It was also facilitated by a pleasant change in the weather. What seemed to be near-constant rainfall in June and July had finally stopped. Instead warm, dry, sunny weather was the norm. For the AAF, it meant that twenty-eight of the thirty-one days of August were operational flying days.[5]

A flank guard, composed of Company K, the 3d Platoon of Antitank Company, and the I&R Platoon, 357th Infantry, with the 2d Platoon, Company A, 607th Tank Destroyer Battalion, followed Weaver's command group. It crossed the IP at 0630 but was not on the road heading south from La Richardiere (D977). Instead they followed a parallel route to the main body and took the Rue de Paris (D976) southeast out of Saint-Hilare and headed for the village of Buais-les-Monts. They reached it at 0915 then went on to Fougerolles-du-Plessis, which they reached at 1000. By 1600, they were 2.5 miles from Gorron where they were warned by French Resistance sources that the town was occupied by a strong German force that supposedly included a Tiger tank, four antitank guns, a company of Fallschirmjäger, and other infantry. This information was relayed to Colonel Barth, who reported it to division, along with the recommendation that a strong reinforcement should be sent to the flank guard before an attempt was made to eliminate the Germans at Gorron. Instead, because of the lack of trucks to send reinforcements, McLain instructed the flank guard to hold in place. However at 2000, the Resistance reported the Germans had withdrawn and the flank guard occupied the town without any further trouble, ending its advance there for the night. The "Tiger" tank disappeared and may have been any type of armored vehicle or even a figment of the French Resistance's imagination.

A Ninth Air Force Air Support Party in late November 1944. They are communicating with an aircraft using the SCR-522 radio mounted in the back of their jeep. U.S. Army SC.

The main body was next in the order of march. It was led by an advance guard under Major Hamilton, commander of the 1st Battalion. Twenty-eight 2.5-ton trucks were picked up in Saint-Hilaire from an unnamed Quartermaster Truck Company at 0600 by the Battalion Motor Officer, 1st Lieutenant Archie L. Todd. They were driven north to load up at the battalion assembly area at La Gandonnière near Juvigny, before driving south again to Saint Hilaire. Despite the 25-kilometer round trip, they got back on the road quickly. Unfortunately, it turned out it was the wrong road.

At 0615, Major Hamilton and the Liaison Officer of the 343d Field Artillery met with General Weaver at the IP south of Saint Hilaire, when they realized the leading element of the advance guard, composed of Company B, 357th Infantry and Company A, 712th Tank Battalion, was nowhere to be found. It was quickly discovered they had taken a wrong turn in the center of town and had driven southeast rather than south. It took a while to turn them around and get them back on the right road to Landivy, where they were ordered to wait for the rest of the column. They got there at about 0900.[6]

The next element of the advance guard was a detachment from Company A, 315th Engineer Combat Battalion, which was hauling bulldozers on trailers. They were there to clear any obstacles or fill road craters discovered by the reconnaissance element if they could not be bypassed. The rest of the 1st Battalion, 357th Infantry (- B) followed with a platoon from the 357th Infantry Antitank Company. It was to assist in direct assaults on German positions initiated by the command group or alternately would envelop or bypass strong opposition if so ordered. They reached the IP at 0800.[7]

The 343d Field Artillery Battalion, which was closely supported by Battery A, 537th AAA Battalion, was the direct support artillery for Task Force Weaver and closely followed the advance guard. In just a few weeks a close relationship had developed between Colonel Riemers's artillery battalion and Captain Lea's antiaircraft battery. The artillerymen noted "Undo Able was high on the list of people that we liked most to have around."

The main body proper was composed of the 357th Infantry (-), with the 712th Tank Battalion (- A & D), Company A (-), 315th Engineer Combat Battalion, Company A, 315th Medical Battalion, and Company A (-), 607th Tank Destroyer Battalion. The 2d Battalion, 357th Infantry and the 3d Platoon of Company A, 607th Tank Destroyer Battalion acted as rear guard. However, they too had been delayed. The rapid American advance meant that few Quartermaster Truck companies were available to haul troops. The fifty trucks allocated to motorize the 2d Battalion failed to arrive on time. General McLain reacted quickly, ordering the three infantry regiments of the division to unload their kitchen trucks and use them instead. It was 0900 before the scrounged trucks arrived, were loaded with troops, and got underway.[8]

Despite all the delays Task Force Randolph moved rapidly south, brushing aside the defenders of roadblocks at La Tannière, Pouillé, and Ernée en route. From Ernée, the road turned east and there was no opposition until, at about noon, the 2d Platoon of the 90th Reconnaissance Troop approached the outskirts of Mayenne. About 800 meters from where the Ernée-Mayenne Road (RN12) turned right to enter town as the Rue Ambroise de Loré, two concealed "tank guns" opened fire and knocked out the two leading armored cars and one jeep, killing five men and wounding others. Major Hamilton immediately ordered the 1st Battalion to detruck and requested the 343d Field Artillery go into position and prepare to support the attack.

While the 1st Battalion prepared to make the assault, Major Hamilton ordered Company B under 1st Lieutenant Burrowes G. Stevens Jr. to eliminate the roadblock. The two leading platoons deployed on either side of the road, each with a medium tank platoon, supported by the Mortar Platoon of the 712th Tank Battalion, and followed by Company B's third platoon. At 1345, they advanced—with General Weaver, who had just arrived, leading the infantry's charge himself, there was a good reason why he was known as "Wild Bill"—and quickly overran the German position. As it turned out there was no organized resistance to the advance, and the roadblock was overrun without any further casualties. It appears the two German "tank guns" had withdrawn or disappeared, much like the mysterious "Tiger tanks" at Gorron. The division G-2 later attributed the encounter to a single antitank gun and "a small group of infantrymen."[9]

The main road from the roadblock ran east before it turned southeast toward the last bridge over the Mayenne River that was still standing. The road bridge was known as the Pont de la Caisse d'Epargne—the "Savings Bank Bridge," after the imposing stone bank building built in 1884 that still sits at the western end of the bridge. The road sloped gently down from the west bank in a straight line for 700 meters to the bridge, which spanned 70 meters, and then ran straight uphill on the opposite bank for another 800 meters, so nearly a mile. A second road bridge on the Rue Saint Martin about 150 meters to the south of the intact road bridge and a railway bridge another 500 meters farther south had both already been destroyed by the Germans at 0420 that morning.

712th Tank Battalion rolls through a French village. The censor has obscured the "Rhino" hedge-cutting device on the front of the tank. U.S. Army SC.

The German defenses on the far side of the river appeared to be strong. Two 8.8-cm Fliegerabwehr-Kanone 37, the dreaded "Flak 88," were deployed less than 200 meters from the American side of the river. On the far side of the bridge the road is known as the Rue Roullois. One gun was on the south side of the road at the corner of the Rue Henri Dunant. The other gun was on the north side, perhaps 25 meters farther east, and was close alongside a brick wall that borders the street. Both could easily fire down the length of the road. Worse, there was also at least one deadly 2cm Flak automatic gun on the street near the 88s. Infantrymen with automatic weapons and small arms were seen on the far side as well. Lieutenant Stevens also believed he could see tanks on the far side of the river. An assault crossing appeared a daunting and deadly task.

An indication of the speed with which Task Force Weaver had advanced was the large number of German vehicles and soldiers that kept heading toward

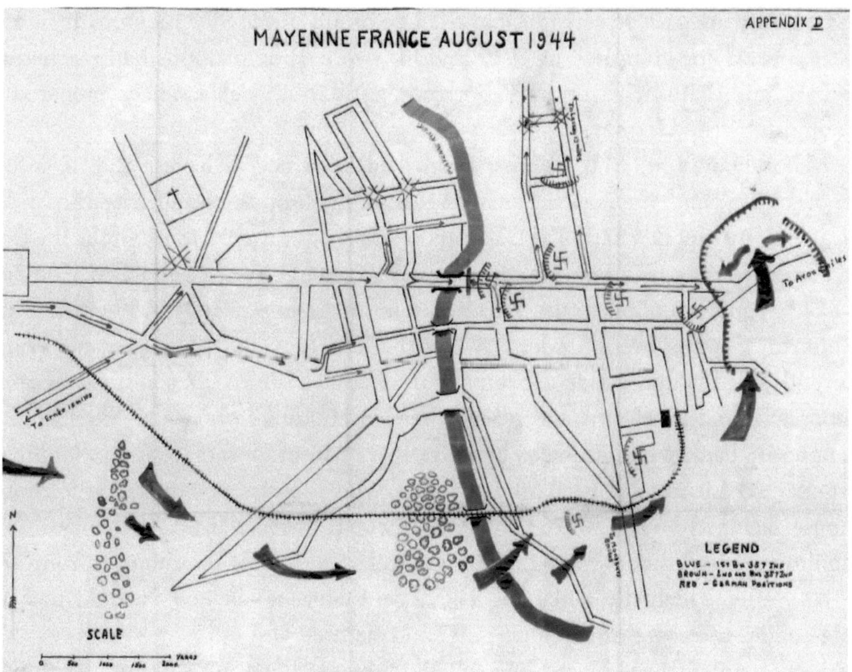

Map 14. The attack on Mayenne,5 August 1944. Note that the scale given on the map is incorrect. The distance to the first road leading north after crossing the bridge should be about 1,500 yards according to the map scale, but in reality it is only 150 yards. Kelly, *The Operations of Task Force Weaver*, Appendix D.

the bridge from roads entering Mayenne from the north, apparently completely unaware that the Americans had cut access to the bridge. The confusion caused by the rapid advance of the Americans was also probably why the Germans did not immediately blow up the last bridge across the Mayenne River. Hamilton ordered the 1st Battalion Antitank Platoon to move its three 57mm guns into positions covering the two main roads entering from Domfront to the north (D23) and Vieille Route d'Ambrières. As the guns crossed the road leading to the bridge the crews came under heavy fire, and one man was killed and two wounded. The gunners exacted a swift revenge on the German vehicles trying to get to the bridge from the north, engaging them at point blank range: "the result was carnage."[10]

Meanwhile, Company B continued to work its way east toward the bridge. They moved through buildings, back alleys, and yards, while supported by and simultaneously escorting the medium tanks of Company A, 712th Tank Battalion, which moved down the back streets to avoid the line of fire of the 88s. Lieutenant Stevens reported to Major Hamilton at 1630 that his two leading platoons had reached the riverbank and that furthermore the bridge was still intact but had been prepared for demolition by the Germans.[11]

Major Hamilton, who Colonel Barth had described as having the "dash of a Stonewall Jackson," was just the man to take the risk of an assault over the bridge. Because Company B, 712th Tank Battalion was now scattered throughout the town and along the river firing on the opposite side, General Weaver attached Company C, 712th Tank Battalion to the 1st Battalion for the bridge assault. Hamilton gave Lieutenant Stevens simple orders: "when the lead tank started out on the bridge, [Stevens's] 2d Platoon was to accompany it." Captain Liford Gibson brought up his Company D machine guns and placed them in buildings where they could fire on the opposite bank. Hamilton also brought up an 81mm mortar section of Company D, under 2d Lieutenant Richard D. Smith, who found a position on the roof of a house facing the river at 1645 where he could observe the German positions. Hamilton ordered the mortars, tanks, and artillery to fire for ten minutes from 1750 to 1800, after which the tanks and Lieutenant Stevens's riflemen would rush the bridge under the cover of machine-gun and rifle fire.[12]

Lieutenant Stevens placed one squad of the 1st Platoon on the upper floor of the bank building where they could fire overhead directly across the river. Under the cover of their fire, the 2d Platoon and a Light Machinegun Section of his Weapons Platoon were able to edge forward to take shelter behind a low stone wall that ran along the right side of the bridge. The rest of the 1st Platoon and the 3d Platoon assembled under shelter nearby to cross the bridge. Two squads of the 2d Platoon, the squad of the 1st Platoon, and the Light Machinegun Section would establish a base of fire, while the remaining squad of the 2d Platoon would cross the bridge led by two tanks from 3d Platoon of Company C, 712th Tank Battalion under Platoon Leader 1st Lieutenant Charles H. Lombardi. Sergeant Neal Stephens's 1st Squad of the 2d Platoon of Company A, 315th Combat Engineers would follow the tanks to disable the German demolition charges—hopefully before the Germans had time to set them off. Then the 3d Platoon, the two squads of the 1st Platoon, and the rest of Company C would follow.[13]

Major Hamilton also ordered Colonel Reimer's 343d Field Artillery into action. Reimer's howitzers drove past the Headquarters of the 712th Tank Battalion and went into battery "close enough so that medium range would clear the town," just 5,000 yards from the river. One of the tankers was overheard quipping, "What the hell kind of war is this when even the artillery medics pass up the tanks?"

When Captain George L. Ingram, the 343d Field Artillery's Liaison Officer with the 1st Battalion, 357th Infantry, called for fire, it was adjusted by an aerial observer, 1st Lieutenant William J. Rhein, in his "Cub" flying over the battlefield. After endless days of rain and low cloud cover had prevented effective aerial observation, the sunny skies meant the artillery "Cubs" could be used to full effect. Rhein and his counterpart flying the second "Cub" of the 343d, 1st Lieutenant Edward C. Hicks Jr., had chosen to take advantage of the excellent weather to remain in the air as long as possible during the advance to Mayenne. The two pilots alternated, with one flying while the other refueled, precariously landing on fields along the route of the column that had not been previously reconnoitered. Every takeoff and landing risked a crash, but luck was with them. When Ingram called it was Rhein's turn aloft and he quickly walked rounds onto the German positions on the far side of the bridge. One round was a direct hit on the 88 on the north side of the Rue Roullois and another hit ammunition piled nearby. The ammunition exploded with a huge bang and a blanket of smoke that engulfed the German position, temporarily stunning and blinding the German gunners. Lieutenant Smith's mortars also began dropping rounds on the German positions, driving the gun crews to cover.

Lieutenant Rhein was awarded the Distinguished Flying Cross for his actions at Mayenne.

A Piper L-4 "Cub" of the V Corps Artillery in August 1944. U.S. Army SC.

First Lieutenant William J. Rhein (Army Serial No 01175555), Field Artillery, United States Army, for extraordinary achievement while participating in aerial flights during the period from 5 August 1944 to 8 August 1944, in France. First Lieutenant Rhein was a liaison pilot for the 343d Field Artillery Battalion, part of the task force which spearheaded the drive of the 90th Infantry Division on Mayenne and Le Mans, France. In order to remain in the air for long periods of time, he landed in fields along the route of the column without prior ground reconnaissance. By refueling on these fields and not returning to his base, valuable time was gained for observation purposes. On 5 August 1944, he adjusted and scored a direct hit on a German 88mm gun across the Mayenne River that was holding up the 1st Battalion, 357th Infantry. The knocking out of this gun and the exploding 88mm ammunition near the gun materially aided our infantry in taking the bridge.[14]

Lieutenant Stevens took advantage of the opportune smokescreen and began the assault.

Everything went smoothly until the time for the jump-off. The Krauts opened up with small-arms about the same time we did, but with about a fifth of our volume. I ordered

> *Lieban's squad over, but the leader, Sgt. Phillips, balked. The situation was critical. The lead tank was rolling down the hill, firing his 75mm cannon on the move. Something had to be done. I said, "Follow me!" in approved Infantry School style and took off across. The whole squad followed me.*[15]

Lieutenant Stevens's leadership got Sergeant Phillips and the ten men of the 1st Squad moving onto the bridge behind Lombardi's tank. They were followed by two other men, Private James D. McRacken and Private Jack E. Bergstrom from Sergeant Stephens's Engineer squad. McRacken and Bergstrom stopped one-third of the way across the bridge. They were frantically cutting the wires leading to the explosives, when Hamilton, observing from the bank building roof, saw both men get hit by what he first thought was a rifle grenade. To Hamilton the two engineers "momentarily seemed to disappear." However, it was not a grenade, it was automatic fire from the 20mm Flak gun, which killed McRacken instantly and tore off Bergstrom's leg.[16]

Private McRacken received the posthumous award of the Distinguished Service Cross for his heroism on the Mayenne Bridge. The townspeople of Mayenne also honored his sacrifice, later covering his body on the bridge with a sheet and strewing it with flowers. A plaque was placed on the bridge after the war to commemorate his service. His Distinguished Service Citation reads,

> *The President of the United States takes pride in presenting the Distinguished Service Cross (posthumously) to James D. Macracken [sic], Private, U.S. Army, for extraordinary heroism in connection with military operations against an armed enemy while serving with Company A, 315th Engineer Combat Battalion, in action against enemy forces on 5 August 1944. Private Macracken's intrepid actions, personal bravery and zealous devotion to duty at the cost of his life, exemplify the highest traditions of the military forces of the United States and reflect great credit upon himself, his unit, and the United States Army.*[17]

Stevens's, Stephens's, and Phillips's men cut the rest of the demolition wires as they raced across until they reached the far bank. They continued up the street into the eastern part of town for about 80 yards, firing at windows and throwing grenades into cellars. When they reached the "first alley" (likely the Rue Quettier) Lombardi's tank continued up the street, while Stevens looked back and realized none of the other troops had followed them. Stevens told Phillips to hold his position, took one man with him, and turned around, recrossing the bridge. When he got to the far bank, he found the 3d Platoon leader "in a blue funk" still huddled

Private James D. McRacken, DSC. 1st Squad, 2d Platoon, Company A, 315th Combat Engineers. Killed in action, 5 August 1944. U.S. Army Engineer School, Fort Leonard Wood, Missouri.

with his men under the protection of the wall along the riverbank. Stevens ordered the platoon sergeant to get the platoon across the bridge and sent the platoon leader to the rear. The platoon promptly moved across, followed by Stevens, who picked up McRacken's bloodied M1 Rrifle and bandolier of ammunition, replacing his captured P-38 pistol, which was out of ammunition. The 1st Platoon and the rest of the 2d Platoon with the Light Machinegun Squad followed shortly afterward along with a second tank from Lombardi's platoon.[18]

With the 2d Platoon and Light Machinegun Squad on the left, the 1st Platoon on the right, and the 2d Platoon in reserve, Stevens's company swept up the hill through town for about 350 meters from the riverbank, where they found Lombardi's tank, which was nearly out of ammunition. While Lombardi's tank returned to the opposite bank to replenish ammunition, the other tank halted to hold the crossroads

Private McRacken's body on the Mayenne Bridge after it was covered in flowers by the townspeople. U.S. Army SC.

and Stevens's company continued another 260 meters to the railroad tracks outside of town. There they were engaged by about forty Germans, supported by a "Mark IV or V tank." Company A was coming across the bridge to his right, so Stevens prepared to take on the "tank" with bazookas, but the Germans withdrew. Stevens's men pushed on another 200 meters past the railroad tracks where they contacted the 3d Battalion, 357th Infantry, which in the meantime had crossed the river on rubber assault boats south of the destroyed railroad bridge. Stevens was lightly wounded during the action and was later awarded a Silver Star.[19]

The main body of the 357th Infantry had detrucked south of town while the 1st Battalion was working its way to the riverbank. The original plan had been for the 2d and 3d Battalion to make an assault crossing of the river while the 1st Battalion fought its way into town, but Hamilton's assault had been so quick they were across before Company A (-), 315th Engineers could inflate its pneumatic boats and get them to the riverbank. The 3d Battalion did not begin crossing until 1920 and did not finish until 2015. The 2d Battalion began crossing at 2015 and did not finish until nearly three hours after the 1st Battalion seized the bridge.

Colonel Barth crossed the bridge and established a forward CP for the 357th Infantry in the Hotel Ferichard, which was also the Task Force Weaver CP, shortly

The disabled 8.8cm Flak gun in Mayenne. The view is looking west toward the bridge. U.S. Army SC.

after 2145. Shortly after dark, at 2215 two German vehicles drove from the north into the town on the west side of the river, crossed the bridge, and parked in front of the Hotel Ferichard without being challenged on the way. The Germans were completely unaware the town was now in American hands, until three of them got out of their vehicle and tried to enter the building. The American CP guards opened fire on them, wounding one and capturing all three. That sparked a firefight with two more Germans in the other vehicles, which the Germans lost. Major Hamilton said that one German officer was "so full of holes that he grotesquely resembled a sieve."[20]

Nor was that the end of it. At about 2300, another German vehicle was stopped outside the Task Force Headquarters, and its occupants were taken prisoner. Then three more arrived, including a truck loaded with troops, which drove in from the north between 0100 and 0250 and stopped outside a café they planned to spend the night at. They parked nonchalantly next to another German truck and got out, only to be quickly surrounded and disarmed by Americans. The "German truck" was a captured vehicle the 357th Infantry Headquarters Company was using to transport the Regimental CP, which they were just setting up in the same café. Just as that encounter was resolved, four other German vehicles were stopped by Company

C, which was still on the western side of the river. Company A was moved to the northern edge of town with one of the 3-inch guns of the 607th Tank Destroyer Battalion, to prevent more such surprises. Two more 3-inch guns and two light tanks of Company D, 712th Tank Battalion were also posted outside the CP to deter further German incursions. Altogether, about thirty prisoners were taken, ten more Germans were killed, and twenty vehicles were seized in these encounters overnight.[21]

The rapid advance of Task Force Weaver, the confidence and decisiveness of its leaders, and the skill and bravery demonstrated by many of the its officers and men in the assault on the bridge were a huge boost to the morale of the 357th Infantry. In one day, the Task Force had advanced 37 miles from the IP to the eastern outskirts of Mayenne, when previous daily advances had sometimes been less than 100 yards. Just twenty-three men were reported as casualties by the 357th Infantry. The two Engineers and five men from the Reconnaissance Troop made a total of about thirty-one, of which just nine were fatal. The success of the 357th Infantry was symptomatic of a new confidence and skill exhibited by the entire division.

While Task Force Weaver raced across the French countryside, the rest of the 90th prepared to follow in its wake. However, the lack of trucks meant they would mostly be marching to their objectives.

The 358th Infantry assembled as CT 8 with its attached 344th Field Artillery; Battery B, 357th AAA Battalion; Company B, 315th Engineer Combat Battalion; Company B, 315th Medical Battalion; and Company B, 607th Tank Destroyer Battalion, on the road leading from La Loriais, northwest of Saint-Laurent-de-Terregatte to Buais-les-Monts, which was the IP. The 2d Battalion crossed the IP at 1230, followed by the 1st Battalion, and then the 3d. From there they marched on a route from Fougerolles-du-Plessis–La Dorée–Levaré–Saint-Denis-de-Gastines to their objective just south of Ernée, 22 miles in just over eight hours. Before dark, elements moved to establish a roadblock 4.5 miles east at Vautorte and south of Ernée.[22]

The 359th Infantry—CT 9—began assembling at 0800 in the area around Saint-Martin-de-Landelles. The march began at 1330 and took the 359th 15 miles through Landivy then south to its objective of La Tannière, 8.5 miles west of Gorron. CT 9 marched with the 915th Field Artillery; Battery C, 537th AAA Battalion; Company C, 315th Engineer Combat Battalion; Company C, 315th Medical Battalion; and Company C, 607th Tank Destroyer Battalion. The 1st Battalion led and reached the march objective at 1945, followed by the rest of the CT, which closed in at 2115. The 1st Battalion settled into a bivouac south of town at La Durantaie, and the 2d and 3d Battalion north of town at Le Mesnil and La Rimboiche, respectively. No resistance on the ground was encountered during the day, but four men were killed, two from Antitank Company and two from Company B, in a Luftwaffe bombing attack early in the morning.

The 90th Division Artillery, with the 345th Field Artillery, and the attached 173d Field Artillery Group with the 961st and 693d Field Artillery Battalion and Battery B, 3d Observation Battalion; the 40th Field Artillery Group with the 731st Field Artillery Battalion; the 537th AAA Battalion (-); and the 607th Tank Destroyer Battalion (-) received the order to move to Mayenne in the wake of Task Force Weaver at 0520. The movement began at 1420 and by 1545 Division Artillery Headquarters was set up in Landivy collocated with the Division Headquarters.

Task Force Weaver captured 5 Wehrmacht officers and 101 men in Mayenne on 5 August, and another 20 men en route to Mayenne, which closely matched the division report of 125 Wehrmacht officers and men, including 9 wounded, captured that day. Those captured by Task Force Weaver included 25 from the Luftwaffe, mostly from the *5. Fallschirmjäger-Division*. The Flak guns were likely from *gemischte Flak-Abteilung 124 (verlegbar)* (124th Mixed AAA Battalion, partly mobile). It had moved to Mayenne from Bordeaux, although three of its batteries had long been stationed in the Channel Islands. Six men were SS, all from *SS-GvB*. The rest were from various Heer units, many of them old adversaries of the 90th Infantry Division, including three from the *77.*, eleven from the *91.*, three from the *243.*, and sixteen from the *353. Infanterie-Division*. What is astonishing is the sheer variety of units the prisoners represented, which covered virtually the entire Allied front. There were twelve men from the *Panzer-Lehr-Division*, which had opposed the VII Corps in COBRA. There were also five men from the *21. Panzer-Division*, which had spent the entire campaign facing the British in the vicinity of Caen, 60 miles to the north, and three from the *363. Infanterie-Division*, which had just arrived from Belgium and was committed at Vire, 37 miles to the north. Perhaps most surprising though was the actual defense of the bridge at Mayenne had been entrusted to *3./Bau-Pionier-Batallion 59*, a company of construction engineers sent to Mayenne from Wimereaux, Belgium, and the guns of *Flak-Abteilung 124*, while the rest of the personnel captured were from units in transit, unaware of the threat from the rapidly advancing American forces.

Which German units were the source of the tanks and assault guns reported both west and east of town remains unclear. Men from the *Stabsbatterie/SS-Panzer-Abteilung 17.*, *2./Sturmgeschütz-Brigade 341*, the *Stabsbatterie/Sturmgeschütz-Brigade 902*, and *8./Panzer-Regiment 130* were all captured in or around Mayenne on

5 August. However, as of 1 August, *SS-GvB* reported that none of its Sturmgeschütz were operational. All the other units had been heavily engaged and were very weak, while the remainder of *Panzer-Lehr-Division* was assembling at Alençon for refitting. It seems most likely that none were from organized units but were straggler vehicles from various sources, all trying to escape the onrushing American forces.

The German high command had intended that Mayenne be strongly defended by the *708. Infanterie-Division*, which like the *363. Infanterie-Division* was just arriving at the front. The *708. Infanterie-Division* was organized as a static occupation division in February 1941 and had been stationed defending the Gironde estuary since June 1941. It was ordered to move north to reinforce the front in Normandy sometime after 25 July. Some elements moved by road and others by train. By 2 August, its leading motorized elements moving by road had reached Angers, about 70 miles south of Mayenne, while the rest had only reached Niort, about 235 miles south of Mayenne. On 5 August, its *Füsilier-Bataillon 708*, *14./Grenadier-Regiment 748* (the Regimental Antitank Company), and a self-propelled Flak platoon were at Laval, while *1./Panzerjäger-Abteilung 708*, with nine self-propelled 7.5cm Marder antitank guns, was at le Lion d'Angers, still en route to Le Mans by train. Five of twelve 8.8cm Pak of *2./Panzerjäger-Abteilung 708, Grenadier-Regiment 728*, *Pionier-Batallion 708*, and *3./Artillerie-Regiment 1708* were on the march from Le Mans through Sillé-le-Guillaume on their way to hold the line of the river at Mayenne. *Grenadier-Regiment 748* (less *14. Kompanie* at Laval) and *4./Artillerie-Regiment 1708* were on the march from Sablé-sur-Sarthe to do the same between Mayenne and Laval. *Sicherungs-Regiment 1* was at Le Mans. The rest of the division was still on its way from Bordeaux.[23]

Finally, a potentially very powerful force was assembling in the area Domfront–Alençon–Trun, the leading elements of *9. Panzer-Division*. It had been refitting in the Avignon area and was quite strong, although it lacked many essential motor vehicles. It was ordered to move north by train on 27 July and by 4 August about 75 percent of the trains hauling the division had been unloaded. It was intended that *9. Panzer-Division* would support the projected attack at Mortain, Unternehmen Lüttich (Operation Liege) by *XXXXVII Panzerkorps*, which was intended by Hitler to drive west to seize the bridges at Avranches and separate TUSA from the FUSA.[24]

However, the German plans began to fall apart when Task Force Weaver seized the bridge at Mayenne intact. Instead of securing the deep southern flank of the German counterattack, Mayenne could become a springboard for American attacks to the north and northeast, cutting the lines of communication and supply of the *XXXXVII Panzerkorps* from Alençon to Domfront. On the night of 5/6 August,

General der Panzertruppen Adolf Kuntzen, commander of the *LXXXI Armeekorps*, was ordered to counterattack with elements of the *708. Infanterie-Division* and *9. Panzer-Division* to retake Mayenne.[25]

6 AUGUST

On the morning of 6 August, General McLain was notified that General Collins had directed General Huebner to cut short the 1st Infantry Division's pause and move to Mayenne. They would relieve the elements of the 90th Infantry Division there, allowing Task Force Weaver to resume its advance eastward, with Le Mans as its next objective. General Haislip's plan for the XV Corps was for a concentric attack by the three divisions of the corps. The 5th Armored Division was finally through the Avranches–Pontaubault bottleneck and would drive east before turning north to attack the city from the south and southeast. The 79th Infantry Division would drive from Laval to attack the city from the southwest. The 90th Infantry Division would attack the city from the west.

General McLain decided to split Task Force Weaver into two elements. Task Force Weaver would drive southeast and then east via Aron–Jublains–Évron–Sainte-Suzanne–Saint-Denis-d'Orques–Coulans-sur-Gée–Chaufour-Notre-Dame–Le Mans. Task Force Barth would drive south through Moulay–Commer–Montsûrs–Sainte-Suzanne–Viviers–Saint-Symphorien–Bernay-Neuvy-en-Champagne–La Quinte–Le Mans. The reorganized Task Force consisted of:

Task Force Weaver

Reconnaissance Echelon:	90th Reconnaissance Troop (- 2d Platoon)[26]
	Company D, 712th Tank Battalion
Advance Guard:	Company A, 357th Infantry (riding on tanks)
	Company A, 712th Tank Battalion
	Battery, 343d Field Artillery Battalion
	Detachment, Company A, 315th Engineer Combat Battalion
Column Command Group:	General Weaver
	Detachment, 90th Signal Company
Main Body:	3d Battalion, 357th Infantry
	712th Tank Battalion (-)
	343d Field Artillery Battalion (-)
	693d Field Artillery Battalion

	Battery A, 537th AAA Battalion
	Company A, 315th Engineer Combat Battalion (-)
	Company A, 315th Medical Battalion
	Company A, 607th Tank Destroyer Battalion (-)
Rear Guard:	Company C, 712th Tank Battalion (- 1st and 3d Platoon)

Task Force Barth

Reconnaissance Echelon:	Intelligence and Reconnaissance Platoon, 357th Infantry
	Reconnaissance Platoon, 712th Tank Battalion
Advance Guard:	Company C, 357th Infantry
	1st and 3d Platoon, Company C, 712th Tank Battalion
Column Command Group:	Colonel Barth
	Regimental Defense Platoon[27]
	Platoon, 357th Infantry Antitank Company
Main Body:	357th Infantry (-)
	345th Field Artillery Battalion
	Detachment, Company A, 315th Engineer Combat Battalion
	1 platoon, Company C, 607th Tank Destroyer Battalion

Both task forces waited until units of the 1st Infantry Division arrived at Mayenne before resuming the advance.

Task Force Barth got moving first, at 1400. Initially the movement was on foot because the trucks for motorizing the task force had been released the previous afternoon and returned to their parent units. Fifty trucks from the 5th Armored Division caught up with Task Force Barth about 6 miles south of Mayenne at about 1600. Motorized again, the Task Force moved forward rapidly, brushing aside slight resistance 3 kilometers north of Montsûrs from elements of the *Sicherungs-Regiment 195,* which was a security unit composed of elderly and limited duty men, capturing twelve or thirteen of them.[28]

The Advance Guard, command group, and 1st Battalion reached Torcé-Viviers-en-Charnie, 4 miles east of Sainte-Suzanne at 1930. Colonel Barth decided to close there for the night but then received word the rest of the Main Body, the

2d Battalion, 357th Infantry and the two artillery battalions had halted north of Montsûrs due to a misunderstanding in their orders. Worse, as the 345th Field Artillery, which was ahead of the 2d Battalion in the column, prepared to go into bivouac at dark between Commer and Montsûrs; they were fired on by a German machine gun in the woods just 800 yards away. General McLain appeared on the scene and brought up the 2d Battalion to deal with the situation, but by 2200 it was apparent the Germans had reoccupied Montsûrs. They had cut the American column in two.[29]

Meanwhile, Task Force Weaver was ordered to move out at 1330 but was delayed by heavy German artillery fire impacting the assembly area and roads on the eastern edge of Mayenne. The Task Force finally got moving at 1500. By 1800 it had advanced just a mile, about halfway to Aron, where it struck elements of the *9. Panzer-Division* advancing from the north and northeast and *708. Infanterie-Division* moving from the east. The two opposing forces had collided in a meeting engagement. The 90th Reconnaissance Troop quickly called in two air strikes on German vehicles approaching from the north and east of Mayenne.

One air strike was directed at German troops north of Mayenne, east of La Haie-Traversaine. Four tanks were reported knocked out from that strike near Saint-Fraimbault-de-Prières. The German unit hit by this air strike was probably *KG Corretti* under Oberst Julius Corretti who had been the commander of *Regiments-Stab zbV. 752*, the headquarters for Osttruppen on the Cotentin Peninsula, then later was retained as a supernumerary officer by *LXXXIV Armeekorps*. *KG Coretti* consisted of fragments of *Panzer-Lehr-Division*: *2./Panzer-Aufklarüngs-Lehr-Abteilung 130*, ten or twelve Panther tanks of *I./Panzer-Regiment 6*, and some Panzergrenadier, with parts of *I./Panzergrenadier-Regiment 11*of *9. Panzer-Division* and *III./Sicherungs-Regiment 1*.[30]

Coming up behind *KG Corettie* was the advance guard of *9. Panzer-Division*, *KG Unger* and *KG Reich*, under Oberstleutnant Dr. Johann Reich, the commander of *Panzergrenadier-Regiment 10*. Only one company of Panzer IV was available as the rest were still unloading from trains at Alençon, 65 kilometers to the east, along with most of the rest of the Division Artillery. The last element of the division present, *Panzer-Aufklarüngs-Abteilung 9*, patrolled north along the Mayenne River to Domfront, covering a front of about 35 kilometers.[31]

The other air strike was directed at a group of ten self-propelled guns, accompanied by infantry, reportedly advancing west on the Rue de la Grange, 650 meters northwest of Aron on the D35 Road. The P-47s claimed seven of the self-propelled guns, but later it was determined they knocked out only four.

After the P-47 strike on La Grange, Company D and the 2d Platoon of Company A, 712th Tank Battalion, which were the point of the Task Weaver column, became heavily engaged outside of Aron. Lieutenant Lund, the 2d Platoon Leader, had his tank knocked out as it neared Aron. Lieutenant Lund was wounded and his driver killed as they evacuated the tank, and his other three crewmen were badly burned. The 3d Platoon moved up in support and advanced into Aron, where one tank was hit by a "enemy bazooka." Its crew escaped with the driver burned on his face and hands. That tank was later recovered and repaired. The 1st Platoon then relieved the 2d Platoon, which withdrew to reload and refuel, followed by the 3d Platoon.

The Germans were estimated to still have six tanks or self-propelled guns in or just west of Aron after the air attack. Four of those were knocked out by the fire of Company A, 712th Tank Battalion and the supporting American artillery. The indefatigable Lieutenant Rhein was again flying his "Cub" and did his best to suppress the German defenses. His Distinguished Flying Cross citation stated,

> *On 6 and 7 August 1944, he adjusted fire on tanks and self-propelled guns ahead of the reconnaissance elements and infantry. His continuous reports on the progress of the leading elements of the column to the task force commander materially aided and speeded the advance of the column.*[32]

The other liaison pilot of the 343d Field Artillery, Lieutenant Hicks, also did his best to suppress the Germans in Aron and was also awarded a Distinguished Flying Cross.

> *First Lieutenant Edward C. Hicks, Jr (Army Serial No 01183537), Field Artillery, United States Army, for extraordinary achievement while participating in aerial flights during the period from 5 August 1944 to 8 August 1944. The 343d Field Artillery Battalion, for which First Lieutenant Hicks was observing, was part of a task which spearheaded the drive of the 90th Infantry Division on Mayenne and Le Mans, France. In order to remain in the air for long periods of time, he landed in fields along the route of the column without prior ground reconnaissance. By refueling on these fields and not returning to his base, valuable time was gained for observation and fire missions. On 6 August 1944, First Lieutenant Hicks was fired on by German 20mm antiaircraft guns from the vicinity of Aron, but he continued to adjust fire on the enemy. During the attack on Aron by the 3d Battalion, 357th Infantry, he adjusted on 2 tanks and 2 self-propelled guns. At Coulans, during a heavy rain, he directed fire on a strongly held position, and, as a result, the advance was not held up and the town was taken. His continuous reporting*

to the task force commander on the advance of the leading elements materially aided the accomplishment of the task force mission. The outstanding services rendered by Lieutenant Hicks reflect the highest credit upon himself and the armed forces of the United States. Entered military service from Oregon.[33]

Another two self-propelled guns were thought to have been knocked out by bazookas of the 357th Infantry in Aron during the night. Despite the success in eliminating the German self-propelled guns, heavy German small arms fire kept Company A, 357th Infantry pinned down and unable to support the further advance of the tanks. General Weaver attempted to outflank the resistance in Aron from the south with the 3d Battalion, 357th Infantry, but they too encountered heavy resistance. Nevertheless, they made slow progress, hampered by counterattacks from a few remaining German "tanks." By 2400, the Germans were pushed out of the town.

Prisoners captured by the 357th Infantry quickly revealed the Germans were intent on recapturing Mayenne. The Regimental S-2 assessed that at least two German battalions with artillery and armored support were opposing Task Force Weaver. He was substantially correct. The *14./Grenadier-Regiment 728* was positively identified by a PW at 2200 and prisoner interrogation made it clear the *III./Grenadier-Regiment 728*, reinforced by a *Pionierkompanie*, a *Panzerjägerkompanie*, and ten to twelve self-propelled guns, had been committed at Aron. While most of the self-propelled guns were accounted for, the threat of *KG Coretti* with reportedly another "40 tanks" remained, while the rest of *708. Infanterie-Division* was continuing to deploy on the line Aron–La Bazoge-Montpinçon–Belgeard as it arrived from Le Mans.[34]

Given the strong opposition found on the original route through Aron, General McLain demonstrated a flexibility never seen from General Landrum. McLain directed General Weaver to stop hammering against the German defenses at Aron and instead withdraw his Task Force to Mayenne. From there, Task Force Weaver was to follow the route of Task Force Barth through Montsûrs to Vaiges and then pick up its original route from Saint-Denis-d'Orques–Coulans-sur-Gée–Chaufour-Notre-Dame–Le Mans, bypassing Aron, Jublains, Évron, and Sainte-Suzanne. Task Force Weaver duly withdrew from Aron to Mayenne at 0300, disengaging from the Germans without much effort. However, it then became embroiled in a fratricidal conflict with the 16th Infantry of the 1st Infantry Division, resulting in several casualties to both divisions before the mistake was sorted out. Task Force Weaver finally settled back into its assembly area on the eastern outskirts of Mayenne for three hours of rest before moving out again.[35]

CT 8 was issued verbal orders by Colonel Stillwell, the division G-3, to advance by foot and motor marching to the southeast. The initial march objective was Alexain and then Montgiroux, where it was planned to build a bridge to span the Mayenne River. From there the regiment was to continue east to Martigné-sur-Mayenne, following behind Task Force Weaver. Company F was motorized and reinforced with a Heavy Machine Gun and an Engineer Platoon as Advance Guard and set off at 0800 from Saint-Denis-de-Gastines, following Troop C, 106th Cavalry Reconnaissance Squadron of the 106th Cavalry Group. The Cavalrymen reached Montgiroux at 1140, where they found the bridge partially destroyed as expected. Elements of the Forces françaises de l'Intérieur (FFI—the armed French Resistance) had attempted to protect the bridge until the arrival of the Americans but had been driven away by elements of *SS-Das Reich*. Two Frenchmen, twenty-five-year-old Maurice David and twenty-seven-year-old Roger Garnavault, were captured at a nearby farm and then were beaten to death by the SS troopers.[36]

Elements of the 537th Treadway Bridge Company arrived at 1415 and began emplacing a bridge. CT 8 closed up on the river at 1630 and the troops were permitted to bathe while bridge construction continued. At 1800, the bridge was completed and the regiment moved on to Chalons-du-Maine, where they had their first encounter of the day with the Germans—a single enemy vehicle that was stopped in flight by three mortar rounds. CT 8 closed in bivouac by around 2030 after advancing 18.5 miles without opposition.

At 0130 on 6 August, the 359th Infantry received orders to deploy one reinforced battalion at 0900 to protect the left flank of the division. It was to prevent any German movements west past a line from Fougerolles-du-Plessis to Saint-Denis-de-Gastines. Another battalion was to move by truck to relieve Task Force Weaver of the responsibility of holding the bridge at Mayenne. The 2d Battalion was given the flank security mission and the 3d Battalion the bridge defense mission—both moving out by 0900. The rest of the 359th remained at La Durantaie. At 1325, the orders were changed: the 2d Battalion was relieved of its defensive mission and it and the regiment were ordered to prepare for a move to an assembly area at Ernée. They began shuttle movement to Ernée at 1415 and were closed in there by 1800. The division then ordered the 359th (-) to move to Chailland and then to Saint-Jean-sur-Mayenne. Earlier in the day, Troop C, 121st Cavalry Reconnaissance Squadron of the 106th Cavalry Group, which was screening the right flank of the 90th and left flank of the 79th Infantry Division, found that although the Germans had blown up the bridge at Saint-Jean-sur-Mayenne on 4 August, they had not left any forces covering the crossing site. They also found the demolition of the bridge was incomplete; there was a 16-foot and a 20.5-foot gap in the bridge deck but otherwise the bridge was intact. French civilians were already working at repairing the bridge and they were soon joined by elements of the 1277th Engineer Combat Battalion, which was in support of the 315th Engineer Combat Battalion. At 2045, the two gaps in the bridge were repaired well enough so that troops and light vehicles could cross, and by 2315 the bridge was strong enough to support the Cavalry's light tanks, which crossed to the east bank.

At Mayenne, the 3d Battalion, 359th Infantry found itself without a mission because the 16th Infantry of the 1st Infantry Division had taken over responsibility to defend the bridge and bridgehead. Instead it remained under division control and followed in the trail of Task Force Barth.

By this time the German situation was rapidly deteriorating. While the *9. Panzer-Division* was assembling north and northeast of Mayenne, elements of the 1st Infantry Division had crossed the Mayenne River against minimal resistance from fragments of German units, including the *5. Fallschirmjäger-Division*, 11 kilometers to the north at Ambrières-les-Vallées and quickly completed a bridge. That threatened the German rear and their line of supply via the N12 to Alençon and left the forward elements of *9. Panzer* vulnerable to encirclement from north and south.

The situation for the *708. Infanterie-Division* was even more dire. The division *Fusilier-Batallion*, its bicycle-mounted "mobile" reserve, was at Laval, 29 kilometers to the southwest of the two battalions of the *728. Infanterie-Regiment* at Aron–Belgeard. The *Fusilier-Batallion 708.* was part of *KG Kuntzen*, a hodgepodge of Heer and Luftwaffe troops, and was overrun and destroyed on 7–8 August by the 79th Infantry Division and 5th Armored Division. Two battalions of the *748. Infanterie-Regiment* with one *Pionierkompanie* had advanced through Évron on the afternoon of 6 August attempting to reach positions to attack Mayenne from the south and east but instead ran into Task Force Barth at Sainte-Suzanne and Montsûrs. It was reportedly supported by as many as twenty Panzer IV attached from *9. Panzer-Division*. The *Sicherungs-Regiment 1*, which had just arrived at Le Mans from Paris on 5 August, was the last major element of the German defense. Its *III. Batallion* extended the line of the *728. Grenadier-Regiment* south from Aron, along the L'Aron River toward Moulay. The *II./Sicherungs-Regiment 1* defended Évron, while the *I./Sicherungs-Regiment 1* defended the Laval to Le Mans highway (D57) at Vaiges.[37]

The supporting units for the German division were also less than ideal in terms of quality and quantity. The *1708. Artillerie-Regiment* had nine batteries, but only one, *3. Batterie* with four ex-French 105mm howitzers, was motorized. The others were all horse-drawn. Three other batteries each had four of the French 105mm howitzers, while two each had four 122mm ex-Soviet howitzers, and three each had four 76.2mm ex-Soviet guns. The *3. Batterie* was at Évron and the *4. Batterie* was at Sainte Suzanne, but *Stab I. Abteilung* and *2. Batterie* were arriving at Le Mans during the night of 6 August, while *5.*, *6.*, *7.*, *8.*, and *9. Batterie* were still en route from Royan. The rest of the Division Artillery—*Stab/Artillery-Regiment 1708*, *Stab/II. Abteilung*, *1.* and *9. Batterie*—were still in Bordeaux as of mid-August and probably never left.[38]

The *Panzerjäger-Abteilung 708* was somewhat more mobile but was split up over a wide area. The nine Marder of *1. Kompanie* were probably still unloading from their trains at Le Mans early on 6 August and were committed piecemeal to the front at Mayenne. The twelve motorized 8.8cm Pak of *2. Kompanie* had been added to the battalion when it left Royan—it was originally a Heerestruppen (Army Troops) unit that was hastily organized and equipped by *1. Armee* in July. The last element of the battalion, *3. Kompanie*, was only partly motorized. Two platoons were equipped with a total of nine horse-drawn 2cm Flak guns and one platoon—the one at Laval—had self-propelled guns, probably four of them.[39]

The hastily organized and incomplete German defenses were a far cry from what the 90th Infantry Division had faced at Mont Castré. The 90th Infantry Division was also a far cry from the battered and discouraged formation it was on the Island. The division was about to exhibit its newfound confidence and expertise in the American way of war: maneuver.

Possibly far more consequential for the operations of the 90th Infantry Division were events occurring this night about 47 miles to the northwest, along a line just east of Sourdeval and Mortain. There, based upon telephone orders issued by Adolf Hitler sometime on 2 August, stood the remnants of five German divisions: *2. Panzer*, *116. Panzer*, *1. SS-Panzer-Division "Leibstandarte SS Adolf Hitler"* (*LSSAH*), *SS-Das Reich*, and *SS-GvB*. They were poised to execute Unternehmen Lüttich. This intention was revealed to the Allied leaders through ULTRA in the late evening of 6 August. Shortly after midnight the German attack crashed into the lines of the 30th Infantry Division at Mortain and parts of the 9th Infantry Division at Sourdeval.[40]

7 AUGUST

Shortly after midnight, Colonel Barth, with his Command Group, including the liaison parties of the 345th and 693d Field Artillery, had stopped in Sainte-Suzanne to make sure the Main Body did not get lost coming through the town. There they were attacked while separated from the 1st Battalion at Viviers. German units began appearing in large numbers south and west of town at dark. The antitank guns with the Command Group shot up some German trucks to the south, but by midnight German infantry had pushed into the town and forced Barth to order the 1st Battalion back from Viviers to restore the situation. However, Hamilton's 1st Battalion was also being attacked, and he could not immediately break contact until that attack was repulsed at 0230. At 0500, the Germans overran one of the antitank guns defending the Command Group. The Command Group was preparing for a last-ditch stand when at 0630 medium tanks from Company C, 712th Tank Battalion and infantry from the 1st Battalion reentered the town and drove the Germans west and south.

There was no escape for the Germans though. As they fled, they ran into the 2d Battalion, 357th Infantry and the 345th Field Artillery, which had broken through the Germans at Montsûrs and headed to Sainte-Suzanne. Many were cut down and others surrendered or fled in confusion. By 1000 on 7 August, the two halves of Task Force Barth were reunited and ready to move on. However, the situation remained confused as fragmented German units continued to blunder into the American line of march. After the tanks and infantry began moving on to Viviers, about 100 yards south of Sainte-Suzanne the 345th Field Artillery was hit by indirect and direct high-velocity gunfire from the woods southeast of town. The 345th went into battery in less than fifteen minutes and began firing battery and battalion volleys at what was reported as fifteen German tanks. The 345th was quickly joined by the 693d Field Artillery and the two battalions proceeded to hammer the German force, which withdrew eastward, leaving four wrecked vehicles smoking in the woods.

A third liaison pilot, this one assigned to the 345th Field Artillery Battalion, was awarded a Distinguished Flying Cross for their service during this period.

> *First Lieutenant Allen T. O'Connor (Army Serial No 0465107), Field Artillery, United States Army, for extraordinary achievement while participating in aerial flights from 6 August 1944 to 9 August 1944, in France. First Lieutenant O'Connor performed outstanding work as a liaison pilot to the 345th Field Artillery Battalion, during the advance from Mayenne to Le Mans, France. Remaining in the air almost continually during daylight hours, he directed accurate artillery fire on the enemy opposing the advance, conducted reconnaissance to the front and flanks, and furnished liaison between adjacent columns. He flew over enemy lines on many occasions under hostile fire. His daring was an inspiration to the front line troops, and his work was a direct contribution to the speed and success of the advance. The services rendered by First Lieutenant O'Connor reflect the highest credit upon himself and the armed forces of the United States. Entered military service from Nebraska.*[41]

By 1200, the 2d Battalion, led personally by General McLain, reached the Command Group in Saint-Suzanne. McLain conferred there with Colonel Barth, informing him of the detour taken by Task Force Weaver. Barth was directed to continue his march east. The 357th's I&R Platoon led off again, followed by the 1st Battalion, as before. They encountered periodic small arms and sniper fire from small groups of disorganized Germans that were quickly dealt with. Near Bernay several German patrols were captured. By 2200, the head of column and 1st Battalion were east of La Quinte, with the 2d Battalion west of town, where they settled into a bivouac for the night. They had advanced 20 miles and were just 8 miles from Le Mans.

Task Force Weaver set off again from Mayenne between 0400 and 0500, through Montsûrs to Vaiges, shortly after 1100. There they found the head of the CT 9 column, which had advanced east from its bridgehead at Saint-Jean-sur-Mayenne at 0915, after another frustrating delay waiting for trucks. The 359th had expected fifty-five trucks in time for them to move out at 0700, but only twenty-seven arrived. Kitchen trucks were again used as a substitute, and CT 9 was finally able to move at 0915. CT 9 and elements of the 106th Cavalry Squadron of the 106th Cavalry Group were engaged with an estimated German "light infantry" battalion at Saint-Jean-sur-Erve farther to the east.

General Weaver ordered Company D, 712th Tank Battalion (-) to Chammes, then south to envelope Saint-Jean-sur-Erve. They reached a point overlooking the town at 1600. The 2d Platoon of Company D and the 90th Reconnaissance Troop were ordered to drive southeast from Vaiges, reconnoitering a possible route to encircle the German forces at Saint-Jean-sur-Erve from the south. The envelopment from the north encountered stiff resistance outside of Chammes. Company D was reinforced by medium tanks from Company A, 712th Tank Battalion and infantry from Company A, 357th Infantry and took Chammes at 2100, but when they tried to move east, they again encountered heavy German fire.

A P-47 strike was called in to bomb and strafe the heavily wooded area east of Chammes where fifteen German tanks were reported, likely the same German group encountered earlier by the 345th Field Artillery. Progress was steady, but slow, and prisoners claimed the woods were held by a reinforced battalion with tank support. A frustrated General Weaver decided the attack had bogged down and ordered the column to backtrack again, reversing its course to Vaiges and then to Saint-Jean-sur-Erve, where they passed through the 359th Infantry at 2200. Little resistance was encountered, and the column halted for the night with its head just east of Saint-Denis-d'Orques.[42]

The German forces were later identified as *2./Fusilier-Batallion 708*, *3.* and *4./Grenadier-Regiment 748*, and a *Pionier* company. It was believed they were supported by a "Btry of 105's and 2-20mm AA guns (used as AT guns) and several S/P guns which were never positively identified."

During the back-and-forth of Task Force Weaver, Dad and Battery A, 537th AAA Battalion continued to follow in trail with the 343d Field Artillery. At 1445, while they were between Vaiges and Sainte-Suzanne, the column was overflown by a dozen FW 190. Curiously, the Germans did not attempt to bomb or strafe the column, but Battery A opened fire on them, shooting down one and claiming damage to another. Other batteries of the 537th claimed two more and all three German pilots were reportedly captured.

For the 358th Infantry, 7 August was another day of marching on foot. At 0700 the head of the column crossed the IP at Chalons-du-Maine, heading for Montsûrs. From there they marched through Livet to an assembly area 2.75 miles northwest of Sainte-Suzanne, where they settled in for the night at 1900. A half hour later, the orders for the next day were received: "Continue March at 0700. Order of March, 2d, 1st, 3d. IP fwd [forward] edge of woods. Rear Bn furnish [left–north] flank motor patrols. Maintain motor contact to protect rear of CT 357." The objective was Le Mans.

By midnight of 7 August, all the 90th Infantry Division was east of the Mayenne. It formed a rough triangle, with a base about 5.5 miles wide from Sainte-Suzanne to Saint-Jean-sur-Erve and extending eastward twenty miles to La Quinte. Considerable German forces had been bypassed or encircled. Roadblocks were stablished north and east of Monstours by the 2d Platoon of Company C, 607th Tank Destroyer Battalion, which destroyed three German halftrack vehicles there at 1900. The 106th Cavalry Reconnaissance Squadron extended the screen eastward to Évron, where they were stopped south of town by strong German resistance.

The German attackers at Sainte-Suzanne were likely parts of the *748. Grenadier-Regiment*, which were trying to move forward to take up positions at Montsûrs. They had no artillery support, very little antitank capability, and were attacked from front and rear by Task Force Barth. The German force at Sainte-Suzzane was crushed, but no G-2 Periodic Report was issued for the period from 1600 on 6 August to 1600 on 7 August and no Prisoner of War or Interrogation Reports were completed, so the number captured can only be estimated. Furthermore, the number of prisoners captured was only given as an approximation on some days of August and does not appear to have ever been reconciled. As many as 190, including the dozen men reported captured from the security battalion at Montsûrs, may have been captured by Task Force Barth. The rest of the *748. Grenadier-Regiment* was now trapped in a pocket east of Chammes between Task Force Barth to the north and Task Force Weaver to the south.

Meanwhile, to the southeast the 79th Infantry Division was probing the southern defenses of Le Mans. Elements of the 121st Cavalry Reconnaissance Squadron of the 106th Cavalry Group got into the city in the afternoon but were pushed out by German counterattacks. Regrouping, the 79th Infantry Division pushed the 313th Infantry into the southern edge of the city by 2100, with the 313th Infantry 5 miles farther south.

Far to the northwest, the German counteroffensive at Mortain was creating anxiety for the senior Allied leadership. In the early morning, General Bradley visited General Patton at TUSA Headquarters to discuss the situation. Bradley was forced to weigh the chances that the German attack might succeed against the advantages gained by reinforcing the XV Corps attack at Le Mans. Any reaction was also subject to the overriding requirement of keeping the ULTRA secret a secret. He finally decided to err on the side of caution and temporarily held elements of the XX Corps in positions where they could counter the German move if necessary.

In fact, the XX Corps divisions already had been ordered to hold in place. Late on the night on 7/8 August, General Patton was woken by his Chief of Staff, Major General Hugh J. Gaffey, with the ULTRA message warning of the Mortain attack. Although Patton thought it was a German bluff, he ordered the 35th Infantry Division held in the vicinity of Notre-Dame-du-Touchet, south of Mortain. The 2ème Division Blindée (2d French Armored Division), which had just completed landing, was held at Saint-James, with a task force deployed to guard the bridges at Saint-Hilaire-du-Harcouët, until 8 August when it was attached to the XV Corps. The newly arriving 80th Infantry Division was held at Saint-Jores.[43]

8 AUGUST

Task Force Weaver resumed its advance east via Joué-en-Charnie–Chassillé–Brains-sur-Gée–Coulans-sur-Gée and ending at Chaufour-Notre-Dame, less than 6 miles from the center of Le Mans. One medium tank of the 1st Platoon, Company A, 712th Tank Battalion was knocked out, but it was later recovered when it encountered a large German force near Chammes as it was moving from its bivouac toward Saint-Jean-de-Erves. Otherwise, the initial German resistance was quite light but became more intense as the march went on. Just east of Joué-en-Charnie they encountered a roadblock at a mined bridge over the Le Palais creek. Engineers rapidly cleared the mines under fire, and the advance guard drove the Germans

Medium Tanks M4A2 and M4A4 and other vehicles of the 2nd Squadron, 12th Régiment de Chasseurs d'Afrique, French 2nd Armored Division (2ème Division Blindée or 2e DB) at a marshalling area in Normandy, shortly after landing on UTAH Beach on 1 August 1944.

defending the roadblock away. At Longnes, two 20mm guns hit and disabled the leading light tank of the 2d Platoon of Company D, 712th Tank Battalion, shaking up the crew, but no one was seriously injured. The rest of the platoon quickly deployed a base of fire that destroyed the two guns and several other vehicles. The remaining three light tanks of the 3d Platoon led the column into Chaufour-Notre-Dame. There one of the 3d Platoon's tanks was hit by friendly fire from Task Force Barth, which was coming up the road from the east, behind the Germans, and its driver was killed. Two more light tanks of the 3d Platoon were disabled in this action.

Task Force Barth had moved southeast at 0900 on the D28 about 4 miles to its junction with the D357 east of Chaufour-Notre-Dame, which was marked as L'Arche on the American maps. General McLain intended for them to cut off the retreat of the Germans falling back in front of Task Force Weaver, while Colonel Bacon's 358th Infantry protected Barth's rear from the concentration of Germans surrounded east of Chammes.

The plan worked to perfection; Barth's Advance Guard reached L'Arche just before the head of the German column fleeing east. There they encountered German troops from an old adversary, *Grenadier-Regiment 1050* of the *77.*

Infanterie-Division, setting up an ambush for Task Force Weaver. Instead the erst-while ambushers were ambushed. Lieutenant Lombardi's 1st Platoon of Company C, 712th Tank Battalion again led the column.[44]

Colonel Barth later described what happened:

> *Just as the leading tank reached the crossroads, it met a German anti-aircraft battery of two self-propelled guns and one 88 trying to escape. Lt, Lombardi, firing his 75 in the lead tank, destroyed about 15 vehicles, four of them pulling AA guns, in about two minutes. The infantry riding on the tanks* [Hamilton's Company C] *took care of over 60 Germans who tried to escape, killing over half of them. This completely blocked the crossroad. I changed the plan and now turned all of Hamilton's battalion west to block. They were already deployed in that direction by the time the fight ended.*[45]

The German forces trapped between Weaver and Barth consisted of "50 enemy tanks plus a large number of vehicles" and was first spotted by XIX TAC aircraft flying reconnaissance at Coulans-sur-Gée. When Task Force Weaver approached, they were met by fire from "high-velocity guns and scattered infantry," as well as a considerable amount of artillery fire. Eliminating the trapped German force required the combined effort of the light and medium tanks of the 712th Tank Battalion, the 357th Infantry, the 343d Field Artillery, and an airstrike. The artillery fire was again observed by the liaison pilots, despite occasional rainstorms. Lieutenant Rhein was in the air again.

> *On 8 August 1944, he observed and adjusted fire during a heavy downpour of rain. First Lieutenant Rhein's outstanding accomplishments reflect the highest credit upon himself and the armed forces of the United States. Entered military service from Illinois.*[46]

The 90th Infantry Division G-2 later reported the vehicles were a mixture of self-propelled weapons as well as tanks. The count included "4-88mm AA-AT towed guns, approximately a Bn of 105mm howitzers, 4-105 AT guns (Inf cannon), 8-20mm AA guns, 50 S/P guns (7.62 cm) and approx. 100 trucks and cars." It is difficult to identify where the mass of self-propelled guns came from given all those of the *Panzerjäger-Abteilung 708* had likely already been accounted for at Aron. The "50 S/P guns" apparently also included at least one Panther tank, some assault guns, and possibly other tanks and armored vehicles, which were later identified when they were cleared from the roadway. The German forces identified included elements of the *Panzerjäger-Abteilung 708* and *Artillerie-Regiment 1708* from *708. Infanterie-Division*, as well as troops identified from *SS-GvB* and *SS-Das Reich*. It likely included remnants of *Panzer Lehr-Division* as well.

While Barth's Advance Guard and 1st Battalion dealt with the trapped Germans he sent his 2d Battalion west toward Le Mans. They also suffered from a fratricidal attack, as the 79th Infantry Division fired their artillery on what was thought to be a German column marching toward Le Mans. Despite that and the resistance of a few German self-propelled guns that were quickly knocked out, the 2d Battalion entered the western suburbs of Le Mans and reached the banks of the Sarther River just after midnight.[47]

Even with the fratricidal incidents, Task Force Weaver and Barth probably suffered fewer than 60 casualties on 8 August; Hamilton's 1st Battalion reported just one man killed and fifteen wounded and the entire 357th Infantry only suffered 30 casualties, of which four were fatal. The 712th Tank Battalion had one man killed and a half-dozen injured. But they inflicted hundreds of casualties on the Germans. An estimated 400 Germans alone were captured, about 230 just by Hamilton's Battalion, but not including some hundred or more captured who were evacuated through the divisional medical channels. Many Germans were killed as well, estimated as 100 just in the trapped column at L'Arche.

The 358th Infantry set off promptly at 0700 as planned, following the route of Task Force Barth. The head of the 358th Infantry column quickly closed up to the rear of the 357th Infantry, reaching them by 0924. When Clarke's column closed up with the rear of Barth's column, Colonel Barth immediately ordered one battalion to advance on Le Mans. It immediately encountered resistance east of the L'Arche crossroads.

At 1400, the columns were overflown by the Luftwaffe but were not attacked, probably because the Germans could no longer determine which of the numerous columns speeding eastward were German and which were American. Ten minutes later, General McLain arrived at the Regimental CP to confer with Colonel Clarke, with two German prisoners he had captured on the way riding in the back of his jeep. McLain told Clarke the 5th Armored Division was to encircle Le Mans from the south, while the 90th encircled it from the north. General McLain ordered the units of Task Force Weaver, Task Force Barth, and CT 8 to halt in place to minimize the chances of further fratricide as the division continued to close up. Positions of the northern and southern columns were sent to each other by all possible means—organic radios, artillery radios, liaisons between the leading elements, and even the artillery "Cubs" were ordered to circle over the leading elements of each group and the L'Arche road junction. It was not until after midnight that the two columns made physical contact after a patrol from Colonel Mason's 3d Battalion, 357th Infantry of Task Force Weaver met with Hamilton's 1st Battalion, 357th Infantry of Task Force Barth at the crossroads.

Meanwhile, the 358th Intelligence and Reconnaissance Platoon confirmed the Germans were still in Le Mans as of 1500. The Engineers with the 358th were ordered to establish roadblocks north and northwest of the city to prevent German advances into or out of Le Mans. However, it was becoming more and more apparent the Germans were in considerable disarray and were losing the ability to control their own troops. The 358th's G-2, Major Falvey, discovered an abandoned German battery of 105mm "guns" at Bernay-en-Champagne on the route of the march and had his I&R Platoon disable them. They almost certainly were the 105mm howitzers of *4./Artillerie-Regiment 1708*. Nor was that the only German loss of artillery that day. At 1100, armed reconnaissance planes from the XIX TAC discovered a column of German horse-drawn artillery southeast of Le Mans and destroyed it. Very likely it was another element of *Artillerie-Regiment 1708*. Another German force trying to escape Le Mans blundered into one of the roadblocks and surrendered after it was fired upon, about forty to fifty prisoners were taken, but many others slipped past in the confusion.[48]

CT 8 had just settled in for the night when at 1935 General McLain ordered Colonel Clarke to "By-pass LE MANS. 2d Bn cross [Sarthe] River NE of LE MANS tonight, with a Bn of Artillery." The troops were hastily roused from their bivouacs and by 2150 were en route to their new objectives. The Intelligence and Reconnaissance Platoon led as usual, followed by the 2d Battalion and then the 1st Battalion, which was to occupy Saint-Pavance and the riverbank to cover construction of a bridge over the Sarthe. When they crossed, the two battalions would occupy the high ground between the river northeast to Sargé-lès-le-Mans, cutting the main roads running north and northeast out of the city. The 3d Battalion would secure the west bank of the Sarthe and protect the artillery, which would deploy in the area northwest and west of La Chapelle-Saint-Aubin. By midnight, the head of the column had reached the Sarthe east of La Chapelle-Saint-Aubin, where it halted to await the arrival of bridging material.

Unfortunately, neither the 358th Infantry's regular engineer support, Company B of the 315th Engineer Combat Battalion, nor the 998th Treadway Bridge Company, which had been given the bridging job, were present at the bridge site at Saint-Pavance. Company B was ordered to move at 1035 but was at Saint-Denis-d'Orques, 23 miles from the bridge site. Worse, at 1120, Captain Midyett of Company B, 315th Engineer Combat Battalion was ordered by the commander of the 315th Engineers to hold in place because the Germans were threatening the road east of Saint-Denis. They did not begin moving until 1435, which was also when the

998th Treadway Bridge Company was ordered to accompany them and both units began slowly moving down the jammed roads toward Le Mans.

For the 359th Infantry, 8 August was a day of hurry up and wait. Just before they began marching east at 0700, General McLain notified Colonel Bacon he was to take his orders from General Weaver. In turn, Weaver then ordered Bacon to hold in place until the columns of Task Force Weaver had cleared Saint-Jean-sur-Erve. Finally at 1100, the regiment was ordered to Saint-Denis-d'Orques, then wait for orders to move on to Le Mans. The regiment with the 1st and 2d Battalion—the 3d was still under division control in reserve at Montsûrs—closed in an assembly area with the head of column at Saint-Denis-d'Orques at 1715. Shortly after, they were ordered on to Chassillé, which the 1st Battalion reached at 2300, where they were ordered to be ready to continue the advance east any time after 0600 the next day.

The 90th Division Artillery and its attached Field Artillery units were much busier on 8 August than it had been on previous days. During the afternoon, the 961st Field Artillery was continually changing its direction of fire to respond to reports of German columns. It initially fired to the southwest on targets reported by Task Force Weaver, then rotated its 155mm howitzers to fire to the northwest at Germans attempting to move against Montsûrs and then due north to fire at Évron. The 731st Field Artillery fired its 155mm guns at Évron as well, which was the first time it had opened fire since landing in France on 18 July. All missions were observed from the air.

Casualties in the 358th Infantry were minor, one killed and three wounded. Nor did the 359th Infantry suffer badly, recording just eight casualties, two fatal, on 8 August. The advance was proving to be less obstructed by German resistance than by traffic jams on the limited road network leading to Le Mans. The number of prisoners accumulating was also becoming problematic and there were few resources to evacuate them to the rear. By nightfall, the 358th Infantry had about 98 German prisoners in its hands that could not be evacuated. Even the Field Artillery was collecting large numbers of prisoners—the 693d captured 132 during the day, including 17 captured in an engagement at its CP late that evening when they also killed 6, wounded 9, and seized 5 German trucks.

Also on 8 August, Omar Bradley seized the opportunity the Germans had given him by failing in their initial attack at Mortain the previous day. With General Eisenhower present, Bradley called Montgomery and secured his approval for a change in plan. Bradley proposed turning the XV Corps north toward Alençon, while the XX Corps extended the American penetration eastward to the Seine. Bradley also requested permission to advance as far as Argentan, 12 miles north of the intra-army group boundary, if necessary. Montgomery happily agreed, especially given that the First Canadian Army had just begun an attack directed southward from Caen toward Falaise, Operation TOTALIZE, which meant there was a strong prospect of cutting off large parts of *7. Armee* and *5. Panzerarmee*.

It is uncertain exactly when this discussion took place because the printed orders do not have a time stamp. While the TUSA "Confirmation of Fragmentary Orders" implementing the change in direction gave 8 August as the date they were issued, the XV Corps did not record the receipt of General Patton's "oral orders" until 9 August at 1130.[49] General Patton recorded the event in his diary as

> *At 0900 Bradley released the 80 & 2 French and the 35th as soon as it is disengaged and I am closing them on Le Mans with a view to attacking North on the axis LE MANS-ALCENON-SEES I would rather head for CHARTRES or DREUX but Bradley won't let me.*[50]

This was the first indication that the Allied generals were diverging in their operational vision for the possible encirclement of the German army in Normandy. Montgomery and Bradley were focused on a short envelopment through Falaise and Argentan. Patton, who just a week earlier had been intent on capturing the Brittany Peninsula and its ports as laid out in the NEPTUNE planning, now saw the possibilities in a deep envelopment directed at crossing the Seine River on either side of Paris and then driving north and northwest to cut the German lines of communication across the Seine. If successful, such an attack could trap most of the *7. Armee* and *5. Panzer-Armee* west of the Seine, pocketing over a quarter million German troops. It was estimated that about twenty-one German divisions west of Argentan and south of Caen were threatened by such an envelopment.[51]

9 AUGUST

Colonel Barth's 2d Battalion, 357th Infantry reached the Sarthe River at 0030, knocking out two German tanks en route. They found the Pont Gambetta, a stone arch bridge built in 1811, intact because the prepared German demolitions had been disabled by the resistance, but they waited until daylight to cross in strength. By 0900, 357th Infantry patrols contacted the 5th Armored Division, which was approaching from the east, and the 79th Infantry Division, which was in the southern half of the city that it had occupied late the previous night. The 2d Battalion settled into a position north of the road to Savigne at Courdoux at 1130, the 3d Battalion moved up on its right and extended the line for about 1,000 yards to the

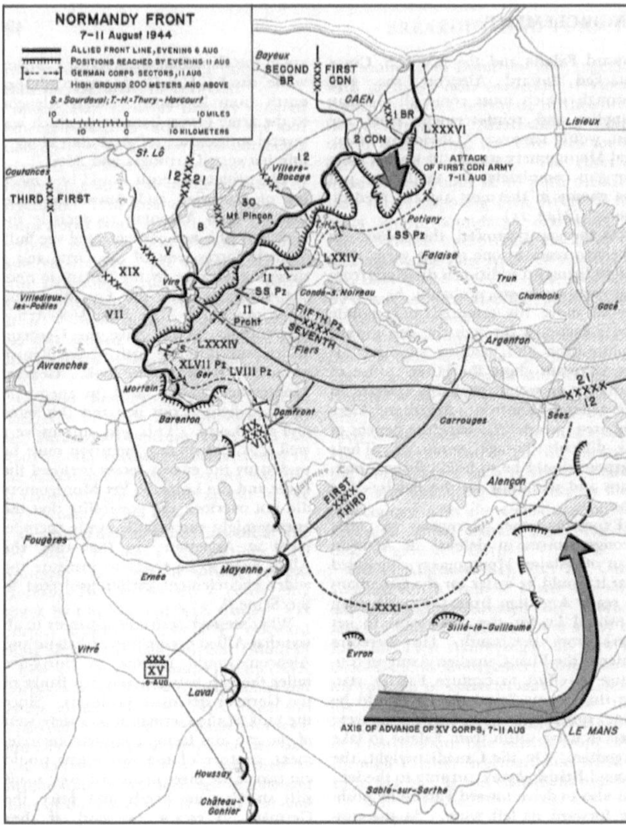

Map 15. Normandy Front, 7–11 August. Blumenson, Map 15.

southeast, and the 1st Battalion, which was released from control of Task Force Weaver, assembled in reserve between Le Cassoir and Les Fouches, astride the road 1,500 yards to the southwest. The Headquarters, 357th Infantry continued to the northeast edge of town where it occupied the Château de la Blancharderie as a CP at noon. Until just a few days earlier, the Château had been the location of the Gefechtsstand of the *7. Armee.*

The 358th Infantry spent an anxious night waiting for bridging material to arrive so they could cross the Sarthe. At 0200, Captain Midyett reported he had yet to receive any bridging equipment. At 0215, Midyett told Clarke he would go ahead and use assault boats to cross, but Clarke worried that without the ability to get antitank guns across the troops would be vulnerable to a counterattack. He decided that the crossing would wait for the start of the bridge construction, but at 0445 the bridging materiel had still not arrived, so Clarke ordered the 1st and 2d Battalion to go ahead and prepare to cross as early as possible with whatever means were available. At 0905, the 2d Battalion finally began crossing the Sarthe, using assault boats and rafts for heavy equipment, and by 1115 it was across with sixteen vehicles, and the 1st Battalion was beginning to cross. At 1330, a light ponton bridge capable of handling up to ten tons was completed, which enabled heavily loaded 2.5-ton trucks and towed artillery to cross into the bridgehead, but not heavier armored vehicles. At the same time two reconnaissance parties from the 998th Treadway Bridge Company finally arrived to select the best construction site for a treadway bridge, which could support heavy armored vehicles. The bridges were quickly emplaced, at 2247, the 133d Engineer Combat Battalion, which was supporting the 315th, reported that two treadway bridges were open at Saint-Pavance.[52]

The 359th Infantry spent another day of marching and battling traffic jams rather than Germans. At 1300, CT 9 was motorized and ordered to move via Notre Dame–Le Mans–Savigné-l'Évêque, passing through the 357th Infantry to secure the road network at Savigné. The 3d Battalion at Montsûrs was released from division control and reserve at 0600 to rejoin the 359th but could not move until 1130 because the traffic on the roads was so heavy. It was after midnight, at 0300 on 10 August, before the 359th closed at Savigné-l'Évêque.

At 1400, the 90th Division Artillery Headquarters and its attached Field Artillery battalions moved from Chassillé to Le Mans. The last of its units crossed the Sarthe into the city at 1900.

The 712th Tank Battalion conducted maintenance for much of the day. The Battalion Headquarters Company, Company C, and Company D bivouacked around Chaufour-Notre-Dame, while Company A was at Coulaines and Company B was at La Cassoir. Company D recovered and repaired two of the four tanks knocked out on 8 August. Between 1800 and 1830, Battalion Headquarters Company, Company C, and Company D moved across the Sarthe and through Le Mans to reunite with Company A and B in the vicinity of Sargé-lès-le-Mans.

With the completion of these movements, the mission assigned to the 90th Infantry Division on 5 August was completed. Task Force Weaver was dissolved at around 1100. As the Division After-Action Report put it,

> *The Division had marched 140 miles in 10 days [62 miles in the four days 6–9 August], fought three hard engagements, and numerous skirmishes. 1,517 prisoners were taken in the five days during the advance from the MAYENNE RIVER to the SARTHE*

One of a series of photographs taken by Captain Oehmichen in Le Mans on 9 August 1944. In this photo he was standing on the modern Rue du Rampart above the Rue Voltaire, looking southeast toward the Place de Jacobins. The column of vehicles is turning north onto the Avenue de Paderborn, heading toward Coulaines or Sargé-lès-le-Mans. The column is probably from the 359th Infantry.

Another photograph taken by Captain Oehmichen of the 90th Infantry Division column moving through Le Mans on 9 August 1944. In this view he was looking northeast at the Place de la République, almost 500 meters south-southwest of his previous location, at another vehicle column with the old Le Mans Renault office building in the background.

> *at LE MANS [only 1,311 were recorded by the Division G-1, the other 206 were probably evacuated through medical channels]. Practically all were from the pocket ST SUZANNE–VAIGES–LE MANS. Many were killed. Our killed, wounded and missing were less than 300. Many tanks, armored and other vehicles were destroyed. The force defending LE MANS was completely destroyed.*

General Weaver was recognized for his outstanding leadership of the task force by the award of an Oak Leaf Cluster to his Distinguished Service Cross. The citation read:

> *Brigadier General William Gaulbert Weaver (ASN: 0-3413), United States Army, was awarded a Bronze Oak Leaf Cluster in lieu of a Second Award of the Distinguished Service Cross for extraordinary heroism in connection with military operations against an armed enemy while serving with the 90th Infantry Division, in action against enemy forces on 17 August 1944. Brigadier General Weaver's intrepid actions, personal bravery and zealous devotion to duty exemplify the highest traditions of the military forces of the United States and reflect great credit upon himself, the 90th Infantry Division, and the United States Army.*[53]

****

Returning to Ducey from Mont-Saint-Michelle we went south to Louvigne-du-Desert, which is truly a desert; there was nothing around for miles except empty fields. On to Landivy, where we discovered road construction. Dad's original route east, the D31, was closed for construction all the way to Mayenne. So we detoured farther east onto the route of Task Force Weaver's Flank Guard, through Gorron, then farther east still into what was the 1st Infantry Division's zone to Ambrières-les-Vallées. From there, we turned south along the west bank of the Mayenne River, approaching Mayenne from the north rather than the west as Task Force Weaver did.

At Mayenne we turned east to cross the bridge, following the same route that led some of the lost German units into the arms of Task Force Weaver. From Mayenne we went south to Montsûrs. However, because the day was getting late and our next stop was in Alençon, instead of following the narrow back country lanes to Sainte-Suzanne we went via the faster route, through Évron to Sainte-Suzanne and then to Saint-Denis-d'Orques and east to Le Mans. We skirted the west side of town, more or less following the route of the 358th Infantry, but instead of delays for bridge building we were met by traffic backups on the A11 and A28, the French Autoroutes toll roads, to Alençon.

Dad's recollection of his five days with Task Force Weaver was one of exhilaration, constant movement, and lack of sleep. The column moved as rapidly and regularly as if on an exercise, until they met resistance when they rapidly deployed, tested the enemy resolve, and either overran them or turned back to seek a new route forward. It seemed like the endless days of standing still in the bocage while it rained were just a bad dream. Dad remembered everyone in Task Force Weaver thought they were leading the American Army to a decisive defeat of the Germans in France.

CHAPTER 11

SOLID SHOULDER OR BROKEN NECK?

10 AUGUST

As of midnight on 9 August, the 90th Infantry Division was in a position north and east of Le Mans, ready to move to the north or east as ordered. The rest of the XV Corps were arrayed around the city. The 79th Infantry Division was to the south, the 5th Armored Division to the east, and the newly arrived 2ème Division Blindée to the north. The French had crossed the Sarthe at Le Mans and were still passing through the 90th Infantry Division. In addition, the 80th Infantry Division, which had just landed in France on 3 August and was at Saint-Jores, was also attached to the XV Corps on 8 August before it was switched to the XX Corps on 10 August and was ordered to secure Le Mans.

On the evening of 9 August, ULTRA confirmed the Germans were still trying to cover their southern flank using the *9. Panzer-Division* and *708. Infanterie-Division*. Then, in the early morning hours of 10 August, ULTRA revealed that instead of cutting their losses and withdrawing from Mortain, Hitler had resolved to renew the attack there. Feldmarschall Günther Adolf Ferdinand von Kluge, Oberbefehlshaber (Supreme Commander) *Heeresgruppe B*, as well as Oberbefehlshaber West ordered the attack continue "probably on the 11th." The troops involved included those already engaged at Mortain, as well as elements of *9. Panzer-Division* and *10. SS-Panzer-Division "Frundsberg,"* which were to the north of XV Corps. Sending them on a futile mission to the west stripped away what little chance the Germans had of preventing the XV Corps from plunging deep into their rear.[1]

General Patton's oral orders for a new axis of advance, which the XV Corps received on the morning of 9 August, were finally implemented early on 10 August. The XV Corps was to turn north, toward Alençon, advancing east of the Sarthe, to seize an initial line Carrouges–Sées. General Haislip relayed his orders to the Corps units at 1000. The advance would be led by the 5th Armored Division on the right (east) and the 2ème Division Blindée on the left (west). The 79th Infantry Division would follow the 5th Armored Division and the 90th Infantry Division would follow the French.

At noon, General McLain issued orders for the division to advance in three columns. The right column was led by the motorized CT 9, followed by the marching 357th Infantry. The center column consisted of the 315th Engineer Combat Battalion and the Division Artillery. The left column was CT 8, with one reinforced battalion motorized as flank protection, followed by the 712th Tank Battalion (-). The 90th Reconnaissance Troop, reinforced with the 1st Platoon, Company D, 712th Tank Battalion, screened the left of the division and maintained contact with the 106th Cavalry Group (-), which screened the Corps left front (north) and flank (northwest and west), moving on the west bank of the Sarthe River. The 80th Infantry Division (-319th RCT) would secure the left and rear of the XV Corps, defending the road junctions at Évron and Sillé-le-Guillaume and the bridges at Le Mans, until it passed to control of the XX Corps. The XIX TAC would again provide the column cover that had proven so effective in the advance on Mayenne and Le Mans.[2]

While it was assumed the attack by the 2ème Division Blindée to the front would eliminate the German threat from that direction, leaving the 90th to mop up behind them, the XV Corps G-2 considered the threat from the left flank to be very real. It was known that all or parts of several German divisions were west of the Sarthe, including elements of the *9. Panzer* and *708. Infanterie-Division*. The detailed assessment was:

> *5 Armd Div faced the 708 on its left flank, 9 Pz in the center, and 130 Pz Lehr Div on its right flank. The 2 French Armd Div reported contact with 9 Pz and scattered elements of previously identified divs. 90 Inf Div captured prisoners from elements of 708 Inf Div, 9 Pz Div, 130 Lehr and 116 Pz Div. PW interrogation reveals 9 SS HOHENSTAUFEN Pz Div possibly in 90 Div sector.*

Liaison with the 2ème Division Blindée was established during the day. The French had advanced rapidly against scattered resistance after passing through the division on 9 August. With the French columns cleared from the front of the division, at 1800, General McLain notified his three CTs that the 90th Infantry Division advance would begin at 0600 on 11 August.

Tactical Organization of the 90th Infantry Division, 10 August 1944

Left Flank Screen	**Screen**		
	106th Cav Gp (-)		
	Left Column	**Center Column**	**Right Column**
Route A	**Route B**	**Route C**	**Route D**
90th Recon Tp 1st Plat, Co D, 712th Tk Bn 3d Bn, 358th Inf (Mtz)	CT 8 358th Inf (-) 344th FA Bn 693d FA Bn Co B, 315th Med Bn 1st Plat, Co B, 315th Engr C Bn Co B, 607th TD Bn Btry B, 537th AAA Bn	90th Division Artillery (-) 40th FA Group 999th FA Bn (8-inch How) 731st FA Bn (155 Gun) 173d FA Group (-) 182d FA Bn (155 How) 961st FA Bn (155 How) 607th TD Bn (-) 537th AAA Bn (-)	CT 9 (Mtz) 359th Inf 915th FA Bn 345th FA Bn Co C, 315th Med Bn Co C, 315th Engr C Bn Co C, 607th TD Bn Btry C & D, 537th AAA Bn
	712th Tk Bn (-)	315th Eng C Bn (-)	CT 7 343d FA Bn Co A, 315th Engr C Bn Co A, 315th Med Bn Btry A, 537th AAA Bn

All regimental and battalion commanders of the division met with General McLain at 1000 for a briefing on the upcoming operations. Colonel Clarke later passed on the gist of General McLain's briefing to the company commanders of the 358th Infantry.

We will now, for a while, move rapidly. Sometimes we will be motorized, sometimes, not. Our direction of move now will be north, then east to the highly prized objective—Paris!

Tho our tremendously valiant record of fighting and victories in the first days of the campaign never reached the public eye, our efforts since have been cited by the War Correspondents and Public Relations writers that have been with us. Now we are getting the publicity we deserve!

General McLain stressed the importance of keeping the "Jerries" moving, never giving them a chance to rest of set up. By doing this, he stated, we can outrun them and out-flank them.

Many times the Germans have been "just a step" behind us, as we very well know. Our experience with their bombers at St. Hiliare is just one instance!

The Division Commander also recommended the use of lesser roads when we go to rear areas. The German operations "zero in" on main roads and cross roads.

The renewed confidence and improved tactical capability demonstrated by the 90th in the previous week was about to be tested again. Although the Division G-1 reported the loss of 143 casualties on 10 August, it seems likely they were catching up on reports from the intense battles of July because the three infantry regiments only reported a combined total of eight casualties. Otherwise, the major action of the day was by T/5 Albert T. Cascio of Gun Section #4, 1st Platoon, Battery D, 537th AAA Battalion.

His Platoon was emplaced about 7 miles north of Le Mans when two excited French civilians approached and told them there were "several Germans" hiding in the woods nearby. The 1st Platoon organized two details to round them up, one detail consisting of T/5 Cascio and two other members of his gun crew. The two groups started off with Cascio's heading directly for the woods and the other circling around to flank them.

When Cascio's group got within about 100 yards of the hedge surrounding the woods they were suddenly met by a volley of small arms fire that forced them to drop to the ground. None were hit, so Cascio rose to a kneeling position and unleashed a burst of thirty rounds from his M3 submachine gun into the hedge. Although he could not see a result, or the enemy, Cascio boldly called on them to surrender, while still kneeling and changing magazines. Immediately about thirty Germans began to filter across the hedgerow into the field. One of the Germans still was armed, so Cascio motioned for him to drop his weapon. Instead the German brought his weapon up to fire, so Cascio fired another burst, killing the armed German and wounding four of the others. The other Germans immediate raised their hands and were soon joined by more who began pouring into the field. When they were all rounded up, Cascio and his two companions had sixty-six Germans on their hands, including four officers, from a Luftwaffe airfield security unit. T/5 Cascio was awarded a Silver Star by General Marshall, who was visiting the ETOUSA, in an awards ceremony held at the end of the month.[3]

The two divisions leading the XV Corps advance had a slightly more difficult day. By 1930, the XV Corps had reached an east-west line running through Beaumont-sur-Sarthe against occasionally strong resistance. Combat Command R, 5th Armored Division lost six tanks and forty men, while the rest of the division had forty-four personnel casualties and an unknown number of tank losses. The 2ème Division Blindée reported the loss of just four tanks and fourteen men, all wounded.

11 AUGUST

CT 9 began its advance promptly at 0600. There was no resistance other than from traffic jams on the roads. Route D started at the IP at Savigné-l'Évêque and then to Chanteloup–Ponthouin–Dangeul–René. By the evening, the regiment had closed up northeast of René.

The traffic on CT 7's Route D was so bad that McLain ordered it to shift west to Route C in front of the Division Artillery column to relieve the congestion on Route D. The 357th Intelligence and Reconnaissance Platoon left at 0430 to mark the new route and the 3d Battalion crossed the IP at Les Fourches in Sargé-lès-le-Mans at 0630. At 1000, the 3d Battalion was 2.5 miles north of Courcebœufs, the 2d Battalion was at Courcebœufs, and the 1st Battalion was 2,000 yards to its south. By 1150, the 3d Battalion was 5 miles north of Ballon-Saint-Mars, when the column was halted for a one-hour break. The hour break became a dead halt at 1310, when word came that the 2ème Division Blindée and 5th Armored Division had collided in a confusion of routes. While waiting, CT 7 closed into an assembly area northwest of Congé-sur-Orne. Finally, the two armored divisions cleared out of the way and at 1930 the march continued to a bivouac area just south of René, where the regiment halted for the night at 2300.

The Division Artillery moved off at 0700 and halted southwest of Ballon by 1000. It remained there until 1600, when it moved northeast of Ballon. That evening, the 40th Field Artillery Group and its battalions was detached from the 90th Division Artillery to prepare for a Corps mission at the Forêt de Perseigne, which is a heavily forested, rugged area east of Alençon that runs generally west to northeast for about 15 kilometers and is about 5 kilometers wide. The XV Corps suspected a sizeable German force was hiding there. General Haislip's solution was to use the Corps Artillery and air support to bombard the exits from the forest, while bypassing it to the west, gambling that any German forces there would be unable to effectively attack the Corps's right flank. Reconnaissance by the 106th Cavalry later that night determined the woods were nearly free of Germans and there was no real threat.

CT 8 moved smoothly into action on the left of the division at 0600. The 3d Battalion moved by truck north along the Sarthe River for 5 miles to the vicinity of La Guierche–Montbizot, where they detrucked to secure the riverbank against any possible German attempt to cross. The trucks then returned to shuttle the 2d Battalion forward to Ballon on the road farther east through Souligné-sous-Ballon, behind the French, at 1000. By 1130, the CT 8 Headquarters was near Lucé-sous-Ballon, and Colonel Clarke decided to hold the CT in place until the French columns cleared the jammed roads ahead. Ten minutes later the French reported the bridge across L'Orthon stream west of Mareschê to Beaumont-sur-Sarthe had been blown by the Germans, but another bridge east of town was still open. CT 8 closed up there between 1230 and 1300, while waiting to cross.

Also at 1300, the 1st Battalion was ordered to secure the crossing of the Orne River at Beaumont-sur-Sarthe. The 1st Battalion reached the vicinity of L'Épinay on the D6 Road at 1335, when it was reported the bridge over the Orne at Beaumont-sur-Sarthe was blown. They reached the town around 1400, crossed to secure the area, and by 1500 had a workable temporary bridge in place. The three battalions of the regiment closed up to the Orne and then marched northeast to Lombray, southwest of René by 2100.

The left flank screening forces led off ahead of the 1st Battalion, 358th Infantry along the river road to the area of Vivoin, northeast of Beaumont-sur-Sarthe. The light tanks of the 1st Platoon, Company D, 712th Tank Battalion extended the screen out to Saint-Germain-sur-Sarthe and Fresnay-sur-Sarthe without encountering any resistance.[4]

Evidence of a hasty German withdrawal was evident along the routes of the division. Newly dug trenches and abandoned positions were found covering the approaches to Ballon. However, the largest actual engagement of the day occurred long before the advance began, at about 0200, and again involved Battery D, 537th AAA Battalion. It was in bivouac with the 345th Field Artillery when a bypassed German unit attempted to pass through the battery area. The men of Gun Section Number 7 repeated the feat of T/5 Cascio the previous day.

The following situation occurring in the 537th AAA AW Battalion (M), attached to the 90th Division, Third US Army, in the vicinity of Nord de Guerre, France, is related as a typical example of the conditions an AAA unit encounters in mobile warfare. While this situation is considered typical the actions of the personnel involved are considered "outstanding."

About 0200, 11 August 1944, Gun Section No 7, 2nd Platoon, Battery "D" was set up in a small field surrounded by hedgerows with sunken roads on the north and east. The 40mm gun was emplaced near the center of the field, with the .50 caliber MG south of it, and a recently procured .30 caliber MG just to the east. The tents of the section were along the eastern hedgerow. The night was clear and the moon was shining. Pvt Honea and Pvt Fetherholf were on duty at the 40mm gun. Suddenly noises were heard in the northern hedgerow, Pvt Fetherholf challenged the noise and was answered by a burst of

Light tanks of Company D, 712th Tank Battalion, advancing north through Lucé-sous-Ballon, about 1300 on 11 August. The church spire is the Église de la Sainte-Trinité (Church of the Holy Trinity) as viewed looking north on the Rue Louis Louaze (D123). They went into an assembly area north of Lucé-sous-Ballon about 1700 and the rest of the 712th Tank Battalion (-) and CT 8 followed them. U.S. Army SC.

fire from rifle and machine pistols and by the explosion of hand grenades. Pvt Fetherholf fell mortally wounded. Pvt Honea dropped to the ground and returned the enemy fire, retiring slowly to take up a position behind the 40mm gun.

The remainder of the section were awakened by the sound of enemy fire and bullets tearing through their tents. Pvt Giamos immediately returned the enemy fire and Pfc Hofley, realizing the seriousness of the situation and without regard for his personal safety, made a dash for the .30 caliber machine gun through heavy enemy fire. He commenced firing the MG at the enemy locations until forced to stop due to the gun jamming. Although he was wounded at this time, he resumed firing with an M-l rifle. During a brief lull, Pvt Giamos reached the 40mm gun, and he and Pvt Honea decided to charge the hedgerow to flush the Germans. Just then three of the enemy, a Sgt and two Pvts, came out of the hedgerow with their hands up. The Sgt could understand some English. He was told to call to his men to surrender, which he did. The enemy did not come forward. It was then that Pvt Giamos and Pvt Honea started toward the enemy positions. No guns were discovered until the third hedgerow was reached, Behind this hedgerow were eleven of the enemy who appeared to be on the verge of shooting the three Germans who had just surrendered and could be seen from this location. By the aggressive actions of Pvt Giamos and Pvt Honea the enemy surrendered. Pvt Giamos left the prisoners with Pvt Honea and made a search of the vicinity discovering two more of the enemy who surrendered without opposition. The total bag of prisoners added up to 16. The number of enemy personnel killed or wounded in this action could not be determined as the section moved before daylight.

During this action, four members of the section were wounded and one killed. The enemy had the advantage of surprise, position, protection, and fire power, but by the courageous and bold actions of the members of this section these advantages were overcome.

As an aftermath of the above action, during General George C. Marshall's recent visit to the Twelfth Amy Group, he attended a 90th Division ceremony, at which time he presented awards for heroism to men of the Division and attached troops. Of the ten awards made, five were given to enlisted men of the attached 537th AAA AW Battalion, which included one Distinguished Service Cross, three Silver Stars, and one Bronze Star, Three of these decorations were for the above action with Pfc Hofley receiving the DSC and Pvts Giamos and Honea receiving each a Silver Star.[5]

For the 90th Infantry Division, the day again involved little or no combat. While the division reported a total of 213 battle casualties for the day, it seems likely the Division G-1 was still reconciling its personnel figures and accounting for losses earlier in the campaign. None of the three infantry regiments reported a single battle casualty or engaging in any combat.

Nor was the intensity of combat very high for the two armored divisions bearing the brunt of the advance, as traffic jams proved to be a greater issue than German resistance. The 5th Armored Division reported just seventy-six battle casualties and the 2ème Division Blindée only a few more: ninety-eight. No tank losses were noted from either division.

Issues other than casualties were of greater concern to the Allied leadership on 11 August. For General Haislip and the XV Corps, the problem was two heavily forested areas that blocked the line of advance and offered potential shelter for German forces. One, the Forêt de Perseigne southeast of Alençon, had already been bypassed to the east and west. The second, the Forêt d'Ecouves, is north of Alençon on the route to Argentan. The two forests straddle the main roads running 18 kilometers east to west and vary from 8 to 10 kilometers from north to south. General Haislip directed the 5th Armored Division bypass the Forêt d'Ecouves to the east of Alençon with CCA and CCR leading and CCB in reserve, while the 2ème Division Blindée was to bypass the Forêt to the west of Alençon.

Major General Lunsford E. Oliver, commander of the 5th Armored Division, followed Haislip's orders exactly. CCR advanced from Bonnétable, bypassing

Mamers to the east and crossed the Sarthe at Le Mêle-sur-Sarthe, ending the night at Essay. CCA moved north from Ballon-sur-Mars to Danguels and then through Courgains, before crossing the Sarthe 5 miles west of Le Mêle-sur-Sarthe. CCB followed in reserve.

The French however failed to follow Haislip's orders. The commander of the 2ème Division Blindée, General Philippe François Marie de Hauteclocque, who went by the nom de guerre "Leclerc," decided to send his three groupement tactique—equivalent to the American combat command—on three routes to the east, west, and through the Forêt. His division was already falling behind the rate of advance of the 5th Armored Division, which caused the massive traffic jams hampering the advance of the 90th Infantry Division. By nightfall, his left-hand column, composed of a single groupement, was still 3 miles south of Alençon, and his right-hand columns with the rest of the division were only as far as Louvigny on the southern edge of the Forêt de Perseigne. To speed up movement the next day, Leclerc ordered the right-hand column to split after passing through the Forêt de Perseigne. One groupement would skirt the Forêt d'Ecouves to the east and head for Sées, in the 5th Armored Division zone, while

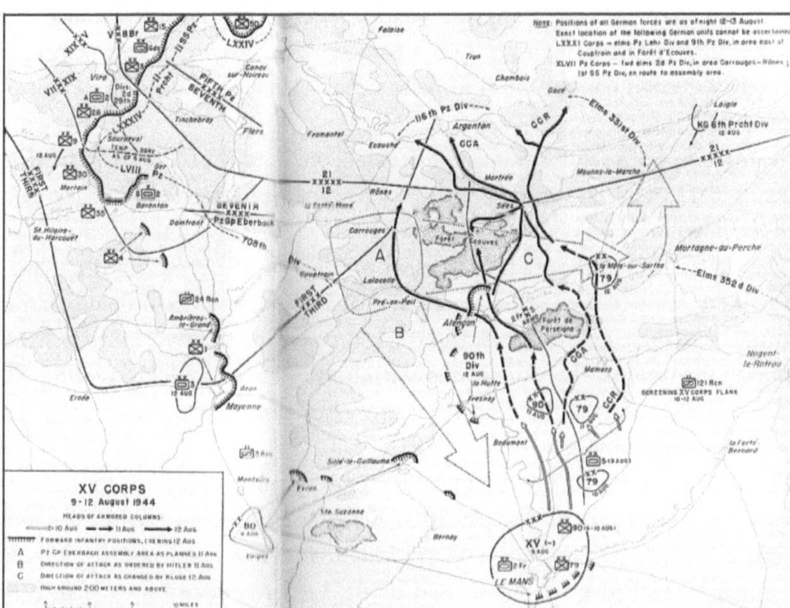

Map 16. XV Corps, 9–12 August 1944. Blumenson, Map 16.

the other would drive straight through the forest. The stage was set for another monumental traffic jam the next morning, which would have far-reaching consequences.[6]

Also, late in the evening of 11 August, ULTRA intercepted several important German messages, but most were not decoded and distributed until the early morning hours of 12 August. One message directed the *116. Panzer-Division*, which was pulling out of the line near Mortain, to a new assembly area. The assembly area given in the message was Alençon, directly in the path of the XV Corps. However, what ULTRA could not reveal was that when Generalleutnant Gerhard Helmuth Detloff, Graf von Schwerin, the commander of the *116. Panzer-Division*, arrived at the Gefechtsstand of the *LXXXI Armee-Korps* southeast of Argentan, he was told that Alençon had fallen and instead his division was ordered to defend Sées.[7]

12 AUGUST

Various disparate events came together in the morning of 12 August to halt the advance north of the XV Corps and delay closing the trap behind the German armies west of Argentan. Early in the morning, the 2ème Division Blindée captured an intact bridge over the Sarthe River at Alençon, entered the city, and sped northward. Groupement tactique Langlade headed west of the Forêt d'Écouves toward Carrouges. Groupement tactique Dio advanced through the Forêt. Groupement tacticque Billotte, which had been in reserve, left Alençon headed directly for Sées as ordered by Leclerc.[8]

Meanwhile, from its positions east of Alençon, Task Force Burton from CCA, 5th Armored Division advanced northwest toward Sées. Reconnaissance elements entered the town around 0800 and by 0900 were advancing on the road to Mortrée. There they encountered the leading element of the *116. Panzer-Division*, a lone battery of artillery. One of the German pieces, a 10.5cm Wespe self-propelled howitzer, opened fire and managed to break the track on each of the two leading American tanks, disabling them. The Americans withdrew to Sées, quickly regrouped, and then maneuvered to strike the German battery position in the flank, almost wiping out the German unit by 1000.[9]

The destruction of the German artillery battery came at a price though: CCA's vehicles were almost out of gas. At 1010, CCA withdrew again to Sées and was preparing to refuel, while CCR was behind it, moving northeast to Aunou-sur-Orne, which it reached by 1100. At that point, Leclerc's decision to push Billotte's task force into the 5th Armored Division zone had its inevitable consequence. Groupement tactique Billotte passed east of the Forêt d'Ecouves and entered Sées, blocking the roads, just as CCA's fuel trucks were trying to move up. The result was a delay of several hours as the traffic jam was unscrambled.

The two Allied armored groups were finally able to continue the advance at around 1500. CCA advanced toward Mortrée on the main road (D958), while Groupement tactique Billotte advanced west out of town on a parallel secondary road. The Allies immediately ran into *Panzergrenadier-Regiment 156* of *116. Panzer-Division*, which was unaware the town was not in German hands. The regiment's two battalions attempted to advance on either side of the Carrouges-Sées road (D908) and were about 300 meters from the town when they realized their predicament and attempted to withdraw into the Forêt d'Écouves. Both battalions, which had no supporting armor or adequate antitank capability, were quickly overwhelmed and fragmented. CCA reported capturing "an entire battalion of enemy troops," and it was ten days before the Germans were able to reassemble the remnants of the regiment at Vimoutiers.[10]

CCA and the French continued the advance northwest and by 1630 were at Mortrée, just 9 miles from Argentan. Northwest of town they ran into Panther and Panzer IV tanks of the *Stab/Panzer-Regiment 16*, which further delayed the Allied advance. One Panzer IV was knocked out in Mortrée and a Panther was lost there when it backed into a building that collapsed onto it. Two more Panthers defended a mined roadblock northwest of town at Hill 209 for another few crucial minutes until one was knocked out and the remaining Panther withdrew. By 1900, the Allied tanks reached the outskirts of Argentan.

However, they were too late. The operations officer (Ia) of the *116. Panzer-Division*, Major Heinz Günther Guderian, had cobbled together a defensive position there by commandeering troops, including two Panther tank battalions, *II/Panzer-Regiment 33* of *9. Panzer-Division* and *I/Panzer-Regiment 24* of his own division. The two battalions between them had more than twenty-five tanks operational and were supported by two or three 10.5cm howitzers, all that was available of the Division Artillery, Luftwaffe *leichte-Flak-Abteilung 90*, and other units from *Flak-Sturm-Regt.1.* and *4.* of *III. Flak-Korps*. Later in the day, *schwere Artillerie-Abteilung 992* with some ex-Soviet 15.2cm gun howitzers also arrived to bolster the defense. However, the dispersal of *Panzergrenadier-Regiment 156* in the morning meant that Guderian had little or no infantry available until later that night, when some of his divisional *Pioniere* arrived in town. The only "infantry" troops initially available were men from a bakery company that he hastily threw into the line. Nevertheless, the intense activity in town and the lateness of the day led the commander of CCA, Brigadier General Eugene A. Regnier, to conclude Argentan was too heavily defended, so he ordered his men to halt on the high ground to the south. Only patrols were sent into town to confirm that the bridges over the Orne were still intact. Argentan would remain in German hands for another week.[11]

CCA captured 275 Germans on 12 August, mostly from *Panzergrenadier-Regiment 156*, while the rest of the division reported capturing another 87. The French reported the capture of 1,000 more from numerous German units, including *SS-Das Reich* and *2. Panzer-Division*, which had also been withdrawn from the salient at Mortain, 80 kilometers to the west. However, the number claimed by the French was probably an exaggeration, given that the total reported captured by the XV Corps was only 771.

While this was going on, the 90th Infantry Division marked time in place until 1050 when Haislip ordered the division to,

> *Advance without delay to complete the capture of ALENCON and advance N through the FORET DE COUVES [sic] and secure the high ground in the vicinity of LA CERCUEIL (2802) and establish contact with the 2nd French Armored Division in the vicinity of CARROUGES.*

CT 9 moved off at 1130, led by the 90th Reconnaissance Troop. It followed a route via René–Les Mées–Rouessé-Fontaine–Bourg-le-Roi–Champfleur–Alencon to Colombiers, northwest of Alençon. The 90th Reconnaissance Troop managed to get ahead of the French columns and contacted the Germans just south of the Forêt d'Écouves at 1515, before the French passed through to lead the advance. CT 9 had the only other contact by the 90th with German forces on 12 August when they were met by small arms fire from units of the *9. Panzer-Division* bypassed by the French at Colombiers. CT 9 captured fifteen Germans there.

Just before setting off, Colonel Bacon changed the commander of his 2d Battalion. He ordered Colonel Gorton to assume the duties of Regimental Executive Officer and appointed Major Leonard C. Dull, the Battalion Executive Officer, as Battalion Commander. The change left the 359th Infantry with all its battalions commanded by majors, Pond with the 1st Battalion, Dull with the 2d Battalion, and Smith with the 3d Battalion. The three made an excellent command team. The thirty-four-year-old Dull was not as driven and mercurial as "Fireball" Pond but was solidly competent. Now Major Smith—he was promoted on 22 July—had gained the nickname "Foxhole," but not because he liked to cower in one. He was adamant that his men dig in solidly every time they halted in a position but was proving to be a gifted tactician and was also exceedingly brave. He had been awarded a Silver

Star for his actions on 8 July and would receive a Distinguished Service Cross for his conduct on 10 January 1945.

CT 7 also began marching on foot at 1130. The 3d Battalion, followed by the 2d Battalion, and then the 1st Battalion marched from its assembly area north to René, then turned left (west) to Chérancé, before turning north to Bois Mocquet to Rouessé-Fontaine and then Bourg-le-Roi, where they halted until 1230 to clear the intersection for the advance of the French. Struggling through heavy traffic, CT 7 finally reached Alençon at 2030, but it was not until 2300 that it closed into an assembly area at Damigny about 3 kilometers north of the city.

While CT 7 and CT 9 were advancing, Haislip changed the 90th's objectives. Instead of advancing through the Forêt d'Écouves it was to halt on the southern edge of the forest. Its primary mission was now to establish and defend the XV Corps bridgehead on the Sarthe and Orne rivers at Alençon.[12]

CT 8 was at La Hutte, 10 miles south of Alençon at 1430 when it was ordered to move to a point just south of that town. The Infantry shuttled by trucks to the new assembly area without incident, but not without receiving some harrowing

Col. Robert L. Bacon, Lt. Col. Leroy R. Pond (DOW 15 January 1945), Lt. Col. James F. Smith, Lt. Col. Donald R. Gorton, Maj. Leonard C. Dull (DOW 15 September 1944). The photo was taken during an awards ceremony at the end of August, while the division was resting after the Battle of the Chambois-Falaise Pocket. U.S. Army SC.

intelligence. French civilians reported at 1630 that there were 100 German tanks at Héloup on the south edge of the Forêt d'Écouves 7.5 kilometers to the northwest. Then over the next hour and a half, more reports from various sources warned that German tanks were to the "immediate front." Finally, at 1815, CT 8 was told that "many Panzer divisions were in the general vicinity, or capable of coming there. Also many Infantry units were reported off to our east flank." Where these reports were coming from is unclear because they did not reflect the reporting by the Divisional G-2 Staff, which reported no enemy armor other than "two SS tanks" seen in the Forêt Domaniale de Réno Valdieu, 27 miles east of Alençon, by a Franco-American civilian who had managed to get from Paris to American lines the day before.

Nevertheless, by the night of 12 August, the Allied armies were well on their way to envelop the German forces west of a line extending from Falaise to Argentan. The First Canadian Army had advanced in a series of hard-fought battles to Moulines, less than 10 miles from Falaise. The XV Corps was on the outskirts of Argentan, less than 13 miles from Falaise. German line of communications to Paris and Germany were reduced to a few secondary roads running from Falaise through Trun to Vimoutiers, which were grossly inadequate to support the operations of the two armies of *Heeresgruppe B* engaged in Normandy.[13]

Bradley's original intention in sending the XV Corps north to Alençon on 8 August was to relieve the pressure from the German counterattack on the VII Corps of FUSA at Mortain. His actions had dovetailed nicely with General Montgomery's intentions with regard to the attack on Falaise by the First Canadian Army. However, while the Canadian advance had been slowed to a crawl by fierce German resistance, Patton's advance had far exceeded all expectations. It had also opened a yawning gap of about 25 miles between the left of the XV Corps at Carrouges and the right of the VII Corps at Ambrières-les-Vallées. That gap weighed on Bradley's mind, especially after ULTRA confirmed the movement of the *116. Panzer-Division* from Mortain to Sées. Nor was that the only indication the Germans were withdrawing from Mortain. As early as midnight on 10 August, the G-2 of the 30th Infantry Division, which was blocking Unternehmen Lüttich at Mortain, believed the Germans had largely completed a withdrawal and only delaying forces were left to their front. Then at 2245 on 11 August, a British intelligence summary stated,

> *Two nights ago [10 August] we said "he must withdraw." It was obvious. Nevertheless all yesterday [11 August] the enemy remained formed up to attack and the Americans were praying he would do so. Five Panzer divisions were in the line, 1 SS in front of*

> *SOURDEVAL SOUTH of VIRE,2 Pz, 116 Pz, 2 SS, 10 SS stretching SOUTH and more armour moving WEST, 9 Pz at DOMFRONT, 500 tanks in all and thirty bns of infantry. Everything it seemed was to be risked on one great throw and Armageddon fought out now. It would have been a noble Gotterdammerung.*
>
> *That was yesterday. Today* [12 August] *there were air reports of scattered MET* [Motorized Enemy Transport] *moving EAST, through FLERS, ARGENTAN and towards BERNAY. Those trickles became a flood this afternoon. At 1715 hrs a column of MET interspersed with troop carriers and tanks was reported moving along a thirty mile stretch of road from 980170* [a point about 7 miles east of Flers on the D924] *to ARGENTAN [a column about 20 miles long] to Q 4651 [a point 10 miles northeast of Argentan] at the unheard of spacing of 20-50 v.t.m.* [vehicles to the mile, that is, there were an estimated 600 to 1,500 vehicles in the column]. *There was movement too NE into ARGENTAN, and on other side roads, all Eastwards. All of the resources pf our air forces have been directed on to these roads.*
>
> *The enemy is withdrawing, and the question is now how much can he get out. For the trap continues to close. A tank battle is raging around NOGENT [Nogent-le-Rotrou], between ALENCON and CHARTRES. Our advance elements are in CHATEAUDUN on the road to ORLEANS, and in BROU, NOGERS, BELLEME and SEES, and on from SEES they are very near ARGENTAN. They are at CRAUCE SOUTH of DOMFRONT and at SR JEAN DES BOIS, SW of TINCHEBRAY. Whoever holds Mortain, and it is uncertain, the enemy is obviously going, and we have already made local advances SOUTH of VIRE and the VIRE-VASSY road. ARGENTN is held in some strength by reinforcements, but it is a long road to protect. He has eight and a half armoured divisions, but some must remain to the last to cover the withdrawal from MORTAIN, others are desperately needed to hold our thrusts at CONDE, at FALAISE and at ARGENTAN. At every one of these places his resistance must of necessity be desperate, while on one clogged blazing road his spare armour moves Eastward. As for the infantry in the line their future rosy for a Heldentod* [hero's death].[14]

Bradley's initial reaction was to authorize Hodges to resume the V and XIX Corps offensive on 12 August, which had been on hold during the crisis of Mortain. They did so but met strong resistance and were unable to advance very far. The VII Corps was also authorized to revert to the offense but required a day to reorganize from its defensive posture, so it would be sometime on 13 August before they could jump off. That left the XV Corps left flank still open to a possible German counterattack on the scale of Unternehmen Lüttich for at least another twenty-four hours.

Meanwhile, Haislip was pestering Patton over what he should do with the XV Corps. In a conference with his staff the morning of 12 August, Haislip had concluded the XV Corps with its four divisions could hold its positions between

Argentan and Alençon and could close the pocket if the Canadians were able to reach Argentan. However, a drive north through Argentan to link up with the Canadians somewhere closer to Falaise would require additional troops.

At 2130 and again at 2150 Haislip messaged TUSA to inform Patton that the XV Corps was in front of Argentan, well past the boundary between the 12th and 21st Army Group established by Montgomery five days earlier. He also told Patton he expected to seize the town no later than noon the next day. Finally, Haislip also reminded Patton of the threat to the XV Corps left and requested additional troops to meet the threat.

Patton, never one to give counsel to his fears, directed his Chief of Staff, General Gaffey, to message Haislip at 0040 on 13 August. Gaffey told Haislip to "push on slowly in the direction of Falaise" and then "continue to push on slowly until . . . contact [is made with] our Allies [the Canadians]." Patton was also planning to assemble the XX Corps at Alençon with the 7th Armored, and the 35th and 80th Infantry Division (-319th RCT), which would largely eliminate the threat of a German attack into the left flank of the XV Corps.[15]

However, the story that Bradley later told about these events is considerably different. In his postwar memoir, Bradley claimed that sometime on the evening of 12 August, Patton supposedly called to tell him what was happening on the TUSA front. Patton reportedly told Bradley, "we have troops in Argentan"—a slight exaggeration—and that they were on their way to Falaise. Bradley's response supposedly was,

> *Nothing doing, you're not to go beyond Argentan. Just stop where you are and build up on that shoulder. Sibret* [Brigadier General Edwin M. Sibert, Bradley's G-2] *tells me the German is beginning to pull out. You'd better button up and get ready for him.*[16]

Instead of authorizing Patton to complete the encirclement of the Germans under what was Bradley's original concept of operations, Bradley now wanted Patton to halt in place. Bradley's reply stunned Patton. On 8 August when Bradley had ordered him north, Patton had protested, arguing that a deeper envelopment directing TUSA to Chartres and Dreux could trap all the German forces west of the Seine. However, Bradley had been adamant in sending the XV Corps to Alençon instead. Now Bradley was changing his mind again.[17]

Notably, this and other similar accounts of this conversation are based solely on Bradley's version of events in his postwar memoir *A Soldier's Story*. Oddly enough, Patton made no mention of the conversation in his diary at the time and the records maintained by TUSA on the subject are incomplete as well. There are also significant inconsistencies in Bradley's account. For example, Bradley said Patton telephoned and spoke to him on the evening of 12 August from TUSA Headquarters "near Laval." However, TUSA Headquarters was not at Laval then. Patton mentioned in his diary that he "drove to our new CP at a point about 6 miles NW of Le Mans" on 12 August. Patton also made no mention of speaking with Bradley or of a change of plans for the XV Corps in his diary entry for the day.[18]

In fact, telephone communications between 12th Army Group Headquarters and TUSA Headquarters at this stage of the pursuit apparently were infrequent. Landline telephone and cable systems were badly overloaded during the pursuit in August as the Signal Corps frantically laid new lines trying to keep up with the rapid advance. In most cases senior Allied commanders met in person or used enciphered cablegrams to preserve security, especially in any communications that might touch on information gained through ULTRA. Patton for one frequently flew to meetings, sometimes piloting himself in a "Cub." In Patton's diary entries he mentions physically meeting with Bradley—one or the other of them driving or flying to the others location—only eight times in the first fifteen days TUSA was operational. In only one diary entry in those fifteen days—on 7 August—did Patton himself refer to making or receiving a telephone call to Bradley, and in that case, he finally decided not to use the telephone to reach him. All communications back and forth from TUSA to XV Corps were also clearly referenced as cable or radiogram messages, which were encrypted, rather than as telephone conversations, in TUSA and XV Corps records. Patton's diary entry about his interaction with Bradley on 12 August is slightly ambiguous because he does not say if they spoke face to face. However, in any case the conversation was not about the halt order at all. Rather, it was about how Patton would commit the XII Corps east of the XV Corps.[19]

The claim that Bradley was being told by his G-2 that the Germans were pulling out is supported by the 21st Army Group appreciation already cited, but it is less clear how universally accepted this assessment was. For example, the SHAEF G-2 Summary, transmitted to the U.S. Army War Department at 1245 on 12 August, stated that there was

> *No evidence of any change in general intention* [by the Germans] *to hold fast in all sectors of present uneconomical lines until forced to withdraw. Appreciate, however, enemy becoming increasingly anxious of open left flank and American exploitation. Until further reinforcements available, enemy may be compelled to thin out armour from Mortain area, accepting further withdrawals in this sector if necessary.*[20]

Finally, it seems inexplicable that Bradley would order Patton to halt on the evening of 12 August, but that Patton would then still direct Gaffey to order Haislip to continue to advance after midnight on 12 August. In fact, the XV Corps did not register receipt of the message ordering the halt until 1415 on 13 August. It appears that Bradley's decision to halt the advance of the XV Corps was made on the morning of 13 August, rather than the night of 12/13 August. That sequence of events fits much more closely with the record.[21]

Evidence for this sequence of events also may be found in the XV Corps After-Action Report for August 1944. On 18 January 1945, General Haislip forwarded a "correction" to the report's Paragraph 25, which covered the events of 13 August. The correction inserted the following sentence into the report.

> *This action* [Patton's directive that the XV Corps "push on slowly in the direction of FALAISE and make contact with Allied forces advancing from the north"] *was being initiated when orders were received rescinding these instructions and directing the Corps to halt on the ORNE.*

At 0950 on 13 August, Brigadier General A, Frankin Kibler, the 12th Army Group G-3, called Major General Francis W. "Freddie" de Guingand, Montgomery's Chief of Staff, on Bradley's behalf to request permission for Patton to cross the interarmy group boundary, which ran south of Argentan, so the XV Corps could seize Argentan and advance on Falaise to meet the British and Canadians. De Guingand consulted Montgomery, who refused permission. Brigadier General Edgar T. "Bill" Williams was present at 21st Army Group Headquarters when the call and discussion occurred. Postwar his account was:

> *Monty said "Tell Bradley they ought to get back." Monty missed closing the sack. He was fundamentally more interested in full envelopment [an encirclement at the Seine] than inner envelopment* [an encirclement at Argentan-Falaise]. *We fell between two stools. He missed the chance of closing the Seine by doing the envelopment of Falaise.*[22]

Then at 1215, Patton called 12th Army Group Headquarters from TUSA Headquarters near Le Mans to ask Bradley if there were any further orders for TUSA. However, Bradley was away from the 12th Army Group visiting Eisenhower, so Patton spoke to Major General Leven C. Allen, Bradley's Chief of Staff. Patton told Allen that the XV Corps was on the 12th Army Group-21st Army Group boundary and had reconnaissance elements north of it. In reply, Allen, not

Bradley, told Patton to halt on that line and consolidate. Patton considered this conversation so critical that he commented in his diary, "A partial stenographic report of this conversation is in the 'Telephone Conversations' [in the TUSA daily journal]."[23]

Nor are the reasons Bradley later gave for the halt order believable. In *A Soldier's Story*, he said,

> *Although Patton may have spun a line across that narrow neck, I doubted his ability to hold it. Nineteen German divisions were now stampeding to escape the trap. Meanwhile, with four divisions George was already blocking three principal escape routes through Alençon. Sees, and Argentan. Had he stretched that line to include Falaise, he would have extended his roadblock a distance of 40 miles. The enemy could not only have broken through, but he might have trampled Patton's position in the onrush. I much preferred a solid shoulder at Argentan to the possibility of a broken neck at Falaise.*
>
> *At the same time I was reluctant to chance a head-on meeting between two converging Armies as we might have done had Patton continued on the Falaise.*[24]

Bradley's postwar excuse appears to be specious at best and dishonest at worst. As we will see, on 13 August, he authorized Patton to send the XX Corps, which Patton had been planning on inserting to protect the vulnerable XV Corps left flank, east toward the Seine, significantly reducing the potential strength of his "solid shoulder." Then, on 14 August, Bradley authorized Patton to send half of the XV Corps forces at Argentan farther east toward the Seine as well, further reducing the strength of the "strong shoulder" to just two divisions. At that time there was no clear indication of a full German withdrawal from the pocket and there was certainly no evidence that nineteen German divisions were "stampeding" eastward. Instead the actual indications from ULTRA were of a deliberate, phased withdrawal from the Mortain salient in order to attack the left of the XV Corps to stabilize the German southern flank.[25]

However the decision was finally made, Bradley forbade any further advance by the XV Corps. When the orders finally reached Haislip at 1415 on 13 August, they even directed he recall any Corps elements that might have gone farther "in the vicinity of Falaise or to the north of Argentan."

While a good argument can be made for blaming the halt order and its result on either of the senior Allied commanders—Bradley or Montgomery—the truth is there was plenty of blame to go around for both. Bradley was mercurial, elated one moment at being out from under Montgomery's thumb, then hesitant and second-guessing himself the next moment. Montgomery, as always, treated both subordinates and peers as his inferiors and failed to recognize how much his own personality flaws were harming the Allied cause. Eisenhower too can be blamed for his overly light touch in commanding Montgomery and Bradley. Patton should be censured as well, given he egged on Bradley's resistance to Montgomery's command, which in part led to the muddled decisions on 12 and 13 August.

13 AUGUST

As already mentioned, just after midnight on 12 August, Patton ordered Haislip to continue to push the XV Corps on slowly in the direction of Falaise. The 5th Armored Division was to cut the roads leading east out of Argentan to Gacé but were not to get tied up in a serious fight for the town itself. The 2ème Division Blindée was directed to move east of the Forêt d'Écouves and was given the task of seizing Argentan. The 90th Infantry Division was to relieve the French positions south and west of the Forêt and consolidate the Alençon bridgehead. The 79th Infantry Division was to remain in corps reserve.

The CT 9 secured Colombieres with the 1st Battalion in the morning. The 2d Battalion extended the line east to Valframbert and the intersection of the N12 and D31 to the southeast. The 3d Battalion covered the right rear of the division with one company deployed to guard a roadblock at Grandchamp 12 miles to the south. At 1415, division ordered the 2d Battalion to advance through the Forêt d'Écouves to positions overlooking the Carrouges–Sées road (D908). It began moving at 1600 and by 2240 was in position at Saint-Hilaire-la-Gérard north of the D908 after an advance of 8 miles against minimal resistance.

CT 7, with the 345th Field Artillery Battalion attached, moved to the northwest onto three hills southeast of Carrouges on the west end of the Forêt d'Écouves between La Roche-Mabile and Corbinière. One platoon of the 1st Battalion encountered a strong German force reported as five tanks and one hundred infantrymen with antitank guns at Corbinière.

The 3d Battalion, 358th Infantry moved up to occupy the 357th's former area at Damigny and tied in with the right of the 357th. The 1st Battalion, 358th Infantry deployed to defend the bridges on the Sarthe at Alençon, while the 2d Battalion, 358th Infantry went into division reserve near the Division CP north of Ballon.

The 5th Armored Division shifted east as ordered and at 1700 was at Gacé. By dark, the 2ème Division Blindée was in position at Carrouges, Écouché-les-Vallées, and west and south of Argentan, the 90th Infantry Division was in a strong position overlooking the Carrouges–Sées road. Farther north, the Canadians were less than

4 miles from Falaise. The Allied trap was nearly complete with only a little over 16 miles separating the Canadians from the Americans.

A real sense of the uncertainty in the Allied ranks about where the Germans were to the front of the XV Corps and where they were moving can be seen in some of the intelligence reports received by the 90th Infantry Division on 13 August. The 358th's I&R Platoon reported Germans in Colombiers at 1115, less than 2 miles to the northwest, although the town was reported secured by CT 9 by 1130. Also at 1115, the Platoon reported a column of "80 horse-drawn vehicles, 40 tanks and 5 heavy trucks" moving northeast from Gesvres, 12 miles to the southwest of Alençon. Then they reported 100 tanks at Radon, just 4 miles to the northeast of Alençon at 1145, which in retrospect was certainly a sighting of French or American tanks. Finally, at 1650, the I&R Platoon reported capturing nineteen Germans, including a Hauptmann (Captain), and killing six more, while releasing a British soldier who was a prisoner, at Saint-Denis-sur-Sarthon, nearly 6 miles to the west of Alençon. Notably, the Germans reported at Gesvres and Saint-Denis-sur-Sarthon were well behind the frontline of CT 7 and CT 9 at the deep left flank and rear of the division.

Even more alarming was the Division G-2 report prepared overnight and issued at 1600 on 14 August. Based upon interrogation of the 206 prisoners captured on 13 August, in addition to the *9.*, *116.*, and *Lehr Panzer-Division*, and *331. Infanterie-Division* previously identified, elements of the *2. Panzer-Division*, *LSSAH*, and an old adversary, *SS-GvB*, were suspected to be in front of the division.

14 AUGUST

General Haislip directed the 90th Infantry Division to mop up the Forêt d'Ecouves, a task that was completed without much incident during the day. The 1st and 3d Battalion, 359th Infantry swept the eastern part of the forest and the 3d Battalion, 357th Infantry swept the western part, rounding up 314 German stragglers from nine different German divisions and miscellaneous other units. The largest haul were 3 officers and 171 men from the *Sicherungs-Regiment 1.*, which until 2 August had been enjoying occupation duties in Paris. Perhaps most disturbing though were the prisoners from the *2. Panzer-Division*. They claimed the division had started to withdraw from positions near Vire on the night of 12 August and were on a "mission of keeping the trap open on the N[orth] and S[outh] and to enable the trapped troops to escape."

All the growing uncertainty in the Allied camp as to German strength, intentions, and locations came to a head on 14 August. Combined with Eisenhower's hands-off command style, Montgomery's growing reluctance to issue peremptory orders to the American forces still nominally under his command, and Bradley's indecisiveness, the result was a series of decisions that prevented the closing of the ring around the German forces in Normandy.

In his Intelligence Summary for 14 August, General Sibret, the 12th Army Group G-2, assessed that only twelve German divisions—five Panzer and seven Infanterie—were threatened with entrapment, west of a line from Argentan to Falaise. He also believed two Panzer and eight Infanterie divisions were either already outside the encirclement or in a position to easily escape. However, it is difficult to see how he arrived at that conclusion. The 12th Army Group situation map for 1200 on 14 August 1944 clearly showed ten Panzer and sixteen Infanterie (including *SS-GvB*) divisions in the battle area, with only nine of them—three Panzer and six Infanterie—east of a line drawn from Falaise to Argentan. Yet even that was not correct. The *OKH* situation map of the same day shows that only elements of *85., 272., 331., 346., 711. Infanterie*, and *6. Fallschirmjäger-Division* were outside the encirclement. All of the others, including all of the Panzer divisions except elements of *116. Panzer-Division*, were still inside the encirclement.[26]

Furthermore, several German formations were not included on the American map. One was the 90th's old adversary, the *91. Infanterie Division*. It had been officially disbanded on 10 August, but its remnants were still in the battle area. Twenty-four men from the division were captured on 9 August, ten more on 10 August, and eight on 14 August. Similarly, the *77.* and *353. Infanterie-Division*, and *5. Fallschirmjäger-Division*, also old adversaries of the 90th Infantry Division, do not appear, nor does the *352. Infanterie-Division*, which was famous for defending OMAHA and GOLD beaches on D-Day and then for the protracted defense of Saint-Lô. Most of the combat elements of the *77. Infanterie-Division* had withdrawn into the fortifications of Saint-Malo along with some remnants of *91. Infanterie-Division*, but the rest were caught in the developing trap. All were considered abgekämpft (fought out) by the Germans, but that large numbers of their personnel were still present is evident from the number of prisoners reported captured from them.[27]

In all, it appears that about twenty-two divisions or equivalents were west of the line Falaise–Argentan. Another four were east of that line but were desperately trying to hold the XV Corps from reaching Argentan, cutting the road running northeast to Trun and Vimoutiers, which was one of the few roads left available to the Germans. Only three of the twenty-two west of the line were in positions to the north outside of the pocket. The Allied leadership estimated that perhaps 100,000 Germans were potentially trapped in the pocket, but that appears to have been based upon an estimate of so-called Gefechtsstärke (fighting strength) and ignored the divisional, corps, and army headquarters as well as the support troops still likely present in the area. Those twenty-six divisions had originally brought about 410,000 men into the battle, while the army and corps headquarters and nondivisional troops accounted for an estimated 132,000 more, and another 30,000 were received as replacements. Overall, it may be that as many as 572,000 troops were committed by the Germans to the Battle of Normandy, not including the numerous Luftwaffe Flak and security troops in the area. By 13 August, Oberbefhlshaber West counted 158,930 of those as casualties, which was probably grossly underestimated. However, even if the casualties amounted to 200,000, it remains likely that about 372,000 German troops remained in France west of the Seine and north of the Loire rivers. It is of course possible that many of the army and corps headquarters and nondivisional troops were already outside the encirclement line moving to escape the envelopment, but that still leaves at least 200,000 unaccounted for. Thus, the Allied estimate of 100,000 Germans potentially trapped was most likely at least half and quite possibly only one-third of the number of German troops actually in the pocket.[28]

Given the growing belief that the bulk of the German forces had already escaped, Montgomery's and Bradley's next actions make some sense. In a letter to Bradley that day, Montgomery explicitly stated the viewpoint of the Allied commanders:

> *Dear Brad, it is difficult to say what enemy are inside the ring, and what have got out to the east. A good deal may have escaped. I think your movement of the 20 Corps should be N.E. toward Dreux. Also any further stuff you can move round to Le Mans, should go N.E. We want to head off the Germans, and stop them breaking out.*[29]

Montgomery's letter played directly into the thinking of Bradley and Patton. Early that morning, Patton flew via Le Mans and Alençon to Haislip's headquarters to review the situation at Argentan.[30] Patton found Haislip

> *Quite pepped up and full of confidence. I told him of my plan to move the XX [Corps] on DREUX and the XII [Corps] on CHARTRES. I then flew back to ST. JAMES [12th Army Group Headquarters] to see Bradley and sell the plan.*
>
> *He took it and even consented to let the XV* [Corps] *move on DREUX the XX on CHARTRES and the XII [Corps] on Orleans. He will let me keep the 80 Div and give Middleton an Inf Div from the 1st Army to replace the 6th AD in Brittany. It is a great plan. Wholly my own and I made Bradley think he thought of it.*
>
> *"Oh what a tangled web we weave when first we practice to deceive."*[31]

Patton, who had wanted to execute a deep envelopment to the Seine but was stymied by Bradley's decision for the shallow envelopment on 9 August, was finally to get his wish. However, Bradley's earlier decision had placed the XV Corps in close contact with the Germans at Argentan, making it difficult, if not impossible, for it to break contact and move east toward the Seine. To do so, Bradley was forced to authorize Patton taking a considerable risk: split the XV Corps into two, sending half of it east and keeping the other half facing the Germans at Argentan. Crucially, either due to simple oversight or perhaps to deliberate contrariness, Bradley failed to inform Montgomery of his decision to split the forces massed near Alençon.[32]

Back at XV Corps late that same afternoon, Patton instructed Haislip to sideslip 2ème Division Blindée to its right (east) to relieve the 5th Armored Division, which would head for Dreux. The 79th Infantry Division, still in corps reserve near Mortagne-au-Perche, would head for Nogent-le-Roi. The 90th Infantry Division

Lieutenant General George S. Patton Jr. This photograph was taken at the Seine River crossing near Mantes-Gassicourt on 26 August 1944. U.S. Army SC.

was directed to move north and tie into the right of the French, extending the line of the two divisions east to Le Bourg-Saint-Léonard. Three of the four corps Field Artillery group headquarters and six of the ten corps Field Artillery battalions would also go east with the XV Corps.

General McLain received the alert order for the new movement at 1600. One CT was to remain protecting the bridgehead at Alençon, while the other two moved east. Later that evening, McLain received Patton's orders from the XV Corps, dividing the corps into two parts. The 90th Infantry Division would relieve the 5th Armored Division in the area northeast of Sées, from Le Bourg-Saint-Léonard to Nonant-le-Pin, by 1100 on 15 August.

15 AUGUST

The movements directed by Generals Bradley and Patton continued in the early morning hours. The XV Corps Headquarters moved to Mortagne-au-Perche, leaving a skeleton staff at Alençon to control the rump of the corps left behind.

The Advance CP and quartering party of CT 9 set off at 0630 to contact CCR, 5th Armored Division and set up near Nonant-le-Pin. The column left its previous positions beginning at 0915, arrived at the assembly area at Nonant-le-Pin at 1130,

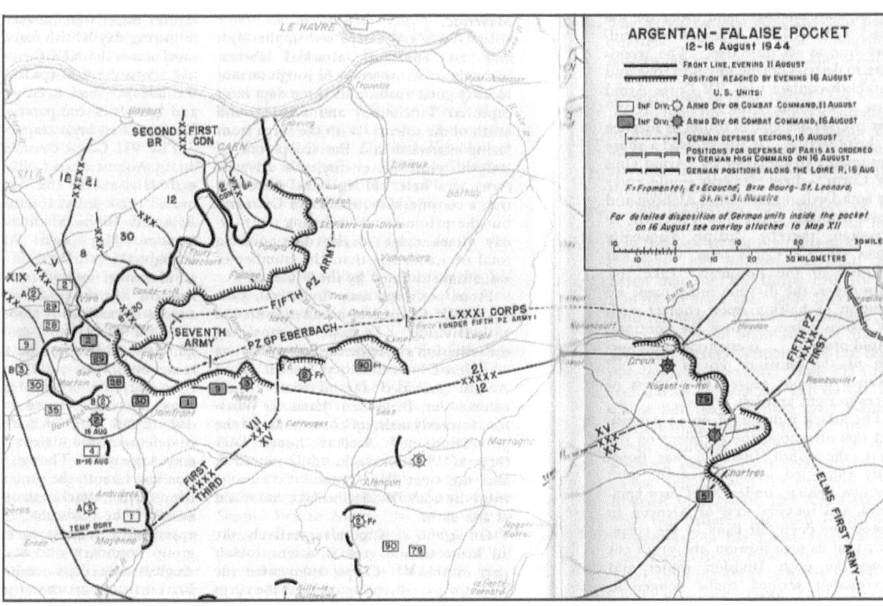

Map 17. Argentan-Falaise Pocket, 12–16 August 1944. Blumenson, Map 17.

and closed into the assembly area at 1600. The 3d Battalion remained in reserve at Nonant-le-Pin with Company L to the east at Le Merlerault. The 2d Battalion, with Company B, 712th Tank Battalion, relieved elements of the 5th Armored Division at roadblocks north and northeast of Nonant-le-Pin. The 1st Battalion, with the 1st Platoon, Company A, 712th Tank Battalion, relieved elements of the 5th Armored Division at Le Bourg-Saint-Léonard. Company A, under 1st Lieutenant Benton R. Fritz, deployed to defend Le Bourg-Saint-Léonard, Company C defended Exmes, nearly 3.5 miles to the east, and Company B, under Captain Donald B. Hutchens, was in reserve at Le Pin-au-Haras. By 2200, CT 9 held a defensive line extending from Le Bourg-Saint-Léonard to Exmes, Croisilles, and Le Merlerault, almost 12 miles. Just how much the loss of the other two divisions of the XV Corps was felt is easy to measure, given that the normal frontage a division was expected to defend was 5 to 9 miles. Major Pond's 1st Battalion alone covered a frontage of 6,000 yards or nearly 3.5 miles.[33]

CT 8, less the 2d Battalion, was in divisional reserve astride the Sées–Nonant-lePin road near Chailloué. The 2d Battalion, less Company E, and the 773d Tank Destroyer Battalion, less Company B, was at Almenêches, 4.25 miles south of Le Bourg-Saint-Léonard. Company E, with Company B, 773d Tank Destroyer Battalion, was on the high ground southeast of Argentan, where the Tank Destroyer's 3-inch M10 Gun Motor Carriages covered the main road running east from the town (D926).[34]

CT 7 remained holding the bridgehead at Alençon and the line of the Carrouges–Sées road (D908). The 1st Battalion held positions defending the western approaches to Alençon with Company A at Saint-Denis-sur-Sarthon, Company B to the south at La Ferrière-Bochard, and Company C in reserve at Condé-sur-Sarthe. The 2d Battalion blocked all the roads leading west from La Roche-Mabile to Corbinière. The 3d Battalion defended the crossroads northeast of L'Être Perreaux and south of La Sevestrie on the Carrouges–Sées road (D908). Late in the evening, Company I was attached to the 2ème Division Blindée and moved to Carrouges.

Several critical ULTRA messages were transmitted from Bletchley Park to the SLUs of the 12th and 21st Army Group and FUSA and TUSA at 2114 on 14 August and 0854 on 15 August. They were decrypts of German messages transmitted just hours earlier, at 1900 and 1700 on 14 August respectively. The first was an appreciation of the general situation by *I SS-Panzer-Korps* and the latter was a discussion between General der Panzertruppen Heinrich Eberbach and

Generalfeldmarschall Kluge. These messages contradicted the Allied command's belief that the bulk of the German forces in the pocket had already been withdrawn. They revealed that *7. Armee* with all or parts of eight divisions and *5. Panzerarmee* with all or parts of twelve divisions were still in the pocket and were only authorized to withdraw farther during the night of 15/16 August. They also confirmed the earlier suspicion that the XV Corps at Argentan was the intended target of a counterattack by *Panzergruppe Eberbach* with elements of as many as eight Panzer divisions.[35]

This news badly rattled General Bradley, who was at the 21st Army Group CP at 1100 for a meeting with Montgomery and the Second British Army Commander, Lieutenant General Sir Miles Dempsey. With both the Second British and First Canadian Army struggling to advance, Montgomery said he would have the Canadians shift focus from Falaise farther eastward, to Trun, where he expected them to link up with XV Corps coming from Argentan. Bradley finally informed Montgomery of his decision to move half of the XV Corps eastward. Not doubt surprised at the unexpected news, Montgomery cautioned Bradley to prepare for the counterattack by *Panzergruppe Eberbach.*

After leaving the meeting, Bradley began to second-guess his decision, allowing Patton to drive farther east with the bulk of TUSA, including half the XV Corps. Later, on the afternoon of 15 August, Bradley met Patton at TUSA Headquarters at Le Mans. According to Patton's diary entry,

> *Bradley came down suffering from an attack of nerves. The Black Market* [Patton's personal code in his diary for ULTRA-derived intelligence] *reports five Panzer Divs at ARGENTAN. I don't believe it so Brad wants me to halt on the line XV at DREUX, XX at CHARTRES, XII at CHATEAUDUN. His motto is, In case of doubt Halt.*
>
> *I will let him stew and tomorrow might get him to let me move.*
>
> *I wish I was Supreme Commander.*[36]

Despite Patton's entreaties, Bradley remained firm in his orders to halt the movement eastward by TUSA. However, Bradley was inexplicably slow to reinforce the position at Argentan. The 80th Infantry Division (-319th RCT) remained attached to the XX Corps but in TUSA reserve. It spent the day assembling in a concentration area at and northwest of Évron with one regiment at Laval. Instead of moving north to Argentan, it was alerted for a movement the next day to join the XX Corps near Châteaudun, 160 kilometers to the east. Despite Bradley's apprehension and his decision to halt the movement of TUSA to the east, the 80th was not actually ordered to move north, to Alençon, until early on 17 August, when it was attached to the V Corps. Once more, Bradley's indecision was hampering the effectiveness of the Allied encirclement.

Nor was Bradley's indecision the only problem Patton had to deal with. He was also having trouble keeping the French in line. General Leclerc was more focused on liberating Paris than he was on holding the line against a German counterattack at Argentan or advancing north to Trun. After reaching Écouché-les-Vallées on 13 August, Groupement tactique Langlade and Groupement tactique Dio at Carrouges had displayed a marked reluctance to continue the attack to the north. Groupement tactique Billotte was in reserve at Sées. Patton noted in the same diary entry that

> *Le Clerc* [sic] *2d French came in very excited. In order to save time I sent the two Eastern Divs of the XV Corps the 5 Armd and 79 on Dreux leaving the French and 90 to hold the Argentan backed by the 80th. Le Clerc wrote me a fool letter in which he said if he was not allowed to be in the advance on Paris he would resign.*
>
> *I told him that he was a baby that I did not propose to have division commanders tell me where they would fight and that any way I had left him in the most dangerous place.*
>
> *We parted friends.*[37]

Despite Patton's words with Le Clerc, the 2nd French Armored Division remained immobile at Carrouges and Écouché-les-Vallées. Farther west, the right of FUSA was finally closing up on the left of TUSA. The 3d Armored Division, on the right of the VII Corps, battled north to Rânes with its objective Fromentel, 10 kilometers to the northwest, against heavy resistance from elements of the *SS-Das Reich*.

****

After a long drive we checked into our next hotel in Alençon. The restaurant, like so many French restaurants we encountered, was not open until 7:00 P.M., so we decided to explore the town. Dad was in search of the famous Alençon lace, thinking he might buy some for Mom. The nice people at the visitor center sadly inform us that the only place to see the lace is in the city museum. It was now so expensive that none was sold in the area but was instead sent to only the best shops in Paris and Monaco. So back to the hotel and restaurant. The meal, like every other meal we had in France, was superb.

During the meal we discussed our options for the next day. Our next hotel in Château-Thierry was a three-and-a-half-hour drive, with part of it through the outskirts of Paris. The next day was also Saturday, so Dad was worried about traffic. Eventually, though, we decided to press on and explore the valley of the Dives and the battlefield at Chambois.

CHAPTER 12

THE BATTLE OF LE BOURG-SAINT-LÉONARD

The climax of the Battle of the Argentan-Falaise Pocket occurred in a triangular area of about 7.75 square miles (20.1 square kilometers) roughly centered on the village of Chambois. The southern point of the triangle was at the village of Le Bourg-Saint-Léonard, the northern point at Mont-Ormel (Hill 262), and the western point at the village of Saint-Lambert-sur-Dive.

In August 1944, Le Bourg-Saint-Léonard was a tiny crossroads town. The southern end of the town ran along either side of the main east-west highway from Argentan to Paris, then known as the RN24 bis (D926). The northern end of town ran on either side of the road to Chambois (D16) and another road ran south to Sées (D16) from the western end of town. Various other smaller dirt farm roads ran cross-country to the southeast, the most important of which paralleled the L'Ure River (D729). About 875 yards (800 meters) east of town another secondary road split off from the RN 24 bis at a Y-junction and ran southeast to Nonant-le-Pin (D926). The road north to Chambois ran slightly uphill through the village to a high point, Hill 172, before it descended into a wide valley. West and northwest of the village was the Forêt de Gouffern, which was crisscrossed by trails and firebreaks, which were a natural avenue of approach for German forces seeking to avoid the section of the RN24 bis running east out of Argentan that was exposed to American and French observation and fire from positions on the high ground southeast of Argentan.[1]

The 1st Battalion, 359th Infantry, under the command of Major "Fireball" Pond, began moving into its positions at 1100 on 15 August and by 1330 completed the relief of the 5th Armored Division units there. Pond placed the 1st and 2d Platoons of Company A in Le Bourg-Saint-Léonard with the 3d Platoon at the Y-junction east of town. Company C was in Exmes. Company B, in reserve, was in the woods just north of the Battalion CP at the Hostellerie du Tourne Bride at Le Haras du Pin about 2.5 miles (4 kilometers) southeast of Le Bourg-Saint-Léonard. The Battalion Heavy Weapons Company D attached one section of heavy machine guns to Company A and one to Company B. Its 81mm mortar Platoon was split, with three in Le Bourg-Saint-Léonard attached to Company A and three attached to Company B. The Battalion Antitank Platoon, with three 57mm towed guns, was with Company B in reserve as well.[2]

Pond also had several attachments to work with. The 3d Platoon, Company C, 607th Tank Destroyer Battalion was at in Le Bourg-Saint-Léonard with four towed 3-inch guns. One section of two guns was in the center of the village with one gun facing down the road to the west and one facing down the road to the north. The other section of two guns was at the Y-junction with one gun about 300 yards west of the junction, facing north, and the other at the junction facing northeast. The 1st Platoon, Company C, 315th Engineers was in reserve with Company B. The 1st Platoon, Company A, 712th Tank Battalion deployed one section of two tanks in Le Bourg-Saint-Léonard and the other section of two tanks in Exmes. The 1st Platoon, 359th Infantry Regimental Antitank Company locations and actions are unclear.[3]

Major Pond had one big problem to deal with in laying out his defenses. His entire Battalion only had access to seven 1:50,000-scale maps of the area. None of his platoon leaders had access to any maps during the engagement. It was not until nearly the end of the engagement, late on 17 August, before additional maps, including some 1:25,000-scale ones, were available.

There was little activity during the afternoon and evening. The Germans occasionally fired a few rounds of artillery at the American positions but otherwise there was no movement or small arms fire directed at them.

16 AUGUST

Company A, 359th Infantry deployed in Le Bourg-Saint-Léonard with its 1st Platoon, under 2d Lieutenant Morency R. Dame, manning a line facing northwest with its right on the church and stretching southwest through an orchard. The 2d Platoon, under 1st Lieutenant Charles A. Schroeder, tied in on the right of the church and extended its line to the northeast across the Chambois road. The Company CP was in the last building on the road heading east out of the village.

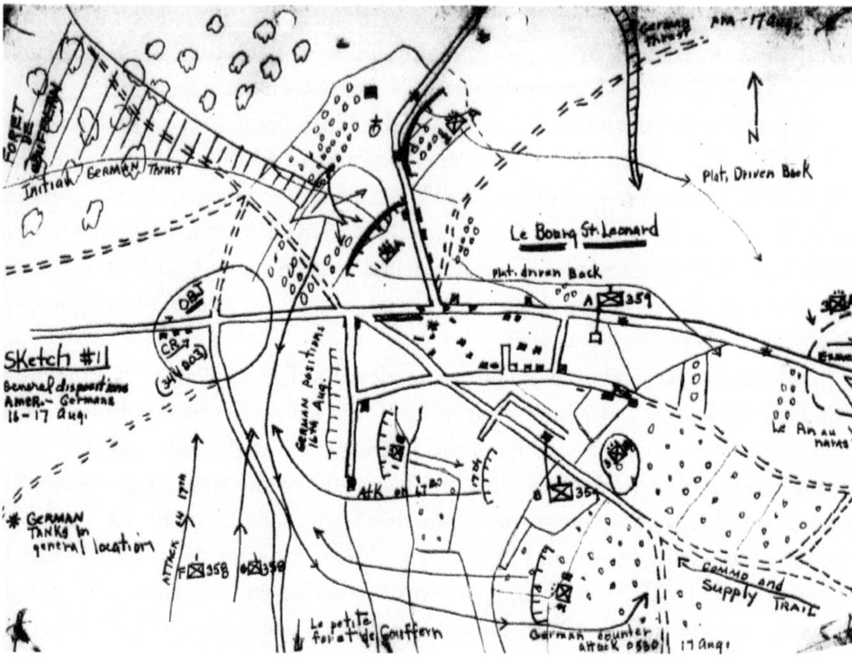

Map 18. The defense of Le Bourg-Saint-Léonard by the 1st Battalion, 359th Infantry, 16–17 August 1944. Jenkins, Sketch #1.

At first light, 2d Lieutenant Vernon W. Cross, the Weapons Platoon Leader of Company A, was with his 60mm mortar section, emplaced in an orchard in the southeast corner of the town. He had placed security teams to the east and south but was surprised by what appeared to be a patrol of about a dozen Germans, approaching from the southwest, which suddenly appeared near the mortar positions. One of the security teams called out for them to surrender, but they turned and ran. A few hasty shots wounded one of the Germans, who was captured and interrogated. He claimed to be a cook and said the group was planning to surrender. In retrospect it seems more likely they were indeed a patrol that was pinpointing the American positions.[4]

Later in the morning at 1035, the Germans began shelling the village and at about the same time the 2d Lieutenant Dame led a patrol of six or seven men through the orchard and into the woods to the northwest. The patrol went 1,000 yards (914 meters) when they ran into a German force estimated as twenty-five to thirty men. A firefight broke out, lasting only a few minutes, when "a helluva lot more Germans" appeared and Dame was slightly wounded in his left hand, which bled profusely. Hopelessly outnumbered, an excited and confused Dame fled with the patrol back to his platoon's position. When confronted with their bloody and obviously rattled leader and what appeared to be a mass of Germans pursuing the patrol, the 1st Platoon fell apart, panicked, and fled to the opposite side of the street where the panic spread to the 2d Platoon. Both platoons then fell back to the east and south near the Company A CP. Without infantry support, the two tank destroyer guns in the center of town were vulnerable to being overrun. The crews managed to withdraw one gun back to the Y-junction, but the other was disabled and left in town. By 1100, the Germans had occupied the west side of town.[5]

At 1300, the Germans renewed the attack, this time with two or three tanks accompanying their infantry. One of the 3-inch guns of the 607th Tank Destroyers knocked out one of the German tanks but in turn was disabled by German fire. The rest of the German tanks and infantry continued to advance east toward the Y-junction, but two tanks were disabled by another 607th Tank Destroyer gun, which then fired HE at the German infantry, forcing them back as well.[6]

3-inch Gun M5 of the 3d Platoon, Company C, 607th Tank Destroyer Battalion. The building is now 7 Place de la Liberté, Le Bourg-Saint-Léonard. Dated 19 August 1944, but probably the same position occupied on 16 August. Personnel are identified left to right as Sgt. Ross E. Gudbaur, Pfc. William J. Pierson, and Cpl. John J. Blair. The soldier barely visible in the doorway to the back was not identified. U.S. Army SC.

Lieutenant Fritz hastily reorganized the 1st and 2d Platoon east of town and sent runners back to bring up the 3d Platoon from the Y-junction. He also notified Major Pond of what had happened. Pond hurried forward to the Company A CP and was there when Lieutenant Fritz began counterattacking at about 1400. Fritz's attack drove the Germans back and he was able to reoccupy the previous positions, but the Germans quickly returned with superior forces, now including some tanks, and drove the Americans back again.

Realizing the Germans were in considerable strength, Major Pond ordered his Executive Officer, Captain David I. Hickman, to bring up Company B and the Engineer Platoon from reserve. The Engineers, directed in place by Pond, took over the defense of the Y-junction. Shortly after, Colonel Bacon came up with elements of the Regimental Headquarters Company and rear elements of the 1st Battalion to further secure the area. He was later awarded the Silver Star for his actions on 16 August.

CITATION: The President of the United States of America, authorized by Act of Congress July 9, 1918, takes pleasure in presenting the Silver Star to Colonel (Infantry) Robert Lynn Bacon (ASN: 0-8657), United States Army, for gallantry in action as Commanding Officer of an Infantry Regiment of the 90th Infantry Division.

On 16 August 1944 while the infantry of his Regiment was fighting in the town of [Le Bourg-Saint-Léonard], France, the enemy delivered a strong double envelopment around the right flank using infantry and tanks. Colonel Bacon, learning of the situation, went forward personally and seeing the envelopment would cut off his leading Battalion, having no formed troops ready to meet the envelopment and while the area was under heavy artillery and small arms fire, he personally gathered together rear elements of this battalion, engineers, and a part of his Regimental CP, quickly organized them into a unit and personally led the attack of this provisional unit against the enemy envelopment, driving them back and securing the road leading into [Le Bourg-Saint-Léonard] from the east. This prevented the cutting off of his leading battalion which was then heavily engaged in the town. Colonel Bacon's disregard for his own personal safety and leadership of the improvised force against a serious enemy counterthrust effectively forestalled it. It set a fine example of leadership to the officers and men of his regiment and is in keeping with the highest standards of the military spirit.[7]

Company B, led by the 1st Platoon under 1st Lieutenant Charles F. Kingsley, moved out at about 1645 and marched up the paved road from Le Pin-au-Haras to a position about 150 yards south of the Y-junction, where they turned left onto the unpaved farm road. On the southeastern outskirts of town, they ran into a force of about two platoons of Germans, deployed, and pushed them back after a short fight, capturing sixteen of them. Captain Hutchens and his Executive Officer, 1st Lieutenant John E. Oram, set up the Company B CP in a walled farmhouse and prepared to counterattack alongside Company A. At 1800, the American attack jumped off with Company A on the right and Company B on the left.

Company A quickly retook its positions, but 1st Lieutenant Henry E. Burness, the Company Executive Officer, was killed. The Germans responded with a renewed attack, throwing in more infantry, tanks, and artillery. The 3d Platoon, Company A was soon threatened by encirclement. One of its BAR men was hit and Lieutenant John Bergstrom, the Platoon Leader, picked up his gun, trying to find a way out, and was killed by machine-gun fire. Bergstrom's Platoon Sergeant took over and with the timely arrival of two tanks from the 712th Tank Battalion he managed to withdraw the platoon back to where it started its attack, near the Company A CP. The Germans pursued with infantry and tanks and forced the evacuation of the CP, except for eight men who retreated to the second floor of the building. The Germans fired a fusillade of rifle shots and threw hand grenades up the stairs calling out, "hands up, or I kill." Private Eugene M. Blythe, one of the Company Headquarters runners, shouted back "fuck you!" as the eight men managed to escape through a back window. Finally, after riffling through the company mail, the Germans seized the Americans rations, cigarettes, and a jeep with a mounted .50-caliber machine gun and fell back toward the town at about 2100.[8]

Company B, still led by Lieutenant Kingsley's 1st Platoon, jumped off and advanced 150 yards farther west, to the crossroads in the center of town, where they encountered a force estimated as two to three platoons of Germans on the other side of the Chambois road. Lieutenant Kingsley deployed his 1st Platoon, while the 2d Platoon, under 2d Lieutenant Edward L. Marks, came up and deployed to its left. The two platoons engaged in a protracted small arms fire contest with the Germans. About 1930, Lieutenant Oram brought up the section of heavy machine guns attached from Company D and placed them on the left flank of the 1st Platoon where they could fire the length of the Chambois road. Captain Hutchens came up as well, at around 1950, but failed to give Kingsley clear orders as to what to do other than hold his position.

However, as darkness set in at around 2130, a burning house about 100 yards to the west provided enough light for the Germans to see the 1st Platoon positions, while at the same time the glare obscured the Germans to the Americans' front. The Germans quickly took advantage, lobbing volleys of hand grenades from no more than 25 to 30 yards away, while harassing the 1st Platoon with automatic weapons and rifle fire. The Germans then brought up a tank on the right of the platoon, somewhere in town, which was able to fire down the road running northwest to southeast, effectively isolating the 1st and 2d Platoon from the Company B CP. Probably about this time, the 2d Platoon fell back about 150 to 200 yards, leaving the left of the 1st Platoon exposed.

By this point, Kingsley had lost all contact with the Company CP as well as the 2d Platoon. He sent a runner, Private First Class Paul P. Dvorok, to try to contact Captain Hutchens, but Dvorok was shot and seriously wounded after going only a few yards. Lieutenant Kingsley decided to pull back the platoon 75 yards to the east, behind a hedgerow that provided cover and better fields of fire. No other men were hit, and the withdrawal was completed between midnight and 0100, effectively ending the engagement for the night. While the Americans no longer held Le Bourg-Saint-Léonard and had lost visibility of the Chambois valley, they still controlled the German escape route east on the RN24 bis.[9]

The 90th Infantry Division G-2 identified the Germans attacking Le Bourg-Saint-Léonard as elements of the *SS-Das Reich*. The combined *II.* and *III./SS-Panzergrenadier-Regiment 3* was estimated to be about 400 strong, supported by as many as five Panzer IV, and one or two batteries of artillery and Nebelwerfer in direct support. In support at Fougy was *SS-Panzergrenadier-Regiment 4.* with an estimated strength of 300. They were also reinforced by ten Panzer IV and a few Panther tanks from *Panzer-Regiment 16* of *116. Panzer-Division*. American accounts of the battle at Le Bourg-Saint-Léonard indicate some Sturmgeschütz were available as well, but it is unclear which unit they were from. In addition, elements of eight other German divisions and numerous smaller units were identified through prisoners of war in front of the 90th Infantry Division and 2ème Division Blindée on 16 August. While some appeared to be withdrawing from the pocket, it was very evident that the Germans were indeed intent on attacking with significant forces to keep the gap at Argentan open. General Bradley's fear of a "broken back" may have been justified, but in light of the strength encountered by the rump of the XV Corps around Argentan, it may be asked why he agreed to Patton's weakening of the "strong shoulder."[10]

In fact, at 1640 on 16 August Hitler had authorized a request made by Feldmarschall von Kluge earlier at 0200 for an immediate evacuation by the *7. Armee* and *5. Panzer-Armee* from the pocket through the gap between Argentan and Falaise. Even before he received that authorization, Kluge conferred with SS-Oberstgruppenführer Hausser and General der Panzertruppen Eberbach on the growing peril the German armies were in. They decided jointly on the counterattack by *SS-Das Reich* at Argentan that began the morning of 16 August and the withdrawal of *7. Armee* east of the Orne River to begin on the night of 16/17 August. At the same time, the Germans also began evacuating the mass of logistical support units—division, corps, and army—that had collected at the base of the pocket, many of them in the woods southwest of Trun and northwest of Le Bourg-Saint-Léonard.

While Bletchley intercepted Kluge's messages from the early morning and had them decrypted and retransmitted to the Allied commanders by 2047 on 16 August and 0211 on 17 August, Hitler's message authorizing the complete withdrawal from the pocket was not intercepted. However, by the evening of 16 August, Bletchley intercepted a message from *Heeresgruppe B* at 1600 ordering an immediate withdrawal of *7. Armee* east of the Orne, which was decrypted and retransmitted at 2048. While that was not evidence of a complete withdrawal by all German forces from the pocket, it could be inferred that such a withdrawal was likely to begin at any moment.[11]

As the 1st Battalion, 359th Infantry battled the Germans in Le Bourg-Saint-Léonard, General McLain was bringing up reinforcements. He ordered Colonel Bacon to move the 3d Battalion, 359th Infantry to Le Pin-au-Haras and then farther north to block the road from Le Bourg-Saint-Léonard to Exmes (D14). At 1840, he directed Colonel Clarke's 2d Battalion, 358th Infantry "to proceed north, through Forest to this side of La Corne [about 1,500 meters south of Le Bourg-Saint-Léonard]. One company to be placed astride road, just north of La Corne and one company to outpost." By 2125, the 2d Battalion, 358th Infantry was in position and Major Lytle, the 1st Battalion, 358th Infantry commander, and Major Schultz, the 2d Battalion, 358th Infantry commander, were at the 359th Infantry CP conferring with Colonel Bacon.

Meanwhile, the 3d Armored Division was finally closed up on the left of CT 7, relieving it of securing the Forêt d'Ecouves. At 1700, the 3d Battalion, 357th Infantry, under division control, was ordered to move to Sées and then to positions northwest of Nonant-le-Pin in reserve. The 1st and 2d Battalion were ordered to assemble in the vicinity of Lonrai, northwest of Alençon, prepared to move northeast the next morning. By 2200, the 357th was closed in its assembly area and further orders were received instructing it to relieve the CT 9 positions northeast of Sées as early as possible on 17 August. However, the 357th Infantry's supporting artillery was already on its way. The 343d and 344th Field Artillery, with Dad's Battery A accompanying them, left early and were in firing positions near Nonant-le-Pin by midday. There one of the howitzers of Battery C, 344th Field Artillery had a "muzzle burst"—a round that detonated early at the muzzle when fired—injuring some of the cannoneers.[12]

Major command changes were also underway. In the afternoon, General Bradley went to FUSA Headquarters, at Domfront, 30 kilometers south of Vire, only to find that General Hodges was away, meeting with General Collins at VII Corps Headquarters, far to the east near Gavron. In his absence, Bradley met with Brigadier General William B. Kean, FUSA Chief of Staff, and Colonel Truman C. Thorson, FUSA G-3, to discuss the future employment of the V Corps. At the time, V Corps was a headquarters without troops after it had been effectively pinched out of the line by the convergence of the XIX Corps and the Second British Army at Vire earlier that day.

Bradley decided he would use now Major General Leonard Gerow's V Corps Headquarters to command Patton's troops at Argentan. Gerow would take command of the 2ème Division Blindée, 80th Infantry Division (-319th RCT), and 90th Infantry Division and would attack north through Chambois to Trun to link up with the Canadian attack conceived by Montgomery the previous day. At 2100, Thorson called Gerow, who was at his headquarters south of Vire, about 80 kilometers northwest of Alençon. Thorson told Gerow to pick eight or ten key staff officers from V Corps Headquarters and report to FUSA Headquarters. Gerow arrived at 2230 and detailed planning began. At 0200 17 August, Gerow set out with his command group in seven jeeps in a driving rainstorm.[13]

Unfortunately, communications and liaison between the FUSA and TUSA headquarters were so poor there were no answers for some of Gerow's very basic questions at the staff conference. When Gerow asked where the locations of the divisions he was to command were, he was told, "we do not know . . . You will have to find them." When he asked what the German situation was, the reply was the same.[14]

Seemingly nothing could be straightforward about the situation at Le Bourg-Saint-Léonard. Uncertain of how long it would take Gerow to reach Alençon, Bradley called Patton at 1900 and ordered him to use the 2ème Division Blindée, 80th Infantry Division (-319th RCT), and 90th Infantry Division to execute the attack on Trun on 17 August. Patton told Bradley he would organize a provisional corps under his Chief of Staff, General Gaffey, to take command of the divisions and execute the attack in the morning. Gaffey left at 2000 in the same rainstorm as Gerow's group and reached Alençon where at 2300 he established the Provisional Corps with the Rear Headquarters elements the XV Corps left behind, the 5th Tank Destroyer Group Headquarters with the 772d Tank Destroyer Battalion, and the 208th Field Artillery Group with four Field Artillery battalions.[15]

Gaffey's orders for the Provisional Corps were to attack on order, any time after 1000 on 17 August, to the northwest to capture Trun. The mission of the 90th Infantry Division was to attack north to seize Omméel and Mont Ormel and the surrounding high ground northeast of Chambois, securing a passage for the commitment of the 2ème Division Blindée. General McLain's plan expected the main effort would be by the 358th Infantry, less two battalions, attacking on the right of the 359th Infantry from Exmes. The 359th Infantry, initially with the 2d Battalion, 358th Infantry attached, was to complete the seizure of Le Bourg-Saint-Léonard and continue its attack north to Hill 129 southwest of Chambois. Then the plans changed again, as Patton noted in his diary:

> *About 2330 Bradley told me to have Gaffey withhold his attack until he Bradley, ordered it. I delivered the order.*
>
> *Life is never dull.*[16]

17 AUGUST

Company A, 359th Infantry regrouped after midnight east of the former Company CP. A platoon-size group of German infantrymen tried to work around the right of the company positions to the Y-junction, but Cross's mortars and fire from the tank destroyer guns drove them back. The Americans followed them, and the rifle platoons reoccupied the Company A CP area and the eastern end of Le Bourg-Saint-Léonard by dawn. Shortly after, a German tank probed into the American lines by driving east along the RN 24 bis toward the Y-junction. It was knocked out by an American tank as it passed the Company A CP.

Two more German tanks were spotted moving south on the Chambois Road into town, where they halted. The 1st Platoon, Company A, 712th Tank Battalion claimed they knocked out one of the German tanks, a Panther, at 0400 and left it burning. Then at 0530, the Germans attempted a double envelopment of the 1st Battalion. One group tried to slip around the right flank of Company A, through the valley that ran parallel to the north of the N24 bis, and another tried the same tactic on the left flank of Company B. About fifteen to twenty Germans were spotted by one of Cross's mortarmen, who informed some American tankers near the Company A CP. They and the heavy machine-gun section attached to Company A brought fire on the Germans, killing and wounding some and forcing the others to retreat. Three Germans, one of them wounded, surrendered.

At around 1330, Company A attacked again and encountered more German tanks, which they managed to force back with bazooka fire. One was disabled and

Lieutenant Fritz, the Company A commander, shot the crew down as they tried to escape. However, the other German tanks forced Fritz to pull his men back again. He managed to get the Company Headquarters, 1st and 2d Platoon, and the attached mortars and machine guns back, but lost control of the 1st Platoon south of the B24 bis. Fritz went back with one of his sergeants to try to contact them and was not seen again, although his sergeant was later found wounded. It was found out later that Fritz was captured and he remained a prisoner until the end of the war. He was awarded a Silver Star for his actions at Le Bourg-Saint-Léonard.

On the left of Company A, the Germans continued their unrelenting small arms fire on the 1st Platoon, Company B, throughout the night. By 0400, the Americans were low on ammunition and hand grenades. Private Raymond D. Knox, who had gotten separated from his 2d Platoon, volunteered to go to the Company CP for help. He managed to get there unscathed and returned at 0430 with as many bandoleers of ammunition and hand grenades as he could carry. Knox told Lieutenant Kingsley that he was to report to Captain Hutchens at the CP at 0600 for orders.

Lieutenant Kingsley tried again to contact the 2d Platoon and finally found them about 100 yards farther to the rear, leaving the 1st Platoon flank exposed, so Kingsley pulled his platoon back to tie in with them. By 0545, the two platoons were in line with the Company CP. Kingsley was talking with Staff Sergeant William Ackerman, the Platoon Sergeant of the 2d Platoon, who was trying to find out "where in the hell" his Platoon Leader, Lieutenant Marks, was when they were joined by the Company Weapons Platoon Leader, 2d Lieutenant George G. Foster. Just then, the Germans opened fire on the CP area from the deep left rear of the 2d Platoon; the Germans had slipped past the American line in the night. It was the typical German tactic to sow confusion in the American lines that had worked so well in June and July, but this time was different. Instead of panicking, heading for the rear, or firing wildly into their own men, the Americans sheltered in place and waited for the storm of German fire to end. The men of the 90th Infantry Division were again displaying a newfound confidence and experience in battle.

Kingsley noted that the positions of the 2d Platoon masked the fire from the 1st Platoon, but neither platoon wavered. After about an hour of intense fire, the German attack stopped, and Kingsley made his way to the Company CP where he found that Captain Hitchens had been killed in the first German volley and Lieutenant Oram had been wounded earlier in the morning. Kingsley, now effectively in command of Company B, went back and made sure the 2d Platoon was tied in with his 1st Platoon and moved the Weapons Platoon to the left rear of the 2d Platoon to prevent another German attempt to outflank them.

At about this same time, around 0600, Major Pond drove up the dirt farm road in a jeep to the Company B CP, which he was also using as his Battalion OP. He was accompanied only by his driver and a second jeep with the Company D commander, 1st Lieutenant Samuel F. Cartwright, and two men from Company D. About 400 yards from the CP the German flanking force previously mentioned opened fire on them with automatic weapons, but without hitting anyone. Pond later said, "we sure cleared out of those jeeps in one hell of a hurry." Pond brought up the 81mm mortars of Company D to try to suppress the Germans but could not get any closer to the Company B CP. Realizing the situation was dire, Pond called his Executive Officer, Captain John S. Fisk, and ordered him to bring up the last battalion reserve, its A&P Platoon. Fisk then gave him the welcome news that a platoon of Company B, 712th Tank Battalion had also just arrived at Battalion Headquarters. Pond responded, "Send them up with the A&P Platoon and make it fast![17]

The tanks, with the A&P Platoon riding on them, arrived at 0600. Pond quickly oriented the tank and infantry platoon leaders on the situation and then mounted one of the tanks himself. At 0615, Pond's counterattack set off, quickly driving the Germans back again. Pond's group reached the Company B CP and reunited with the remnants of Company B at about 0800. Shortly after, Kingsley returned to the Company CP and found Major Pond, who ordered him to prepare to attack at 1230, again with Company A and B abreast. Company B's objective was still the crossroads on the west side of town, which they were to hold until relieved by the 2d Battalion, 358th Infantry, which was coming up from the south.

However, about 1100 the Germans opened a heavy artillery barrage and attacked again with tanks and infantry. Company B was out of bazooka ammunition, so Kingsley left the German tanks to be dealt with by the American tanks and tank destroyers and had his men concentrate on the German infantry. The German attack ended about 1230 and after an hour delay Company B, along with Company A, began its attack, supported by three tanks and the attached Company D heavy machine guns. After an hour of steady progress, the American attack had advanced 300 yards and contacted Company F, 358th Infantry, which was advancing from the west, leading the 2d Battalion, 358th Infantry, which was coming up to reinforce the position.

Other additional reinforcements were coming up as well. One platoon of Company C, 359th Infantry, Company B, 712th Tank Battalion, and Company A and C, 773d Tank Destroyer Battalion with twenty-three self-propelled 3-inch M10 Gun Motor Carriages, joined Company A and B at 1445. The 2d Battalion, 358th Infantry also came up from the southwest, with the 1st and 3d Platoon,

Company C, 773d Tank Destroyer Battalion, ready to support the attack and relieve the 1st Battalion, 359th Infantry once the town was secured. Colonel Randolph, commander of the 712th Tank Battalion, personally led Company B, 712th Tank Battalion into the action.[18]

At 1600, seven M10 of the 1st and 3d Platoon, Company A, 773d Tank Destroyers fired into the southern edge of town for five minutes before the 1st Battalion, 359th Infantry attack jumped off again. Company A, 359th Infantry with the platoon of Company C, 359th Infantry, Company C, 773d Tank Destroyer Battalion, and the 1st Platoon, Company A, 712th Tank Battalion, again drove west into town. Company B, 359th Infantry, with Company A, 773d Tank Destroyer Battalion, and Company B, 712th Tank Battalion advanced into town from the south.

The additional tank and tank destroyer support invigorated the attack. The 3d Platoon, Company A, 773d Tank Destroyer Battalion, supported by tanks, entered the southern part of town under heavy German artillery fire and knocked out three Panzer IV. The 3d Platoon knocked out two more Panzer IV that attempted a counterattack. However, snipers took a toll on the tank destroyer men in their open-topped gun carriages. By the end of the battle, two men were killed and twelve wounded in Company A, 773d Tank Destroyer Battalion. The 3d Platoon, Company C, 773d Tank Destroyer Battalion accounted for another Panzer IV on the east side of town and in exchange lost one M10 and had two men wounded.

By 2000, the crossroads west of town and the southern part of Le Bourg-Saint-Léonard were secured. At midnight, Company B, 359th Infantry was relieved by Company E, 358th Infantry, and marched back to Le Pin-au-Haras to reorganize. Orders took longer to reach Company A and before they were relieved another man was wounded by German artillery fire just before midnight.

Considering the intensity of the action, the 1st Battalion, 359th Infantry casualties were surprisingly light. Out of six officers and 158 men, Company A had two officers and three men killed, one officer captured, ten men severely wounded, fourteen men lightly wounded and evacuated, and a few others lightly wounded that remained on duty. Company B had only a few fatal casualties. Out of a strength of five officers and 163 men, Captain Hutchens was killed, and five men were missing, one of whom returned to duty a few days later. Otherwise, twenty-three men were seriously wounded, including Lieutenant Orem, and six were lightly wounded and evacuated. Hardest hit was the platoon of Company C, which had four men killed, one officer, the Platoon Leader 2d Lieutenant Armand DeMaio, and eight men seriously wounded, and seven men lightly wounded and evacuated.[19]

Major Schulz, commanding the 2d Battalion, 358th Infantry, received an award of the Distinguished Service Cross and Major Pond, commanding the 1st Battalion, 359th Infantry received his second award of the Distinguished Service Cross for their actions at Le Bourg-Saint-Léonard.

CITATION: Major Robert H. Schulz, United States Army, was awarded the Distinguished Service Cross for extraordinary heroism in connection with military operations against an armed enemy while serving with the 90th Infantry Division, in action against enemy forces on 17 August 1944. Major Schulz's intrepid actions, personal bravery and zealous devotion to duty exemplify the highest traditions of the military forces of the United States and reflect great credit upon himself, the 90th Infantry Division, and the United States Army.[20]

CITATION: Lieutenant Colonel (Infantry) Leroy R. Pond (ASN: 0-370275), United States Army, was awarded a Bronze Oak Leaf Cluster in lieu of a Second Award of the Distinguished Service Cross for extraordinary heroism in connection with military operations against an armed enemy while serving with the 1st Battalion, 359th Infantry Regiment, 90th Infantry Division, in action against enemy forces on 16 and 17 August 1944. Lieutenant Colonel Pond's intrepid actions, personal bravery and zealous devotion to duty at the cost of his life [the citation confused his death on 15 January 1945 from wounds suffered 14 December 1944, with the action at Le Bourg-Saint-Léonard], exemplify the highest traditions of the military forces of the United States and reflect great credit upon himself, the 90th Infantry Division, and the United States Army.[21]

Colonel Randolph of the 712th Tank Battalion also received the Distinguished Service Cross for this action.

CITATION: The President of the United States of America, authorized by Act of Congress, July 9, 1918, takes pride in presenting the Distinguished Service Cross (Posthumously) to Lieutenant Colonel (Cavalry) George B. Randolph (ASN: 0-227591), United States Army, for extraordinary heroism in connection with military operations against an armed enemy while serving as Commanding Officer of the 712th Tank Battalion, 90th Infantry Division, in action against enemy forces in France, on 17 August 1944. On that date, Colonel Randolph personally led a tank company into action against the enemy-held town of Le Bourg St. Leonard, France, inspiring his men by his bold, fearless leadership. As the battle grew in intensity he moved from tank to tank, heedless of his own safety, personally directing the fire of the tank crews and supporting infantry. On the following morning during a desperate enemy attack, Colonel Randolph, although wounded, led a counterattack so aggressively that the enemy was routed and the town secured. His inspiring leadership, and his courage and supreme devotion to duty exemplify the highest traditions of the military forces of the United States and reflect great credit upon himself, his unit, and the United States Army.[22]

While the 2d Battalion, 358th and 1st Battalion, 359th Infantry were battling it out at Le Bourg-Saint-Léonard, the CT 7 began its movement from the left to the right of the division zone at 0700. The 1st Battalion left Lonrai and drove northeast via Colombiers–Radon–Sées and detrucked at Chailloué. By 1200, it relieved elements of the 359th Infantry and assumed blocking positions in reserve at Croisilles, Le Taillis Saint-Sauveur-Lendelin, Le Merlerault, and Nonant-le-Pin. The 2d Battalion was shuttled forward next and by 1430 Company F relieved the 359th Infantry at Gacé. Company G relieved Company K, 359th Infantry at Exmes 1645 and Company F went into reserve 2,000 yards to its south.

General Devine also reoriented some of the divisional Field Artillery battalions to bring them closer to the gap between Le Bourg-Saint-Léonard and Trun, through which elements of twenty or more German divisions were finally beginning to flee eastward. At 0700, the 915th, 344th, and 345th Field Artillery were ordered to move farther northwest of Nonant-le-Pin, closer to Le Haras du Pin. The 343d Field Artillery, with Dad's Battery A, was ordered to move as well and started at 2030. Their destination was the farm fields around the church at La Cochère, about 5 kilometers northwest of Nonant-le-Pin and 2 kilometers south of Le Haras du Pin. En route, they experienced something that was all too common during the Normandy campaign: an attack by friendly aircraft.

Sometime earlier that day, two P-38J15 "Lightning" fighter bombers of the 430th Fighter Squadron, 474th Fighter Group, IX TAC took off from their base at Landing Ground A-11, near Saint-Lambert south of Isigny-sur-Mer. Each aircraft was fully armed with a 20mm and four .50-caliber machine guns and two 500-pound bombs. Aircraft Serial Number 43-28725 was flown by 1st Lieutenant Robert Gustave Loft. The other was flown by Loft's wingman, 2d Lieutenant Marshall Hanna. Their mission was to fly a dive-bombing and strafing mission against German positions near Bernay. The pilots flew a course of 110 degrees to reach Bernay through 8/10ths cloud cover, a 5,000-foot cloud base, and good visibility.[23]

A half hour after the 343d Field Artillery and Battery A got on the road, they noticed two aircraft circling above them. Dad's four M16B began tracking the aircraft, but they were quickly identified as American P-38s. However, as the aircraft approached, both made a low firing pass at the American column. According to the account by the 343d Field Artillery,

The second came in too low, shearing the tops of four telephone poles and hitting Baker Battery's 4th gun section truck with its wing and propeller. Four men were killed and two injured during the strafing. The men killed were T/4 John Burkhart, Pfc. Henry Maul, Pfc. Fred D. Weyl, Jr., and Pvt. Tony A. Vigil. The plane crashed and burned about 250 yards from the road. The pilot was killed in the crash and burned beyond recognition, but his dog tags identified him as an American pilot.

That story, while it described a sad series of events all too common in warfare, also appears to conceal some of the reality of what happened that night. Problematically, there are numerous discrepancies in this account.

For example, Lieutenant Hanna said that Loft crashed at 2030, while Battery A gave the time as 2100. However, that simply glosses over the major issue with the AAF account—the two aircraft were over 30 miles off course, far south of their assigned target at Bernay. To end up where Loft crashed, they had to fly a course of about 130 degrees, not 110 degrees. Worse, Lieutenant Hanna testified that the crash site was 1 mile east of La Goulafrière, which is about 20 miles northeast of the actual crash site. The two pilots were completely mistaken about their location, which helps explain why they believed the American column they attacked was German. Given that neither plane bombed, but only made a strafing attack, it also seems likely that they had already expended their bombs on another target and were only attacking a target of opportunity.[24]

Nor does the account of the 343d Field Artillery match with Hanna's description of events, which was that "[Loft] climbed above the overcast and came down on his bomb run at approximately 350 MPH and went into the ground bursting into flames."[25] The problem with that is that Hanna implied that only Loft attacked, when it is clear from the accounts on the ground that both attacked. It is also clear from the 343d Field Artillery account that Hanna attacked first, followed by Loft. It is also unclear why Hanna described Loft's attack as a "bomb run" when it was evident that they had already expended their bombs.

The answer to this enigma is simple and was given by Dad, who was an eyewitness—he recalled running over to the crashed aircraft and seeing the recovery of Loft's dog tags, which confirmed that the pilot and aircraft were American. He remembered, just as in the 343d Field Artillery account, that both aircraft made a firing pass on the column. In that pass four men in Battery A, Sergeant Franklin F. Newcomb, Corporal John F. Reddington, Private First Class Lawrence A. Moore, and Private Lawrence Bradley, one of the M16B gun crew, were all lightly wounded by ricocheting fragments from the aircraft's 20mm and .50-caliber rounds.

Reddington was lightly wounded enough that he returned to duty the same night, but the others remained in the casualty clearing station until the next day when they returned to duty as well. It may have been that Loft and Hanna were trying to suppress the "German" antiaircraft guns before they made another pass.[26]

According to Dad's account, the two aircraft then circled and made another pass at the column. Dad recalled that as soon as the aircraft opened fire, the Battery A M16Bs fired in return. One aircraft, Hanna's, broke off the attack. The second was either hit by the fire from Battery A, struck the poles, and crashed or the fire momentarily distracted Loft, who struck the poles trying to avoid the fire, and crashed. Either way, Dad stated firmly, "he made a second pass at us, and we opened fire on him; we shot him down."[27]

While it may seem shocking that Dad was so matter-of-fact regarding a fatal friendly fire incident, it was far too common an occurrence and the subject of considerable bitterness on the part of the ground forces to the air forces. Even General Patton had experienced the problem. Three days earlier on 14 August he recorded just as matter-of-factly in his diary, "One of our own P-47's strafed the cross roads [*sic*] near Hq getting a tank carrier. It was shot down."[28]

Ironically, also on 17 August, the Allied Expeditionary Air Force, in overall tactical command of the air support effort in France, ordered the bomb safety line "entirely removed from the pocket west of the narrowing Falaise-Argentan gap, and theoretically air activity over the beleaguered enemy in that area ceased." The reason for shifting the bomb line east was to protect Allied ground forces from accidental air attacks, which had become a bone of contention between the ground and the air commanders. Air Chief Marshall Sir Trafford Leigh-Mallory, commander of the Allied Expeditionary Air Force, had long opposed fixed bomb lines, claiming they restricted the effectiveness of close air support and denied the tactical air forces excellent target opportunities, allowing many enemy troops to escape. He preferred a less cautious policy, allowing fighter-bombers to attack identified targets at will. The problem with that, illustrated repeatedly in the Normandy campaign, as in Dad's case, was that identification of targets—and even basic navigation—was problematic for many of the young pilots flying missions.[29]

By 14 August, Leigh-Mallory had come to a remarkable conclusion. He had decided that the battle of Normandy had been won and was over. He dictated in his daily diary,

> *My own view is that the chances of the Hun getting out have no gone. Inside [the pocket] of course he is being harried by the fighter-bombers which have clobbered and clobbered*

and clobbered. But the opportunity of wiping out the German Army as they streamed back over the roads in headlong retreat doesn't look as though it will come my way. It is possible that they might last incise the pocket for as much as a week or ten days. They are almost surrounded. When that army in the pocket has gone, what can the Hun do? He will, I suppose, try to hold the Seine for a short time but he has no more troops, or certainly, none of any value, and with the large forces at our disposal, we shall be able to continuously to outflank him.[30]

Leigh-Mallory was so convinced the campaign was over that on 15 August he ceased dictating entries for his diary, stating,

He now regarded the campaign in France and Western Europe (as far as the air was concerned) as won and his eyes were turning in the direction of the Far East whither he was shortly to proceed.[31]

Leigh-Mallory was promoted to air chief marshal on 16 August and was appointed Air Commander-in-Chief of South East Asia Command effective 1 November but was killed in an aircraft accident on 14 November 1944 before he could assume command his new command in Burma. His body was not recovered until June 1945. His older brother George famously disappeared attempting to scale Mount Everest in June 1924, and his body was not discovered until 1999.[32]

On the morning of 17 August, Montgomery flew to Bradley's headquarters at Saint-James, where they discussed how to trap the Germans. The town of Falaise had fallen to the 2d Canadian Division that morning. During the discussion, both agreed to move the bomb safety lines east of the Argentan-Falaise gap. Given his assumption that the campaign was essentially over, Leigh-Mallory acquiesced with little protest.[33]

However, the shifting of the bomb safety lines did not, as some have inferred, halt all air attacks on the pocket. Rather, it meant that air attacks were banned west of the line Argentan-Falaise, although there is anecdotal evidence that some still occurred there as well. Critically, on 17 August the four-mile stretch of the Dives river between Trun and Chambois was still within the bomb lines.[34]

The Dives River, while barely a narrow stream, was deep and its banks were steep-sided. It was only easily crossed by vehicles at four bridges at Trun, Magny, Saint Lambert-sur-Dives, and Chambois, and the two bridges at Magny the crossed the Dives and a tributary were narrow farm road crossings that were unlikely to support heavy armored vehicles. There were also fords: one at Magny, three at Sainte

Lambert, one at Moissy, and two east of Chambois. The fords were passable to foot traffic and light vehicles but were more problematic for heavier vehicles. Years later, a French historian remarked of the ford at Moissy,

> *It was a ridiculously small crossing for the might of a powerful army—a ford for washer-women who crossed by laying a plank from one bank to the other. By pouring tanks and vehicles into it, Seventh Army would fill the deep riverbed, and soldiers would kill each other fighting to cross the bridge. . . . The Allied artillery and air forces pounded this semi-paralysed mass unceasingly.*[35]

At Trun, another narrow farm lane bridge, the Pont de Chalets (D247) was damaged by two Tiger tanks attempting to cross it on 14 August and was impassable for vehicles. During the day, tens of thousands of German vehicles of all types were reported heading for the Dives crossings. One Ninth Air Force fighter-bomber pilot reported, "the whole goddam German Army was moving through this gap.[36]

While all this was transpiring, the command situation at Argentan became even more confused. As Patton recorded in his diary,

> *At 0730 Gerow called from Gaffeys Hq N of Argentan* [sic, Alençon] *saying he was there with a small staff ready to take command. I told him that since Gaffey had arranged the attack which might come off at any moment Gaffey should run it and he, Gerow, could take over as opportunity afforded.*[37]

However, Gerow objected for several reasons. The Germans still had control of Le Bourg-Saint-Léonard at that time, which was part of the intended line of departure for the attack towards Chambois and Trun. Gerow was also still uncertain of the terrain and dispositions of friendly and enemy troops and was not happy with Gaffey's scheme of maneuver, which envisaged the 90th attacking on the right, the 2ème Division Blindée attacking on the left, and the 80th remaining in reserve to reinforce the attack as it developed. Gerow wanted to attack with all three divisions abreast but also wanted to wait for the arrival of his V Corps Artillery Headquarters and additional reinforcing artillery battalions, which could not get there until late in the day.[38]

At this point the confused lines of command and poor communications between the far-flung headquarters led to an impasse. Gaffey was under orders from Patton to hold up the attack until further notice. Gerow was uncertain whether he was transferred from Hodge's to Patton's command. The two sat at Alençon waiting for someone to tell them what to do. However, Patton too was at an impasse. The unreliable landlines were down again and the risk of interception by the Germans meant that such an important conversation could not be made over the radio. Patton noted,

> *I could only talk to Bradley on the radio which is too dangerous, so decided to fly up. I could not get off till 1200 due to Fog.*
>
> *Arrived at Hq 12 AG at 1250.*
>
> *Hodges arrived and Bradley told his plans. To turn over the 90-80-2 F to Gerow who would attack in conjunction with 1st Army. This is sound.*
>
> *Before leaving I told Gay [Brigadier General Hobart R, Gay, TUSA Deputy Chief of Staff for Administration and the Acting Chief of Staff in Gaffey's absence] that if I called him on the Radio and said "Change Horses" it would mean for Gerow to take over. I phoned at about 1445 and added attack at once same objective.*[39]

When Patton arrived at the 12th Army Group Headquarters, Bradley was still deep in discussions with Montgomery and could not see him, but Hodges, who was also there, clarified what had been decided the previous night at FUSA Headquarters. Bradley had shifted the boundary between FUSA and TUSA to the east. The V Corps was still under FUSA and the three divisions assigned to TUSA—2ème Division Blindée, 80th and 90th Infantry—were attached for operations to FUSA. Most importantly, Gerow was to run the attack on Trun.

Patton then radioed Gay and ordered "change horses" and then added "thence on", probably intending for that to lend some urgency to the order. Gay, possibly confused, asked what Patton meant by that and Patton then replied, "another Dunkirk." Patton was obviously trying to convey the urgency to Gay, but it was to no avail. When Gay telephoned Gaffey and Gerow to pass on Patton's order, Gerow became confused, asking what "change horses" meant and if the order came from Bradley or Patton. Gay clarified the order was from Patton, but that Bradley was with him when it was issued. With that, Gerow took over, and the Provisional Corps was dissolved. Gaffey returned to TUSA Headquarters. By then it was afternoon, and the V Corps attack was deferred to the next day.[40]

Unfortunately, Bradley in his postwar memoirs used this incident completely out of its original context as part of his effort to make Montgomery and his British and Canadian Army commanders appear dilatory and indecisive compared to Patton and himself. He claimed Patton's remark was made on 12 August, which was when he called to tell Bradley he had elements in Argentan, rather than five days later on 17 August. Bradley also claimed that Patton said, "let me go on to Falaise and we'll drive the British back into the sea for another Dunkirk." After Bradley's memoir was published it led to a furious response from Montgomery and then the repetition of that fictitious phrase in numerous secondary sources to this day.[41]

****

Dad's matter-of-fact account of the crash of Lieutenant Loft has always left me wondering which version of the story was the "truth"? Was it "friendly fire" or an "accident"? The available ground and air records leave the "truth" open to interpretation. Was it a "bomb run," as the Air Force records have it? Or was it a "strafing run," as the Ground Forces records have it? Had Loft and Hanna already expended their 500-pound bombs in an earlier attack? If they were still abroad Loft's plane when it crashed, they almost certainly would have exploded, but no mention was made of that by any of the eyewitnesses. Finally, why were the two pilots so far off course and why did they ignore the recognition panels?

As far as Dad was concerned, I think he believed his M16B shot Loft down or at least caused him to crash. At the same time, he expressed no guilt about it, because as far as he was concerned it was Loft's or Dad's men's lives that were at stake. Dad chose his own men.

CHAPTER 13

CLOSING THE CHAMBOIS–FALAISE POCKET

18 AUGUST

The Germans harassed the Americans at Le Bourg-Saint-Léonard throughout the early morning hours with artillery and Nebelwerfer fire. When Company A, 359th Infantry was finally relieved by Company G, 358th Infantry at 0300 the area was struck by a barrage of twenty to thirty Nebelwerfer rockets, which destroyed one of the M10s of the 773d Tank Destroyer Battalion, killing three of its crew and severely wounding two other crewmen. Another rocket barrage struck just as Company A, 359th Infantry was ready to move out, lightly wounding Lieutenant Schroeder, although he remained on duty, and seriously wounding six and lightly wounding two men of his 2d Platoon. Another three men were lightly wounded but remained on duty. The heavy shelling also disabled two tanks of the 1st Platoon, Company A, 712th Tank Battalion.

Gerow's attack finally kicked off at 0800. On the right, the 3d Battalion, 359th Infantry led off, accompanied by Company B, 712th Tank Battalion and the 3d Platoon, Company C, 773d Tank Destroyer Battalion, attacking to the northwest toward Chambois from a line of departure along the Le Bourg-Saint-Léonard–Exmes road. The 3d Battalion objective was Hill 129, about 1,200 meters west of the Le Bourg-Saint-Léonard–Chambois road, and the roads to the northeast of Chambois. They quickly reached the bend in the Le Bourg-Saint-Léonard–Chambois road, east of Fougy, where they were fired on by tanks and infantry to the east and northeast and by tanks and vehicles to the west near Fougy. The 1st and 2d Platoon, Company A, 712th Tank Battalion and the 2d Platoon, Company C,

773d Tank Destroyer Battalion firing from Le Bourg-Saint-Léonard knocked out one tank near Fougy at 1100 and the advance continued. By 1800, they were astride the road, about 500 meters west of Le Haut Fel, where they halted for the night.[1]

The 2d Battalion, 359th Infantry initially held its positions at Le Bourg-Saint-Léonard, supporting the 3d Battalion by fire, and then followed the 3d Battalion to advance to take positions near the road bend. The 1st Battalion completed reorganizing at Le Pin-de-Haras and then moved back to Le Bourg-Saint-Léonard, taking the place of the 2d Battalion.

On the left, the 1st Battalion, 358th Infantry attacked north on an axis from Méguillaume toward Sainte-Eugénie but met considerable resistance on the Argentan–Le Bourg-Saint-Léonard road (D926). It was midday before it was able to cross the road and get into the Forêt de Gouffern but resistance remained strong, and an added problem was created when white phosphorus artillery rounds started a major forest fire. Major Nichols, the Regimental S-3, ordered the 1st Battalion hold south of the road at 1646, but Major Lytle ignored him and kept urging his men on. Fourteen minutes later Lytle reported Company A had managed to work its way 500 yards into the woods and was making steady progress. By 1910, the 1st Battalion had pushed through about halfway to Sainte-Eugénie, but Major Lytle was complaining he was having trouble getting his supporting tanks to move up. Finally, the 2d and 3d Platoon, Company C, 712th Tank Battalion jumped off in support of Lytle's infantry and some more progress was made, but at 2220 Lytle was told to hold on to what ground his men had gained and renew the attack at 0800.

The 2d Battalion, 358th Infantry pushed west along the Argentan–Le Bourg-Saint-Léonard road from the crossroads to the west of Le Bourg-Saint-Léonard with the mission of clearing the road and then following the 1st Battalion. The slow advance of the 1st Battalion left them in the rear, and at 2220 they were ordered to halt in place as well, defending the forest road that had been cleared by the 1st Battalion and maintaining contact with the 359th Infantry to the east and the 80th Infantry Division (-319th RCT) to the west.

The 3d Battalion, 358th Infantry remained in division reserve for most of the day near Le Pin-au-Haras. Then it marched to the Y-junction. One company was sent about 2,000 meters to the northeast onto Hill 137 to secure the right rear of the 359th Infantry.

The 358th Infantry made significant progress in the battle to clear the Forêt de Gouffern, hampered by the fanatical German resistance, the confusing terrain, and the slow advance of the 80th Infantry Division on its left. Colonel Clarke was awarded a Distinguished Service Cross for his actions this day:

Lieutenant Colonel Christian Hudgins Clarke, Jr. (ASN: 0-18213), United States Army, was awarded the Distinguished Service Cross for extraordinary heroism in connection with military operations against an armed enemy while serving with the 90th Infantry Division, in action against enemy forces on 18 August 1944. Lieutenant Colonel Clarke's intrepid actions, personal bravery and zealous devotion to duty exemplify the highest traditions of the military forces of the United States and reflect great credit upon himself, the 90th Infantry Division, and the United States Army.[2]

By retaining its hold on Le Bourg-Saint-Léonard, the 90th Infantry Division gave the American Field Artillery a perfect opportunity to demonstrate its power. From Hill 172 at the north end of Le Bourg-Saint-Léonard, artillery observers could see all the way to Chambois. From Hill 148 near Villebadin, north of the Le Bourg-Saint-Léonard–Exmes road (D14), they could see all the way to Villedieu-lès-Bailleul on the Argentan-Trun road (D916). Eleven divisional and four separate artillery battalions were now in place and began firing at the growing number of targets as the Germans tried to escape the pocket. As the 90th Division Artillery described it, "enemy targets were plentiful, and General Devine had every available gun ready to fire at all times." However, it was also a sad day for the Division Artillery. Around 1100, Devine's Executive Officer, Lieutenant Colonel John B. Daly, and his driver, T/5 Francis Dolan, were driving north out of Le Bourg-Saint-Léonard when they ignored warnings from the 2d Platoon, Company C, 773d Tank Destroyer Battalion about a German Panther tank that was firing from a position on the Chambois road.

Captain Laughlin E. Waters, commander of Company G, 359th Infantry, who was there and also warned the pair, described what happened:

During the day, a major [Laughlin mistook Daly's tarnished oak leaf insignia for that of a major] *from a different unit, with a driver and jeep, came into Le Bourg and brusquely demanded an assessment of the situation. This was laid out for him, including pointing out to him the German tank. Notwithstanding the major took off down D16 toward Fel-Chambois and in line with the tank. One round from the tank took the lives of both men.*[3]

The Allied tactical air forces also continued to hammer the German columns. They were concentrated on the Argentan-Chambois road (D113) and the network of small country lanes running from Putanges-le-Lac on the Orne River to the gap, over which the remnants of the *7. Armee* and the German rearguards were attempting to escape. The American artillery observers noted numerous British Typhoon fighter-bombers strafing German vehicles on the roads from 1800 to 1900. The 2d

British Tactical Air Force "bombed on [*sic*] area 8000 meters long by 3500 meters wide, until dark in the area of Villedieu-lès-Bailleul."

Also on 18 August, the Canadians seized Trun and cut the German retreat route there across the Dives River. The actions of Major David V. Currie, commanding C Squadron, 29 Armoured Reconnaissance Regiment (The South Alberta Regiment) of the 4th Canadian Armoured Division, were as critical as the American effort to the eventual closure of the pocket. Late that night he led a combat group of just 175 men, fifteen tanks, and four self-propelled 17-pounder antitank guns in an attack on Saint Lambert-sur-Dives. As they approached the village, two of his leading tanks were knocked out. Currie went forward himself to rescue the crews and make a reconnaissance of the German defenses in the village. He then concentrated his battle group on Hill 117, just to the north of the village, where he was joined by the Regimental Headquarters Troop and "B" Squadron of the South Alberta Regiment.[4]

Another Allied division was closing in on Chambois from the north as well—the Pierwszy Polska Pancerna Divisia or "1st Polish Armoured Division" under Major General Stanislaw Maczek. It landed in France on 30 July and was assigned to the II Canadian Corps of First Canadian Army. After its introduction to combat on 7 August it battled its way forward and crossed the Dives northeast of Falaise at Jort on 16 August. On 17 August, it pushed generally southeast, paralleling the advance of the 4th Canadian Armoured Division to its right. At 1750 on 17 August, Lieutenant General Guy Simonds, commander of the II Canadian Corps, ordered Maczek to take Chambois.

By the morning of 18 August, the Polish Division Headquarters, service units, and the Division Artillery were near Jort. The rest of the division was deployed in two brigade groups:

The 10 Brygada Kawalerii Pancerna or "10th Armored Brigade" was under command of Colonel Tadeusz Majiewski and consisted of three battle groups and supporting units. Battle Group Zgorelski was under command of Major Wladislaw Zgorelski of the 10 Pulk Draganow or "10th Dragoon Regiment"—a mechanized infantry battalion. He also had under his command the 24 Pulk Ulanow or "24th Lancer Regiment," which was a tank battalion, and one towed antitank battery. It was about 1,800 meters south of Grandmesnil. Battle Group Koszutski was under command of Lieutenant Colonel Stanislaw Koszutski of the 2 Pulk Pancerna or "2d Armored Regiment." He also had under command the 8 Batalion Strzelców or "8th Rifle Battalion." It was about 7.5 kilometers to the west of Zgorelski's group. The last brigade element was nominally the divisional reconnaissance regiment, 10

Pulk Strzelców Konnych or the "10th Mounted Rifle Regiment" under Major Jan Maciejowski. It, reinforced with two self-propelled antitank batteries, was observing the German columns fleeing Falaise between Crocy and Trun and the Canadians pursuing them.

The 3 Brygada Strzelców or "3d Rifle Brigade" was under command of Colonel Marian Stanislaw Wieronski. It consisted of two battle groups and supporting units. Battle Group Stefanowicz under the command of Lieutenant Colonel Aleksander Stefanowicz of the 1 Pulk Pancerna or "1st Armored Regiment"—another tank battalion—also had under command two companies of the Batalion Strzelcow Podhalan'skich or "1st 'Highland' Rifle Battalion" and a towed antitank battery. Battle Group Szydlowski, under command of Lieutenant Colonel Zdzislaw Szydlowski of the 9 Batalion Strzelców or "9th Rifle Battalion," also had the 1st "Highland" Rifle Battalion (-) under command and a towed antitank battery.

Maczak ordered Major Maciejowski and the 10th Mounted Rifle Regiment to reconnoiter Chambois by going cross-country directly southeast using farm lanes. By 1650 it was about 1 kilometer from the town when it was attacked by Allied aircraft, which thought they were Germans. They withdrew north and settled in positions on Hill 124, which was about two kilometers north of Chambois and about 2.25 kilometers east-northeast of the bridge at Saint Lambert.[5]

Battle Group Zgorelski was ordered to move to the area south of Louvières-en-Auge and Le Ménil Girard. Its mission was to interdict the German traffic on the roads leading from Trun to Chambois. It set off at 0400 but was delayed by irrigation ditches crisscrossing the countryside until some local farmers showed them the route. By 2030, they were in position and immediately engaged in a fierce firefight with the Germans fleeing Trun and crossing the Dives at Saint Lambert.

Battle Group Koszutski was to head directly for Chambois at 1930 on 17 August, driving through the night and bypassing German resistance as necessary. Unfortunately, Koszutski misheard Champeaux for Chambois and drove east rather than southeast. By the time Maczek realized they had gone the wrong way they were embroiled in a battle with elements of the *2.* and *9. SS-Panzer-Division "Hohenstaufen"* of the *II. SS-Panzer-Korps*, which was assembling for a counterattack to hold the gap open, near Les Champeaux. Worse, Koszutski's vehicles were low on fuel and ammo, and its resupply had been sent to Le Hameau Bourdon, 8 kilometers south, on its expected path. Maczek ordered Battle Group Szydlowski to reinforce Koszutski, who was hard pressed by the SS. However, they did not find him at Champeaux—his Battle Group was still lost and turned out to be 2 kilometers south of Les Champeaux and 2 kilometers east of Écorches. The 1st "Highland" Rifle Battalion (-) eventually found them there.[6]

Battle Group Stefanowicz was to seize Hill 262 North, Hill 252, and Hill 262 South, reinforced by Battle Group Szydlowski. This hill mass, Mont Ormel to the locals, runs north and south in the shape of what Maczek called a "caveman's club," in Polish "maczuga"—literally translated as a "mace"—and the name stuck. The Chambois–Vimoutiers road (D16) passes through Maczuga, which dominates the road and the Dives River valley to the west and southwest. Szydlowski's Battle Group was well on its way when Maczek diverted it to rescue Koszutski's lost column. By nightfall Koszutski and Szydlowski were in the vicinity of Bourdon–Écorches about 3.5 kilometers northwest of their objective.

With Koszutski delayed and out of position, late that night Maczek changed his plans. He ordered Zgorelski to take over the mission to seize Chambois. Koszutski would instead reinforce the attack on Mont Ormel.[7]

By nightfall, three Allied divisions were converging on the Dives River between Saint Lambert and Chambois, threatening the last possible exits for the Germans from the pocket. There was barely 3.5 miles (5.6 kilometers) from the bridge at Magny, now under Canadian control, and the bridge at Chambois. Only the bridges at Chambois and Saint Lambert-sur-Dives and the ford at Moissy were still passable for escaping German vehicles. About 4.25 miles (6.8 kilometers) separated the Americans from the Canadians, while unbeknownst to them the Poles were just 1.25 miles (2 kilometers) north of Chambois.

Later that evening, General Gerow ordered the 80th and 90th Infantry Division to continue the attack the next morning. Possibly upset by what was perceived as a lack of interest by the French to participate in the attack that day, Gerow attached Groupement tactique Langlade to the 90th Infantry Division. General Leclerc and Colonel De Langlade met with General McLain at the 90th Infantry Division Headquarters at 2300. McLain ordered the French to attack

> *Along all available roads from Exmes to the north and northwest. This in order to first capture the high ground around Omméel and to prevent the enemy from using the road from Chambois to the east. Thereafter, in cooperation with the 3d Battalion, 358th Infantry to take possession of the high ground immediately northeast of Chambois and to prevent the enemy from using the road from Chambois to Mont Ormel.*

The German situation was becoming more precarious by the hour. *Panzergruppe Eberbach*, effectively just *XXXXVII Panzer-Korps*, was attempting to hold the southern shoulder of the pocket while simultaneously covering the withdrawal of *7. Armee*. The artillery of the *116. Panzer-Division* was nearly out of ammunition, so all that remained was turned over to the few remaining howitzers of the firing batteries. A Nebelwerfer brigade supporting the division was also completely out of ammunition. The few remaining vehicles of the Division Artillery and Nebelwerfer brigade were loaded with wounded and evacuated during the night through Chambois. There they collected the rest of the division rear services and withdrew to Broglie. That left a few hundred infantrymen of *Panzer-Grenadier Regiment 60,* perhaps a dozen tanks of *Panzer-Regiment 16,* and a handful of reconnaissance troops of *Panzer-Aufklärungs-Abteilung 116*, "reinforced" by scattered remnants from numerous divisions holding the line from Moulins-sur-Orne to Omméel, almost 28 kilometers of front, which was an impossible task. To "fill" the gap between the Panzer-Grenadiers fighting the 358th Infantry in the Forêt de Gouffern and the troops of *Panzer-Aufklärungs-Abteilung 116* at Chambois and Omméel, a few Panzerjäger and some Pioniere were sent to defend Aubry-en-Exmes. From Moulins-sur-Orne to Nécy, another 9 kilometers of front, was held by *LSSAH* and *2. Panzer-Division*. It seems likely they were in a similar state as the other two divisions of *XXXXVII Panzer-Korps*.

The headquarters of *7. Armee* was at Villedieu-lès-Bailleul. Its two corps, *II. Fallschirm-Korps* and LXXXIV Armee-Korps, now only consisted of the remnants of *3.* and *5. Fallschirmjäger-Division* and *84.* and *353. Infanterie-Division*. They had just crossed the Orne River the night of 16/17 August and had continued to march east during 17 and 18 August under almost constant air and artillery attack.

5. Panzer-Armee was covering the withdrawal of the *LXXIV Armee-Korps* and the remnants of four other divisions: *89.*, *276.*, *277.*, and *356. Infanterie-Division*. with *I. SS-Panzer-Korps* while *II. SS-Panzer-Korps* was preparing to attack southwest from Vimoutiers with the *SS-Das Reich* and *SS-Hohenstaufen* to hold the pocket open. From Nécy to Crocy another 8 kilometers was held by *12. SS-Panzer-Division "Hitler Jugend"* (*SS-HJ*). Trun had been held by *KG Rauch* of *21. Panzer-Division* and its *KG Luck* extended the line of *I. SS-Panzer-Korps* northeast to Vimoutiers, while *Panzer-Aufklärungs-Abteilung 21* reinforced the screen covering the withdrawal across the Orne River. In "reserve" was *SS-Frundsberg* at Villedieu-lès-Bailleul.[8] By late evening, *SS-Das Reich, SS-Frundsberg, 21. Panzer-Division*, and *SS-GvB* had all essentially escaped the encirclement, as had many of the rear elements of the other mobile divisions as well as the rear elements of the corps and armies.[9]

Nevertheless, it is evident from prisoner-of-war identifications that substantial elements of other divisions were still trapped in the cauldron. Later, on the evening of 19 August, the leader of the 90th Infantry Division G-2 Interrogation Prisoner of War Team, 1st Lieutenant Herman D. Shickman, noted,

> *In the last 36 hours PWs from 21 Divs as well as several AA, Corps and Army units were taken. Most PWs had become detached from their units during the intense Arty or Air bombardment and had been stragglers for a period from one to ten days before capture. Only a few of these units ever opposed our Div, but as the gap narrowed they were squeezed into our hands.*

Two decisions were made during the day by the Allied Expeditionary Air Forces that limited the impact of airpower on the pocket in the following days. The attacks by friendly aircraft on the Poles were not the only such incidents that day; Canadian troops in Trun also complained of being attacked by American Thunderbolts. As a result, Leigh Mallory ordered a new inter-Tactical Air Force boundary running from L'Aigle–Évreux–Vernon with the Ninth U.S. Air Force operating to the south and the 2nd Tactical Air Force to the north. Major General Hoyt S. Vandenberg, commanding the Ninth Air Force, protested and an exception was made for American ground forces making requests for air support on their side of the pocket, but an unnecessary layer of complexity had been added to the already complex process of providing air support. Perhaps the most crucial decision made on 18 August was to limit the extent of Allied air strikes southwest of Vimoutiers. On 19 August, no Allied air strikes were to be permitted inside the pocket due to the increasing difficulty of distinguishing between friend and foe west of the line Trun–Chambois.[10]

19 AUGUST

The 3d Battalion, 358th Infantry began its attack early in the morning under direct control of the 90th Division Headquarters. They assembled in an area south of Hill 212, about 1,000 meters north of Le Pin-au-Haras, then advanced quickly north at 0800 toward its objective, the high ground northeast of Chambois. By mid-morning Company K seized Hill 129, just south of the Dives and the Chambois–Gacé road (D13), after knocking out a Panzer IV and two halftracks. At 1300, Colonel Bealke aggressively pushed Company K and L onto the high ground to the north of the Chambois–Gacé road where they had good observation of the Chambois–Vimoutiers road (D16) and the German traffic fleeing toward Mont

Ormel. Another unidentified tank and some other vehicles were knocked out en route. A counterattack at 1530 was repelled and the battalion pushed on at 1900 with Company K on the left and Company L on the right to positions blocking the Chambois–Vimoutiers road west of La Frênée and 0.5 mile from Chambois. The desperate Germans attacked again trying to open up the road. As the battalion *Battle History* later recounted,

As the two companies reached the NE road they set up roadblocks and waited. Company L very soon thereafter knocked out two trucks, killing 20 Germans and taking 31 prisoners. Then two tanks attacked Company L and drove them back one hedgerow. Captain Bryan called for more men, ammunition and bazooka rounds from Lt. Col. Bealke at the OP immediately behind him. He also had his artillery observer put fire on the Germans attempting to flee CHAMBOIS by the NE road.

A column consisting of six tanks, 20 to 30 trucks, towed guns, ambulances with machine guns in them and other vehicles came down the road. For two hours an all-out fight raged. It was in this action that Pfc, Caldwell and Pfc. Giebelstein, both from Company K knocked out four tanks with five rounds of bazooka fire.

During the day about 320 Germans were captured, over 100 killed and 11 tanks, eight self-propelled guns as well as numerous other vehicles were destroyed.

Both Caldwell and Giebelstein were decorated with the Distinguished Service Cross for this action.

Private First Class, GEORGE J. CALDWELL, 34767036, Company K, 358th Inf. Rgt., 90th Division, U.S. Army. For extraordinary heroism in connection with military operations against an armed enemy. On 19 August 1944, in the vicinity the CHAMBOIS, FRANCE, Private CALDWELL was serving has one member of a two-man rocket launcher team, advancing with elements of the 358th Infantry Regiment against determined enemy resistance. When several enemy tanks approached, the two men moved from position to a position exposed to enemy fire, and calmly held their fire until the enemy came within close range. Expending only five rounds of ammunition, they destroyed four tanks. The heroic actions of Private CALDWELL, and his companion, and their courageous devotion to duty exemplify the highest traditions of military forces of United States.

Private First Class, WALTER C. GIEBELSTEIN, 37663847, Company K, 358th Inf. Rgt., 90th Division, U. S. Army. For extraordinary heroism in connection with military operations against an armed enemy. On 19 August 1944, in the vicinity the CHAMBOIS, FRANCE, Private GIEBELSTEIN was serving as one member of a two-man rocket launcher team, advancing with elements of the 358th Infantry Regiment against determined enemy resistance. When several enemy tanks approached, the two men moved from position to a position exposed to enemy fire, and calmly held their fire until the enemy came within close range. Expending only five rounds of ammunition, they destroyed four tanks. The heroic actions of Private GIEBELSTEIN, and his companion, and their courageous devotion to duty exemplify the highest traditions of military forces of United States.[11]

The attached 1st Platoon, Company B, 773d Tank Destroyer Battalion was stopped for a time by what they called the "12-Foot Creek"—the Dives River—and were late getting forward to join Bealke's infantry at the roadblocks. Later, the infantrymen somewhat disparagingly said, "The attached platoon of tank destroyers arrived at the end of the battle, but managed nevertheless, to knock out one tank." The tank destroyermen of the 1st Platoon in turn claimed destroying two tanks, two ammunition trucks, a staff car, and a house full of Germans, as well as firing HE rounds into the mass of Germans struggling to escape the pocket. The rest of Company B of the 773d decided not to wait to cross the Dives and instead moved west to Fel, where they were able to fire across the river. The 2d Platoon claimed another Panzer IV there. As Major Falvey, the 358th Infantry S-2, later described it,

The 3rd Bn. of the 358th near Chambois was surrounded by Germans trying to escape. Some tried to fight, but most tried to swarm toward the east, and guns of the 3rd Bn. were hot from continuous fire at easy targets. The killing was terrible. Toward evening, Col. Bealke ordered his men to stoop shooting except in self-defense, because they were running out of ammunition.

As it was getting dark, the Colonel was trying to get his defense lines set up for the night. He had Capt. Clive Jaffray helping him with the task. Jaffray was trying to get the [1st Platoon, Company B, 773d Tank Destroyer Battalion] *in the defense line and was motioning three to move to a certain location when he suddenly realized he was trying to coax three German tanks into our lines. The tanks were immediately knocked out by our* [Tank Destroyers]. *We all had a good laugh out of Jaffray trying to do this.*[12]

The 3d Battalion, 359th Infantry continued its advance on Hill 129 at 0800 but was halted short of it by friendly fire. The Americans blamed Canadian and British artillery firing from the northwest, and after a series of back-and-forth radio messages a "no fire" line was agreed to, allowing the 3d Battalion to continue the advance. It reported knocking out numerous tanks and other armored vehicles, as well as capturing and destroying truckloads of German personnel trying to escape on the Bonménil–Chambois road (D113) northwest of Hill 129.

Up to that point Colonel Bacon intended for the 1st Battalion to pass through the 2d Battalion and continue the attack north to the south bank of the Dives, where it would control the roads in Chambois by fire only. However, at 0930, Bacon decided that Pond's 1st Battalion was still too weak after its two-day battle at Le Bourg-Saint-Léonard and changed his plan. Instead he sent Major Dull's 2d Battalion to occupy Chambois, while Major Smith's 3d Battalion secured the high ground from Hill 129 to Le Bas Fel on the south side of the Dives. Pond's 1st Battalion was to occupy Fougy and Hill 149 on the north edge of the Forêt de Gouffern, tying into the left of the 3d Battalion.

The 2d Battalion was still engaged in a firefight with some Germans on Hill 149 and had to disengage before it could reorganize and move north. One company was left to cover the withdrawal and hold Hill 149 until the 1st Battalion relieved them. While reorganizing, Major Dull sent patrols toward Chambois, but it was 1430 before the 2d Battalion began its advance. By 1600 they were on the southern bank of the Dives and Dull sent patrols into town. They quickly returned though as intense artillery fire—believed to be friendly—impacted the town. It took over half an hour before the fire was halted.[13]

Finally, at about 1730 the 2d Battalion advanced, with Company E and the 2d Platoon, Company C, 773d Tank Destroyer Battalion on the left of the Le Bourg-Saint-Léonard–Chambois road (D16) and Company G on the right of the road with a platoon of tanks from the 2ème Division Blindée. Company F was in reserve, following Company E. Scouts discovered the bridge on the Le Bourg-Saint-Léonard–Chambois road that crossed a stream south of the Dives was blocked by a wrecked Panther tank, so Company E and the tank destroyers shifted west onto the Bonménil–Chambois road, entering Chambois from the southwest rather than the south. Company G went northeast and crossed the Dives at a ford northeast of Le Haut Fel about 1 kilometer from the center of Chambois. The terrain sloped steeply uphill through apple orchards from the ford, which made the French tanks reluctant to cross. They instead turned east toward the main body of Langlade, which was now near Omméel, and never returned. It later turned out that De Langlade was acting on secret orders given to General Leclerc from General de Gaulle to hold his division in readiness for a dash toward Paris. In the end, only a minor element of Groupement tactique Langlade joined the 3d Battalion, 358th Infantry at La Frênée, but that was the sole French contribution to the fighting during the day.[14]

Captain Edward R. Lienhart led Company E into Chambois with the 1st Platoon advancing up the main street, across the Dives, and then to the east end of town. The 3d Platoon advanced on their left and secured the northern part of town, while the 2d Platoon and Company Headquarters did a house-by-house mop-up, which netted forty prisoners. The streets were littered with destroyed and abandoned vehicles—on the main street running north alone there were at least two Panther tanks, three halftracks, and many miscellaneous vehicles—and dozens of dead bodies, both men and horses. The Company CP was set up near the center of town and the men dug in.[15]

To the right of Company E, when Company G reached the Chambois–Gacé (D13) road the intensity of the fire from all directions increased. Captain Waters was reluctant to turn west toward Chambois as ordered without knowing what was to his front and rear, so he held his men along a hedge on the south edge of the roadway and went alone to the east to reconnoiter the situation. He then saw an individual, dressed in what he thought was a British uniform, step into the middle of the road. It was Major Zgorzelksi of the 10th Polish Dragoons. The American 12th Army Group and British 21st Army Group had just made contact.

At 0920, Major Zgorzelksi's group had advanced on Hill 137, 1,800 meters west of Hill 262 North, and captured it at 1200. After securing the area and reorganizing, the 24th Lancers pushed on to the hill to the south of Coudehard downslope from Mont Ormel. Major Zgorzelski with the 10th Dragoons continued to push south toward Chambois while the 24th Lancers advanced toward La Frênée. The two quickly lost contact with each other and the battle groups at Mont Ormel. Zgorzelski and the 10th Dragoons instead met Major Maciejowski and the 10th Mounted Rifles, which were still about a kilometer north of Chambois holding Hill 113. Shortly afterward, at about 1930, Major Zgorzelski met Captain Waters.[16]

Meanwhile, Stefanowicz's two Highlander infantry companies led the assault on Hill 262 North, followed by the 1st Tank Regiment, which drove up a narrow, winding road (D242) past the Manoir de Boisjois—known as Zameczek or the "Hunting Lodge" to the Poles—to Hill 262 North and engaged in a fierce battle there with Panther tanks. Koszutski, finally reoriented, occupied Hill 240, about 2 kilometers northwest of the Manoir de Boisjois, and sent Szydlowski to reinforce the defenses. Szydlowski was ordered to take Hill 262 South but by the time he arrived at Coudehard it was too dark.

While the 2d Battalion, 359th Infantry secured Chambois, the 3d Battalion moved up in support. Company L crossed into Chambois and advanced up the road toward Saint Lambert where they contacted a Canadian patrol. Company K deployed in Le Bas Fel, while Company I remained on Hill 129.[17]

As night fell, the situation around Chambois remained confused. Zgorzelski's 10th Dragoons occupied the northwestern part of Chambois, while Dull's men

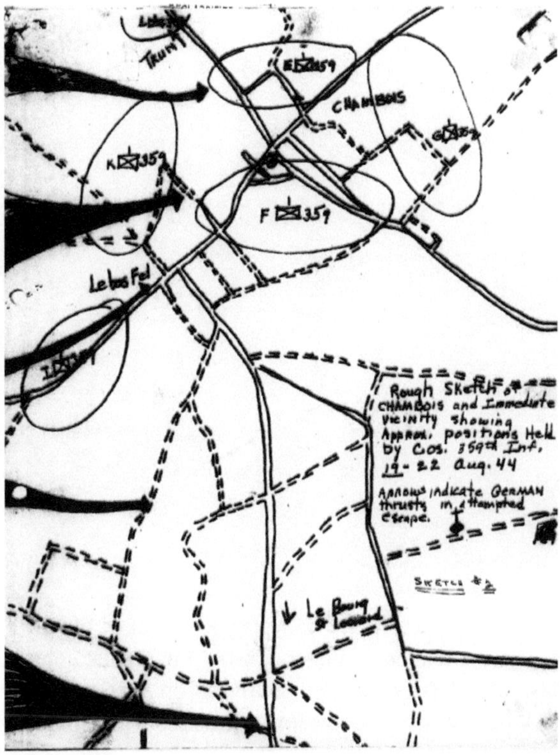

Map 19. The 359th Infantry closes the Gap, 19–22 August 1944. The dark arrows are the main German escape routes. "2d Battalion Action at Chambois," Sketch #2.

occupied the rest of the town and secured the bridge on the Dives and the southern suburbs of Le Bas Fel. However, it appears neither Major Dull nor Major Zgorzelski were aware that Bealke's 3d Battalion, 358th Infantry was just to the northeast at La Frênée. Zgorzelski and Maciejowski had also lost contact with the main body of their division as well. Antitank support was limited to the 3-inch M10 GMC of the 1st Platoon, Company C, 773d Tank Destroyer Battalion at Le Bas Fel and the 2d Platoon in Chambois. Between them they claimed the destruction of "two Mark V [Panther], eight Mark IV and two Mark III tanks, one SP gun and 20 other vehicles." The 3d Platoon, Company A, 712th Tank Battalion was also in support of Dull's attack. During the approach march to Chambois they shot up haystacks and a farmhouse, but it is uncertain if they entered the town. They reportedly settled into a holding position, probably at Le Bas Fel for the night.[18]

Major Leonard C. Dull and Lieutenant Wladyslaw Klaptocz of the 10th Polish Dragoons point at the map where their units linked up on 19 August. The scene was staged on 20 August. Major Dull died of wounds suffered on 15 September and Lieutenant Klaptocz was later killed in action on 4 November 1944 in Holland. U.S. Army SC.

On the left of the 359th Infantry, the 358th Infantry (-) continued to struggle with the mass of Germans seeking to flee from Argentan through the Forêt de Gouffern. The 1st Battalion on the left pushed into the forest headed for Bonménil at 0800, still supported by the 2d and 3d Platoons of Company C, 712th Tank Battalion. However, the failure of the 80th Infantry Division to secure the woods between Bordeaux and Crennes left its left flank exposed, slowing progress. The 2d Battalion also encountered fierce resistance as it slowly advanced on Sainte-Eugénie supported by the 1st Platoon of Company C, 712th Tank Battalion.[19]

Nevertheless, by about noon, both battalions had managed to clear the woods. The 1st Battalion advanced toward Bonménil "to wait for Germans—then to blast them." Soon they were doing just that, firing at masses of Germans to the west as they came out of the woods fleeing northeast on the Argentan–Chambois road (D113). The 2d Battalion came up on the right rear of the 1st Battalion. Company F covered the rear of the 1st Battalion, while Company E and the tanks of the 1st

Platoon, Company C, 712th Tank Battalion fired into the valley. The firing was so intense it soon was noted the tanks were running out of ammunition.

By 1320, Lieutenant William Matthews, a liaison pilot for the 344th Field Artillery, reported that at least 1,000 German vehicles of all types was moving north of Bonménil and requested fire on it. He was told by the Fire Direction Center to "wait" while they finished "computing." Matthews replied, "Wait?! Let's have more shootin' and less computin'!"

The left flank remained a concern for the 358th Infantry because the 80th Infantry Division continued to run into fierce German resistance. Major Lytle reconnoitered the road leading northeast from Crennes to Bonménil (D113) at 1730 and reported "quite a bit" of Germans were still on the road attempting to escape. Colonel Clarke asked for additional help from division to secure the flank and at 1930 brought forward the regimental cooks to guard the road leading east out of Argentan. Finally, late that evening, the 2d Battalion, 317th Infantry of the 80th Infantry Division managed to cut the Argentan–Bonménil and Argentan–Trun roads (D916) by securing the southern slope of Hill 213 north of Argentan.

The day was relatively quiet for the 357th Infantry. At 1345, the 3d Battalion was assigned to division reserve and moved to a position about 2,000 yards north of Le Pin-au-Hara. Company L was sent forward between the right of the 1st Battalion, 359th Infantry at Fougy and Hill and the 3d Battalion, 359th Infantry on Hill 129. Company L deployed astride a farm road that ran southeast from Villedieu-lès-Bailleul to Exmes. The 2d Battalion at Exmes and Croisilles was relieved by the main body of Groupement tactique Langlade, which shifted east, and the battalion assembled in reserve at Ginai. The 1st Battalion remained around Nonant-le-Pin.

It was the opposite experience for the Division Artillery, which had one of its busiest days of the war. Between 0600 and 1630, the attached 186th Field Artillery Battalion alone reported firing 915 rounds of 155mm, which was an extraordinarily high rate of fire for a 155mm howitzer battalion. For the period from 17 to 19 August, Division Artillery reported firing a total of 9,031 rounds of all types into the pocket, with 95 percent of the missions observed. That was nearly half of all rounds expended by the Division Artillery during the entire month of August, which was 20,667 rounds. In the same period, the 345th Field Artillery fired 2,961 rounds of 155mm, 1,000 rounds on 18 August alone. The 343d Field Artillery fired 2,242 rounds of 105mm. Between them, the 344th and 915th fired 3,828 rounds of 105mm.[20] Dad's recollection was of incessant firing; from their position in the fields

An OP, probably near Le Bourg-Saint-Léonard. Although they are calling for artillery fire, most of the officers are Infantry, so it is likely either the 3d Battalion, 359th Infantry or the Regimental OP. Still from a film dated 19 August 1944, Tech 4 W. J. Tomko, 166th Signal Photo Company, Detachment 8, Falaise Gap.

west of Le Pin-au-Haras they could see or hear dozens of artillery batteries firing to the north.

During the day as many as twelve additional battalions of Field Artillery joined the battle as elements of the V Corps Artillery arrived and five went into action with the 90th Division Artillery. The plethora of artillery battalions meant that individual German targets were subjected to fires from one to six battalions of artillery each. From the opposite side of the gap, relatively fewer Polish and Canadian artillery were able to fire because both those divisions had outrun the range of its supporting artillery in its lunge forward that day.[21]

Lieutenant Matthews, the liaison pilot for the 344th Field Artillery, wrote down his observations on 19 August:

> *On the morning of the 19th I took off to register a battalion, just as I cleared the hills looking into the valley, I saw the roads alive with vehicles of every description. Immediately fire was brought down on the road crossing just to the north of Ste. Eugénie and the progress of the vehicles was stopped in that vicinity. Fire was falling in several places in the valley, however, several trucks pulled to the sides of the road and moved around the stalled vehicles, then headed north towards Chambois and St. Lambert-Sur-Dives, which were under fire at the time. Every place where there were more than four vehicles grouped,*

artillery fire would drop. Those trucks that were still trying to escape through Chambois were piling up, caught our fire. . . .

The road east of Bailleul was blocked and the trapped vehicles began to move into the fields, the roads through Tournai-Sur-Dives were blocked also, and then the roads were forgotten. Vehicles flooded out into the fields and it looked like a stampede of cattle. . . .

A large body of vehicles, trucks, tanks, SP guns, grouped south of Tournai, numbering around 200 or more. It looked as if they wanted to give up, but then they started firing, and I called for artillery. After what seemed like hours, it was actually minutes, the group of vehicles turned into Tournai. The roads were blocked and they assembled in the woods just south of town. Artillery hammered the woods until the assembly area was a mass of burning vehicles. Black smoke obscured our vision and prevented further fire at this point. The enemy gathered his vehicles along hedgerows, under trees, or out in the open. No cover was too small, but it still was not enough. Continued pressure from the rear forced them to try and move. . . .

Moving out into the open, and in regular lines, were several regiments of horse drawn artillery, carts and wagons. They came forward as our first rounds landed right on them. The line wavered north of the fire and continued on. Several volleys landed right in the column and the line turned at right angles and headed north. It was a slaughter. Horses would fall and stop a wagon. Many were running away, some would turn right into the fire, others gathered in the shelter of an old rock quarry to escape but immediately artillery fire drove them out. They turned south into a crossroad just southeast of Tournai-Sur-Dives and the road was soon blocked by fire. More units piled up on top of them and soon it was impossible to turn the horses. Then it became a shambles. Horses loose and running everywhere. Some teams still hitched to caissons and wagons and one or more killed in the traces. All semblance of organization had ceased at this point. . . .

Vehicles were still headed northeast towards the once formed outlet, the creek, but none could be seen making their way past it. Very late in the day, another column of trucks and vehicles tried to make Tournai-Sur-Dives. They were already blocked and turned south into other stopped vehicles. Breaks were in the column as they tried to dodge the fire, but soon they came to a halt, and as it grew dark only occasional movement could be seen. Grouped vehicles in Villedieu Les Balleul were given as interdiction for the night.

On the Canadian side of the shrinking gap, they occupied the eastern bank of the Dives at Magny, cutting the escape route over the narrow farm bridges there. Many Germans were captured, including Oberst Otto Gerlach, who was commanding the remnants of *708. Infanterie-Division* in the pocket. More important, Major Currie slipped his battle group into Saint Lambert-sur-Dives at 0635, without artillery support. The Regimental Headquarters and "B" Squadron on Hill 117 provided covering fire, while Currie's troops quickly secured the northern half of the village.

However, they were unable to make headway against a fanatical German defense of the southern half. In the evening, Company C of the Argyll and Sutherland Highlanders of Canada joined Currie's force and attempted to push south toward the ford at Moissy but were stopped by machine-gun fire and returned to the village.[22]

The incessant artillery fire was turning the German retreat into a rout. While some units trapped in the pocket retained a semblance of organization, others were beginning to disintegrate. As Lieutenant Shickman of the 90th Infantry Division Interrogation Prisoner of War Team put it,

> *The description of the retreat by PWs varied from orderly withdrawal, during which the unit marched at night and took up position in daytime, to a complete rout under the motto "every man for himself." For the last 12 hours it was obviously a confused flight when the Germans jumped on any vehicle that had a space and ran the gauntlet of our Arty fire.*

However, the poor working relationship between Eisenhower, Montgomery, and Bradley was now bearing its poisonous fruit. Eisenhower as Supreme Commander had failed to keep a firm hand on his contentious subordinates. Montgomery as Ground Forces Commander had tried his best not to antagonize his American allies but without success. He assumed mostly a hands-off policy in his dealings with Bradley and the other American generals, making suggestions rather than giving orders whenever possible, while trying his best not to condescend to them, which went against his very nature. Perhaps ironically, not only did that not work—by the first week of August Montgomery was almost universally loathed by the American generals in France—but it was partly Montgomery's failure to employ his signature "firm grip" on the breakout battle that led directly to Bradley's poor decisions and lack of decisiveness at the critical points.

The result was that of the 200,000-plus German troops likely in the pocket on 14 August when the German withdrawal began, by the night of 19/20 August there were probably no more than 125,000 in the trap. All of them were heading directly for the last possible crossing places on the Dives River, with the last organized remnants of the Panzer and SS-Panzer divisions leading the breakout. The bridge at Saint Lambert was barely 2.5 kilometers from the bridge at Chambois, with the ford at Moissy halfway between them. Currie at Saint Lambert had fewer than one hundred men and a dozen tanks. The 10th Mounted Rifles on Hill 113 overlooking the ford at Moissy were not much stronger, and the bridge at Chambois was defended by the equivalent of just two weak battalions from two different armies of two different Allies that did not share a common language. The real battle to close the pocket would be fought on 20 and 21 August.[23]

For the Germans, on the morning of 19 August, SS-Oberstgruppenführer Hausser, the *7. Armee* commander, had left his Gefechtsstand in a quarry on the eastern edge of Villedieu-lès-Bailleul and headed for the Gefechtsstand of the *116. Panzer-Division* in the tiny village of Montmilcent, less than 2.5 kilometers away. The near-constant threat of air attack and artillery fire slowed him such that he did not reach his goal until noon, just as more artillery rounds impacted the area. Also present were General der Panzertruppen Eberbach and General der Panzertruppen Hans Freiherr von Funck, commanding the *XXXXVII Panzer-Korps*. Nearby too was the headquarters of Generalleutnant Otto Elfeldt's *LXXXIV Armee-Korps* and SS-Brigadeführer Kurt Meyer's *SS-HJ*, which were collocated in a farmhouse near La Londe. Because the *I. SS-Panzer-Korps* had evacuated the pocket the night before, Meyer's SS troops were now commanded by Elfeldt's Korps as were the remnants of *LSSAH*. Both Elfeldt and Meyer made the hazardous journey through the artillery fire to the conference as well.[24]

Hausser agreed with Generalleutnant Gerhard Helmuth Detloff Graf von Schwerin, the commander of the *116. Panzer-Division*, that the situation was hopeless and authorized a breakout that night. Funck offered a plan to break out in two columns, which would attack in concert with an attack by the *II. SS-Panzer-Korps* to reopen an escape corridor through Mont Ormel to Vimoutiers. The right-hand (eastern) column under Elfeldt's *LXXXIV Arme-Korps* would execute a breakout at Chambois after midnight with the *LSSAH* and elements of the *116. Panzer-Division*, reinforced by the remaining tanks of *SS-HJ*. They would be followed by the *XXXXVII Panzer-Korps* with the *SS-Hohenstaufen* and *2. Panzer-Division* and what remained of a half-dozen or more infantry divisions.[25]

The left-hand (western) column under Meindl's *II. Fallschirm-Korps* with the *3.* and *5. Fallschirmjäger-Division* would execute a similar breakout at Saint-Lambert and Moissy, followed by the unarmored elements of *SS-HJ* and then the *LXXIV Armee-Korps* with the organized remnants of the *276.*, *277.*, and *326. Infanterie-Division*. The remaining mobile elements of the *SS-HJ* would act as the rearguard to the north and west and *116. Panzer-Division* would do the same to the south.[26]

The planned *II. SS-Panzer-Korps* attack on 19 August was delayed by heavy air attacks from the British 2nd Tactical Air Force on 18 and 19 August. The British fighter bombers concentrated on Vimoutiers and badly disorganized the hasty refitting of the *SS-Das Reich* and *SS-Hohenstaufen*. However, elements of the *SS-Panzer-Grenadier Regiment 3.* and the *SS-Panzer-Aufklärungs-Abteilung 2* were able to work their way forward from Saint-Pierre-la-Rivière to Hill 262 South and secured it, limiting the ability of Bealke's men at La Frênée to control the road from Chambois to Vimoutiers.[27]

20 AUGUST

Shortly after daybreak. between 0500 and 0700, the Americans began detecting the German breakout attempt. Company I, 359th Infantry on Hill 129 just south of Chambois reported a column of vehicles approaching their position from the west. The 1st Platoon, Company C, 773d Tank Destroyer Battalion opened fire with its three M10 GMC (one was disabled the previous day) in a firefight that lasted about two hours. The tank destroyers claimed the destruction of two Panther, three Panzer IV, one Panzer III, and ten other vehicles, while killing at least forty Germans, for the loss of one M10.

The German column then turned left toward Chambois but recoiled from the fire of Company F, 359th Infantry and the 3d Platoon, Company B, 773d Tank Destroyer Battalion at Le Bas Fel. The 2d Platoon, Reconnaissance Company, 773d Tank Battalion captured six Germans there and one interesting piece of equipment, "an elaborate cipher device" that was "turned into Corps and flown to England for examination." It was almost certainly an Enigma machine.

Part of the German column turned again and headed south, skirting the right of the 3d Battalion, 359th Infantry. However, it ran into Company L, 357th Infantry, which took a further toll of it before the Germans were able to slip past them headed toward Exmes. By that time, the column was reportedly reduced to just a few halftracks loaded with infantry, which managed to get within 200 yards of the Headquarters, 357th Infantry just west of Exmes. Regimental Headquarters personnel and elements of Groupement tactique Langlade reported finishing off the last remnants of the column there.

One of the tanks in the column did manage to slip unnoticed across the bridge into Chambois at 0700 and drove toward the Company E position. Sergeant Ross N. Boatwright finally noticed it and opened fire with his rifle on the Germans riding on the back of the tank. The tank retreated under a hail of bazooka rockets but sped away unhurt.

What was probably yet another fragment of this column turned northeast and may have crossed the Dives at Avenelles before it ran into the 3d Battalion, 358th Infantry. The group, consisting of "several truckloads of troops, two tanks, and an undetermined number of halftracks," attempted to break through the American line at 0930, nearly reaching the Battalion CP. The Battalion Headquarters personnel deployed bazooka teams and its .50-caliber machine guns to halt the German attack. Over 250 prisoners were captured, but one halftrack reportedly escaped and captured four jeeps, ten medical personnel, and two men from the A&P Platoon

"Lined up in front of a wrecked German tank and displaying a captured swastika, is a group of Yank infantrymen of the 90th Div. who were left behind to 'mop-up' in Chambois, France, last stronghold of the Nazis in the Falaise Gap area, August 20, 1944." U.S. Army SC. Probably men of the 359th Infantry in Chambois. The presence of the Black soldier is often questioned, but he was likely part of the OP Party of the 333d Field Artillery (Cld), which was in support of the 90th Infantry Division and 359th Infantry at this time.

before it was knocked out by the 2ème Division Blindée. For the rest of the day, Bealke's battalion reported nearly constant attacks from inside and outside the pocket. In the afternoon, the battalion was contacted by an officer from the Polish 10th Mounted Rifle Regiment, who asked the Americans to take the 750 prisoners they held. The Poles were also in desperate need of food and ammunition. That night the Americans evacuated the Poles' captives, which had swollen to 1,027, including Generalleutnant Otto Elfeldt, commander of the *LXXXIV Armee-Korps*. Bealke's men also sent to the rear another 531 Germans they had captured, but the Americans were unable to provide the requested supplies for the desperate Poles.[28]

By 0800, Field Artillery observers supporting the 358th Infantry reported spotting a 3-mile-long column just south of Tournai-sur-Dive, which was probably Elfeldt's *LXXXIV Arme-Korps* column assembling for its breakout attempt.

Unfortunately, the 90th Infantry Division request for air strikes on the column was denied. They were told the air was "too thick," which must have been confusing, because the troops on the ground reported the weather as "warm and clear." At 0825, the 2d Battalion, 358th Infantry reported another column was moving out of Argentan and requested the "air corps be sent up," but no action was noted.

In fairness to the Air Forces, the XIX TAC did complain that air operations that day were affected by rain and low cloud cover over their bases in the Cotentin and closer to the coastline. However, other factors were also at play. The shifting of the intra-Tactical Air Forces boundary on 18 August had added an unnecessary layer of complication to the already complicated air support request system. Also, the attention of Eisenhower, Montgomery, and Bradley was already shifting from the encirclement battle at Chambois to the possibilities of a deeper envelopment and crossing of the Seine River, ironically, about ten days after Patton had advocated that course of action.

Possibly as a consequence of the commander's meeting, Allied tactical air support was shifted from what was later known as the "Pocket," which was the area west of the line Falaise–Argentan, and the "Shambles," which was the area east of the line Falaise-Argentan, to the "Chase," which was the area from Vimoutiers to the Seine River crossings. On 20 August, most of the Ninth Air Force's effort was directed at the Seine River: the IX Bomber Command sent sixty-one medium bombers to attack troop and equipment concentrations waiting in the Forêt de La Londe to be ferried across the Seine at Rouen, while fighter bombers of the IX and XIX TAC flew armed reconnaissance missions along the Seine and escorted the medium bombers and aircraft on supply and evacuation runs bringing in fuel and evacuating wounded.[29]

The British 2d Tactical Air Force was similarly distracted by the effort to interdict the Seine—only two RAF missions over the battle area were remarked upon by the 90th Infantry Division on 20 August. One was at 1500, when surrender leaflets intended for the Germans were dropped by a British plane on the front lines of the 358th Infantry. The other was also reported by the 358th Infantry at 1623, when British aircraft were bombing a German tank concentration north of a line roughly from Bailleul to Chambois.

Yet another problem was the ongoing confusion on the part of the Allied command about just where and what German forces were still trapped. It may be significant that when later mapping the encirclement in August 1945, the USAAF drew the American phase line of 19 August as running from just north of Pierrefitte on the Argentan–Falaise road (D958) to Trun and then to Gacé, which bore little relation to the reality on the ground. It misplaced where the gap between the Allied pincers was, putting it between Falaise and Trun rather than between Trun and Chambois. It also badly misunderstood which German units were inside and outside the pocket, placing *SS-HJ* outside the pocket but *SS-Das Reich* and *SS-Hohenstaufen* inside the pocket, when the opposite was actually the case.[30]

At noon, at least three more tanks assembled outside of bazooka range from the infantrymen in Chambois and Le Bas Fel and outside the arc of fire of the tank destroyers on Hill 129 and in Chambois. The 2d Battalion mortars brought the tanks under fire and managed to hit one, but nevertheless they advanced toward Chambois. The 2d Platoon of Company E was forced to withdraw to shelter along the riverbank while bazooka teams stalked the German tanks. One bazooka team finally managed to knock out the leading tank, a Panther, and the others withdrew.

The next German attempt at Chambois was with 100 infantrymen supported by 20mm antiaircraft guns. The Company E machine guns were temporarily out of commission with overheated barrels, so the 2d Battalion mortars fired 108 rounds on the 20mm guns, silencing them. The 3d Platoon Leader, 1st Lieutenant Albert L. Budd, called for artillery fire on a Handi-Talkie radio to the Company E CP where Captain Lienhart relayed the request to the 915th and 345th Field Artillery Battalion. The fire halted the German movement. Shortly afterward two M10 GMC from the 2d Platoon, Company C, 773d Tank Destroyer Battalion were brought up to fire on another suspected tank sheltering behind a barn but were unable to spot it. Sergeant John D. Hawk of Company E, who had already been wounded while helping to stalk the tanks in the earlier encounter, helped direct the tank destroyer's fire when their first shots missed because of the obscuring terrain. At one point Hawk told one of the gunners to fire by aiming just over the top of his head. For this and other actions during the day, Hawk was later awarded the Medal of Honor, the first of four by members of the division during World War II to be awarded it.[31]

> *The President of the United States of America, in the name of Congress, takes pleasure in presenting the Medal of Honor to Sergeant John Druse "Bud" Hawk, United States Army, for conspicuous gallantry and intrepidity in action above and beyond the call of duty while serving with Company E, 2d Battalion, 359th Infantry Regiment, 90th Infantry Division. Sergeant Hawk manned a light machinegun on 20 August 1944, near Chambois, France, a key point in the encirclement which created the Falaise Pocket. During an enemy counterattack, his position was menaced by a strong force of tanks and infantry. His fire forced the infantry to withdraw, but an artillery shell knocked out his gun and wounded him in the right thigh. Securing a bazooka, he and another man*

stalked the tanks and forced them to retire to a wooded section. In the lull which followed, Sergeant Hawk reorganized two machinegun squads and, in the face of intense enemy fire, directed the assembly of one workable weapon from two damaged guns. When another enemy assault developed, he was forced to pull back from the pressure of spearheading armor. Two of our tank destroyers were brought up. Their shots were ineffective because of the terrain until Sergeant Hawk, despite his wound, boldly climbed to an exposed position on a knoll where, unmoved by fusillades from the enemy, he became a human aiming stake for the destroyers. Realizing that his shouted fire directions could not be heard above the noise of battle, he ran back to the destroyers through a concentration of bullets and shrapnel to correct the range. He returned to his exposed position, repeating this performance until two of the tanks were knocked out and a third driven off. Still at great risk, he continued to direct the destroyers' fire into the Germans' wooded position until the enemy came out and surrendered. Sergeant Hawk's fearless initiative and heroic conduct, even while suffering from a painful wound, was in large measure responsible for crushing two desperate attempts of the enemy to escape from the Falaise Pocket and for taking more than 500 prisoners.[32]

The well-directed fire on the German position led to a German soldier approaching the positions of the 2d Platoon with a white flag. The German was escorted to Lieutenant Budd and handed the American a note from a major who commanded the opposing German infantry. The note was an offer of parley. Budd demanded the Germans surrender and the major came forward personally with an interpreter to negotiate. At that point Budd pressed the issue and demanded the remaining German tanks surrender as well. At about 1400, the German tank commander agreed, Budd ordered his artillery support to check fire and 500 Germans, including the major, the tank commander, and four other officers surrendered. Many were wounded and thirty of the prisoners were employed as stretcher bearers evacuating the wounded throughout the night.[33]

While all this was going on, the rest of Company E and Company F in Chambois were fully occupied trying to prevent the Germans from breaking through the center of town. Another M10 GMC from the 2d Platoon, Company C, 773d Tank Destroyer Battalion was positioned next to the Company E CP where it was able to fire down the road to Saint Lambert. It fired on what was described as a "205mm self-propelled artillery gun," which was advancing on the line of the 1st Platoon of Company G on the northwest edge of town. The German vehicle, which was probably a Hummel 15cm self-propelled howitzer was quickly dispatched. The same M10 followed up by destroying a halftrack and eventually twenty-five other vehicles that were approaching on the same road, leaving a 600-yard-long trail of destruction from the outskirts of Chambois almost to Moissy. One halftrack was destroyed just 35 yards from the M10 and just 25 yards from the Company E CP. They were all likely vehicles that had crossed at the Moissy ford.[34]

More halftracks and other vehicles continued to approach from the direction of Moissy and Saint Lambert during the afternoon and evening. They were all dispatched by the tank destroyers or by the infantry's bazooka, rifle grenades, or 57mm antitank guns. By nightfall, the 359th Infantry estimated they had knocked out 80 tanks and 400 other vehicles, inflicted over 800 casualties in killed and wounded, and captured about 2,600 Germans. That night, the men around Chambois watched as artillery continued to pound targets to the north and east and were astonished to see both British and German aircraft dropping parachutes to the north and west. The British planes were dropping supplies to the surrounded Poles on Mount Ormel, while the German planes were doing the same for their troops in the pocket.[35]

Captain Lienhart was awarded a Distinguished Service Cross for his leadership on the two critical days of 19 and 20 August.

> *Captain (Infantry) Edward H. Lienhart, United States Army, was awarded the Distinguished Service Cross for extraordinary heroism in connection with military operations against an armed enemy while serving with the 2d Battalion, 359th Infantry Regiment, 90th Infantry Division, in action against enemy forces on 19 and 20 August 1944. Captain Lienhart's outstanding leadership, personal bravery and zealous devotion to duty exemplify the highest traditions of the military forces of the United States and reflect great credit upon himself, the 90th Infantry Division, and the United States Army.*[36]

Major Dull was not cited for his actions at Chambois, perhaps because unlike Lienhart, he did not survive for very long after the battle. On 15 September 1944, the 2d Battalion attacked Fort Jeanne d'Arc outside of Metz and Major Dull was severely wounded by artillery or mortar fire just as the attack began. He died of his wounds later that day and was awarded a Silver Star, posthumously, for his actions.[37]

To the left of the 359th Infantry, Major Lytle was pessimistic about the 1st Battalion's prospects after the fierce resistance it encountered the previous day. At 0410, he informed Colonel Clarke that Bonménil was strongly held and there were German tanks spotted in the town. The Germans fired quadruple and single 20mm antiaircraft guns against the American advance, and although the 1st Battalion had not suffered severe casualties it was disorganized and would not be able to advance again until 1200. Nevertheless, by 0755 Company C was reported in Bonménil as

A Hummel 15cm schwere Feld-Haubitze self-propelled howitzer on one of the roads leading out of Chambois, taken by Captain Oehmichen, probably on 21 or 22 August 1944. It is possibly the same one knocked out by the 2d Platoon, Company C, 773d Tank Destroyer Battalion.

the German breakout attempt began. They were met by a German medical officer who asked for a cessation of the artillery fire so that he could evacuate 200 wounded. The request was passed to the Division Headquarters for a decision.[38]

The 1st Battalion's advance was probably eased by the German evacuation as yet another major column attempted to drive east from Bonménil, skirting the flank of the 1st and 2d Battalion, 358th Infantry at 0900. It was most likely parts of *2.* and *116. Panzer-Division*. Scouts guiding the 1st Platoon, Company A, 773d Tank Destroyer Battalion, which was moving up to relieve the 1st Platoon, Company C, about 1,000 meters south of Hill 129, spotted the Germans and alerted the tank destroyers. The four M10 GMC went into hasty firing positions and ambushed the surprised Germans. The ensuing engagement went on for an hour and was extraordinarily one-sided. The Americans suffered the loss of just two men, both wounded. After nearly three more hours of combing the fields and silencing the last German resistance, it was discovered the four tank destroyers had knocked out one Panther, seven Panzer IV, one self-propelled gun, two self-propelled 20mm antiaircraft guns, sixteen armored halftracks, eighteen halftrack prime movers, twenty-nine trucks, ten Volkswagen cars, ten field pieces, four Nebelwerfer launchers, nine command and reconnaissance cars, one field kitchen, three horse carts with horses, and eight motorcycles. In addition to many killed and wounded, 220 Germans were captured.

A view of one of the roads leading out of Chambois, taken by Captain Oehmichen, probably on 21 or 22 August 1944. In the left foreground is the remains of a Panzer IV, which appears to have had the front of its turret blown off from an internal explosion.

It is likely the 3d Platoon, Company C, 773d Tank Destroyer Battalion at Fougy also had a hand in this action. It reported firing on what was probably the same column from 0800-1130. The 1st Platoon then moved to positions on the south end of Hill 129 and reported knocking out two more Panzer IV at 1830.

To the right rear of the 1st Battalion, Schulz's 2d Battalion, 358th Infantry was asked by the 359th Infantry at 0700 to fire on five German tanks trying to slip out to the east along the southern slope of Hill 129. They were likely yet another part of the column that had struck Company I of the 359th Infantry and the 1st Platoon, Company C, 773d Tank Destroyer Battalion on Hill 129. At the same time, there were still more German troops and vehicles milling about in the Forêt de Gouffern, which led Lieutenant Colonel Stillwell, the Division G-3 to admonish Clarke's Executive Officer, Lieutenant Colonel Loomis, "be sure to clean out the woods today."

However, it was becoming increasingly clear that while some German units remained organized and were attempting to break out in front of the 358th Infantry, many others were simply trying to surrender. Colonel Munson, who was at one of the 344th Field Artillery's OPs directing fire, said at 0950 that he had counted

Another view of one of the roads near Chambois, taken by Captain Oehmichen, probably on 21 or 22 August 1944.

thirty-seven Germans with white flags. At 1015, General McLain authorized a ceasefire along the front of the 358th Infantry. However, in a sign of just how confused the situation was, ten minutes after McLain's order was issued, Major Schulz reported five "Tiger tanks" were getting into position to fire on the 2d Battalion. They too were likely part of the column that was battling the 1st Platoon, Company A, 773d Tank Destroyer Battalion.

Major Lytle's 1st Battalion finally secured Bonménil at 1100 and began to arrange the evacuation of the German aid station. Then, in a remarkable turn of events, a German column led by a tank encountered two or three jeeps of Company B, 315th Medical Battalion in the woods behind the 2d Battalion at 1155. The Germans did not fire on them but forced the medics to dismount and the Germans drove off in the jeeps. Nevertheless, plans for the ceasefire continued, with the time set as 1345 to 1430. The lull in the artillery fire began as scheduled at 1345 and almost immediately hundreds of Germans began surrendering. Not everyone was happy about the ceasefire though. The 358th recorded comments such as "My God—and such shots!" and "We chase 'em all over France, and now—!" Despite the complaints, the ceasefire held and at 1400 ten trucks were sent to help haul the large numbers of prisoners to the rear with the 359th's cooks as guards. So many Germans were surrendering that Major Wallace, the 2d Battalion Executive Officer asked the ceasefire to be extended and so the artillery fire was ordered to hold off indefinitely.

"'IKE' INSPECTS THE WORK OF HIS MEN IN FRANCE—Gen. Dwight D. Eisenhower, supreme commander of the Allied expeditionary forces, inspects an overturned German tank left by a roadside in France by the retreating enemy." U.S. Army SC. General Eisenhower toured the Falaise Pocket on 26–27 August, stopping to view this Königstiger of *schwere Panzer-Abteilung 503*, just west of Vimoutiers.

At 1448 the 80th Infantry Division reported it had seized Crennes. By that time, they had also cut the Argentan–Trun highway (D918) in two places and were meeting little resistance. However, Major Falvey, the 358th Infantry S-2, warned that a column of German tanks from Argentan was heading for the left flank of the 1st Battalion and it could be seen that they were not flying white flags. At 1515, the ceasefire ended when that column opened fire. Twenty-five minutes later, the leading elements of the 80th Infantry Division finally contacted the 1st Battalion, 358th Infantry at the village of Miguillaume, which the 358th called an "unnamed town," closing the gap in the Forêt de Gouffern that had caused so many problems for the men of the 358th Infantry. The ceasefire had netted about 400 prisoners. Fighting sputtered on into the evening, mostly random bursts of artillery fire, some of it suspected to be from the 80th Infantry Division. By 2225, the number of prisoners had grown to 1,800.

For the 357th Infantry, the day was quiet again. At 0850, the 2d Battalion was placed under division control and moved to Silly-en-Gouffern as a reserve for the 358th Infantry. The 3d Battalion, minus Company L, was ordered motorized

90th Infantry Division troops advancing, photo dated as 20 August 1944. Probably men of the 358th Infantry in the Forêt de Gouffern. U.S. Army SC.

five minutes later and moved to a position south of Fougy to intercept one of the numerous German columns reported to be breaking through the lines of the 358th and 359th Infantry in the valley between Le Bourg-Saint-Léonard and Chambois. However, at 0945, just as the 3d Battalion (-) was preparing to move, the Germans were reported to be abandoning and burning their vehicles and dispersing into the woods. The 3d Battalion (-) then moved to Hill 137, 2,000 yards northeast of Le Bourg-Saint-Léonard, to cover the roads there. Around 1500, Company L tied in again with the rest of the 3d Battalion. The final act of the day was at 1650 when the regiment was warned that another German column was forming up to attack from the northwest, but fifteen minutes later it was discovered they were on foot under white flags. It was the column of German prisoners captured by the Poles and Americans, led by Generalleutnant Elfeldt, making their way to captivity.

For the Germans, the breakout actually began before midnight on 19 August, as the *3. Fallschirmjäger-Division* set off from its assembly area in the woods north of Montabard at 2230. Thirty minutes after midnight they reached the mill 1 kilometer southeast of Magny and crossed the Dives northwest of Saint Lambert. Although they were intermittently harassed by tank and machine-gun fire from the Canadian position on Hill 117 and Currie's men on the north edge of Saint Lambert they managed to slip through the gap and reached Coudehard by first light. From there, some of them joined in with the attacks by *SS-Das Reich* and *SS-Hohenstaufen* that pushed the Poles south from Boisjois—although the Poles managed to keep a tenuous hold on the Hunting Lodge—onto Hill 262 North, opening a narrow route to Champosoult and out of the pocket.

The remnants of the *SS-HJ* followed the Fallschirmjäger. Those on foot mostly took the same route across the Dives at the mill, but the remaining vehicles were forced to attempt the bridge crossing at Saint Lambert or Chambois. In the darkness many vehicles managed to get across the bridge at Saint Lambert, but as day broke Major Currie's men opened fire on them. Vehicles were hit and destroyed or damaged, some burning out on the bridge. Others, confused, turned toward Trun or Chambois and were quickly dispatched by the Canadians, Americans, and Poles. By the time the units of the *LXXIV* and *LXXXIV Armee-Korps* reached the Dives it was daylight. What was described as waves of thousands of Germans eventually pushed Currie's men back to the north and western parts of Saint Lambert, away from the bridge, but Currie tirelessly kept his men firing at the Germans and continued to direct the incessant artillery fire on them. The South Albertas War Diary described what happened.

> *At about 0800 hrs waves of German infantry began moving against the positions. It could hardly be called an attack as there was no covering fire plan, simply a mass movement of riflemen.*
>
> *RHQ tanks were moved to better fire positions and began to mow down the advancing Infantry.*
>
> *Similar activity occurred on "B" and "C" sectors, "B" Sqn finding themselves defending the axis of an enemy attack and "C" Sqn busily engaged in knocking off Infantry on their front sending back an additional 200 PW at 0930 hrs.*
>
> *A little later the situation at RHQ began to get out of hand as there were just too many infantry. The CO ordered "A" Sqn to move into the position to sp RHQ and with this the enemy broke and fled.*
>
> *From a PW it was ascertained that the idea behind the attack was a mass recce to find any holes in our lines to enable the large forces trapped in the pocket to find a way through.*
>
> *The casualties inflicted on the enemy by RHQ troop alone were two–three hundred killed and wounded and one hundred PW taken.*
>
> *"C" Sqn reported that the POLISH ARMD RECCE UNIT was in CHAMBOIS and by 1600 hrs "C" Sqns bag of prisoners had amounted to 500. They knocked out a Panther tank and reported their position firm except for a few snipers in the vicinity.*

The men became tired and the CO asked if relief could be sent, infantry particularly being needed.

"C" Sqn freed 12 American PW from the Jerries and put them to work with ground weapons.

German wounded in the Regt'l area by this time amounted to three hundred and evacuation became difficult. The MO did an excellent job of work with the assistance of more ambs being sent from Bde.

The Jerries sent over a request for us to remove their wounded from a hospital in the vicinity and a party was sent out under a red cross flag to size up the situation. It proved to be a trap and Lieut BURNS and 3 other ranks were killed. Later 500 German wounded were passed through our lines.[39]

Most of the last few operational tanks and assault guns of the *SS-HJ* and the few Tiger I tanks of *schwere SS-Panzer-Abteilung 102* also attempted to breakout at Saint Lambert. Two Tiger, two Panther, five Panzer IV, three Flakpanzer, and two Jagdpanzer formed up near the village of Roc at 2000 on 19 August. Most apparently failed to escape. One of the Tiger I may have escaped only to end up in the Seine River when it slipped off a ferry. Photographic evidence shows at least four Panther tanks were lost in the vicinity of Saint Lambert: one identified as *1. SS* and one as *9. SS*, the other two may well be the two from *12. SS*. Four Panzer IV may also be found in photographs at Saint Lambert but all from *LSSAH*, a fifth that was destroyed in the center of town with its turret blown off is not identified, and at least one Jagdpanzer IV was lost at Saint Lambert.[40] The destruction was later described as,

One Panther tank was still on the Dives Bridge where it had been hit, while another had been pushed off the bridge into the ditch. There were two knocked-out Panthers near the Mairie and a Tiger with its turret blown off on the main street and another at the southern crossroads hit by the 103rd Battery gunners. Across the river in the orchards and farm fields there were more than a dozen knocked-out German tanks or SPGs and three more were found in the north end of the village. Burned out trucks, halftracks and armoured cars littered the streets and lanes of St. Lambert and the area around it.[41]

Motorized elements of the *1. SS, 10. SS, 12. SS,* and *2. Panzer-Division*, as well as the motorized and horse-drawn elements of the Infanterie divisions tried to cross at the Moissy ford. Eventually, the approach and exit at the Moissy ford became so congested that fights broke out between the soldiers desperate to escape. Vehicles became mired or broke down and were abandoned or were disabled by the incessant artillery fire. As the day wore on the rain that had plagued the airfields to the north also began to fall, making crossing even more difficult. Other motorized and horse-drawn units attempted what they hoped were possible crossing places along the riverbank; most of them were unsuccessful. Tanks and other armored vehicles also attempted to cross there as well, probably with limited success. Photographs show five Panther tanks in the area between Le Château d'Aubry-en-Exmes and Moissy and another Panther on the road from Moissy to Mont Ormel. More remarkably, a RAF low-level reconnaissance photo taken of the area on 22 August shows approximately 140 or more vehicles, including at least 1 other Panzer IV, 12 armored half-tracks, 119 miscellaneous motorized and horse-drawn vehicles, and eight guns, all in an area of about 500 by 500 meters, centered on the ford.

Chambois was where most of the remaining German armored vehicles attempted to escape. Ten Panther tanks, including one from the *9.* and two from the *116. Panzer-Division* have been identified from photographs in and around Chambois and Fel. Another, identified as from the *116. Panzer-Division*, was on the road between Chambois and Mont Ormel. Other photos show three Sturmgeschütz and a Panzer IV, from unknown units, destroyed in a column on the streets of Chambois. Many other vehicles were scattered along the roads leading to and from Chambois.

Wrecked German vehicles scattered around the ford at Moissy. The view is looking south. TNA AIR 37/1231.

The destruction near the Moissy ford from the ground. TNA AIR 37/1231.

Some parts of *116. Panzer-Division* did evade the American cordon between Le Bourg-Saint-Léonard and Chambois and managed to escape eastward out of the pocket. Major Helmut Bochnig, commander of *Panzerjäger-Abteilung 228*, led the remnants of his battalion out in the morning without orders. It was probably part of the column that struck the 3d Battalion, 359th Infantry on Hill 129. Hauptmann der Reserve Friedrich Graf von Brühl led Gruppe Brühl, with the five remaining Panzer IV of *Panzer-Regiment 16.* and other vehicles, to safety in the afternoon after losing two tanks. The remaining parts of the division assembled that night south of Saint Lambert. By dusk, enough of the mass of destroyed and damaged vehicles were cleared from the Dives bridge to enable the last fifty vehicles of the division to cross. By then, there were no tanks or assault guns remaining but two assault guns from an unknown unit appeared and were tasked to lead the breakout column. One almost immediately turned the wrong way toward Trun before it was knocked out by Currie's men. The other, followed by the remnants of the division, slipped across the Dives bridge and managed to reach the German lines near Champosoult by dawn the next morning.[42]

21 AUGUST

The last day of battle for the 90th Infantry Division in the pocket was something of an anticlimax. The fight had gone out of the remaining German troops trapped west of the Dives and hundreds simply laid down their arms and went meekly into captivity.

The 357th Infantry continued to mop up and did not suffer any casualties. In the early afternoon, elements of the British 11th Armoured Division began passing through the 357th's positions as it prepared to renew the British attack to the north and east. For the two days, 20 and 21 August, the 357th reported capturing approximately 1,700 prisoners.

For Bealke's 3d Battalion, 358th Infantry, the day became an international affair. The Americans established firm contact with the battered Polish units on Hill 262 North and Mont Ormel. A reconnaissance and liaison detachment from the 4th Canadian Armored Division arrived from Saint Lambert. Then liaison detachments from the British 11th Armoured Division and 50th Northumberland Infantry Division arrived to coordinate the handover of the American positions to the British troops. The battalion rounded up another took 83 prisoners, which brought its three-day total to 933. In the same period, they counted 15 tanks and about 40 halftracks, trucks, and other vehicles knocked out by the battalion.

The rest of the 358th Infantry continued combing through the forest, rounding up German stragglers and by the end of the day had collected more than 700. They also reported some interesting events. At 0815 the 2d Battalion S-2 reported "something falling from planes" under white parachutes. He could not tell if they were men or supplies but identified the aircraft as C-47s in U.S. markings. At 0830, the 90th Infantry Division reported the 537th AAA had shot down a "Heinke 11" ([*sic*], Heinkel 111) carrying 75mm and 88mm ammunition at the same time that the 2d Battalion S-2 reported what they thought to be those same aircraft as dropping thirty-six red and blue parachutes. The 2d Battalion sent out a patrol to investigate but the Division G-2, Lieutenant Colonel Boswell, thought they were dropping supplies to the Poles. Everyone was warned to positively identify aircraft before firing at them.

The 359th Infantry spent the day consolidating positions and rounding up prisoners. By the end of the day, they had contributed at least 2,400 German officers and me to the total.

Medics of the 359th Infantry use a captured German SdKfz 251 halftrack to transport wounded Germans. Vicinity of Chambois, probably 21 August 1944. U.S. Army SC.

The 90th Infantry Division reported hearing a BBC Radio announcement that "fighting and rioting" had broken out in Paris at 0930. Meanwhile, two German field hospitals complete with staff and patients were evacuated through the 90th's lines during the day and a total of 857 men from eleven different Panzer and Panzergrenadier divisions were rounded up as well. Another 221 men from the *3.* and *5. Fallschirmjäger-Division* were counted, along with 1,691 men from thirteen different Infanterie divisions. Finally, 525 men were captured from various nondivisional units and from five different corps headquarters, for a grand total of 3,294 men, including 98 listed as "Russians" and 2 as "Italians." There were also 80 officers captured, for a finally total of 3,374 officers and men. Late that afternoon, the V Corps notified the 90th to arrange for relief by the 50th British Infantry Division. The 90th Infantry Division's part in the Battle of the Chambois-Falaise Pocket was over.

AFTERMATH OF A BATTLE, THE GERMAN CASUALTIES IN THE CHAMBOIS-FALAISE POCKET

The 90th Infantry Division G-2 Section recorded the material losses inflicted on the Germans on 25 August, while the division was still in the area. Some losses were no doubt double-counted, but in general the figures appear reasonably accurate, given that the counts made by the British No. 2 Operations Research Section and the 197 Infantry Brigade Battlefield Clearance Group after the battle did not cover the area south of the line of the Argentan–Chambois–Gacé road, which is where the 90th Infantry Division fought. The area searched by the British only covered the area north of the 90th Division's battles on 17–18 August and part of the battles of 19–21 August. The British counted "358 tanks and S.P. guns," 4,715 "tracked vehicles, lorries and cars," and an estimated 491 towed antitank, antiaircraft, and field guns and howitzers.[43]

General Maczek reported the German material loss to his Polish troops as,

55 tks and armoured vehs, (incl 14 Panthers, 6 Tigers, 12 Mk IV, 5 Mk III, 2 Mk II), 2 guns SP (88 mm), 14 armoured cars, 44 guns (various types), 38 armoured tracked vehs for tp [troop] transport, 207 Motor vehs, 152 horse-drawn vehicles.[44]

Part of the problem with being more certain with these figures is that while the Germans reported the number of tanks, assault guns, armored vehicles, and other vehicles lost on a monthly basis by theater for 1944, it is obvious the collapse of the German forces in France in August 1944 led to most of the losses that month getting counted in September. For example, they reported the loss of only 124 Panzer of all types in the West in August, but 1,340 in September. Similarly, they reported only 141 self-propelled and assault guns of all types lost in the West in August, but 653 in September. Loss figures for other armored vehicles and motor vehicles follow this same pattern.[45]

90th Infantry Division G-2 Tally of Enemy Material Destroyed 16–22 August 1944

Division Units:	Tanks	S/Ps	Artillery	Motor Vehicles	Miscellaneous
359th Inf	41	40	–	141	–
358th Inf	31	–	–	976	–
915th FA	7	16	42	596	328 Horse-Drawn Vehicles
344th FA	34	10	43	612	421 Horse-Drawn Vehicles
345th FA	5[46]	8		200	–
Attached Units:					
607th TD	36	–	9	53	–
712th Tk	50	123	42[47]	408	13 Motorcycles, 2 Nebelwerfer
773d TD	104[48]	51	28	284	–
Total	308	248	164	3,270	764

The German personnel losses are also difficult to pin down. On 24 August, the Division Prisoner-of-War Cage was about 1,200 meters northeast of the church in Marmouillé just west of the highway (D438) along the railroad tracks. By then, the division had processed 15,546 prisoners to date since 8 June, and 12,472 since the crossing of the Mayenne on 6 August. Included in the total were 1,405 wounded processed through medical channels.[49] Also included in the 90th Infantry Division total were 317 Germans captured by the division but processed and evacuated by the 80th Infantry Division. The 80th captured 1,204 prisoners in its battle at Argentan from 18 to 23 August, not including those it evacuated by the 90th.

The 2ème Division Blindée reported evacuating 451 prisoners on 14–15 August. The 90th Infantry Division evacuated another 491 captured by the French.

The Polish count of German prisoners was more problematic. General Maczek recorded the capture of 87 German officers, including Generalleutnant Elfeldt, four Oberst, and two Oberstleutnant, and 3,576 enlisted men from 14 through 23 August but did not include an estimated 50 officers and 1,400 enlisted men he believed were evacuated through American lines. American records indicate the 90th Infantry Division only evacuated 1,027 Germans captured by the Poles. British records provide little clarification. The 21st Army Group recorded 3,324 prisoners captured by the Poles 14–23 August, including 1,953 evacuated through American lines.[50]

To the northwest at Saint Lambert, the South Alberta's reported capturing at least 2,100 Germans and estimated they had killed another three hundred and wounded five hundred during the four days from 18 to 21 August. Altogether, the Canadian 4th Armoured Division reported the capture of 5,880 Germans in the period from 14 to 24 August.

Note that the total estimated 46,986 captured by the Allies in the battle is somewhat lower than thc 50,000 usually given. That is partly due to the period used—historians may argue exactly which date the battle began and ended—but also because that count excludes many prisoners captured by the elements of Allied armies not directly engaged in the battle, such as TUSA, which was engaged in Brittany and along the Loire and Seine. If the start date for the battle used is 10 August—when the XV Corps began moving north to meet the Canadians, then the total prisoners captured by the Allies increases to about 25,458 for the 12th Army Group—12,591 of those by the 90th Infantry Division—and 29,727 for the 21st Army Group, totaling 55,185.

It is more difficult to calculate the number of Germans killed, wounded, and missing who were not prisoners of war. In the confusion of the collapse of the

Weary men of the 90th Division MP Platoon relax in Château-Thierry. U.S. Army SC.

Westheer, the German casualty accounting system fell apart. Through 13 August, the Germans reported their total casualties since 6 June as 158,930 officers, enlisted men, and Hilfswilliger. Later, a 10 January 1945 analysis attempted to reconcile the losses and reported 35,454 casualties in June, 104,798 in July, and 148,443 in August. That would imply that for the period from 14 to 31 August, German losses were around 129,765.[51]

22 AUGUST–4 SEPTEMBER 1944

On 22 August, the division assembled south of the Argentan–Exmes road and began a period of rest and rehabilitation of men and equipment that lasted until 26 August when it rejoined TUSA, attached to the XX Corps, at Fontainebleau. The division marched rapidly to rejoin the fight, crossing the Marne Rive at Château-Thierry on

29 August and assembled around Reims on 31 August. On that same date, General McLain was promoted to Major General, Army of the United States.

****

The decision we made to go ahead and take the time to explore the Chambois-Falaise Pocket battlefield was the right one. The morning was beautiful as we drove north from Alençon through Sées and Nonant-le-Pin. Continuing north we turned west along the Dives at Gacé and followed the narrow valley to Chambois. We stopped for pictures at the Donjon and then turned north to the Memorial Montormel Museum, which lies just west of the D16 about 1,000 meters south of Hill 262 North on the western slope of the hill.

The museum was one of the best battlefield museums I have seen. The displays presented the events of the battle in a lucid, easy-to-follow format. It occupies its site without overwhelming it, with much of the structure built into the hillside with panoramic viewing windows looking out at the valley of the Dives. From the museum you can see Chambois to the south, Trun to the west, and Falaise on the northwest horizon. It is easy to understand why this terrain feature was so critical to the events of the battle.

As we left, Dad signed the guest register with his name and World War II rank and unit. I signed below him for myself and the boys, giving thanks to Dad and his peers for what they did in those dark years.

From the museum we continued on to Vimoutiers, then turned back to Trun before driving on to Argentan. From Argentan we turned east on the N26, skirting the south edge of the Forêt de Gouffern and drove into Le Bourg-Saint-Léonard, before heading on to Le Pin-au-Haras and then Nonant-le-Pin again. This took us past where the 343d Field Artillery and Battery A were attacked by the two P-38, driving in the opposite directions that Dad had followed.

Then it was on to Verneuil d'Avre et d'Iton, Chartres, and then Château-Thierry, where we checked into our hotel at 5:30 P.M. Château-Thierry was also where our expedition ended with an exploration of the World War I battlefield, including Belleau Wood, just 11 kilometers away. However, Château-Thierry was not the end of Dad's war. He, Battery A, and the 90th Infantry Division still had eight months and twelve days of battle before Victory in Europe Day on 8 May 1944.

CHAPTER 14

EPILOGUE

THE 90TH INFANTRY DIVISION AND ITS ATTACHMENTS REMAINED AT REIMS through 4 September as it was delayed by the widespread shortage of gasoline in TUSA. During this period of forced inaction, the division's men rested and indulged in champagne. Finally, enough gasoline arrived to motorize CT 7, including the 343d Field Artillery and Dad's Battery A, and get it on the road to Verdun on 5 September. Led by the 90th Reconnaissance Troop and Company C, 712th Tank Battalion, they moved through Verdun to Étain, where the rest of the division joined them, shuttling forward on 6 September as gasoline supply permitted.

By this time, the hasty pursuit of the collapsing German forces and the start and stop caused by the gasoline shortage had badly disjointed the Allied armies. While the orders to the 90th Infantry Division from the XX Corps, which it was now attached to, was to advance to capture Thionville and establish a bridgehead there over the Moselle River, it was supposed to do so by advancing behind the 7th Armored Division. However, the 90th noted late on 6 September that "it was soon ascertained that no elements of the 7th Armored Division were operating in our zone." The 7th Armored Division was driving east as well, but its northernmost column followed a route from Étain through Conflans-en-Jarnisy to Doncurt-les-Conflans. The 7th Armored Division route was diverging to the southeast, away from the 90th Infantry Division.

The 90th was also supposed to secure the north flank of the XX Corps and maintain contact with the V Corps of FUSA, which was moving forward to insert between the XX Corps and the VII Corps. However, only the leading elements of the V Corps had arrived and were at Sedan, Charleville-Mézières, and Rocroi. There was a gap of about 50 miles (80 kilometers) between the 90th Infantry Division and the V Corps that was only lightly patrolled by elements of the 90th Reconnaissance Troop and the attached Troop B, 43d Cavalry Reconnaissance Squadron.

The confusion and exposed northern flank left the 90th Infantry Division potentially vulnerable to a German counterattack. The battle that ensued on the night of 7/8 September demonstrated conclusively that the 90th Infantry Division was no longer the hesitant, easily confused, and frightened unit that had fought in Normandy in June and July. That night, the *106. Panzer-Brigade* slipped past outposts in the dark and struck the 90th Division Headquarters and Division Artillery Headquarters. However, instead of panicking, the division acted decisively to defeat them, effectively destroying the German attackers. The total number of prisoners captured by the 90th and its attachments was about 830, while at least twenty-four German tanks and fifty-four halftracks were destroyed as well. Losses of the 90th Infantry Division numbered only about eleven killed and sixty wounded.

Dad continued to serve with Battery A, 537th AAA Battalion after the Battle of Mairy. In late September they came up against the defenses of the fortress city of Metz and began a campaign to reduce it that took months. However, by the time Metz fell to American forces on 13 December 1944, the 90th was farther east of the city on the Saar River, battling the Germans and miserable weather.

One of Dad's most memorable wartime experiences occurred during this time. In early November, the 90th Infantry Division skirted the fortified city of Metz to the north, executed an assault crossing of the flooded Moselle River, and broke through the Maginot Line. Then, in a week of heavy fighting from 25 November to 2 December 1944, the it pushed forward 6 miles to the west bank of the Saar River. During the night of 2/3 December, Company C, 357th Infantry occupied Rehlingen, overlooking the river. Roads were swept for mines and the 359th Infantry closed up on the river to the north. The Germans held the fortified line known as the Westwall, which the Americans called the "Siegfried Line," on the east bank. The division's next mission was an assault crossing of the fortified river line, one of the most difficult and dangerous types of attack.

To the south, on 3 December the 95th Infantry Division managed to establish a tenuous hold on the east bank of the Saar by capturing an intact bridge over the river at Saarlautern in a coup de main. Under the XX Corps plan, the 95th would then sweep north, clearing the east bank of the river to the vicinity of Rehlingen, which would allow the 90th to cross the river and reinforce the attack.[1] Unfortunately, the 95th Infantry Division attack stalled in vicious fighting to maintain the Saarlautern bridgehead when the Germans threw in their reserves. On the evening of 3 December, "the long expected order came from Corps: Cross within zone at earliest practicable hour." The 90th Infantry Division would have to make its own river assault, without any intact bridges in its zone of operations.

General George C. Marshall (in light-colored trench coat) while on his tour of the ETOUSA, 8–14 October 1944. On the right is Major General McLain and in the center is Major General Walton H. Walker, the commander of the XX Corps. The other officers are unknown. This meeting probably took place on 10 or 11 October, just a few days before McLain left the 90th Infantry Division to take command of the XIX Corps. U.S. Army SC.

General McLain was relieved on 15 October 1944 in order to take command of the XIX Corps. His replacement, the equally competent Major General James A. Van Fleet, began contingency planning for an assault crossing of the river between Merzig and the twin towns of Pachten-Dilligen on the night of 2 December.[2] The terrain on the German side from opposite the town of Rehlingen northwest to Merzig was a high, steep, sparsely wooded hill mass. It was extensively covered by pillboxes and trenches, but exact details were hidden by the extensive undergrowth. General Van Fleet decided to assault the river southeast of Rehlingen where the terrain was more moderate and appeared to be less well fortified.[3]

However, while the high ground the Americans held allowed excellent observation across the Saar to their objectives, it was also so rugged that it restricted access forward to the river to the roads following the valleys of the Itzbach and the Wallerfangerbach. Van Fleet assigned the crossing from Siersberg east along the Itzbach to the north of Pachten-Dilligen to CT 7.[4] The crossing from Wallerfangen northeast to Pachten-Dilligen was assigned to CT 8. CT 9 would be in reserve and hold the extended northern flank of the division to where it joined the line of the 3d Cavalry Group, which guarded the left of TUSA to its connection with FUSA near Remich in Luxembourg.

Normally, the Saar was only 200 feet wide along most of its course, but the heavy autumn rains had caused it to flood its banks. Most of the old river course to the north of Rehlingen, known as the Kondeler Bach and Alte Saar, were flooded, creating an additional loop in the river. The Germans had blown up the bridge crossing the Saar at Rehlingen on 2 December, just before Company C, 357th Infantry got to the town. In 1979, General DePuy, who took command of the 1st Battalion on 4 December 1944, described the opposition his battalion faced in this attack.

> *The Siegfried Line ran along the river with some of the pillboxes right at the water's edge. And, halfway across the flood plain was a railroad track up on an embankment; under that embankment there were more pillboxes. Then the flood plain extended further to the woodline and hills beyond. I guess from the river to the hills it was a half mile, a quarter of a mile to the railway embankment, and a quarter of a mile to the road at the foot of the wooded hills. At the road there were another line of pillboxes and back up in the woods there were still more pillboxes and concrete shelters.*
>
> *So, there were three lines of pillboxes, plus some scattered ones up in the woods. Up on top of the hill, on the left flank, there was a highway intersection, not really a major one but an important one for that area. Well, anyway, my job was to cross the river, get on that hill and block that major road junction on the left flank of the division's bridgehead.*[5]

During the day on 3 December, the 2d and 3d Battalions of the 357th Infantry moved up behind the 1st Battalion and assembled in the valley in the area of Siersberg–Hemmersdorf–Büren. General Van Fleet met with all the company, battalion, and regimental command and staff officers of CT 8 at the Regimental CP at Veckering, France, to orient the officers on Van Fleet's plan and the combat team's role in the assault crossing. At 2100, CT 8 was alerted for movement on 4 December from Veckering to an assembly area at Gisingen, west of Wahlerfangen. Immediately after receiving the alert, CT 7 and 8 received Division Field Message Number 4, which directed the timing of its movement and directed both to conduct reconnaissance of the proposed crossing sites and positions for direct fire weapons, including for attached and supporting direct fire units. CT 8 included Company A, 712th Tank Battalion and Company B, 81st Chemical Mortar Battalion with Company B, 773d Tank Destroyed Battalion in support. CT 7 included Company C, 712th Tank Battalion, and Company C, 81st Chemical Mortar Battalion with Company A 773d Tank Destroyer Battalion was in support.[6]

The flooded Saar River viewed from the American side to the west of Rehlingen. The photo was probably taken from the area of Eimersdorf. Rehlingen is obscured in the upper right, just above the smoke. U.S. Army SC.

One other unit brought into the direct fire support plan for the crossing was the 537th AAA Battalion. General Van Fleet had his G-3, Lieutenant Colonel Richard Stillwell, call upon Colonel Recer for recommendations on how his battalion could support the attack while still performing its primary antiaircraft mission.[7] Recer decided to use the water-cooled .50 caliber machine guns of two batteries and four of the M16B of one battery for direct fire of the German pillboxes across the river. Eight of the .50 caliber water-cooled guns from Battery D were placed in two positions near Elmersdorf, with each in a well-dug position sited so they could fire to the northeast onto pillboxes northwest of Rehlingen. The other eight .50 caliber guns and the four M16B from Battery A were placed in Rehlingen to fire on pillboxes across the river to the north and east. The Battery A guns were organized as a Provisional 3d Platoon and placed under Dad's leadership.[8]

At 0400 on 5 December, Dad began leading the eight machine-gun crews and their heavy loads of guns, tripods, ammunition, and cooling water cans into

Rehlingen. Working as much as possible under cover and concealment from the German positions on the other side of the river, they placed the guns in the windows of eight different buildings selected so they could be accessed out of sight of the German positions, but with visibility and fields of fire on their pillbox targets. Each machine-gun position was reinforced with sandbags and camouflaged with whatever material they could find. The four M16B were driven up in the dark and parked in the streets behind buildings that sheltered them from view and direct fire from across the river. Routes to primary and alternate firing positions were planned so the M16B could move to fire at targets either to the north or to the east. By the late evening of 5/6 December, the positions were prepared and Dad and his men settled in to wait for the time they were directed to open fire.[9]

CT 8 executed its movement to assembly areas for the assault on 4 December, taking up much of the day. CT 9 was also moving, taking over its extended front on the division left. During the day, Colonel Julian H. George, commanding CT 7 because Colonel Barth was severely wounded in October, and his battalion commanders conducted a reconnaissance of the proposed crossing sites and firing positions. Crucially, George's S-3, Major DePuy, remained at the Regimental Headquarters in Hemmersdorf. Sometime after Colonel George returned, Colonel Charles A. Carrell, who had taken over the 1st Battalion after Major Hamilton was severely wounded in September, walked into the Regimental CP and announced that "he couldn't take it anymore" and walked back out again. He was later evacuated for exhaustion. According to DePuy, the no doubt astonished George

> *Waved his finger at me and said, "Go to the 1st Battalion." And, to this day, I don't know exactly what he wanted me to do—whether he wanted me to go down and take command or just what he wanted me to do. But, in any event, I went down and sent a message back that I had taken command of the battalion. They already had orders to cross the river in a day and a half or two days.*[10]

The final day of planning and preparation for the assault was 5 December. General Van Fleet met again with his command and staff to finalize plans for the operation. CT 7 and 8 would attack abreast, with CT 7 on the left and CT 8 on the right. CT 7 would cross with the 1st Battalion under Major DePuy on the left and the 2d Battalion on the right. CT 8 would cross with the 3d Battalion on the left and the 1st Battalion on the right. Once a bridgehead was established, the Engineers would emplace footbridges, then build heavy ferries to transport tanks, tank destroyers, and other heavy weapons across until vehicle bridges could be put in.

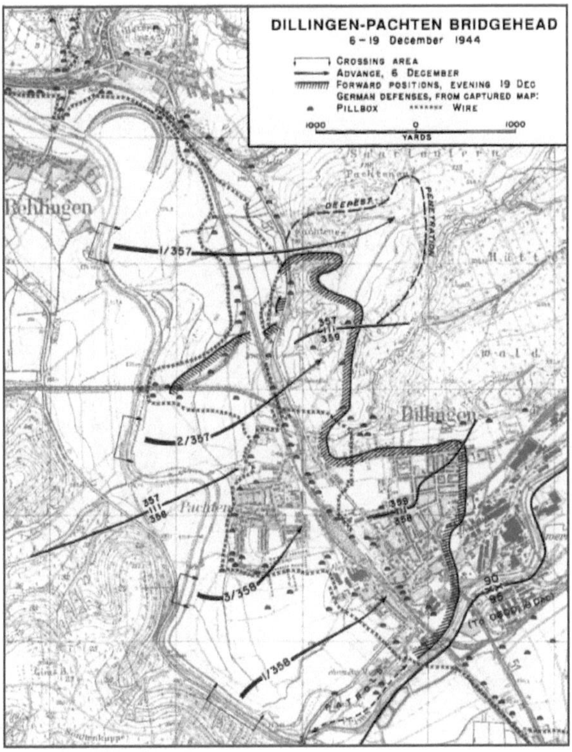

Map 20. The Dillingen-Pachten Bridgehead 6–19 December 1944. Dad's machine guns were positioned along the north edge of Rehlingen to the right of the destroyed bridge in the upper left corner of the map. Cole, *Lorraine Campaign*, Map XLI.

Critically, although plenty of artillery units were available, it was decided that there would be no artillery preparation preceding the assault by the leading battalions. The initial attack would depend on stealth and surprise to get the vulnerable assault boats and their cargo across the river. However, there was one problem. Colonel Stillwell apparently had not told Colonel Recer that. Instead Colonel Recer understood that his guns had a dual mission. One was to suppress the German pillboxes opposite Rehlingen. The other was to act in concert with the supporting weapons of the 359th Infantry to distract German attention from the actual crossing site upstream. Because of that misunderstanding, Recer assigned a specific time for Dad to open fire with his guns—0415, just as the assault boats would begin crossing the Saar.

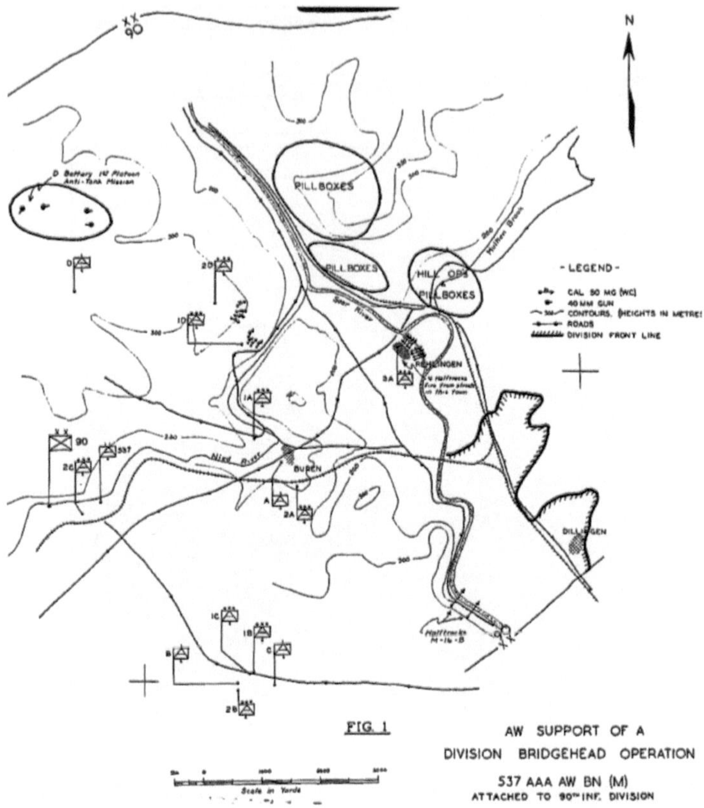

Map 21. AW (Automatic Weapons) Support of a Division Bridgehead Operation.

Between 0250 and 0300 the four assault battalions began moving to the river, where they linked up with the Engineers with the assault boats. On schedule at 04015 as they assembled on the banks of the Saar, preparing to embark the assault boats, Battery A opened fire on the German pillboxes with its eight .50 caliber machine guns. Nor were they the only ones in Rehlingen to open fire. The 3d Platoon, Company A, 773d Tank Destroyer Battalion, which had deployed west of Dad's position in what is now, ironically, the Schützengemeinschaft—the Rehlingen-Siersburg municipality's shooting club—also opened fire on two of the pillboxes north of the river. Taken unawares by the sudden fusillade, Major DePuy became furious. As he later recalled the events,

What happened is that we had the boats lined up about 100 yards from the river. The engineers had put them there and we had engineer tape leading from the assembly areas to the boats. After they picked up as boat, each squad was to go straight to the river, get in, and go and do all of those good things that I talked about. Well, just about the time the first two companies got to the boats and were picking them up, about two machine pistols fired from the other side of the river and the whole goddamned town of Rehlingen lit up. All the.50 calibers, all the tanks and all the tank destroyers were firing tracers. It lit up the whole Saar River Valley and it woke up every defender for 5 miles. . . . The crossing was hairy because I initially made a horrible mistake. In the little town of Rehlingen, which was right on the near riverbank, I infiltrated in a platoon of quad .50s mounted on the back of half-tracks. I wanted them there just in case we got stopped in the middle of the river by pillbox fire and weren't able to get across. Well, my mistake was that I gave the antiaircraft lieutenant in command of that platoon responsibility for deciding when to open fire. I actually thought I had given that responsibility to the commander of the tanks; I also had a tank platoon and a tank destroyer platoon in there, and some .50 caliber machine guns from the battalion trains. In other words, I had that town loaded with firepower, but what I didn't have, was clear responsibility as to whom would decide when to use it. You see my orders were, "Don't open fire unless we're getting heavy fire from the pillboxes on the river." Well, it turned out that heavy fire to me and heavy fire to that lieutenant from the antiaircraft platoon, who had never been on the front-line in his life, was quite different.[11]

General DePuy's recollections in 1979 were vivid and detailed but they were also memories of events thirty-five years in his past and were prone to the errors and confabulations common to memory. For example, there were no "tanks" in Rehlingen, only tank destroyers. DePuy did not order Dad's guns into Rehlingen, they were sent there by Colonel Recer, acting on the instructions of Colonel Stillwell, not Major DePuy. Nor were they "attached" to DePuy's battalion or the 357th Infantry, they were still attached to the 343d Field Artillery but were in support of the 357th Infantry for the river crossing. The same was true for the tank destroyers in Rehlingen; they were also not attached but were in support of the 357th Infantry.

The 90th's Operational Report described the incident somewhat differently from DePuy's later recollection.

Only on the extreme Division left in the zone of the 1st Battalion 357th Infantry was there any enemy reaction to the activity on the near bank; and this due to the accidental firing of a multiple 50 caliber anti-aircraft gun positioned in Rehlingen.

Hugh Cole, the author of the official Army history of the Lorraine Campaign, also described the incident, again somewhat differently.

> *Surprise was complete, except for an incident on the left where the accidental firing of some .50-caliber machine guns in Rehlingen brought hostile fire down on the 1st Battalion of the 357th.*[12]

A few years before General DePuy was interviewed, Dad read Cole's account and gave me his recollection of those events. He remembered that his Provisional Platoon and Battery A were in support of the crossing. Shortly after his guns opened fire on the pillboxes north of Rehlingen, an officer in a jeep sped into Rehlingen where he angrily asked Dad why his guns had opened fire against orders. Dad heatedly responded that he was following orders and showed him the message form he had jotted Colonel Recer's timing on. Dad then sarcastically asked if they were supposed to cease firing now that the operation had already started. The unknown officer turned and left without a word. Dad had never seen the officer before and never saw him again and nothing ever came of the incident.

I have tried to deduce who the officer DePuy sent to accost Dad was, but he remains unknown. It certainly was not Major DePuy because he was busy at the river's edge getting his battalion ready to cross. It may have been DePuy's S-3, Captain McAlister. More curious though is why DePuy later thought the incident was of such major consequence. DePuy himself said that the Germans opened fire first on the crossing with "two machine pistols" before the firing by Dad's Platoon and the tank destroyers began. DePuy also claimed that the firing "woke up every defender for 5 miles," while Cole said the firing "brought hostile fire down on the 1st Battalion of the 357th." Except DePuy also recalled his battalion only suffered two casualties in crossing the river, while the Division Operations Report simply remarked that DePuy's battalion suffered "brief confusion caused by enemy mortar and artillery fire which greeted the outburst of the multiple .50 caliber mentioned above."[13]

In fact, all four assault battalions had a relatively uneventful crossing of the river. It was when they got to the other side that things began to fall apart. While the initial German response was weak and uncoordinated, they reacted swiftly to the American success. By the end of the day, German artillery and mortar fire on the crossing places was intense, accurate, and increasing in volume. Worse, plans to use chemical smoke to obscure the bridge-building and ferry operations were only partly successful as the wind refused to cooperate, blowing away the man-made fog.

Some tanks and tank destroyers managed to ferry across, and more troops crossed by boat and footbridges, but artillery and mortar fire kept damaging or destroying the Engineers' work. It was also difficult to get supplies across the swift-moving water, so carrying parties were organized to haul supplies by hand across the river. Each of the batteries of the 537th supplied one officer and five enlisted men for the task, starting on 11 December. The duty was arduous and potentially dangerous, four men were wounded slightly while working the carrying parties, and Dad considered the 3d Platoon lucky to stay in Rehlingen.

However, the position in Rehlingen was no picnic either. On 7 and 8 December, Dad's men were subjected to constant mortar and artillery fire, but thanks to their well-prepared positions only two were slightly wounded and only one of the M16B suffered minor damage. Artillery and mortar fire continued intermittently until the night of 19 December, when the Germans fired very heavy concentrations that continued into the next day, disabling two of the machine guns. Throughout, Dad remained intent on his mission suppressing the German pillboxes and supporting the 357th Infantry fighting on the other side of the river. His bravery and attention to duty was later recognized with a promotion to 1st lieutenant, effective Christmas Day, and with the award of a Bronze Star Medal.

> *Richard C. Anderson, O525336, First Lieutenant, Coast Artillery Corps, 537th Antiaircraft Artillery Automatic Weapons Battalion, United States Army. For heroic service in support of operations from 10–22 December 1944 in the vicinity of Rehlingen, Germany. While his battery was using their weapons as flat trajectory guns in support of an infantry battalion, First Lieutenant Anderson deployed his 50 caliber machine guns in strategic positions. He repeatedly subjected himself to enemy artillery and mortar barrages as he moved from one gun position to another, directing their fire against the foe's positions, facilitating the advance of the infantry. His heroic service was in accordance with military tradition. Entered Military Service from Pennsylvania.*[14]

The amount of ammunition expended by the 3d Platoon was staggering. On 6 December they fired 8,000 rounds, then at least 76,000 more from 7 through 22 December. On 18 and 19 December they fired 20,000 rounds each day. Including the eight machine guns of Battery D and occasional firing by the other batteries, 245,000 rounds of .50 caliber were expended by the 537th AAA Battalion between 5 and 22 December 1944.[15]

One of the more curious of Dad's wartime recollections was of Rehlingen when they were firing those copious amounts of ammunition. Such sustained fire

Engineers working on one of the heavy ferries at Wallerfangen during the crossing attempt. One problem was that the flooded river left the banks very shallow, and the ferries kept grounding far from shore. This also appears to be one of the few times that the chemical smoke screen was not dispersed by the wind along the river. U.S. Army SC.

consumed a lot of the cooling water used in the machine guns as it steamed away. Dad's gun crews first resorted to the old soldier's method of replacing the water—they peed into the water cans—but that was only a stopgap. They were then faced with the problem of hauling heavy water cans forward, along with ammunition, increasing the backbreaking supply runs they had to make every night, until one of Dad's soldiers made an astonishing discovery. The water was still running in some of the buildings in Rehlingen!

That solved their cooling water problem and also gave them access to two things that were even better: flush toilets and a bathtub. The intact bathtub even had a coal-fired water heater. The only problem was it was on the second floor of the building and shellfire had blasted away most of the wall facing the German side of the Saar, exposing the bathroom to the field of fire of one of the German pillboxes. Occasionally one of Dad's men would sneak into the bathroom at night to try to heat some water for bathing but always without success. Dad and his men became so irritated at the German pillbox that they repeatedly tried to suppress it, but also without success. After one "serenade" from all eight of their water-cooled machine guns and a couple of the M16B the German machine gun in the pillbox opened fire again in just a few minutes. During the entire two weeks they were in Rehlingen they were never able to silence that irritating German pillbox for long. Surprisingly, in 1969 we were able to locate that pillbox, in the underbrush by the river, close to the north side of the replacement bridge. It was easy to identify it because the entire face of it was pockmarked with tiny craters, small divots caused by the impact of numerous .50 caliber rounds. Dad laughed and wryly commented, "well, at least we were hitting it . . . It didn't do much good, but we were hitting it."

However, it was all for nothing. On 16 December 1944, the Germans executed a surprise attack to the north in the Ardennes. Within forty-eight hours the situation became critical, and on 18 December, in a conference at Luxembourg City, General Bradley instructed Patton to halt the Saar offensive and prepare to intervene to support FUSA. Bradley's decision was confirmed by General Eisenhower the next morning at Verdun, when Patton confidently told Eisenhower, "he could start a piecemeal attack in three days, a co-ordinated attack in six." Eisenhower directed Patton hold his front with just the XX Corps, while the XII Corps with the 26th and 35th Infantry Division and the III Corps with the 4th Armored and the 80th Infantry Division moved north. All XX Corps offensive operations were to cease.[16]

The order to prepare to evacuate the bridgehead reached the 90th Infantry Division on the afternoon of 19 December. The withdrawal began that night and was completed by 1040 on 22 December. The withdrawal was executed so skillfully that the Germans only became aware of it about forty-five minutes before the last ferry load left. Only two tank destroyers, two tanks, one jeep, and one truck were left behind disabled, and all were destroyed before the last boats left. The 3d Platoon withdrew from Rehlingen at 1600.

The 90th went into an assembly area where its various units, especially the 357th and 358th Infantry, reconstituted and absorbed replacements. One memorable feature of this period for Dad was when one of the 537th AAA Battalion cooks somehow scrounged a commercial ice cream machine from one of the towns in Waldwisse and put it into operation. He collected powdered milk, powdered eggs, and sugar from rations and started to make ice cream. Soon word got out and the 537th started cranking out ice cream for other units.

The 90th Infantry Division, with its usual attachments as well as the 3d Cavalry Group, remained on the defensive from 22 December 1944 through 5 January 1945. They held an extended line from the area north of Schengen to the Saar River

"These soldiers of the 357th Regiment, 90th Infantry Division, were fighting Nazis last night across the Saar River near Dillingen. They have just received word that they are part of 64 Yanks who will be granted a thirty day furlough at home plus 2 months travel time. All have received the Purple Heart and numerous other decorations for outstanding acts of courage. L to R, (sitting) . . . T/Sgt. Thomas L. Chamberlain, Kansas City, Mo.; S/Sgt. Merle A. Welfare, Ledyard, Ia.; Sgt. Joseph Dorner, New England, N.D.; and L to R (Standing) . . . S/Sgt. Ed Melton, Haskell, Tex.; Pvt. James Jirles, Aphens, Tenn.; S/Sgt. Albert J. Apple, Bottom, Tex.; S/Sgt. Victor E. Wold, Friday Harbor, Wn.; and T/Sgt. Albert E. Lambright, Amarillo, Texas. (Λ). 357th Regt., 90th Inf. Div. Dillingen, France" (original Signal Corps caption). U.S. Army SC.

opposite Merzig and then south to the Nied River. The division prepared an extensive obstacle barrier in case the German counteroffensive spread south and hunkered down in the cold and wet winter weather.

Finally, on 6 January 1945 at 0230, the division received orders to move north. Under tight security—unit markings on vehicles were obscured, the famous "T/O" patch on uniforms was covered, and they traveled mostly at night to avoid German observation—they drove 50 miles to an assembly area southeast of Bastogne. Conditions were miserable. It was bitterly cold, the roads were snow-clogged, and little shelter was available.

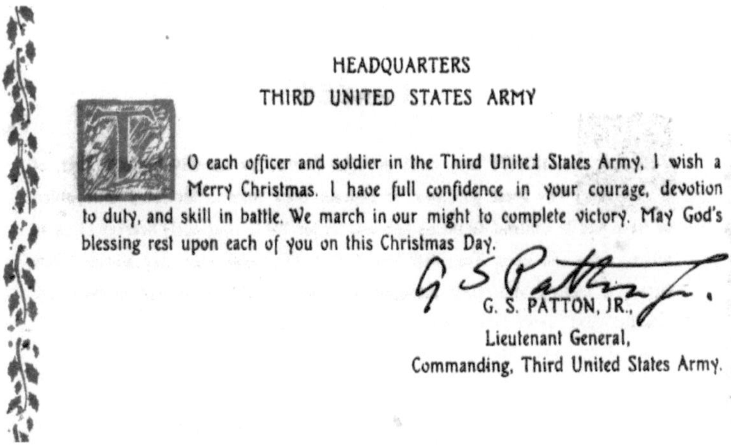

HEADQUARTERS
THIRD UNITED STATES ARMY

TO each officer and soldier in the Third United States Army, I wish a Merry Christmas. I have full confidence in your courage, devotion to duty, and skill in battle. We march in our might to complete victory. May God's blessing rest upon each of you on this Christmas Day.

G. S. PATTON, JR.,
Lieutenant General,
Commanding, Third United States Army.

Patton's Christmas Message to the soldiers of TUSA.

Dad remembered it as the coldest winter he ever experienced. He recalled the roads were so slick with ice that engineers rigged heavy winches at the top of hills to haul chains of vehicles up before lowering them down, so they would not lose control and crash. Despite such measures, Dad watched a Sherman tank of the 712th Tank Battalion careen out of control on an icy road, spinning helplessly like a top when it lost traction before ending in a ditch.

The 90th Infantry Division settled into place behind the exhausted 26th and 35th Infantry Division and General Van Fleet carefully planned its attack. On 9 January, CT 7 and CT 9 Infantry passed through the 26th Infantry Division and knifed deeply into the German lines. The Germans temporarily slowed the advance on 10 January, but CT 9 executed a night attack that unhinged the German defenses. The 90th continued to hammer the German defenses until 14 January, when they joined hands with troops of the 6th Armored and 35th Infantry Division attacking from Bastogne to the west. The rest of January was occupied in a slogging advance eastward to the Westwall, restoring the original frontline as it was before the German counteroffensive.

In February 1945, the division battled through the defenses of the German frontier. Skillful infantry tactics learned in the battles at Metz and along the Saar were used to pry the Germans out of the fortified defenses of the Westwall.

At the end of February, the 90th Infantry Division was placed in SHAEF Reserve and settled in behind the lines near Winterspelt, Germany. On 4 March 1945, the division went on the offensive again, attacking without a preparatory

PRAYER

ALMIGHTY and most merciful Father, we humbly beseech Thee, of Thy great goodness, to restrain these immoderate rains with which we have had to contend. Grant us fair weather for Battle. Graciously hearken to us as soldiers who call upon Thee that armed with Thy power, we may advance from victory to victory, and crush the oppression and wickedness of our enemies, and establish Thy justice among men and nations. Amen.

The reverse side of Patton's Christmas Message was his famous Christmas Prayer. He requested it from the TUSA Chief Chaplain, James H. O'Neill, on 8 December and had copies printed and distributed to every soldier in the Third Army. Dad kept his as a souvenir.

artillery barrage. By 6 March, the division advanced 24 miles and established a bridgehead southwest of Gerolstein, Germany, that was 1.5 miles deep. A week later, after advancing another 45 miles against increasingly spotty German resistance, the Tough 'Ombres crossed the Moselle River at Brodenbach, south of Koblenz. From there, the 90th headed southeast along the west bank of the Rhine toward Bingen and Bad Kreuznach.

For Dad, the advance through the Rhineland was as exhilarating as the advance of Task Force Weaver. One of his clearest memories was the day a German staff car tried to pass their column while it was halted on the road. One of the American vehicles pulled into the road, blocking the Germans' route. Infuriated, one of the German officers jumped out and started to loudly berate the driver who had the effrontery to get in his way. He was so absorbed by his rage at being delayed that it took him a few moments to realize that the soldier he was dressing down was not German. A few minutes later, the disconsolate Germans were left disarmed at the side of the road, waiting for escort to the Division Prisoner-of-War Cage. Adding insult to injury, they were forced to endure the taunts and catcalls of Dad's men as they sped past the dejected Germans when the column resumed its march.

Dad's Battery A reached Kratzenburg, Germany, 4 miles west of the Rhine River, south of Boppard on 18 March 1945. The next day, they shifted 32 miles

The coldest winter ever. Brigadier General James A. Van Fleet, standing center, near his CP at Isenborn, Esch-sur-Sûre, Luxembourg, circa 9 January 1945. U.S. Army SC.

south to Gensingen on the Nahe River, south of Bingen. There they prepared to support the 90th in a potentially much tougher river crossing than the Saar—they were to execute an assault crossing of the Rhine River on the afternoon of 23 March. However, by the evening of 18 March Dad was no longer with them. At some point during the day, he reported to the Battalion Aid Station complaining of excessive fatigue and weakness. The medical officer took one look and told him, "Dick, see that cot there? I want you to get in it and stay there until further notice—you're severely jaundiced and need rest so your liver can recover." Dad had contracted hepatitis A, probably from contaminated food or water. That evening he was evacuated to the 201st General Hospital at Verdun to recuperate. There he developed a love for ice cream, as ice cream was one of the daily treats offered in the hepatitis ward to help build up the strength of the men.

While Dad was recovering, the 90th Infantry Division executed the assault crossing of the Rhine River on schedule. They advanced past Darmstadt and on

The coldest winter ever. One of the M16B of the 537th AAA Battalion in the snow during the Battle of the Bulge. U.S. Army SC.

toward the east and an expected junction with the Soviet forces advancing west into Germany. On 4 May, the 90th accepted the surrender of the last remnants of the 11. Panzer-Division at Všeruby, Czechoslovakia, northwest of Pilsen. It was the last major act by the division in World War II, although fighting continued as some German remnants refused to surrender. Shortly after 0923 on the morning of 7 May 1945, the 90th Division Headquarters received a cable from SHAEF Headquarters.

A representative of the German High Command signed the unconditional surrender of all German land, sea and air forces in Europe to the Allied Expeditionary Forces and simultaneously to the Soviet High Command at 0141B Central European Time 7 May 1945 under which all forces will cease active operations at 0001B 9 May 1945.

All offensive operations by Allied Forces will cease. Troops will remain in present positions. . . . Due to difficulties of communication there may be some delay in similar orders reaching enemy troops, so full defensive precautions will be taken. . . . No release will be made to the press pending announcement by the three governments.

Eisenhower

s/0923

A few hours earlier, Eisenhower had sent a much more succinct message to the American and British Combined Chiefs of Staff: "***The mission of this Allied Force was fulfilled at 0241, local time, May 7th, 1945.***"

Dad was still in hospital at Verdun when Germany surrendered. He finally rejoined the 537th on 27 May, nearly three weeks after the war in Europe had ended. By then they had moved to Indersback, about 8 miles southeast of Landau on the Isar River. From 5 to 13 June, Dad was on temporary duty as the Platoon Leader of a provisional truck platoon organized with twenty-nine enlisted men from Battery A. They spent the week using most of the Battery's motor vehicles hauling displaced Czechs, Germans, Austrians, and Italians, from camps in Czechoslovakia,

The coldest winter ever. One of the .50 caliber water-cooled machine guns of the 537th AAA Battalion in the snow during the Battle of the Bulge. They had to put antifreeze into the water condensers to keep it from freezing. U.S. Army SC.

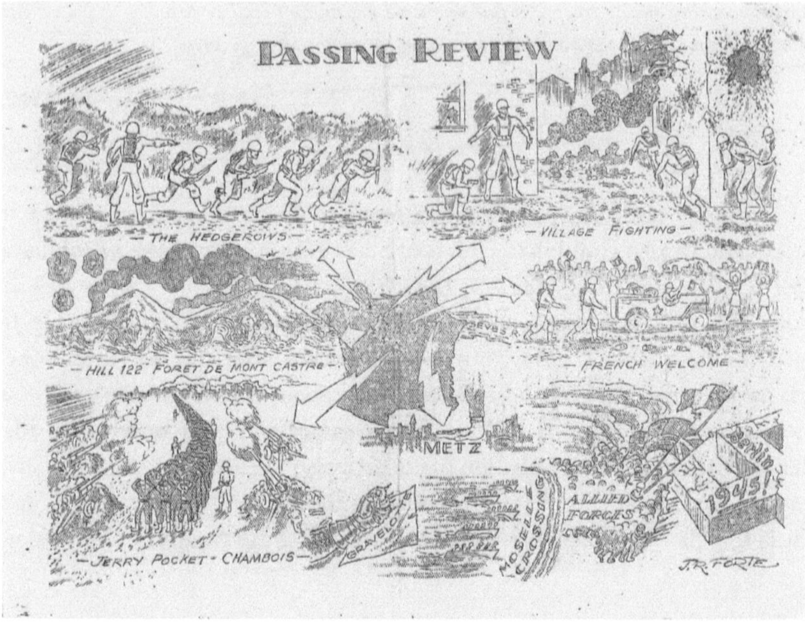

Carry On Newsletter of the 90th Infantry Division, January 1945. This copy was kept by Captain Oehmichen.

Germany, Austria, and northern Italy, back to their home country. On 21 June, Dad was assigned as the 2d Platoon Leader, but he spent little time in that job. On 13 July, he was relieved from assignment to the 537th AAA Battalion and was reassigned to the 12th Tank Destroyer Group at Le Havre. He was heading home to the States.

The next day he was in Paris, where he spent 680 francs—about $5.70—at the famous nightclub Le Lido Le Plage de Paris. It was established in 1928 as "La Plage" or "the beach," the "beach" being an indoor swimming pool and champagne bar in the basement of 78 Avenue des Champs-Elysees. It was styled after the Lido of Venice, complete with marble columns and gondolas. Although it was very popular, it was forced to close in 1933 during the Great Depression but reopened three years later—without the swimming pool—as a nightclub cabaret with the lengthy name of "Le Lido La Plage de Paris." In 1946, it changed ownership, and the name was shortened to simply "Le Lido."[17]

Dad's stay in Paris was short. He had time to climb the observation platform of the Arc de Triomphe and the Eiffel Tower to see the city, but by 18 July, he was at

Dad and Lieutenant Colonel Beo W. Recer, commander of the 537th AAA Battalion. Unknown location, probably late March 1945.

Le Havre, assigned to the 772d Tank Destroyer Battalion as a Platoon Commander in Company A.

The 772d departed Le Havre on 20 July on the S.S. *Sea Robin*, which was a Liberty ship rebuilt as a troop transport able to carry 2,045 passengers. She was just as crowded as the *Queen Mary* but much smaller and much slower as well. *Sea Robin* was only capable of 16 knots and took eight days to cross to New York, arriving on 28 July. The next day Dad was at Camp Shanks and immediately sent a telegram to Mom in Arizona: "Back in States. Feeling Fine. Furlough Soon. Love. Dick." They reunited in Phoenix in early August, when Dad was first able to see his little girl, Connie, who was nearly a year old.[18]

However, Dad was not out of the Army, and his war was not yet over. The 772d Tank Destroyer Battalion—and Dad—were slated to participate in the

Dad with Colonel Recer again. Probably at Indersback after the end of the war. Note the windshield damage on the 2.5-ton truck.

proposed invasion of Japan. They would be part of Operation CORONET, which was planned for March 1946, following an initial invasion, Operation OLYMPIC, scheduled for 1 November 1945. He was still on furlough, "for purpose of rehabilitation, recuperation, and recovery," when the atomic bombs were dropped on Hiroshima on 6 August and Nagasaki on 9 August. President Truman announced the surrender of Japan on 14 August and Emperor Hirohito broadcast his surrender message on Tokyo Radio on 15 August. Yet despite the end of the war, the country was still officially in a state of emergency. Dad reported as ordered to Camp San Luis Obispo, California, on 7 September 1945, only to find that the 772d Tank Destroyer Battalion had moved to Camp Shelby, Mississippi. After a long and uncomfortable train ride, he rejoined the battalion at Camp Shelby and was made an Assistant Provost Marshal, supervising the steady stream of soldiers being discharged from the Army. His turn finally came on 9 October 1945, when he was granted terminal leave and release from active duty. For Dad, the war was finally over.

Immediately postwar, while still technically on leave from the Army, Dad worked for a short time for Phelps Dodge Mining in Globe, Arizona, and then as a metallurgist for Kaiser Iron and Steel in Fontana, California. After his discharge, in April 1946, Dad, Mom, and Connie returned to Phoenix when he was offered a

Plage de Paris in its heyday when the pool was still open, circa 1928–1933.

job as a draftsman for the new architectural firm of Guirey & Quist. However, Dad found himself dissatisfied with the 9 to 5 life of an office worker and civilian life quickly lost its appeal. He applied for a return to active duty, which was granted on 9 February 1947, shortly before my sister Linda was born. Dad left for Fort Holabird, Maryland, to attend the Army Intelligence School. Mom, Connie, and Linda joined him there in April. From Maryland, he then traveled to Japan as part of the Army of Occupation, and then spent the next twenty-two years at various assignments—as a student at Fort Sill, as an ROTC instructor at the University of Michigan, as a Battery Commander at Fort Knox and in Hanau Germany with the 3d Armored Division, where Connie desperately spent our last year there trying to track down and meet Private First Class Elvis Presley. From Germany, Dad went to an assignment at the Pentagon, followed by an unaccompanied year in Korea—we stayed in D.C. Then there was duty as an advisor to the South Carolina NG, before his final duty station with the V Corps Artillery in Darmstadt, Germany.

Retirement from the Army led to working in real estate in Northern Virginia until I left the nest and my parents retired permanently to the Sea Islands of South Carolina. They enjoyed life there until Dad decided to make the trip that eventually resulted in the writing of this book.

Back in the States again. Mom and Dad celebrate their second wedding anniversary at the Adams Hotel in Phoenix, Arizona, 17 August 1945, two days after VJ-Day.

Three years after we returned from France, Dad enlisted me for another special project. In going through his personnel files, he discovered that he had been recommended by Captain Alfred L. Lea for a second award of a Bronze Star, and he asked me to help him follow up on it. After filling out a few forms and waiting for nearly a year and a half the U.S. Army Human Resources Command Military Awards Branch approved the award of the Bronze Star Medal (First Oak Leaf Cluster) for "Meritorious Service in connection with military operations against the enemy in Germany during the period 11 February 1945 to 8 May 1945."[19]

Over his twenty-seven-year Army career, Dad's awards included: the Legion of Merit, the Bronze Star Medal with "V" Device and Oakleaf Cluster, the Army Commendation Medal, the American Campaign Medal, the European-African-Middle Eastern Campaign Medal with Silver Campaign Star, the World War II Victory Medal, World War II Army of Occupation Medal (Germany and Japan), and the National Defense Service Medal.

The 90th Infantry Division and its attached nondivisional units, including the 537th Antiaircraft Battalion, Automatic Weapons (Mobile) were awarded credit for five campaigns during World War II: Normandy, Northern France, Ardennes-Alsace, Rhineland, and Central Europe.[20] They were also awarded the French Croix de Guerre with Palm. The 90th's citation read:

> *A magnificent unit which particularly distinguished itself during the combat of 9 to 19 November 1944 on the Moselle and the Sarre Rivers. After having crossed the Moselle River by open attack, the unit seized the fort of Koenigsmacker, capturing many prisoners. Although violently counterattacked, nevertheless the unit continued its advance over heavily mined ground, penetrating deeply into the Maginot Line, taking by storm, strong positions defending Metz, attaining all the objectives which had been assigned to it.*[21]

Collectively, the officers and enlisted men of the 90th Infantry Division and its attachments were awarded 4 Medals of Honor, 72 Distinguished Service Crosses, fourteen Legions of Merit, 1,459 Silver Star Medals, 50 Soldier's Medals, 5,705 Bronze Star Medals, 120 Air Medals, and 4 Distinguished Flying Crosses. However, that actually undercounts the number awarded inasmuch as every single Infantryman awarded the Combat Infantryman's Badge and every Medic awarded the Combat Medic's Badge were retroactively eligible for award of a Bronze Star Medal for meritorious service postwar. There were also a reported 18,460 officers and men who were wounded in combat, who would have been eligible for an award of the Purple Heart Medal, as were the 2,963 reported killed in action.[22]

NOTES

ACKNOWLEDGMENTS

1. A mess sergeant is an enlisted man working in the enlisted or officer mess and is not a rank.
2. https://www.goldenarrowresearch.com
3. https://www.echodelta.net/mbs/eng-welcome.php

CHAPTER 1. DAD AND THE WAR

1. "Civil War Veterans' Card File, 1861–1866," *Pennsylvania State Archives, United States Census of Union Veterans and Widows of the Civil War, 1890*, NARA microfilm publication M123 (Washington, D.C.: National Archives and Records Administration, n.d.); RG-19 Records of the Department of Military and Veterans' Affairs, *Registers of Pennsylvania Volunteers, 1861–1865*, Volume 4, p. 474.
2. David was the great-uncle of John Wesley Culp, who famously was working in Virginia on the outbreak of the Civil War, enlisted in the 2d Virginia of the Stonewall Brigade, and was killed in the Battle of Gettysburg on 3 July somewhere in the area of Benner's Hill-Brinkerhoff Ridge-Christian Benner's Farm (owned by Wesley's cousin), likely within sight of Culp's Hill and his family's farmhouse.
3. "CW/VFM-50: Kendlehart Letter," Gettysburg College, Musselman Library, *Special Collections.*
4. David also got Burns his other job as part-time constable. It has always struck me as fitting that one reason often given for the Confederate advance on Gettysburg on 1 June was so the many barefoot Rebels could find footwear at a supposed "shoe factory" in town. As far as I can find, David's small operation was the only such business there.
5. The group included Tillie Pierce, Sally and Jenny Myers, Alice Powers, sisters Florence and Sophia Culp, Mary Culp (their cousin), Dora Fleming, Anna Garlach, Sally McClellan, Belle McElroy, Ann Jane Powers, Amanda Reinecher, Carry Young, Irene Weisich, and Anna and Lydia Zeigler. See Sarah Sites Rodgers, *The Ties of the Past: The Gettysburg Diaries of Salome Myers Stewart, 1854–1922* (Gettysburg, PA: Thomas Publications, 1996).
6. The retreat began shortly after midnight. Karlton Smith, "'Such a night is seldom experienced . . .' James Longstreet and the Retreat from Gettysburg," *2010 Gettysburg Seminar* (Gettysburg, PA: National Park Service, 2010); *History of Cumberland and Adams Counties, Pennsylvania* (Chicago: Warner, Beers & Co., 1886), pp. 357–358. This account says that David met with General Meade on 4 July, but it was actually 5 July.

7. A second two-year commitment after the first was optional and a minority of men chose to attend as civilians; in the class of 1943 there were 92 civilian and 414 cadet graduates, thus about 18 percent were civilians. There was also a small number of women attending; just 25 graduated in the class of 1943, about 4 percent of the class.

8. Virginia Military Institute and the Johns Hopkins University in Baltimore, Maryland, were also feeder schools for these units. ROTC graduates were commissioned into the Officer Reserve Corps (ORC) and were assigned to these units. In turn, the units were affiliated with active RA units for summer training. The pre–World War II Army organization is exhaustively detailed in four volumes by Lieutenant Colonel (Ret.) Steven E. Clay, *U.S. Army Order of Battle, 1919–1941* [in four volumes], (Fort Leavenworth, KS: Combat Studies Institute Press, 2010).

9. The VPI team mascot is a tom turkey, thus the "Gobblers" nickname at the time. The VPI cheer was written in 1896 by a senior, O. M. Stull, who called it the "Hoki," which was a nonsense name he made up. Later, an "e" was added and in the 1970s the VPI team nickname changed to the "Hokies."

10. VPI's Yearbook shows the Coast Artillery cadets practicing on 14-inch, 12-inch, 6-inch, and 155mm coast defense guns, 3-inch and .50 caliber AA guns, as well as pistols and rifles. Infantry cadets practiced with rifles, pistols, machine guns, and obsolete M1917 Light Tanks. VPI, *The Bugle* (Blacksburg, VA, 1940, 1941, 1942, and 1943).

11. The senior military colleges of the United States included the Citadel at Charleston, South Carolina; Texas A&M University at College Station, Texas; Virginia Military Institute at Lexington, Virginia; and Norwich University at Northfield, Vermont. "A History of the Corps of Cadets," *Virginia Tech.*

12. Reverend Pinkerton died 11 January 1949 at Rochester, Pennsylvania. *The Pittsburgh Press* (Pittsburgh, PA), Wednesday, January 12, 1949, p. 32.

13. The notation "Mobile" indicated there was a prime mover for each of the battalion's guns. A Battalion that was "Semi-Mobile" (SM) usually only had a single prime mover for each battery of four guns and movement was done by shuttling back and forth from one location to another. A battalion that was "Self-Propelled" (SP) was armed with self-propelled gun carriages and did not use separate prime movers.

14. Camp Bradford was first established to train Navy Construction Battalions—Seabees—then to train LST crews, but was also part of larger amphibious training base that later became the Navy's Amphibious Base–Little Creek and is now the Joint Expeditionary Base–Little Creek.

15. In typically mixed-up Army fashion, the Battery A, 537th AAA AW Battalion MR of 2 December recorded Dad's assignment as of 1 December, which was when Colonel Recer assigned him to the Battery. The XIII Corps order assigning him to the 537th was dated 29 November. May E. Arbuckle, Chapter 2, "Camp Atterbury in Dorothy Riker," in *Indiana in World War II: The Hoosier Training Ground* (Indiana: Indiana War History Commission, 1952).

16. Civilian Production Administration, *Official Munitions Production of the United States by Months, July 1, 1940–August 31 1945,* (Washington, D.C.: War Production Board, 1947), p. 252; Robert R. Palmer, Bell I. Wiley, and William R. Keast, *The Procurement and Training of Ground Combat Troops* (Washington, D.C.: U.S. GPO, 1947), p. 465.

17. In a sample of 32 cabarets in 1944–1945 it was found that only eleven made no changes to their live music offerings, while five ceased offering live music at all. John Copeland, "Some Effects of the Changes in the Federal Cabaret Tax in 1944," *Proceedings of the Annual Conference on Taxation under the Auspices of the National Tax Association*, Vol. 38 (1945), pp. 321–339.

18. *Queen Mary Record of Wartime Cruises, 1944.*

19. Headquarters, ETOUSA, "AAA in Ground Roles (SECRET)," *Anti-Aircraft Artillery Notes, No. 10*, 27 December 1944, p. 6.

20. FM 9-223, *Twin Cal. .50 Machine Gun Mount M33 and Multiple Cal. .50 Machine Gun Mount M45* (Washington, D.C.: War Department, 27 July 1944).

21. Dad kept a mimeographed list of "London Restaurants and Clubs" recommended by the Billeting Office, Central Base Section, SOS ETOUSA, but failed to note which restaurant he went to.

22. Dad kept the proprietor's business card. The former hotel is now two private residences.

23. The Battery A MR called it "Burley House."

24. The time required to cross the Channel is based upon other, similar follow-up crossings by LST in this period. The time of arrival is taken from those similar accounts but matches my Dad's recollection, as well as the time of unloading, which was probably around the same time as that recorded by Battery B, 2145 hours, in its postwar history. Battery B, 537th AAA AW Battalion, *UNDO BAKER, Narrative of the Combat Experiences of Battery "B," 537th AAA AW Battalion during Continental Operations* (Pasadena, CA: Tripp Print. Co., 1946), p. 1.

25. The 343d Field Artillery Battalion had the same experience when they landed on 8 June. 343d Field Artillery Battalion, *Mission Accomplished 343rd F.A. Battalion* (Regensburg, Germany: Friedrich Puster, November 1949), p. 13.

26. The 537th was scheduled to land on D+5 with 538 O & EM and 104 vehicles. The Battalion Residual, 279 O & EM and 101 vehicles was scheduled to land on D+19 but did not land until 30 June (D+24) and did not join the battalion until 2 July (D+26). First U.S. Army, *OPLAN NEPTUNE*, Annex 3, Consolidated Build-Up Priority Troop List "A," p. 12, First United States Army Revised Consolidated Troop List "B," p. 3; 343d FA Bn, *Mission Accomplished*, p. 14.

27. Details on the operations on UTAH Beach may be found in "Notes on UTAH Beach and the 1st Engineer Special Brigade" (compiled 20 October–7 November 1944), Records of the ETOUSA ADM File 359A, pp. 57, and 88–93.

CHAPTER 2. THE 90TH INFANTRY DIVISION

1. Clay, *Volume 4. The Services*, Appendix C; Col. Forrest L. Marion, USAFR (ret.) and Col. Jon T. Hoffman, USMCR (ret.), *Forging a Total Force, The Evolution of the Guard and Reserve* (Washington, D.C.: Historical Office, Office of the Secretary of Defense, 2018), p. 22.

2. Marion and Hoffman, *Forging a Total Force*, pp. 22–23.

3. Clay, *Volume 1. The Arms*, p. 265.

4. John Sloan Brown, *Draftee Division* (Novato, CA: Presidio Press, 1998), pp. 18–20; Frank Gilchrist, *History of the 315th Engineer Combat Battalion of the 90th Infantry Division* (NP: July 1949), p. 1.

5. While the AUS encompassed the RA, NG, and OR, it also designated units raised specifically for wartime service, temporary officer wartime ranks (brevets), and personnel drafted for wartime service. Public Law 242, *National Defense Act of 1920*, as amended 1940.

6. Shelby Stanton, *World War II Order of Battle* (New York: Galahad Books, 1991 [1984]), seriatim; see also the individual unit histories.

7. Michael E. Weaver, *Guard Wars* (Bloomington: Indiana University Press, 2010), p. 72.

8. An excellent overview of the MTP may be found in Ken Roberts Greenfield, Robert R. Palmer, and Bell I. Wiley, *The Organization of Ground Combat Troops* (Washington, D.C.: Office of the Chief of Military History (OCMH), 1947, and in Brown, *Draftee Division*.

9. Romie L. Brownlee and William J. Mullen III, *Changing an Army: An Oral History of General William E. DePuy, USA Retired* (Washington, D.C.: GPO, ND [1979]), p. 8.

10. Brownlee and Mullen, *Changing an Army*, p. 7.

11. Robert R. Palmer, *Mobilization of the Ground Army*, AGF Historical Section Study No. 4 (Washington, D.C.: U.S. GPO, 1946), p. 4.

12. Major Constantine J. Blastos, *Judgement of Units* (Fort Leavenworth, KS: CGSC Student Papers, 1966), p. 27.

13. Blastos, *Judgement of Units*, p. 27; *Camp Barkeley News* (Camp Barkeley, TX), vol. 1, no. 38, ed. 1 Friday, November 6, 1942, p. 3.

14. Major Benjamin L. Bradley, USAF, *Searching For Competence: The Initial Combat Experience of Untested U.S. Army Divisions in World War II—A Case Study of the 90th Infantry Division, June–July 1944* (Fort Leavenworth, KS: CGSC Student Papers, 2004), p. 8, n. 24; Franklin Delano Roosevelt (FDR) Presidential Library, *President's Secretary's File (PSF)*, Box 84, War Department—Henry L. Stimson, 1942, Memorandum for the President, Box 84, Subject: Temporary Promotions, 22 June 1942; Hugh M. Cole, *The Ardennes: Battle of the Bulge* (Washington, D.C.: OCMH, 1965), seriatim; Office of the Theater Historian, *Order of Battle of the United States Army World War II, European Theater of Operations* (Paris, France: December 1945), p. 333; Col. Harold J. "Jack" Meyer, *Hanging Sam, A Military Biography of General Samuel T. Williams* (Denton: University of North Texas Press, 1990), seriatim; Ted Gittinger, "Oral History Interview with Samuel T. Williams," Association for Diplomatic Studies and Training (Austin, TX: Lyndon Baines Johnson Library, 2 March 1981), p. 4.

15. Lt. Joe Abrams, *A History of the 90th Division in World War II*, 90th Division Association, 1946 (Nashville, TN: Battery Press, reprint, 1999), p. 2; *The Camp Crier* (Camp Atterbury, Indiana), Friday, November 19, 1943 (vol. 2, no. 9), p. 3; Glen C. Cangelosi, M.D., "The Washington Artillery Enters the 20th Century, Fit Via Vi," *The Washington Artillery, A Lineage of Honor*, 2004. On 6 May 1944, General Lewis became Artillery Officer, ETOUSA, and after the war was commander of the 7th Armored Division and later commanded the XIX Corps Artillery. "Chronology," 14 March–25 August 1944, ADM 70, Historical Section, ETOUSA, Records of the ETOUSA; *Breaching the Siegfried*

Line, Headquarters XIX Corps, 12 January 1944; Theater Historian, *Order of Battle*, pp. 333 and 481.

16. Palmer, Wiley, and Keast, *Procurement and Training*, p. 465; Blastos, p. 7.

17. Blastos, seriatim.

18. John B. Wilson, *Armies, Corps, Divisions and Separate Brigades* (Washington, D.C.: U.S. GPO, 1999), pp. 163, 165, and 172.

19. Jean R. Moenk, *The History of Large-Scale Army Maneuvers in the United States, 1935–1964* (Washington, D.C.: U.S. GPO, 1969), pp. 96–98.

20. Wilson, *Armies, Corps, Divisions*, p. 182.

21. "Cld" was the standard Army abbreviation for "Colored," which at the time was the segregated Army's designation for units made up of Black enlisted soldiers and white officers. The term is not used here in any pejorative way but is simply how units were designated at the time.

22. *Camp Barkeley News* (Camp Barkeley, TX), vol. 2, no. 25, ed. 1 Friday, August 6, 1943, p. 4.

23. *Dominion Monarch* had the unique vessel designation of "QSMV" for "Quadruple-Screw Motor Vessel"; she had four massive diesel engines each driving a single propeller. Reuben Goosens, "QSMV Dominion Monarch," www.ssmaritime.com; Rowland W. Charles, *Troopships of World War II* (Washington, D.C.: The Army Transportation Association, 1947), p. 313. Convoy information and number of troops embarked are taken primarily from the Arnold Hague Convoy, Ports, Arrivals/Departures, and Ship Movements data bases at *Convoy Web.*

24. As built, the *Kungsholm* had accommodations for 209 first class, 395 second class, and 940 third class passengers. Charles, *Troopships*, p. 291.

25. Charles, *Troopships*, p. 311.

26. The *Dominion Monarch*, *John Ericsson*, and *Athlone Castle* carried the bulk of the division's officers and men, but not all were embarked on the same ship their unit was on. Some officers and men were attached to other units, and the maximum use was made of space on the ships, so some traveled on other ships. There were also personnel of other units assigned to the ETOUSA traveling on board these ships, principally troops assigned to the VIII Corps. The *Edmund B. Alexander* was originally the Hamburg-Amerika Line ocean liner *Amerika*, which was first interned and then seized by the United States in World War I. She was renamed *America* and was used as a troop transport. After a few years as an American ocean liner, she was laid up until October 1940 when she was renamed the *Edmund B. Alexander* and was turned over to the Army as a floating barracks. In May 1942, she was converted from coal to fuel oil and substantially rebuilt to carry 5,159 troops. She had 5,296 troops aboard. HMT *Stirling Castle* was completed for the Union-Castle Line for its South African Royal Mail Service in 1936. She was converted to carry 4,981 officers and men in 1940. She had 5,038 troops aboard. Charles, *Troopships*, pp. 20, 326.

27. The number of troops on board one of the transports, the *Duchess of Bedford*, is not known. The other seventeen transports had 57,395 officers and men aboard.

28. U.S.S. *Robinson* returned to New York on 27 March and was sent to the Pacific. Arnold Hague's listing for Convoy UT-10 includes the U.S.S. *Cincinnati* and *Chemung* as part of the convoy, which is an error. FDR Presidential Library, *Map Room Papers*, Box 114,

MR410 Sec. 18 Locations of U.S. Naval Forces, March 1944 and MR410 Sec. 19 Locations of U.S. Naval Forces, April 1943.

29. ETOUSA, *Station List*, 30 April 1944.

30. Abrams, *90th Division*, p. 3.

31. Total strength of the Advance Detachment, Group A, and AA was 3,798 O & EM, with 547 vehicles. There was also a Group C, 359th Infantry, which consisted of kitchen and bath trains of Service Company, the Headquarters G-1 personnel section, and the regimental nonessential residuals, which were to land after the assault phase. The Division Main Body consisted of 9,313 O & EM with 1,300 vehicles. The Division Residuals were scheduled to land with 254 O & EM and 66 vehicles on D+9 and 938 O & EM and 245 vehicles on D+11. First U.S. Army, *OPLAN NEPTUNE*, Annex 3, Consolidated Build-Up Priority Troop List "A," pp. 7, 8, 18.

32. David G. Chandler and James L. Collins, eds., *The D-Day Encyclopedia* (New York: Macmillan Library Reference, 1994), p. 348.

33. John Colby, *War from the Ground Up* (Austin, TX: Nortex Press, 1991), p. 485; DePuy, *Changing an Army*, p. 35.

34. MacKelvie addressed the 357th Infantry on 29 May. Lieutenant General Omar N. Bradley, "Letter to Eisenhower, 14 June 1944," NARA RG 491, *MacKelvie 201 File*, Records of the Secretary, General Staff, Records of Headquarters, ETOUSA, Correspondence Relating to Individuals; Chandler and Collins, *The D-Day Encyclopedia*, p. 348.

35. The 37 Motor Transport Vessels transporting the preloaded buildup forces from the Bristol Channel ports were Liberty ships converted to haul vehicles and personnel. On average, each was loaded with 527 O & EM and 149 vehicles, which included wheeled guns and trailer.

36. Only four of the nine MT transporting the Main Body of the 90th have been positively identified.

37. The number of Army personnel aboard the U.S.S. *Susan B. Anthony* is calculated by subtracting the number of Navy crewmen, 40 O and 378 EM, from the total number aboard. "Report of Loss of the U.S.S. Susan B. Anthony," *US Navy War Diaries*, Fold3. The total Army personnel planned for was 2,193. Appendix I, "Preloaded Build Up Bristol Channel Ports," File 603ff—*Western Base Section, Final Report*, 12 June 1944. The complete personnel loading plan has not been found.

38. Company A landed at 1400, Company B at 1630, Company C at 1730, and Company D at 2000. *MR* 6 June 1944, 1st Battalion, 359th Infantry; Company M landed at 2030 from LCI 527 and Atcuson's death was not recorded until 3 July when the MR noted he was "Fr dy [From duty] to KIA a/o [as of] 6 June 44."

39. The other three transports of Convoy LBP 1 were the USAT *George W. Goethals*, *General George S. Simonds*, and *Borinquen*; Meyer, *Hanging Sam*, p. 10.

40. 90th Infantry Division, G.O. No. 17–44, dated 23 June 1944.

41. *Narborough* (Captain-Class Frigate K578) was an American-built Buckley-class Destroyer Escort, DE-569, Lend-Leased to the Royal Navy, which named her. She was commissioned 21 January 1944, and NEPTUNE was her first major operation. She sustained minor damage in going alongside *Anthony* to take off the survivors. She was decommissioned and returned to the U.S. Navy 4 February 1946 and scrapped 14 December 1946. Captain

Class Frigate Association; Meyer, *Hanging Sam*, p. 10 gave the British ships name incorrectly as the *Nedbrough*.

42. Colby, *War*, p. 25.

43. Norman Ohler, *Blitzed: Drugs in Nazi Germany* (Boston: Houghton Mifflin, 2017), seriatim.

CHAPTER 3. BAPTISM OF FIRE

1. Historical Division, War Department, *UTAH Beach to Cherbourg (6 June–27 June 1944)* (Washington, D.C.: Historical Division, 1947), pp. 2–3; Commander Task Force 122, *NEPTUNE Monograph*, 1 April 1944, pp. 29–30.

2. *(LL)* was the German abbreviation for *Luftlande* or "Air Mobile." The division was originally organized for possible airborne operations and was partially equipped with specially designed weapons and equipment intended for air transport. *UTAH Beach*, pp. 7–10.

3. Meyer, *Hanging Sam*, p. 64; Gordon A. Harrison, *Cross-Channel Attack* (Washington, D.C.: OCMH, 1950), p. 401; Ronan, p. 7.

4. Colonel Stilwell was often mistaken for the son of Major General Joseph W. "Vinegar Joe" Stilwell, but in fact they were not closely related. Meyer's account of MacKelvie's inaction and mental state appears to have been derived from interviews with the Division G-2, Lieutenant Colonel James Boswell, in 1985. Meyer, *Hanging Sam*, pp. 64–65.

5. Andrew Rawson, "The Divisional Commander in the U.S. Army in World War II: A Case Study of the Normandy Campaign, 6 June 1944 to 24 July 1944," M. Phil. thesis (Department of Modern History, College of Arts and Law, The University of Birmingham, June 2011), pp. 3–4; see also Stephen R. Taafe, *Marshall and His Generals: U.S. Army Commanders in World War II* (Lawrence: University Press of Kansas, 2011), seriatim.

6. Mary Lee Stubbs and Stanley Russell Connor, *Armor-Cavalry Part I: Regular Army and Army Reserve* (Washington, D.C.: OCMH, 1969), p. 39.

7. A measure of the inexperience of the 90th Division may be seen in its reports for 10 June. It reversed the deployment and positions of the 357th and 358th Infantry.

8. An "initial point" or "IP" was a "point at which a foot march or motor movement is formed by the successive arrival of the units that finally make up the column. The initial point is usually a crossroads, or other place easy to locate, where the head of the column is to pass." War Department, *TM 20-205, Dictionary of United States Army Terms* (Washington, D.C.: War Department, 18 January 1944), p. 143.

9. Ronan, *Operations of the 3rd Battalion, 357th Infantry*, pp. 7–8.

10. Ronan, *Operations of the 3rd Battalion, 357th Infantry*, p. 9; Colby, *War*, pp. 7 and 149.

11. Ronan, *Operations of the 3rd Battalion, 357th Infantry*, pp. 10–11.

12. AOK 7 Ia Nr. 3116/44 g.Kdos. 15.6.1944, NARA RG 242, T312, R1565, F001048.

13. Library of Congress [hereafter LOC], *George S. Patton Papers: Diaries, 1910–1945*; Original; 1944, May 31–October 2, p. 595. Note the text of Patton's original handwritten diary entries are used. The later typewritten version is very different and in many cases was altered to make Patton appear in a better light or more prescient. It is also not clear which of the later alterations was made by Patton and which by other editors after his death. See Daniel Feldmann, "Fixing One's History: George S. Patton's Changes in his Personal Diary," *War in History*, vol. 28, no. 1, January 2021.

14. Every American Infantry Regiment included a Cannon Company of towed, short-barreled 105mm Howitzers M3, which was intended to be the regimental commanders "personal artillery." However, the towed guns were unwieldy and rarely used for direct fire, where tanks were more suitable, so frequently simply acted as a fourth battery for the regiment's direct fire artillery battalion.

15. Brownlee and Mullen, *Changing an Army*, p. 10.

16. The Division G-1 Summary completed in September 1944 reported 967 German prisoners captured by the division in June, including 399 for the period 8 June through 14 June, whereas the G-2 Daily Reports only accounted for 77 from 8 through 14 June.

17. Ronan, *Operations of the 3rd Battalion, 357th Infantry*, pp. 12–13. Note that a CP was the location of the unit headquarters and its signal communications center. When the commander was not at the CP, his Executive Officer was expected to be there. The CP location was selected for concealment and defilade where it was protected from enemy fire and an alternate CP site was also usually selected for contingencies. An OP was a location or locations from which the unit commander could observe and command operations in the attack and was also where the unit's S-2 and Artillery Liaison personnel would be located. See FM 7-40 *Rifle Regiment* and FM 7-20 *Infantry Battalion*.

18. Ronan, *Operations of the 3rd Battalion, 357th Infantry*, p. 12.

19. Ronan, *Operations of the 3rd Battalion, 357th Infantry*, pp. 12–13.

20. Ronan, *Operations of the 3rd Battalion, 357th Infantry*, pp. 13–14.

21. Ronan, *Operations of the 3rd Battalion, 357th Infantry*, pp. 14–15. The Company K commander was later killed-in-action.

22. Captain Pay, the commander of Company B, 746th Tank Battalion witnessed Collins's visit to the 357th and it is also mentioned in the 746th Tank Battalion After-Action Report, but not the 357th Infantry After-Action Report.

23. Ronan, *Operations of the 3rd Battalion, 357th Infantry*, p. 16.

24. Ronan, *Operations of the 3rd Battalion, 357th Infantry*, p. 16.

25. Meyer, *Hanging Sam*, p. 71. The visit by Collins, MacKelvie, and Williams is not mentioned in the 358th Infantry *History*, but is confirmed by the memoir of General Williams ADC, Major (later Lieutenant Colonel) Eames Yates. It is unclear if they met at the 358th Infantry CP or the Division CP.

26. The large number of wounded lost to the regiment were due to the liberal evacuation orders in place at the time. Most were only lightly wounded but were still evacuated to field hospitals for treatment.

27. The average daily attrition rate for a U.S. Army division in World War II was about 1 percent, while rates of 3 percent to 8 percent were found in periods of extremely high intensity combat. Trevor N. Dupuy, *Attrition: Forecasting Battle Casualties and Equipment Losses in Modern Warfare* (Fairfax, VA: HERO Books, 1995), p. 42, Figure 25, and p. 44, Figure 26.

28. TUSA, G.O. No. 66-44.

29. Chandler and Collins, *D-Day Encyclopedia*, p. 348. Note this incident does not appear in other sources, but the entry was written by Frank Norris, Orwin Talbott, and Eames Yates, all of whom were officers in the division and some of whom would have personally witnessed it.

30. What was referred to as a "bazooka" in the After-Action Report was probably a round from an 8.8cm Raketenpanzerbüchse 54 "Panzerschreck" (Tank's Terror) or a Panzerfaust (Tank Fist).

31. Ronan, *Operations of the 3rd Battalion, 357th Infantry*, p. 16.

32. TUSA, G.O. No. 105-44.

33. Meyer, *Hanging Sam*, p. 73.

34. The 359th Infantry glossed over its loss of direction, but the tankers' account makes it clear it happened.

35. The most complete account of the 82d Airborne's battle with the *Panzer Ausbildungs und Ersatz Abeilung 100* are two internet articles by Niels Henkemans, posted 23 March 2007 and subsequently updated through 2017, at the *Missing-Lynx* discussion group.

36. "Thomas W. Lasher," *American Battle Monuments Commission.*

37. TUSA, G.O. No. 90-44.

38. Abrams, *The 90th Infantry Division in World War II*, p. 3.

39. The 746th Tank Battalion departed the NYPOE on 29 January 1944. Hechler, *History of the Armored Force*, pp. 46–54; Greenfield, Palmer, and Wiley, *The Organization of Ground Combat Troops*, pp. 416–417.

40. *FM 17-36 Employment of Tanks with Infantry*, p. 21; *Sup. No. 1* (Washington, D.C.: War Department, 13 March 1944).

41. Stanton, *Order of Battle*, seriatim.

42. 90th Infantry Division, G.O. No. 549, 15 June 1945.

43. The piecemeal arrival of the German units into the battle, the fragmenting of the German front, and the deaths of so many senior officers make the evolution of the German command in the Cotentin difficult to follow.

44. The date and timing of MacKelvie's relief is unclear. The Division After-Action Report for 12 June ends with "Major General Eugene M. Landrum assumed command of this Division on this day." Meyer says it happened at the Division CP "in the morning" of 13 June, Meyer, *Hanging Sam*, p. 72. However, on 14 June, Collins wrote to Bradley informing him he had relieved MacKelvie "upon oral authority granted by you this date." That Collins obviously meant 13 June rather than the date of his letter has only added to the confusion as to when MacKelvie was actually relieved. It is also a likely indication that General Collins was tired as well, otherwise he would have caught his own error. The full text of Collins's letter may be found in Meyer, *Hanging Sam*, pp. 72–73.

45. Colby, *War*, pp. 475–476.

46. *Official Army Register*, 1945, p. 541; *An Historical and Pictorial Record of the 87th Infantry Division in World War II* (NP: 1945), p. 18.

47. Colby, p. 149.

48. Ronan, *Operations of the 3rd Battalion, 357th Infantry*, p. 16.

49. "Coffin Corner" was the intersection of the Rue du Moulin (D69) and the Rue de La Pesquerie. Colby believed a German headquarters was located nearby, which explained the desperate defense. Colby, *War*, p. 44; Magnuson was later transferred to the 134th Infantry, 35th Infantry Division. Major James A. Huston, *Biography of A Battalion: The Life And Times of an Infantry Battalion in Europe in World War II* (Pickle Partners Publishing, 2016). Domries landed as a captain commanding Company G, 357th Infantry. Ronan, *Operations of the 3rd*

Battalion, 357th Infantry, pp. 9–10. He was promoted to major on 12 July and was reassigned as Battalion XO on 6 August.

50. Colby, *War*, pp. 44–46.

51. Colby, *War*, p. 47.

52. *Seventh Army Kreigstagbuch* (KTB) (War Diary), [trans.] 14 June 1944.

53. *Seventh Army Kreigstagbuch* (KTB) (War Diary), [trans.] 14 June 1944; Niklas Zetterling, *Normandy 1944, German Military Organization, Combat Power and Organizational Effectiveness* (Winnipeg, Canada: J. J. Fedorowicz Publishing, Inc., 2000), p. 230.

CHAPTER 4. CHANGE OF MISSION

1. The "Terre-de-Beauval" was a large family farm now identified as the GAEC (Groupement Agricole d'Exploitation en Commune) de Beauval.

2. Colby, *War*, p. 47.

3. Major Buchanan later received the Bronze Star Medal. Department of the Army G.O. No. 19-48, p. 4; George O'Hara, "Burying the Dead" in Beverly Levine, ed., *World War II, We Were There: An Anthology* (San Jose, CA: Writer's Showcase, 2001), p. 136.

4. Colby, *War*, pp. 49–50.

5. Colby, *War*, p. 49. Eames Langdon Yates was born in Ohio on 31 March 1924. In 1947, he received a RA commission and retired in 1962 as a lieutenant colonel.

6. Colby, *War*, p. 50.

7. TUSA, G.O. No. 10-45.

8. Costain was born in Minnesota on 29 March 1911 and graduated from West Point as a 2d lieutenant in the Field Artillery on 12 June 1934. He was promoted to 1st lieutenant, RA, 12 June 1937; captain, AUS, 3 October 1940; major, AUS, 1 February 1942; and lieutenant colonel, AUS, 31 December 1943. *Official Army Register*, 1944, p. 195. Novelli later recalled that Costain may have said either "we're going forward" or "I'm going forward." *Upstarts*, Appendix "What Happened on 15 June."

9. The strange actions and death of Colonel Costain are covered in detail in *Upstarts*, pp. 21–24, 31, and Appendix "What Happened on 15 June." Moore, author and editor of *Upstarts*, believed Costain had a premonition of his own death. Costain's Silver Star citation is in 90th Infantry Division G.O. No. 20-44, dated 29 June 1944. Respass survived and was recovering at his home in Alexandria Virginia in August 1944. He died of cancer in February 1990. *Washington Star*, 22 August 1944; *The Washington Post*, February 9, 1990.

10. TUSA, G.O. No. 76-44.

11. TUSA, G.O. No. 100-45.

12. Aaron Elson, "My name is . . . I was wounded at . . . ," transcript of 358th Infantry Regiment 1993 Annual Luncheon, *World War II Oral History*, 24 April 2024.

13. Colby, *War*, p. 49.

14. Dupuy, *Attrition*, p. 42, Figure 25, and p. 44, Figure 26. As a comparison, the reinforced 1st Infantry Division suffered a casualty rate of 11.6 percent for the single day of 6 June 1944, which is one of the highest daily rates recorded by the U.S. Army in World War II. A count of the 357th's daily casualty lists shows at least 46 were killed, wounded, missing, or injured 10–16 June. T/O&E was 140 officers.

15. There is an extensive body of literature on the problems and limitations of the U.S. Army replacement system in World War II. See General Board Report No. 3, *Reinforcement System and Reinforcement Procedures in European Theater of Operations*, United States Forces European Theater, 1945; Leonard L. Lerwill, *The Personnel Replacement System in the U.S. Army* (Washington, D.C.: Department of the Army, 1954), pp. 438–477; Eric William Klinek, *The Army's Orphans: The United States Army Replacement System in the European Campaign, 1944–1945*, PhD diss. (Philadelphia, PA: Temple University, 2014), pp. 170, 257–258, 270, 290, and 313. An alternative point of view that highlights the strengths of the individual replacement system is Robert S. Rush, *Hell in Hürtgen Forest: The Ordeal and Triumph of an American Infantry Regiment* (Lawrence: University Press of Kansas, 2001).

16. Colby, pp. 484–496.

17. Colby, pp. 496–503.

18. Harrison, *Cross-Channel Attack*, pp. 413–414.

19. Curiously, many sources, such as *Utah Beach to Cherbourg*, state the 47th Infantry had reached Saint-Sauveur-de-Pierrepont, but the town was not liberated until 4 July.

20. Georges Bernage, *The Battle for the Cotentin Peninsula* (Barnsley, South Yorkshire: Pen & Sword Military, 2018).

21. Eitner was given command of *KG 265. Infanterie-Division* the previous day as one of Hellmich's last orders because its commander, Oberstleutnant (Lieutenant Colonel) Jäger was considered too hesitant and unsure of himself. KTB KG 265.ID, 18.6.44.

22. NARA RG 242, T312, R1565, F001381, AOK 7 Ia Nr. 3454/44 g.Kdos 27.6.44.

23. "La Hardellerie" was possibly a farmhouse or crossroads.

24. Colby, *War*, p. 87.

25. Prétot-Sainte-Suzanne was always referred to simply as Pretot in American records.

26. TUSA, G.O. No. 28-45.

27. TUSA, G.O. No. 4-46. Taylor retired from the Army 25 March 1946 as a captain, AUS, with a line-of-duty disability.

28. European Centre for Medium-Range Weather Forecasts, *Revisiting the Meteorology of the D-Day Period, using a Modern Analysis and Forecasting System*, 6 June 2014.

29. The divisional G-3 report account simply does not match its G-2 report. The only regimental commander possibly captured by the division in June was Oberst Sylvester von Saldern-Brallentin, commanding *Grenadier-Regiment 1057.* of the *91. Infanterie-Division.*

30. In Colby, *War*, pp. 86–87, Hamilton recalled he rejoined the regiment on 23 June. The 357th Infantry HQ MR of 7 July gives Jensen's date of relief as 25 June, although the Division G.O. 44-35 says it was 10 July, while the 1st Battalion HQ MR of 12 and 21 July gives Hamilton's date of command as 27 June and his date of assignment as 24 June.

31. Colby, *War*, p. 88.

32. The Bayerische Flugzeugwerke Bf 109 was usually referred to by the Allies as the Me 109 after its designer, Willi Messerschmitt. The designation given in the original reports will be used in this work.

33. "Yons" is the crossroads hamlet of Les Yons about 2.25 miles east-southeast of Port-Bail at the intersection of the D147E Road and the D132. Niels Henkemans, email to author, 11 August 2024; Lore Oehmichen, "Memorial Biography for Herbert K Oehmichen," 2018–2024, www.theritchieboys.com, and "Captain Herbert K Oehmichen, World War II. 90th Infantry Division," https://www.facebook.com/HKO90THWWII.

34. *Official Army Register*, 1945, p. 654.

35. *The Caine Mutiny* was released ten years later in 1954.

36. Aaron Elson, *Armored Fist: The 712th Tank Battalion in the Second World War* (Stroud, UK: Fonthill Media, 2013), Chapter 3; Janet Miller Simkins, "LTC Samuel Whitside 'Whit' Miller," *Find a Grave*, accessed 8 August 2022.

37. Elson, *Armored Fist.*

38. LOC, *Patton Papers*, p. 571; *Official Army Register*, 1956, Vol. 1, p. 590; Simkins, "LTC Samuel Whitside 'Whit' Miller."

39. All Quartermaster Service Companies, Black or white, were essentially labor organizations, typically assigned to do manual labor and the "dirty work" other units did not do, while identifying the dead and collecting personal effects was the work of the Quartermaster Graves Registration Company, all ten of which in Normandy were white units. The 3d Platoon, 603d Quartermaster Graves Registration Company performed that duty for the 90th Infantry Division in Normandy.

CHAPTER 5. CALVARY ON MONT CASTRÉ

1. Storms affecting unloading over the beaches continued to plague the Allies through the summer. Bad weather on 21 and 22 July reduced the July average cargo unloaded daily by about 85 percent, delaying the start of Operation COBRA, and another storm on 2 and 3 August reduced it by over 90 percent. More storms struck on 15 and 16 August. Unloading across UTAH Beach was affected by bad weather in about one out of every ten days from D-Day until the end of August 1944. ETOUSA File 583f-g—ADSEC, Communications Zone Vol IV—Operational History, Oct 1943-July 1945, p. 36; File 359A—Utah Beach, "Notes on UTAH Beach and the 1st Engineer Special Brigade" (Compiled 20 October–7 November 1944), pp. 141–144; and Roland J. Ruppenthal, *Logistical Support of the Armies*, Volume I: May 1941–September 1944 (Washington, D.C.: OCMH, 1954), p. 475; F.O. 1 (revised), 1 July 1944; First U.S. Army, *Report of Operations I*, p. 82; VIII Corps, After-Action Report, July 1944, p. 2; 90th Infantry Division, *Report of Operations, After-Action Report, July 1944*, p. 2; Martin Blumenson, *Breakout and Pursuit* (Washington, D.C.: OCMH, 1961), pp. 40–44.

2. The 86th Chemical Mortar Battalion was armed with rifled 4.2-inch mortars firing HE and chemical smoke (white phosphorus) rounds up to 4,400 yards; the 333d Field Artillery Group (Cld) was unique in that it commanded both Black and white Field Artillery battalions while in Europe. In total, the 48 Field Artillery pieces of the 90th Infantry Division would be reinforced by a further 156 howitzers and guns. Blumenson, *Breakout and Pursuit*, p. 55.

3. The origins of the ruins are hazy. Some sources link them to a nearby earthwork dating to before Caesar's Gallic wars but usually called "Caesar's Camp." However, the "castle" was actually built by William the Bastard of Normandy, later William the Conqueror, in the middle of the eleventh century. The small size of the "castle"—just 14 by 14 meters—indicates it was probably a simple watchtower. It was partially demolished in 1204 but continued in use as a local defensive shelter during the Hundred Years War. https://www.castles.nl/Castré-castle.

4. Blumenson, *Breakout and Pursuit*, pp. 53–55.

5. A fought-out (Abgekämpftes) battalion was defined as fewer than 100 effective riflemen, weak (Schwaches) was 100 to 200 effectives, average (Durchschnittliches) was 200 to 300 effectives, medium (Mittlestärkes) was 300 to 400 effectives, and strong (Stärkes) was more than 400 effectives. Zetterling, *Normandy 1944*, seriatim.

6. The German term Erst-Ausstattung is similar to the American Army's "basic load." It was the amount of ammunition carried by the tactical units and its supply trains, as well as what was carried by the division supply units. For a 1944-type infantry division it amounted to just under 711 metric tons: 119 tons for light infantry weapons, 205 tons for heavy infantry weapons, 126 tons for antitank guns, 236 tons for artillery, and 25 tons of illumination and signal munitions, engineer munitions, and smoke munitions. Bundesarchiv-Militärarchiv (BAMA), Freiburg, Germany, RH 3/V135, 255, 259, and 368, *1.Mun.-Ausstattung der verschiedenen Div. in to.* [First Ammunition Issue of various divisions in tons].

7. The origin of the cadre confused the 90th Division G-2 initially when two of the first prisoners from *Fallschirmjäger-Regiment 15* captured on 6 July carried documentation for *Fallschirmjäger-Regiment 3* and *4*, which were known to still be in Italy. The other two regiments of the division were not committed to the battle until mid-July.

8. Beaucoudray is a commune east of Villebaudon and not the village of Beau-Coudray between Le Plessis and Les Belles Croix. As of 1 July, the division had 26 Panther, 50 Panzer IV, 36 Sturmgeschütz, and 31 artillery pieces operational. Reardon, *Defending Fortress Europe*, pp. 82, 89, 92; Zetterling, *Normandy 1944*, pp. 321–325.

9. Blumenson, *Breakout and Pursuit*, p. 47 gives the date of Dollman's death as 28 June and the cause as heart attack, probably based upon *The New York Times* report of 3 July 1944, "Nazi Commander Killed in France; Col. Gen. Friedrich Dollmann Was in Charge at Front, Hitler Announcement Reveals," while Carlo D'Este, *Decision in Normandy* (New York: Penguin Books, 2004), pp. 241–242, and Hubert Meyer, *The 12th SS, Vol I* (Mechanicsburg, PA: Stackpole Books, 2005), p. 425, say he committed suicide in the early morning hours of 29 June; however, *7. Armee* Generalstabsartz (Army Medical Officer) Dr. Scheppokat's report to Ob.West dated 28.6.1944 gave Herzschlag (heart attack) as cause of death and Dollmann's personnel file also gives 28 June as the date of death.

10. Mahlmann, p. 15; Blumenson, *Breakout and Pursuit*, p. 59; *German War Diary, 7th Army, Translation, Vol 1*, 30 June–3 July.

11. Kit C. Carter and Robert Mueller, *U.S. Army Air Forces in World War II, Combat Chronology 1941–1945* (Maxwell AFB, AL: USAF Historical Research Center, 1973), 3 July 1944; AAF, *Ninth Air Force, April to November 1944, Army Air Forces Historical Studies No. 36* (AAF Historical Office, Hq, AAF, October 1945), p. 119.

12. The Château de Sainte Suzanne and Église Sainte-Suzanne were always referred to collectively as just Sainte Suzanne, while Le Carrefour Saint-Jores was known as the "crossroads north of Saint Jores" by the Americans because the maps in use did not distinguish between them.

13. TUSA, G.O. No. 89-44.

14. "Unterstellungsbefehl für die SS-Pz.A.A. 17 vom 5.7.1944," M. Wind and H. Günther, *Kriegstagebuch Götz von Berlichingen, 30. Oktober 1943 bis 6. Mai 1945* (München, Germany: Schild-Verlag, 1993).

15. The battalion was tactically subordinated to *91. Inf.-Div. (LL)* but was administratively part of the Ersatzheer, the Replacement Army, on 1 June. It performed Replacement

(Ersatz) and Training (Ausbildungs) duties, thus its title. BAMA RH 10/149; 82d Airborne Division, *G-2 Report No. 84*, 022200-032200 July 1944; 90th Infantry Division, *OB Report No. 20*, 030001-042100 July 1944.

16. Colby, *War*, p. 476.

17. Phil Nordyke, *All American All the Way, From Sicily to Normandy, A Combat History of the 82nd Airborne Division in World War II* (Minneapolis: Zenith Press, 2009), pp. 391–396.

18. United States Army, *The Cross of Lorraine: A Combat History of the 79th Infantry Division, June 1942–December 1945* (NP: 1946), pp. 31–32.

19. Benbrook, from Fayetteville, Arkansas, was promoted to major as the Executive Officer of the 2d Battalion, 359th Infantry in September 1942. He became commander of the 3d Battalion on 17 June, when General Landrum relieved Lieutenant Colonel Lawrence, who in turn had assumed command from Lieutenant Colonel James E. Casey, when Casey was wounded on 12 June, but little else is known of him. *Camp Barkeley News* (Camp Barkeley, TX), vol. 1, no. 30, ed. 1 Friday, September 11, 1942, p. 7; Balkoski, *UTAH Beach*, p. 299; Letter, Brigadier General Robert E. Dunlop, Acting Adjutant General, to Mrs. Aline Benbrook, 31 October 1944.

20. TUSA, G.O. No. 204-45.

21. Department of the Army, G.O. No. 27, April 19, 1948.

22. TUSA, G.O. No. 88-44.

23. The previous S-3, Major Nichols, was wounded on 14 June and evacuated. Major Wallace arrived as a replacement on 16 June. Nichols returned to duty on 21 July.

24. Third Army, G.O. No. 97-44.

25. Nordyke, *All American All the Way*, pp. 400–404.

26. United States Army, *The Cross of Lorraine*, pp. 32–34.

27. Reardon, *Defending Fortress Europe*, p. 148, Zetterling, *Normandy 1944*, pp. 321–323.

28. The hamlet at the crossroads is named La Peignerie in wartime maps but is now known as Montsenelle. The east end of the Mont Castré ridgeline was usually referred to as the "NE nose of the Foret" by the 90th Infantry Division. The Camp de Cesar near there dates to prehistoric early Iron Age Gallic tribes rather than the Romans as folklore would have it. Pierre Giraud, Cyril Marcigny, Anthony Lefort, et al., "Les sites fortifiés de hauteur de La Tène finale en Basse-Normandie," in Philippe Barral, Bernard Dedet, Fabien Delrieu, et al., *L'Âge du fer en Basse-Normandie. Gestes funéraires en Gaule au second-âge du fer* (Besançon, France: Presses universitaires de Franche-Comté, 2011), pp. 73–94.

29. Third Army, G.O. No. 71-44.

30. Reardon, *Defending Fortress Europe*, p. 199.

31. Reardon, *Defending Fortress Europe*, pp. 149–150.

32. The XIX Corps attack did not begin until 7 July.

33. Alfred D. Chandler et al., *Papers of Dwight David Eisenhower, The War Years, Vol III* (Baltimore: The Johns Hopkins Press, 1970), pp. 1971–1972.

34. Chandler et al., *Papers of Dwight David Eisenhower*.

35. Cullum No. 5876; findagrave.com/memorial/122759414/robert-lynn-bacon; Colby, *War*, p. 490. Bacon's first Silver Star was with the 90th and the second with the 95th.

36. GSGS 1:50,000 Map 6E/5—Le Haye Du Puits.

37. Why Hill 122 was referred to as 120 is unknown but is another sign of the confusion in the division.

38. Reardon, *Defending Fortress Europe*, pp. 152–153.

39. Colby, *War*, p. 123.

40. "Heroic Exploits of Scurry County Captain Told at Memorial Services," *Abilene Reporter-News* (Abilene, TX), Saturday, September 2, 1944, p. 15; "Captain Woodrow R. Allen," *Heart of Texas Veterans Memorial*.

41. LOC, *Patton Papers*, p. 595.

42. Once in reserve, the 82d Airborne Division would prepare for withdrawal from France to England for reconstitution.

43. LOC, *Patton Papers*, p. 596.

44. The only record of Williams's outburst was made by Eames Yates in an interview in 1987 with Colonel Harold J. Meyer, *Hanging Sam*, Note 6, Chapter 7, pp. 87, 88, and 171.

45. Of 11,770 officers and men on D-Day, the 82d lost 5,436: 1,142 killed or died-of-wounds, 2,373 wounded, 840 missing or captured, and 1,081 evacuated sick or injured. Nordyke, *All American All the Way*, p. 406.

46. Colby, *War*, p. 126.

47. Traditionally there is no company lettered "J" in the U.S. Army. The 121st Cavalry was part of the 106th Cavalry Group, which was attached to the VIII Corps.

48. LOC, *Patton Papers*, pp. 600–601.

CHAPTER 6. VICTORY ON MONT CASTRÉ

1. The T/O&E figures were as of 15 July 1943. The strengths were revised downwards as of 30 June 1944, but as of 10 July 1944, the change had not yet been effected in the ETOUSA.

2. Mouloir is French for "Grinder," which reflects the narrow rockiness of the stream. Once it runs downhill to the southeast from Mont Castré it turns generally northeast to a junction with the Sèves River near Baupte.

3. Colonel Bealke thought it was 1600, which is probably much too early. Colonel Taylor said it was 1750, which is probably much too late. In the confusion of the battle different participants recorded different times for events, most of which contradict one another. These times are the best estimate of the author based upon the conflicting reports.

4. A house now appears to be built on the rocky knoll.

5. Major Oehlesen was relieved 9 August 1944 and transferred to Headquarters, 12th Army Group. The Battalion Adjutant was the S-1. His name is unknown for certain, but it was probably Captain Clive P. Jaffray. Loomis commanded the 1st Battalion from 7 to 11 July while its commanding officer, Major Albert Seeger, was given a rest. Seeger was promoted to lieutenant colonel effective 10 July.

6. The A&P Platoon was primarily concerned with transporting ammunition to the battalion's companies but also assisted in setting up and digging in the battalion CP and OP.

7. War Department, G.O. No. 34, dated 25 March 1947.

8. TUSA, G.O. No. 88-44.

9. TUSA, G.O. No. 89-44.

10. TUSA, G.O. No. 89-44 (12 November 44).

11. BAMA RW 6v.-570.

12. Zetterling, *Normandy 1944*, p. 323. Other elements of the division, *KG Wisliceny*, were attached to the *Lehr Panzer-Divisio*n and were not included.

CHAPTER 7. "THEY GOT THE WRONG MAN"

1. *Hansen Diary*, 13 July 1944, Box 4, U.S. Army Historical Education Center, Carlisle, Pennsylvania.

2. Chandler et al., *Eisenhower, The War Years*, p. 2024. Roosevelt is often mistakenly named as the Assistant Division Commander of the 4th Infantry Division on D-Day. He was not; that post was held by Brigadier General Henry A. Barber Jr.

3. Omar N. Bradley, *A Soldier's Story* (New York: Random House Modern Library, 1999 [1951]), p. 333.

4. Meyer, *Hanging Sam*, p. 89. Meyer gave no reference for the source for this account of the confrontation or the exact date it occurred, but it seems likely it originated from Meyer's interview with Eames Yates in 1987.

5. Brownlee and Mullen, *Changing an Army*, p. 31.

6. Gene Currivan, "U.S. 90th Plays Historic Role: Army Identifies Unit That Did Some of the Heaviest Fighting in Normandy Battles," *The New York Times*, July 19, 1944.

7. The Rangers were mentioned in a detailed account of their role at Pointe du Hoc on 12 June 1944. Lewis Hawkins, "Courageous American Rangers Silence Deadly Nazi Shore Battery, Nearly Half of Them Die," *The San Bernardino County Sun* (San Bernardino, CA), Monday, June 12, 1944, p. 3. The 29th Infantry Division was mentioned before 15 June 1944. Philip S. Heisler, "Landing Yanks Met Foe on Maneuvers," *The Evening Sun* (Baltimore), Thursday, June 15, 1944, p. 2.

8. The VIII Corps After-Action Report for July lacks considerable detail on operations and makes no mention of when Landrum's plan was presented to Middleton or when it was approved.

9. Colonel Cornog was assigned to command the 36th Armored Infantry Regiment of the 3d Armored Division. He was killed in action leading his regiment on 9 August 1944, although his grave gives the date as 10 August. Blumenson, *Breakout and Pursuit*, p. 487.

10. On 18 July, Division Artillery ammunition expenditure was restricted by FUSA to 14 rounds per piece. On 21 July, the division received an additional allotment of 4,500 rounds of 105mm and 900 rounds of 155mm, while 450 rounds of 155mm were received by each of the reinforcing Field Artillery battalions. 90th Division Artillery, After-Action Report, 18 and 2 July 1944. The normal day of supply for the 105mm was 20 rounds and for the 155mm 10 rounds per day. The prescribed load—the ammunition carried in battalion tactical and ammunition resupply vehicles—for each of the division's 105mm battalion was 2,196 rounds and for each 155mm battalion was 1,800 rounds. FM 101-10, *Organizational, Technical, and Logistical Data*, 1 August 1945.

11. Wood's nickname was short for "Professor," which was given him at West Point, where he tutored many other cadets.

12. The 90th's G-2 report identified the aircraft as an *FW 190.*

13. Ian Kershaw, *Hitler 1936–1945: Nemesis* (New York: W. W. Norton, 2000), p. 693.

14. *The Guardian*, "Hitler's Six-Minute Broadcast: No Commands of 'Usurper Groups' Must Be Obeyed," Friday, 21 July 1944.

CHAPTER 8. COLLAPSE ON THE ISLAND

1. Colby, *War*, p. 140.

2. Brig. Gen. Raymond E. Bell Jr., U.S. Army (ret.), "Tough Time for Tough Hombres," *World War II* [magazine], February 2000.

3. Friedrich Freiherr von der Heydte, *A German Parachute Regiment in Normandy: Operations of the 6th Fallschirm Regiment, 6 June–15 August 1944*, FMS MS B-839, p. 32.

4. Alexander Uhlig, "A Fallschirmjäger's Reflections on Fighting in the Normandy Bocage," Drop Zone Virtual Museum, ND; Walther-Peer Fellgiebel, *Elite of the Third Reich, The Recipients of the Knight's Cross of the Iron Cross 1939–1945: A Reference* (Solihull, UK: Helion & Company Limited, 2003), p. 347; Colby, pp. 144–145.

5. Zetterling, *Normandy 1944*, pp. 321–322, 324; Heydte, *German Parachute Regiment*, pp. 30–32.

6. TUSA G-2, *Annex No 2 to Accompany G-2 Periodic Report No 41*, 22 July 1944. However, the 12th Army Group Situation maps for the period 15–22 July 1944 consistently placed *SS-Das Reich* in reserve rather than in the front line. LOC, *12th Army Group Situation Maps*.

7. Although General Landrum was frequently accused of commanding from his headquarters bunker, in this case it was very clear he was forward directing the course of the assault.

8. The After-Action Report says Company F, but this may be a typo because Company F was already in action.

9. The Château de Saint-Germain-sur-Sèves is a late fifteenth- and early sixteenth-century brick and stone fortified residence.

10. Colby, *War*, p. 140. Falvey was promoted to major on 12 July.

11. TUSA, G.O. No, 41, 19 February 1945.

12. Major Schulz came ashore on D+2 as a captain commanding Company D, 358th Infantry.

13. Bauer was killed in action on 16 March 1945 while flying as an observer in a "Cub" piloted by 1st Lieutenant Jack Hester, also of the 344th Field Artillery. They were shot down by a Luftwaffe fighter over Halsenbach, Germany. Sydney G. Gumpertz, *The Jewish Legion of Valor* (New York: [self-published], 1946).

14. It seems likely that "2 platoons" was a typo for "2d platoon," which added to the confusion.

15. Colby, *War*, p. 140.

16. It appears this account may have partially condensed the events of the night of 22 July with those of the morning of 23 July.

17. Colby, *War*, p. 140.

18. 8th Infantry Division, G.O. No. 118-44.

19. The "heavy" MG42 machine gun was the same gun and caliber as the "light" MG42, 7.92mm, but was mounted on a heavy tripod, with a telescopic sight and elevation and traverse mechanisms that could be adjusted to fire the gun very accurately at much longer ranges than were possible with the "light" version, which was bipod-mounted.

20. Neither of these attacks were recorded by the 358th Infantry at the time. The timing was reconstructed by Falvey after the war from extensive interviews of both American and German participants, including Uhlig. Colby, *War*, pp. 141 and 548.

21. Bell, "Tough Time"; Blumenson, *Breakout and Pursuit*, p. 84 and n. 11, p. 84.

22. T/O&E 7-11, *Infantry Regiment*, 26 February 1944, including Change No. 1 30 June 1944, called for three chaplains in the regiment. The third chaplain of the 358th Infantry, Captain James M. Hamilton, performed a similar mission in a different area during the truce and did not cross the river. Hamilton was a Protestant, a member of the Disciples of Christ, but not much else is known of him. One of the litter bearers was later identified as Private Elwin Stevens of Rutland, Vermont. *St. Albans* [Vermont] *Daily Messenger* [newspaper], Monday, August 21, 1944.

23. Sara M. Stohler, "Captain Edgar H. Stohler, U.S. Army Chaplain in World War II" (self-published, ND).

24. The German captain may have been Hauptmann Horst Trebes, commanding the *III. Bataillon*, who massacred thirty-one Greek civilians at Kondomari and Kandenos, Crete, 2–3 June 1941. In July 1941, while in a drunken stupor, he accidentally shot and killed Oberjäger Karl Polzin, holder of a Ritterkreuz (Knight's Cross) for the assault on Eben Emael in May 1940. Trebes was court-martial and stripped of his own Ritterkreuz awarded for Crete. He was killed 29 July 1944 in an American air attack during the withdrawal from the Island. Robert Kershaw, *The Hill: The Brutal Fight for Hill 107 in the Battle of Crete* (Oxford: Osprey Publishing, 2024), pp. 318–322 and 331–332.

25. The number of men rescued varies by source. Falvey mentioned sixteen and Esser forty. It is unknown how many wounded Captain Hamilton rescued. Stohler, "Captain Edgar H. Stohler."

26. Ball was born 9 July 1904 in Alabama and graduated from Auburn in 1926, after which he joined the AP. He retired in 1958 and died on 7 October 1992. *The Tennessean* [newspaper], Wednesday, October 14, 1992. Dodd was born in 1910 and died in 2005 but aside from the many sketches done for the AP during the war and for various pulp magazines such as *Police Detective* and *True Fact Crime* postwar not much is known of him. The current whereabouts of the painting is unknown. Joel Bohy, "Howell Dodd: Illustrator and War Correspondent," *Cranston Herald* [Cranston, RI], Wednesday, July 13, 2022.

27. 90th Infantry Division, G.O. No. 93, 19 October 1944.

28. Robert W. Black, *The Battalion: The Dramatic Story of the 2d Ranger Battalion in WW II* (Mechanicsburg, PA: Stackpole Books, 2006), pp. 16, 70–71, 78–79.

29. La Forge had landed in Normandy as a captain commanding Company A, 358th Infantry. On 13 June 1944, he was appointed Battalion Executive Officer in place of Seeger, who had become Battalion Commander after the death of Spike Nave. La Forge was promoted to Major on 4 July 1944.

30. 90th Infantry Division, G.O. No. 42, 20 August 1944.

31. Heydte, *German Parachute Regiment*, p. 36.

32. LOC, *Patton Papers*, p. 622; Blumenson, *Breakout and Pursuit*, pp. 309–311.

33. Uhlig, "A Fallschirmjäger's Reflections on Fighting in the Normandy Bocage"; Prisoner of War Camps in Devizes During World War II, *Devizes Heritage.*

CHAPTER 9. PROBLEM DIVISION?

1. No written record of such a staff recommendation appears to exist in the records of the 12th Army Group, but both General Bradley and General McLain mentioned it in their postwar writings. Bradley, *A Soldier's Story*, p. 297; McLain letter, *Army Combat Forces Journal*, 16 March 1954. LOC, *Patton Papers*, p. 618.

2. Bradley, *A Soldier's Story*, p. 298.

3. W. F. Kerr and Ina Gainer, *The Story of Oklahoma City, Oklahoma: "The Biggest Little City in the World,"* Vol. 3 (Chicago: S. J. Clarke, 1922), pp. 422–426.

4. Roy P. Stewart, "Raymond S. McLain: America's Greatest Citizen Soldier," *Chronicles of Oklahoma*, vol. 59, no. 1, Spring 1981, p. 7.

5. McLain had succeeded Key as Commanding General of the 70th Field Artillery Brigade when Key became Commanding General of the 45th Division. Clay, *Volume 1. The Arms*, p. 241; Rawson, *Divisional Commander*, pp. 121–122.

6. Key was Provost Marshal of the ETOUSA from June 1943 through May 1943, then Commanding General of the Iceland Base Command until 4 December 1944, when he was assigned to the U.S. Control Commission for Hungary.

7. Chandler et al., *Eisenhower, The War Years*, pp. 1795–1796.

8. Stewart, "Raymond S. McLain," p. 13.

9. D'Este, *Patton*, p. 387.

10. Frank James Price, *Troy H. Middleton: A Biography* (Baton Rouge: LSU Press, 1974), pp. 206–207.

11. Bradley, *A Soldier's Story*, p. 298; Stewart, "Raymond S. McLain," pp. 13–14.

12. For example, Lieutenant Colonel Charles M. Schwab was Executive Officer of the 357th Infantry from D-Day until given command of the 2d Battalion, 357th Infantry from 6 to 9 August, when he was transferred to Headquarters 12th Army Group, but there is nothing otherwise to indicate he was one of the "sixteen."

13. Chandler et al., *Eisenhower, The War Years*, p. 2080.

14. Van R Mayhall, *Cranking Up a Fine War: A Louisiana Soldier from Boot Camp to General's Aide* (Austin, TX: Byren Lee Press, 1999), pp. 136–137; Stewart, "Raymond S. McLain," p. 14.

15. Anon., *On the Way: A Historical Narrative of the Two-Thirtieth Field Artillery Battalion Thirtieth Infantry Division, 18 February 1942 to 8 May 1945* (Poessneck i. Thuer., Germany: Fr. Gerold Verlag, ND [1945]), p. 10.

16. Stewart, "Raymond S. McLain," p. 14.

17. Mayhall, *Cranking Up a Fine War*, p. 188.

18. As of late July 1944, General Bradley was still wearing two hats as commander of both the 1st U.S. Army Group and First U.S. Army. As part of the FORTITUDE deception plan the Germans had been surreptitiously informed that General Patton was the 1st U.S. Army Group Commander, but it was felt that when the Germans inevitably became aware he was in France commanding the TUSA, it would be necessary to create a logical alternate Army Group commander and McNair was selected for the role. The 1st U.S. Army Group was redesignated as the 12th U.S. Army Group, effective 14 July 1944, but it did not become operational until 1 August 1944. 12th Army Group, *Report of Operations (Final After Action Report), 12th Army Group, Volume I, Summary* (12th Army Group, 31 July 1945), p. 6.

19. Blumenson, *Breakout and Pursuit*, pp. 273–278.

20. Blumenson, *Breakout and Pursuit*, pp. 317–321.

21. Blumenson, *Breakout and Pursuit*, pp. 424–425.

22. LOC, *Patton Papers*, pp. 630–631.

23. Mayhall, *Cranking Up*, p. 145.

24. The publication of the pamphlet was noted in the After-Action Report of the 3d Battalion, 358th Infantry on Wednesday, 3 January 1945.

25. It appears in the entry for the division in Theater Historian, *Order of Battle*, so was well recognized by July 1945.

26. One Quartermaster Truck Company drawn from Third Army and one drawn from the 5th Armored Division were used to motorize the 357th Infantry. They were to be returned as soon as the 357th Infantry detrucked.

CHAPTER 10. TASK FORCE WEAVER

1. La Richardiere does not appear on modern maps. The intersection is the modern traffic circle intersection of the D30-D977-D977E, 780 meters south of the center of Saint-Hilaire-du-Harcouëtt.

2. Captain Boyd L. Brown, *The Operations of the Task Force Weaver (90th Infantry Division) in the Attack on Mayenne, France, 5–6 August 1944* (Fort Benning, GA: The Infantry School, Advanced Infantry Officers Course, 1949–1950), pp. 6–7.

3. David N. Spires, *Airpower for Patton's Army, the XIX Tactical Air Command in the Second World War* (Washington, D.C.: Air Force History and Museums Program, 2002), pp. 52–60.

4. Allied vehicles were identified by a large 144-inch by 30.5-inch colored aircraft recognition panel. In August, the air recognition panel color used was cerise—a bright fluorescent red. The other colors, which were rotated according to schedule, were yellow and orange. Spires, *Airpower*, pp. 67–68.

5. While a few sorties were flown on some days, 21, 29, and 30 August were considered "unflyable." *Air-Ground Teamwork on the Western Front, the Role of the XIX Tactical Air Command during August 1944* (Washington, D.C.: Center for Air Force History, reprint 1992), originally published as Office of Assistant Chief of Air Staff, Intelligence, *Twelve Thousand Fighter-Bomber Sorties: XIX Tactical Air Command's First Month of Operations in Support of the US Third Army in France* (Washington, D.C.: Hq, AAF, 1945), hereafter *Air-Ground Teamwork*, pp. 37, 40, and 42.

6. Brown, *Task Force Weaver*, p. 9.

7. Brown, *Task Force Weaver*, pp. 7–8.

8. It appears the 5th Armored Division trucks were those that failed to arrive because they were noted as arriving in Mayenne on 6 August; see below. There were nineteen kitchen trucks per regiment, so they were able to supply more than enough trucks. Kelly, *Task Force Weaver*, p. 6; FM 101–10, p. 44.

9. Colby, *War*, pp. 178–188.

10. Colby, *War*, p. 180.

11. Hamilton said the bridge had been rigged with eight "500-pound aerial bombs," while a modern account says it was "a 125kg [275-pound] bomb and 15 cases of dynamite." Either was likely sufficient to demolish the bridge completely. Colby, *War*, p. 179.

12. Brown, *Task Force Weaver*, p. 11; Colby, *War*, p. 180.

13. Colby, *War*, pp. 180, 182, and 186.

14. HQ ETOUSA, G.O. 130-44, 26 December 1944.

15. Colby, *War*, p. 186.

16. Colby, *War*, p. 181; "'James McRacken Day' Abroad Has Special Meaning for Hays Resident," *The Hays Daily News* (Hays, KS), Monday, August 7, 1961, p. 1. Although Lieutenant Stevens said that "only" the two Engineers followed his men, it appears the rest of Stephens's Engineer squad was busy disarming the explosives at the entrance to the bridge and was simply not seen by Stevens in the confusion. Sergeant Stephens was awarded a Silver Star for the action. Thanks to Vincent Orrière for the identification of Private Bergstrom.

17. HQ, USFET, G.O. No 43-47. The citation for Private McRacken's DSC spells his name as "Macracken." However, his family name is McRacken and that spelling is used here. McRacken's remains were later exhumed and reburied at Alloway Cemetery, Red Springs, Robeson County, North Carolina.

18. Colby, *War*, pp. 186–187.

19. Colby, *War*, pp. 187–188. Stevens was lightly wounded during the action on 5 August. He was wounded a second time later in the war.

20. The location of the Hotel Ferichard is unclear; it does not exist under that name today. Based on a sketch map drawn by Lieutenant Stevens, it appears it was probably in the large building at 1 Rue Quettier.

21. The number and location of these encounters with German stragglers is difficult to pin down, given the contradictory accounts and vague statements about where they happened. It seems likely the German force at Gorron was one of the elements that attempted to escape through Mayenne that night. Brown, *Task Force Weaver*, p. 18; Kelly, *Task Force Weaver*, p. 8; Colby, *War*, p. 182.

22. Note that the 90th Division After-Action Report erroneously reported the movement of the 358th Infantry for that of the 359th Infantry and vice versa.

23. Only twenty-five of thirty-seven trains carrying the division had unloaded at Le Mans by end of day on 7 August. Zetterling, *Normandy 1944*, pp. 160, 205–206, 209–210, 289–291, and 386–387; NARA Microfilm RG 242, T314, R1594, Frame 0000006.

24. Zetterling, *Normandy 1944*, pp. 330–331. The Germans consistently used XXXXVII rather than the more conventional XLVII in designations.

25. Kunzen's corps had only been ordered to move to Normandy on 3 August and was still moving from Canteleu, near Rouen, to Le Mans, on 5 August. Reardon, *Defending Fortress Europe*, p. 244.

26. The 2d Platoon was reorganizing from the previous day's action.

27. No such organization was authorized under T/O&E, but many regiments organized one for practical reasons.

28. As of 1 June 1944, *Sicherungs-Regiment 195* was headquartered at Rennes and comprised three battalions of Landdeschützen—literally "State Riflemen"—mainly conscripts from the Landwehr (thirty-five to forty-five years old, that is, those born between 1894 and 1904 at the start of the war) and the Landsturm (over forty-five years old, that is, those born in 1894 or earlier at the start of the war). It is uncertain which battalion or battalions were at Laval and Montsûrs, but men from *5.* and *6. Kompanie* were reported captured at Laval, so it was likely the *4. Kompanie* at Montsûrs. Zetterling, *Normandy 1944*, p. 160; NARA, Microfilm RG 242, T314, R1594, Frame 0000005-6.

29. Colby, *War*, pp. 188–189; Kelly, *Task Force Weaver*, pp. 9–10.

30. Zetterling, *Normandy 1944*, p. 389. The exact composition and strength of *KG Coretti* is difficult to pin down. *Lehr* reported twelve Panther tanks operational as of 1 August, but it is unclear if they had reached Mayenne. American reports mention the presence of Panther tanks—as well as "Tiger" tanks—but they could not have been from *9. Panzer-Division* because its Panther Abteilung was at Trun, about 80 kilometers to the northeast, on 4 August and was intended for the Mortain counterattack. Elements of *Sturmgeschütz-Brigade 341* may also have been attached.

31. *KG Unger* was under the command of Major Heinz Unger with *I./Panzergrenadier-Regiment 10*, *4./Panzer-Regiment 33* with Panzer IV tanks, and *Panzer-Pionier-Batallion 86*, less *3. Kompanie*. It appears Oberst Reich's commanded Unger as well as the rest of his own regiment, reinforced by *Stab I./Panzer-Regiment 33*, *3./Panzer-Artillerie-Regiment 102*, and *3./Panzer-Pionier-Batallion 86*. NARA, Microfilm RG 242, T314, R1594, Frame 0000006.

32. HQ ETOUSA, G.O. 130-44, 26 December 1944.

33. HQ ETOUSA, G.O. 130-44, 26 December 1944.

34. NARA, Microfilm RG 242, T314, R1594, Frame 0000006.

35. Kelly, *Task Force Weaver*, p. 11.

36. Thanks to Vincent Orrière for the additional details of the FFI participation in this action and the SS atrocity.

37. *Sicherungs-Regiment 1* was similar to *Sicherungs-Regiment 195*. Zetterling, *Normandy 1944*, p. 160.

38. Zetterling, *Normandy 1944*, pp. 290–291.

39. Zetterling, *Normandy 1944*, pp. 288–291.

40. Ralph Bennett, *ULTRA in the West* (New York: Charles Scribner's Sons, 1979), pp. 111–115.

41. HQ ETOUSA, G.O. 130-44, 26 December 1944.

42. Kelly, *Task Force Weaver*, pp. 11–12.

43. A description of Bradley's decision making, carefully worded to protect the ULTRA secret, may be found in Bradley, *Soldier's Story*, pp. 372–375. The account also makes Bradley's decisions appear more of a gamble than they were and makes Patton's decision to hold the three divisions in place seem as if it was Bradley's. A more evenhanded account may be found in Mark J. Reardon, *Victory at Mortain* (Lawrence: University Press of Kansas, 2002), pp. 178–179. Patton's original account is in LOC, *Patton Papers*, p. 639. The 2ème Division Blindée was organized from Free French forces in North Africa on 24 August 1943; its organization and equipment were similar to an American armored division but with some unique features and designations. Theater Historian, *Order of Battle*, pp. 273, 557.

44. The *77. Infanterie-Division* was reorganizing again at Le Mans, but its combat strength was only about that of a small battalion.

45. Colby, *War*, p. 192.

46. HQ ETOUSA, G.O. 130-44, 26 December 1944.

47. Colby, *War*, p. 192.

48. It is possible this is the same report as that for the Germans at Coulans-sur-Gée engaged by Task Force Weaver, only mistakenly entered as southeast rather than southwest of Le Mans.

49. TUSA, *AAR Vol I*, p. 24 and Annex No. 2, p. IV; XV Corps, *Action Against Enemy, Reports After, 31 July to 31 August 1944*, 9 August.

50. LOC, *Patton Papers*, p. 639.

51. D'Este, *Patton*, pp. 642–643; Martin Blumenson, *The Battle of the Generals* (New York: William Morrow & Co., 1993), pp. 189–190.

52. The bridge was probably put in by the 513th Engineer Light Ponton Company of the 1101st Engineer Combat Group. The 315th Engineers were also supported by the 133d Engineer Combat Battalion of the 1101st Group.

53. TUSA, G.O. 75-44, 17 August 1944.

CHAPTER 11. SOLID SHOULDER OR BROKEN NECK?

1. Kluge replaced Rundstedt as Oberbefehlshaber West on 2 July. He assumed his "second hat" as Oberbefehlshaber Heergruppe B on 19 July after Erwin Rommel was wounded in an air attack on 17 July. Bennett, *ULTRA in the West*, pp. 118–119.

2. The 319th Infantry RCT was detached under corps command specifically to secure the bridgehead at Le Mans and later at Angers. It did not rejoin the division until 28 August. Theater Historian, *Order of Battle*, p. 272.

3. Headquarters, ETOUSA, "Gallantry in Action," *Anti-Aircraft Artillery Notes, No. 3*, 8 November 1944, pp. 3–4.

4. There was further evidence this day of the problems American units were having in correctly identifying place-names in France. The 1st Platoon, Company D, 712th Tank Battalion gave its location as Saint-Germain-*de-la-Coudre*, which was on the opposite flank of the division, when it was actually at Saint-German-*sur-Sarthe*.

5. Headquarters, ETOUSA, "Gallantry in Action," *Anti-Aircraft Artillery Notes, No. 2*, 1 November 1944, pp. 5–6.

6. Blumenson, *Breakout and Pursuit*, pp. 498–499; Blumenson, "General Bradley's Decision at Argentan."

7. Bennett, *ULTRA in the West*, pp. 120–112; Heinz Günther Guderian, *From Normandy to the Ruhr with the 116th Panzer Division in World War II*, translated by Ulrich Aberle, Esther Aberle, and Keith E. Bonn (Bedford, PA: The Aberjona Press, 2001), p. 76.

8. La Fondation Maréchal Leclerc de Hauteclocque, "Bataille de Normandie."

9. Guderian, *From Normandy to the Ruhr*, pp. 76–77. Note the German and American accounts are very contradictory with regard to the timing of these events.

10. Guderian, *From Normandy to the Ruhr*, p. 79.

11. The other infantry regiment of the division, *Panzergrenadier-Regiment 60*, was holding a weak security line west of Argentan. Guderian, *From Normandy to the Ruhr*, p. 80.

12. No time was given for the receipt of this order in the 90th Infantry Division After-Action Report, and there is no mention of it in the XV Corps After-Action Report, but it likely was around 1400.

13. Colonel C. P. Stacey, *The Victory Campaign, Volume III, Official History of the Canadian Army in the Second World War* (Ottawa: Queen's Printer and Controller of Stationery, 1966), pp. 236–237.

14. The [British] National Archives, WO 171/440, 7 Armd Div, *Intelligence Summary No 63 (Based on information received up to and including 2359 hrs 12 Aug)*, Part I., A, Situation.

15. The 35th was released from attachment to the V Corps of First U.S. Army on 5 August and was attached to the XX Corps on 6 August. On 12 August it was at

Notre-Dame-du-Touchet, about 150 kilometers from Le Mans by road. The 80th Infantry Division was attached to the XX Corps and on 10 August was at Amné, just west of le Mans. The 7th Armored Division was attached to the XX Corps on 10 August and was assembling at Louvigné-du-Désert after landing in France across OMAHA and UTAH beach on 8–10 August.

16. Bradley, *A Soldier's Story*, p. 376.

17. LOC, *Patton Papers*, p. 639.

18. LOC, *Patton Papers*, p. 644.

19. Such travel and personal meetings were recorded on 1, 2, 4, 5, 9, 10, 14, and 15 August. LOC, *Patton Papers*, pp. 628–649 and seriatim. Even Martin Blumenson, who wrote numerous well-researched accounts of these events, was contradictory on this point. In *Breakout and Pursuit*, he made no mention of a telephone conversation with Patton on the night of 12/13 August, nor did he mention such a conversation in "General Bradley's Decision at Argentan." It was only in *The Battle of the Generals* that Blumenson returned to the supposed telephone conversation, by repeating Bradley's account from *A Soldier's Story.*

20. Major General Kenneth Strong, the SHAEF G-2, was British, as was a large part of his staff, thus the British spelling of "armor." FDR Presidential Library, *MR 300, Sec. 6 France*, From SHAEF (Forward) to War Department, Part 3 of trans of FWD 12801 DTG 121545.

21. It is difficult to understand how Bradley got his account so badly scrambled unless we assume he was deliberately rewriting the record, as he had done after the short bombing in Operation COBRA. Blumenson explains the discrepancy by theorizing that there was a second conversation that was not logged by either 12th Army Group or TUSA Headquarters, which seems unlikely. *The Battle of the Generals,* pp. 207–208.

22. Quoted in Richard Lamb, *Montgomery in Europe, 1943–1945* (New York: Franklin Watts, 1984), p. 171. Bradley denied ever making the request (Bradley, *Soldier's Story*, p. 376).

23. LOC, *Patton Papers*, p. 649. Unfortunately, in writing the two-volume *Third Army After-Action Report* at the end of the war, the anonymous authors ransacked the Army Headquarters files for documentation. In the aftermath, many of the supporting document files, including the "Telephone Conversations," were misplaced and have not been found. As Martin Blumenson put it, "most of the [*Third Army After-Action Report*] official supporting documents seem to have vanished" (Blumenson, *Breakout and Pursuit*, p. 707), which is also what this author found when exploring the TUSA records at NARA.

24. Bradley, *A Soldier's Story*, p. 377.

25. Bennett, *ULTRA in the West*, pp. 121–122.

26. LOC, *12th Army Group Situation Maps*, 14 August 1944; BAMA RH 2-KART/10942, *Generalstab des Heeres.- Lagekarten*, 9 August 1944.

27. Henkemans, *Defending Normandy*, p. 217 and seriatim. A modern analysis of the effectiveness of the 12th Army Group G-2 Section is Trygve J. Smidt, "Intelligence in Support of Military Operations: What Was the Role of US Military Intelligence in the Falaise Pocket Battle August 1944?" (thesis, Norwegian National Defence University, Spring 2013).

28. Zetterling, *Normandy 1944*, pp. 28–29. Postwar the USAAF studied the German retreat and estimated that as of 19 August about 309,000 German troops with 47,000 motor vehicles and 800 tanks and assault guns were still west of the Seine and north of the Loire. USAAF, *Third Phase Tactical Air Operations in the European Theater 5 May 1944–8 May 1945*

(The Army Air Force Evaluation Board in the European Theater of Operations, August 1945), p. 128.

29. Blumenson, *The Battle of the Generals*, p. 218.

30. The flights, in two "Cubs," covered nearly 190 miles in the day. In his diary, Patton noted, "I admit that I never cared to do anything less and the fact that every one [*sic*] seemed assured we were going to be shot down by friends & foes did not tend to confidence." LOC, *Patton Papers*, p. 646.

31. LOC, *Patton Papers*, pp. 646–647.

32. Martin Blumenson argued that Bradley's growing antagonism toward Montgomery's command of American troops in Normandy combined with Patton's flattery of Bradley in the aftermath of the success of COBRA was a major factor in the decisions Bradley made during this period. Blumenson, *The Battle of the Generals*, pp. 220–222.

33. W/O Carl Jenkins [90th Division Historian], "The Gap at Chambois—Aug 15–22, 1944," and Jenkins, "1st Bn Action at Le Bourg St. Leonard," *Combat Interviews*, Box 19064, Folder 194, Chambois Gap. NARA RG 407, Entry 427A. Pond was promoted to major effective 22 July. The Combat Interviews were conducted between 26 August and 5 September.

34. The 773d Tank Destroyer Battalion had just landed in France on OMAHA Beach on 7 August. It was attached to the XV Corps and the 5th Tank Destroyer Group on 10 August and reached Le Mans on 12 August. The rest of the battalion was at Aunou-le-Faucon with the 1st Platoon, Company A 1 mile to the southwest and the 3d Platoon, Company B 1 mile to the east.

35. The divisions already assembled near Argentan were *2.*, *9.*, and *116. Panzer*, *LSSAH*, and *SS-Das Reich*. Eberbach was promised *21. Panzer*, *SS-Hohenstaufen*, and *SS-Frundsberg* as reinforcements. Attacks by the XIX Corps pinned the *SS-Frundsberg* in place and attacks by the Canadians diverted the *21. Panzer*. Bennett, *ULTRA in the West*, pp. 121–122; Reardon, *Defending Fortress Europe*, pp. 246–247.

36. LOC, *Patton Diaries*, pp. 648–649. This was a personal meeting rather than a telephone or radio conference.

37. LOC, *Patton Diaries*.

CHAPTER 12. THE BATTLE OF LE BOURG-SAINT-LÉONARD

1. Jenkins, "1st Bn Action at Le Bourg St. Leonard."

2. Captain David Hickman, "Operations of the 1st Battalion, 359th Infantry, 90th Infantry Division, in closing the Falaise-Argentan Gap and Defense of Le Bourg St. Leonard, 14–19 August 1944" (Northern France Campaign) (Personal Experience of a Battalion S-3), Infantry School Advanced Officer Class Number 1, 1949–1950.

3. The location of the Platoon Leader's tank was not given. It may have been at the 1st Battalion CP in La Haras du Pin. Hickman, "Operations of the 1st Battalion, 359th Infantry."

4. Cross mixed up some events in his account, and there is some conflict between his description of this early incident and other accounts of the action but there does not appear to be any reason to doubt it occurred. "Interview with 2nd Lt. Vernon W. Cross, Weapons Platoon Leader, A Co, 359th Infantry, 90th Division, 26 August 1944," *Combat Interviews*.

5. "Action of 3rd Platoon, Co C, 607th TD Bn in Battle of Falaise Pocket," 2 September 1944; Jenkins, "1st Bn Action at Le Bourg St. Leonard." Slightly different versions of events are found in the 359th Infantry After-Action Report, and interviews with the participants, including Major Pond, Captain Hickman, and Lieutenant Cross. For example, different accounts have Cross's patrol advancing, 200, 800, or 1,000 yards into the woods.

6. "Action of 3rd Platoon, Co C, 607th TD Bn in Battle of Falaise Pocket."

7. Headquarters, 90th Infantry Division, G.O. No. 57, 10 September 1944.

8. Jenkins, "Interview with 2nd Lt. Vernon W. Cross." Cross claimed that shortly afterward both Company A and B counterattacked again, but there is no other corroborating evidence to support that.

9. Lieutenant Kingsley identified the tank as a "Tiger," to which the interviewer noted, "most of the men to whom we talked called all German tanks Tigers, irrespective of whether they were or not. . . . They were still jumpy and on edge at the time of the interviews." Jenkins, "B Company action 1630 Aug–16th to 2400 17th Aug," *Combat Interviews.*

10. Guderian, *From Normandy to the Ruhr*, p. 83; German documents indicate the *116. Panzer-Division* had five Panzer IV, three Panther, and eight Sturmgeschütz operational on 13 August, which closely matches American accounts. It also had as many as eight artillery batteries available, which matches American reports that the German artillery occasionally fired battalion volleys in the battle. Zetterling, *Normandy 1944*, pp. 324–325.

11. Bennett, *ULTRA in the West*, pp. 122–124.

12. 343d Field Artillery Battalion, *Mission Accomplished*, p. 19; *Combat History of the 344th Field Artillery Battalion*, p. 14.

13. William C. Sylvan, Francis G. Smith Jr., and John T. Greenwood, ed., *Normandy to Victory, The War Diary of General Courtney H. Hodges and the First U.S. Army* (Lexington: The University Press of Kentucky, 2009), pp. 97–99; Blumenson, *The Battle of the Generals*, p. 234 says there were only three jeeps in the group, which is probably incorrect.

14. Blumenson, *The Battle of the Generals*, p. 234.

15. The Field Artillery battalions were the 691st (105mm howitzer), the 186th (155mm howitzer), 989th (155mm gun), and the 240th (155mm gun).

16. LOC, *Patton Papers*, p. 652.

17. Jenkins, "1st Bn Action at Le Bourg St. Leonard," pp. 7–8.

18. One M10 of Company A had been knocked out by mines on the march to Le Bourg-Saint-Léonard.

19. The losses amounted to a daily casualty rate of 9.1 percent in Company A and 10.1 percent in Company B. Average daily loss for a company-sized unit in World War II was estimated as 21.0 percent and for a battalion-sized unit was 9.5 percent. Dupuy, *Attrition*, p. 42.

20. Headquarters, TUSA, G.O. No. 90, 1944.

21. Headquarters, TUSA, G.O. No. 10, 1945. Pond was promoted to lieutenant colonel on 31 August. Headquarters, 1st Battalion, 359th Infantry, *MR*, 31 August 1944.

22. Headquarters, TUSA, G.O. No. 84, 20 April 20, 1945.

23. USAAF, *Missing Air Crew Report, 43-28725*, 18 August 1944.

24. Hanna made no mention of an earlier attack in his statement. USAAF, *Missing Air Crew Report, 43-28725.*

25. USAAF, *Missing Air Crew Report, 43-28725*, 18 August 1944.

26. Loft was awarded the Distinguished Flying Cross and Purple Heart, both posthumously. "Lt. Robert E. [*sic*] Loft Services Tonight," *Brooklyn Eagle* (Brooklyn, New York), Wednesday, October 27, 1948, p. 13.

27. Dad did not say who gave the order to open fire, although it was likely either Lieutenant Lindell or Dad.

28. LOC, *Patton Papers*, p. 646.

29. Wesley Frank Craven and James Lea Cate, eds., *The Army Air Forces in World War II, Volume Three, Europe; Argument to V-E Day, January 1944 to May 1945* (Chicago: University of Chicago Press, 1951), p. 254; Sir Trafford Leigh-Mallory, "Despatch," Fourth Supplement to the *London Gazette* of December 31, 1946, p. 66.

30. TNA AIR 37/784, *Air Commander-in-Chief, AEAF, Air Chief Marshall Leigh-Mallory: Air Commander-in-Chiefs Diary of Events*, 14 August 1944. Leigh-Mallory dictated the diary to Hilary St. George Saunders of the Ministry of Information.

31. TNA AIR 37/784, *Air Commander-in-Chief, AEAF*, 15 August 1944.

32. *The London Gazette (Supplement)*, 29 August 1944. p. 3995.

33. The last resistance at the Ecole Superieure in the center of town ended at 0200 18 August. Stacey, *Victory Campaign*, p. 250; Blumenson, *The Battle of the Generals*, p. 245; Sir Trafford Leigh-Mallory, "Despatch," p. 66.

34. For example, Blumenson, *The Battle of the Generals*, p. 239 and *Breakout and Pursuit*, p. 505.

35. Eddy Florentin, *The Battle of the Falaise Gap* (London, Elek Books, 1965), p. 233.

36. *Trun 1944*, http://trun.free.fr/1944.htm; AAF Historical Office, *Ninth Air Force April to November 1944, Army Air Forces Historical Studies No 36* (Hq, AAF, October 1945), p. 172.

37. LOC, *Patton Papers*, p. 652.

38. Blumenson, *The Battle of the Generals*, pp. 234–235. The two different schemes of maneuver may be found in the two 90th Infantry Division Field Orders of the day. *FO # 21*, 170300B August 1944 is Gaffey's original order and *FO # 22*, 171800B August 1944 is Gerow's revised order.

39. LOC, *Patton Papers*, p. 652

40. Blumenson, *The Battle of the Generals*, pp. 235–236

41. Bradley, *Soldier's Story*, p. 376; For the controversy that ensued postwar, see, for example, Terry Brighton, *Masters of Battle: Monty, Patton and Rommel at War* (London: Penguin Books, 2009). It also appears as part of the dialogue in the movie *Patton*, for which Bradley was senior technical advisor.

CHAPTER 13. CLOSING THE CHAMBOIS-FALAISE POCKET

1. Note there were two hills designated 129 in the area, one west and one east of the Le Bourg-Saint-Léonard–Chambois road. The 3d Battalion objective was Hill 129 west of the Le Bourg-Saint-Léonard–Chambois road.

2. TUSA, G.O. No. 103 (1944),

3. Colby, *War*, p. 227.

4. Stacey, *Victory Campaign*, p. 256.

5. The Poles were attacked multiple times by Allied aircraft during the Normandy Campaign. They were hit by Allied heavy and medium bombers on 8 August in Operation

TOTALIZE and on 14 August during Operation TRACTABLE. The Poles incurred 204 casualties in the second bombing, 48 killed, 103 wounded, and 53 missing. Major-General Stanislaw Maczek, "The 1st Polish Armoured Division in Normandy," *Canadian Military History* 15, no. 2 (2006), p. 62.

6. *SS-Das Reich* had withdrawn to Ticheville to hastily reorganize after its abortive counterattack at Le Bourg-Saint-Léonard.

7. Maczek, "1st Polish Armoured Division," pp. 64–67.

8. Guderian, *From Normandy to the Baltic*, pp. 86–87; Meyer, *The 12th SS*, pp. 72–73, 94–98; Reardon, *Defending Fortress Europe*, pp. 251–252.

9. The *7. Armee* ordered the *17. SS* to withdraw to Metz for rebuilding on 18 August. "Div.-Befehl für die Verlegung in den Raum Metz vom 18.8.1944," in Wind and Günther, *Kriegstagebuch*.

10. The National Archives (UK), AIR 41/67, *The Liberation of NW Europe: Vol IV, The Break-out and Advance to the Lower Rhine June–Sept. 1944*, p. 105.

11. TUSA, G.O. No. 90-44.

12. Falvey apparently thought the 3-inch M10 GMC of the 773d Tank Destroyers were tanks of the 712th Tank Battalion. Colby, *War*, p. 225.

13. None of the 90th Division Field Artillery battalions admitted to being the culprit. It may have been one of the supporting corps battalions. It may have been a corps interdiction mission laid out when the plan was to control the town by observation and fire rather than occupying it.

14. The 3d Platoon, Company A, 712th Tank Battalion was supporting the 359th Infantry that day but not the 2d Battalion. Captain Waters, commander of Company G, 359th Infantry, was adamant the tanks were French. Colby, *War*, p. 228.

15. Colby, *War*, p. 236.

16. Maczek, "1st Polish Armoured Division," p. 67.

17. "2d Battalion Action at Chambois."

18. Company B and the rest of Company A were still reorganizing from the hard-fought two days of battle at Le Bourg-Saint-Léonard. By 2200 19 August only forty-four of the Battalion's 75mm-armed Medium Tanks M4 were operational. Three more had been written off and seven were in long- or short-term repair. NARA RG 492, *ETOUSA Armored Fighting Vehicle and Weapons Section, Daily Tank States*, 19 August 1944.

19. The inexperienced units of the 80th Infantry Division were pinned down by intense fire from mobile 2cm and 3.7cm Flak guns deployed on the high ground north of Argentan and northwest of Bordeaux. Captain William L. Koob Jr., "The Operations of the Antitank Company (Reinforced), 317th Infantry (80th Infantry Division) Northeast of Argentan in the Closing of the Argentan-Falaise Gap, 17–20 August, 1944" (Northern France Campaign), Class Number II, 1949–1950, pp. 11, 29.

20. An expenditure of about fifty-seven to ninety-one rounds per howitzer per day was typical for the U.S. Army in a large-scale offensive operation during World War II. However, rates double that could be achieved over short periods of time. Historical Evaluation and Research Organization, *Memorandum for Captain Denton West, Subject Artillery Fire and Effect, US Ninth Army, Roer River Crossing, February 23, 1945* and *Search for Historical Records of High-Rate Artillery Fire in Combat Situations*, September 1983. The 90th Infantry Division

expenditure for the month of August was 3,939 rounds of 155mm, 14,598 rounds of 105mm M2, and 2,130 rounds of 105mm M3.

21. The five additional battalions with the 90th are not identified in the available records. The three 25-pdr Field Regiments supporting the 4th Canadian Armoured Division spent the day displacing forward. The Polish artillery was apparently out of ammunition until it was resupplied late in the day from American sources. That left just two British Royal Artillery Medium Regiments with thirty-two 5.5-inch gun-howitzers within range that were able to fire. Historical Section (G.S.), Army Headquarters, *Canadian Participation in the Operations in North-West Europe, 1944, Part III: Canadian Operations, 1–23 August*, AHQ Report No. 65, 23 December 1953, p. 87.

22. The *708. Infanterie-Division* commander, Generalmajor Edgar Arndt, with the few parts of the division that had not reached Le Mans earlier in August, was at Montargis, south of Paris and east of Orléans. Stacey, *Victory Campaign*, p. 256; Alexander Fitzgerald-Black, "Right in Their Way, Major David Vivian Currie, VC and the Battle for St. Lambert-sur-Dives," *Project 44*.

23. Forrest C. Pogue, *The Supreme Command* (Washington, D.C.: OCMH, 1954), p. 215.

24. Hubert Meyer did not note Funck's or Schwerin's presence, but Heinz Günther Guderian did. On the other hand, Guderian's account implied only Hausser and Funck were present. It seems likely all were there at some point.

25. The column included all or parts of *84., 89., 271., 275., 343., 352., 353., 363.,* and *708. Infanterie-Division*. They had little organization or combat effectiveness, but they and various nondivisional units likely accounted for about one-third to one-half of the troops remaining in the pocket.

26. The accounts from two participants of this conference—Guderian and Meyer—differ on whether it was intended that the *2.* or *116, Panzer-Division* execute the initial breakout. Guderian says that Hausser initially wanted the *116. Panzer* to join *LSSAH* but that Funck intervened to have the *116. Panzer* hold while the others attacked to break through. Guderian, *From Normandy to the Ruhr*, pp. 86–87; Meyer, *The 12th SS*, pp. 98–100.

27. Meyer, *The 12th SS*, pp. 73; AIR 41/67, pp. 106–107.

28. Elfeldt was not named but was described as a "Major General commanding the German 49th Infantry Division." Elfeldt had commanded the *47. Infanterie-Division* and Generalleutnant in the Wehrmacht was equivalent in rank to major general in the U.S. Army.

29. The IX TAC flew about 200 sorties; the XIX TAC flew 388 combat and 36 reconnaissance sorties. *Air-Ground Teamwork on the Western Front*, p. 37; *Combat Chronology*, 20 August 1944; *Ninth Air Force, April to November 1944*, pp. 171–173, 186–194; AIR 41/67, p. 107.

30. *Third Phase Tactical Air Operations*, p. 127, "Figure 31, German Retreat Across the Seine, Phase Lines."

31. Colby, *War*, p. 237. The other Medals of Honor were to Private First Class Foster J. Sayers for actions on 12 November 1944, Technical Sergeant Eugene Everhart for actions on 12 November 1944, and Corporal Edward A. Bennet for actions on 1 February 1945. Sayers was killed in the action that resulted in his award; the others all survived the war.

32. War Department, G.O. No. 55, July 13, 1945.

33. Colby, *War*, p. 238.

34. Colby, *War*, p. 238.

35. Colby, *War*, p. 239. While the count of "tanks" was likely an exaggeration, to an infantryman any vehicle with a semblance of armor and a gun was a "tank."

36. TUSA, G.O. No. 216, 1945.

37. "Leonard Charles Dull," *Find a Grave*.

38. A figure of "1200" German wounded was mentioned in other sources of this incident but in context it appears that was a typo for "1–200", that is, between 100 and 200. At 0930. They were described as "four ambulances and 80 men, plus wounded" and at 1015 as "200 german [*sic*] wounded and the aid station."

39. South Alberta Regiment (29 Armoured Reconnaissance Regiment), *War Diary*, 20 August 1944.

40. Meyer, *The 12th SS*, pp. 76–77; various amateur studies have been done of ground and aerial photography of the area identifying vehicles by type and occasionally by unit. See, for example, *Axis History Forum*, https://forum.axishistory.com/viewtopic.php?f=47&t=19525&start=240&hilit=chambois+photos and *Missing Lynx* https://www.tapatalk.com/groups/missinglynx/stug-iii-g-photo-in-chambois-t325991-s10.html.

41. Donald E. Graves, *South Albertas: A Canadian Regiment at War* (Toronto: Robin Glass Studios, 1998), p.173.

42. Guderian, *From Normandy to the Ruhr*, p. 87. As of 22 August, the *116. Panzer-Division* had four Panzer IV and three Jagdpanzer IV operational. *I./Panzer-Regiment 24* also rejoined the division with eleven operational Panther.

43. The figures are adjusted for the probable number there based upon the different counts made. [British] No. 2 Operations Research Section, *Operational Research in North West Europe: The Work of No 2 Operational Research Section with 21 Army Group June 1944–July 1945*, "Enemy Casualties in Vehicles and Equipment during the Retreat from Normandy to the Seine," O.R.S. Report No. 15, 1945, p. 88.

44. Maczek, "1st Polish Armoured Division," p. 70.

45. BAMA RH 3/368, Bestandsmeldungen über gepanzerte Kraftfahrzeuge, Panzer und Sturmgeschütze. 1944.

46. Four Panther and one Panzer IV.

47. Twenty-five field pieces, thirteen 88mm guns, and four antitank guns.

48. Seventy-one Panzer IV, twenty-six Panther, five Tiger, and two Panzer III.

49. Later the figure was revised to 13,208.

50. Maczek, "1st Polish Armoured Division."

51. Hilfswilliger or HiWi were volunteer auxiliaries, usually recruited from Soviet prisoners of war, but also including French, Italians and other nationalities. *Ob. West Ia, KTB and Anlagen*, June 1–5, 1944, NARA T311, R24, F9013~, *KTB and Anlagen*, 6–30 June 1945, R24 and 25, F9176~, *Anlagen z. KTB*, July 1–30 September 1944, R28, 29, and 30, F4098~; *Heeresartz i. OKH, Gen.Stb. d. Heer/Gen.Qu.*, NARA T78, R414, F383228-383229.

CHAPTER 14. EPILOGUE

1. The commanding officer of the 379th Infantry, which captured the bridge, was Colonel Bacon, formerly the 359th Infantry commander.

2. "Editorial Note on Inspection Trip to France, 8–14 October 1944," *The Papers of George Catlett Marshall*, ed. Larry I. Bland and Sharon Ritenour Stevens, vol. 4, "Aggressive

and Determined Leadership," June 1, 1943–December 31, 1944 (Baltimore and London: The Johns Hopkins University Press, 1996), pp. 624–626.

3. Cole, *Lorraine Campaign*, pp. 512–513.

4. Three towns, Rehlingen to the north, Siersberg to the south, and Büren to the east, are now combined as the municipality of Rehlingen-Siersberg.

5. Brownlee and Mullen, *Changing an Army*, p. 54.

6. 81st Chemical Mortar Battalion, *Unit History of the 81st Chemical Mortar Battalion* (NP: ND), Chapter XI.

7. The records are unclear when this meeting took place and whether it was in person or by phone. It seems clear that it was sometime between 2 December, when the 90th Division Operations report notes that the emplacement of direct fire supporting weapons along the 359th Infantry front began, and the night of 4/5 December, before Battery A was ordered to emplace the guns in Rehlingen.

8. Headquarters, ETOUSA, "Air Support of Bridgehead Operations," *Anti-Aircraft Artillery Notes, No. 10*, 27 December 1944, pp. 6–7.

9. Although the 90th Infantry Division Operations Report says the emplacement of supporting weapons for the crossing began on 2 December "all along the front," the Battery A MR for 5 December states clearly it was at 0400 that the 3d Platoon moved to Rehlingen.

10. Brownlee and Mullen, *Changing an Army*, p. 52. DePuy actually took command of the 1st Battalion on the night of 4 December, about thirty hours before the leading boats of the assault started across the river.

11. Brownlee and Mullen, *Changing an Army*, pp. 56–57.

12. Cole, *Lorraine Campaign*, p. 561.

13. Twelve years after the 1979 interview, DePuy wrote that the river crossing "worked perfectly" and "There were virtually no casualties." Colby, *War*, p. 161.

14. 90th Infantry Division, G.O. No. 102, 4 February 1945. Note that the "V" for valor Bronze Star device was not authorized until 22 December 1945, otherwise Dad's award would have included the "V" device.

15. Reported expenditures by the 3d Platoon, Battery A were: 2,000 on 7 December, 6,000 on 8 December, 4,000 on 9 December, 1,000 on 12 December, 10,000 on 17 December, 20,000 on 18 December, 20,000 om 19 December, and 10,000 on 20 December. No expenditures were recorded on 10–11, 13–16, or 21–22 December.

16. Hugh Cole, *The Ardennes: Battle of the Bulge* (Washington, D.C.: OCMH, 1965), pp. 486–488.

17. *Secret Follies*, "L'histoire du Lido de Paris."

18. *Arnold Hague Ports Database*.

19. U.S. Army Human Resources Command, Military Awards Branch, *Permanent Orders 323-45*, 18 November 2004.

20. The temporal and geographic areas for the U.S. Army campaigns of World War II are defined in War Department, G.O. No. 24, Campaigns, World War II—List of Battles and Campaigns, dated 4 March 1947.

21. Department of the Army, G.O. No. 24, Units Entitled to Foreign Decorations, dated 10 December 1947, pp. 37 and 88.

22. Department of the Army, *Change 13 to AR 600-45*, 4 November 1947.

www.ingramcontent.com/pod-product-compliance
Ingram Content Group UK Ltd.
Pitfield, Milton Keynes, MK11 3LW, UK
UKHW041412011026
8983IPUK00009B/9

9 780811 778336